COMMUNICATION AND ORGANIZATIONAL BEHAVIOR
Text and cases

THE IRWIN SERIES IN MANAGEMENT

CONSULTING EDITOR   JOHN F. MEE   *Indiana University*

Communication and organizational behavior

TEXT AND CASES

WILLIAM V. HANEY, Ph.D.

The Traffic Institute
Northwestern University

President, Management Development Consultants
Wilmette, Illinois

1973 · Third Edition
RICHARD D. IRWIN, INC. *Homewood, Illinois 60430*
IRWIN–DORSEY LIMITED *Georgetown, Ontario*

Third Edition

First Printing, January 1973

ISBN 0-256-00224-X
Library of Congress Catalog Card No. 72-90776
Printed in the United States of America

Every writer is a product of his experiences. In the case of this book so much is due to the author's contact with one outstanding personality that special mention must be made of it. The author is deeply grateful for eight years of study and friendship with the late

PROFESSOR IRVING J. LEE

of Northwestern University. Those who have been stimulated by his writings and inspired by his person will recognize his influence. It is to the continuation of his teachings and values that this book is respectfully dedicated.

Foreword

New developments in the philosophy and practice of management depend upon the communication process for the implementation of new concepts and the intelligent integration of new research findings into the dynamic process of management. The practice of management responds to the factors and forces that emerge from the changing values and priorities in the environment.

Since the publication of the first edition of this classic text on the subject of communication and its relationship to organization behavior in 1960, the concept of the world environment has changed from that of a "Cowboy Economy" to one of a "Spaceship Economy." There is increasing concern among the people of the world about the influence on their life styles of population explosions, available food supply, pollution increments, natural resources depletion, and the steady increase in industrial output. Those responsible for the management and administration of business and governmental affairs are struggling to respond to the developing demands of consumerism, affirmative personnel actions, corporate social objectives, medical and health care delivery, urban deterioration, minority groups, and numerous other results that stem from an impinging scientific society.

The development of management thought and practice requires an understanding and an application of communication skills and proficiencies. Unless those who practice and teach the concepts and the skills of management and organization theory are competent to perform the communication function, the promises of the new developments and innovations may not be realized. As the decade of the 1970s unfolds, some exciting and identifiable innovations in management thought and practice are developing concurrently with the expansion of the new "knowledge industry."

Results-oriented management, long-range strategic objective setting and policy formation, and strategic planning are all based upon the communication system that provides a way of thinking for advanced management practices. Current interest in the application of the theories of organization development and organization effectiveness requires the web of communication processes in some type of information system for effective results. Control theory and control systems are impotent unless they are supported by viable communication systems.

Throughout the ensuing decade, the work and play environment for increasing numbers of people will be characterized by changes in society that will involve more complex social and economic institutions. However, the individual is the basic unit in all forms of organized activity. His behavior decrees the course of economic growth and social progress. His survival and success depend largely upon his initiative, creativity, flexibility, and adaptability. His influence on the behavior of others stems from the knowledge, skills, and values of communication that he acquires and applies.

Dr. William V. Haney presents a logic of communication in this third edition of his book that can be learned, taught, and applied by individuals who interact with other individuals in organizations such as business, government, military, hospital, and educational institutions. An appreciation of the values of both written and oral communication is basic for the satisfying and successful career of any individual working or preparing for work in a growing and complex industrial and scientific society.

JOHN F. MEE
Mead Johnson Professor of Management
Graduate School of Business
Indiana University

Preface

THIS BOOK is designed for communicators—for people who deal with other people in organizations such as business, government, military, hospital, and educational institutions. It was written for use in college courses, management-development seminars, supervisory training programs, adult education classes, and individual self-study.

*   *   *

Beyond a general updating the major changes in the third edition are an extensive revision of Chapter 6: "The Inference-Observation Confusion," Chapter 7: "Bypassing," Chapter 8: "Allness," and Chapter 10: "Polarization." In view of the increasing destructiveness of polarization and the "pendulum effect" in community, national, and international affairs, Chapter 10, especially, required restructuring and amplification.

There is somewhat more emphasis on the *application* of concepts and on *techniques* for preventing or correcting miscommunication.

Some new cases, such as "Preston Lee, C.P.A." have been added to provide opportunities for more detailed analyses of communication behavior.

Discussion questions have been added to each chapter for two purposes:

—to provide a self-examination of sorts on the key concepts involved in the respective chapter.

—to suggest further ramifications, implications, and applications of those concepts.

Finally, the bibliography has been updated. A systematic review of recent literature leads to an inescapable conclusion. The body of knowledge in the broad areas of communication and organizational behavior has been markedly increased. In terms of *quantity*—which is overwhelming—and *quality*—which is impressive if not uniform—there has probably been more solid development in these areas in the last decade alone than in the entire previous history of their study. And well there might for considering the "world of miscommunication" (see page 4) we appear to be being drawn inexorably into "the race between education and destruction." To paraphrase William F. Buckley, Jr.: "Communication may not save us but without communication we will not be saved."

The book continues to consider communication in the *organizational* setting and in terms of a broad *behavioral* base for the communicative act. The communicator, after all, is a complex being with feelings, values, attitudes, perceptions, needs, and motives. To examine his communication behavior apart from "the whole man" and apart from his interpersonal relations is not only artificial but misleading. Moreover, society is becoming progressively *organized*—thus an inspection of the impact of the organization upon the individual and his communicating is necessary.

*   *   *

According to its title, this book is about *communication*. The title will appear appropriate or inappropriate, I suppose, to the extent that the reader's visualization of "communication" coincides with the author's. Perhaps it would be helpful to indicate what this book is *not* about. It does not, for example, deal with much of the subject matter usually developed in texts of public, conversational, conference, and business and professional speaking. It does not serve the purposes of texts of composition or of business writing, reports, and letters. Nor is it a book on reading or listening. These vital aspects, phases, and media of communication are treated skillfully and thoroughly in many fine works. Some of them are listed in the bibliography at the end of this book.

The book *is* concerned with the less familiar but equally critical phases of communication which are common to all of the modes of human interchange above. It focuses on what it is that happens *inside* a communicator *before* and *as* he talks, writes, and so forth, and *as* and *after* he listens, reads, etc. Some might call these processes "thinking" and dissociate them from the communication experience. Others, including this writer, have felt no need to make such a distinction and, indeed, question the wisdom of drawing an arbitrary line between "thinking" and "communicating." It seems to this writer that perceiving, evaluating, visualizing, and interpreting are as involved in the communication process as are phonation, articulation, spelling, and grammar.

The book is also about *organizational behavior*—human behavior in the context of a human organization. That organizational behavior and communication are inextricably interwoven is a major thesis of the opening chapters.

Accordingly, the book is organized as follows:

Part I deals with the organizational setting in which communication occurs. Part II discusses the behavioral basis of the communicative act with special reference to the roles that perception and motivation play in communication. A basic model of communication is detailed in Chapter 5, "The Process of Communication." The model describes communication as a serial process involving the phases of encoding, sending, medium, receiving, and decoding. Each step, like a link in a chain, is crucial. Because they are by far the least understood, this book focuses on the encoding and decoding phases.

Each chapter in Part III deals with one or more "patterns of miscommunication" which arise in the encoding and/or decoding phases. These miscommunications stem largely from various fallacious assumptions unconsciously held by the communicators—be they speakers or writers, listeners, or readers. The usual chapter format in Part III includes a definition of the miscommunication pattern(s), the range and types of their consequences, some of their probable causes, and finally, the suggestion of techniques for correcting the miscommunications and for preventing their recurrence.

THE CASES

If the book's purpose were only to provide the reader with a body of information and theory about communication it would seem sufficient to restrict it to the textual material. The fond hope, however, is that readers will be able to use the book to move beyond the level of acquaintance with content to the improvement of their own communication performance. And this is the function of the cases. Some suggestions on using the cases are in Chapter 1, "Introduction."

ACKNOWLEDGMENTS

With respect to the first edition, my deepest appreciation goes to M. Kendig, Director of the Institute of General Semantics, Lakeville, Connecticut, for her critical discussion of the draft of most of the chapters, and to Robert R. Hume, National Science Foundation, Washington, D.C., for his invaluable editorial assistance with the final manuscript.

I want to thank the students of Northwestern and DePaul Universities and the executives, supervisors, and professionals of numerous business, professional, government, and military organizations in management development seminars here and abroad who permitted me to share theories and techniques with them.

Principally among these organizations were Abbott Laboratories, Agway, Allegheny Ludlum, Allis Chalmers, The American Group of CPA Firms, Anaconda, Ashland Oil, Carter Oil, Caterpillar Tractor (domestic and international), The Executive Committee, Firestone, IBM (domestic and international), Inland Steel, Internal Revenue Service, International Nickel, Liberty Mutual Insurance, McCann-Erickson, MacNeal Memorial Hospital, Mead Johnson, Metropolitan Life, Mobil Oil (domestic and international), Motorola, New York Life, Northrop, Pillsbury, President's Association (American Management Association), Price-Waterhouse, RCA, Standard Oil of Indiana, Swift, Teletype, U.S. Departments of Air Force, Army, Health-Education-Welfare, Navy, Public Health, and State, Weiss Memorial Hospital, Western Electric, and Zenith Radio, and the Ecole des Hautes Etudes Commerciales. In addition there were the executive development programs conducted by the American Hospital Assn., the American Institute of Baking, the Bank Marketing Assn., the Brookings Institution, Cornell University, DePaul University, Emory University, Management and Business Services, National Assn. of Mutual Savings Banks, Northwestern University, Northwestern's Traffic Institute, Notre Dame University, the Ohio State University, Oklahoma State University, Pepperdine University, UCLA, the University of Chicago, the University of Illinois, and the U.S. International University.

I am especially indebted to Standard Alliance Industries, Inc., that, with whole-hearted cooperation, has permitted me in the roles of director, researcher, and consultant to explore without inhibition organizational communication and relationships.

I am grateful to the Ford Foundation for a research fellowship that, with the assistance of the Graduate School of Industrial Administration, Carnegie Institute of Technology, enabled me to do a good deal of the behavioral research. Special thanks go to colleagues who read part or all of the manuscript and offered valuable suggestions. They include: Professors Warren G. Bennis (Massachusetts Institute of Technology); John F. Mee (Indiana University); Joseph S. Moag (Northwestern University); Victor H. Vroom (Carnegie Institute of Technology); and Karl F. Weick (University of Minnesota).

Much gratitude goes to my wife, Arlene, who somehow managed to shield me from our wonderful but active sons and daughters— five in all.

Finally, and it should go without saying, any errors and shortcomings in this book are uniquely my own and undoubtedly result from good advice unheeded.

Wilmette, Illinois   WILLIAM V. HANEY
December 1972

Contents

4.   **Motivation and communication** 133

A motivation model. Frustration: *Conflict.* Kinds of needs: *Primary and secondary needs. Some finer delineations.* The value of motivation theory. Epilogue.

5.   **The process of communication** 179

Communication process model: *Encoding. Transmission. Medium. Reception. Decoding.* A serial process: *Encoding and decoding—the subtle phases.*

Part III
PATTERNS OF MISCOMMUNICATION

6.   **The inference-observation confusion** 211

The uncalculated risk. Observational and inferential statements. Correctives: *Step one: Awareness. Step two: Calculation.* Questions: *Creativity. Decisiveness.*

7.   **Bypassing** 245

Definition: *Same word—different things. Different words—same thing.* Some consequences: *The range of consequences. Immediate consequences.* The underlying mechanism: *The fallacy that words have mono-usage.* The fallacy that *words* have meanings. Deliberate bypassing: *Gobbledygook.* Correctives: *Be person-minded—not word-minded. Query and paraphrase. Be approachable. Be sensitive to contexts.* Postscript.

8. **Allness** 294

Two false assumptions. The process of abstracting. Allness defined. Craving for certainty. Modes of allness. Deliberate deception. Summing up. Correctives. Challenging a myth: *Action* and *viability.* Profile of viable men.

9. **Differentiation failures I (indiscrimination)** 332

"Hardening of the categories": *Stereotypes.* The battle of the categories. Language: A contributing factor. Correctives: *Become sensitive to differences.* The values of seeing similarities.

10. **Differentiation failures II (polarization)** 355

Definition: *Contradictories. Contraries. Polarization.* Consequences: *Deluding ourselves. Deluding others. The pendulum effect.* Polarization in America. Contributing factors: *Similar grammatical form. Neglect of middle ground.* Correctives: *Detect the contrary. Specify the degree—apply the how-much index. Separate the double contraries. Guard against the pendulum effect.* Epilogue.

11. **Differentiation failures III (the frozen evaluation)** ....

The case of Frank. The assumption of nonchange: *Changes in people. Changes in business. The influence of language.* Correctives: *Internalize the premise of change. Apply the when index.*

CASES

12. **Intensional orientation I (a general statement)** ....

The Graham University tax case. Intension and extension. Intensionality: Some manifestations. Correctives.

CASES

13. **Intensional orientation II ("pointing" and "associating")** ....

The "pointing-associating" confusion: *Euphemisms and dysphemisms.* "Name calling": *The double burden. Living up to the labels. Living down the labels. Positive labels.* "Associative" bypassing. A possible misunderstanding. Correctives: *The "pointing-associating" confusion. "Name calling." "Associative" bypassing.*

CASES

14. **Intensional orientation III (blindering)** ....

Some consequences: *Delayed solutions. Undesirable solutions.* Correctives:

Remember, defining-neglecting. Does my definition blinder me? How to recognize our blinders.   .

CASES

15. **Undelayed reactions** 490

Three classes of behavior: I. Reflex responses. II. Voluntary responses. III. Reflexlike responses. The problem of undelayed reactions. Correctives: Instantaneous action—rarely necessary. The habit of delay. Advance preparation for emergencies. Anticipate the undelayed responses of others. A group technique.

CASES

Part IV
OVERVIEW AND BIBLIOGRAPHY

16. **Overview** 517

Introduction. Organizational climate and communication. Perception and communication. Motivation and communication. The process of communication. Inference-observation confusion. Bypassing. Allness. Differentiation failures: I. Indiscrimination. II. Polarization. III. The frozen evaluation. Intensional orientation: I. A general statement. II. "Pointing" and "associating." III. Blindering. Undelayed reactions.

Part one

Communication and organizational behavior

1

Introduction

It is eminently clear that effective communication is essential in business, in governmental and military organizations, in hospitals, schools, communities, homes—anywhere people deal with one another.[1] It is difficult, in fact, to imagine any kind of interpersonal activity which does not depend upon communication in one form or another.

The concern for communication in business, in particular, has grown enormously. Among the scores, if not hundreds, of factors responsible for this burgeoning interest must surely be the insights being developed by management. Today's administrator is aware that the efficiency of a group depends to a great extent on how well the efforts of its individual members can be coordinated. But he also appreciates that coordination does not just "happen." He realizes, for example, that satisfactory communication is necessary if he and his employees are to achieve understanding and cooperation; if he is to cope with the problems which come with geographical decentralization and departmental specialization; if he is to present a desirable image of his organization to its various publics. In dealing with these and many other concerns the modern administrator has become, characteristically, a *communicator*. Studies indicate that aside from

---

[1] The newly established Council of Communication Societies recently published a directory listing 64 *associations*—not *organizations* but *associations of organizations*—concerned in some fashion or other with communication!

3

communicating—speaking, writing, listening, reading, and thinking (*intra*personal communication)—an organization's top administrator does virtually nothing! The typical executive spends about 75 percent of his time communicating and about 75 percent of this time in individual, face-to-face situations.[2] Even middle- and lower-manage-

FIGURE 1–1
A world of words

2 C. S. Goetzinger and M. A. Valentine, "Communication Channels, Media, Directional Flow and Attitudes in an Academic Community," *Journal of Communication*, March 1961, pp. 23–26, and "Communication Patterns, Interactions and Attitudes of Top-Level Personnel in the Air Defense Command," *Journal of Communication*, March 1963, pp. 54–57.

ment personnel devote the bulk of their working hours to the processes and problems of communication.[3]

With all this increased interest, one might expect improvements in the communicative process. And, indeed, there has been fantastic advancement—in some areas. With the aid of modern electronic equipment it is possible to send, receive, process, store, retrieve, and reproduce prodigious amounts of information with incredible speed—and reach unlimited numbers of people in the process.

Quantity, speed, and coverage, however, are not the only requirements of communication. It is also imperative that we communicate *clearly* and *precisely*. But, in contrast to the technological improvements, progress toward greater *understandability* has come much more slowly. It is still quite possible for persons to fail to understand one another, even though they speak the "same" language; for firms to snarl orders and lose customers' confidence; for nations to break off diplomatic relations and even declare wars because of distortions in communication.

Consider the world of words we have been living through in recent years. (See Figure 1–1.) These words and phrases, among others which have dominated the news the past five years, suggest the tension and conflict that characterized the period. Taken *in toto* they depict a world in *flux*. However, it is not *just* change—but the *acceleration* of change which has so sorely tested our ability—and willingness—to communicate with one another.

With communications satellites we can now be in audiovisual contact with any place on Earth.[4] Yet, frequently it appears that our *interpersonal communication practices* as distinguished from *communication technology* have regressed.

Have we lost sight of the fact that the *ultimate* senders and receivers of messages, regardless of the sophisticated intervening apparatus, are *human beings?* To reiterate, how far have we progressed in understanding what happens *inside* people as they communicate—or fail to communicate? Adler is none too comforting:

How far can we overcome the imperfections of language?
Only slightly.
How far can we keep the relations of our thoughts and our feelings in good order?
Very slightly.

---

[3] Milton M. Mandell and Pauline Duckworth, "The Supervisor's Job: A Survey," *Personnel,* Vol. 31 (1955) , pp. 456–62.

[4] And *off* the Earth, recalling the excellent color telecasts from recent moon landings.

How far can we go to create a common background of knowledge and experience for all men?

Not very far.

How much can we attain the idea of each man perfectly understanding himself without psychosis or neurosis to any degree?

Not very much.

How many of us are willing, every time we talk to another human being, to expend the effort to really do it well?

Few of us or, if ever, few times.

How many of us are free from all neurosis and in perfect possession of the moral and the intellectual virtues?

As you answer that question you will see that I am not exaggerating when I say that a fifty per cent success in the process of communication would be very good, indeed. We probably do not come near that now.[5]

It is small wonder that John B. Lawson, a top executive of the Philco Corporation, was moved to comment:

I am appalled at the almost organized, perverse ability of businessmen to misunderstand each other and to remain ill informed while in the midst of the biggest information explosion man has ever known. . . . Poor communications cost companies billions a year in ill-conceived actions based on misunderstandings and baseless rumors. If our corporations are to grow in size and complexity, then our managers will have to become articulate.[6]

As veteran Federal Mediator Douglas Brown put it: "At least 99 percent of the union-company difficulties I deal with either start with or are complicated by poor, inadequate, or omitted communication."

Just what happens when men talk together, when they write, when they read? Why are they sometimes so unsuccessful in exchanging their thoughts clearly, understandably, and effectively? When Green speaks, why does White fail to "get" him, even though White tries to understand? How is it possible for an executive, earnestly wanting to communicate with his employees, to make costly errors in terms of money and morale? How is it that a military commander can issue orders which can be misinterpreted so as to lead to incalculable disasters? This is the nature of the problems which concern us in this book.

---

[5] Mortimer Adler, "Challenges of Philosophies in Communication," *Journalism Quarterly*, Vol. 40, No. 3 (Summer 1963) , p. 452.

[6] *Steel: The Metalworking Weekly,* June 28, 1965, p. 29.

PLAN OF THE BOOK

The organization of this book is something like a funnel beginning with the large end and leading down to the small hole at the bottom. After this introductory chapter, Chapter 2 deals with the large and complex *organizational setting* in which communication plays such a vital role and then focuses on that critical aspect of the organization, its *"climate,"* with which communication performance is inexorably intertwined. Chapters 3 and 4 set out the behavioral base in which the *individual* is examined as an organism whose behavior (including his communication behavior) is profoundly influenced by his perceptions and motivations. In Chapter 5 we investigate that special but critical behavior called *communication.* Chapters 6 through 15 detail numerous *patterns of miscommunication*—recurrent modes of self-deception and inaccuracy which lead to misunderstanding, confusion, and conflict. Each chapter describes a pattern of miscommunication, examines its prime causes, and recommends strategies and techniqes for preventing or correcting its occurrence. Chapter 16, the overview, consists of a concluding rationale for the book and a summary of its key concepts.

THE CASES

The late communication authority, Irving J. Lee, used to say that the road to becoming a competent practitioner of communication (and of the prevention and correction of miscommunication) was marked by five milestones. First, one acquaints himself with the subject matter—the studies, the theories, and the methods. In other words he acquires the current knowledge of the field. Second, he acquires the ability to recognize and learn from proficiencies and shortcomings in the communication of others. Third, and more difficult, he comes to perceive and understand them in his own behavior. Fourth, he develops skills for improving his own communication. Fifth, and by far the most formidable accomplishment, he learns to prescribe for the communicative problems of others.[7]

---

[7] Lee listed these "steps" in their order of difficulty rather than suggesting they be strictly adhered to chronologically. He never insisted, for example, that Step One had to be mastered before practicing Step Two, and so forth. Nor did he discourage one's developing skills on two or more levels simultaneously. However, some accomplishment at Step One should facilitate development at Step Two; learning at Step Two should aid in accomplishing Step Three, and so on.

The textual part of this book, at most, can only contribute to the reader's realization of Step One. The cases which follow each of the succeeding chapters, however, give him the opportunity to practice at the level of Step Two.[8]

Most of the cases are simply reports of actual happenings in which communications somehow went awry. They are offered because there is often a decided gap between one's intellectual *acquaintance* with a subject matter and his *internalization* of it. The cases afford the opportunity to move beyond a superficial knowledge of the patterns of miscommunication to a more profound and enduring awareness and understanding of them.

It is suggested that the reader will benefit from the cases to the extent that he "bores into them." He should not be content with an appraisal of the obvious. To the cases he should bring questions rather than preconceived answers:

What is going on in the case? What has happened?
Why did it occur? What are the *underlying assumptions* of the communicators involved?
What could have been done to prevent the communication failure or at least to diminish its consequences?
What can be done now?
What procedures, techniques, measures would you suggest to prevent a *recurrence* of this type of miscommunication?[9]

The cases were allocated to the chapters because they appeared to this writer and to many of his students (all of the cases have been "class tested") to exemplify in some manner the content of the chapter to which they are appended. This is not to suggest that other pat-

---

[8] Explorations into Steps Three and Four may be within grasp for some at this point. It is recommended, however, that Step Five be approached with considerable caution and constraint. In all candor, Step Five may be something of a will-o'-the-wisp. Communication habits are often so deeply rooted that change may take place only at the volition of the individual himself. For one to attempt to change another may arouse the other's defenses and lead to resistance. (Defense against change is discussed more fully in Chapter 3, "Perception and Communication.") Change, if any, would likely be superficial and temporary at best.

Given the requisite of volition, perhaps the best one can do is to try to provide a nonthreatening environment wherein the other person can perform Step Four for himself (see Carl Rogers and Richard E. Farson, *Active Listening* at the end of Chapter 3 in this regard).

[9] For a more detailed problem-solving, decision-making format see the "Pattern of Analysis, Decision, Action, and Learning," G. L. Bergen and W. V. Haney, *Organizational Relations and Management Action* (New York: McGraw-Hill Book Co., 1966), pp. 23–30.

terns of miscommunication (including those described elsewhere in this book or in other works) cannot or should not be perceived in the cases. On the contrary, the reader is encouraged to probe, to examine, to analyze, and to dissect as far as his insights and skills will permit.

In sum, the purpose of this book is not unlike that of medical training. While there is no pretense of turning out "Doctors of Communication," there is the earnest hope that the reader, after acquiring some background from a given chapter, will proceed to develop a heightened sensitivity to the communicative processes of others and, perhaps, to his own. And it is genuinely hoped that he will begin to acquire or reinforce awarenesses and techniques for avoiding and coping with these patterns of miscommunication in "real life."

DISCUSSION QUESTIONS

1. What conclusions do you draw from the "World of Words" on page 4? How do they bear on *your* life?

2. ". . . it is not *just* change—but the *acceleration* of change which has so sorely tested our ability—and our willingness—to communicate with one another." (p. 5) How do you react to that statement? What do you anticipate for the future? Will the situation improve, worsen? Why? How?

3. Some people feel that Adler's assessment (pp. 5–6) is unnecessarily gloomy. What do you think?

4. In view of Chapter 1, "Introduction," and the Preface and the Foreword, what is this book about? What is it *not* about? What value might the book have for you?

5. What do you think of Lee's five-step procedure toward becoming a more competent practitioner of communication? Why might Step 5 be considered a "will-o'-the-wisp"?

6. "There is often a decided gap between one's intellectual *acquaintance* with a subject matter and his *internalization* of it." (p. 8) Do you agree? Why or why not?

7. What is the best way to get maximum value from the use of cases in this book?

8. "The souls of emperors and cobblers are cast in the same mold. . . . The same reason that makes us wrangle with a neighbor causes a war twixt princes."

—Michel de Montaigne

"We are in such great haste to construct an electric telegraph between Maine and Texas. But it may be that Maine and Texas have nothing to communicate."

—*Henry David Thoreau*

What possible bearing might these statements have on Chapter 1?

2

Organizational climate and communication

FOR BETTER OF WORSE society is becoming progressively organized. Fewer and fewer people are self-employed. Individual enterprisers—craftsmen, merchants, farmers, and professionals—are disappearing from the scene. Virtually everyone finds himself temporarily or permanently involved in organizations—schools, churches, hospitals, government agencies, business and military organizations—the list is almost endless.

But just what is an organization?

First, it consists of a *number* of people—anywhere from two on up.

Second, it involves *interdependence*. If you had 1,000 artisans each of whom designed his product, purchased his materials, manufactured, sold, and shipped the product, and so on, you would not have an organization—you would have 1,000 enterprises. Individuals are *interdependent* when the performance of one person affects and is affected by the performance of others—e.g., when one man designs the product, another purchases the materials, a third manufactures the product, and so forth.

Interdependence calls for *coordination*—activities to assure that the individual functions will be carried out in order that the objectives of the organization will be achieved.

And, coordination requires *communication*. *Genesis* describes how the building of the Tower of Babel was disrupted by the "confound-

11

ing of tongues." When men no longer had a common language, when they were unable to communicate, they could not work together.

TRENDS

Communication, then, is a *sine qua non* of the organization. Consider now what is happening in our organizations.

1. They are getting *larger*. The trend toward business through internal growth, merger, and acquisition is unmistakable. Three automobile firms dominate an industry in which there were once scores of manufacturers. The "Big Three" catalog chain stores— Sears, Penneys, and Montgomery Ward—handle about a third of all general merchandising sales—almost as much as all other conventional department stores combined.[1] Federal Trade Commission Chairman Paul Rand Dixon predicts that the top 20 grocery chains will increase their sales from a current 35 percent of the market to 80 percent by 1984 if present trends continue.[2]

2. They are becoming more *complex*. The simple line organization of authority and responsibility is often inadequate to cope with the growing complexities of many of today's organizations[3] in which an individual reports to one superior for one function, to another for another activity, and so on. Complicated? Yes, but necessary. For when the organization's objectives become more demanding, a more complex grouping of its skills and resources may be imperative.

3. A closely related trend is the increasing demand, due to international as well as domestic competition, for even *greater efficiency* and *quality* in the production of goods and the provision of services.

4. And society is beginning to impose other *requirements* upon its organizations. For one, there has been growing concern about mental health in our country. Some spokesmen feel that the structure and climate of today's organization are in many respects inimical to the mental health and emotional development of its

---

[1] "The Giants Put on More Muscle," *Business Week*, July 23, 1966, pp. 72, 73, and 74.

[2] Ibid., p. 72.

[3] For a lucid exposition on organizational overlays see J. M. Pfiffner and F. P. Sherwood, *Administrative Organization* (Englewood Cliffs, N.J.: Prentice-Hall, Inc., 1960), especially chapter 2.

members.[4] They call for a serious reappraisal of and, where advisable, significant changes in our organizations.

Moreover, the organization's members, particularly its younger members, are expecting more of their employers. They insist upon higher compensation, yes, but they also demand greater satisfaction *on the job* for their psychological needs. This widespread demand for a revised *organizational climate* will be discussed more fully later in this chapter.

In sum, when we consider the nature of an organization and the growing trends of largeness, complexity, demand for greater efficiency, and so on, one conclusion is eminently clear: Today's organization requires *communication performance* at an unprecedented level of excellence. And chief among the demands made upon our organizations is the increasing necessity for an *organizational climate* compatible with the psychic needs of the organization's members. We will now examine a managerial philosophy which is designed to establish and maintain such a climate.

SUPPORTIVE CLIMATE

"I know I'm supposed to 'know my people' but business is just *too* good. Pressure for output is tremendous, the labor market is drum tight, and turnover is high. I simply don't have *time* to know my people." The complaint is pervasive.

Even supervisors who have the time insist that people are more difficult to understand, more complex; their needs are less directly satisfiable by the boss. Moreover, their expectations of their employer are high and growing higher—in terms of psychic as well as material rewards.

In consequence of these changes a new, more subtle industrial revolution is in process and it is leading to a serious reexamination of the role of the manager and of the organization. After inspecting considerable experimental and empirical evidence Likert concludes:

---

[4] See, for example, Chris Argyris, *Personality and Organization* (New York: Harper & Bros., 1957) and *Interpersonal Competence and Organizational Effectiveness* (Homewood, Ill.: The Dorsey Press, 1962); Herbert A. Shepherd, "An Action Research Approach to Organization Development," *Management Record*, 1960; Charles R. Walker and Robert Guest, *Man on the Assembly Line* (Cambridge, Mass.: Harvard University Press, 1952); Charles R. Walker, Robert R. Guest, and Arthur Turner, *Foreman on the Assembly Line* (Cambridge, Mass.: Harvard University Press, 1956); and William F. Whyte, *Money and Motivation* (New York: Harper & Bros., 1955).

The leadership and other processes of the organization must be such as to ensure a maximum probability that in all interactions and all relationships with the organization each member will, in the light of his background, values, and expectations, view the experience as supportive and one which builds and maintains his sense of personal worth and importance.[5]

He added that "the superiors who have the most favorable and cooperative attitudes in their work groups display the following characteristics . . . as perceived by the subordinate":

. . . He is supportive, friendly, and helpful rather than hostile. He is kind but firm, never threatening, genuinely interested in the well-being of subordinates and endeavors to treat people in a sensitive, considerate way. He is just, if not generous. He endeavors to serve the best interests of his employees as well as of the company.

. . . He shows confidence in the integrity, ability, and motivations of subordinates rather than suspicion and distrust.

. . . His confidence in subordinates leads him to have high expectations as to their level of performance. With confidence that he will not be disappointed, he expects much, not little. (This again, is fundamentally a supportive rather than a critical or hostile relationship.) [6]

Trust and performance

The key to Likert's ideal appears to be *trust*. By and large high trust tends to stimulate high performance—so say the overwhelming majority of over 4,200 supervisors I have questioned in 29 organizations of varying kinds and sizes. These supervisors feel that a subordinate generally responds well to his superior's genuine confidence in him. He tries to justify his boss's good estimate of him. And, axiomatically, high performance will reinforce high trust for it is easy to trust and respect the man who meets or exceeds your expectations. (See Figure 2–1.)

"But how can I develop trust under today's pressures and complexities?" Too frequently the cycle is vicious rather than virtuous. Unable to "know his people," the supervisor is unwilling to trust them and fails to provide for a supportive relationship. More often than not the subordinate responds with minimal compliance and resentment. "If that's all he thinks of me I might as well give it to him—I

---

[5] Rensis Likert, *New Patterns in Management* (New York: McGraw-Hill Book Co., 1961), p. 103.

[6] Ibid., p. 101.

won't get credit for doing any more." Low performance, under these circumstances, reinforces low trust and the system is self-perpetuating. (See Figure 2–2.)

FIGURE 2–1	FIGURE 2–2
Constructive cycle	Destructive cycle

HIGH TRUST → HIGH PERFORMANCE

LOW TRUST → LOW PERFORMANCE

Trust and communication.   The trust-performance cycles suggest an interesting parallel—the mutual dependency of a trusting relationship and effective communication performance. When the organizational climate can be characterized as trusting and supportive, communication practice is generally good. There are a number of reasons for this.

First of all the members of such an organization, relatively speaking, have no ax to grind, nothing to be gained by miscommunicating deliberately. The aura of openness makes possible candid expressions of feelings and ideas. Even faulty communication does not lead immediately to retaliation, for others are not prone to presume malice on the offender's part, but instead "carry him"; compensate for his errors. Moreover, a lapse in communication is viewed not as an occasion for punishment but as an opportunity to learn from mistakes. Obviously, effective communication will do much to reinforce and enhance an existing trusting climate. But if communication performance begins to falter repeatedly the trusting relationship may be jeopardized. People begin to wonder if the slipups are inadvertences or did the other fellow have something in mind. When self-fulfilling prophecies of intrigue and suspicion emerge the organization may be in for trouble.

Conversely, when the climate is hostile and threatening communication tends to suffer—not only is there a tendency toward miscommunication with malice aforethought but in such an atmosphere true feelings are suppressed lest one be punished for revealing them. When an organization member slips no one "carries him"—on the contrary he may serve as a useful scapegoat for others who seek temporary relief from criticism of themselves. By and large one's communication (as well as his behavior in general) is dominated by the need to protect himself rather than the desire to serve the interests of the organization. Unfortunately, when the climate is unhealthy even letter-perfect communication practice can be inadequate, for if another *wishes* to misunderstand or to be misunderstood he can do so readily as will be demonstrated in the Patterns of Miscommunication chapters in this book.

Breaking the cycle

There are two general ways of breaking the destructive cycle and converting it to the constructive cycle of Figure 2–1. First if the subordinate can respond to a low-trusting superior with high performance, if he can resist resigning himself to his supervisor's low regard for him, he stands a chance of eventually winning the boss's respect. (See Figure 2–3.)

FIGURE 2–3
Breaking cycle on subordinate's initiative

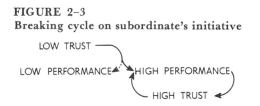

However, the ability to withstand a low-trust atmosphere for a prolonged period requires considerable strength and maturity on the subordinate's part which suggests that the response is possible but not probable.

Parenthetically, if the superior's low-trusting attitude is primarily a function of external conditions, such as temporary pressure for production, rather than of his own personality, say, a tendency toward paranoia, the prognosis is more favorable.

The other approach lies in the superior's ability to respond to low performance with high trust. (See Figure 2–4.)

This presents a paradox. How, indeed, can you trust one who has not demonstrated his trustworthiness? And *can* you "con" a low pro-

FIGURE 2–4
Breaking cycle on superior's initiative

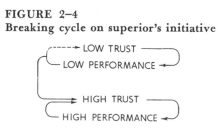

ducer into high performance by making him believe you regard him highly? Or will he conclude that he is being manipulated?

A RECONCILIATION

No one has reconciled this seeming contradiction more adroitly than the late Douglas McGregor.[7] Unfortunately, McGregor has not been uniformly interpreted so let me briefly review his conceptions as I understand them.

He contrasted two general modes of thought about how a manager should manage (people). "Theory X" was his notion of the traditional and still largely current philosophy of management. "Theory Y" was the emerging theory which promises to integrate the goals of the organization and its members. There has been some confusion about the theories mainly because some readers fail to discriminate between *theory* and *practice*.

Theory X

The *theory* of Theory X in essence holds that the so-called average man is *inherently* (and therefore unalterably) *immature*—that he is *innately* lazy, irresponsible, gullible, resistant to change, self-centered and thus indifferent to organizational needs, and so forth. The managerial *practice* in dealing with such persons is to apply external controls (harshly or paternalistically or firmly but fairly, etc.). External control is clearly appropriate for dealing with truly immature individuals. We "externally control" infants, for example, and without such "management" they would perish.

While conceding that men are quite capable of immature behavior McGregor argued that such behavior and attitudes are not manifestations of their inborn nature but the *product of their experiences*. Treat people as if they were children, he said—and thus chronically underestimate them, distrust them, refrain from delegating authority —and they respond as children.

Thus, in reacting to a myth (people are unchangeably immature) with external controls, managers have stimulated subordinates' behavior which in turn perpetuated the myth and seemingly justified their practice, for the more one controls the more he *has* to control

---

[7] Douglas McGregor, *The Human Side of Enterprise* (New York: McGraw-Hill Book Co., 1960).

—and, as goes the old Chinese expression, "he who rides a tiger can never dismount."

Hierarchy of needs

What, then, is the *nature* of the "average man"? Very much the same as any other man's—and McGregor draws on Abraham Maslow's "Hierarchy of Needs"[8] to support his case.

Maslow holds that we are all constituted in such a way that we *normally* seek satisfaction (and thus are motivated) through a *sequence* of needs:

Physiological Needs—the needs to eat, drink, rest, be protected from the elements, etc.—the "tissue needs."

Security and Safety Needs—respectively, the needs to be free of the *fear* of physiological deprivation and of the *fear* of physical danger.

Social Needs—the needs to belong, to be accepted, to be loved, etc.

Ego Needs—the needs to be respected, to be "somebody," to gain recognition, prestige, status, etc.

Self-fulfillment Needs—the need to realize one's fullest potential in whatever guise it may take—among the modes of self-fulfillment are religion, altruism, education, power, and artistic expression.

Two propositions pertain: The upper level needs (social, ego, self-fulfillment) *ordinarily* will have little or no motivating effect upon the individual until his lower level needs (physiological and safety-security) have been reasonably satisfied. This suggests there is little point in running off to developing nations to preach democracy and free enterprise (or any other abstraction) to people who are literally starving—they can't hear *at that level*. George Bernard Shaw noted: "I can't talk religion to a man with bodily hunger in his eyes."

Conversely, once the lower level ends are at least reasonably fulfilled they become inoperative on the premise that a satisfied need is no longer a motivator of behavior. The individual is thus open to motivation from the upper level needs—or in the words of Will Rogers, "It is easy to be a gentleman when you are well fed."

And the latter state of affairs is precisely what prevails today in the United States, asserted McGregor. For the first time in history the *masses* of a nation, excepting depressed minority groups, pockets of

---

[8] Abraham H. Maslow, *Motivation and Personality* (New York: Harper & Bros., 1954).

depression, and so on, have had their physiological and safety-security needs at least reasonably satisfied and are now susceptible to motivation from their higher level needs.

But American management, according to McGregor, could not thwart these upper level needs more if it tried. He felt managers were failing to understand the change that has occurred in people. Many managers still insist on attempting to motivate in the ways which

FIGURE 2–5
Utility of money for need satisfaction

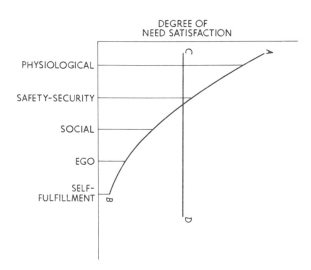

were quite effective when people were preoccupied with their physiological and safety-security needs.

The utility of money. Take the dollar, for example. Let it be clear, first of all, that neither McGregor nor any other behavior scientist has claimed that money is an unimportant motivator. Consider, however, that no one has a *need* for dollars as such—that money is a *tool,* a most versatile tool which can be *used* to satisfy needs. However, the utility of a given dollar amount to satisfy *diminishes* as one ascends the hierarchy of needs. (See Figure 2–5.)

A–B represents the degree of need satisfaction hypothetical Joe Bachelor[9] could obtain on $20 a day. *C–D* represents the minimal sat-

---

[9] Joe Married would be a more complex example.

isfaction level for each of his needs. If satisfaction falls below this line Joe is "hurting."

Twenty dollars might be more than enough to satisfy Joe's physiological needs—i.e., to have three square meals, a comfortable room, warm clothes, and so forth. If Joe is reasonably frugal and banks part of his $20 they can do a fair job of alleviating his acute security needs. How well his social needs are met is largely dependent on how much Joe needs to "belong" and upon the "dues" of the group from which he desires acceptance. If Joe insists on "buying" ego satisfaction—say, through the purchase of a new Cadillac every other year—he will probably find the price exorbitant and thus his $20 will leave him basically frustrated in this department. And as for self-fulfillment. . . .

Perhaps you felt that as Joe moved into the upper levels of the need hierarchy the notion of using money to "buy" satisfaction was singularly inappropriate. How can one *buy* genuine respect, for example? Which is precisely the point. Even with unlimited funds Joe will find it impossible to *buy* all of his satisfaction—the higher he goes in the need hierarchy the more he will have to *earn* his satisfactions and money becomes increasingly irrelevant.

Thus a management which relies largely or exclusively on monetary rewards to coax productivity from its employees is using an increasingly ineffectual means of motivation provided its people have their lower level needs basically satisfied.[10]

The Ford story.   There is a distinct irony in all of this. Consider the case of Henry Ford. Ford became eminently successful by implementing the concepts of the assembly line operation and interchangeable parts. Jobs became highly specialized portions of larger, more complex tasks. How did Henry entice a grown man to work for him, screwing in Bolt 14 all day long? Simple—if the man were living marginally, and many were—just pay him $5 a day (twice as much as the going rate) and he would be delighted to put in his purgatory time to gain a bit of financial breathing room. But workers were not the only ones who had to play restrictive, externally controlled roles. Managers, generally, were deprived of the freedom to manage—to exercise authority, to make decisions.

---

[10] The role of money in motivating performance is a very complex one for money is primarily symbolic. It means rather different things for different people. For good synopses of current thought about money as a motivator, see Chapter 5, "The Impact of Money: William F. Whyte," and Chapter 14, "The Money Motive," in Saul W. Gellerman, *Motivation and Productivity* (New York: American Management Association, Inc., 1963).

Ford has been characterized as the arch-authoritarian but no one can deny his success—two thirds of the automobile market by the early twenties. But he was to pay a price for his "one-man-showman-ship." The story of the near collapse of the company is a long and involved one[11] but the moral is clear. Men will submit to strict external control when there is no effective escape and when the controller has the power to satisfy their needs. In Ford's case dollars proved highly successful in motivating people when their predominant needs were at the lower end of the hierarchy. But as the base of wealth broadened, as the dollars came in, these needs began to be satisfied to the extent that they were no longer the individual's exclusive preoccupation. Ironically, the very success of the methods—external controls and good wages—eventually undermined their own utility as motivating agents as the needs to which they were eminently suited became fulfilled. The Ford story differs from industry in general only by degree. McGregor epitomized the situation:

Management by direction and control whether implemented with the hard, soft, or the firm but fair approach—fails under today's conditions to provide effective motivation of human effort toward organizational objectives. It fails because direction and control are useless methods of motivating people whose physiological and safety needs are reasonably satisfied and whose social, egoistic and self-fulfillment needs are predominant.[12]

Theory Y

Thus a new management theory was necessary—one based on more valid premises about human nature and motivation. Whereas Theory X held that the "average man" was unalterably immature, the *theory* of Theory Y is essentially that he is at least *potentially* mature.

The *motivation*, the *potential* for development, the *capacity* for assuming responsibility, the *readiness* to direct behavior toward organizational goals are present in people. . . .[13]

---

[11] See Peter Drucker, "The Ford Story," chap. 10 in *The Practice of Management* (New York: Harper & Bros., 1954).

[12] Douglas McGregor, "Adventures in Thought and Action," Proceedings of the Fifth Anniversary Convocation of the School of Industrial Management, Massachusetts Institute of Technology, Cambridge, Mass., April 9, 1957. Published by M.I.T., June 1957, p. 28.

[13] Ibid. Italics are mine.

The managerial *practice*, therefore, should be geared to the subordinate's *current level of maturity with the overall goal of helping him to develop, to require progressively less external control, and to gain more and more self-control.* And why would a man want this? Because under these conditions he achieves satisfaction *on the job* at the levels, primarily the ego and self-fulfillment levels, at which he is the most *motivatable.*

Thus Theory Y would lead to management practices which would work *with* rather than *against* the grain of human nature. The goal of management under Theory Y, then, is to "arrange organizational conditions and methods of operations so that people can achieve their own goals best by directing *their own* efforts toward organizational objectives."[14] See Figure 2–6 for a summary of Theory X and Theory Y.

Flexibility. Possibly the prime misunderstanding of Theory Y is that some equate it with the soft version of Theory X—a sort of sugarcoated or manipulative system.[15] Thus, some writers have advocated a "Theory Z"[16] which calls for the use of external controls with some people and various degrees of self-control with others.

Theory Z is quite unnecessary. Theory Y permits access to the full range of management approaches from external to self-control. *Where* on the spectrum to peg one's approach depends on his judgment of the subordinate's current state of development. For example, if he is new, inexperienced, rather close supervision and guidance may be necessary initially. But external control gradually decreases as the individual learns to make decisions and take action on his own. The two theories might be epitomized as follows:

THEORY X: John, I want you to be able to swim. However, you cannot swim. Therefore, do not go into the water until you can swim.

The illustration is absurd but not irrelevant. The net result is that John does not learn to swim, remains undeveloped and dependent

14 Ibid.

15 To suggest the prevalence of this interpretation of Theory Y, see: Joe D. Batten, "Bare Knuckle Management or Fist-in-Glove Management?" *Factory,* October 1965, pp. 104–5; Robert N. McMurry, "Are You the Kind of Boss People Want to Work for?" *Business Management,* August 1965, pp. 59–60; and D. G. Leeseberg, "Management's Dilemma—Theory 'X' -v- Theory 'Y,'" *The Chicago Purchaser,* August 1966, pp. 30–34.

16 J. M. Rosenfeld and M. J. Smith, "The Emergence of Management Theory Z," *Personnel Journal,* Part I (October 1965), and Part II (November 1965) and John E. Megley, "Management and the Behavioral Sciences: Theory Z," *Personnel Journal,* Vol. 49, No. 5 (May 1970), pp. 216–21.

FIGURE 2-6

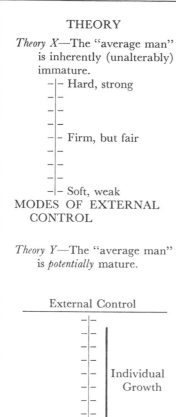

THEORY

Theory X—The "average man" is inherently (unalterably) immature.

—|— Hard, strong
—|—
—|—
—|—
—|— Firm, but fair
—|—
—|—
—|—
—|— Soft, weak

MODES OF EXTERNAL CONTROL

Theory Y—The "average man" is *potentially* mature.

External Control

Individual Growth

Self-Control
BALANCE OF EXTERNAL AND SELF–CONTROL

RESULTING PRACTICE

Therefore, it is necessary to control and motivate him *externally*. While the manager may have a *range of modes* by which to apply controls, he has no choice as to *whether* external control will be imposed. The *theory* of Theory X precludes anything other than external control.

However, external controls tend to perpetuate themselves for they keep men immature, emotionally undeveloped, unable to shoulder responsibility, etc.

Therefore, select the *appropriate balance* between external control and individual freedom commensurate with the individual's *current stage* of development. A new dimension is now open. It is no longer only a question of *how* to administer external control but of *how much* is desirable.

The overall objective is to build the constructive cycle (see Figure 2–1): Given skillful coaching and the opportunity to grow (less external control; more freedom to exercise his initiative, to make decisions, etc.), the individual will indeed be motivated to grow (because growth renders satisfactions particularly at the ego—and self-fulfillment need levels).

Thus by growing he will become more capable of responsible, more self-controlled behavior which serves the best interests of his organization as well as his own. In sum, the more growth—the more self-control; the more self-control —the more growth; etc.

upon his superior—which is what the superior may have had in mind at least unconsciously in the first place.

THEORY Y: John, I want you to be able to swim. However, you cannot swim. Therefore, I shall teach you and let you practice in three feet of water. If you show some prowess there you may try five feet, and so on.

The key to the art of managing under Theory Y is the ability to *trust appropriately*. *Chronic undertrusting* leads to apathy or resentment and the conditions which generally prevail under Theory X. *Overtrusting* can be equally destructive. To carry the swimming analogy further, the overtrusting manager throws John into 10 feet of water. Since John is *currently incapable* he begins to sink and the boss must rescue him. There tends to be two destructive consequences: (1) John's self-confidence has been destroyed or at least badly battered, (2) the boss's confidence in John may be destroyed and he may be sorely tempted to run back to rigorous external control—("you'll never get a chance to fail me again!")—with the ensuing pattern of John's nondevelopment, failing to recognize that it was his own faulty judgment which triggered the fiasco.

FREEDOM–ORDER "DICHOTOMY"

In perspective, some traditional management philosophers and managers seem to have been burdened with a myth—that freedom (of the individual to satisfy his needs) and order (coordination to achieve the organization's objectives) existed as polar opposites on a single continuum—that freedom would be attained only at the expense of order and vice versa. (See Figure 2–7.)

Business management has attempted to work out its role at various points along this continuum—hard, soft, firm but fair—(see Figure 2–6) but generally has gravitated toward the high order—low freedom end. The rationale appears to have been essentially as follows:

1. Free enterprise has been demonstrably effective in motivating high quality and quantity performance. . . .

FIGURE 2–7
The freedom-order "dichotomy"

FREEDOM   ORDER

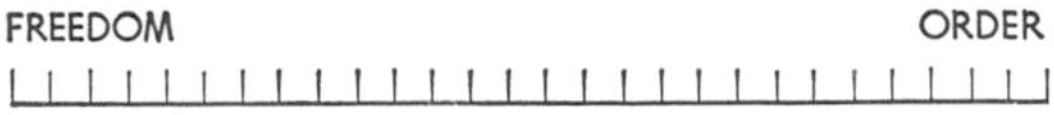

"No one works harder than the man who is in business for himself."

2. But economic and technological reasons require complex, interdependent, well-ordered organizations.

"You can't produce automobiles economically on a shoestring."

3. No. 1 and no. 2 appeared to be in conflict and no. 2 has usually prevailed.

"Let everyone work for himself when and in the manner he wishes—*chaos!*"

4. Thus the institution has generally striven for coordination often at the cost of passivity and antagonism on the part of its employees.

A true dilemma faces managers. On the one hand, we have the force for logic, order, and control, and on the other, the need for the freely responsive, the creative, and the impulse for change.

In industry, the most immediate necessity is for logical planning, doing, and controlling. Our ideas of organizational structure, job simplification and control systems require, and tend to develop, submissive, dependent performance. Sometimes active or passive revolt is generated. More often an appalling measure of unhealthy dullness is the result.

In addition, our sense of ethical and social concern is deeply distressed by the problem of the individual subordinated to the organization. I assume that it is *not* simple acquiescent, conforming, or apathetic performance we would like to see, but lively interest and sense of excellence.[17]

Mr. Richard's word choice is unfortunate for the situation is *not* a "true dilemma." (In fairness, the remainder of his article describes how he and his company have evaded the "dilemma's" horns.) It is becoming increasingly clear that freedom and order are not necessarily extremes on a single continuum but can exist as two distinct dimensions. (See Figure 2–8.)

Real-life counterparts for the four quadrants might be: (*A*) Dacca during the terrorism following the brief India-Pakistan war of 1971—low order and very little freedom in the sense that many citizens could not walk down the street without extreme danger. (*B*) The stereotypic Polynesian idyll where life is presumably sublime but little is

---

[17] James E. Richard, "A President's Experience with Democratic Management," *Occasional Paper Series,* No. 18 (Chicago: Industrial Relations Center, The University of Chicago, 1960.) Abstracted in *The Executive,* November 1960.

FIGURE 2-8

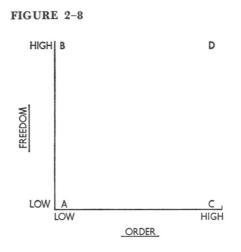

accomplished. (*C*) Stalin's Russia and Hitler's Germany. And (*D*)? There is increasing evidence that it or something approaching it in organizations is a possibility.

Integration of goals

(*D*) will be possible, according to Theory Y, when there is an alliance of individual and organizational goals. The prospect: the organization will encourage the individual to participate more fully in decision making, in determining the destiny of the organization—to provide him significantly more *freedom* to "be in business for himself"—i.e., to satisfy his needs but in such a way as to maintain the *order* necessary to achieve the goals of the organization. Thus he will simultaneously work at satisfying his own psychic needs and contribute maximally to his organization's objectives—in McGregor's words, a true "integration of goals."

But will it *work*? There is increasing evidence that it will. The most publicized Theory Y venture in industry has occurred in Non-Linear Systems, Inc., a medium-sized manufacturer of electronic instruments and test systems, located near San Diego, California.

The ensuing revolution at NLS took place at all levels but is most striking on the floor of the factory. First, Kay [owner and president] threw out time cards and put all production workers on salary—at 60¢ an hour higher than the prevailing wage in San Diego. Then he tore down the assembly line, which carried electronic equipment through wiring, soldering, testing, inspection, and packaging, and replaced it with 16 independent production units of six or seven workers each.

With an electronic technician as captain, members of each team are free to organize and work as they wish. They can decide to break the work down and specialize in different assembly operations, or they can decide that each man should take an entire product unit through every phase of the operation, including test and final checkout, himself.

First results were to boost morale—"sky high," . . . and disrupt production. It took three months to get output back up to the old assembly line level—but now Kay figures it's at least 30% higher.

There have been other tangible benefits. As skills increased, rejects dropped almost to nil. NLS eliminated the job of inspector. Customer complaints fell 70%. With 16 assembly teams instead of one production line, NLS gained flexibility. Where it used to take eight to 10 weeks to crank up for a new model, now it takes two or three.

Given their heads, some employees bore out the theorists—they expanded their work roles, showed unsuspected talents. Former hourly wage earners now are writing their own assembly instructions. All 16 initial team captains have moved up to more responsible positions.[18]

Vectors

To express the concept of goal integration somewhat differently permit me to oversimplify a business firm by dividing it into two groups—management and workers.

Figure 2–9 depicts a fairly typical relationship between the respective goals of management and workers and the resultant attainment of the goals of the organization to which both groups belong. *A–B* represents the organization's objectives (e.g., to maintain and enhance its wealth-generating capabilities). The "organization," for our purposes here, is an abstraction—neither management nor workers nor the two groups combined. The vector, *A–C,* is management's aim —largely compatible but not totally congruent with the organization's. Managers—first-line supervisors through board chairman—are after all individuals with needs and motives of their own. Vector *A–D*

---

[18] From "When Workers Manage Themselves," *Business Week,* March 20, 1965. Reprinted by permission. For further accounts of the Non-Linear experience see Arthur H. Kuriloff, "An Experiment in Management—Putting Theory Y to the Test," *Personnel,* November–December 1963 and Abraham H. Maslow, *Eupsychian Management: A Journal* (Homewood, Ill.: The Dorsey Press, Inc., 1965). For an example of how one larger firm (Union Carbide) has attempted to implement Theory Y see Aileen L. Kyle, "Employee Commitment to Company Goals," *Management Record,* September 1962, pp. 2–10.

FIGURE 2-9

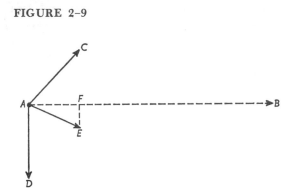

is the workers' goal—relatively self-centered and apathetic insofar as the organization's objectives are concerned. The resultant vector, *A–E*, represents their combined accomplishment and *A–F* represents the degree of the attainment of organizational objectives. The results are not inspiring but payrolls are met, creditors are paid, shareholders receive dividends, and earnings may be retained for future commitments. The situation could be significantly better or appallingly worse. (See Figure 2–10.)

The net organizational accomplishment *A–F* is nil or even negative. Note that both vectors have swung farther away from *A–B*. For

FIGURE 2-10

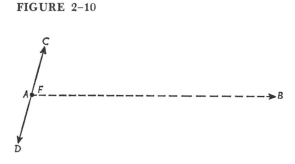

each group, in periods of emotionality such as a strike, are quite capable of disregarding the organization's welfare as well as their own in order to thwart the "enemy."

It seems to me that the prime promise of Theory Y is that its basic premises and resultant management practices will lead to an organizational climate in which the goals of both manager and worker (*A–C* and *A–D*, respectively) will be more closely aligned with those of the organization $(A–B)$. (See Figure 2–11.) Thus $A–F$, the degree of attainment of the organization's objectives, will be markedly greater.

FIGURE 2–11

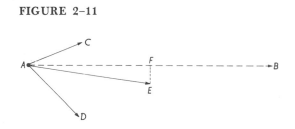

Through *participatory management* (the broader sharing of authority) workers will identify more closely with the firm for basically the same reason top management identifies with it now. The organizational setting will offer them more opportunity for satisfying their needs—especially those at the ego and self-fulfillment levels. And this, by and large, has been the open secret of motivating anyone at any time—offering him the opportunity to satisfy his needs. It is axiomatic, however, that when the needs change so should the means for satisfying them.

PROBLEMS OF IMPLEMENTATION

To be sure, there are some very substantial problems associated with the implementation of changes growing out of the Theory Y rationale. One is the evitable expense of transition. Recall that the participative management approach at Non-Linear Systems, Inc., exacted a toll. The initial consequences of their changes were to boost morale "sky-high"—and disrupt production! It took three months to return production to its former rate.

Another problem arises when behavioral changes are attempted in the middle and lower echelons of an organization without reinforcement from above. "How can I be a Theory Y manager when I report to a Theory X boss?" and "How can I delegate authority when the boss doesn't delegate it to me?" are plaintive cries of many managers participating in management seminars in which Theory Y is suggested.

This is probably only symptomatic of a more profound obstacle to the full implementation of Theory Y. Theory Y, in essence, calls for the fullest sharing of authority possible. Consider our current system of progression. Is it not, other factors being equal, the power-oriented individual who rises in our organizations? Participative management approaches, however, are asking such individuals to *relinquish* the very means of need satisfaction they strove so diligently to acquire. Maslow's hierarchy of needs suggests that a solution to this seeming dilemma lies in the prospect of the executive finding even greater need fulfillment in the *sharing* of power and the development of his own and subordinates' skills.

McGregor was not unmindful of such obstacles.

Only the management that has confidence in human capacities and is itself directed toward organizational objectives rather than toward the preservation of personal power can grasp the implications of this emerging theory. Such management will find and apply successfully other innovative ideas as we move slowly toward the full implementation of a theory like Y.[19]

Clearly Theory Y management, eupsychian management, enlightened management, or whatever one cares to call it, has exciting potential. But it also places markedly greater demand upon the manager's abilities to analyze and predict human behavior (his own included), to "know his people," and to communicate (encode and decode messages). The refining of these skills is this book's principal purpose.

We have considered the organization and the climate it generates. We will now turn to the individual and examine some of the perceptual and motivational aspects of his communication behavior.

DISCUSSION QUESTIONS

1. "For better or worse society is becoming progressively organized." (p. 11) How do you feel about this trend? What benefits and drawbacks are associated with this tendency? What special kinds of problems are arising in this regard and what can be done to cope with them?

2. "Some spokesmen feel that the structure and climate of today's organization are in many respects inimical to the mental health and emotional development of its members." (pp. 12–13) Do you agree, disagree with those "spokesmen"? More specifically, what might they be objecting to?

3. ". . . A new, more subtle industrial revolution is in process . . ." (p. 13) What was intended by that statement? What is contributing

---

[19] McGregor, "Adventures in Thought and Action," p. 29.

to this "revolution"? Is the "revolution" broader than just "industrial"?

4. Rensis Likert is quoted on page 14: "The leadership . . . and importance." How does this strike you as a managerial philosophy? Is it too idealistic? Will it work? Does it have sufficient regard for organizational needs? If you were employed in an organization which adhered as closely as possible to these ideals would you be effectively motivated to produce? If *you* were the boss how would this philosophy affect *your* people?

5. Re: the constructive and destructive cycles. Are they valid, i.e., do high trust and high performance *generally* tend to reinforce each other? Do low trust and low performance *generally* tend to reinforce each other? If high performance tends to follow high trust why don't managers simply start "high-trusting" their subordinates—even if they don't mean it?

6. What is the relationship between *trust* and *communication* in an organization?

7. "He who rides a tiger can never dismount." How does that statement relate to this chapter?

8. Maslow's *Hierarchy of Needs:* Does it explain and predict human behavior to your satisfaction?

9. According to McGregor most employees in the United States have had their physiological and safety-security needs at least reasonably satisfied. Do you agree? If so, what are the implications of this to managers and others who are concerned with the motivation of people?

10. "A management which relies largely or exclusively on monetary rewards . . . is using an increasingly ineffectual means of motivation provided its people have their lower level needs basically satisfied." (p. 20) Discuss. How does the "Ford Story" relate to the above statement?

11. In accord with Theory Y, managerial *practice* "should be geared to the subordinate's *current level of maturity with the overall goal of helping him to develop, to require progressively less external control, and to gain more and more self-control."* (p. 22) Is this realistic? Will it *work?* Does it have limitations?

12. Discuss the freedom-order "dichotomy." Under what conditions could these qualities coexist?

13. What are some of the problems associated with the *implementation* of changes called for by Theory Y?

14. What does this chapter on "organizational climate" have to do with *communication?* What special challenges confront the manager who attempts to implement Theory Y?

15. Write an essay on "organizational climate" discussing the relationship among the destructive and constructive cycles, Theories X and Y, external and internal control, the hierarchy of needs, the freedom-order "dichotomy," and the integration of goals.

CASES

Drexel Electronics Company[20]

The Drexel Electronics Company, a nationally known firm, specialized in the manufacture of communications equipment. One of its larger plants was located in a nearby suburb of a large West Coast city. Some 800 people were employed in this plant, engaged in the production and minor assembly of metal parts from sheet and bar stock. Finished parts were sent to another plant for final assembly. Local sales, public relations, and general office departments were maintained on the premises in addition to the personnel, time study, engineering, and maintenance departments. Ninety percent of the employees were engaged in the 10 production and materials handling departments.

One of the production departments, small parts, was supervised by Fred Schultz, assisted by two foremen. Some 40 men and women worked in small parts on the day shift. Another 35 on the night shift were supervised by the night foreman. Workers in this department were classified into 12 grades according to skill and seniority. The lower grades, 1 through 3, were composed mainly of younger workers who had little experience or technical skill. Their work consisted of deburring, straightening, and assembling small parts with simple hand tools. The middle grades, 4 through 6, consisted of skilled workers who did more complex work, while grades 7 through 12 were reserved for inspectors, setup men, assistant foremen, and foremen.

Although production in this department was on an individual or job-order basis, a weekly bonus determined by the total production of the department was added to the base wage for each job grade. This group bonus plan was employed wherever feasible throughout the plant.

In July, Jack Marcell, 18, a recent high school graduate, applied for employment at Drexel Electronics. The personnel manager told Jack that the prime factor in advancement was ability and that superior workers had been known to make grade 7, the lowest grade of inspector, after five years of service. Seniority, he said, played only a secondary role and was generally rewarded with pay increases rather than with advancement in rank.

Marcell was assigned to the small parts department. The day he reported for work, Schultz took him aside for a brief interview, confirmed the personnel manager's statements about advancement, and added that all women began in grade 1, while men started in grade 2. He explained that all new workers were hired on a trial, or probationary, basis.

The maximum probationary period was five months. If a worker had attained the department standards of quantity and quality of production before the end of this period, he was considered to be on a permanent basis with the firm. Otherwise, he was released. An exceptional producer could be promoted to grade 3 anytime after a minimum probationary period of five weeks. Grade 3 represented a raise in base pay and work of a more complex, less monotonous nature. Schultz said the company's probation policy was designed to give ample opportunity for the "late bloomer" to prove himself and yet permit the unusual worker to advance as rapidly as his ability and production warranted.

Each worker was required to turn in a "factor time summary" at the end of each working day. This sheet showed the job orders on which the employee had worked, actual hours worked on each job, the standard rate for each, the number of parts finished, and the standard hours produced. Jack soon learned that management expected the average worker on his job to produce 8 to 10 standard hours[21] per day, while a superior worker produced 10 to 12 standard hours per day.

---

21 A "standard hour" was a measure of production. For example, if the standard rate for a particular piecework job had been set at 100 pieces per hour, then a standard hour on that job would be 100 pieces. A worker who turned out 120 pieces would have produced 1.2 standard hours of work. The group bonus was computed at the end of the week. A worker who produced 50 standard hours for the week was paid his base hourly wage for the 40 hours. His standard hours over 8 per day (10 in

Most of the job rates seemed hard to "make" to Jack, but he learned quickly and was soon producing seven to eight standard hours per day. Within several weeks, he learned from other workers that there were certain "gravy" jobs" which came through the department quite often. These jobs carried unusually low standard rates in relation to the amount of hand finishing necessary to complete the part. Low rates were often caused by improved manufacturing procedures in one or more of the departments which processed the parts before they reached small parts, thus making certain small parts jobs easier, although the rates remained unchanged. On such jobs, it was possible to produce 18 or 20 standard hours per day. Furthermore, these hours could be "saved up" and turned in anytime during the week. If a worker had a "gravy job" on Monday, for example, he might turn out 20 standard hours of work. However, he would report only 12 hours and save the other 8 hours to spread over the remaining days of the week. Thus, it would be possible for him to report 12 hours for each of the five days of the week, even though he had produced only 10 standard hours on each of the other four days.

It became obvious to Jack that the "saving" technique was designed to conceal the "gravy jobs" from the time study department. It was clear that only the foremen and Fred Schultz were in a position to detect these jobs. The actual starting and stopping times on each job were not revealed by the timecards sent to the payroll department but only by the route sheets or individual and group productivity reports which were forwarded to the production department. But he never heard Schultz or any foreman mention the "soft touches" to anyone except their older workers.

FOREMAN: Joe [a senior employee], I got a light one coming up. Do you need it?

JOE: Well, no—I've had a few of them already this week, so I don't need it. Why don't you give it to Tom [a younger employee]? He's had some rough ones. He'll need the hours.

In order to "even up" for the week, it seemed to Jack that many "gravy jobs" were given workers who had handled a series of jobs with tighter rates. However, the distribution of the easier jobs was not entirely determined by worker need. Although all workers re-

---

this case) were "thrown into the pot" along with the excess hours of the other workers. The "pot" hours were divided equally each week among the workers, regardless of grade. Pay for these hours varied with the bonus rate for each worker's grade (approximately 80 percent of his base rate) .

ceived "gravy jobs" occasionally, those closest to the senior workers and foremen were assigned appreciably more than average. This group appeared to be favored over eight younger men who ate and took their breaks together, without much contact with Schultz, the foremen, and the other workers. One of the foremen expressed what he said was the general feeling toward the "out group." "They're our poorest workers. They're always complaining. The only thing they're looking for on this job is the almighty buck. They have the lowest output in the department, and if you turn your back for two minutes, they're off sneaking a smoke or goofing off in some other way. They're just punks and wise guys in my book."

Not all young workers were in the "out group." Jack Marcell found no difficulty in making friends with his co-workers and foremen. Before long, he was getting his share of "gravy jobs," which made it possible for him to turn in 12 standard hours per day much of the time.

At the end of the fifth week of Jack's employment at Drexel Electronics, Fred Schultz called the boy aside to tell him that he was pleased with his work and that he was being promoted to grade 3. As Jack expressed his gratitude, Schultz added, "You'd better keep this under your hat. There are two other men in the department who have been with the company four months but are still in grade 2."

Jack did not mention his promotion to his co-workers, but they soon noticed that Jack was doing more advanced work. Carson and Welles, young grade 2 men with more seniority than Jack, went to see Schultz in his office and complained bitterly.

Schultz drew a breath and said acidly, "You men knew the rules when you came in here. If you don't like it, you know where the door is."

East-Ohio Communications System[22]

The East-Ohio Communications System, an independent telephone company, served a portion of eastern Ohio. The company had

[22] All names and organizational designations have been disguised. Northwestern University cases are reports of concrete events and behavior, prepared for class discussion. They are not intended as examples of "good" or "bad" administrative practices. Copyright, 1955, by Northwestern University. Printed by permission.

seven districts. Each district served five or six towns or cities. A communications manager was in charge of each district. In each town, an office manager was responsible for the switchboard office. Under the office manager were assistant office managers (AOMs), who supervised switchboard operations. The office manager, AOMs, and switchboard operators were women.

In March, between quarters, Prof. Richard Cart of Northwestern University had the following conversation with Mr. Gregory Jergens, communications manager of the Garretsville, Ohio, district of the East-Ohio Communications System:

JERGENS: We have a problem in Newton Falls which may be of interest, Professor Cart.

CART: What sort of problem?

JERGENS: The service ratings have been very low. Perhaps I should explain what a service rating is. In our company, we have men who go to various towns and sample switchboard operations in order to determine how efficient the service is. Such items as slow answers and wrong numbers are recorded as errors. Slow answers are the chief fault in Newton Falls. An operator is supposed to answer a call within 10 seconds after the sending party picks up his receiver to place the call. If there is no response in 12 seconds, an error is charged against the office service rating.

The men who do the rating sample about 500 calls a month from various telephones within the office area. Then they give the district a rating, which is a percentage of error-free calls to total calls sampled.

A good rating is about 94. Newton Falls was just rated 84 and has been getting poor ratings periodically for more than a year now. As a result, there has been a great deal of pressure on Mrs. Swanson, the office manager at Newton Falls, and on her AOMs.

CART: They don't know what's wrong?

JERGENS: We've all been working on it. A few weeks ago, I sent my assistants, Steve Hieber and Ron De Kamp, to Newton Falls to interview the operators and to try to find out what the trouble is. Ron and Steve concluded that the operators are upset because AOMs plug into the boards and take calls. The operators complain of not being given a chance. They resent interference by AOMs on the switchboards.

CART: That's a tough situation for all of you.

JERGENS: I went to Newton Falls with Steve and Ron. We had a very unfortunate occurrence, however. While we were talking to Mrs. Swanson and some of the AOMs, Ron De Kamp noticed one AOM, Miss Johnson, taking a call at the switchboard. Without thinking, he blurted out, "See, that's what we mean. Look at Miss Johnson over there taking a call. There's the trouble."

Ron shouldn't have done this. It's not good human relations. You can't just tell a person he is wrong. You can't scold him. You have to talk to the employee and try to get him to realize his mistakes. It must come from him if there is going to be any kind of cooperation and desire to do good work.

CART: Did the incident have repercussions?

JERGEN: Yes, it did. Later, when I greeted Miss Johnson in the hall, she sort of mumbled under her breath. I asked her what was wrong. "Nothing," was the reply, and with that she walked away. Later in the afternoon, I noticed Miss Johnson sitting by herself in the conference room. I walked up to her and said I didn't want to pry, but if she would like to discuss her problem, I would be happy to listen. She said, "What good is it to try and do anything around here? You're only reprimanded for it later." Apparently, she hadn't overheard Ron's remark, but some-one told her about it later. She was very upset. As a matter of fact, Miss Johnson is rough on her employees. She reprimands them and often threatens them. I listened to her and then asked if she could see how wrong it was to reprimand someone instead of listening to their story. I explained that nothing was accomplished by reprimands except anger and hostility. This was an excellent opportunity to get a point across. I spoke to Ron about the incident later in the district office. He apologized and said he realized he had made a mistake.

CART: Do you feel the operators' complaints about AOMs taking calls get at the basic problem?

JERGENS: Partly, but I'm sure this isn't the whole story. The more I think about it, the more I'm convinced it's a human relations problem. Say, how would you like to go to Newton Falls with me tomorrow?

CART: I would like that very much.

The next day, Professor Cart accompanied Mr. Jergens to Newton Falls. After Cart had been introduced to Mrs. Swanson, the switch-board office manager, the following conversation took place:

JERGENS: Professor Cart and I were discussing the possibility that em-ployee attitudes or other human relations problems may be causing the low rating here, Mrs. Swanson.

SWANSON: I'm beginning to think so.

JERGENS: Would you care to give us an example, Mrs. Swanson?

SWANSON: Well, the attitudes of some of the operators could be caus-ing the trouble. I've been concerned about them. It's difficult to put your finger on any one thing.

JERGENS: Could you tell us an incident which would illustrate what you have in mind?

SWANSON: A few days ago, I was coming up the stairs to the switchboard room with two of the AOMs and the union president. At least five operators turned around from their work to see what was going on. We can't have this sort of thing. An operator cannot answer calls when she's looking at something else.

JERGENS: Don't you feel such a reaction is the normal thing for a person, Mrs. Swanson? Everyone is curious to see what's going on around him. A quick look wouldn't disturb anything too much, would it? Do you really feel it would prevent answering a call in 12 seconds?

SWANSON: They're not always quick glances, Mr. Jergens. By the time an operator turns around to see what's going on and then turns back to her board, she could miss 12 seconds.

JERGENS: It's possible. But do you really feel we can stop this? Curiosity is pretty normal, especially when people walk into a room. Don't you think so?

SWANSON: I guess so. But service can be interrupted.

CART: Do operators turn around and stare long enough to slow answering time?

SWANSON: It happens.

JERGENS: We shouldn't have that. But do you really feel we can stop a quick glance, Mrs. Swanson?

SWANSON: I don't know. But it's serious when four or five operators turn around at once.

JERGENS: Do you want to post notices on the bulletin board? I've seen some in other offices which say, "Are you a swivel head?"

SWANSON: That may have been useful a long time ago. But notices won't do any good now. And turning around isn't the only thing. There's a good deal of talking on the job.

JERGENS: Of course, we are not going to try and stop a greeting or comment when an operator comes on duty, are we?

SWANSON: Oh, no. I'm referring to excessive chatter which disturbs everyone.

JERGENS: We can't have that. And yet we don't want to merely tell them to keep quiet, do we?

SWANSON: No.

JERGENS: I think we should talk to each operator. We should listen to them in order to get their suggestions for overcoming the situation. The operators should feel they are taking part in the solution. Realization of the causes of the difficulty should come from them. With this realization will come a desire to improve. When employees are allowed to participate, they are thereby motivated with a desire to do a better job. A sense of importance and a sort of team spirit emerges. When one is able to see problems more clearly, you have set the stage for self-correction.

Group discussions would also be a good idea. When a group decides for itself, a team atmosphere is created. There is a group desire or motivation to correct the situation. They pull together to get at the bottom of the difficulty, see their mistakes, and establish means of overcoming them. The group creates a good deal of acceptance for the solution, since the solution comes from its members. We might hold short discussions of a few minutes' duration as each new shift comes on duty.

I did a similar thing in another district. Every month, I would visit each switchboard office with a chart showing a summary of service rating fluctuations. A few operators would gather around the chart, and I would ask what they thought we could do to improve our answering time. I think the discussions did a lot of good. Everyone had a desire to improve the situation, and the solutions to the problems came from them. The desire to improve must come from them. Would you like to try this, Mrs. Swanson?

SWANSON: Yes.

JERGENS: You feel individual and group discussions may help?

SWANSON: We can try. I'll talk to my AOMs. Something happened recently which I wanted to discuss with you, Mr. Jergens. Last Monday, one of the operators, Mrs. Frankel, asked Miss Manion (an AOM) if she could take a couple of hours off on Wednesday. She works the 12:30 to 6:30 P.M. shift. Miss Manion told Mrs. Frankel she could have the time if she switched shifts with another operator. She told Mrs. Frankel her board couldn't be left unattended for a couple of hours. Mrs. Frankel said she would get someone. But she also said she had to have the time off. On Tuesday, Mrs. Frankel had not yet arranged to switch shifts. At 12:30 on Wednesday, she called the AOM and said she wouldn't be in for a couple of hours. She had not gotten a replacement. Miss Manion told her not to bother to come in at all that afternoon, as a replacement was being put in her position. Mrs. Frankel said she was taking the time whether anyone liked it or not.

JERGENS: How's her attendance been?

SWANSON: Very poor.

JERGENS: What did she need the time for?

SWANSON: To go downtown with her son to buy a camera for him.

JERGENS: What do you want to do?

SWANSON: That's what I wanted to talk with you about.

JERGENS: Don't you feel she has been punished enough by being replaced on Wednesday? She lost the day's pay. Don't you want to talk to her?

SWANSON: Yes. I don't want to let the situation go by. I know why she didn't get a replacement. She would have had to switch with an operator on the 7:30 A.M. to 12:30 shift. Mrs. Frankel just didn't want to get up that early.

JERGENS: Well, do you think we might practice the listening technique here? I'm sure if you interview her and let her do the talking, she will realize she's wrong. Don't you think so, Mrs. Swanson?

SWANSON: I have to do something.

JERGENS: Would you rather reprimand her or warn her that we won't tolerate this sort of thing?

SWANSON: No, but I don't want to let it go by. Then they get the attitude they can do these things, because nothing happens anyway.

JERGENS: You're right. But we have to be understanding. If you listen to her, she will realize her mistake. And it will come from her. It must come from her if there is going to be a desire to do a better job. She may tell the other operators you talked to her. She will say you were kind and she realizes how wrong she was. Isn't this the best way, Mrs. Swanson?

SWANSON: Yes. But I also believe people are different, Mr. Jergens. I think we have to treat them differently.

JERGENS: That's right. But the desire to improve must come from them. You cannot accomplish this by telling them or by warning them, can you?

SWANSON: I guess not.

JERGENS: You will try to interview the operators and hold the discussion sessions with them, won't you, Mrs. Swanson?

SWANSON: Yes, but I'll speak to my AOMs about it first.

JERGENS: Fine, and I think everything should be discussed—supervision, talking on the job, and looking away from the board.

SWANSON: As far as supervision is concerned, you must realize we are all under a good deal of pressure because of our poor service ratings.

JERGENS: I agree with you, Mrs. Swanson. This is a difficult situation. (*Pause*) Well, if you will both excuse me, I have some important phone calls to make. Perhaps the two of you would like to discuss the problem further while I am gone.

(*Mr. Jergens left the room.*)

CART: This is quite a situation.

SWANSON: You know, Professor Cart, I like Mr. Jergens very much. He is a very fair and honorable man. But I can't say I agree with some of his ideas on handling employee problems.

CART: How's that?

SWANSON: Well, much of our trouble stems from an attitude among operators that it doesn't make much difference what one does, because no one will do anything about it anyway.

CART: They feel they can get away with things?

SWANSON: They feel management is sort of "wishy-washy." To the operators, management is nice but nothing more. So operators do what they please. I think we should be firm.

CART: You should let them know where they stand?

SWANSON: Management is a combination of fairness and firmness. Employees shouldn't be allowed to get away with questionable behavior. After all, the slow answering is affecting the whole office. When operators do things which cause slow answers, they should be told about it.

CART: The entire office could suffer from the poor service record. Operators should know that their questionable actions will not be tolerated.

SWANSON: That is exactly how I feel. The operators know when someone is called in because of something she did. But the way things are now, someone will ask her, "What happened?" The answer is, "Nothing. They were very nice, but nothing happened." In other words, management people are a bunch of suckers.

I think this is bad. Well, take Mrs. Frankel, for instance. She will be interviewed, and I will listen to her. But I can't let her leave my office before I am sure she realizes such behavior will not be tolerated in the future. Maybe she will realize her mistake by my listening to her, and maybe she won't. In either event, I have to be firm. Then when the other operators ask her what happened, she will tell them I meant business. There should be an attitude of: "Management means what it says, and it won't tolerate any fooling around."

CART: Employees should feel that you mean what you say.

SWANSON: Exactly. Our AOMs are wishy-washy and confused. They don't know how to handle the "problem child." Not one of them would tell an operator to turn around and to stop talking. AOMs know such tactics are not accepted by higher management. The AOMs talk to operators and ask how they feel about this or that. There is no firmness at all. So the operators continue to behave in the same manner.

Why, if I did something wrong and wasn't called on it, I would feel I could do the same thing again. What would there be to stop me? No one would do anything, anyway. Our operators feel this way. Firmness is not approved. I preach the "golden rule" to my AOMs, Professor Cart. But I think firmness is appreciated, too. An employee respects a superior who is firm. This makes a good leader. There is no confidence or respect for a confused, wishy-washy superior.

Employees know they can walk all over such a person. We shouldn't be nasty. But we can be firm and still be fair.

Listening is good in its place. An employee with a problem should be able to go to her superior for help. But people are different, and you cannot deal with them all in the same way.

CART: Listening and group discussion won't help the present situation?

SWANSON: Not when an operator knows she can get away with anything. I don't mind quick glances round, and I don't mind when operators greet one another. But I do mind when four or five operators turn

When Dalton wanted any change made, he simply requested that it be done. He often explained in some detail how it could be done expeditiously and effectively. As a rule, his action was taken with a minimum of discussion with the people immediately affected. Some executives felt the timing of changes was unpredictable.

For the past two years, the company's net profit had been below the industry's figures. During the 59 years of its existence, Atlas Publishing Company had consistently shown a profit, but the net profit percentage of both sales and investment had gradually decreased during the past decade. Several Atlas publications had doubled their advertising volumes in the last 10 years, but competitors had "stolen" large advertising accounts from others. Junior executives believed some of these publications had not kept up to date with developments in the interests, habits, and attitudes of their readers. In their judgment, competitors had recognized these changing trends and had revised their periodicals to meet readers' needs.

The record showed that Mr. Dalton was by no means opposed to change. He had personally initiated many modifications in editorial policy. Several staff people, however, told Arthur Dalton's son, Ben, that the reasons for these changes were not always clear to others in the business.

The consolidated balance sheet and P and L reports of Atlas Publishing were prepared monthly by the controller and distributed to the president, the business manager, and members of the board of directors. Arthur Dalton told his management group that he knew when the expenditure of money was justified and when it was not. Since he had a substantial personal investment in the business, he felt that "frills," as he called them, should be kept to a minimum. For example, advertisements occupied a large portion of the front covers of several Atlas publications, reducing the amount of space available for the title and contents of the publication. In the opinion of many in the trade, some of these ads were unsightly and gave a negative impression to readers. Most competitors had abandoned this practice long ago in favor of attractive four-color illustrations relevant to the contents of the issue. Their covers were designed to create a favorable "publication image," a term used frequently in the trade. It was Dalton's opinion that his competitors were wasting space and money on "window dressing," with loss of potential advertising revenue. Discussion and documentation by other executives had not succeeded in convincing Dalton that Atlas should give the prevalent trade practice a try.

around and stare at something or someone, and I do mind excessive talking about goodness knows what.

CART: It must be frustrating.

SWANSON: I'm plenty frustrated. I almost feel as if I will explode at times. I know we can do something about the situation. And yet, we are told to listen and not reprimand. So the situation continues to exist. This is nerve-racking.

(*Mr. Jergens returned to the room with his hat and coat.*)

JERGENS: Sorry to rush off, but I have to get back to the office.

(*Jergens and Cart said good-bye to Mrs. Swanson and departed.*)

"My case against Paul Brown"[23]
JIMMY BROWN AND MYRON COPE

In the summer of 1957, when I first arrived in the Cleveland Brown's training camp in the town of Hiram, Ohio, a burly man named Lenny Ford took me aside and gave me a few words of advice.

"Rookie," he said to me, "if you want to get along here, listen to what I'm telling you.

"First," he said, "when you're running through plays in practice, always run twenty yards downfield. Don't just run through the hole and then jog a few steps and flip the ball back. The man doesn't like that. Run hard for twenty yards, even if you feel silly.

"Second," Lenny Ford told me, "keep your mouth shut when he speaks to you. When he tells you how to run a play, run it the way he tells you. If you have an idea for improving the play, keep it to yourself. Suggestions make the man mad. If you're pretty sure you can make more ground by changing the play, change it in the *game*. Don't change it in practice. Run it your way in the game and hope it works, and if it does, don't say anything. Just make your yardage and act like it was a mistake."

Lenny was telling me to behave in a way that sounded kind of childish to me, but I wasn't about to mistake him for an idiot. He was a feared man in professional football. I kept listening.

[23] From *Off My Chest* by James N. Brown and Myron Cope. Copyright © 1964 by James N. Brown and Myron Cope. Reprinted by permission of Doubleday & Company, Inc.

"Also," he went on, "don't start any conversations with the man. Don't *initiate* anything. You see something wrong, let it go. He does all the talking here."

The man being described by Lenny Ford was, of course, Paul Brown, our head coach. Working for Paul Brown in the ensuing years, I became the highest-salaried player in the history of football and have continued upward. My salary this season is more than $50,000. And thanks in part to my football reputation, I've earned substantial money in business, in broadcasting and in the movies. So I suppose I should be able to say some nice things about Paul, and the truth is, I can. But I'm afraid I'll never rank as one of his leading admirers.

In 1962, I told Cleveland clubowner Art Modell that if Paul Brown remained as head coach in '63 I wanted out. Trade me, I told Modell, or I'll quit. I was not the only player to make such a threat. Nor did I relish taking a stand against Paul. I don't think it can be seriously questioned that among all of America's coaches this pale, tight-lipped little man was far and away the genius of modern postwar football. He was the Browns' first coach, and they were named for him. His teams thoroughly dominated the old All-America Conference, then won six straight divisional titles in the National Football League. An original thinker and painstaking organizer, Paul Brown made the Cleveland Browns one of the most astonishingly successful organizations in the history of commercial sports. Then, sadly, they declined. My six years under Paul were as much as I could stomach. . . .

Although I was billed as Paul's star performer, I had no relationship with him. I wanted to, but his aloofness put him beyond approach. Yet curiously, during my rookie season I thought Paul was a great guy. Far from being the grim man Lenny Ford warned me about, Paul dazzled me with compliments and solicitude. I led the league in rushing that year with 942 yards, and we won the Eastern Division title. I had every reason to expect that I would always be happy working for Paul. But I didn't realize at the time that Paul followed a pattern in his handling of men—a pattern in which, at an almost predictable moment, he would turn off his amiability as decisively as a plumber turns off the warm water with a twist of his wrench.

Given a rookie who had outstanding promise, Paul would flatter and cajole him. But after the rookie proved himself and got accli-

mated in his first season, he became little more than a spoke in the wheel. I became Paul's big brute, the man who would slug out yardage for him. It seemed to me that he thought of me as nothing more than a weapon. I felt he had no interest in me as an individual.

Fair enough, I did not hanker to be babied. Yet in the atmosphere that Paul created, his players inevitably became robots. You played hard, but you concerned yourself almost entirely with your own performance. "I've done *my* job," you told yourself. When a teammate scored a touchdown, you didn't go out of your way to hug him or pat him on the fanny. When the ball changed hands, you went to the bench and sat there in silence. You cared, but the action on the field moved you to no demonstration of emotion. You were as close to being a mechanical man as a football player can get.

And as the NFL developed a balance of power that made every game a tough one, it became obvious that robots no longer would do. The Browns lacked spirit. It is my honest opinion that in Paul Brown's last five years as coach—five years in which we were also-rans every season—every one of those five squads, given its fair share of breaks and a feeling of enthusiasm, could have won the championship. . . .

Atlas Publishing Co.[24]

All improvements and changes at Atlas Publishing Company had, for years, been initiated and directed by Mr. Arthur Dalton, the business manager. Atlas published a variety of monthly trade and general business periodicals. It was Dalton's practice to make most of the decisions personally on problems which arose during the day's work. Some of his associates said that they often suggested changes and improvements in the various magazines but, they felt, Dalton rarely listened. One of the department heads said, "Arthur believes, because of his experience in directing the business, that he knows what should be done, what shouldn't, and when."

---

[24] All names and organizational designations have been disguised. Northwestern University cases are reports of concrete events and behavior, prepared for class discussion. They are not intended as examples of "good" or "bad" administrative practices. Copyright, 1960, by Northwestern University. Printed by permission.

Mr. Dalton often said that he maintained an "open door" policy. His executives could come to see him on problems whenever necessary. He didn't have to agree with them, he said, but they could secure his opinion on any subject at any time.

When some of the younger, college-trained executives met at luncheon, they often discussed their feelings about Dalton's arbitrary behavior. It seemed to them that substantive changes in the magazines might be accomplished more effectively through long-range planning. When decisions were made on a day-to-day basis, many areas, they felt, received no attention, while others were treated almost as pet projects.

Arthur Dalton had often said, "When we have the money, we'll spend it on things that are necessary. When we haven't the money, even important projects will just have to wait." One of the executives, who had studied modern magazine-business methods, thought that some improvements could be considered capital items, to be depreciated over a period of years rather than charged wholly against current income. He held the opinion that, in some instances, it might be wise for the company to borrow money for improvements instead of postponing them indefinitely merely because working capital was needed for day-to-day operations.

Dalton's son, Ben, started work with Atlas Publishing upon graduation from Yale. On the eighth anniversary of his employment with the organization, Ben was named business manager, and his father became president. Arthur Dalton told Ben that, from then on, the operating responsibilities of the publishing company were his job. Arthur Dalton planned to concern himself primarily with broad matters of policy and community affairs.

Ben realized he had moved up swiftly through the organization. He was only superficially acquainted with many of the magazines' operating problems. He decided that he needed a firmer basis than his own experience on which to start to make major decisions. He told one of his friends that he intended to make use of the know-how of other, more seasoned executives.

Ben also recalled the opinions younger executives had expressed from time to time at luncheon meetings. He decided to encourage his staff to participate in decision making. He began to consult regularly with his associates and encouraged them in turn to consult with him. To give this idea more than lip service, he appointed a Management Committee, consisting of major heads of departments, including editorial, circulation, production, advertising, and sales promotion.

After several meetings, Ben proposed that the committee develop a long-range program for improving the business. He asked each committee member to submit projects which, in his judgment, should be initiated within the coming 12 months, plus other projects which he thought were desirable but could be deferred until the following year.

Within a month, the Management Committee agreed on a·consolidated list of projects which they felt were important enough to be given top priority. The estimated cost of these improvements for the next fiscal year was in excess of $500,000. The program included:

1.   Changing magazine formats to achieve a modern appearance
2.   Hiring additional writers and upgrading salary scales
3.   Maintaining a Washington sales office and editorial correspondent
4.   Using more pictures, which would require additional and more up-to-date photographic equipment
5.   Using four-color pictures, as well as selling four-color advertising
6.   Offering more merchandising services to back up advertising sales
7.   Conducting research on readership, magazine image, and buyer motivation
8.   Creating a new magazine to meet growing needs in a related industry

Ben was shocked by the report. He was sure that no more than $300,000 could be appropriated for the coming 12-month period and that it would be difficult to persuade his father and the board of directors to go along with even this amount. He did not believe he could or should decide personally which items should be deferred for another year or two. All the items had been marked by the Management Committee as "high priority." As he studied the list, Ben himself agreed all were important.

Ben finally decided against launching a new magazine at this time. This alone would require an outlay of $250,000 the first year. If this project were implemented now, other urgent improvements would necessarily be tabled.

Ben explained to the committee, "Perhaps we have set our sights too high." He asked them to review the list again to determine which items should be given top priority so that a final decision could be made at the next meeting, one week later.

The committee readily accepted this assignment to prune the original proposals. They agreed on a "special priority" list of projects totaling $200,000. The group also concluded that all of the work could not be included in the allocations for the next 12 months. However, if $100,000 were authorized for each of the next two years, most of the recommended action could be initiated. This plan met with unanimous approval. The business manager decided he was ready to discuss it with his father.

The following day, Ben presented to his father the $200,000 program of improvements for the next two years. Arthur Dalton exploded, "We simply can't afford it, Ben. Why is this necessary now? Some of these things may need attention, but we just can't tackle them with our working capital situation in the shape it is. What else have you been dreaming up, Ben?"

Ben explained that he was not alone in feeling that these improvements were necessary. He told his father about the Management Committee he had set up to work with him in planning the needs of the business. Mr. Dalton sputtered, "How long has this Management Committee been going on? Why take the valuable time of all these people? How long did it take the group to arrive at these recommendations? If you had come to me in the first place, we could have worked this out in less than an hour and at a much lower cost than $200,000."

Arthur Dalton studied the complete list more carefully. He concluded that it might be reasonable to spend $100,000 for several items which he agreed were urgently needed. He blue-penciled the remaining proposals as he said, "Some of the other directors may be more liberal, but I personally can't justify spending more than $100,-000 for improvements."

Ben went back to his office. He looked out the window and pondered the future effectiveness of his Management Committee and his own future with Atlas Publishing.

Mayhall House

Mayhall House is an independent men's dormitory on the campus of a large Midwestern university. The grade average of the dorm was one of the lowest of any house on campus. This was mainly because almost all of our 65 residents were majoring in either engineering or commerce—generally acknowledged as the most difficult schools in the university. And, of course, we had our share of "goof-offs"—five or six fellows who had ability but had never been able to apply themselves to their studies. We chalked them up as immature and hoped they would "see the light" before their academic probation ran out. But as long as they didn't disturb anyone we felt we could get along with them.

As a matter of fact, there was very little "horsing around" in the house. I[25] had visited a number of the other dorms and was surprised to see college men, or rather "boys," running up and down the halls yelling and chasing one another and playing silly pranks on one another. As I said, I had always considered our house remarkably calm and dignified—until this year. Now, you wouldn't know it. Everyone's calling it "Mayhem House."

The situation has become so out of hand that it's difficult to know how to describe it, but I'll try to start at the beginning.

When we started school in September, two important events (at least to me) occurred. I was elected president of Mayhall House, and a new counselor moved in. His name was John Morrison, 23, a graduate student in theology. John seemed to be very pleasant but made it clear in his first meeting with the residents of the house that he had heard our grade average was low and hoped we could raise it. He gave quite a pep talk and said if we would all pull together, we might put Mayhall near the top of the list.

I agreed with this, but I didn't see how there could be much improvement, in view of the fact that most of us were in the toughest schools.

The first evidence that John meant what he said occurred when he established his "closed-door policy." The fellows had the custom of leaving the doors of their rooms open and occasionally talking across the corridor to one another. If John happened to be passing by, he would simply close the doors without saying a word. I suppose he thought the fellows would take the hint, but they only got sore about the situation and started doing more "transcorridor communicating." It got to be quite a joke. John would start at one end of the corridor and close 10 sets of doors as he walked to the other end. Two minutes after John was gone, all the doors would be open, and the talking

---

[25] An undergraduate student with whose permission this case is published.

would start in again—only louder and more of it. On one occasion, a student yelled, "Go to hell, John!" after John had closed his door. John opened the door again and put the student on formal warning.

Next was the radio episode. About the middle of November, John posted a notice:

> In order to provide proper study conditions, no radios will be turned on after 7 P.M.; effective this date.

This seemed high-handed and unnecessary to me. Radios had never been a problem in the house before. A few students liked to study with some soft music in the background. But if anyone objected, they would turn their radios off.

The fellows seemed to accept this as a challenge. The same night the notice was posted, about seven or eight men turned on their radios to get them warmed up but not loud enough for anyone to hear.

Then one radio blared up full blast for a second and was quickly snapped off. John came bolting down the corridor to find the radio. When he got near the room, another radio blared up for a moment at the opposite end of the hall. John wheeled and streaked back. At this moment two other radios opened up, and John started twirling around in circles! It was the most ridiculous thing you ever saw, and the fellows couldn't help bursting out laughing.

John was furious. "All right, *children!* If you can't take proper care of your *toys,* someone will have to take care of them for you!"

He then started moving from one room to the next, confiscating the radios. It took him about two hours, but he picked up every radio in the house, put them in a storeroom, and locked the door. Maybe the seven or eight pranksters deserved this, but he took *all* the radios—mine included!

Well, that was the sign for open warfare. What happened then was one continuous nightmare. The next night, somebody brought some firecrackers into the house, and the mayhem started! Someone tied a firecracker to a burning cigarette and laid it in front of John's door. A few minutes later, the cigarette burned down and ignited the firecracker, John threw open his door, and not a soul was to be seen. He was fit to be tied. That was a night to be remembered! All night long, about every 10 minutes, a firecracker went off somewhere—outside the dorm, in the corridor, in somebody's room, or outside John's door! John didn't even come out.

The next day it snowed, and that night it was snowballs. I won't go into the gory details, but the end result was the damage of various property, including five broken windows!

This, of course, brought in the dean of men. I was surprised that he hadn't come in before. I guess John never mentioned our situation to him. The rest is history. John has been transferred to another house, and we are on social probation for the rest of the semester.

Part two

The behavioral basis of communication

3

Perception and communication

"This is nothing. When I was your age the snow was so deep it came up to my chin!"

Reprinted from Redbook *with the permission of cartoonist, Gerry Marcus.*

DAD IS RIGHT, of course—*as he sees it*. And in this seemingly innocuous self-deception lies one of the most interesting and perhaps awesome aspects of human experience: *We never really come into direct contact with reality*. Everything we experience is a manufacture of our nervous system.

While there is never a perfect match between reality and one's perception of it, the *range of disparity* between reality and perception is considerable. When an engineer is measuring, testing, and the like, usually with the aid of precise gauges and instruments, his perceptions may be an extremely close approximation of reality. This is basically why bridges, tunnels, and skyscrapers not only get built but generally stay built.

But when the engineer, or anyone else, is relating to and communicating with other human beings,—when he is operating in a world of feelings, attitudes, values, aspirations, ideals, and emotions—he is playing in a very different league and the match between reality and perceptions may be far from exact.

Just what is going on and just what is this concept "perception" we have been alluding to so casually? "Perception" is a term we perhaps shouldn't be using at all. There seems to be very little agreement as to what it entails. It evidently is a complex, dynamic, interrelated composite of processes which are incompletely and variously understood. Allport, for example, describes some 13 *different* schools of thought on the nature of perception, listing, among others, core-context theory, gestalt theory, topological field theory, cell-assembly, and sensory-tonic field theory.[1] In the face of such irresolution I will be so bold as to define perception in unsophisticated language as the process of *making sense out of experience—of imputing meaning to experience.*[2]

Obviously what kind of "sense" one makes of a situation will have great bearing on how he responds to that situation so let us examine the phenomenon more closely.

A MODEL OF PERCEPTION

March and Simon suggest a model (see Figure 3–1) which seems well supported by research. First of all, they regard man as a complex, information-processing system—"a choosing, decision-making, problem-solving organism that can do only one or a few things at a time,

---

[1] F. H. Allport, *Theories of Perception and the Concept of Structure* (New York: John Wiley & Sons, Inc., 1955).

[2] Perception has been defined as "the more complex process [as distinguished from sensation] by which people select, organize, and interpret sensory stimulation into a meaningful and coherent picture of the world." B. Berelson and G. A. Steiner, *Human Behavior: An Inventory of Scientific Findings* (New York: Harcourt, Brace & World, Inc., 1964), p. 88.

and that can attend to only a small part of the information in its memory and presented by the environment."[3]

They argue that one's behavior, through a short interval of time, is determined by the interaction between his *internal state*[4] (which is largely a product of one's previous *learning*) at the beginning of the interval and his *environment*.

FIGURE 3–1

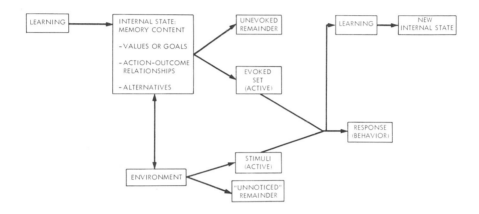

When the interval is very short only a small part of one's internal state and a small part of his environment will be active, i.e., will significantly influence his behavior during the interval. In information theory terms, the eye can handle about 5 million bits per second, but the resolving power of the brain is approximately 500 bits per second. *Selection* is inevitable. How, then, are these active parts determined? As stated above, they are selected through the interaction of one's internal state and his environment at the beginning of the time inter-

---

[3] J. G. March and H. A. Simon, *Organizations* (New York: John Wiley & Sons, Inc., 1958) , p. 11.

[4] His internal state is mostly contained in his memory which "includes [but is not limited to] all sorts of partial and modified records of past experiences and programs for responding to environmental stimuli." Thus, the memory consists, in part, of:

a) Values or goals: criteria that are applied to determine which courses of action are preferred among those considered.

b) Relations between actions and their outcome: beliefs, perceptions, and expectations as to the consequences that will follow from one course of action or another. . . .

c) Alternatives: possible courses of action.

Ibid., pp. 10–11.

val. The active part of the internal state is called the *set*[5] which is evoked by the environment leaving the *unrevoked remainder* which plays no significant role in affecting the behavior at that time. Similarly, the active part of the environment is selected by the internal state and is called the *stimuli;* the residue is the "unnoticed" remainder. Munn gives a relevant illustration:

> I once had a colony of white rats in the attic of the psychology building. One afternoon I found several rats outside of their cages. Some were dead and partly eaten. It occurred to me that, however the rats had escaped, they must have been eaten by wild rats. I went downstairs to get some water and was climbing the stairs again when I saw before me, and directly in front of the cages, a large wild gray rat. It was standing tense and trembling, apparently having heard me ascend the stairs. Very slowly I raised a glass jar that was in my right hand, and aimed it at the rat. Much to my surprise, the animal failed to move. Upon approaching the object, I discovered it to be a piece of crumpled-up-grayish paper. Without the set induced by my suspicion that gray rats were in the attic, I should undoubtedly have seen the paper for what it was, assuming that I noticed it at all.[6]

Let us examine Munn's behavior, asserting a chain of *sets* and *stimuli.* To start at an arbitrary point, he was *set* to notice the white rats among other reasons because they were presumably why he went to the attic in the first place. Thus, the partly eaten white rats readily became *stimuli* which in turn triggered still another *set*—the expectation of wild gray rats. Any part of his environment which bore a reasonable resemblance to a wild gray rat thus became a candidate for becoming his new *stimuli.* The crumpled paper qualified. It was not only selected as a *stimulus* (supposedly it had been part of the "unnoticed remainder" of the environment on his first trip to the attic) but was interpreted as a wild gray rat.

The result of the interplay of environment and internal state is one's *response* (behavior) and his *internal state* at the beginning of the next time interval. This new internal state can be considered as modified by the *learning* derived from the experience of the previous interval.

Just what is active or passive in one's internal state and environ-

---

[5] *Set* is generally regarded as the readiness of the organism to respond in a particular way.

[6] Norman L. Munn, *Psychology: The Fundamentals of Human Adjustment* (Boston: Houghton Mifflin Co., 1947), p. 327. Reprinted by permission.

ment is a function of time, among other factors. For a very short period, there will be very few active elements in set and stimuli. For a longer period, a larger portion of the memory content will likely be evoked and a large number of environmental events will influence behavior at some time during the interval. Thus, phrases such as "definition of the situation" and "frame of reference" are more appropriate than "set" in discussing longer time periods.

If one's response is a function of interrelated variables it follows that a variation in any or all of them would normally affect the response. Therefore we shall examine some of these variables in greater detail.

Differing environments

Hold up a die between us. If you see three dots I will see four. As obvious as it should be, the phenomenon of differing environments, which would preclude our receiving the same stimuli, seems to contribute to a great deal of unnecessary and destructive conflict.

I have had the rewarding experience of serving for several years as a consultant to the Federal Mediation and Conciliation Service. Any number of the commissioners, men who are constantly concerned with union-management controversies, have asserted to me that a significant portion of the lack of communication, understanding, and harmony between the two parties stems from the simple fact that neither side is given full and direct access to the private environment— including the pressures, complexities, and restrictions—of the other. Thus, from the very outset of the negotiation the parties are exposed to substantially different environments and therefore are, in many respects, responding to different stimuli.

Differing stimuli

Presume a mutual environment and there is still no guarantee that your responses and mine will be influenced by the same stimuli. Our respective evoked sets will have a considerable bearing on which parts of the environment will significantly impinge upon us as stimuli. Munn's story of the rat is a case in point.

Differing sensory receptors

Another reason why parts of the environment either never become stimuli or are experienced differently is that our sensory "equipment" varies. It has long been recognized that individuals differ markedly in sensory thresholds and acuity. While there has been gratifying progress in the prevention, correction, and amelioration of sensory limitations there is still much to be learned.

An interesting demonstration of differing sensory "equipment" is to give a bit of paper to each person in a group and request each to determine the taste of the paper. The group does not know it but the paper is impregnated with phenylthiocarbamide (PTC). If the group is representative, a significant portion will experience a distinctly bitter sensation. But some will taste it as sweet, others as sour, and still others as salty. And about half will find it utterly tasteless!

PTC, a chemical used by geneticists to trace heredity traits, reveals dramatically that we simply do not all inherit identical sensory "apparatus." Add to this variations of the nervous system due to disease and injury and it is clear that our senses are inclined to be neither infallible nor uniform. I have a personal example to contribute in this regard. I have had a few mild disputes with my wife who "alleged" a shrill whistle in the television set. Since I did not hear it I denied that it existed. Somewhat later I had an audiometric examination and discovered that, like many others who were exposed to artillery noise during the war, I had lost the capacity to hear tones of extremely high pitch.

Differing internal states

One's *internal state* is the product of his *learning processes* and it is obvious that the "lessons" acquired by one person can differ markedly from those of another. Imagine a number of individuals observing a man drinking liquor. If the observers are candid and sufficiently representative we can expect a gamut of reactions. Some will regard the man as sinful; others as extravagant. Others will associate his drinking with friendliness and congeniality. Some will view it as a character flaw—a way of avoiding unpleasantness, running from problems. Still others may perceive it as a relaxant. And people in the distilling industry—and the Alcohol and Tobacco Tax Division of the Internal Revenue Service—may relate it to a job!

For a more dramatic example of the role of learning compare cultures. One's culture is an extraordinarily effective teacher. First, it teaches us unrelentingly—every waking moment. Second, it is a most subtle, even insidious teacher—which detracts not at all from its effectiveness. Immersed in it constantly, we are seldom conscious of what it has been teaching us until we contrast its lessons with those taught by other cultures. The perceptive traveler, for example, as he visits foreign countries learns a good deal about *himself* and the special lessons his culture has taught him.

For example, anthropologists tell us that we learn from our respective cultures how to perceive a misbehaving child. This is revealed by how we speak to the child. English-speaking people generally consider misbehavior as "bad" or "naughty," a suggestion of immorality, and admonish the child with "Johnny, be *good!*" Italian- and Greek-speaking people say the equivalent. The French, however, tend to say "Jean, sois sage!"—be *wise*. Their culture teaches that the child who misbehaves is being stupid, foolish, imprudent, injudicious. The Scandanavians have another concept expressed by the Swedish, "Jan, var snell!" and the Norwegian, "Jan, ble snil!"—be *friendly*, be *kind*. Germans have learned still differently. With them it is "Hans, sei artig!"—*get back in step*. *Sei artig* is literally "be of your own kind"—in other words, "conform to your role as a child."[7]

Clearly, individuals from these various cultures could observe the same child misbehaving but regard him very differently because they had been *trained* to do so. Grant that different people learn different "lessons" from life and it is readily apparent that individualized learning plays a subtle but critical role in one's communication with others.

Differing evoked sets

One's set, according to the model, is dependent upon three other variables: that which is available in the internal state, the stimuli which trigger the set, and, though less directly, the processes of learning. March and Simon clarify the role of learning in this regard:

When one of these elements (values or goals, action-outcome relationships and alternatives) is evoked by a stimulus, it may also bring into the evoked set a number of other elements with which it has become associated through the learning processes. Thus, if a particular goal has been achieved on previous occasions by execution of a particular course of

---

[7] L. Sinclair (ed.), "A Word in Your Ear," *Ways of Mankind* (Boston: Beacon Press, 1954), pp. 28–29. For a fascinating account of cultural differences interfering with interpersonal communication see E. T. Hall, *The Silent Language* (Garden City, N.Y.: Doubleday & Co., Inc., 1959).

action, then evocation of that goal will be likely to evoke that course of action again. Habitual responses are extreme instances of this in which the connecting links between stimulus and response may be suppressed from consciousness. In the same way, the evocation of a course of action will lead by association to evocation of consequences that have been associated with the action.[8]

This helps to account for the apparent self-perpetuating nature of sets which others have observed.

Our concept of causal texture implies that definitions and relations, once they have been adopted, influence interpretations of subsequent events. Early definitions of the conditions under which a task will be accomplished are apt to take precedence over later definitions.[9]

. . . the tendency to distort messages in the direction of identity with previous inputs is probably the most pervasive of the systematic biases.[10]

Sebald confirmed a hypothesis "that largely only those meanings are being perceived and recalled which reinforce prior images."[11] He also suggested "that selective distortion takes place in order to screen out dissonant features—features which are apt to disturb pre-conceived images."[12]

The concept of differing sets helps to explain the abyss which so frequently separates superiors and subordinates. A man looking downward in an organization may often have a very different set from the man below him looking up. For example, Likert reports that 85 percent of a sampling of foremen estimated that their men "felt very free to discuss important things about the job with my superior." However, only 51 percent of their men shared this view.[13] Seventy-three percent of the foremen felt they "always or almost always get subordinates' ideas" on the solution of job problems. Only 16 percent of their subordinates agreed with this appraisal.[14] Ninety-five percent

---

[8] March and Simon, *Organizations,* p. 11.

[9] H. B. Pepinsky, K. E. Weick, and J. W. Riner, *Primer for Productivity* (Columbus, Ohio: The Ohio State University Research Foundation, March 1964), p. 54.

[10] D. T. Campbell, "Systematic Error on the Part of Human Links in Communication Systems," *Information and Control,* Vol. 1 (1958), p. 346.

[11] H. Sebald, "Limitations of Communication: Mechanisms of Image Maintenance in Form of Selective Perception, Selective Memory and Selective Distortion," *Journal of Communication,* Vol. 12, No. 3 (September 1962), p. 149.

[12] Ibid.

[13] Rensis Likert, *New Patterns in Management* (New York: McGraw-Hill Book Co., 1961), p. 47.

[14] Ibid., p. 53.

of the foremen said they understood their men's problems well but only 34 percent of the men felt that they did.[15]

The gulf between superiors' and subordinates' sets is documented further by Maier[16] who reports a study of 35 pairs from four large firms. A pair consisted of a manager, third echelon from the top, and one of his immediate subordinates. Each partner in each pair was questioned regarding the subordinate's job. On only one aspect was there substantial agreement—the content of the subordinate's duties. However, there was little agreement on the order of importance of these duties. There was only fair agreement on the job's requirements and almost complete disagreement on their priority ranking. Finally, there was virtually no agreement on the problems and obstacles of the subordinate. These findings were discussed with all participants. Several months later a questionnaire was sent to each participant asking if the superior and his respective subordinate had gotten together to discuss their differences. Only 22 pairs replied. Six of them agreed that they had gotten together; nine agreed that they had not; and seven pairs could not agree on whether they had or had not gotten together![17]

In summation

The perception model suggests why it is impossible for one to be in simple, direct contact with reality, why he lives in a personalized world and why, in the words of St. Paul, "We see through a glass darkly." Indeed, there are a number of interrelated variables (differing environments, stimuli, sensory receptors, internal states, and evoked sets) which intervene between perception and reality. Thus, individuals are led to respond differently to events and, in general, complicate the process of communication enormously—particularly *if the role of such factors is ignored or misunderstood.*

. . . the prime obstacle of every form of communications . . . is simply the fact of *difference.* On this point most serious students of communication are in agreement, the great gap is the gap in background, ex-

---

[15] Ibid., p. 52.

[16] N. R. F. Maier, "Breakdown in Boss-Subordinate Communication," *Communication in Organizations* (Ann Arbor, Mich.: The Foundation for Research on Human Behavior, 1959).

[17] The reader may wish to test the influence of sets upon him by viewing the perceptual (*not optical*) illusions on pages 81–84.

perience, and motivations between ourselves and those with whom we would communicate.

It is a gap that will remain. . . . But if we cannot close the gap, we must at least acknowledge it. For this *acknowledgment of difference* is the vital preface to all the efforts that follow. . . .[18]

DEFENSIVENESS

The "acknowledgment of difference"—a simple phrase but how difficult to practice! Perhaps the most appropriate adjective to describe much of the behavior of people communicating and relating to one another in organizational settings would be *defensive*. A fundamental reason for defensive behavior appears to be the inability of so many people to *acknowledge differences*—differences between their perceptions and reality and differences between their perceptions and those of others. Their prevailing, albeit largely unconscious, presumption is that "the world is as I see it." He who harbors this notion will find life continuously threatening for there are many others who share his notion—but not *his "world!"* Such people find it perpetually necessary to protect their "worlds" and to deny or attack the other fellow's.

Admittedly, the premise that one deals only indirectly and often unreliably with reality can be disturbing. To those who crave a certain, definite, and dependable world (and that includes all of us in varying degrees) the admission that we respond only to *what it appears to be* rather than *what it is* necessarily lessens our *predictability* about the "real world." Even those who *intellectually accept* the perception model and the roles that stimuli, set, learning, and so on, play in determining responses may have difficulty converting the concept into performance. A good test of the extent to which one has truly internalized such awareness occurs when he becomes emotionally involved with others.

For instance, suppose you and I work in the same organization and we observe Joe, one of our colleagues, taking home company supplies —such as paper pads, paper clips, and pencils—not in large quantities but it is obvious to us that he will not use them exclusively for official purposes. He will let the children have them, use them for his private affairs, and so on.

Now, let us say that you are the product of a rigorous, religious up-

---

[18] "Is Anybody Listening?" *Fortune,* September 1950, p. 83. The italics are mine.

bringing. It is likely that you will be *set* to regard Joe as dishonest. But suppose that I have none of your training and that the only part of my background that is particularly relevant was the three years I spent in the Army in World War II. There I learned a code that was unwritten but very pervasive. It was in effect, "You may rob the Army blind!—but you must not steal a nickel from another serviceman." I would be quite inclined to regard Joe as honest and could readily consider his acquisitions as normal perquisites.

Let us examine the *communication* issue. (Permit me to disregard the moral issue without denying that there is one.) Consider the tremendous difficulty you and I would have in discussing Joe if in our increasingly vehement statements—"Joe's dishonest!" "No, he's not!" —we failed to realize that neither of us was talking about *Joe*. We were talking about *you* and *me* and our *respective* "inside-the-skin" experiences. Our respective worlds were different from the outset and there was no reason to expect them to be identical—and no *rational* reason to have to protect them. Why, then, did we protect them so ardently?

Let us begin with an assertion: Most reasonably mature people can tolerate fairly well differences in value judgments, opinions, attitudes, points of view—so *long as they can recognize them as such.* If I can realize that your "reality" is not the same as mine then your statement about *your* "reality" is no threat to *mine*.

But no one can tolerate differences on matters of objectivity—matters which submit to corrorable measurement and are capable of general agreement. To illustrate, suppose you and I have a mutual superior and he comes to us and says: "This may sound silly but I'm serious. I want you two to estimate the length of that 2 $\times$ 4 over there (about 20 feet away) on the ground. You have to estimate because you can't use any kind of measuring device and you can't get any closer to it than you are now. Now, I want a good estimate and only one between you—so get to it!"

(Now suppose the piece of lumber is actually 7 feet long but neither of us knows this.) So we start sizing up the situation and you say, "Looks about 6½ or 7 feet." And I say, "No, no—you're way short— that's a lot closer to 14 feet!" Unless you had admirable constraint you would probably blurt out, "You're crazy!"

Now, why were you moved to feel I was crazy?

Was it not partly because my statement was at least a slight threat to your sense of reality and, therefore, your sanity? In other words if

(I said *if*) I were indeed right—i.e., if the board actually were 14 feet and everything were twice as big as you perceive it—would you not begin to have serious misgivings about *your* "contact with reality"? "You're crazy!", then, is your understandable if impulsive way of defending yourself against an attack on your sanity.

Actually, we would be unlikely to have such a disparity (unless one or both of us *were* losing touch with reality) because our perceptual lessons, when we initially learned to perceive the inch, the foot, and the yard, were likely to have been very similar regardless of where or when we learned them. And even if we were to disagree on matters such as distance, speed, and weight we could resolve our differences by using standardized measuring devices.

But when we encounter Cezanne and Dali, Tolstoi and Faulkner, Mozart and Cole Porter, we are unlikely to have had identical learning experiences and where is the "standardized measuring device"? Will someone resolve a controversy with "Why, that Van Gogh is 87 percent beautiful!"? Even professional critics are unable to provide universally acceptable and applicable criteria.

The point is that not only can we not tolerate differences in matters of objectivity (but what differences there may be are generally minor or resolvable by objective measurement) but we cannot accept differences on matters of subjectivity (value judgments, opinions, and so on) if we unconsciously *treat them* as matters of objectivity. There are many important aspects of our lives such as art, music, architecture, religion, politics, morals, fashions, food, economic and political theory, which (1) are not taught to us in standardized lessons and (2) are not, by and large, measurable by standardized scales or gauges. It is in such areas that we find it easiest to threaten one another. And when one is threatened he tends, if he does not run, to fight back—the threatener is now threatened and bootless conflict generally follows.

Defensiveness appears to be so pervasive and potentially so destructive to organizational communication and interpersonal relationships that we shall examine it in more detail in terms of the communicator's *frame of reference*.

Frame of reference

Frame of reference is the term March and Simon used for longer intervals of time in lieu of "set." It has been defined as:

A system of standards or values, usually merely implicit, underlying and to some extent controlling an action, or the expression of any attitude, belief, or idea.[19]

Carl Rogers offers several propositions[20] which serve as a rationale for the validity and utility of the frame of reference construct.

1. *Every individual exists in a continually changing world of experience of which he is the center.*

Rogers holds that each of us is at the core of his own world and everything else is happening, developing, occurring about him— (not unlike Ptolemy's homocentric notion of the earth as the center of the universe). It is painfuly obvious that man is the most egocentric organism on earth, and surely no one can be more self-centered than the human infant. The baby will outgrow much of this, of course, but hardly all of it. But it would seem that one who is approaching emotional maturity has already recognized that egocentrism is a substantial part of being human. Once one accepts this frailty he is in an excellent state to begin to compensate for it and to grow beyond it. The truly arrogant person, however, is the man or woman who has never made and perhaps cannot make this admission. For so long as one can shield himself from a recognition of his fallibility, he need not expend energy in growing and he need not submit to the unknowns and possible pain of *change.*

2. *The individual reacts to his world as he experiences and perceives it and thus this perceptual world is, for the individual, "reality."*

Rogers put quotes around *reality* to indicate that it is not the "real" reality. Consider these definitions of perception: "The point of reality contact, the door to reality appraisal!";[21] the "structuring of stimuli"[22] and the "organization of stimuli";[23] and "the way in which the person structures his world and himself."[24] But regardless

---

[19] H. B. English and A. C. English, *A Comprehensive Dictionary of Psychological and Psychoanalytical Terms* (New York: Longmans, Green & Co., 1958).

[20] Paraphrased from C. R. Rogers, *Client-Centered Therapy* (Boston, Mass.: Houghton Mifflin Co., 1951), pp. 483, 484, 487, 494.

[21] G. S. Klein, "The Personal World through Perception," *Perception: An Approach to Personality*, ed. R. R. Blake and G. V. Ramsey (New York: The Ronald Press Co., 1951), pp. 328–29.

[22] C. M. Solley and G. Murphy, *Development of the Perceptual World* (New York: Basic Books, Inc., Publishers, 1960), p. 26.

[23] F. A. Beach, "Body Chemistry and Perception," Blake and Ramsey, *Perception*, p. 56.

[24] U. Bronfenbrenner, "Toward an Integrated Theory of Personality," ibid., p. 207.

of how invalid and incomplete it may be, one's personalized reality is the only one he has and therefore the only one to which he responds.

3. *The individual has one basic tendency and striving which is to actualize, maintain, and enhance himself.*

Roger writes of the *actualizing tendency* as "the inherent tendency of the organism to develop all its capacities in ways to serve to maintain or enhance the organism. It involves not only the tendency to meet . . . 'deficiency needs' for air, food, water, and the like, but also more generalized activities. . . . It is development toward autonomy and away from heteronomy, or control by external forces."[25] He subscribes to Angyal's statement: "Life is an autonomous event which takes place between the organism and the environment. Life processes do not merely tend to preserve life but transcend the momentary status quo of the organism, expanding itself continually and imposing its autonomous determination upon an ever increasing realm of events."[26]

More specifically, Rogers refers to *self*-actualization. We will discuss his concept of the self-image later in this chapter and for the moment will merely suggest that much of the individual's perceiving is in the service of preserving or enhancing his self-image.

According to Frenkel-Brunswik:

It would appear that we do not always see ourselves as we are but instead perceive the environment in terms of our own need. Self-perception and perception of the environment actually merge in the service of these needs. Thus, the perceptual distortions of ourselves and the environment fulfill an important function in our psychological household.[27]

The role of *needs* and *motivation* in influencing perception and therefore behavior is clearly important enough to require the separate chapter which follows this one.

4. *Therefore, the best vantage point for understanding another's behavior is from that person's internal frame of reference.*

This conclusion follows logically from Rogers' preceding proposi-

---

25 C. R. Rogers, "A Theory of Therapy, Personality, and Interpersonal Relationships, as Developed in the Client-Centered Framework," *Psychology: The Study of a Science*, Vol. 3, *Formulations of the Person and the Social Context*, ed. Sigmund Koch (New York: McGraw-Hill Book Co., 1959) , p. 196.

26 A. Angyal, *Foundations for a Science of Personality* (New York: Commonwealth Fund, 1941) .

27 Else Frenkel-Brunswik, "Personality Theory and Perception," chap. 13 in Blake and Ramsey, *Perception*, p. 379.

tions but this does not necessarily make it easy to utilize the frame of reference concept. The individual's internal frame of reference *is* his subjective world. "Only he knows it fully. It can never be known to another except through empathic inference and then can never be perfectly known."[28]

Probably the greatest single deterrent to one's accurately visualizing another's frame of reference is his *own*. An analogy will suggest why this is so.

Analogy of the box

Visualize each of us as the sole and constant tenant of a box with a top, a bottom, and four sides. There is just one window in this box—one's frame of reference, loosely speaking—through which he views the outside world.

A restricted window. This suggests immediately that one's view is restricted—he cannot see what is happening in back of him, above, to the sides, and so forth. One obviously cannot be ubiquitous and therefore his view is inevitably limited. But there is another restriction that he can overcome to an extent—the *size* of the window. We all have our "narrownesses"—our areas of naïveté. I, for example, was born and reared in a suburb. Suppose you are a country boy and we go out to a farm. We would share the same environment but I would expect that your stimuli and evoked sets would greatly outnumber mine. You would have the preparation, the memory content, to make so much more significance out of the experience than I.

But I have the capacity to learn. Given the time and provided I have the motivation I can acquire some of your sophistication. In short I can *expand* my window.

Stained-glass window. Not only is one's window frame restricted (but expandable largely at his will) but it also does not contain a pane of clear glass. It is rather like a stained-glass church window with various, peculiarly shaped, tinted, and refracting lenses. In one's frame of reference these lenses are his experiences, biases, values, needs, emotions, aspirations, and the like. They may all be distorting media to an extent but are we powerless to overcome these distortions? Hardly, but let us establish one point first.

Does anyone grow up with a clear window? Can anyone be without

---

[28] C. R. Rogers, "A Theory of Therapy . . . ," *Psychology* . . . , p. 210.

bias for example? Quite unlikely, for everyone had to be born at a particular time and in a particular place. Thus he was exposed to particular people and situations all of whom and which taught him *special* lessons regarding values, customs, mores, codes, and so on.

But again man has viability and the capacity to adjust and compensate—he can *clarify* his window. A pencil in a glass of water appears to bend abruptly but if one *understands* something about the nature of refraction he can compensate for the distortion, aim at where the pencil appears not to be, and hit it. So it is more profoundly with a man himself—if he can *understand himself* he can *compensate* for his distorted frame of reference and, in effect, clarify his window.

The self-image

But there is at least one potentially formidable obstacle in the way of a man's truly understanding himself. We return to Carl Rogers for this. A key concept of the Rogerian therapeutic approach is the premise that as a person grows up he develops a *self-image* or *self-concept* —a picture of himself. Hayakawa asserted: "The mode of human behavior is not self-preservation but self-concept. The self-concept is who you think you are and the self is who you are. Values determine people's self-concept and self-concept determines social experience."[29] Rogers uses *self, concept of self,* and *self-structure* as terms to refer to

the organized, consistent conceptual gestalt composed of perceptions of the characteristics of the "I" or "me" and the perceptions of the relationships of the "I" or "me" to others and to various aspects of life, together with the values attached to these perceptions. It is a fluid and changing gestalt, a process, . . . The term self or self-concept is more likely to be used when we are talking of the person's view of himself, self-structure when we are looking at this gestalt from an external frame of reference.[30]

On coping with guilt.   The self-image helps to explain how one copes with guilt.

One of man's most compelling needs, is the need to justify himself. Moreover, most us tolerate guilt very poorly. Guilt is painful— acutely so. Therefore, as pain-avoidance organisms most of us have devised highly facile and sophisticated means for eliminating or di-

29 S. I. Hayakawa, participating in the 1965 Student Symposium, "Spectrum of Perspectives," Northwestern University.

30 C. R. Rogers, "A Theory of Therapy . . . ," *Psychology,* p. 200.

minishing the pain of guilt. Test this assertion, if you can tread a painful route, by tracing back to an event in which you did something that you *knew* was *wrong;* that you *could not justify* by rationalizing that the end warranted the means; and that *was not beyond your control.*

Most of us have great difficulty remembering such events objectively and yet almost all of us have been guilty of them. The pain of guilt is so noisome that we have developed great skill in justifying our behavior before, during, or after the act.

At the core of this behavior appears to be the overriding motive to "actualize, maintain, and enhance" one's self-image. It is clear that the individual can distort experience to satisfy this powerful need. For example, suppose Mike treats Tom unjustly—at least as Tom perceives it. Tom will likely become angry and want revenge. If Tom were to analyze himself he might find that what he wants most of all is for Mike to experience remorse, true contrition—the pain of guilt —at least commensurate with the pain he inflicted upon Tom. However, Mike, as a pain-avoider, has already begun to justify his behavior and is unlikely, therefore, to tender a sincere apology. Failing to receive evidence of Mike's acceptance of his own guilt, Tom may be moved to retaliate in kind or to attempt to wrench an apology from Mike. In either event, Tom's behavior, as Mike perceives it, is sufficiently obnoxious to complete his self-justification. "You see how Tom is acting? That _____ deserved to be treated that way in the first place!"

No matter how unreasonable, irrational, or immoral another's behavior may appear to us it is generally a good assumption that it is quite reasonable, rational and moral *in his world.* Epictetus wrote: "The appearances of things to the mind is the standard of action of every man."

One's self-image is perhaps most profoundly important to the individual in the sense that it serves as *his contact with himself.* In fact, when he talks or thinks about *himself* he is usually not referring to his limbs, torso, and head but rather to an abstraction he usually labels as "my *self.*" Thus, it is by his self-image that he *knows* himself.

Images of others. But we also need to know and understand others and thus we form images of them as well—particularly those with whom we are most interdependent—parents, spouse, children, superiors, subordinates. Such image formation, whether one is conscious of it or not, requires considerable energy output and the marshaling of much psychological intelligence about the individual of whom one is forming an image. The prime motive for the effort is that we need to build a good base for understanding and predicting the behavior of the other person. And only by predicting the other's behavior reasonably accurately can we confidently control our own behavior and deal effectively with the other person.[31] This helps to explain why one becomes confused and upset when another's behavior suddenly contradicts his image of that other person. He has lost or risks the loss of his base for predicting and thus for controlling himself in dealing with the other.

And this holds even when the other's behavior is *more favorable* than anticipated. Suppose you have a superior—a father, a teacher, a boss—who is a veritable tyrant. And suppose one day he greets you with a broad smile, a friendly clap on the back, and an encouraging comment. Is your initial response—"Wonderful, the old buzzard has finally turned over a new leaf!"? Or is it—"What's he up to now!"? As a friend in business put it, "You can work for an s.o.b.—provided he's a *consistent* s.o.b.! It's the one who turns it on and off unpredictably that gives you the ulcers!"

Self-image challenged.   Now if we are troubled by another person's jeopardizing our predictability about him then how much more traumatic is it for one to have his *own self*-image challenged. He stands the risk of losing the ability to predict, control, and *know himself*. It is difficult to imagine a greater internal upheaval than suddenly not to *know oneself—to lose contact with oneself*. It may

---

31 The process we call *forming impressions of personality* is sometimes called *person perception.* Bruner [J. S. Bruner, "Social Psychology and Perception," *Readings in Social Psychology,* ed. E. Maccoby, T. M. Newcomb, and E. L. Hartley (3d ed.; New York: Henry Holt, Inc., 1958), pp. 85–94] has argued that the "process of perception tends, in general, to accomplish two things: (1) a recording of the diversity of data we encounter into a simpler form that brings it within the scope of our limited memory; (2) a going beyond the information given to predict future events and thereby minimize surprise." Roger Brown, *Social Psychology* (New York: The Free Press, 1965), p. 611.

Social psychologists, in particular, have been concerned with how we perceive or infer the traits and intentions of others. For a sampling of experimental and theoretical works in "social perception" or "person perception" see: I. E. Bender and A. H. Hastorf, "On Measuring Generalized Empathic Ability (Social Sensitivity)," *Journal of Abnormal and Social Psychology,* Vol. 48 (1958), pp. 503–6; V. B. Cline and J. M. Richards, Jr., "Accuracy of Interpersonal Perception—A General Trait?", *Journal of Abnormal and Social Psychology,* Vol. 60 (1960), pp. 1–7; F. Heider, *The Psychology of Interpersonal Relations* (New York: John Wiley & Sons, Inc., 1958); W. C. Schutz, *FIRO: A Three-Dimensional Theory of Interpersonal Behavior* (New York: Holt, Rinehart & Winston, Inc., 1960); R. Taft, "The Ability to Judge People," *Psychological Bulletin,* Vol. 52 (1955), pp. 1–23; R. Tagiuri and L. Petrullo (eds.), *Person Perception and Interpersonal Behavior* (Stanford, Calif.: Stanford University Press, 1958).

not be inaccurate to say that our mental hospitals are full of people who have lost contact with themselves more or less permanently.

It is no wonder, then, that the loss of a self-image is generally warded off at almost any cost. And yet few of us have gone through life unscathed. Anyone who has experienced a deeply traumatic experience at one time or another—whether related to a parent, a spouse, a child, school, religion, vocation, narcotics, alcoholism, job security, illness, injury, lawsuit—will probably find on retrospection that his self-image was being severely threatened.

A PERSONAL CASE.   My own experience is a case in point. As a high school freshman I hit upon chemical research for a career. I suppose this was encouraged by an older boy I admired who also aspired to chemistry. He had built a laboratory in his basement so, of course, I had to have one too. I remember collecting hundreds of jars and bottles and scores of other treasures that might somehow be useful in my lab. I can also recall spending hour after hour thoroughly enjoying mixing potions of every description—and some beyond description. (I recall without quite so much relish the time I brewed some chlorine and nearly gassed myself unconscious!)

I *devoured* the chemistry course in my junior year. I must admit feeling rather smug during this period for I had a ready answer to the recurrent question, What are you going to be? Most of my friends had either a hazy answer or none at all. My self-image in this regard was forming and solidifying.

I was graduated from high school during World War II and immediately entered the service. Somehow the Army gave little shrift to young men who were long on aspiration but short on experience and consequently I had three years of singularly nonchemical experience —but this did not dissuade me. Finally, the war ended and I was discharged. I immediately enrolled in a chemical technology program at a university reputed for this field.

Suddenly, reality began to catch up with my self-image. I had not realized that a chemist was also expected to be a pretty fair mathematician. I had done well enough in high school math courses but the last three years were nonmathematical as well as nonchemical. At any rate I foolishly disregarded the math refresher course (my self-image said I didn't need a "crutch") and charged headlong into college algebra where I was in competition with students fresh from high school math. While I was rusty, it would be unfair to say that I didn't get the math; I did get it but about a week after the exams, which is poor timing! Net result—the first *D* I had ever received in my life. What was the consequence—did I trade in my self-image for a new model? Hardly; rather than yield, I fought tenaciously and found a ready explanation for my plight: Aside from the Army's causing me to "forget my math" the instructor "had it in for me." Among other evidences he had a Scottish name and I was convinced he was anti-Irish!

I was practicing what some writers call "perceptual defense," a form of perceptual distortion which "demonstrates that when confronted with a fact inconsistent with a stereotype already held by a person, the perceiver is able to distort the data in such a way as to eliminate the inconsistency. Thus, by perceiving inaccurately, he defends himself from having to change his stereotypes."[32] Haire and Grunes suggest that we "blinder" ourselves to avoid seeing that which might trouble us.[33] As communication authority David K. Berlo paraphrased the Bible—"Seek and ye shall find—whether it is there or not!"

The next quarter? A *C* in math. This instructor had an Irish name but he didn't like me either! (I suspected he was from *Northern* Ireland!) In the middle of the third quarter and another math *D,* my self-image had withstood all the onslaught from harsh reality that it could. And for two to three weeks (at the time it seemed like six months) I was in a state of unrelieved depression. I became very nervous and had difficulty eating, sleeping, and studying (which only intensified my problem). Figuratively, a large section of my self-image had been shot away and *I had nothing to replace it.* The most appalling aspect of the experience was that I realized that *I didn't know myself.* To give the story a happy ending I took a battery of aptitude tests, changed to another major, and very gradually began to construct another self-image.

Resistance to image change.   Anyone who has undergone such a traumatic experience will understand why the individual generally resists image change—particularly sudden change. And herein lies one of the greatest obstacles to the full development of an effective communicator and, for that matter, an effective person. The central premise of an excellent book[34] by psychiatrist Karen Horney is that

---

32 S. S. Zalkind and T. W. Costello, "Perception: Some Recent Research and Implications for Administration," *Administrative Science Quarterly,* September 1962, p. 227.

33 M. Haire and W. F. Grunes, "Perceptual Defenses: Processes Protecting an Original Perception of Another Personality," *Human Relations,* Vol. 3 (1958), pp. 403–12.

34 Karen Horney, *Neurosis and Human Growth: The Struggle toward Self-Realization* (New York: W. W. Norton & Co., Inc., 1950).

the neurotic process is a special form of human development which is the antithesis of healthy growth. Optimally, man's energies are directed toward realizing his own potentialities. But, under inner stress, he becomes estranged from his *real self* and spends himself creating and protecting a false, idealized self, based on pride, but threatened by doubts, self-contempt, and self-hate. Throughout the book the goal of liberation for the forces that lead to true self-realization is emphasized.

Take the case of a high school friend. After graduation he, too, went into the service but was more fortunate (in a sense), for the Army put him through three years of an engineering curriculum. Then the war was over and he was discharged. But he decided he did not care for engineering and could not bring himself to take a final year of course work to earn an engineering degree. And yet he could not bear the thought of starting all over again in another field. The net result was that, for all practical purposes, he did nothing. He took a clerical job in a nearby insurance firm and has been there for 27 years. Through the years, his perhaps largely unconscious philosophy of life has evidently been: "I can't stand another failure [he probably regarded not completing the engineering degree as a failure] and one sure way not to lose a race is not to enter it." In sum, here is a man who apparently has protected his invalid self-image at the cost of a stunted life.

The handicap of inaccurate self-knowledge and the unwillingness to reconstruct a more realistic self-image seem to be very widespread. In 20 years of organizational research and consulting I have known scores, if not hundreds of men (and some women), particularly in the middle echelons of their organizations, who seemed to have all the requisites for continued success: intelligence, education, experience, drive, ability, ambition. But they had one vital failing—*they did not know themselves.* The image they held of themselves was pitifully out of phase with that which they were projecting to others. They seemed chronically annoyed and/or bewildered by the reactions of others to them. What was happening? As unrealistic as their self-images were it was nevertheless too threatening to entertain contrary cues from other people. Fending off the reactions of others variously as "those malicious/crazy/misinformed/ornery/perverse/stupid people!" they had been successful in perpetuating and even reinforcing their respective self-myths. Thus, they ineffectualized themselves; squandered their nervous energies in a kind of internal conflict, protecting their fallacious self-images.[35] The masterful Robert Burns captured the poignancy of self-deception almost two centuries ago.

> Oh wad some power the giftie gie us
> To see oursels as ithers see us!
> It wad frae monie a blunder free us,
>   An' foolish notion.

ON COPING WITH DEFENSIVENESS

We have discussed defensive behavior as a critical obstacle to effective interpersonal communication. What, in the final analysis, are people defending *against?* In a word, *perceived threat*—the threat of change or harm to their self-images, to their personalized worlds. This would suggest that whatever reduced perceived threat would reduce the need to defend against it—to enable one to reduce his defenses accordingly. What threat-reducing techniques or approaches, then, are available to us?

After an eight-year study of recordings of interpersonal discussions, Jack Gibb delineated two communication climates—one threatening ("defensive") ; the other nonthreatening ("supportive") . (See Table 3–1.) Incidentally, Gibb's "supportive climate" is quite in keeping

TABLE 3–1
Categories of behavior characteristic of supportive and defensive climates in small groups*

Defensive climates	*Supportive climates*
1. Evaluation	1. Description
2. Control	2. Problem orientation
3. Strategy	3. Spontaneity
4. Neutrality	4. Empathy
5. Superiority	5. Equality
6. Certainty	6. Provisionalism

* Jack R. Gibb, "Defensive Communication," *Journal of Communication*, Vol. 2, No. 3, Sept. 1961, p. 143.

with Likert's "supportive relationship" and McGregor's Theory Y as discussed in Chapter 2.

---

[35] This is why Brouwer was moved to write: "Manager development means change in the manager's self-image." Paul J. Brouwer, "The Power to See Ourselves," *Harvard Business Review*, Vol. 42, No. 6 (November–December 1964) , p. 156.

Gibb defined his paired categories of perceived behavior as follows:[36]

Evaluation. To pass judgment on another; to blame or praise; to make moral assessments of another; to question his standards, values and motives and the affect loadings of his communications.

Description. Nonjudgmental; to ask questions which are perceived as genuine requests for information; to present "feelings, events, perceptions, or processes which do not ask or imply that the receiver change behavior or attitude."

Control. To try to do something to another; to attempt to change an attitude or the behavior of another—to try to restrict his field of activity; "implicit in all attempts to alter another person is the assumption of the change agent that the person to be altered is inadequate."

Problem orientation. The antithesis of persuasion; to communicate "a desire to collaborate in defining a mutual problem and in seeking its solution" (thus tending to create the same problem orientation in the other); to imply that he has no preconceived solution, attitude, or method to impose upon the other; to allow "the receiver to set his own goals, make his own decisions, and evaluate his own progress—or to share with the sender in doing so."

Strategy. To manipulate others; to use tricks to "involve" another, to make him think he was making his own decisions, and to make him feel that the speaker had genuine interest in him; to engage in a stratagem involving ambiguous and multiple motivation.

Spontaneity. To express guilelessness; natural simplicity; free of deception; having a "clean id"; having unhidden, uncomplicated motives; straight-forwardness and honesty.

Neutrality. To express lack of concern for the welfare of another; "the clinical, detached, person-is-an-object-of-study attitude."

Empathy. To express respect for the worth of the listener; to identify with his problems, share his feelings, and accept his emotional values at face value.

Superiority. To communicate the attitude that one is "superior in position, power, wealth, intellectual ability, physical characteristics, or other ways" to another; to tend to arouse feelings of inadequacy in the

---

[36] Jack R. Gibb, "Defensive Communication," *Journal of Communication*, pp. 142–48.

other; to impress the other that the speaker "is not willing to enter into a shared problem-solving relationship, that he probably does not desire feedback, that he does not require help and/or that he will be likely to try to reduce the power, the status, or the worth of the receiver."

Equality. To be willing to enter into participative planning with mutual trust and respect; to attach little importance to differences in talent, ability, worth, appearance, status, and power.

Certainty. To appear dogmatic; "to seem to know the answers, to require no additional data"; and to regard self as teacher rather than as co-worker; to manifest inferiority by *needing to be right,* wanting to win an argument rather than solve a problem, seeing one's ideas as truths to be defended.

Provisionalism. To be willing to experiment with one's own behavior, attitudes, and ideas; to investigate issues rather than taking sides on them, to problem solve rather than debate, to communicate that the other person may have some control over the shared quest or the investigation of ideas. "If a person is genuinely searching for information and data, he does not resent help or company along the way."

It would appear that if one were to offer another the most supportive climate possible his behavior should be descriptive, problem oriented, spontaneous, and so on, and should avoid attempting to evaluate, control, employ stratagems, and so forth. But the situation is a bit more complex.

First of all, the above are *perceived* behaviors. Therefore, the *perceptions* of the *perceiver* rather than the *intentions* of the perceived will be the final arbiter as to how defensive or supportive the perceiver regards the climate. Moreover, as a person becomes more defensive he becomes less able to assess accurately the motives, values, and emotions of the other person. Conversely, as he grows less defensive, the more accurate his perceptions become.[37]

The more "supportive" or defense reductive the climate, the less the receiver reads into the communication distorted loadings which arise from projections of his own anxieties, motives, and concerns. As defenses are reduced, the receivers become better able to concentrate upon the structure, the content, and the cognitive meanings of the message.[38]

---

[37] J. R. Gibb, "Defense Level and Influence Potential in Small Groups," L. Petrullo and B. M. Bass (eds.), *Leadership and Interpersonal Behavior* (New York: Holt, Rinehart & Winston, 1961), pp. 66–81.

[38] J. R. Gibb, "Defensive Communication," *Journal of Communication*, p. 142.

Another qualification on Gibb's classifications is that while the defensive categories *generally* arouse defensiveness and the supportive categories *ordinarily* generate defense reduction, the *degree* to which these responses occur depends upon the *individual's level of defensiveness* as well as the *general climate of the group at the time.*[39]

Still another qualification is that the behavior categories are *interactive.* For example, when a speaker's behavior appears *evaluative* it ordinarily increases defensiveness. But if the listener feels the speaker regards him as an *equal* and is being direct and *spontaneous,* the evaluativeness of the message might be neutralized or not even perceived. Again, attempts to *control* will stimulate defensiveness depending upon the degree of *openness* of the effort. The suspicion of hidden motives heightens resistance. Still another example, the use of *stratagems* becomes especially threatening when one attempt seems to be trying to make strategy *appear spontaneous.*

Openness

A central theme running throughout Gibb's findings is the importance of *openness*—the willingness to be receptive to experience. Rogers considered openness as the polar opposite of defensiveness.

In the hypothetical person who is completely open to his experience, his concept of self would be a symbolization in awareness which would be completely congruent with his experience. There would, therefore, be no possibility of threat.[40]

One who is open to experience evaluates threat more accurately and tolerates change more graciously. This is why the frame of reference concept can be so helpful in reducing defenses and in keeping them low. Because the frame of reference obviates the mine-is-the-only-valid-world presumption it makes defense of one's personalized world unnecessary. Nondefensive, one is not compelled to attack or counter-attack—thus he is more able to contribute to a supportive climate in his relations with others.

In a supportive climate people are more able to explore their own and each other's decision premises[41] and thus get down to the real

[39] J. R. Gibb, "Sociopsychological Processes of Group Instruction," N. B. Henry (ed.), *The Dynamics of Instructional Groups* (Fifty-ninth Yearbook of the National Society for the Study of Education), (1960), Part II, pp. 115–35.

[40] C. R. Rogers, "A Theory of Therapy . . . ," *Psychology,* p. 206.

[41] H. A. Simon, *Administrative Behavior* (2d ed.; New York: The Macmillan Co., 1957).

grounds of controversy (or to discover that there was no real basis for conflict). Even if there are genuine differences, under conditions of openness people themselves are more capable of dealing with them maturely.

Rogers offers this practical suggestion:

The next time you get into an argument with your wife, or your friend, or with a small group of friends, just stop the discussion for a moment and for an experiment, institute this rule. "Each person can speak up for himself only *after* he has first restated the ideas and feelings of the previous speaker accurately, and to that speaker's satisfaction." You see what this would mean? It would simply mean that before presenting your own point of view, it would be necessary for you to really achieve the other speaker's frame of reference—to understand his thoughts and feelings so well that you could summarize them for him. Sounds simple, doesn't it? But if you try it you will discover it one of the most difficult things you have tried to do. However, once you have been able to see the other's point of view, your own comments will have to be drastically revised. You will also find the emotion going out of the discussion, the differences being reduced, and those differences which remain being of a rational and understandable sort.[42]

SUMMARY

We have depicted human behavior as the product of the internal state of the individual and the environment in which he finds himself. His behavior, then, is only indirectly a response to reality. One who cannot tolerate this basic uncertainty of life and who assumes *his world is the only real world* may find that "world" in almost constant jeopardy. Closed and defensive he may respond to the "threats" with irrational attack and/or flight.

We have conceded that many organizations are populated to an extent with more or less defensive (and thus often aggressive) people. Therefore, the challenge to anyone who aspires to be an effective leader or member of an organization (or more broadly, wishes to live an emotionally mature and deeply satisfying life) might be phrased as follows:

---

[42] C. R. Rogers, "Communication: Its Blocking and Its Facilitation," a paper originally prepared for delivery at the Northwestern University Centennial Conference on Communications, held in Evanston, Illinois, October 11–13, 1951. Reproduced here from the Northwestern University *Information*, Vol. XX, No. 25.

1. Can he come to accept that *his* and everyone else's "reality" is subjective, incomplete, distorted, and unique? Can he, therefore, muster the courage to become open and nondefensive—to permit even contrary cues to reach him and to begin to revise, update, and make more valid his self-image?

2. Having clarified his own frame of reference can he learn to assess accurately the frames of reference of others? Can the manager, for example, realize the simple but profound truth that his subordinates' worlds have him in it as a boss—his world does not?

In the next chapter we will now consider how needs and motives affect one's perceptions and thus his responses to experience. In general, we will examine their influence upon his behavior. Then in Chapter 5 we will focus on that particular and critical kind of behavior we call "communication," with emphasis on the self-deceptions to which we are all more or less subject.

SETS

The following illusions illustrate the role of visual *sets* in distorting perception.

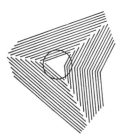   

Is the circle round or lopsided?   Are the center circles the same?

Is the vertical dimension of the hat equal to or
greater than the horizontal?

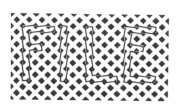

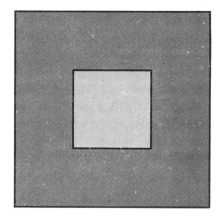

Are the letters parallel?

Are the checkers parallel?

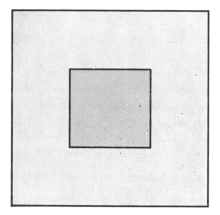

Note how the backgrounds determine set in perceiving the center squares which are the same shade of gray.

In these illusions the principal set is to perceive the *two-dimensional depictions* as *three-dimensional objects*.

Trichotometric indicator bracket

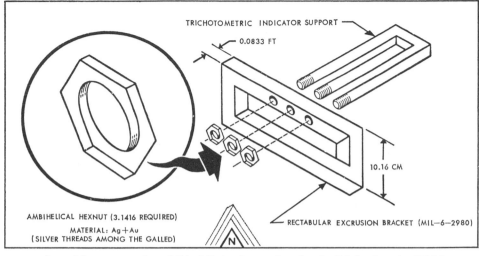

TRICHOTOMETRIC INDICATOR SUPPORT

0.0833 FT

10.16 CM

AMBIHELICAL HEXNUT (3.1416 REQUIRED)
MATERIAL: Ag+Au
(SILVER THREADS AMONG THE GALLED)

RECTABULAR EXCRUSION BRACKET (MIL—6—2980)

An article was recently published listing instructions for the fabrication of a "Trichotometric Indicator." However, it seems that some difficulty is being experienced with the brackets which attach the indicator. As an aid toward fabricating the indicator brackets, the above illustration has been provided. It will be noted that in attaching the bracket to the indicator, a special ambihelical hexnut is used. The application of this nut is rather unique in that any attempt to remove it in the conventional manner only tightens it. Because of this design, the nut must be fully screwed on before it can be screwed off.

Sources: The illusions on p. 81 and the three workmen on p. 82 are reprinted with permission from *Observation . . . Perception* published by E. I. du Pont de Nemours & Co., Wilmington, Delaware.

The "impossible staircase" is reprinted with permission from L. S. Penrose and R. Penrose, "Impossible Objects: A Special Type of Illusion," *British Journal of Psychology,* 49, 31 (1958).

The "Trichotometric Indicator Bracket" courtesy NAA "Operations & Service News." From *Approach,* May 1965.

DISCUSSION QUESTIONS

1. What is the point of the cartoon on page 55?

2. "We never come into direct contact with reality." (p. 55) What was meant by that statement? Do you agree?

3. If perception can lead to "a meaningful and coherent picture of the world" (see footnote 2, p. 56), does that suggest that *meaning* does not exist until perception has taken place?

4. Discuss Munn's experience with the "wild gray rat" in terms of the perception model in Figure 3–1.

5. Recalling the illustration of the misbehaving child as he was perceived by people from differing cultures (p. 61), what special prob-

lems confront United Nations members and others who communicate cross-culturally?

6. Concerning the role of learning in perception Sebald concluded "that largely only those meanings are being perceived and recalled which reinforce prior images" and "that selective distortion takes place in order to screen out dissonant features—features which are apt to disturb pre-conceived images." (p. 62)

   Do these assertions seem reasonable? What implication do they have for interpersonal communication? What can we do to cope with these phenomena in ourselves?

7. Regarding Carl Rogers' propositions pertaining to the frame of reference concept, do you agree with each of these assertions? Do they lead logically to the conclusion (proposition 4)?

8. Regarding the "Analogy of the Box": This is a *figurative* analogy designed to clarify rather than to prove. In what respect do you feel it is an accurate (or inaccurate) depiction?

9. The motive of "actualizing, maintaining, and enhancing" one's self-image (p. 68): How important is this motive? What bearing does it have upon our communicating with others? What does it have to do with guilt feelings?

10. Among the motives listed for forming images of others are the needs to understand, predict, and deal with the behavior of others. Are there other motives?

11. According to Horney (p. 75), under inner stress one becomes estranged from his *real self* and spends himself creating and protecting a false, idealized self, based on pride, but threatened by doubts, self-contempt, and self-hate. Does that strike you as a valid assertion? What might it have to do with communicating with and relating to others?

12. "In a supportive climate people are more able to explore their own and other's decision premises and thus get down to the real grounds of controversy." (pp. 79–80) Do you regard this as a reasonable generalization? If so, *why* is it so?

ARTICLE

Active listening[43]

CARL R. ROGERS AND RICHARD E. FARSON

SECTION ONE—THE MEANING OF ACTIVE LISTENING

One basic responsibility of the supervisor or executive is the development, adjustment, and integration of individual employees. He tries to develop employee potential, delegate responsibility, and achieve cooperation. To do so, he must have, among other abilities, the ability to listen intelligently and carefully to those with whom he works.

There are, however, many kinds of listening skills. The lawyer, for example, when questioning a witness, listens for contradictions, irrelevancies, errors, and weaknesses. But this not the kind of listening skill we are concerned with in this booklet. The lawyer usually is not listening in order to help the witness adjust or cooperate or produce. On the other hand, we will be concerned with listening skills which *will help* employees gain a clearer understanding of their situations, take responsibility, and cooperate with each other.

Two examples

The kind of listening we have in mind is called "active listening." It is called "active" because the listener has a very definite responsibility. He does not passively absorb the words which are spoken to him. He actively tries to grasp the facts and the feelings in what he hears, and he tries, by his listening, to help the speaker work out his own problems.

---

[43] Reproduced by special permission of the authors and The University of Chicago's Industrial Relations Center.

To get a fuller picture of what is meant by active listening, let us consider two different approaches to the same work problem.

Example No. 1

FOREMAN: Hey, Al, I don't get this production order. We can't handle this run today. What do they think we are?

SUPERVISOR: But that's the order. So get it out as soon as you can. We're under terrific pressure this week.

FOREMAN: Don't they know we're behind schedule already because of that press breakdown?

SUPERVISOR: Look, Kelly, I don't decide what goes on upstairs. I just have to see that the work gets out and that's what I'm gonna do.

FOREMAN: The guys aren't gonna like this.

SUPERVISOR: That's something you'll have to work out with them, not me.

Example No. 2

FOREMAN: Hey, Ross, I don't get this production order. We can't handle this run today. What do they think we are?

SUPERVISOR: Sounds like you're pretty sore about it, Kelly.

FOREMAN: I sure am. We were just about getting back to schedule after that press breakdown. Now this comes along.

SUPERVISOR: As if you didn't have enough work to do, huh?

FOREMAN: Yeah. I don't know how I'm gonna tell the guys about this.

SUPERVISOR: Hate to face 'em with it now, is that it?

FOREMAN: I really do. They're under a real strain today. Seems like everything we do around here is rush, rush.

SUPERVISOR: I guess you feel like it's unfair to load anything more on them.

FOREMAN: Well, yeah. I know there must be plenty of pressure on everybody up the line, but—well, if that's the way it is . . . guess I'd better get the word to 'em.

There are obviously many differences between these two examples. The main one, however, is that Ross, the supervisor in the second example is using the active-listening approach. He is listening and responding in a way that makes it clear that he appreciates both the meaning and the feeling behind what Kelly is saying.

Active listening does not necessarily mean long sessions spent listening to grievances, personal or otherwise. It is simply a way of approaching those problems which arise out of the usual day-to-day events of any job.

To be effective, active listening must be firmly grounded in the basic attitudes of the user. We cannot employ it as a technique if our fundamental attitudes are in conflict with its basic concepts. If we try, our behavior will be empty and sterile and our associates will be quick to recognize this. Until we can demonstrate a spirit which genuinely respects the potential worth of the individual, which considers his rights and trusts his capacity for self-direction, we cannot begin to be effective listeners.

What we achieve by listening

Active listening is an important way to bring about changes in people. Despite the popular notion that listening is a passive approach, clinical and research evidence clearly shows that sensitive listening is a most effective agent for individual personality change and group development. Listening brings about changes in people's attitudes toward themselves and others, and also brings about changes in their basic values and personal philosophy. People who have been listened to in this new and special way become more emotionally mature, more open to their experiences, less defensive, more democratic, and less authoritarian.

When people are listened to sensitively, they tend to listen to themselves with more care and make clear exactly what they are feeling and thinking. Group members tend to listen more to each other, become less argumentative, more ready to incorporate other points of view. Because listening reduces the threat of having one's ideas criticized, the person is better able to see them for what they are, and is more likely to feel that his contributions are worthwhile.

Not the least important result of listening is the change that takes place within the listener himself. Besides the fact that listening provides more information than any other activity, it builds deep, positive relationships and tends to alter constructively the attitudes of the listener. Listening is a growth experience.

These, then, are some of the worthwhile results we can expect from active listening. But how do we go about this kind of listening? How do we become active listeners?

SECTION TWO—HOW TO LISTEN

Active listening aims to bring about changes in people. To achieve this end, it relies upon definite techniques—things to do and things to avoid doing. Before discussing these techniques, however, we should first understand why they are effective. To do so, we must understand how the individual personality develops.

The growth of the individual

Through all of our lives, from early childhood on, we have learned to think of ourselves in certain, very definite ways. We have built up pictures of ourselves. Sometimes these self-pictures are pretty realistic but at other times they are not. For example, an over-age, over-weight lady may fancy herself a youthful, ravishing siren, or an awkward teenager regard himself as a star athlete.

All of us have experiences which fit the way we need to think about ourselves. These we accept. But it is much harder to accept experiences which don't fit. And sometimes, if it is very important for us to hang on to this self-picture, we don't accept or admit these experiences at all.

These self-pictures are not necessarily attractive. A man, for example, may regard himself as incompetent and worthless. He may feel that he is doing his job poorly in spite of favorable appraisals by the company. As long as he has these feelings about himself he must deny any experiences which would seem not to fit this self-picture, in this case any that might indicate to him that he is competent. It is so necessary for him to maintain this self-picture that he is threatened by anything which would tend to change it. Thus, when the company raises his salary, it may seem to him only additional proof that he is a fraud. He must hold onto this self-picture, because, bad or good, it's the only thing he has by which he can identify himself.

This is why direct attempts to change this individual or change his self-picture are particularly threatening. He is forced to defend himself or to completely deny the experience. This denial of experience and defense of the self-picture tend to bring on rigidity of behavior and create difficulties in personal adjustment.

The active-listening approach, on the other hand, does not present a threat to the individual's self-picture. He does not have to defend it. He is able to explore it, see it for what it is, and make his own decision as to how realistic it is. And he is then in a position to change.

If I want to help a man reduce his defensiveness and become more adaptive, I must try to remove the threat of myself as his potential changer. As long as the atmosphere is threatening, there can be no effective communication. So I must create a climate which is neither critical, evaluative, nor moralizing. It must be an atmosphere of equality and freedom, permissiveness and understanding, acceptance and warmth. It is in this climate and this climate only that the individual feels safe enough to incorporate new experiences and new values into his concept of himself. Let's see how active listening helps to create this climate.

What to avoid

When we encounter a person with a problem, our usual response is to try to change his way of looking at things—to get him to see his situation the way we see it, or would like him to see it. We plead, reason, scold, encourage, insult, prod—anything to bring about a change in the desired direction, that is, in the direction we want him to travel. What we seldom realize, however, is that, under these circumstances, we are usually responding to *our own* needs to see the world in certain ways. It is always difficult for us to tolerate and understand actions which are different from the ways in which *we* believe *we* should act. If, however, we can free ourselves from the need to influence and direct others in our own paths, we enable ourselves to listen with understanding, and thereby employ the most potent available agent of change.

One problem the listener faces is that of responding to demands for decisions, judgments, and evaluations. He is constantly called upon to agree or disagree with someone or something. Yet, as he well knows, the question or challenge frequently is a masked expression of feelings or needs which the speaker is far more anxious to communicate than he is to have the surface questions answered. Because he cannot speak these feelings openly, the speaker must disguise them to himself and to others in an acceptable form. To illustrate, let us examine some typical questions and the type of answers that might best elicit the feeling beneath it. (See page 90.)

These responses recognize the questions but leave the way open for the employee to say what is really bothering him. They allow the listener to participate in the problem or situation without shouldering all responsibility for decision making or actions. This is a process of thinking *with* people instead of *for* or *about* them.

Passing judgment, whether critical or favorable, makes free expression difficult. Similarly, advice and information are almost always

Employee's Question	*Listener's Answer*
Just whose responsibility is the tool room?	Do you feel that someone is challenging your authority in there?
Don't you think younger able people should be promoted before senior but less able ones?	It seems to you they should, I take it.
What does the super expect us to do about those broken-down machines?	You're pretty disgusted with those machines, aren't you?
Don't you think I've improved over the last review period?	Sounds as if you feel like you've really picked up over these last few months.

seen as efforts to change a person and thus serve as barriers to his self-expression and the development of a creative relationship. Moreover, advice is seldom taken and information hardly ever utilized. The eager young trainee probably will not become patient just because he is advised that, "The road to success in business is a long, difficult one, and you must be patient." And it is no more helpful for him to learn that "only one out of a hundred trainees reach top management positions."

Interestingly, it is a difficult lesson to learn that positive *evaluations* are sometimes as blocking as negative ones. It is almost as destructive to the freedom of a relationship to tell a person that he is good or capable or right, as to tell him otherwise. To evaluate him positively may make it more difficult for him to tell of the faults that distress him or the ways in which he believes he is not competent.

Encouragement also may be seen as an attempt to motivate the speaker in certain directions or hold him off rather than as support. "I'm sure everything will work out O.K." is not a helpful response to the person who is deeply discouraged about a problem.

In other words, most of the techniques and devices common to human relationships are found to be of little use in establishing the type of relationship we are seeking here.

What to do

Just what does active listening entail, then? Basically, it requires that we get inside the speaker, that we grasp, *from his point of view,* just what it is he is communicating to us. More than that, we must convey to the speaker that we are seeing things from his point of view. To listen actively, then, means that there are several things we must do.

Listen for total meaning

Any message a person tries to get across usually has two components: the *content* of the message and the *feeling* or attitude underlying this content. Both are important, both give the message *meaning*. It is this total meaning of the message that we try to understand. For example, a machinist comes to his foreman and says, "I've finished that lathe set-up." This message has obvious content and perhaps calls upon the foreman for another work assignment. Suppose, on the other hand, that he says, "Well, I'm finally finished with that damned lathe set-up." The content is the same but the total meaning of the message has changed—and changed in an important way for both the foreman and the worker. Here sensitive listening can facilitate the relationship. Suppose the foreman were to respond by simply giving another work assignment. Would the employee feel that he had gotten his total message across? Would he feel free to talk to his foreman? Will he feel better about his job, more anxious to do good work on the next assignment?

Now, on the other hand, suppose the foreman were to respond with, "Glad to have it over with, huh?" or "Had a pretty rough time of it?" or "Guess you don't feel like doing anything like that again," or anything else that tells the worker that he heard and understands. It doesn't necessarily mean that the next work assignment need be changed or that he must spend an hour listening to the worker complain about the set-up problems he encountered. He may do a number of things differently in the light of the new information he has from the worker—but not necessarily. It's just that extra sensitivity on the part of the foreman which can transform an average working climate into a good one.

Respond to feelings

In some instances the content is far less important than the feeling which underlies it. To catch the full flavor or meaning of the message one must respond particularly to the feeling component. If, for instance, our machinist had said "I'd like to melt this lathe down and make paper clips out of it," responding to content would be obviously absurd. But to respond to his disgust or anger in trying to work with his lathe recognizes the meaning of this message. There are various shadings of these components in the meaning of any message. Each time the listener must try to remain sensitive to the total meaning the message has to the speaker. What is he trying to tell me? What does this mean to him? How does he see this situation?

Note all cues

Not all communication is verbal. The speaker's words alone don't tell us everything he is communicating. And hence, truly sensitive listening requires that we become aware of several kinds of communication besides verbal. The way in which a speaker hesitates in his speech can tell us much about his feelings. So too can the inflection of his voice. He may stress certain points loudly and clearly, and may mumble others. We should also note such things as the person's facial expressions, body posture, hand movements, eye movements, and breathing. All of these help to convey his total message.

What we communicate by listening

The first reaction of most people when they consider listening as a possible method for dealing with human beings is that listening cannot be sufficient in itself. Because it is passive, they feel, listening does not communicate anything to the speaker. Actually, nothing could be farther from the truth.

By consistently listening to a speaker you are conveying the idea that: "I'm interested in you as a person, and I think that what you feel is important. I respect your thoughts, and even if I don't agree with them, I know that they are valid for you. I feel sure that you have a contribution to make. I'm not trying to change you or evaluate you. I just want to understand you. I think you're worth listening to, and I want you to know that I'm the kind of a person you can talk to."

The subtle but most important aspect of this is that it is the *demonstration* of the message that works. While it is most difficult to convince someone that you respect him by *telling* him so, you are much more likely to get this message across by really *behaving* that way—by actually *having* and *demonstrating* respect for this person. Listening does this most effectively.

Like other behavior, listening behavior is contagious. This has implications for all communications problems, whether between two people, or within a large organization. To insure good communication between associates up and down the line, one must first take the responsibility for setting a pattern of listening. Just as one learns that anger is usually met with anger, argument with argument, and deception with deception, one can learn that listening can be met with listening. Every person who feels responsibility in a situation can set the tone of the interaction, and the important lesson in this is that any behavior exhibited by one person will eventually be responded to with similar behavior in the other person.

It is far more difficult to stimulate constructive behavior in another person but far more profitable. Listening is one of these constructive behaviors, but if one's attitude is to "wait out" the speaker rather than really listen to him, it will fail. The one who consistently listens with understanding, however, is the one who eventually is most likely to be listened to. If you really want to be heard and understood by another, you can develop him as a potential listener, ready for new ideas, provided you can first develop yourself in these ways and sincerely listen with understanding and respect.

Testing for understanding

Because understanding another person is actually far more difficult than it at first seems, it is important to test constantly your ability to see the world in the way the speaker sees it. You can do this by reflecting in your own words what the speaker seems to mean by his words and actions. His response to this will tell you whether or not he feels understood. A good rule of thumb is to assume that one never really understands until he can communicate this understanding to the other's satisfaction.

Here is an experiment to test your skill in listening. The next time you become involved in a lively or controversial discussion with another person, stop for a moment and suggest that you adopt this ground rule for continued discussion: Before either participant in the discussion can make a point or express an opinion of his own, he must first restate aloud the previous point or position of the other person. This restatement must be accurate enough to satisfy the speaker before the listener can be allowed to speak for himself.

This is something you could try in your own discussion group. Have someone express himself on some topic of emotional concern to the group. Then, before another member expresses his own feelings and thought, he must rephrase the *meaning* expressed by the previous speaker to that individual's satisfaction. Note the changes in the emotional climate and the quality of the discussion when you try this.

SECTION THREE—PROBLEMS IN ACTIVE LISTENING

Active listening is not an easy skill to acquire. It demands practice. Perhaps more important, it may require changes in our own basic attitudes. These changes come slowly and sometimes with considerable difficulty. Let us look at some of the major problems in active listening and what can be done to overcome them.

The personal risk

To be effective at all in active listening, one must have a sincere interest in the speaker. We all live in glass houses as far as our attitudes are concerned. They always show through. And if we are only making a pretense of interest in the speaker, he will quickly pick this up, either consciously or unconsciously. And once he does, he will no longer express himself freely.

Active listening carries a strong element of personal risk. If we manage to accomplish what we are describing here—to sense deeply the feelings of another person, to understand the meaning his experiences have for him, to see the world as he sees it—we risk being changed ourselves. For example, if we permit ourselves to listen our way into the psychological life of a labor leader or agitator—to get the meaning which life has for him—we risk coming to see the world as he sees it. It is threatening to give up, even momentarily, what we believe and start thinking in someone else's terms. It takes a great deal of inner security and courage to be able to risk one's self in understanding another.

For the supervisor, the courage to take another's point of view generally means that he must see *himself* through another's eyes—he must be able to see himself as others see him. To do this may sometimes be unpleasant, but it is far more *difficult* than unpleasant. We are so accustomed to viewing ourselves in certain ways—to seeing and hearing only what we want to see and hear—that it is extremely difficult for a person to free himself from his needs to see things these ways.

Developing an attitude of sincere interest in the speaker is thus no easy task. It can be developed only by being willing to risk seeing the world from the speaker's point of view. If we have a number of such experiences, however, they will shape an attitude which will allow us to be truly genuine in our interest in the speaker.

Hostile expressions

The listener will often hear negative, hostile expressions directed at himself. Such expressions are always hard to listen to. No one likes to hear hostile action or words. And it is not easy to get to the point where one is strong enough to permit these attacks without finding it necessary to defend himself or retaliate.

Because we all fear that people will crumble under the attack of genuine negative feelings, we tend to perpetuate an attitude of pseudo-peace. It is as if we cannot tolerate conflict at all for fear of the damage it could do to us, to the situation, to the others involved. But of course the real damage is done to all these by the denial and suppression of negative feelings.

Out-of-place expressions

There is also the problem of out-of-place expressions, expressions dealing with behavior which is not usually acceptable in our society. In the extreme forms that present themselves before psychotherapists, expressions of sexual perversity or homicidal fantasies are often found blocking to the listener because of their obvious threatening quality. At less extreme levels, we all find unnatural or inappropriate behavior difficult to handle. That is, anything from an "off-color" story told in mixed company to seeing a man weep is likely to produce a problem situation.

In any face-to-face situation, we will find instances of this type which will momentarily, if not permanently, block any communication. In business and industry any expressions of weakness or incompetency will generally be regarded as unacceptable and therefore will block good two-way communication. For example, it is difficult to listen to a supervisor tell of his feelings of failure in being able to "take charge" of a situation in his department because *all* administrators are supposed to be able to "take charge."

Accepting positive feelings

It is both interesting and perplexing to note that negative or hostile feelings or expressions are much easier to deal with in any face-to-face relationship than are truly and deeply positive feelings. This is especially true for the businessman because the culture expects him to be independent, bold, clever, and aggressive and manifest no feelings of warmth, gentleness, and intimacy. He therefore comes to regard these feelings as soft and inappropriate. But no matter how they are regarded, they remain a human need. The denial of these feelings in himself and his associates does not get the executive out of the problem in dealing with them. They simply become veiled and confused. If recognized they would work for the total effort; unrecognized, they work against it.

Emotional danger signals

The listener's own emotions are sometimes a barrier to active listening. When emotions are at their height, when listening is most necessary, it is most difficult to set aside one's own concerns and be understanding. Our emotions are often our own worst enemies when we try to become listeners. The more involved and invested we are in a particular situation or problem, the less we are likely to be willing or able to listen to the feelings and attitudes of others. That is, the more we find it necessary to respond to our own needs, the less we are able to respond to the needs of another. Let us look at some of the main danger signals that warn us that our emotions may be interfering with our listening.

Defensiveness

The points about which one is most vocal and dogmatic, the points which one is most anxious to impose on others—these are always the points one is trying to talk oneself into believing. So one danger signal becomes apparent when you find yourself stressing a point or trying to convince another. It is at these times that you are likely to be less secure and consequently less able to listen.

Resentment of opposition

It is always easier to listen to an idea which is similar to one of your own than to an opposing view. Sometimes, in order to clear the air, it is helpful to pause for a moment when you feel your ideas and position being challenged, reflect on the situation, and express your concern to the speaker.

Clash of personalities

Here again, our experience has consistently shown us that the genuine expression of feelings on the part of the listener will be more helpful in developing a sound relationship than the suppression of them. This is so whether the feelings be resentment, hostility, threat, or admiration. A basically honest relationship, whatever the nature of it, is the most productive of all. The other party becomes secure when he learns that the listener can express his feelings honestly and openly to him. We should keep this in mind when we begin to fear a clash of personalities in the listening relationship. Otherwise, fear of our own emotions will choke off full expression of feelings.

Listening to ourselves

To listen to oneself is a prerequisite to listening to others. And it is often an effective means of dealing with the problems we have outlined above. When we are most aroused, excited, and demanding, we are least able to understand our own feelings and attitudes. Yet, in dealing with the problems of others, it becomes most important to be sure of one's own position, values, and needs.

The ability to recognize and understand the meaning which a particular episode has for you, with all the feelings which it stimulates in you, and the ability to express this meaning when you find it getting in the way of active listening, will clear the air and enable you once again to be free to listen. That is, if some person or situation touches off feelings within you which tend to block your attempts to listen with understanding, begin listening to yourself. It is much more helpful in developing effective relationships to avoid suppressing these feelings. Speak them out as clearly as you can, and try to enlist the other person as a listener to your feelings. A person's listening ability is limited by his ability to listen to himself.

SECTION FOUR—ACTIVE LISTENING AND COMPANY GOALS

"How can listening improve production?"

"We're in business, and it's a rugged, fast, competitive affair. How are we going to find time to counsel our employees?"

"We have to concern ourselves with organizational problems first."

"We can't afford to spend all day listening when there's a job to be done."

"What's morale got to do with production?"

"Sometimes we have to sacrifice an individual for the good of the rest of the people in the company."

Those of us who are trying to advance the listening approach in industry hear these comments frequently. And because they are so honest and legitimate, they pose a real problem. Unfortunately, the answers are not so clear-cut as the questions.

Individual importance

One answer is based on an assumption that is central to the listening approach. That assumption is: the kind of behavior which helps the individual will eventually be the best thing that could be done for the group. Or saying it another way: the things that are best for the individual are best for the company. This is a conviction of ours, based on our experience in psychology and education. The research evidence from industry is only beginning to come in. We find that putting the group first, at the expense of the individual, besides being an uncomfortable individual experience, does *not* unify the group. In fact, it tends to make the group less a group. The members become anxious and suspicious.

We are not at all sure in just what ways the group does benefit from a concern demonstrated for an individual, but we have several strong leads. One is that the group feels more secure when an individual member is being listened to and provided for with concern and sensitivity. And we assume that a secure group will ultimately be a better group. When each individual feels that he need not fear exposing himself to the group, he is likely to contribute more freely and spontaneously. When the leader of a group responds to the individual, puts the individual first, the other members of the group will follow suit, and the group comes to act as a unit in recognizing and responding to the needs of a particular member. This positive, constructive action seems to be a much more satisfying experience for a group than the experience of dispensing with a member.

Listening and production

As to whether or not listening or any other activity designed to better human relations in an industry actually raises production—

whether morale has a definite relationship to production is not known for sure. There are some who frankly hold that there is no relationship to be expected between morale and production—that production often depends upon the social misfit, the eccentric, or the isolate. And there are some who simply choose to work in a climate of cooperation and harmony, in a high-morale group, quite aside from the question of increased production.

A report from the Survey Research Center[44] at the University of Michigan on research conducted at the Prudential Life Insurance Company lists seven findings relating to production and morale. First-line supervisors in high-production work groups were found to differ from those in low-production work groups in that they:

1. Are under less close supervision from their own supervisors.
2. Place less direct emphasis upon production as the goal.
3. Encourage employee participation in the making of decisions.
4. Are more employee-centered.
5. Spend more of their time in supervision and less in straight production work.
6. Have a greater feeling of confidence in their supervisory roles.
7. Feel that they know where they stand with the company.

After mentioning that other dimensions of morale, such as identification with the company, intrinsic job satisfaction, and satisfaction with job status, were not found significantly related to productivity, the report goes on to suggest the following psychological interpretation:

People are more effectively motivated when they are given some degree of freedom in the way in which they do their work than when every action is prescribed in advance. They do better when some degree of decision-making about their jobs is possible than when all decisions are made for them. They respond more adequately when they are treated as personalities than as cogs in a machine. In short if the ego motivations of self-determination, of self-expression, of a sense of personal worth can be tapped, the individual can be more effectively energized. The use of external sanctions, or pressuring for production may work to some degree, but not to the extent that the more internalized motives do. When the individual comes to identify himself with his job and with the work of his group, human resources are much more fully utilized in the production process.

The Survey Research Center has also conducted studies among

---

[44] "Productivity, Supervision, and Employee Morale," *Human Relations*, Series 1, Report 1 (Ann Arbor, Mich.: Survey Research Center, University of Michigan).

workers in other industries. In discussing the results of these studies, Robert L. Kahn writes:

In the studies of clerical workers, railroad workers, and workers in heavy industry, the supervisors with the better production records gave a larger proportion of their time to supervisory functions, especially to the interpersonal aspects of their jobs. The supervisors of the lower-producing sections were more likely to spend their time in tasks which the men themselves were performing, or in the paper-work aspects of their jobs.[45]

Maximum creativeness

There may never be enough research evidence to satisfy everyone on this question. But speaking from a business point of view, in terms of the problem of developing resources for production, the maximum creativeness and productive effort of the human beings in the organization are the richest untapped source of power still existing. The difference between the maximum productive capacity of people and that output which industry is now realizing is immense. We simply suggest that this maximum capacity might be closer to realization if we sought to release the motivation that already exists within people rather than try to stimulate them externally.

This releasing of the individual is made possible first of all by sensitive listening, with respect and understanding. Listening is a beginning toward making the individual feel himself worthy of making contributions, and this could result in a very dynamic and productive organization. Competitive business is never too rugged or too busy to take time to procure the most efficient technological advances or to develop rich raw material sources. But these in comparison to the resources that are already within the people in the plant are paltry. This is industry's major procurement problem.

G. L. Clements, president of Jewel Tea Co., Inc., in talking about the collaborative approach to management says:

We feel that this type of approach recognizes that there is a secret ballot going on at all times among the people in any business. They vote for or against their supervisors. A favorable vote for the supervisor shows up in the cooperation, teamwork, understanding, and production of the

---

[45] Robert L. Kahn, "The Human Factors Underlying Industrial Productivity," *Michigan Business Review,* November 1952.

group. To win this secret ballot, each supervisor must share the problems of his group and work for them.[46]

The decision to spend time listening to his employees is a decision each supervisor or executive has to make for himself. Executives seldom have much to do with products or processes. They have to deal with people who must in turn deal with people who will deal with products or processes. The higher one goes up the line the more he will be concerned with human relations problems, simply because people are all he has to work with. The minute we take a man from his bench and make him a foreman he is removed from the basic production of goods and now must begin relating to individuals instead of nuts and bolts. People are different from things, and our foreman is called upon for a different line of skills completely. His new tasks call upon him to be a special kind of a person. The development of himself as a listener is a first step in becoming this special person.

---

[46] G. L. Clements, "Time for Democracy in Action' at the Executive Level," an address given before the A.M.A. Personnel Conference, February 28, 1951.

CASES

On a certain blindness in human beings[47]

WILLIAM JAMES

Some years ago, while journeying in the mountains in North Carolina, I passed by a large number of "coves," as they call them there, or heads of small valleys between the hills, which had been newly cleared and planted. The impression on my mind was one of unmitigated squalor. The settler had in every case cut down the more manageable trees, and left their charred stumps standing. The larger trees he had girdled and killed, in order that their foliage should not cast a shadow. He had then built a log cabin, plastering its chinks with clay, and had set up a tall zigzag rail fence around the scene of his havoc, to keep the pigs and cattle out. Finally, he had irregularly planted the intervals between the stumps and trees with Indian corn, which grew among the chips; and there he dwelt with his wife and babes—an axe, a gun, a few utensils, and some pigs and chickens feeding in the woods, being the sum total of his possessions.

The forest had been destroyed; and what had "improved" it out of existence was hideous, a sort of ulcer, without a single element of artificial grace to make up for the loss of Nature's beauty. Ugly, indeed, seemed the life of the squatter, scudding, as the sailors say, under bare poles, beginning again away back where our first ancestors started, and by hardly a single item the better off for all the achievements of the intervening generations.

Talk about going back to nature! I said to myself, oppressed by the dreariness, as I drove by. Talk of a country life for one's old age and for one's children! Never thus, with nothing but the bare ground and one's bare hands to fight the battle! Never, without the best spoils of

47 From *Essays in Faith and Morals,* by William James (New York: Longmans, Green & Co., Inc., 1943). Reprinted by permission.

culture woven in! The beauties and commodities gained by the centuries are sacred. They are our heritage and birthright. No modern person ought to be willing to live a day in such a state of rudimentariness and denudation.

Then I said to the mountaineer who was driving me, "What sort of people are they who have to make these new clearings?" "All of us," he replied. "Why, we ain't happy here, unless we are getting one of these coves under cultivation." I instantly felt that I had been losing the whole inward significance of the situation. Because to me the clearings spoke of naught but denudation, I thought that to those whose sturdy arms and obedient axes had made them they could tell no other story. But, when *they* looked on the hideous stumps, what they thought of was personal victory. The chips, the girdled trees, and the vile split rails spoke of honest sweat, persistent toil and final reward. The cabin was a warrant of safety for self and wife and babes. In short, the clearing, which to me was a mere ugly picture on the retina, was to them a symbol redolent with moral memories and sang a very paean of duty, struggle, and success.

I had been as blind to the peculiar ideality of their conditions as they certainly would also have been to the ideality of mine, had they had a peep at my strange indoor academic ways of life at Cambridge.

The cocktail party[48]

The following conversation occurred between Fred Lyons and William Baird at a cocktail party. Both men were in their early thirties. Lyons had been practicing dentistry for six years, and Baird had just been graduated from law school. Both were veterans of World War II and had received G.I. Bill benefits toward their college educations. Each, however, had worked part-time to supplement his income during his years in college. They had known each other on a casual basis for about a year.

LYONS: Well, Bill, I hear you're about to take your bar examination. What are your plans if you get by them?

---

[48] Adapted from a case prepared by Eleanor Lynch Roeser. Printed by permission.

BAIRD: There's no *if* about it, Fred. But to answer your question, I'm lining up a practice right now.

LYONS: Do you mean to tell me you have no doubts about passing the bar?

BAIRD: None, really. This is the way I look at it: I attended one of the better law schools in the country and I was one of the better men in my class. So I really don't have any qualms at all.

LYONS: *(Slightly sarcastically)* And I suppose you have no qualms about succeeding in law, in general.

BAIRD: No, I'm really quite confident that I'll make a go of it.

LYONS: Well, buddy, you've got a lot to learn. [He then began to recount at length some of his own difficulties and disappointments in starting in his profession.] And when you come right down to it, it's a plenty tough uphill climb to establish a reputation and a following. Frankly, Bill, you're going to have trouble attracting a clientele with this superconfidence of yours.

BAIRD: There's where you're dead wrong. A man has to have assurance and confidence in himself or no one else will have confidence in him. Do you think a person would want his legal problems handled by a fellow who didn't give the appearance that he was dead certain he knew what he was doing?

LYONS: To be honest, I think the average man would be repelled rather than attracted by this attitude. Your client, the man on the street, wants to feel that his lawyer is his type of man. You've got to speak his language in order to convince him you understand his problem. Here, I'll give you a test. Suppose I come to you with a problem. [He then posed a legal question concerning income tax.] How would you handle it?

BAIRD: I can't give you an opinion on that. I'd have to have a good many more facts and I'd have to study them.

LYONS: Now, do you see? Be honest with yourself, Bill. You don't have the experience and if you parade around with that cocksure attitude of yours, you're not going to get to first base.

BAIRD: *(Both men were somewhat angered by now.)* Now, listen, Fred. Law is a science of the mind. Dentistry is more of a mechanical science where you might expect to solve some problems immediately. And even in dentistry you can't pass judgment on an oral problem without an examination and maybe even an X-ray.

LYONS: Well, all I can say, Bill—if you don't learn a more humble approach; if you don't bring your speaking and attitude down to the level of the average man, you're asking for trouble.

BAIRD: Well, if you ask me, the "average man" isn't going to have much confidence in anyone who is *too* average.

The afternoon was "saved" by a third person who broke into the conversation and managed to switch the subject to baseball.

An evening at the Leningrad Ballet[49]
TOM BURNAM

Valerie didn't seem to want us to go to the ballet. She was the young, bright, and extremely attractive Intourist guide assigned to the three American couples in a party of some forty foreign travelers at the Hotel Oktober in Leningrad. The others were mostly Finns, who had left Helsinki on the same train with us two days before.

The subject of the ballet came up at breakfast. Valerie frowned slightly. "I don't know that you would particularly enjoy the production," she said. This surprised us. Valerie, like any good guide, was not one to downgrade the attractions of her city, and Leningraders are even more proud of their ballet than they are of their magnificent baroque subway. Rivalry with Moscow has a good deal to do with it. Leningrad's subway is newer, its ballet older than Moscow's.

"What is the ballet tonight?" one of the wives asked.

"It is a modern one," Valerie said.

"Oh, that's fine," I said. "I can take ballet or leave it alone; but given a choice, I would prefer 'Billy the Kid' to 'Sleeping Beauty.'"

"But what's it *about?*" insisted Carl Root.

"It has to do with colored people," said Valerie. "You might find it rather dull." I am sure that she was not being sardonic; though she was not without humor, there was no malice in her. I am sure also, now, that she herself had not seen the production. At any rate, we all must have jumped to pretty much the same conclusion, although none of us said a word about it.

"I'd like to see it," said Carl. "Can you get us tickets?"

"Well, yes, I suppose so," said Valerie. "How many would you like?" She was not enthusiastic.

"Six, I suppose," said Carl. We all nodded.

"Excuse me," said a woman seated at a nearby table. "I have overheard. May I, too, get a ticket?" This was Frau Schmidt, small, ener-

---

49 From *The Reporter*, October 25, 1962, pp. 45–47. Reprinted with permission.

getic, and German, who had elected to join our group on at least an informal basis, since like us she spoke neither Finnish nor Russian. She was a widow, traveling alone, and we learned that she was that rare phenomenon in Europe, a woman professor complete with Ph.D. Valerie turned to answer her, and I saw on our young guide's face, very briefly, that slight shadow Russians still show, as if not able to help themselves, in the presence of Germans.

"I believe I can get seven tickets," said Valerie, including Frau Schmidt indirectly.

That evening we hurried through dinner, knowing that taxicabs can be a problem in Leningrad, as they can also be in Manhattan.

[After a hectic taxi ride we were in front of the theater.] Like much of Leningrad, the theater is 18th-century baroque and does not spare the curlicues. It is a handsome place; the auditorium is spacious, acoustically superb, and quite comfortable. Our seats were good ones. There was a flimsy little program, in blue ink on white paper six by four inches. Though the language had begun to lose some of its strangeness, the letters to look less like a curious form of mirror writing, we could make nothing of the title. Anyway, I thought, it is about colored people.

It was, all right. Scarcely had the production got under way than we had seen (*a*) a Negro, evidently a student, realizing that his happy college days were over and he was back home when he was brutally pushed to the ground on a railroad-station platform; (*b*) a beefy caricature of a planter, in shorts and carrying a golf club, lording it over the field hands; (*c*) a fearful, tremulous, secret, and foredoomed affair between the blonde daughter of the brutal plantation owner and the young Negro home with his B.A.

You must remember that so far as we could know we were the only Americans in the very large audience; we were almost in the center of the sold-out house, in seats we had taken away from Russians, one might say, and we felt very conspicuous. All around us, we could notice members of the audience studying us discreetly, turning to whisper to their companions; above, in the balconies, we seemed invariably to catch someone's eye if we looked up. Certainly there was nothing overtly impolite about it, but I suppose it must have got to us a little.

Anyway, I am sure that as the first act progressed, we all stopped really *seeing* it; or we saw it through the glass of our Americanism, with a rising sense of tension. Of course the dancing and the music were superb; the Russians simply do not permit themselves anything less in their ballet. The audience, caught up in the production, frequently interrupted with bursts of applause. By the time the first-act curtain fell at last, to really thunderous handclapping and cheers, I was almost beginning to feel that the loud approval of the audience, the very smiles and bows of the prima ballerina, were somehow directed at us.

At intermission time in Russia a queer kind of promenade goes on, like the Grand March at a high school's Senior Ball. Several abreast, often with arms linked, those of the audience who do not stay in their seats move solemnly around and around the lobby, which is usually large enough and bare enough to permit this kind of entr'acte exercise. The six of us rose while Frau Schmidt stayed in her single seat a row or two away. But we did not feel like joining in the promenade, so we stood at its vortex, while the Russians wheeled around us like slow-motion hostiles circling a wagon train.

"Let's get out of here," said Carl's wife, Lois, "it's fairly obvious this thing is full of blatant anti-American propaganda. Do *you* feel comfortable in this audience?" She nodded at the solemn promenaders around us.

"You afraid they'll turn on us, or something?" Carl asked. "Russians don't act that way. At least, not unless they're told to."

"Oh, I know it," said Lois. "I'm not really frightened, I guess. It's just—well, uncomfortable. Did you see that set? It was absurd. I suppose it was meant to represent the American South, but what in the world was that big billboard, or whatever it was, supposed to mean?"

"The one with the giraffe?" Carl said. "That's all they know about America. Like Coleridge putting tigers on the Susquehanna."

The set had a ramshackle tarpaper hut with Negro children gathered around it, the billboard, and a modern building in the background.

"What was that sign that said something like 'Afrikan'?" I asked.

"Must be Russian for 'Negro,' " said Lois. "That was supposed to show how the schools are segregated, I imagine."

At this point the warning bell sounded, and the promenaders broke up their march to return to their seats. Our group followed.

"You go ahead," I said to my wife. "I want to buy a souvenir program." But the elderly woman who had been selling the programs shook her head: she was sold out. As I turned away, a young Russian with the look of a student about him was at my elbow.

"Please," he said in English, "take my program."

"Permit me, then, at least to pay you what it cost," I said.

"No, no," said the Russian youth. *"Nyet."* Russians speaking English sometimes seem to lapse into *"nyet"* when they really mean it.

"But this is not fair," I said; I knew the program had cost him thirty kopecks.

The youth smiled. "You are a guest," he said. "We do not see so many Americans in Leningrad, especially at this season." His smile seemed almost to be making amends for something. "Do take it; I insist."

I could not, without rudeness, push the issue further. I thanked him and hurried on in.

Frau Schmidt was in my seat, talking to the others. She rose at once and moved back to her own. Carl and Lois and my wife seemed somewhat subdued. I raised my eyebrows questioningly, and my wife said, "Do you know what Frau Schmidt just told us?"

"She can read Russian, just a little," Carl said.

There was a pause. "Well?" I asked.

"The damn thing has nothing at all to do with America," Carl said. "It's about Africa. Africa, and all the troubles in the Congo, and apartheid, and so on."

"I suppose we should have figured it out long ago," Lois said. "The giraffe and all. I just thought they didn't know any better than that about the South. Everything falls into place now."

And everything did, then and for the remaining two acts. The burden of secret defensiveness we had carried in the first act—indeed, since our morning talk with Valerie—fell away. Nobody was out after us; though we still could not follow the story line precisely, it was obvious that the pith-helmeted tyrants were the Belgians, the Boers, and (possibly) the British. Our reaction to the rest of the ballet, in retrospect, amuses me and saddens me a little, too. For we enjoyed what followed, I must say, enormously. Something like "Give 'em hell!" must have shown on our faces as we watched the violent plot unfold: this was just the kind of treatment apartheid deserved, by God.

When it was all over, to crashing applause and cheers, with flowers pelting onto the stage in true Russian fashion, everyone in the auditorium standing, the dancers returning again and again, we were all right up there on our feet with the rest of the audience, cheering and clapping. When at last we turned to thread our way out, we nodded and smiled to others in the crowd, who nodded and smiled back in the friendliest possible fashion.

Is this man mad?[50]

Imagine that the individual described in the following brief case history came to you for treatment. How would you diagnose his ailment and what therapy would you recommend? . . .

All through childhood, K. was extremely meditative, usually preferred to be alone. He often had mysterious dreams and fits, during which he sometimes fainted. In late puberty, K. experienced elaborate auditory and visual hallucinations, uttered incoherent words, and had recurrent spells of sudden coma. He was frequently found running wildly through the countryside or eating the bark of trees and was known to throw himself with abandon into fire and water. On many occasions he wounded himself with knives or other weapons. K. believed he could "talk to spirits" and "chase ghosts." He was certain of his power over all sorts of supernatural forces.

THE ACTUAL DIAGNOSIS

Believe it or not, K. was not found insane, nor was he committed to the nearest institution for the mentally ill. Instead, in due course, he became one of the leading and most respected members of his community.

How this strange turn of events could come about may become more plausible to you if we supply an important bit of information that was purposely left out of the case history above.

K., we should have told you, was a member of a primitive tribe of fishermen and reindeer herders that inhabits the arctic wilderness of Eastern Siberia. In this far-off culture the same kind of behavior that we regard as symptomatic of mental illness is considered evidence of an individual's fitness for an important social position—that of medicine man or shaman.

The hallucinations, fits, manic episodes and periods of almost complete withdrawal that marked his early years were considered signs that he had been chosen by some higher power for an exalted role. His behavioral eccentricities were, in fact, prerequisite to his becoming a shaman, just as balance, solidity, self-confidence and aggressiveness are prerequisite for the young man who hopes to be successful in American business.

Sociologists and anthropologists explain that shamanism serves two

---

50 *State of Mind*, published by Ciba Pharmaceutical Products, Inc., Summit, N.J., Vol. I, No. 1 (January 1957). Reprinted by permission.

socially useful purposes in Siberian society. In the first place, it provides an approved outlet for the person of unstable temperament. It allows him to let off steam through an emotionally satisfying dramatic performance in which he summons spirits and manipulates the supernatural. In the second place, shamanism provides entertainment for other tribesmen and welcome relief from the monotony of their bleak environment.

Business customs from Malaya to Murmansk[51]

H. K. ARNING

The cultural differences between nations have developed on the basis of religious, political, and economical traditions. Some of them may appear unimportant to the foreigner—but ignorance about them can be dangerous to the success of business operations abroad. It is worthwhile, therefore, to look at some of the areas in which international marketers may experience difficulties that can be embarrassing or costly—and that in some cases can cost the company further business.

Personal manners

Business outside North America follows rather conservative rules, and the personal appearance, including dressing habits, are more formal than in Canada or the United States. To arrive at a business appointment without coat and tie indicates lack of respect in any country, but particularly in Asia the question of respect is more important than in many other parts of the world. One can always take off his coat if everybody else does, but as a rule it is advisable to keep on the formal side. Physical attitudes can also be important: For example, it is considered rude in Southeast Asia, particularly in Thailand and Laos, to display the sole of the foot or to sit with the legs crossed. In the same area it may be considered offensive to place your hands on your hips; many Chinese will regard it as signifying that you are angry.

---

51 *Management Review*, October 1964. Reprinted by permission.

Physical contact should be avoided throughout the Middle and Far East. Handshaking is commonly accepted in most of the Asian countries, but particularly in India and Thailand the initiative in this respect should be left to the national hosts, who often regard any physical contact with strangers—even handshaking—as distasteful. In Moslem countries, avoid linking arms or putting your arm around the shoulders of your wife; it may be unlawful, and would in most cases cause some embarrassment, since such physical contact is regarded as a private matter that should be confined to private quarters.

There is a sharp contrast between the attitude toward physical contact in large parts of the Middle and Far East on the one hand, and Latin America on the other. Again, it is undoubtedly helpful to let the host take the lead. Foreign visitors to Latin American countries have often attempted to avoid the repeated embracings, but such attempts are as a rule misunderstood by the local nationals, who interpret them as a sign of reserved attitude—which in turn breeds distrust. The same applies to a certain extent in respect of the distance between the faces. Asians will as a rule prefer a substantial distance compared to North American standards, while Latin Americans tend to be more comfortable with a distance of just a few inches. Thus, a businessman from North America may easily appear to be crowding in Asia, and give the impression of running away from his host in Latin America—neither of which is conducive to a relaxed business climate.

No trespassing

The European concept of privacy may sometimes appear unreasonably exaggerated to North Americans. Europeans consider it distasteful to talk about their family in the office or the plant, and it is not usual to meet colleagues on a social basis after business hours; family, evenings, and weekends are private matters that most Europeans prefer to keep separate from business. People may live for twenty years in the same house without ever inviting their neighbors over for a cup of coffee or a drink; they are courteous and friendly to each other, but they preserve their privacy. Such attitudes may possibly explain why the American-style cocktail party has not gained very wide popularity in Europe.

First names are seldom used outside the Western hemisphere, possibly because of the differentiation of the word "you" which occurs in many languages. The polite form of "you" expresses respect, while the familiar form is more intimate and is employed only within the family or between very close friends. For business purposes the respectful form is used almost without exception, and to combine it with first names would be comparable to saying Mr. Bob or Mr. Jim in English. The resentment against use of first names is particularly evident among North Europeans, who often will feel embarrassed when business acquaintances infringe on what they consider strictly private.

Dinner at eight

In most countries it is not customary to invite nonrelatives to dinner at home; business acquaintances are entertained in clubs or restaurants. To receive an invitation to a private home is a great honor, and it should be kept in mind that an Indian, for example, never extends such invitations for the purpose of furthering business aims; that would be a violation of sacred hospitality rules. The codes in this respect vary with geographical areas and, generally speaking, only Australasia and the Scandinavian countries come fairly close to North American practices. A detail worth remembering overseas, especially in Scandinavia and the Netherlands, is the custom that the visitor brings some flowers or a box of confectionery to the hostess when he is invited to dinner. The cost or size of the gift is not important; it is the courtesy that matters.

All over the world it is usually appreciated when foreigners follow local eating customs. Often, local food can be very worthwhile, and to experiment with chopsticks, for example, can be highly entertaining—particularly for the host. It is a practical exercise in applied good will, and if you give it an honest try and prove that you cannot manage, your host will not be offended if you ask for knife and fork. It may be useful to remember that Chinese dinners usually consist of eight courses, and that the guest is supposed to remain hungry throughout the seven first ones. The eighth course is usually fried rice or noodles, and at that stage it is customary for the guest to help himself to a modest quantity, thus indicating that he has had enough; otherwise the host will order still further dishes. In Chinese homes it is common practice that the guest will respectfully decline to be the first to help himself from any course, no matter how much the host insists. In Scandinavia it is proper etiquette to shake hands with the hostess thanking her for the meal when the dinner is over. It is much appreciated when foreign visitors are aware of this courtesy.

The Asian attitudes to consumption of alcohol range from partial prohibition in India to various degrees of liberal drinking in Chinese and Japanese company. Contrary to common belief, the local brews are not very potent, and although the principle of temperance is highly recommended, it may be wise to follow the hosts even into simulating a slight degree of intoxication. Complete abstinence from drinking is often regretted, but it is also respected.

In this context, it should be noted that in an Asian society where a rigid code of formality has been deeply ingrained from childhood, the relaxing effects of alcohol may perhaps be more appreciated than in Western societies; for business purposes there may be special reasons to keep that in mind.

In Mediterranean countries and in Latin America, it is rare indeed to see intoxicated people in public. The nationals of these countries are proud of their wines and they enjoy them frequently, but in modest quantities. Scandinavians are said to be heavy drinkers, but that reputation is hardly justified, at least not in business circles.

Pride and status

In countries that recently have obtained political independence, the government and its policies are a matter of considerable pride. Most people will be delighted for an opportunity to explain political and also religious questions to foreigners, but it is advisable to avoid unfavorable comparisons with other systems or religions. There is little satisfaction and still less business to be derived from hurting the host's pride or from questioning his religious convictions.

Some North American businessmen tend to judge business acquaintances abroad on the basis of their status symbols. Many times such judgments are made subconsciously or automatically, and it may be useful to keep in mind that the yardsticks abroad are different. The top floor is not necessarily the executive suite; in Japanese department stores, the top floor is reserved for bargain counters. The location and size of the office or the carpeting of the floor may be subject to practical, legal, or climatic considerations. In fact, in a number of countries the nationals will flatly deny that they have any system of material status symbols at all. There may be many reasons for that, among which could be mentioned that differences in caste or class may make such symbols distasteful; sometimes the language or diction will express status, sometimes the name or title will indicate proud traditions or great wealth. Family, relatives, connections, and friendships are in most cases by far the most important status symbols and, actually, materialistic symbols would often be completely out of place.

Business manners

Through the centuries, it has been a custom in most countries that the eldest son follow the line of his father in career fields such as civil service, the armed forces, and certain professions. The introduction of communism brought an abrupt end to such bourgeois traditions in Eastern Europe. Presently, however, there are indications that the former aristocracy in the communist countries quietly continue their old traditions: the medical families still raise doctors, and the off-spring of the merchant clans join the state trading monopolies. This does not in any way imply a change in the communist doctrine, but it is noteworthy that some of the old and proud traditions are carried forward, notably the sense of honor and integrity that prevailed in business circles in Russia, Poland, Hungary, and Czechoslovakia before the communist upheaval. At that time, the East European countries were in many respects similar to the conservative Western Europe, and some of the old cultural attitudes are still recognizable. Due to the nature of the political system, however, the businessmen have not been exposed to the modifying influence of frequent contact with foreigners, and consequently, they often appear rigidly formal, which is evident in their dress, speech, and observance of traditional business rituals—as well as in their meticulous fulfillment of contract obligations.

Behind the Iron Curtain

Westerners sometimes find it difficult to appreciate that import and export agencies in the East European countries are part of the enormous communist civil service, and considerable time is required before a decision can be made on a Western business proposal. Plans and suggestions have to be approved by a seemingly endless number of committees, and in some cases it has happened that several years have elapsed before a final word is forthcoming.

Russian negotiators often have formal training in both bargaining and chess playing, which may explain why every move they make is so carefully planned. They never seem to get tired, and their negotiating skills may often test the Westerner's professional and human endurance. When agreement on one point apparently has been reached, they may start the next day by going through all the same motions again, pinning down every little detail. As purchasing agents they are shopping all over the world for the most advantageous deals, and they are fully aware that the centralization of the communist purchasing functions put them in a favorable bargaining position: The orders are not numerous, but they are sizable.

Late deliveries are a nuisance in most countries, but they may be more than that for East Europeans: A delay of just a few days may upset their quota system, and thus deprive them of their bonus. Western suppliers who are unable to meet the rigid communist system of quotas and deadlines will be unlikely to receive new or additional orders.

Little white lies

It may not be pleasant to learn that truth is a relative matter, which actually is the case in a number of countries both in the Far East and in Latin America. Form may be more important, and it is obvious that that may complicate regular business transactions. If the foreign visitor is pressing hard to obtain an agreement, he may find that his host will sign the deal just to be pleasant, and without any intention of keeping to the contract. Similarly, and particularly in the Far East, it may be considered rude to say straightforwardly that the Westerner's product or service is unsuited for the Oriental customer's purpose, and the sale may be kept hanging in the air simply because the buyer does not want to be unpleasant.

When a trader in the Middle East asks a price that is twenty times higher than what he actually expects to obtain, we have a situation where the buyer obviously will be pleased when he has managed to haggle the price down to size. Both seller and buyer have made a good deal, and both are satisfied. Pleasantries are considered important, and the time required is immaterial.

Both in Latin America and in the Orient it is customary to spend considerable time talking around the business on hand, sometimes about completely irrelevant matters. One of the reasons for this habit is a traditional distrust of foreigners, which they try to overcome by developing a first stage of friendship before they come down to business. It should be noted in this context that friendships in many parts of the world are considered obligations to a much greater extent than is customary in North America and that such obligations may imply substantial help over and beyond what may be agreed on in the contract. (This is one of the reasons why business with relatives and close family friends has priority over any other business in most parts of the world.)

From here to eternity

In Japan, it is not unusual to have long periods of silence in the middle of negotiations. Although it may be nerve-racking, it usually pays off handsomely if the Westerner can restrain himself enough to outwait the silence of his hosts. It may take thirty minutes, perhaps more, but in the meantime his silence is negotiating for him, usually better than he could do orally. Sometimes Oriental businessmen take advantage of the fact that time has become almost an obsession in Western countries. A Japanese once said that Westerners have a most convenient weakness: If they are kept waiting long enough they will agree to almost anything. Consequently, negotiators visiting Japan will often be asked how long they have planned to stay. Once that is known, they will be pleasantly entertained, while negotiations are kept inconclusive until a couple of hours before they are scheduled to leave, when the real business starts. Another aspect of time is the common lack of punctuality for business appointments in the East. The Westerner will learn that an hour or two is just an insignificant slice of eternity.

In fact, the question of punctuality is considered liberally in most parts of the world except in Northern Europe, where it is customary to arrive before the scheduled time. To be late for a business appointment in Northern Europe is often regarded as so disrespectful that it may hamper subsequent business relations.

Cash and credit

The terms of payment in many countries follow rules that are different from what is commonplace in North America. In Japan, it is not unusual to regard ninety-day or six-month promissory notes as cash payment. Good customers of Chinese business houses have an almost unlimited credit. A Chinese does not want to ask a rich man for money, and consequently the renowned Chinese tailors in Hong Kong may wait for years before they issue a bill to Westerners living in the Crown Colony. On the other hand, a Chinese is highly reluctant to grant credit to strangers, even if he knows that the customer has an important position in a large business corporation and carries fully satisfactory credit credentials. There are old and deeply ingrained traditions which form the reasons for this apparently contradictory attitude.

For exporters it may be useful to remember that interest rates in Asia often range from 8 to 12 percent per year for bank loans—in Latin America, from 1 to 2 percent per month. A liberal extension of credit may therefore be a strong sales argument in both areas. In Europe, the cost of capital is comparable to North American levels.

In most of the Orient, entertainment bills should be checked before they are paid. It is not at all unusual to overcharge foreigners, and if one only starts to add up the items, the bill will frequently be taken away for correction. In a number of Asian countries, the price for smaller services should be agreed on in advance, as the negotiating right is forfeited when the service has been performed. It may be rather embarrassing, for instance, when taxi drivers in the Middle East at the end of the trip start arguing at the top of their voices and with arms raised over the head, claiming a fare that is many times higher than what you are used to or might have agreed on before you hired the taxi.

Bribes or gifts?

Bribery is a relative matter, depending on the country and the circumstances. In Asia, the practice of giving gifts follows local rules which are too complicated to be discussed here. It should be noted, however, that in a number of countries civil servants are notoriously underpaid, and it is more or less understood that they perform certain services against a reasonable reward, provided receipts are not required. Such services may consist of such things as speeding up the handling of applications, arranging meetings with higher officials, cutting red tape, or extending the validity of visas and import licenses. It is highly advisable, however, to ask reliable advice, preferably from your consular service, before doing anything that might be construed as compromising the integrity of a civil servant abroad. What may be common practice in one country may be severely penalized in another.

Advertising abroad

A substantial amount of literature about international advertising is available in North America, but as almost all of it is intended for West European or Latin American markets, it may be useful to mention a few points that should be taken into consideration when advertising is prepared for communist countries and for the Far East.

Marketing of Western consumer products in the Soviet Union may not be so remote any longer, and it may be worthwhile to note that since consumer articles have been in short supply for a long time in Eastern Europe, there has been no need to advertise whatever was available. However, advertising has been resorted to in order to dispose of slow-moving or substandard articles, and that has to a certain extent brought advertising into disrepute. The situation would make marketing difficult for Western businessmen who are accustomed to rely heavily on advertising, and it would appear to be advisable to put stress on quality and guarantees if an advertising campaign is to be launched.

Another difference between Western and communist advertising is in the use of female models: East Europeans regard as distasteful the use of models to attract attention for commercial purposes. An enterprising Russian garment manufacturer was recently criticized in *Pravda* because he used models in advertisements for bathing suits. The display of naked skin was, in *Pravda's* opinion, a sign of degeneracy.

Some elaborate advertising campaigns that have been launched in Asia have turned out to be complete failures because the marketers did not research and explore beyond the conventional data, particularly regarding the religions and superstitions of the countries concerned. Asia is composed of so many countries, religions, languages, and cultures that only wide diversification of the advertisements and a careful selection of media will render satisfactory returns.

There may even be a diversity of languages within the boundaries of the same country: the Commercial Manager of Air India, Mr. S. K. Kooka, has suggested that advertisers may use the Tamil language in South India, Hindi in North India, and Gujerati around Bombay. Also, it is almost impossible to translate directly from an alphabetic language into the characters and symbols of Chinese and Japanese, and still retain the same message.

The choice of illustrations is largely influenced by religious factors, for pictures of birds or animals or animal products may have specific religious connotations. Even pictures of people have to be selected to fit the cultural environment of the local market.

Lucky colors

Colors have to be used with utmost care. To the Chinese, red is a lucky color; the Thai would prefer yellow for the same reason. The combination of purple and green is acceptable in several Asian countries, supposedly from the time when the leaders of the Shinto religion wore those colors. On the unfortunate side, the combination of black, white, and blue is suggestive of a funeral to the Chinese. Throughout the Far East there is a substantial amount of what Westerners usually call superstition connected with almost any color or combination of colors. For business purposes, superstition has to be respected; one cannot ignore it.

There are many pitfalls in international business that are caused by cultural differences, and to be trapped in one of them may have undesirable and sometimes costly consequences. Among foreign businessmen there is a small but increasing awareness of the existence of such differences, and over the long run the most extreme of them may be modified so that the gap is lessened. It is important, however, that visitors do not openly attempt to speed up any such development or to change the cultural habits of the local nationals. Such attempts will understandably be resented, and the repercussions on business will hardly make them worthwhile. Even when people are imitating knowingly, they like to feel that they have developed something themselves, and to tear down their illusions in that respect does not serve any useful purpose—at least not as far as the cultural differences that affect international business are concerned.

Preston Lee, C.P.A.[52]

The day was a cold one even for February but the sky was cloudless and sunlight streamed through the window of Professor Robert

---

[52] All names have been disguised.

Dillon's study. Dillon was entertaining two old friends, Wallace Borden and Frank Compton.

"When you finish with a situation like we went through with Preston Lee, and look back on it, you are never sure you did the right thing," said Wallace Borden. "It just makes you sick when a promising young man, who might have developed into a partner, leaves you for a routine job as a payroll auditor in an insurance company."

Wallace T. Borden was the partner in charge of the Oklahoma City office of J. D. Rodman & Co., C.P.A.s, the headquarters office of which was located in Ft. Worth, Texas. There was also an office in Austin, Texas. The firm enjoyed an excellent reputation and was particularly well known in the oil industry which provided a majority of its clients. The Oklahoma City office was opened in 1956, with Borden in charge, and since that time it had grown slowly but steadily. In 1963, Frank Compton, an outstanding member of the professional staff, became the second resident partner in Oklahoma City. In 1972 there were five men on the professional staff in that office.

Preston Lee was 22 when he joined the firm in August 1968 at a salary of $8,800. He had graduated from the University of Oklahoma three months earlier and had then served a short tour of duty in the Air Force as required by the agreement under which he had been helped through college. A good looking young man over six feet tall and weighing over 200 pounds, Lee had earned a B+ average on his major, accountancy, and a B— average overall.

He had taken the C.P.A. examination in May 1968, while still in college and secured a condition. In November he took the examination again, and passed it. When he resigned in December 1971 his salary was $11,500 and he was due for a raise.

Wallace Borden tells the story

Professor Dillon gazed vacantly out the window of his study. Then he turned to Borden:

DILLON: How did all of this happen?

BORDEN: Before I tell you about Preston Lee, I should mention some related matters. In my opinion, salaries paid by the Oklahoma City office have been and are comparable to those paid by other C.P.A. firms in Oklahoma City. We are pretty much in the middle bracket. The University tells us that most of their graduates are going out at higher than our starting salary. But most of these men are going out of Oklahoma— many of them to the East—so it is hard to compare.

It is our policy to hire men right out of college and develop them, so of course it is rare for them to have taken the C.P.A. exam when hired. Press Lee was an exception. Of course, we put some pressure on the men to get their certificates and apparently the amount of pressure we put on has a lot to do with how many qualify. In 1968 when Lee passed the exam he was the only man on the staff who actually had the C.P.A. but today they all have it. I am talking about staff of course, not partners.

In a few cases, we have really put on the heat. For example, in July 1971 we told Condon and Burke, our two oldest men (see exhibits), that we weren't giving them a raise because they hadn't got their C.P.A.'s, and that their future with the firm didn't look very bright unless they got busy and qualified. Burke passed the exam in November 1971 and Condon quit in January 1972 to become comptroller of a construction firm.

Preston Lee: The first year

When Press Lee came with us, Condon and Burke had been with the firm for several years and were our in-charge staff men. Most of their work was with clients with whom they had established relationships.

Lee had been with us only a few months when I had to throw him in on a mess. The accounting department of one of our clients broke down, and Condon and Burke were both tied up, so Lee went in under my supervision. A key person had left the client's employ and the records were messed up. Press moved right in and every time I checked, which was frequently at first, I found he was on top of it so I began to relax my supervision. He brought the job out in good shape and, naturally, we developed confidence in him and began pushing him along.

We don't usually give a man so much responsibility so fast but in May 1969 we had two senior men leave us [see exhibit]. One of them, Corcoran, had been unable to pass the C.P.A. exam. The other, Graham, was a C.P.A. but he didn't quite measure up to our standards.

Shortly after the job I just mentioned we were called in by one of our clients. The comptroller is a C.P.A. and he has strong ideas about being audited by a non-C.P.A. In spite of the fact that Press Lee was just out of college, he and this comptroller got along fine and he was the only one who was permitted to do the audit. Naturally, this puffed him up.

A difference of opinion over professional ethics

I think it was in his second year with us, that Press began to feel that our firm was lacking in aggressiveness—that we were self-satisfied and didn't have the hustle to expand the practice. He told us that he thought the firm should get much more active in social affairs, particularly at country clubs—giving parties to drum up more clients—and that he thought he should have an expense account to cover the cost of lunches and drinks for clients' personnel and others. He pointed to the fact that some of the Oklahoma City offices of the big national firms were doing just that and that one had started a new office and in six years it had grown to a professional staff of about 50 men.

DILLON: Was that so?

BORDEN: Well, yes, we see the partners of that firm in the clubs and hotels talking to our clients. They are getting themselves well known and putting ideas in people's heads about the wonderful job they are doing, giving them brochures such as the one on the federal income tax —tips for oil companies. They have been passing these out around town in fairly substantial quantities.

We discussed the question of professional ethics with Press and his feeling seemed to be that they were doing it, and no one was telling them they couldn't, and if we didn't do it too we would lose out—in fact we had lost out, according to him.

Along toward the end of 1970 we were at a clients' Christmas party and Press had quite a few drinks under his belt—not really out of control—and he was talking to a business associate of the client. This fellow hit it off real well with Press. They both got pretty high, and started talking about auditing, and Press said to him, "Why the hell don't you bring your audit over to our firm and let us take care of you," and the man said, "Well, I am just going to do that." As a matter of fact, his auditor is a good C.P.A. friend of ours, and that sort of thing is apt to be interpreted in several ways, none of which we would like, particularly, as far as the profession is concerned. So we discouraged Lee from talking to the guy anymore and he was pretty unhappy, I'll tell you. Here he had some business all lined up and we threw cold water on it. He was really upset.

So we weren't about to give him an expense account. We didn't think it was the proper thing to do with such a young man. We had serious reservations about whether we could control it adequately, or his behavior either. And then there was the effect on the other staff men.

So, you see, from Press's standpoint we were just old fogies.

By the end of 1970 we rated Lee as probably having more potential than either Condon or Burke who were many years his senior. Our problem was to get his attitude straightened out, and get him working the way they were. They were primarily trying to build the firm and accomplish the work assigned to them in a way that would please the client and the partners. Press was much more concerned with selling himself to the client, and in many cases his success at this was outstanding; he made friends easily. He was on friendly terms with the other members of the staff except Condon, though it was true that there was a little problem because they began to feel that he was getting breaks that they weren't. There was an undercurrent of jealousy among the other staff men, and Condon and Lee were openly hostile.

Lee had been able to pass them in his technical competence in many areas; to a considerable extent he knew more and was doing a better job. And he was a C.P.A. and until May 1971, when Burke got it, none of them was.

Except for the problem between Condon and Lee, the relations between the men on the staff weren't bad. Ours had always been a pretty open office with usually good-natured ribbing going on all the time. Corcoran, Graham and Lee became fairly close friends and played golf, bowled and partied together quite a bit. Condon and Burke did not join in this very much; Condon, particularly, avoided it presumably because he didn't drink.

Except for Lee, none of the men ever expressed any reluctance to work together, nor disparaged the abilities of others, at least not to me.

After Press was notified that he had passed the C.P.A. we suggested that he take on some community work and he joined some Jaycee committees. He always did everything with a lot of enthusiasm—or with none; when he went flat he went really flat—so he got in the middle of their Christmas progam for orphans and was active in an election campaign, and what with one thing and another I think he might have been president if he had kept pushing, but he didn't. His interest cooled off and he dropped it. Press is like that; hot one minute, cold the next.

Just before New Year's, 1970, Press married an attractive young lady named Charlotte.

The summer of 1971

Because we knew that the staff thought we had been giving Press more than his share of favors, we were really surprised at what happened in our counselling interview in July 1971. We review our staff people twice each year, try to assess their progress, and look at their salaries. However, we use the long form evaluation sheet [see exhibit] only at the end of the year.

So in July 1971 we talked with Press and told him that from our point of view he was making progress, that we had no particular comments to make at that time about strengths or weaknesses, and that we were raising his salary $25 a month. He sort of leaned back in his chair and said: "Same old raise, huh? There is no progress."

DILLON: How do you account for his reaction?

BORDEN: Frank here thinks that many of our problems stemmed back to Graham. Graham's father was a union man who apparently believed that employers took advantage of their employees and withheld most of the fruits of their labor. Graham had some of his father's ideas. For example, I understand that he said that staff people should receive substantially all of the net fees which they generated and that partners should get their compensation from the fees that their work produced. He favored more holidays, longer vacations and more fringe benefits. I think Lee was influenced by Graham and this may have had something to do with his "same old raise" reaction.

We were very surprised. We had just raised him to $11,500 against Condon and Burke at $12,000. He was raised $2,700 in three years. At the same time that we had given him a raise, we had given them none but he didn't know that, at least not then. After the interview, he walked out into the staff office and, in typical Press Lee fashion, said to Condon and Burke: "Well, I got a $25 raise. How much did you guys get?"

As they hadn't been raised, this caused some difficulty.

I suppose he thought his rate should go up to the same level as Condon and Burke, in spite of the big difference in age and experience. He stated that he thought he was better than they were. His attitude was the thing that bothered me—not his competence. He was handling responsible jobs well but we felt his relations with the clients were a bit immature. He was always kidding with them; he seemed to us to be a bit shy on professional attitude. But we thought he just needed to mature a bit.

In the conference he said that he didn't feel that he should be asked to work under Condon and Burke any more; that he was doing as good work as they, and carrying as much responsibility and that he was a C.P.A. and they weren't.

I recalled that when we had put him on a job with Burke in charge he hadn't cooperated very well. It was obvious that he didn't intend to take direction from Burke. We had never had this particular difficulty with him until 1971. During the first two years that he was with us he took supervision in good shape.

Not long after the interview he went out and interviewed the local office of a national C.P.A. firm. I have a good friend who interviewed him. Apparently Press felt he had a lot of specialized tax knowledge about the oil industry which he wanted to sell to them. He made some remarks about J. D. Rodman being a nonaggressive, dead-end firm and was rather taken aback when my friend told him that they had the highest respect for us. They said they had no opening in Oklahoma City but might be able to get him a job in Kansas City, but he didn't want to move to Kansas City, so that was that.

Opening an office in Stillwater

We had been wanting for some time to open an office in Stillwater, as we had a number of clients there, including a couple of good ones that kept pressing us to set up service locally. Finally one of them went so far as to build a new building with space in it planned for us, so we had a partners' meeting and agreed to do it, with Robert Golden, a younger partner from the home office in Ft. Worth, in charge.

The idea was, of course, that Golden would move to Stillwater. At the firm picnic, in August, Bob Golden's wife, Gloria, got to talking to the other wives and said that she had no desire to move to Stillwater and had no intention of doing so.

Gordon Campbell, our managing partner in Fort Worth, got wind of this. Here he had an office, and nobody to put in it. For various reasons, none of the other partners in Fort Worth could move and there was no staff man that seemed appropriate.

Campbell phoned me and asked whether Condon or Burke would be interested in going to Stillwater. I said they had the capacity all right but they didn't have their C.P.A. and so that was dropped. So I said that it seemed to me that Preston Lee was a possibility; that he had the personality and drive to make a new office go, and would do a good job if someone stood behind him to keep him from going off the deep end. I pointed out that he felt himself at a dead end in Oklahoma City and he might welcome the opportunity. We kicked the idea around a bit and Gordon said: "Why don't you check with Lee and see if he's interested?"

I said I didn't want to mention it to him unless it was pretty sure that he would get the opportunity if he wanted it and Gordon said that of course he understood that.

DILLON: So then you talked with Lee?

BORDEN: Yes, Frank Compton and I took Press to lunch. We told him that the firm definitely was going to open an office in Stillwater and that Bob Golden was the logical man to go but apparently he didn't want to. Would he be interested? We said we didn't know for sure that it would develop for him but that he was a strong candidate among others.

Press asked about compensation and we told him that this hadn't been discussed but that we were sure consideration would be given to the expenses involved in moving; that he would have an opportunity to grow and that his compensation would grow accordingly. We told him that he wouldn't be a partner and that we wouldn't guarantee that he would ever be a partner, but that the opportunity was definitely there.

So he talked to his wife and they decided it would be great. She had gone to school in Stillwater and hadn't finished so she would go back to school and finish up, and they made plans bang, bang, bang. I called

Gordon and he said, "Fine. Send him down to Ft. Worth to talk and send his wife with him."

But the next morning Gordon called and he was really upset. He had gone down to the office early and Bob Golden came in and said he was looking forward to going to Stillwater and his wife was very enthusiastic about it, too. So of course the only thing he could do was call me and say he was sorry and that there was no point in Press coming to Ft. Worth.

So Frank and I got Press in and explained to him about Golden: that he was the logical man to go and that after further consideration he had decided to go. We expressed to Press the thought that his having been so strongly considered was a great compliment as most of the other men were older than he was, with more experience. We told him that another opportunity would come along and that we thought he had a great future with the firm.

Gordon Campbell was in town a few weeks later to see a client and he and I took Lee to lunch and Gordon told him he was sorry about the way things had worked out, but that he had had to make the decision on the basis of the welfare of the firm as a whole, that Lee had received very careful consideration and had been a strong candidate, and that in a few years, with a bit more experience, he would be an even stronger candidate. Gordon told Press he had a big future with the firm and that there would be another opportunity coming along.

The last three months

DILLON: What happened then?

BORDEN: Three weeks later Press came into my office and told me he had considered the situation every way he knew how and that he had arrived at the conclusion that there was no future for him in the firm and that there was no alternative for him but to resign.

So we asked him: "Well what do you have in mind?"

And he said, "Nothing. I'm going out and get a job."

Frank and I spent a good deal of time, jointly and separately, with Press. We both told him quite bluntly that he was just plain wrong and making a mistake. There was opportunity—there was a future for the firm and he was a part of that future. We told him that of course we were not proposing to hand him a big job or a partnership on a silver platter but he could earn one through his own efforts. We weren't going to divide up the present situation and just hand him a slice but he could build a share for himself, in time. You don't become a partner because you are a nice guy; you become a partner because you earned it.

I think that he had hoped to pressure us into a substantial raise or a junior partnership or something. I don't know if this is right or not.

Communication broke down and I was guessing, but I think perhaps when he said he was quitting that he didn't intend to leave, but was applying pressure.

I think he wanted a rating equal or superior to Condon and Burke and he wanted equal money. I think he wanted to be on a par with them and he didn't want them telling him what to do. If we had given this to him I really don't know whether we would have had problems with Condon and Burke or not; I am just not sure. But I don't care to give in to that kind of pressure, and anyway it is against the policy of the firm.

The upshot was that we didn't offer him anything at all, except advice that he was being premature. Then he talked around that he could get a better job somewhere, where there was more opportunity. He made a trip to Billings, with his wife, and they didn't welcome him with open arms the way he expected. The man's wife was in the hospital and he kept the Lee's waiting around and in the end didn't offer him the comptrollership that Press thought he would get, and that was a blow. Another company offered him $5,000 for six months as an internal auditor, but that was temporary, and it wasn't a vice presidency, and Press was insulted.

In the meantime he had done a great deal of talking about the wonderful job he was going to have and then, when he had more trouble than he expected, he talked to everyone about his troubles. I guess he was getting rather desperate.

So finally the California Insurance Company offered him $12,100 as a payroll auditor in San Francisco, and they told him that, with his C.P.A. and all, it was a wonderful opportunity for him to move into an executive spot, and he took it and moved out of town. Up to the time that he actually gave notice Frank and I kept trying to convince him to stay, but when he resigned, why of course, we quit.

Comments by Frank Compton

COMPTON: The two senior men, Graham and Corcoran, who left our staff in May 1969 may have had something to do with Press Lee's later behavior. During his first six months on the job, Lee worked closely with them and under their supervision. Both men seemed to have a lot of personal problems. Both were rather negative toward their work and apparently believed that the firm owed them opportunities which it failed to provide. Both had a strong dislike for Condon. I would say that Lee was never able to reconcile their adverse opinion of the firm and what they regarded as their inability to progress in such a firm, with our enthusiasm for its potential.

I had several talks with Lee about his negative attitude, which seemed to be focusing on Condon. Just before he told us he was leaving the firm, he said to me in one of our talks that he could not work with Condon and therefore could not be in the same organization.

I talked with him about attitude and the need to be able to work with most anybody—whether a fellow employee, or client, or client's employee —and about team work and what it meant to be part of an organization. I suggested that some problems take time and patience to work out in fairness to everyone.

He agreed to consider whether he should change his ways, but later told me he had decided that it was unnecessary.

We thought Press had a big future ahead of him, with us. But, obviously, he didn't think so.

Incidentally, after he resigned but before he left town, he came into the office a good deal and had coffee with us, or just talked. Early in January, after Condon gave notice, Press was having coffee with me and he mentioned the news about Condon leaving and said: "Maybe I shouldn't have quit."

BORDEN: So that's the story, Bob. One always thinks, maybe if we had done it differently. . . .

Two days later Dillon received a note from Borden:

Dear Bob,
Just to round out the Press Lee affair here's the gist of a phone call I had with California last month. Frank and I would be quite interested in your views on this situation after you've had a chance to mull it over.

Sincerely,

Wallace

Memorandum for the file, January 21, 1972

Mr. Davis, personnel manager of the California Mutual Insurance Company, called to ask about Preston Lee. They are considering hiring him as an internal auditor.

I told Mr. Davis that:

Lee's reputation for honesty and integrity is excellent.
Clients have complimented us on his ability to work with their employees.
There is some resistance to supervision by the immediate supervisor.
His judgment needs maturing but overall is good.
He is dependable, and has no bad habits which have affected his work; apparently he handles his finances and family affairs well.

He has an excellent record on committee work in the Junior Chamber of Commerce and seems to have leadership qualities.

Mr. Davis asked if we would hire him back. I said no, that our experience is that a man who quits for a supposed advancement does not possess qualities necessary to become a partner and usually is not a satisfactory employee.

W. T. Borden

J. D. Rodman & Co. professional staff salary roll

	Lee	Condon (in-charge senior)	Burke (in-charge senior)	Knowles (junior)	Cowan (junior)	Graham (in-charge senior)	Corcoran (in-charge senior)
7/1/71							
Rate	$11,500	$12,100	$12,100	$10,900	$10,900		
Up	300	None	None	300	300		
1/1/71							
Rate	11,200	12,100	12,100	10,600	10,600		
Up	300	300	300	300	300		
7/1/70							
Rate	10,900	11,800	11,800	10,300	10,300		
Up	600	300	300	600	600		
1/1/70							
Rate	10,300†	11,500	11,500	9,700	9,700		
Up	300	300	300				
7/1/69							
Rate	10,000	11,200	11,200				
Up	600	300	300				
1/1/69							
Rate	9,400*	10,900	10,900			$12,100‡	$11,500
Up	600	600	900			300	900
7/1/68							
Rate	8,800	10,300	10,000			11,800	10,600§
Up							
CPA certificate							
Cond.	May '68	May '70	May '70	Nov. '70		Nov. '67	Several
Passed	Nov. '68	——	Nov. '71	May '71	Nov. '70	May '68	——
Resigned	Dec. 18 1971	Jan. 6 1972				May 7 1969	May 21 1969

* Advanced to semi-senior rating.

† Advanced to senior rating.

‡ First raise since 7/1/67.

§ Regular prior raises: $25 each six months.

STAFF EMPLOYEE RATING SHEET: PRESTON LEE
(Ratings for 1969-70-71 are all summarized on this form.)

	Improvement Needed	Meets Normal Requirements	Exceeds Expected Performance
1. Working papers & tax returns: Presentability of work			
A Completeness	✓1969	✓1970	✓1971
B Conciseness		✓✓✓ 69-70-71	
C Neatness		✓✓✓ 69-70-71	
D Clearness		✓✓✓ 69-70-71	
E Adequately cross referenced		✓✓✓ 69-70-71	
F Properly indexed & dated		✓✓✓ 69-70-71	
G Sheets initialed		✓✓✓ 69-70-71	
H Accuracy of detailed work		✓✓ 69-70	✓1971
I Accuracy of final results		✓✓✓ 69-70	
2. Technical ability:			
A Knowledge of accounting and auditing theory		✓1969	✓✓70-71
B Application of accounting and auditing theory on job		✓1969	✓✓70-71
C Inquiry into clients accounting systems and internal control, etc.		✓1969	✓✓70-71
D Ability to prepare financial statements and schedules		✓✓✓ 69-70-71	
E Knowledge of income tax laws	✓1969	✓✓70-71	
F Application of income tax law in preparing tax returns		✓✓✓ 69-70-71	
3. Application to work:			
A Completing assignments in allotted time		✓✓ 69-70	✓1971
B Attention to broad phases of assignment		✓✓69-70	✓1971
C Ability to organize work		✓✓69-70	✓1971
D Initiative on job		✓1969	✓✓ 70-71
E Attention to pertinent detail		✓✓69-70	✓1971

	Improve-ment Needed	Meets Normal Require-ments	Exceeds Expected Performance
4. Sense of responsibility:			
A Loyalty to firm			
1. Does he try at all time to sell firm?		√√ 69–70	√1971
2. Does he have pride in the firm and in knowledge that he is an essential part of the organization?		√√ 69–70	√1971
B Carrying out instructions			
1. When given specific instructions does he follow through?		√ 1969	√√ 70–71
C Self-reliance on job			
1. Does he try to find answer before asking?		√1969	√√ 70–71
D Dependability			
1. Does he get to work on time?		√√√ 69–70–71	
2. Does he look after jobs assigned to him?		√√69–70	√1971
3. Ability to work without supervision	√ 1969		√√ 70–71
4. Does he follow instructions?	√ 1969		√√ 70–71
E Cooperativeness			
1. Willing to work overtime when necessary			√√√ 69–70–71
2. Willing to travel when necessary on work days, evenings, or Sundays		√√√ 69–70–71	
3. Does he cooperate on job with supervisor?		√√ 69–70	√1971
4. Does he accept advice and decisions?		√√69–70	√1971
5. Professional qualifications:			
A Effectiveness in meeting and dealing with clients		√ 1969	√√70–71
B Judgment in presenting problems to superiors		√√69–70	√1971
C Education or training for public accounting		√√√ 69–70–71	
D Accuracy of judgment or decisions		√√√ 69–70–71	
E Effectiveness in presenting ideas or facts to superiors		√√√ 69–70–71	

	Improve- ment Needed	Meets Normal Require- ments	Exceeds Expected Performance
F Ability to adapt education and training to company policies and procedures		✓ 1969	✓✓ 70-71
G Ability to write		✓✓✓ 69-70-71	
H Ability to speak		✓✓✓ 69-70-71	
I Professional interest (C.P.A. associations, clubs, sports, etc.)	✓ 1969	✓1970	✓ 1971

6. Personal characteristics

	Improve- ment Needed	Meets Normal Require- ments	Exceeds Expected Performance
A Personal appearance		✓✓✓69-70-71	
B Dependability		✓✓ 69-70	✓1971
C Personality		✓1969	✓✓70-71
D Relations with:			
1. Staff		✓✓✓ 69-70-71	
2. Supervisors		✓✓✓ 69-70-71	
3. Principals		✓✓✓ 69-70-71	

7. Based on the staff member's work during the past six months, do you think he is qualified to perform:

	Light	Average	Heavy
1. Senior work	✓1969	✓1971	
2. Semi–senior work		✓✓ 69-70	
3. Junior work			✓ 1969

8. When the staff member has worked on your jobs, have you discussed with him:
   1. Good work he has done — Yes
   2. Poor performance — Yes
   3. Deficiencies which you think he can correct — Yes
   4. Steps that can be taken to correct deficiencies on that or other jobs — Yes

9. In "8" above, what was the staff member's reaction to your comments?

Antagonistic	Indifferent	Receptive
		✓✓✓ 69-70-71

10. Are you glad, satisfied, or unhappy when this staff member is assigned to your jobs?

Unhappy	Satisfied	Glad
		✓✓✓ 69-70-71

11. Does he have potential for advancement in our firm?
   ✓ 1969   Yes
   ✓ 1970   Yes
   ✓1971   Yes

4

Motivation and communication

In the preceding chapter we briefly considered the effects of needs, physiological and psychological, upon perception and thus upon communicative behavior. Indeed, their influence is so pervasive and telling that they deserve at least a chapter if we are to consider adequately communication in a behavioral setting.

Recall that March and Simon cited the *evoked set* and the *stimuli* as the major determinants of human behavior[1] through a short interval of time. In terms of communication behavior, the audible vibrations from the speaker's mouth or the visible light waves reflecting from the writer's manuscript may constitute the central *environment* for the receiver. But the receiver provides the *internal state* or *memory content* from which the *sets* are evoked. The *sets*, in turn, tend to determine what parts of the *environment* will be "permitted" to become *stimuli*—i.e., to play a significant role in determining the response.

Thus, it is clear that whatever contributes to the *set*[2] of a commu-

---

[1] J. G. March and H. A. Simon, *Organizations* (New York: John Wiley & Sons, Inc., 1958), pp. 9–11.

[2] The *evoked set,* the reader will recall, is the active portion of the individual's *internal state* or *memory content,* which in turn consists of *values* or *goals, action-outcome relationships,* and *alternatives.* Thus, in their specific concern with organizations, March and Simon analyzed the *"motivation to produce* as a function of the *character of the evoked set* of alternatives, the *perceived consequences of evoked alternatives,* and the *individual goals* in terms of which alternatives are evaluated." Ibid., p. 53.

nicator, be he sender or receiver, may affect the total *communicative act*. We shall now examine the important role that *needs* play in influencing sets and internal states, generally.

"Relevance to one's needs is the most important determinant of one's personal view of the world."[3] Whatever these needs and their respective intensities may be at a given moment can influence one's behavior—even at the physiological needs level. Market researchers, for example, conclude that one tends to buy significantly more in a supermarket when he is hungry than directly after a full meal! A bachelor friend tells me that he prepares his own breakfast and packs his lunch before going to work. He discovered that he had to make an adjustment because his lunch was either too abundant or too skimpy depending upon whether he packed it *before* or *after* eating breakfast!

According to Murphy:

Needs determine how the incoming energies are to be put into structural form. Perception, then, is not something that is first registered objectively, then "distorted." Rather, as the need pattern shifts, the stage is set, minute by minute, for quasi-automatic structure-giving tendencies that make the percept suit the need. The need pattern predisposes to one rather than another manner of anchoring the percept to one's needs. Needs keep ahead of percepts.[4] The perceived world pattern mirrors the organized need pattern.[5]

And Solley and Murphy contend: "Needs of a moment prepare the individual for the perception of the next moment."[6]

The potency of needs in affecting perception has been demonstrated frequently. "The stronger a state of need in a person, the more strongly he will be perceptually set toward aspects of the field relevant to that need."[7] The early experiments on hunger were the forerunners of a host of studies supporting this assertion. Sanford,[8] for exam-

---

[3] H. J. Leavitt, *Managerial Psychology* (rev. ed.; Chicago: University of Chicago Press, 1964), p. 36.

[4] G. Murphy, *Personality: A Biosocial Approach to Origins* (New York: Harper & Row, 1947), pp. 377–78.

[5] Ibid., p. 351.

[6] C. M. Solley and G. Murphy, *Development of the Perceptual World* (New York: Basic Books, Inc., Publishers, 1960), p. 64.

[7] D. Krech and R. S. Crutchfield, *Elements of Psychology* (New York: Alfred A. Knopf, Inc., 1958), p. 96.

[8] R. N. Sanford, "The Effects of Abstinence from Food upon Imaginal Processes: A Further Experiment," *Journal of Psychology*, Vol. 3 (1937), pp. 145–59.

ple, reported that hungry persons will complete words such as
ME_____ more frequently as food words such as MEAT or MEAL
than will nonhungry people. And McClelland and Atkinson observed
that hungrier subjects "saw" more food objects in very unstructured
stimuli than did less hungry subjects.[9]

A MOTIVATION MODEL

It may be helpful to consider more specifically the role of *motivation* in human behavior. Leavitt[10] provides such a model which he
derives from three basic premises:

1. Behavior is *caused*. The things we do don't "just happen"—there
   are always underlying reasons. This does not mean, necessarily,
   that these reasons will be apparent even to the individual who is
   so behaving.
2. Behavior is *directed*. In the ultimate sense there is no aimless behavior. We are always pursuing some goal or other. Again, there
   is no necessity to assume that one is conscious of his goals or that
   he is approaching them most efficiently.
3. Behavior is *motivated*. Underlying what we do are motives, drives
   which provide the energy to attain or at least to move in the
   direction of the goal.

Relate these three ideas, says Leavitt, and you have a system for
understanding behavior (see Figure 4–1):

With the help of these ideas, human behavior can be viewed as part
of a double play from cause to motive to behavior-toward-a-goal. And, it
is also helpful to think of the three as generally forming a closed circuit.
Arrival at a goal eliminates the cause, which eliminates the motive,
which eliminates the behavior.[11]

---

9 D. C. McClelland and J. W. Atkinson, "The Projective Expression of Needs, I.
The Effect of Different Intensities of Hunger-drive on Perception," *Journal of Psychol-
ogy,* Vol. 25 (1948), pp. 205–22. See also: L. Postman and R. S. Crutchfield, "The Interaction of Need, Set, and Stimulus-Picture in a Cognitive Task," *American Journal of
Psychology,* Vol. 65 (1952), pp. 196–217. For other studies supporting the contention
that motivation influences perception see: J. C. Gilchrist and L. S. Nesberg, "Need and
Perceptual Change in Need-Related Objects," *Journal of Experimental Psychology,*
Vol. 44 (1952), pp. 369–76; and R. Levine, I. Chein, and G. Murphy, "The Relation of
the Intensity of a Need to the Amount of Perceptual Distortion: A Preliminary Report," *Psychological Bulletin,* Vol. 13 (1942), pp. 282–91.

10 Leavitt, *Managerial Psychology,* pp. 7–12.

11 Ibid., p. 8.

FIGURE 4–1
A basic model of behavior*

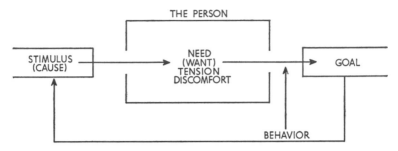

* H. J. Leavitt, *Managerial Psychology* (rev. ed.; Chicago: University of Chicago Press, 1964), p. 9. For a more elaborate and detailed model of behavior see V. H. Vroom, "Motivation—A Point of View," chap. 2 in *Work and Motivation* (New York: John Wiley & Sons, Inc., 1964). "In the model, choices by persons among alternative courses of action are hypothesized to depend on the relative strength of forces. Each force is in turn hypothesized to be equal to the algebraic sum of the products of the valence of outcomes and expectancies that the outcomes will be attained."—p. 28.

One's empty stomach sends neural impulses which the individual perceives as "feeling hungry"; the hunger feeling is the motive which directs energy toward food seeking; if the effort is successful the individual fills his stomach with food thus eliminating the hunger feeling. If he now ceases to seek food and thus fails to consume food for several hours the hunger feelings will reappear and the cycle will be repeated.

This cyclical process is basically the same regardless of the type of needs. Suppose a man is psychologically "hungry" (e.g., has a need for freedom from fear of physical deprivation or a need for acceptance and/or esteem from others). He now has the motive for seeking satisfaction for his "appetite" and if his resultant behavior is successful he fills his psychological "stomach" and ceases for the time being to be "hungry." And he is quite prone to become hungry in this sense all over again if his psychological appetites are not recurrently appeased.

The analogy breaks down to an extent here for it is quite apparent that some psychological appetites, varying with the individual, are rarely if ever sated. But they can be momentarily and partially satisfied and the cause—motive—behavior-toward-a-goal cycle decreases in intensity if it does not halt altogether.

Homeostasis is the "tendency of motivated behavior to maintain a balanced condition within the organism"[12]—an equilibrium. Hebb defined homeostasis as "the process by which a constant internal state is maintained in the organism."[13]

. . . the ultimate condition of man can be thought of as an equilibrium condition in which he need not behave. This ultimate will be unattainable as long as one fly after another goes on landing on man's rump to stir up some new need and to force him to go on swishing his tail.[14]

There appears, at this writing, no dearth of flies in man's environment—nor any danger of their extinction.

FRUSTRATION

No discussion of human motivation would be adequate without a consideration of frustration—"the state of the organism resulting when the satisfaction of motivated behavior is rendered difficult or impossible."[15] The sources of frustrating obstacles include the environment, other people, our own personal defects or limitations, and conflict situations.

Generally speaking, when one is confronted with an obstacle he becomes aggressive. If he is confident of himself his aggression is ordinarily directed toward the obstacle. If he is unsure of himself and pessimistic about his ability he tends to direct his aggression inward upon himself—perceives himself as blameworthy, inadequate, and so forth. The key to the direction of his aggression, then, is his self-concept as we discussed in the previous chapter.

"Many obstacle situations are depriving rather than frustrating because the obstacles do not seem insurmountable or the goals are not central to the self."[16] One will experience fewer frustrations, therefore, if he has a larger repertoire of alternate routes around blocks or because his self-confidence is sufficient to obviate his proving himself every time he meets a problem. Intimately related are one's aspirations. If they are commensurate with one's abilities then frustration will be less frequent. To the extent that they are beyond his capaci-

---

12 N. L. Munn, *Psychology: The Fundamentals of Human Adjustment* (4th ed.; Boston: Houghton Mifflin Co., 1961) , p. 710.

13 D. O. Hebb, *A Textbook of Psychology* (Philadelphia: W. B. Saunders Co., 1958), p. 164.

14 Leavitt, *Managerial Psychology,* pp. 10–11.

15 Munn, *Psychology,* p. 710.

16 Leavitt, *Managerial Psychology,* p. 52.

ties he will tend to experience frustration and perhaps ultimately—if the thwarting is chronic—demoralization. Let us remind ourselves that self-confidence is generally a product of repeated success, but that success is what we perceive it to be.

Conflict

A more severe species of frustration is conflict—a seemingly escape-proof frustration.

Conflict [is] . . . a pulling in two directions at the same time. The obstacles one meets are not brick walls but drags that pull back as one goes forward . . . frying-pan-and-fire situations, or donkey-between-the-bales-of-hay situations.[17]

Conflict situations involve choosing and decision making and are generally of three types: *approach-approach*—the individual is between two equally attractive alternatives and to move toward one would pull him away from the other; *avoidance-avoidance*—one is between two equally unattractive or repulsive alternatives so that in escaping from one he moves closer to the other; *approach-avoidance* —the individual is both attracted and repelled by the same object.[18] *Frustration tolerance,* the ability to retain normal reactions under stress, varies greatly among individuals. Some are quite capable of maintaining problem-solving actions directed toward constructively resolving the conflict in which they find themselves. Others are more prone toward compensatory or subterfuge reactions. Some of these resemble *homeostasis,* a form of physiological compensatory activity which strives to maintain a constant state. Their prime purpose is not to solve problems but to cushion the ego (one's feelings of self-esteem) against threats of deflation. These ego-defensive reactions include: *fantasy* (wish-fulfilling dreams, day-dreaming, etc.) ; *projecting* (imputing one's thoughts and desires to others) ; *rationalization* (finding "justifiable" reasons for our behavior or convincing ourselves that the goal is really undesirable—assuming the "sour grapes" atti-

---

[17] Ibid., p. 53.

[18] For a detailed treatment of conflict see: K. Lewin, *A Dynamic Theory of Personality* (New York: McGraw-Hill Book Co., 1935) ; the chapters by Finger, Lewin, Liddell, and Miller in *Personality and Behavior Disorders,* ed. J. V. Hunt (New York: The Ronald Press Co., 1944) ; N. R. F. Maier, *Frustration* (New York: McGraw-Hill Book Co., 1949) ; and L. A. Festinger, *A Theory of Cognitive Dissonance* (Stanford, Calif.: Stanford University Press, 1962).

tude) ; *repressing* (attempting to ignore, deny, or forget troublesome things) ; *regressing* (reverting to childish ways) : *identifying* (becoming ego-involved with others) ; *blaming others* (excusing ourselves by finding others responsible for our failures—"scape-goating") ; *overcompensating* (trying to overcome one's deficiencies, to "make up" for one's failings—but in an excessive manner) ; *sublimating* (getting indirect but socially acceptable satisfaction) .

The list is neither inclusive nor mutually exclusive, but it does suggest some of the unconstructive responses to frustration.[19]

How, then, can one really resolve his conflicts? A conflict *is* a conflict because one *perceives* it to be one. "Frustration is a state of the organism, not an external condition."[20] "A conflict exists for a person because to him certain needs seem mutually exclusive."[21] Therefore he can resolve a conflict by (1) finding a *new* way to satisfy both needs simultaneously, (2) reducing his valuation of one need or the other or (3) reorganizing the situation so that it is perceptually no longer a significant conflict.

Let us now examine in more detail the human need system which is so subject to frustration and conflict.

KINDS OF NEEDS

What can we say with confidence about motivation? Is there any rhyme or reason to man's needs? Are there any grounds for predicting man's behavior on the basis of his needs?

There is general agreement that man's needs are somehow orga-

---

[19] Some of the most promising work in the area of conflict has been published under the heading of *cognitive dissonance* (see, for example, Festinger, ibid.) . "According to this theory, when there is disagreement or conflict between two elements of cognition or between elements of cognition and behavior, the person is motivated to alter the situation in the direction of congruence. For example, according to this theory, if a person is in a situation in which he publicly states ideas that are contrary to his private beliefs, or if he behaves in a manner that does not fit with his attitudes and values, he will experience discomfort. Moreover, he will be motivated to change his beliefs, his values, or his behavior in order to bring about a state of concordance. It is as though the dissonance produces a state of tension in the organism and he feels the need to alter conditions in his psychological world in order to achieve a harmonious relationship among elements of his cognition." Anthony Davids, "The Relationship of Cognitive Dissonance Theory to an Aspect of Psychotherapeutic Practice," *American Psychologist*, May 1964, Vol. 19, no. 5, p. 329.

[20] Krech and Crutchfield, *Elements of Psychology*, p. 307.

[21] Leavitt, *Managerial Psychology*, p. 66.

nized—that they fall into some sort of pattern. There are considerable differences of opinion, however, on the nature of the pattern.

Primary and secondary needs

Some investigators consider the physiological needs as *primary* and those which involve obtaining their satisfaction at a later time as *secondary*. Hunger, then, would be classified as a primary need whereas saving food for future hunger or saving money for the subsequent purchase of food would exemplify secondary drives. Secondary drives may depend upon previous frustration or what the individual has learned from others about the need to anticipate future needs. This is not to say that all human motivation is physiologically grounded, i.e., directly linked to physiological needs. Allport considers

. . . adult motives as infinitely varied, and as self-sustaining, *contemporary* systems, growing out of antecedent systems, but functionally independent of them. Just as a child gradually repudiates his dependence on his parents, develops a will of his own, becomes self-active, and self-determining, and outlives his parents, so it is with motives. Each motive has a definite point of origin which may possibly lie in the organic tensions of infancy. Chronologically speaking, all adult purposes can be traced back to these seed forms in infancy, but as the individual matures the tie is broken. Whatever bond remains is historical, not functional.[22]

Some finer delineations

Granting the division of motives into physiological and nonphysiological camps, other writers feel finer delineations of needs can be made.

Langer

Langer distinguished three classes of needs: physical, social, and egotistic.[23] Physical needs are the "tissue" needs.

. . . the needs that are built into the organism as a result of the way the body is constructed. In this class we would put the needs for

---

[22] G. W. Allport, "The Functional Autonomy of Motives," *The Nature of Personality: Collected Papers* (Reading, Mass.: Addison-Wesley Publishing Co., Inc., 1950), p. 58.

[23] W. C. Langer, *Psychology in Human Living* (New York: Appleton-Century, 1943).

food and water, for air, temperature control, sleep, elimination, and the like.[24]

Social needs are those which are satisfied only in relationships with other people. The so-called affiliation drive or the need to associate with others is an example.

The evidence of the operation of the need for affiliation at work is not hard to find. We see it in many studies of morale and in casual observations showing the importance that is placed on "a good bunch" at work, and most of us have chosen at one time or another to sacrifice certain aspects of a particular job in order to take advantage of the presence of a preferred group of people at some other job. . . . The force of the need for affiliation in the industrial situation becomes even more clear when we see the compelling effectiveness with which a group can put pressure on one of its members who, let us say, exceeds the tacit group-set level of production. When he goes to the locker room or the washbasin and finds that conversation stops and people turn away from him, or when he walks alone repeatedly, the deprivation provides a potent force to bring him into line.[25]

Other species of social needs include the needs to give and receive affection and nurturance—to care for others and to be cared for.

Egotistic needs are distinguished from social needs by their orientation. The former needs, even though others are instrumental in gratifying them, are directed towards the maintenance or enhancement of one's ego or one's self. To achieve; to be important, dominant, autonomous; to be "somebody," are some of the goals of egotistic needs and recognition, prestige, esteem, fame, status, and reputation are some of the common means for gratifying these needs.

Krech and Crutchfield

Krech and Crutchfield consider needs from the standpoint of their *purposes* and assert that "every activity of the individual can be regarded as governed by one or a combination of four general aims: *survival, security, satisfaction, stimulation.* He aims to stay alive, to keep safe, to feel enjoyments, to experience new stimuli."[26] These they group into two categories. They consider survival and security as *deficiency motives*—the needs to negate deficit, disruption, and dis-

---

[24] Mason Haire, *Psychology in Management* (2d ed.; New York: McGraw-Hill Book Co., 1964), p. 29.

[25] Ibid., p. 31.

[26] Krech and Crutchfield, *Elements of Psychology,* p. 278.

comfort and to preclude or escape from danger, threat, and anxiety. The epitome of these motives is *tension-reduction*.

Satisfaction and stimulation are *abundancy motives*. Their end, in a sense, is *tension-increase*. The two main classes, then, are the avoidance of dissatisfaction and the attainment of satisfaction. See Table 4–1.

TABLE 4–1
The human motives

Listed in this table are some of the principal human motives, classified under the general aims of survival and security (deficiency motives) and satisfaction and stimulation (abundancy motives). Under these general headings the motives are further classified according to whether they mainly pertain to the body, to relations with the environment, to relations with other people, or to the self.

	Survival and security (deficiency motives)	*Satisfaction and stimulation* (abundancy motives)
Pertaining to the body	Avoiding of hunger, thirst, oxygen lack, excess heat and cold, pain, overfull bladder and colon, fatigue, overtense muscles, illness and other disagreeable bodily states, etc.	Attaining pleasurable sensory experiences of tastes, smells, sound, etc.; sexual pleasure; bodily comfort; exercise of muscles, rhythmical body movements, etc.
Pertaining to relations with environment	Avoiding of dangerous objects and horrible, ugly, and disgusting objects; seeking objects necessary to future survival and security; maintaining a stable, clear, certain environment, etc.	Attaining enjoyable possessions; constructing and inventing objects; understanding the environment; solving problems; playing games; seeking environmental novelty and change, etc.
Pertaining to relations with other people	Avoiding interpersonal conflict and hostility; maintaining group membership prestige, and status; being taken care of by others; conforming to group standards and values; gaining power and dominance over others, etc.	Attaining love and positive identifications with people and groups; enjoying other people's company; helping and understanding other people, being independent, etc.
Pertaining to the self	Avoiding feelings of inferiority and failure in comparing the self with others or with the ideal self; avoiding loss of identity; avoiding feelings of shame, guilt, fear, anxiety, sadness, etc.	Attaining feeling of self-respect and self-confidence; expressing oneself; feeling sense of achievement; feeling challenged; establishing meaningful place of self in the universe.

D. Krech and R. S. Crutchfield, *Elements of Psychology* (New York: Alfred A. Knopf, Inc., 1958), p. 279.

Herzberg, et al.

Herzberg, Mausner, and Snyderman[27] suggest a similar dichotomy in their study of accountants and engineers. They contend that man has both *growth* needs and *avoidance* needs. They report that certain job factors ("motivators") have potency for satisfying *growth needs*. These include achievement, recognition, the work itself, responsibility, and advancement. Other job factors ("hygiene factors") were important largely for their capacity to *dissatisfy* the individual—and thus trigger his *avoidance needs*. These included company policy and administration, supervision-technical, salary, interpersonal relations-supervision, and working conditions. The motivators were associated with one's job *content* whereas the hygiene factors were related to the job *context* or environment. The major conclusion of the study was that the job factors capable of satisfying growth needs were largely irrelevant to avoidance needs and the job factors related to the avoidance needs were of little or no consequence with respect to growth needs. For example, management's improvement of substandard working conditions will ameliorate avoidance needs but will be ineffective in motivating the worker to greater productivity and creativity.

When these [hygiene] factors deteriorate to a level below that which the employee considers acceptable, then job dissatisfaction ensues. However, the reverse does not hold true. When the job context can be characterized as optimal, we will not get dissatisfaction, but neither will we get much in the way of positive attitudes.[28]

All we can expect from satisfying the needs for hygiene is the prevention of dissatisfaction and poor job performance.[29]

Maslow

Motive classifications such as Langer's and Krech and Crutchfield's may be useful in sorting out the myriad behavioral acts we encounter but they are not, in themselves, very useful in predicting future behavior.

Abraham Maslow presents a model[30] (which we touched upon in

---

[27] F. Herzberg, B. Mausner, and B. Snyderman, *The Motivation to Work* (2d ed.; New York: John Wiley & Sons, Inc., 1962).

[28] Ibid., pp. 113–14.

[29] Ibid., p. 115.

[30] Abraham H. Maslow, *Motivation and Personality* (New York: Harper & Bros., 1954).

Chapter 2) which purports to be such a predictive base. While he slices the loaf a bit differently, his five needs are not unlike Langer's three. Maslow's needs are: *physiological* (parallel to Langer's "tissue" needs) ; *safety and security* (the need to be free of the fear of physical danger and deprivation) ; *social* (like Langer's social needs) ; ego (like Langer's egotistic needs, except that Maslow distinguishes ego needs which are satisfied publicly [esteem from others] from those which are satisfied privately [self-esteem]) ; and *self-fulfillment* (the ultimate need—to realize one's fullest potential as a human being; to be creative in the broadest sense of the term) .

The principal distinction of Maslow's model is that these needs exist in a prepotency pattern, a hierarchy of needs, as depicted in Figure 4–2:

FIGURE 4–2
Maslow's hierarchy of needs

Maslow's basic propositions:

1. *The lowest unsatisfied needs must be sufficiently appeased before the needs above them normally become operative, i.e., are able to motivate the individual.*

Ordinarily, until a man's physiological needs are reasonably satisfied none of those above will significantly influence his behavior. A desperately hungry man may risk his life, to say nothing of his honor, for food. Even Jesus who preached from the mount, "Man does not live by bread alone," was clearly aware of the importance of bread to man for he fed the multitudes.

When the physiological needs are sufficiently appeased man begins to be concerned with future deprivation as well as with present and future danger. Say a hungry man, motivated to work for food, is rewarded with a meal. But now he continues to work. Clearly he is working—not for another meal, for he could not eat it now if he had it—but for the *assurance* of the next meal which he does not yet physically crave. To stretch the point it might be argued that some men, particularly those scarred by earlier poverty, are working today predominantly for the assurance of meals 20 or 30 years from now.

And so it is, progressively, as the needs at one level are sufficiently satisfied the level immediately above begins to play a role in one's behavior.

The more specifically human needs at the higher end of the scale cannot be satisfied—indeed, they cannot even be felt—until the basic physical and psychological needs have received their proper satisfaction. Thus, love casts out fear—but only where circumstances are favorable. Hunger and stress, if sufficiently prolonged, cast out the very possibility of love. And along with the possibility of love they cast out the possibility of experiencing, and *a fortiori* of satisfying any of the intellectual or emotional needs at the higher end of the scale. For certain individuals it may be possible to feel and satisfy certain of the more specifically human needs and to actualize some of their potentialities as symbol-manipulators, in a state of more or less complete lovelessness and isolation. But for most people and in most circumstances the actualization of their specifically human potentialities can be achieved only when the basic physical and psychological needs have been satisfied, only when they have enough food, enough safety, enough sense of belongingness, enough respect and enough love. Nature and nurture are always synergic. Unfavorable surroundings make it impossible for even the most highly gifted individuals to actualize their potentialities. Bad nurture will starve or smother, will mask or distort, the best of natures. Conversely a poorly endowed individual cannot be made by even the best environment to actualize potentialities which he does not possess. To achieve success, the eugenist must be a social reformer, the social reformer a eugenist.

We see, then, that it is only in a favorable environment that the inborn potentialities of the individual can be actualized.[31]

2. *To the extent that needs are satisfied they will become inoperative, i.e., they cease to motivate the individual for a satisfied need is no longer a motivator of behavior.*

As previously stated, the hungry man who has eaten is no longer hungry thus his subsequent work efforts are temporarily not motivatable by hunger. And, in fact, if he is completely improvident, as many animals are, he will cease to work altogether until hunger feelings reappear sufficiently to motivate him again to attain food. Most of us, of course, are not so casual about the future and our security needs (e.g., to be free of the *fear* of hunger) continue to impel us.

---

[31] Aldous Huxley, "Human Potentialities," *Bulletin of the Meninger Clinic,* Vol. 25, No. 2. (March 1961) , pp. 54–55.

Some qualifications.   Perhaps this discussion of the Maslow model suggests that the prediction of human behavior is merely a matter of discovering where a person currently is on the need hierarchy so as to determine where he will jump next. Unfortunately, the situation is more complex for the *sequence* of *need occurrence* and the *sequence of need satisfaction are not necessarily the same.* However, if we impose a few *qualifications* on the need hierarchy the model gains applicability.

MULTIPLE LEVELS.   First of all, the dotted lines separating the need levels suggest that the "boundaries" of the levels are very permeable and that one may move up and down the "ladder" rapidly. Within a typical day a man working in a factory may be motivated at one time or another at all five need levels. He certainly becomes physically hungry at least three times a day; he is (or should be) concerned about his safety as he operates a machine—and he may experience anxiety about his family's financial security; he may do or refrain from doing many things to maintain or gain social acceptance by his associates; at the same time he may be striving for advancement and/or deriving a sense of achievement from what he is currently doing; he may even have some thoughts about his ultimate destiny, his contribution to mankind, and so forth.

NEED CONFLICT.   Not only is there considerable mobility up and down the hierarchy of needs during even a relatively short period of time, but it is quite possible for a person to be motivated by two or more need levels simultaneously. When his needs are sufficiently strong and/or urgent and yet cannot be satisfied simultaneously there may be *need conflicts.*[32] Take the familiar case of the individual "bucking for promotion." If his methods do not coincide with the

---

[32] "In many cases we have constructed situations that pit these need-satisfactions against one another, rather than harnessing them together, so that the result is a conflict that detracts from the motive force of each need and places the worker in a frustrating situation. An example of this kind of situation was referred to before, in the case where an incentive-pay system promises a worker more physical need-satisfaction in return for more work, but does it only at the expense of his social need-satisfaction if he violates the group culture by exceeding the group norm of production. When such a situation is allowed to occur, the amount of dollars-and-cents pay that has to be paid out to produce unit increase is disproportionate to the return, if it can be effective at all in producing an increase. It is equivalent to driving with the brakes on. It is inefficient in the extreme, and in many cases the situation can be restructured so that the social need-satisfaction is accomplished in return for the same behavior as the increased physical need-satisfaction. Whenever the group can be brought to see higher production levels as a group goal, for instance, the two motives will work together instead of against one another." Haire, *Psychology in Management,* pp. 35–36.

codes of his peer group he is likely to be made aware of his "deviant behavior" in no uncertain terms, with the group threatening him with various sanctions. Here is the classic conflict of social and ego needs. Will he resist the group and if necessary suffer their punishments? Or will he relinquish his goal of promotion, tuck in his wings, and rejoin the group?[33] Maslow's hierarchy of needs would suggest he will take the latter alternative, for social needs appear to be more primary than ego needs, but the situation is not quite so predictable as we shall presently discuss.

MODIFYING FACTORS.   There are at least two factors which suggest why the Maslow model cannot be applied literally in every situation. They are the presence of *varying appetites,* which can be partially accounted for by the concept of *dependency,* and the role of *self-discipline.*

Varying appetites.   There is no doubt that physiological need requirements vary from person to person. Some people simply require less sleep, food, protection from the elements, and the like than others. There is ample evidence to suggest that our need requirements vary at higher levels as well. Recall the man striving for promotion? A major determinant of his response to group pressure may be just how much of a social need appetite versus an ego need appetite he has. If he has learned to seek satisfactions primarily within himself rather than through or from others he may find it fairly easy to shrug off the group and proceed on his course.

In addition we must ask, does he have alternative need-satisfaction routes? Can he, in this case, sufficiently satisfy his social needs through *other groups*—on or off the job—and thus for *this situation* present limited social needs?

Dependency.   The concept of dependency helps to explain why the "appetites," the width of the bands, particularly the social and ego bands, seem to vary so much among individuals. Consider that the human infant comes into the world with a fairly well-developed set of needs and an almost completely undeveloped set of means for sat-

---

[33] Of course there are often escapes from this seeming dilemma. He may be able to convince his group that his *end* is acceptable. For example, he needs the additional income for extraordinary expenses—family medical bills, and so forth. Or he may modify his *means* of approaching his goal so that they will be acceptable to the group. The able student often faces a similar peer response to his seeking good grades. He may be able to justify his efforts by explaining that he needs good grades to enter graduate school, and by studiously avoiding unacceptable means for attaining good marks such as "apple-polishing."

isfying them. In other words, he is necessarily *dependent* upon *others* to satisfy these needs. What seems to be critical in the personality development of the child is whether his dependence is associated primarily with satisfying or with dissatisfying experiences.

If the infant's needs are usually *satisfied promptly and sufficiently by others* and if this becomes a generalized pattern through his formative years he will tend thereafter to rely upon *others* for need satisfaction—to develop a broad *social-needs* band. If, however, his needs are normally *not* so satisfied and this pattern is repeatedly reinforced he will come to rely less upon others and more upon *himself* for the satisfaction of his needs and so develop a broad, demanding *ego-needs* band.

Extreme dependency thus serves as a lever for initiating other kinds of needs. To the extent that dependency yields ready satisfaction of existing needs that one cannot satisfy independently—to that extent one's feelings are likely to be positive, friendly, affectionate, protective, grateful, and one is likely to develop strong *social* needs. To the extent that dependency does not satisfy, but rather frustrates—to that extent one is likely to develop feelings of anger and hostility and to wish more strongly for independence and automony, to develop strong egoistic needs.[34]

In actuality, the infant's needs can neither be completely frustrated (or he would not survive) or completely satisfied (mother is only human). As a consequence, he will develop both social and egoistic needs but there is likely to be a dominance of one over the other. In any event, a conflict tends to develop between the two needs:

As a result of this juxtaposition—the fact that the infant is born with a set of needs, but is dependent on any agent to satisfy them—there grow up simultaneously, two contradictory groups of drives—one in the direction of dependence and one in the direction of independence.[35]

Self-discipline. The second factor which complicates the use of the model is, in old-fashioned language, willpower. An individual can refrain from indulging his food and sleep needs to a degree. It is reasonable to assume that he can deny himself satisfactions at the subsequent need levels as well. Our friend seeking the promotion may decide to suffer his group's "slings and arrows" in anticipation of a compensatory reward. This does not mean he is without social needs or that they are meager—he may simply be capable of suppressing them.

---

[34] Leavitt, *Managerial Psychology,* p. 21.

[35] Haire, *Psychology in Management,* p. 38.

This may help to explain people such as Albert Schweitzer, Tom Dooley, and Mohandas Gandhi—men who seemingly lived primarily at the self-fulfillment level. Among possible speculations: were these men with iron wills who were capable of deferring or more or less permanently denying the gratification of their more material needs? were their lower needs relatively "narrow bands" to begin with? was the wine of self-fulfillment so heady that the lower need satisfactions became pallid by comparison?

The Pike in the Tank. It can be argued that some people seem to be quite content to attain a modicum of satisfaction at the lower two or three levels. They seem to have no "ambition," no drive to "get somewhere" or to "be somebody." Is it possible that these people were "behind the door when the needs were passed out"? Not likely. But it is quite possible that they have *learned not to try to satisfy* some of their needs.

I recall dimly an experiment our undergraduate biology professor described to us. It involved a tank of water about 12 feet long, 4 feet deep, and 4 feet wide. A glass partition was inserted separating the tank into two 6-foot segments. Then a Northern Pike, who had been deprived of food for some time, was placed in one compartment and a bucket of minnows was poured into the other. The pike immediately rushed for the minnows and bumped his nose, which hurt, I presume. But he was persistent and continued to bump his nose, if he were an average Northern, about 165 times. At this point he *stopped trying*. He apparently had "learned" that to seek saitsfaction for his needs resulted not only in a thwarting of his hunger drive but pain as well. The experimenter could now remove the partition and the minnows (who were evidently more stupid than the pike) swam into the other section but the pike wasn't having any—*he had learned his lesson.* And in most cases he would starve to death amidst abundance!

My memory is vague on the experiment and it may be apocryphal but it offers a provocative analogy. Substitute a child for the pike and substitute childhood experiences for the tank. Now suppose this child has a certain colored skin, or a certain shaped nose, or a certain last name, or a physical impairment, or he comes from "the wrong side of the tracks." Now suppose that this child tries to achieve some social or ego satisfaction and "bumps his nose." He is a human being and therefore learns much more rapidly than the pike *to stop trying— that way at least.* Hopefully he learns other ways of dealing with the obstacle, such as were discussed in the sections on frustration and conflict.

But suppose instead he generalizes his painful, failing experiences, and, by way of defense, *denies his needs*. In effect, he learns to *stop trying altogether*. Incidentally, since humans learn by concept as well as by stimulus, he can learn this lesson *vicariously* from others (his parents, older brothers and sisters, friends) who have also learned the lesson—directly or vicariously.

It is likely that later in life when the child has become an adult the mere opportunity for need satisfaction is often insufficient to overcome decades of conditioning. He may have to undergo a thorough and prolonged process of *relearning*—of coming to accept that not only does he *have* the needs but that he is potentially *capable* of satisfying them.

Validity versus simplicity. The imposition of qualifications upon the Maslow model of needs has two consequences: (1) they have hopefully increased the model's validity in accounting for human behavior; (2) they have complicated its use as a predictive tool suggesting that ordinarily it cannot serve as a simple template to predict Joe's next move. The model in no way dispenses one who would communicate effectively with people from perceptive analysis, from "knowing his people." But if the tradeoff has been validity at the cost of simplicity the bargain would appear to be a good one.

THE VALUE OF MOTIVATION THEORY

Much of this discussion of motivation, need models, and conflicts can be broadly categorized as theoretical. So let us pause to consider the practicality, indeed, the inevitability of theory. Theory is a most practical matter. For without theory—without underlying beliefs, assumptions, premises, and so on—we would be unable to act save through our reflex and autonomic responses. "Theory and practice are inseparable."[36]

If one is to communicate with others, serve as a subordinate, manage others, and the like, he must have *some kind of theory*—valid or not, conscious or not—about human motivations and relationships. Otherwise he will be unable to function at all. If we are to control or to influence behavior—our own at any rate—we must be capable of predicting reasonably accurately the responses of others—and of our-

---

[36] D. McGregor, *The Human Side of Enterprise* (New York: McGraw-Hill Book Co., 1960), p. 6.

selves. This is the essential reason we form images of others and of ourselves as discussed in the previous chapter.

The objective of this chapter is not to "sell" any particular theory.[37] Rather it is to urge that the reader bring *his* "theory" to the surface and examine its premises consciously and critically—to do this rather than to make decisions, to take action, and to communicate on the basis of unconscious, unexamined, and, possibly, untenable theory.

It is possible to have more or less adequate theoretical assumptions; it is not possible to reach a managerial decision or take a managerial action uninfluenced by assumptions whether adequate or not. The insistence on being practical really means, "Let's accept *my* theoretical assumptions without argument or test." The common practice of proceeding without explicit examination of theoretical assumption leads, at times, to remarkable inconsistencies in managerial behavior.[38]

EPILOGUE

The objective of placing this and the previous chapters into a book on communication is that the act of interpersonal communication never occurs in a vacuum. In its simplest format it is one man communicating out of his personalized world of feelings, perceptions, values, and needs to another man in *his* world. To treat communication merely at the level of techniques, devices, and media is to imply an unseemly simplicity for a very complex process. To understand human communication as fully as possible we must attempt to understand the communicator himself, the relationships between him and those with whom he communicates, and the organizational setting in which they may be communicating. Mason Haire summarizes the challenge to the communicator.

There are three outstanding basic facts that we must remember if we are going to be able to understand human behavior. The first is that the environment itself does not provide an organization. If we make a sepa-

---

[37] For excellent distillations, evaluations, and syntheses of studies and theories of motivation and productivity see V. H. Vroom, *Work and Motivation* (New York: John Wiley & Sons, Inc., 1964), and Saul Gellerman, *Motivation and Productivity* (New York: American Management Association, Inc., 1964) . The former is a comprehensive, well-documented compendium of the literature while the latter, written for a more general audience, highlights the major contributions to motivation theory.

[38] McGregor, *The Human Side* . . . , p. 7.

ration between the physical world outside of us, on one hand, and the psychological environment, or the world we see on the other, we come to see that the order and organization is not in the physical stimulus but in the observer, and that one of man's greatest problems is to make sense of his environment. The second fact is that man's behavior depends, not on what is actually out there, but on what he sees; not on the way the world is actually organized, but the way he organizes it. This is at first a deceptively simple point, but it is possible that more misunderstanding in human relations arises from this than from any other single factor. The third point is, related to the other two: man has a great deal of anxiety attached to his organization of the world. Man's environment is not organized in itself; he must organize it. His organization determines his behavior. His behavior and its appropriateness to the environment determine whether he will be successful or unsuccessful—in many cases, whether he will survive or not. For this reason, he is reluctant to give up any organizations that seem to work, because of the danger that is involved in being lost in a disorganized environment.[39]

The communicator's "behavior and its appropriateness to the environment" is the central concern of this book. In Chapter 5 we will make a specific examination of the process of human communication.

DISCUSSION QUESTIONS

1. "Needs keep ahead of percepts." (p. 134) What did Murphy mean by this?

2. Leavitt's behavioral model (p. 136): Does it explain human motivation to your satisfaction? Can you visualize any motivated behavior which would not be accounted for by this model?

3. Herzberg's major conclusion was that the growth and avoidance needs were *different* needs. The need to be happy is different from the need not to be unhappy. Moreover, the two needs are related to different job factors. For example, the elimination of subpar physical working conditions cannot be expected to have a significant impact on productivity. Assuming these conclusions to be valid, what implications do they have for managers? For educators? For the leaders of the executive and legislative branches of federal, state, and municipal governments?

4. Give examples of need conflict involving various of Maslow's needs, e.g., physiological and safety-security; social and ego; ego and self-fulfillment.

---

[39] Haire, *Psychology in Management,* pp. 40–41.

5. What does the "dependency" concept have to do with varying appetites?

6. The Maslow hierarchy of needs—in general, does it account for human behavior to your satisfaction? What do you think of various qualifications imposed upon the model? Are they necessary?

7. Re: Herzberg's motivational and hygiene factors and Maslow's hierarchy of needs. Do these theories regarding needs and motivation appear to be compatible? How or how not?

8. Langer, Krech and Crutchfield, Herzberg, Maslow—can their various classifications of needs be reconciled?

9. What do you think of Haire's "three outstanding basic facts that we must remember if we are going to be able to understand human behavior"? (pp. 151–52)

CASES

The accident[40]

E. C. ST. JOHN

The scene is the personnel office of an industrial firm. Bill, the personnel manager, is questioning the second shift printing foreman about an accident which had occurred the previous night. Pete, the printing foreman, is a middle-aged man who has come up from the ranks. He is conscientious, energetic, and proud of his production record.

"Bill, I don't know what makes these guys pull these crazy stunts," Pete said as he lit his cigarette. The cuticles of the hand holding the match were stained from years of washups and make-readys on the presses. "You front office guys are always harping on this 'Why do accidents happen?' business too much anyway," he continued. Leaning forward in his chair eager to make his point, he waved a finger under the personnel manager's nose. "Accidents are bound to happen," he stated. "I've been trying to tell you ever since you came to this plant. You take this one you're asking about now. Ross just did a dumb thing, that's all. He knew better than to adjust the gate on the hopper while the press was running but he just didn't think. Stupid, I guess."

"Stupid?" the personnel manager questioned.

"Oh, I don't mean stupid really," Pete continued. "He's got more education than I have and when it comes to figuring he's tops but last night he just didn't care."

"It must have played the devil with your production to have a man almost lose his finger. Beside the time taken getting him to first aid, you had to run the press a man short," Bill said.

"Well, no," Pete said as he tapped his cigarette out. "You see when

---

[40] All names have been disguised. Printed by permission.

they came in I cornered the whole bunch and told them we had this big beer ad run to get out and I wanted these presses running red hot. I remember telling Ross he wouldn't have time to worry about that baby that's coming soon, cause we were gonna hang up a record for the first shift to shoot at. I had to climb him a little later for taking so long with his make-ready. Then at lunch break he said he was having trouble with his register. I told him not to kid me, I'd run presses when he was reaching for a bottle and I knew he could finish that order if he wasn't too lazy. He didn't get hurt until about an hour and a half after lunch. By then we had two thirds of the order run, so by holding the guys for half an hour, we finished it."

"You say he hurt his hand because—" Bill questioned. "—Cause he's just plain careless," Pete interrupted.

"O.K. Pete," the personnel manager said quietly, "I think I understand."

Arno Annello, machinist[41]

The standards department of the Schoonway Machine Company recommended that Arno Annello, who operated a battery of automatic gear-cutting machines, be discharged for failure to attain required minimum production as set by the standards department. The foreman in whose department Annello was employed objected to the recommendation. The matter was placed before the production manager for final decision.

Arno Annello came to this country from Finland. He had received the equivalent of a grade school education in his native land but had practically no knowledge of the English language. He secured a job as a floor cleaner in the Schoonway plant. He showed himself to be industrious and thorough, and the foreman of the milling and gear-cutting department became interested in him. One day he suggested to one of Annello's friends that the floor sweeper should apply for a better job. When Annello heard this, he signified his desire to become an operative of the automatic sharpening machines. These machines were used to sharpen the teeth of cutters after the cutters were

41 Reprinted by permission from *Introduction to Industrial Management,* by Franklin E. Folts, Copyright 1949, McGraw-Hill Book Company.

otherwise finished. They were automatic in operation, and with proper setup there was very little danger of spoiling the work. The foreman or an experienced assistant personally supervised each setup. The operative inserted and removed the work, started and stopped the machines, and dressed the emery wheels when necessary. He operated from four to eight machines, depending on the character of the work.

When a vacancy occurred in the department, the foreman decided to give Annello a chance, and obtained his transfer (on trial) from the cleaning department. Over a period of several months, Annello, with the assistance of the foreman, became proficient in operating the machines, and was given a permanent job. For the next two years Annello showed steady improvement. He became known in the department as a first-class operative of automatic cutter-sharpening machines and finally developed into a skilled machine setter. While he improved as a machinist, Annello showed no aptitude in mastering the English language, and any extended or involved conversation had to be handled through an interpreter. The foreman, however, believed that Annello had the makings of a first-class machinist and was willing to put up with this inconvenience.

The company decided to install a new battery of gear-cutting machines for milling the teeth in cutters, and the foreman was confronted with the task of getting additional operatives to run these machines. The work of operating the automatic gear-cutting machines required considerably more skill than was necessary to run automatic cutter-sharpening machines. The machine attendant had to set up the indexing mechanism for the cutter blank, set the tooth-milling cutter at the correct distance off the center line of the blank, see that the cutter was properly sharpened, and set the machine for the correct stroke. The machine fed and indexed automatically, but considerable care was necessary on the part of the operative to keep the indexing at exactly the proper adjustment. The foreman approached Annello with the suggestion that he prepare himself to work on the new machines. Annello was highly pleased and put in all his spare time trying to familiarize himself with the work. He succeeded so well that by the time the machines were finally installed the foreman felt that Annello was sufficiently qualified and gave him a place on the new battery. Here Annello worked along with the other workmen, all of whom had been trained at one time or another by the foreman. He appeared to do average work and was well liked by the other men.

The standards department of the Schoonway Machine Company decided to institute a series of studies relative to the operations of gear-cutting machines for milling teeth in cutters. After the routine research had been made, the standards engineer announced the minimum amount of output which a worker must attain in order to be considered efficient. No bonus could be earned until this standard was exceeded.

During the period in which the studies were made. Annello was nervous. He appeared unable to keep his machine in proper adjustment. The pieces which he turned out were inferior in quality, and the total number gradually fell below the point at which the minimum standard was finally set. Engineers from the standards department, knowing that Annello was a protégé of the foreman, sought to ascertain the cause of his trouble, but he was unable to make an intelligible explanation. They warned him of the seriousness of the situation. For several days there was no change. Then, at the suggestion of the foreman, time study men retimed Annello, in an endeavor to find the cause of his failure. His showing was worse than ever. The engineers began to question whether or not he had the native ability to do the work. The head of the standards department expressed that doubt to the foreman. The foreman insisted that Annello was a first-class workman. The standards department believed that the foreman was prejudiced because he did not object when they suggested that Joseph Smith be discharged. Smith had been employed on the new battery for about the same length of time as Annello and his output was not so low.

With their watches concealed in their pockets so as not to arouse Annello's suspicion, the time study men clocked him for a third time. Still he showed no improvement. After that, the standards department became insistent that Annello be discharged. The foreman was obdurate, and the standards department appealed to the production manager for a final decision. The latter listened to the recommendations of the standards department and to the objections which the foreman raised, and then made a ruling that at the end of one week the standards department was to make another clocking of Annello's work. If it still was unsatisfactory, the foreman was to be given an additional week in which he could take any measures he chose in attempting to bring the machinist's work up to standard. If he failed to do this within the allotted period, Annello was to be fired for inability to attain the minimum standard.

At the end of the first week the new timings were made. Annello showed no improvement. When the foreman received this information, he went to Annello accompanied by a friend of the latter's, who acted as interpreter. The foreman told the machinist that his work was coming along well and that he had no need to fear the time study men, that they would bother him no more. He said he would see to it personally that nothing happened to Annello and that as long as he tried his best he always could have a job with the Schoonway Machine Company. Annello thanked the foreman profusely and said that he always tried to do his best. The next morning he appeared at work smiling and happy. His output for the day was just at the minimum standard, but the quality was excellent. The next day his output increased. At the end of the week he was earning a good bonus. Six months later the standards department, as well as the foreman, rated him as the best worker on the automatic gear-cutting machines.

The Crown Fastener Company[42]

During the summer between his junior and senior years at Dartmouth College, Edgar Hagan took a job as a student trainee with The Crown Fastener Company, a medium sized manufacturer and distributor of nuts and bolts. The training program Hagan was placed in consisted of four weeks in the company warehouse, four weeks in the company factory, and two weeks in the company offices. There were five students in the program, all of whom had the understanding that they would receive jobs as salesmen with the company after two summers in the program.

On the first day of work all five of the trainees met in the office of John Cusick, the superintendent of the warehouse. Cusick was a man in his middle thirties, a former decorated Navy veteran, and a graduate of Dartmouth College. After outlining the work program for the next four weeks and assigning each of the trainees to a specific de-

---

[42] Case material of the Harvard Graduate School of Business Administration is prepared as a basis for class discussion. Cases are not designed to present illustrations of either correct or incorrect handling of administrative problems.

Copyright ©, 1955 by the President and Fellows of Harvard College (Ea-C 265; ICH 3H14). This case also appears on pages 411–14 in *Organizational Behavior and Administration* by Paul R. Lawrence and John A. Seiler (rev. ed.; Homewood, Ill.: Richard D. Irwin, Inc., 1965). Reprinted by permission.

partment for the first two weeks, he offered this advice to them: "Fellows, I would be very careful in my relationships with the employees here if I were you. The majority of the people here are a pretty crude bunch. Their work is pretty much physical and routine in nature, and as a result, we can afford to hire men of generally low intelligence. They're all either Italians, Poles, or Negroes from the slums, and they're tough customers. So watch out for your valuables, and don't start any trouble with them."

For the first two weeks, Hagan was assigned to the sixth floor, hexagon nut department, under the supervision of Guildo Bovanni, a man who had been with the company since its inception twenty-two years before. Bovanni, a short but extremely powerful man, spoke in broken English and had quite a difficult time reading any material with which he was not previously familiar. When Cusick introduced Hagan to Bovanni he said: "Guildo, this is Edgar Hagan, a college trainee who'll be with us for the summer. I've decided to have him work here for the first two weeks and I'd like you to teach him all you know about nuts. Give him all the odd jobs you have so he'll get experience with as many different types of nuts as possible. Well, good luck, Hagan. We'll get together again soon."

After Cusick had left, Bovanni said to Hagan. "A college boy, eh? I'll learn ya about nuts, but I'll do it my way. I guess Cusick there thinks I can learn ya in two weeks what I've learned in twenty years. Christ! Don't pay no attention to him. We'll start ya helping the packers so ya can work with the nuts we ship most of. You'll be lucky if ya can learn them in two weeks. Then each day I'll try to learn ya a few of the nuts we don't see very often."

Hagan was amazed that each of the nine employees in the hexagon nut department quickly told him almost the same thing as soon as he was alone with them. Typical of these comments was this statement by Ted Grant, an elderly Negro packer: "If I were you, I'd stay on the good side of Guildo. He's one hell of a good foreman and really knows his stuff. He can teach you more about nuts and bolts than any guy in this place. Work hard for him and you'll get along swell here."

Hagan did his best to follow this advice and soon found that Bovanni was spending more and more time with him. He was very surprised when on Friday, Bovanni said: "Grab your lunch and let's go eat across the street." Bovanni regularly ate his lunch in a little bar across from the warehouse with a group of about seven other foremen.

The conversation ranged from families to sports but soon settled on Cusick. Hagan was amazed at this because he, a newcomer, was there, and interpreted this to mean that Bovanni must have spoken to the men, saying that he was "OK." It was quickly obvious that Bovanni was the leader among this group, and when he summed up the conversation in the following manner everyone seemed in complete agreement with him. "Cusick tries hard. He's tried to improve things here but he hasn't had the experience. He must be able to handle Charley Crown,[43] though, look at the money he's got us for new equipment. But, Christ, then he screws up and buys the wrong stuff. He just don't know what to do and won't listen when we tell him."

On Friday of Hagan's first week, Cusick issued a bulletin stating that all forms used in the routing of materials in the warehouse would be changed to a slightly more complicated type on which material locations could be designated more precisely. The bulletin was handed out to all warehouse employees with their pay envelopes at the close of work Friday. Included was a group of the new forms. The bulletin simply stated that the change was to be made and requested that each man familiarize himself with the new forms over the week end so that he could use them correctly on Monday. The men just took the material and stuffed it into their pockets in their haste to catch their street cars home.

On Monday morning everyone in the hexagon nut department quickly went to work distributing the backlog of materials that had been delivered on Saturday, making a note of each shipment's ultimate location. As was the practice in this department, all of the department personnel met at Bovanni's desk at 10:30 A.M. to give this information to Bovanni so that he could copy it onto the formal forms which went to the office for inventory control. Bovanni claimed he used this procedure so that all the forms would be uniformly filled out and not mutilated by the men carrying them around as they worked. It was quite obvious, however, that his main purpose for insisting on this procedure was that he wanted to know where every shipment on his floor was located, so that when orders came through from the office he could tell the men exactly where the material ordered was located, from memory. Hagan had been constantly amazed by Bovanni's ability to remember exactly where, within each tier and row, a certain shipment was located. This ability had been built up over a period of years, and Bovanni was obviously quite proud of it.

---

[43] The president of The Crown Fastener Company.

At the Monday morning meeting there was a considerable differ-ence of opinion among the various department personnel as to how the locations should be entered on the new forms. Bovanni insisted that it should be done in the same manner as before, where the aisle and tier of each shipment was recorded, while most of the other men protested that additional information was to the exact location within each aisle and tier should be noted. Bovanni argued that this would provide unnecessary detail and would only confuse things. He was quite adamant about this, and the other men quickly acceded to his point of view.

The next morning Cusick came up to the sixth floor and walked directly to Bovanni's desk. He said in quite a loud voice: "Guildo, you're filling out the forms all wrong. Didn't you read the notice? You're still doing it the old way, and that's just what we're trying to get away from. Do you think we would go to all this trouble only to have things done in the same old way? Now you've really got the of-fice all fouled up. We need new forms on all the materials you re-ceived yesterday. You'd better get at it right away so they can make orders out on some of that material."

Guildo was sitting at his desk, looking up a catalogue number, while Cusick was talking to him. He was obviously getting madder and madder as Cusick spoke. Finally he broke in: "Look, Mr. Cusick, this department never had no trouble with its locations before. We've been getting along fine. Why do you have to foul us up by making us change everything? I've been running this department for one hell of a long time, and I guess to Christ I know as much about it as you do. Why don't you handle the top brass and let me handle my depart-ment. As long as I get the work done, what do you care how I do it? When those orders come through, I'll be able to find those kegs just like I always have."

CUSICK: "That's the trouble with you, Guildo, you only think of your-self. I've made this change in the entire warehouse. You're the only one bitching about it. From now on the office wants a complete record of exactly where everything is. Now, dammit, as long as I'm running this warehouse we're going to do it my way!"

Bovanni was getting madder all the time: "Listen, Cusick, you may run this warehouse, but I run this floor. Nobody really needs to know those locations except me, and you know it. The way we're doing things here works fine, and you know it. Why pick on me? Why don't you go climb on some of the other boys that don't get their work done? Why come nosing around here telling me how to do my job?"

Cusick moved around next to Bovanni and put his hand on Bovanni's shoulder: "Calm down, Guildo, remember who's boss here. I won't stand for your talking to me that way. Now just calm down and quit shouting."

BOVANNI: "Wait a second. Who started the shouting? You come up here and broadcast to everyone that I don't know what I'm doing. I've run this floor for ten years, and you can't tell me how to do my job. Don't tell me to calm down, and take your Goddamn hand off me!"

CUSICK (*patting Bovanni's shoulder*): "There's no sense in your getting all steamed up about this. You know damn well you're going to end up doing it my way."

BOVANNI: "Get your hand off my shoulder!"

CUSICK: "Let's not argue about it, you're wrong and you know it!"

BOVANNI: "Take your hand off my shoulder before I slug you!"

CUSICK (*leaving his hand on Bovanni's shoulder*): "Listen, no one talks to me that way. I won't stand for any punk telling me what to do. You'd better learn your place around here!"

BOVANNI: "You heard me! Get your hand off me!"

CUSICK (*with his hand still on Bovanni's shoulder*): "Hold on, Mac—."

Bovanni then whirled and hit Cusick squarely on the shoulder, knocking him back into a stack of kegs. Cusick recovered his balance and walked away, saying: "Okay, buster, if that's the way you want it. . . ."

"Vicious rumor tortures Garfield Ridge"[44]

LOIS WILLE

No one knows who first whispered it. Or why. Or when.

It started to grow slowly, in several places almost at once. It was heard in a drive-in restaurant near W. Archer and S. Austin. In a music class at the high school a block away. At a coffee klatsch in the kitchen of a bungalow across from the school.

Then, suddenly last Wednesday night, the rumor exploded over

---

44 *Chicago Daily News*, November 1, 1966, pp. 1 and 8. Reprinted with permission.

the quiet Garfield Ridge neighborhood on Chicago's Far Southwest Side:

A white girl, according to the story, had been raped by three Negro boys.

The place: A boy's washroom in sleek new John F. Kennedy High School, 6325 W. 56th St. Some say it was the third floor, some swear it was the second.

The time: At noon Tuesday, according to one version. At 2:20 P.M., when the last lunch period ends, according to another.

The victim: Unknown. Ask hundreds of students and parents and they all say something like, "I talked to someone who knows a good friend of hers but I don't know her name. . . ."

"Absolutely unfounded," says Capt. Martin T. O'Connell, commander of the Chicago Lawn District.

For nearly six days his detectives have checked and rechecked every aspect of the rumor. Aided by clergymen, businessmen and teachers, they have interviewed a majority of Kennedy's 3,292 students.

On Monday night O'Connell concluded, "This is a vicious rumor. Totally untrue."

But in the neat bungalows of Garfield Ridge, there are families who grabbed at it hungrily—and now they won't let it go.

Steamed by the rumor, hundreds of students marched around John F. Kennedy School, screaming, "Be a Nazi lover, not a nigger lover."

Their mothers stormed into the school office, demanding that their little girls be sent home.

Five members of the American Nazi Party moved in, distributed hate handbills and were arrested by police and cheered by women on street corners.

The heartbroken Kennedy principal, Dorothy V. Sauer, says she still believes the 192 Negro students are well integrated among the 3,100 white students and adds:

"But one mother told me, 'This has been festering for a long time.' "

Here, pieced together by police, Miss Sauer and the students, is the anatomy of the rumor:

Last Tuesday morning a white girl on her way to Hubbard High School, 6200 S. Hamlin, ran away from three Negro boys who had been talking to her on a corner.

She fell as she ran and skinned her arm. At the school, the girl was given a bandage.

About noon on Tuesday police headquarters at 1121 S. State received an anonymous call from a young-sounding girl who said, "Something is going to happen this afternoon at Kennedy High School."

Police combed the three-story building that afternoon, thinking it may have been a bomb threat.

Also at noon on Tuesday two white girls got into a hair-pulling fight over a boy at a hamburger shop near the school. The two were picked up by police in a cruising squad car and returned to school.

Somehow, out of these three isolated incidents, the rape rumor was born.

Miss Sauer, a pretty, hard-working young woman who has been Kennedy's principal since it opened three years ago, first heard the story at 2:20 P.M. Wednesday.

"Some boys, student leaders, told me about it," she said. "They were concerned and wanted the story stopped."

Over the school public address system, Miss Sauer invited anyone "with any information about a serious incident" to see her. No one came.

"I called police youth officers at that point," she said. "That's when they began their investigation."

Late that afternoon and through the evening, parents began to call her: Was it true a girl was raped? What was she doing about it? Well, if it wasn't true—how did the story get started?

School Supt. James F. Redmond called about 9 P.M. He, too, had heard the rumor.

A group of worried students came to see her: Had she heard there was a student demonstration scheduled for 10:30 A.M. the next day?

At 10 P.M., Miss Sauer finally left her office.

About that same time, a Southwest Side group, the Taxpayers Council, was listening to Waukegan Mayor Robert Sabonjian in Polonia Grove Hall, 6400 S. Archer.

The council and Sabonjian, a write-in candidate for the Senate, share a goal: Kill open-housing legislation.

Sabonjian was followed by Walter Douglas, an officer of the Murray Park Civic Assn. He told the audience of 800 that he had just received a telephone call informing him that a white girl had been raped by three Negro boys at Kennedy school.

He said he was "not sure the incident was verified," but gave a telephone number that supposedly belonged to the girl's family.

Hundreds called the number that night. The confused woman who answered said she had no children at Kennedy and knew of no rape.

Capt. O'Connell, who had sent two detectives to observe the Taxpayers Council meeting, now blames Douglas for "giving momentum to the rumor."

"After that, it spread like wildfire," he says.

The *Daily News* tried to reach Douglas for comment, but learned from his wife that he had gone to New York on a business trip and could not be reached.

She said Douglas is an "engineer" and declined to tell where he works.

At 9:30 A.M. Thursday Miss Sauer told students over the public address system that the rape story had been thoroughly investigated by police and was not true.

But at 10:30 A.M., right on schedule, several hundred students poured out of Kennedy and began their march and their chants of hate.

"It's terrible, the coloreds are taking over the school," screamed a pretty green-eyed blond, Linda Surdej, 17, of 5238 Mayfield.

But isn't it true that the 192 Negro students come only from LeClaire Courts, an old housing project near Midway Airport—and one that hasn't grown for 10 years?

"Just wait," she replied. "In another year it'll be like Lindblom— 98 per-cent colored."

"They're getting so bossy," added her girl friend, Debbie Nowak, 15, of 5710 W. 57th St.

"You look at them funny and they call you white trash."

One girl, asked to trace the origin of her hatred of Negro students, said a "nigger girl" hit her shoulder when the girl opened her locker door.

"I called her a name and now everytime she sees me she hisses 'white trash,' " the girl said.

Clumps of housewives lined the sidewalk to watch the marchers, and every so often one would call out: "That's right." Or, "You tell them, honey."

One mother beamed, "Our children are standing up for their rights. Why don't the niggers have their own high school?"

But the great majority of Kennedy's 3,292 students did not demonstrate. When the last lunch period ended at 2:20 P.M., most of the marchers were back in class.

Over the weekend the Nazi literature appeared.

Monday morning, as the five Nazis tried to pass out more literature, they were arrested. Police also dispersed about 30 housewives who had gathered on the street opposite the high school.

John L. Waner, a heating contractor and past president of the Garfield Ridge Chamber of Commerce, said he thinks the worst is over now. And how did it begin?

"It certainly came from outside sources," he said. "This is a wonderful, peace-loving community."

"He's really coming!"[45]

Charlie Thorp, with 15 years of management experience with the Darron Company, was regarded as "company-minded," cooperative with associates, and a good operator. When his bookkeeper retired, Thorp hired John Pasek to replace her. It soon became apparent that Pasek's ambition was to become a salesman. John was a likeable young man; so when an opening occurred Charlie recommended to Bob Norlach, district manager, "that John, given the opportunity and the leadership, has the qualities that could be developed to make him a successful salesman in my area."

Norlach, Thorp, and Pasek met to discuss the job and its performance standards and to arrive at a mutually acceptable budget. Pasek was installed as a salesman.

Norlach asked for periodic progress reports on John and Charlie invariably responded: "He's really coming! He is ahead of budget in both new accounts and volume of sales during the period. He's right on target."

After six months of favorable reports on young Pasek Charlie visited Norlach and complained: "We gotta get rid of John. His production stinks. He has not performed up to standard or budget."

Norlach was astounded: "But haven't you been reporting to me how well John has been doing? Why the sudden change in your evaluation of his performance?"

---

45 All names have been disguised.

Charlie answered: "I just wanted to encourage him. I figured that if I reported his real output he'd be getting a lot of pressure and he might never shape up. So I was crediting him with all my own new sales and reporting that to you."

Pat's story[46]

Statistical background

Education:
    8½ years parochial grammar school
    4 years high school: 1 year prep and 3 years commercial (change of course—financial reasons)
Home:
    Average American family—father a guard, mother a housewife
    8 children, me being the oldest
Recommended for job by: Office practice teacher
Original position:
    Steno
Other positions:
    Savings teller—which afforded me the chance to learn bonds, Christmas Club, All Purpose Club, trial balances, figuring interest, and a few other odd jobs.
    Mortgage teller & processing out-of-state loans.
    Floater—used in whichever department was busiest.

Appointed branch manager

After three years with the bank, I was transferred to a new branch where I worked with an assistant treasurer and another girl.

Six months after being at the branch, Mr. Wirtz, our assistant treasurer, went on vacation and I was temporarily in charge. About two days before his return, Mr. Stockton, our bank president, appeared and asked me if I thought I could run the branch indefinitely.

Before he finished the question, I had already answered, "Yes." I was a little frightened, but not very disturbed in that Mr. Wirtz, who

---

[46] All names have been disguised.

had been with the bank for 37 years, had to depend on me for all the mortgage questions and there was very little that I didn't know about savings.

Most of the first month was spent trying to make Ellie, my co-worker and friend, accept me as her boss. By this time, we had acquired Fred, who migrated from the main office. Even though he was 65 and taking orders from a 22-year-old dame, I had fewer personality conflicts with him than I did with Ellie.

But we became a happy little family of three for several years.

During this time my home life and work life were happy and it was rare when I wasn't smiling. In fact most of the customers would comment when they came in and I wasn't kidding or laughing. They'd think I was sick or something.

Promoted to treasurer

On February 1st, Mr. Stockton came over for his usual weekly visit. Over the years, we had become the closest of friends. He had plenty of faults and was sometimes very unreasonable, but knowing him and his good qualities, I grew to love him. If something were to happen to him tomorrow, I would feel as badly as if it were my own dad.

Well, he flatly stated that he had a problem and could I spare a few minutes. In the past, we had discussed problems at the main office. This time he said he was at a loss to correct the situation. Morale, in plain English, stunk. I assumed it was the usual gab and proceeded to the lunch room with him. There he made his announcement that Ted Roberts, our treasurer, had given one month's notice, at which time he would go to a competitor.

I thought to myself, "God help us. We'll have to close the doors." I immediately asked Mr. Stockton if he had tried to convince Ted to reverse his decision. He said he did, but I can't imagine him trying very hard, knowing he would be too proud to admit to Ted that the bank needed him.

Mr. Stockton said frankly he didn't know what he should do.

Mr. Wirtz, with all his years at the bank, couldn't qualify. Six years ago, when Les Talmage, our senior assistant treasurer, died and he tried it, he was out for five months with a nervous breakdown. Juan Balboa, our other assistant treasurer in the mortgage department, was fairly new there and Stockton hadn't very much confidence in him yet.

The vice president, who was being groomed to take Stockton's job, as he was nearing retirement, had been let go in January because of lack of aggressiveness and productivity, and there was no one else he could turn to except me.

"Me! I don't know, Mr. Stockton, I just don't know!" Ted was always crabbing about how he got everyone's operational problems, how stupid his help was, and how bad his ulcers were getting, and besides, I still depended on Ted for certain technical questions.

Mr. Stockton said he had approached the board of investment and really built me up, and he and they decided I could do it. Well, I don't know how these men, whom I never saw, except at clambakes could evaluate my capabilities. I've known me for 29 years and I don't know what they are.

But here was a man who didn't care that I was only a 22-year-old female when he made me branch manager and at 26½ made me an assistant treasurer, telling me in a round about way that he needs me. Right now I couldn't live with myself if I didn't at least try. Sink or swim, I made up my mind in a matter of 10 minutes, that I'd try to get as much knowledge from Ted as possible before he left.

Learning the job

The very next day I presented myself at the main office, where Ted was instructed to inform me as to his duties and try to teach me the things I didn't know.

Well, I certainly was discovering there was a hell of a lot I didn't know. And being so content in my own little world at the branch, I never took the initiative to learn things that didn't pertain to branch operations.

After one day as Ted's understudy, I went home very depressed and immediately went to bed and laid there for 6 or 7 hours, telling myself to throw in the towel and at the same time giving myself all the reasons why I couldn't.

What would my folks think! They were so excited about the idea that in the very near future I could very possibly be treasurer. And my kid sisters and brothers all patting me on the back saying, "We know you can do it, Pat." And last, but not least, I will have failed my boss in his efforts to help me advance. ("God, I can't throw in that towel; I'd rather die first.")

My second day was worse. While Ted is explaining, I'm not really getting it because I'm constantly thinking, "I've got to get this in a month, I've got to cram 35 years' experience into one month."

When I returned home that evening, I very quietly went to my room, closed the door, and had a damn good cry. Not only did it seem there were three million jobs being funneled through Ted's desk, but three million questions from the tellers. It seemed like they couldn't blow their own noses without checking with Ted to find out how to do it.

I couldn't help thinking that if these interruptions didn't stop, I'd never catch on to anything.

After one week of depression, tears, frustration in not grasping this information quick enough, I was determined to tell Mr. Stockton to forget it. I don't want to go nuts like Mr. Wirtz, and I don't want to lay awake nights tossing and turning.

Determined and convinced, I marched into Mr. Stockton's office the next day and said, "Mr. Stockton, I . . . !" and with this he said, "Well, how's my girl doing? You certainly haven't smiled much this week, but you're a worry wart—take your time, be yourself, you're smart and you'll get it."

Well, what could I say, but— "One thing good that's happened to me is I've lost nine pounds this week and I could stand to lose about 20 more." We both laughed and I marched out, undetermined and unconvinced.

My morale was fairly good for one day and one day, only.

Three weeks of lying in bed every night, going over the day's instructions, saying, "What the hell is this amortization all about? Depreciation on the buildings and the furniture and amortizing our insurance over the life of the policy. God help me, when he leaves, I'm going to look like the world's biggest jerk! With me running the show, in two months time we'll have to close down."

Ted didn't help very much, telling me nice goodies like, "Forget it, kid, when bookkeeping is out, you won't get anything done. That goof in the back room has been doing this job for 16 years and she still doesn't know where to look when she's out."

Gee, bookkeeping was out practically everyday. When do I get to do my work? And besides, I don't know where to look myself. I don't know a thing about the general ledger except which column to put the amortization and accrued interest in, and that's providing I know what the hell amortization and accrued interest is by the time he leaves.

By the time the final week rolled around, no one in my family cared to come in contact with me. Trying to hold my tears and temper at work made my home life pretty miserable, too. Even my folks were discouraging me, saying things like, "The money and the job aren't worth it!" "You look awful; you better tell Mr. Stockton you can't handle it."

I made up my mind that I had to relieve tension and work somewhere. At this time I owned my own house. Keeping house, clothing, the whole business was getting me down. It seemed I was too tired to even wash my face before going to bed, let alone take care of the problems a house can give you. I decided to sell.

Well, that was a doozy of an idea! Now I had people bothering me with phone calls, plus selling furniture. Boy, I was beginning to look like death warmed over. Now. I no longer dreaded going to work, but home, too.

In the final week, Ted showed me how to reconcile the computer sheets, payroll, trustee reports, state tax, computation, recording new securities, report for estimated earnings, who to collect rent from on our parking lot and when to pay the board of investment and the board of trustees.

I was beginning to think I'd have to work seven days a week at 20 hours a day. Not only had I never done most of this stuff, 80 percent of it I had never seen before.

Prior to my arrival, both Ted and Mr. Wirtz had handled it, along with our vice president, who had been fired, and Mr. Wirtz was now managing our new branch.

I was now making noontime visits to the nearest church, purchasing horoscope books and resorting to palm readers. I don't really know if I was praying for success or just to keep from going nuts.

My horoscope books were all out of kilter. On days when my cycle was supposed to be high at work, it couldn't have been lower. When it said my cycle would be low, I was truly afraid to even go to work.

Friends and associates were now calling my folks, asking if I was feeling all right. When I found out, it made me afraid for myself. I had the feeling I must be acting a little crazy or something for them to notice. I don't think I smiled once during the entire training. Little did I know, I wouldn't be smiling for some time to come.

Ted seemed touched when I started crying when he said good-bye. I don't think he knew I was crying for me.

The weekend prior to my being on my own was spent in bed. If I didn't know better at the time, I would have thought I was pregnant, for I was having morning sickness (which lasted for several weeks).

The first day on her own

My first day on my own was hell. All the young help decided that Pat was a soft slob, so let's hit her with gripes we were afraid to mention to Ted.

It was the first of the month and we were getting all our coupons and interest checks in, which had to be recorded on the bookkeeping sheet and check books, plus sitting on my desk were the usual monthly reports, all of which were going to be done by me for the first time on my own.

Mr. Stockton left at 11:00 for his usual Monday meeting.

As soon as he was out the door, Ann from the mortgage department approached me.

ANN: Gee, Pat, I was wondering about our Blue Cross.

ME: Wondering about what?

ANN: How come the bank will pay the family plan for the guys but not the girls?

ME: That's our policy, I guess.

ANN: But, when I get married in four months, my husband will still be in school and I'll be the main support, so why won't they pay?

ME: Did you ask Ted? I really don't know very much about it. It's one thing he didn't mention.

ANN: Well, he was always so busy, I didn't want to bother him.

At this point, I thought this kid had insulted me. What does she think I've been doing, sitting here picking my nose?

ME: Well, I can talk it over with Mr. Stockton and see about it.

ANN: It isn't a fair policy, after all, if they can spend $52.80 a month on David, who's a jerk, why can't they spend it on me? I do more than my share.

ME: Ann, I've got 9,000 things piling up, please let's not discuss this any further. I will find out for you.

Well now I can get back to work!

MARIA: Pat?

ME: (*Now what?*) Yes, Maria.

MARIA: Do you suppose we could have a suggestion box?

ME: Sure, why not, it sounds great.

Flora than approached me to inquire whether or not she could keep a dentist appointment which was scheduled in three more weeks. She had already gotten Ted's consent, but he was no longer there and she needed mine. I answered, "If I'm still alive in three weeks, you have my permission. If I don't make it, you'll have to check with the next guy."

By this time, it's 11:30 and everyone seems to be puzzled as to what lunch hours they were to take. Everyone wants to eat with their friends. I was beginning to think, "If I went in the vault and took those guns out of joint control, these people wouldn't have to worry about eating."

As everyone bickered over the schedule, I decided that tonight, when I got home, I'd have to make one up and post it, but that wasn't helping me today. After looking over the situation and looking at the top of my desk, I decided to let them work it out themselves, provided some of them stayed to wait on the counter.

Every item I put on the bookkeeping sheet was questionable. I kept running to the back room to ask Flora if it looked right. I thought this would save me the time of having to check last month's work to see how it was done, but Flora went and got last month's work to check. I thought to myself: this is the blind leading the blind.

It was now 12:15 and instead of my desk looking a little better, it gradually got worse. Everything that these people got that seemed a little different and would take some thinking was thrown on my desk, plus both interoffice envelopes from the branches were lying there for the contents to be distributed among the help. After sorting the contents of the envelopes, it was now 12:30. Well, at least I've gotten two things off this desk.

Boy, when Mr. Stockton gets back at 1:00, he's going to think I was goofing off for two hours.

At 12:30 the janitor appeared on the scene.

ERNIE: Pat, I've got this can of 30 W oil down in the basement and the paper on the boiler calls for 20 W oil, do you think it would make much difference?

ME: Ernie, about the only differences in oil that I know of is real olive oil and Mazola oil and that difference to me is the taste. Maybe we should taste the oil and see.

ERNIE: You made a funny!

ME: Did I? That's the first one in a whole month.

ERNIE: All kidding aside, what do you think?

ME: I think, there are two people in this bank that know very little about 20 W and 30 W oil, so I would suggest you buy whatever oil the boiler calls for. I doubt that it will cause us bankruptcy.

ERNIE: Okay, Pat. Can you give me the money right now? I don't have any on me and I'll bring back the receipt.

ME: Sure. Tell Charlie what you need and he'll give it to you.

God, it's five of 1:00 and Stockton is due back and I've accomplished practically nothing.

As I finally get settled down to figure out what to do next, Flora comes out to make the grand announcement of the day: "Pat, bookkeeping is out $1.67."

A fantastic thought flashed through my mind: Maybe I could put Flora in the boiler room and get Ernie to do the bookkeeping.

I gave Flora a consoling half smile. If I could smile, she might watch for my crowsfeet and not see my tears. "Well, let's start hunting."

I at least had Charlie to rely on. Ted seemed to have fed him a lot of info that the rest of the help didn't get.

ME: Hey, Charlie, would you mind helping us look for $1.67?

CHARLIE: Cripe, I've got my own crap sitting here to do and besides, when the heck are you going to take my teller window away so I can devote my time to this important stuff?

ME: Look, Charlie, we'll consider that possibility later, but unless we can find $1.67, we'll never leave here tonight.

CHARLIE: Well, in that case, I'll help out.

I thought to myself, "If I didn't need this bratty 24-year-old, I'd kick him in the a——."

It was now 1:15 and we were in the middle of our search, when Mr. Stockton popped in.

STOCKTON: Having problems?

ME: I really don't know, we've just started looking.

STOCKTON: What have you checked?

ME: Well, I've started adding the check books, but I don't know what Charlie has checked. He's out front.

STOCKTON: I guess you've got everything under control.

ME: Yes, more or less.

As Charlie did the directing (which I might add, was his bag) we checked just about every possibility. It was now 2:15 and neither Flora nor myself had had lunch.

I decided we should get out for a few minutes, anyway, just to help us clear our heads.

Me: Charlie, keep looking. Flora and I are going to lunch. Check with the mortgage department again, it's probably something over there. Ask Juan to go over everything. We're running out of places to look in savings.

Charlie: If he'd get off his butt, instead of having those idiot kids checking for him, we might get results.

As I was thinking the very same thing, myself, I kept my mouth shut and proceeded toward the door.

Teller #1: Pat, the coin machine is jammed. I can smell something burning.

Me: You're right, it's the motor. Is it shut off?

Teller #1: No, I didn't think it would make a difference!

God, what did I ever do to deserve such a fate?

By the time I handcranked the cylinder and removed it from its place, it was 2:35. By 2:45 it was put back together again and I finally got out the door.

I didn't spend my lunch hour with Flora, but instead went to Saint Mary's Church about six blocks away. On my way back I grabbed a sandwich and a coke.

At 3:15 I returned only to find the very same situation. We looked and looked and finally I threw in the towel.

The help usually get out at 4:00 and it's 3:55.

I'll have to tell Mr. Stockton we can't find it.

Me: Mr. Stockton, we've checked everything. I don't know where else to look.

Stockton: Things will be clearer tomorrow. Everybody will be fresh in the morning; we'll look then. Start closing up.

Fresh? He's got to be kidding! The way I've been sleeping, I'll be dead tomorrow. (For a moment, I thought that might be a blessing.)

That night on my way home, I bought a bottle of rum. By 9:00 I was soused. I crawled into bed and finally got a good night's sleep.

The next two days

I wasn't tired the next morning, but I sure as hell was nauseated. I arrived at work early.

As cocky as Charlie was and as much as I wasn't too crazy about him—he was in early, too.

We started from scratch, checking everything step by step. I had accomplished a bank first! Never in the history of our organization, had the daily statement been out for two days. In fact, it had never been out for one.

Plus two days' work still sitting on my desk. Finally, on the third morning, after Flora finished blocking her mortgage cards, she announced that the cards were $1.67 out. Juan had made a wrong correction on the back of the control sheet.

I was so happy for the moment, I couldn't really be mad with Juan. It wasn't too long after, though, that it hit me that none of this guy's work had been interrupted and nothing was piled on his desk, plus the fact that he left on time with everyone else. I don't think I had ever boiled to the point I was boiling at that moment.

I decided from then on I would take one day at a time and stop worrying.

The next day I started off in a pretty good mood. I decided this place was not going to get the best of me.

My problem this day was Mr. Stockton. He must have gotten up on the wrong side of the bed. It seemed everything he looked at was fouled up. Boy, I certainly hadn't seen this side of him for a good number of years. As he proceeded to tell me how messy everything was, I noticed the item to which he was referring had been wrong for two years.

"Look Mr. Stockton, I don't mind being bawled out for my own mistakes, and I make plenty. That's something that has been handled wrong for two years and I'll try to correct it but do not wish to be criticized for it."

This didn't set too well, as he grabbed his hat and coat and mumbled about no one having any respect for his authority and walked out.

I just felt crushed. I don't believe he realized in the slightest just what I was facing and feeling. It seemed that I would never catch on to all the detailed things.

Showdown with Stockton

After two months of trial and error, I gained more and more confidence. This didn't last very long, I'm afraid.

The third week of June Charlie gave two weeks' notice. Maria, our secretary, got a better paying job. Another teller was being sent to our branch and another teller from our new branch quit on the spot.

In one month's time, I had five new savings tellers, three of which had less than one month's experience.

Being short of experienced help, I had to train the new help in as short a time as possible. I'll have to admit their instruction was very poor and I was now being interrupted every two minutes with questions.

I went through another two months of turmoil. Mr. Stockton was getting complaints, that the help in his organization was giving out wrong information to customers, both over the counter and the telephone. That really went over like a lead balloon and I was certainly bawled out.

I finally got up enough nerve to lay the cards on the table.

"Mr. Stockton, I am not a miracle worker. Just an average person. Before I arrived, things were pretty mixed up. At that time, you had an assistant treasurer making $11,000; a treasurer making $16,000; and a vice president making $22,000. They all leave and I replace them for $13,000. I'm not complaining about the money, but I only have one head, two hands, and a limited amount of time in the day. I have come to the conclusion that I haven't complained enough for you to recognize all of our problems. I ask nothing of you, except consideration. Before screaming, look at the entire picture. I realize we're preparing to merge with another bank and that's why we're not replacing our officers, but the load is getting me down. Especially in that you think this place can run just as efficiently now as it has in the past."

He smiled and said I was right and he was irritable lately because he, too, was doing a lot more than he had for quite some time.

My little speech cleared the air and has made it a lot easier on both of us.

The pressure eases

In October, Juan gave two weeks' notice. He had worked for the bank we were to merge with and wasn't too crazy about going in that direction. He left for a competitive bank.

My brother was next in line in mortgages and was made assistant treasurer.

We have moved along and things have been looking better the last three months.

We have, however, been refused our merger by the commissioner, so many changes will be coming about.

I have some good ideas for improvement that I hadn't tried due to the anticipation of a change anyway. Now I want to move.

There are two things which I have come to realize. Most important is the realization that these people are not goofs or idiots.

For example, in 16 years, when bookkeeping was out, it was taken away from Flora and the search was done by the officers in charge. She therefore never had the opportunity to look for herself and broaden her knowledge in that area. I'd say if it hadn't been for Flora I probably would have fallen on my face when I came to the general ledger. She has become more independent and less of a burden on me.

The moral is—make them more efficient, let them think for themselves and ask for ideas.

The second important thing is to make each and everyone feel that their job is important and explain to them why.

Through staff meetings, I find that the kids are volunteering a tremendous amount of their ideas and time.

Morale has really picked up.

And, now that I've stopped fumbling around in the dark, I want to make as many changes as possible to make our organization as smooth running and as pleasant as possible.

I would honestly say that I feel at this moment should any great change occur in my life again, I will face it and should I fall, be able to pick myself up and start again.

I'd like to add that I really love banking and am now enjoying every minute of it. I have a small ulcer, which I acquired five months ago, but it's all worth it.

5

The process of
communication

Now to focus on that critical, challenging, sometimes agonizing human process—communication. Let us begin by examining a very simple, mundane communication experience. Say we have two men, A and B, in an office. A feels warm and asks B to open a window, which he does. We can discuss these events in terms of a model of the communication process.[1]

COMMUNICATION PROCESS MODEL

Encoding

Consider the steps in this incident. First A had a *need*—he felt warm, uncomfortable. Next, he went through a remarkable (for such a simple situation) problem-solving sequence in which he decided among other things how best to satisfy his need without thwarting other needs; whether to take the action himself or to ask another to do it; and, if he decided to enlist the aid of another, how best to ap-

---

[1] See Figure 5–1. For more detailed models of the communication process see: D. K. Berlo, *The Process of Communication* (New York: Holt, Rinehart & Winston, Inc., 1960); C. Shannon and W. Weaver, *The Mathematical Theory of Communication* (Urbana, Ill.: University of Illinois Press, 1962), p. 5; and W. Schramm, "How Communication Works," *The Process and Effects of Mass Communication*, ed. W. Schramm (Urbana, Ill.: University of Illinois Press, 1954), pp. 3–26. See also: Robert S. Goyer, "Definitions of Communications;'" Special Report No. 25, Center for Communication Studies, Ohio University, September 1970.

proach the other person; what time to communicate; what communication medium to use; what choice of words, tone of voice, rate and loudness of speaking; and so forth.

Since the experience is a familiar one and if B is well known to A much of A's choice making was routinized, carried on by conditioned responses—i.e., he need not be *conscious* of making many of these choices.

A has been going through the process of *encoding* a message—perceiving his experiences and formulating a series of symbols with which to *express them.* The "code" part of *encoding* is important, for "code" as we are using it is a system of *symbols* and a symbol is something that *stands for something else.*

Experience cannot be transmitted as *experience:* it first must be translated into something else. It is this something else which is transmitted. When it is "received" it is translated back into something that *resembles* experience.[2]

[2] Anatol Rapoport, *Science and the Goals of Man: A Study in Semantic Orientation* (New York: Harper & Row, 1950), p. 42.

The very most the communicator can do is to *represent* his feelings, ideas, desires, values, and the like with symbols.

(Permit me now to depart from our discussion of the communication model to make a lengthy but important digression.)

Experiential isolation

In other words, each of us is experientially isolated from all others. Thomas Wolfe, from the viewpoint of a baby in a crib, captures this insularity.

He understood that men were forever strangers to one another, that no one ever comes really to know any one, that imprisoned in the dark womb of our mother, we come to life without having seen her face, that we are given to her arms a stranger, and that, caught in that insoluble prison of being we escape it never, no matter what arms may clasp us, what mouth may kiss us, what heart may warm us. Never, never, never, never, never.

He saw that the great figures that came and went about him, the huge leering heads that bent hideously into his crib, the great voices that rolled incoherently above him, had for one another not much greater understanding than they had for him; that even their speech, their entire fluidity and ease of movement were but meagre communicants of their thought or feeling, and served not to promote understanding, but to deepen and widen strife, bitterness, and prejudice.[3]

Complacency

Considering our state of isolation communication is *indeed* a challenge. And yet there appears to be a general denial, albeit unconsciously, of this truism. For several years I have been asking people in organizations how they assessed their communication performance as compared to that of others. Specifically I asked, by anonymous questionnaire:

"In terms of the abilities to understand others and to be understood by others how do you compare with—(*a*) your superior?— (*b*) your subordinates?—(*c*) people at your rank?—(*d*) your department as a whole?—(*e*) your organization as a whole?" I have questioned over 6,000 people in universities, business firms, military units, government agencies, hospitals, and so on, and in some cases every individual in the organization was included. The main conclusion of

---

[3] Thomas Wolfe, *Look Homeward, Angel* (New York: Charles Scribner's Sons, 1929), p. 37. Reprinted by permission.

the study was that virtually everyone felt he was communicating *at least as well* as and, in many cases, *better than* most everyone else in the organization!

Most people readily admit that their organization is fraught with faulty communication but it is almost always "those other people" who are responsible. With such complacency about personal communication practices it is small wonder that communication performance in organizations remains depressingly mediocre. The term *complacency* may suggest a superficial condition which can be ameliorated by "just getting people to become a little more humble."

Actually, the problem is a function of the individual, the organizational structure, and the nature of communication, itself. Many individuals find the admission of communication inadequacy tantamount to admitting inadequacy as a person. And recalling the discussion of the self-image in Chapter 3 it is clear how threatening this confrontation can be. Moreover, organizational processes are generally such that it is often extremely difficult to pinpoint responsibility for a miscommunication. Indeed it is likely that a number of people cumulatively contributed to the breakdown. Accordingly, it is extremely difficult to assess blame accurately; few, if any, are aware of their full contribution to the confusion—thus the motivation to upgrade communication performance is generally lacking.

Still another factor inducing complacency about one's communication is the nature of the process, itself. Consider these aspects, among others: First, communication success (or failure) is a *product of the behavior of two* (or more) *people*. Since no one person has total control over the communication process, its success cannot be measured solely in terms of how well one speaks or writes—or how the other person listens or reads. Conversely, it is generally very difficult to isolate and thus to measure an individual's communication performance because it is so intertwined with that of another.

Second, there is often no objective or clear-cut criterion for communication success. If I try to jump a crossbar at five feet I will receive an immediate and unequivocal feedback (if I am still conscious) as to my success—or lack of it. But in communication the feedback from my recipient may not necessarily be either immediate or unequivocal (e.g., even if he does not understand me he may be reluctant to admit it) .

Finally, consider the false assurance that wishful *intra*personal communication (the talking we do to ourselves) can generate—

"It's clear, logical, rational to me—he's *bound* to see it the same way!"

In sum, people in organizations, generally, seem to be unwarrantedly and dangerously complacent about their communication performance. This is partially because of factors in the individual, the organization, and the communication process which tend to shield the individual from recognizing and/or accepting how deficient his performance actually is. And when one is unable or unwilling to acknowledge a deficiency, he is hardly in a position to do anything constructive about it.

Transmission

Back to the communication model. A's message has been or is being encoded. The next step is to make it available to B. A chooses to speak—(a memo, "Dear B: Re: window. Please open," doesn't seem quite appropriate here).

Some neural impulses are sent from the brain to the abdominal muscles (for air power), the larynx (for phonation), and the articulatory organs (jaw, teeth, tongue, glottis, lips, and so forth) and A is now *transmitting*. Transmitting what? Words? Thoughts? Meanings? Ideas? Feelings? The message? No—vibrations—simply compressions and rarefications of molecules in the air.

Why not *words?*

Parenthetically, why *not* say words are coming out of A's mouth? And just what is a word? Consider this: Hydroherphamorphastyklebackasoriumperpendercularosis. Was that a *word?*

It *is* (or was) a word and here is the silly but true story to support it: It happened 35 years ago. About a hundred of us had arrived at summer Boy Scout camp in southern Michigan. The campmaster assigned us to tents—eight boys to the A tent, and eight boys to the B tent, and so on—and instructed us to choose a name for our tent (patrol) which began with the letter of the tent. We were to be ready to use these names at the evening retreat ceremony.

Retreat came and the patrol leaders, one by one, strode out in front of their patrol and reported in: "All members of the Armadillo Patrol present or accounted for"; "All members of the Bear Patrol . . ."; and so on. H tent (ours) had been unable to agree on a name for our patrol so when his turn came our patrol leader stepped forward and out of desperation and disgust, reported: "All members of the *Herphamorpha* Patrol present or accounted for!" Nonsense, of course, but it received something we hadn't expected—a loud, appreciative guffaw from the other patrols!

The following morning at reveille, it was the "Hydroherphamorpha Patrol"—another chortle—and on it went getting a new syllable or so at each retreat and reveille. It probably would have gotten longer but camp was only for two weeks!

The point is that that noise *became a word*—*nonsense* became *sense*. When that noise was made or heard, *meaning* was occurring— people were *understanding* something—*communication* was taking place. A word, after all, is a *subjective* matter. When one is born into his particular linguistic culture he acquires (without knowing it at the time) a host of previous *agreements* as to what would be *meant* or *understood* when certain sounds were made or heard or when certain marks were put on a piece of paper or seen there. In the chapter on *Bypassing* we shall discuss the sometimes grim and costly consequences of the fact that many of the agreements are by no means airtight.

Medium

The vibrations occur in a *medium*—usually air. Of course, there are numerous modes of transmitting—speaking, writing, gestures, raised dots on Braille cards, and so on—with media to match.

Reception

The vibrations now reach B's ears and he *receives* these physical stimuli which, in turn, are relayed to the brain via an intricate combination of processes in the form of electrochemical-neurological impulses.

Decoding

We do not fully understand what happens at this stage but we understand even less what is yet to happen. Somehow B converts these impulses into symbols and the symbols into meaning. In a word, he *decodes.*

How successful has the communication been? The prime criterion for judging the success of a deliberate communication is the extent to which *B's decoding matches A's encoding.*

A SERIAL PROCESS

It is quite obvious that mismatches occur sometimes with extremely costly, even fatal consequences.

The process of communication is extremely susceptible to distortion and disruption because, among other reasons, it is a *serial process* —a step-by-step process. If you are interested in interfering with or preventing a communication, you need attack it at only *one phase* for as a chain the entire process is as strong as its weakest link.

A's communication to B could be faulty if: A did not *transmit* adequately, e.g., did not speak distinctly or slowly or loudly enough; or they were trying to communicate in an environment where there were *competing vibrations* such as in a forge shop or around a jet engine (B could scarcely distinguish A's feeble vocal vibrations from the barrage of noise assaulting his tympanic membranes) ; or B had *reception* difficulty, e.g., a hearing loss.

Transmission, medium, and reception are critical phases of the communication process (each phase is) but this book will not deal with them. I am presuming that the great majority of its readers do not have horrendous problems in the physiological transmission and reception of communication stimuli.[4] I presume, too, they do not ordinarily encounter serious barriers in the physical media they use.

Even when one has difficulties in the middle three phases of the communication process, he generally has one or two important advantages. First, he is usually *aware* that he is indeed *having a problem* in his communications and furthermore he has a good idea *where it lies*.

Encoding and decoding—the subtle phases

But when he has problems in his encoding and decoding he often has *neither* of these advantages. We know relatively little about what really happens *inside* a communicator as he sends or receives messages, and herein lies the irony I alluded to in Chapter 1. To reinforce the point:

In the last two decades, particularly, we have witnessed incredible advances in communication "hardware"—computers, magnetic tapes, television, lasers, and many others.

Information technology has developed machines capable of performing highly complex manufacturing tasks such as assembling automobiles.

---

[4] There are skilled practitioners in the areas of speech and audiological therapy, opthalmology, and so on, available to deal with difficulties in these functions.

FIGURE 5-2

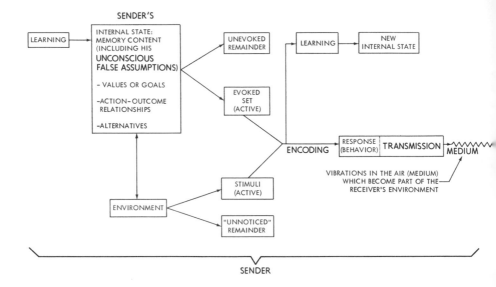

Doctors can dial an electrocardiogram to a computer in Washington, D.C. which can analyze it faster and sometimes more accurately than a human mind. The Japanese are already printing a morning newspaper from the TV set. John Diebold who coined the word *automation* and originated most of its basic concepts predicts that within five years we will be able to communicate with anyone on earth and see them in 3-D color—that within a decade machines will have vocabularies of 7500 words and be able to obey voice commands in any language—that machines will enable an amputee to raise his artificial arm simply by thinking about it.[5]

The irony is that while investing billions in communication research—and receiving commensurate return—we have virtually ignored the *equally critical end processes*. Ultimately, there are *human* encoders and decoders no matter how much sophisticated instrumentation we place between them. The computer people have a phrase for it, GIGO—Garbage In, Garbage Out.

The incongruity is hardly a new one as evidenced by the wry Josiah Stamp of England's Inland Revenue Department, 1896–1919:

---

[5] For a good resumé of the astounding development in communication "hardware," see a series of articles by E. B. Weiss, "A Revolution in Communication," *Marketing Insights,* issues of November 14, 21, 28, 1966, December 5, 1966, and January 16, 23, 1967.

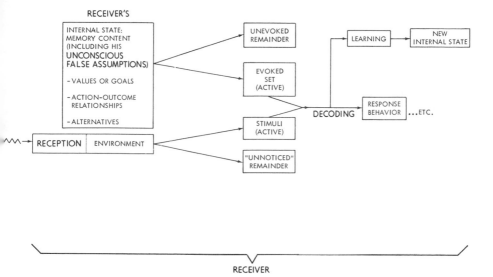

RECEIVER

The government are very keen on amassing statistics. They collect them, add them, raise them to the nth power, take the cube root and prepare wonderful diagrams. But you must never forget that every one of these figures comes in the first instance from the village watchman, who just puts down what he damn pleases.

And so the emphasis in this book will be on encoding and decoding mainly because they are the least understood. To set the stage, examine Figure 5–2 for a superimposition of the communication model upon the general behavioral model (see page 57) we discussed in Chapter 3. Note that the consequence of the sender's behavior (e.g., audible vibrations assuming he communicates by speaking) becomes part of the receiver's environment from which they may be abstracted as stimuli and, coupled with the receiver's sets, contribute to his decoding. Thus, one's behavior, including his communication behavior as sender and receiver, is most immediately the product of his sets *and* stimuli. Clearly, our responses to stimuli are not determined exclusively by the stimuli themselves. One's perception of pain is illustrative.

Dr. Henry K. Beecher, during World War II, was able to make comparative studies of soldiers and male civilians undergoing pain from similar operations. He found that only 32 percent of the soldiers (all of whom had been wounded in combat) said "Yes" when asked if the pain was severe enough to require something for relief. On the other hand, 83 percent of the civilians recovering from non-combat operations (despite the fact that the surgical trauma is less than in combat operations) asked for a hypodermic injection for relief.[6]

Stimuli alone did not account for differences in response; the *meaning* that the pain had for the patient was a very considerable factor in determining the extent of his suffering. Unbolstered by the assurance of security if disabled and by the glory of having served his country and his outfit and by the sense of relief at having escaped a far greater calamity, the civilian patient apparently perceived his pain as markedly more severe than his uniformed counterpart.

One's sets which, as discussed in Chapter 3, select and are determined by his stimuli, have a direct bearing on his behavior. The triangles below are a case in point. Read these phrases:

Almost everyone reads these as "Snake in the grass." "Busy as a beaver," and "Paris in the spring." But look again—it is "Snake in the *the* grass," and so on. Why do we read them incorrectly? There are probably several *sets* in operation. Consider that these are very familiar phrases. Let someone say "snake in the————" and "grass" will immediately occur to most of us. Another is our habit of reading clusters of words rather than word-by-word, and thus we are more prone to skip over individual words—especially those to which our responses have been deeply conditioned such as the short articles "a" and "the." Chances are that we would have caught the trick if "important" words such as "snake," "grass," "beaver," and so on, had been repeated. Again, the separation of the repeated words, which is

----

[6] Henry K. Beecher, "Relationship of Significance of Wound to Pain Experienced," *Journal of the American Medical Association,* Vol. 161 (August 25, 1956), p. 1609.

seemingly legitimatized by triangles, could have thrown us off. The same words stretched out on a straight line don't fool as many people. We could have been misled, too, by our predisposition to gloss over apparent "typographical errors."

One's sets are derived from his memory content which includes his values, goals, attitudes, habits, and other consequences of what he has learned from his experiences. Among such factors are what we shall call the individual's *assumptions*. Let us return to Messers A and B to illustrate the role of assumptions.

Suppose in transmitting his desire about opening the window, A chose to say: "Let's get a breath of fresh air in here!" By this he intends to express simply that he feels warm and that he would like B to open the window. Now note some of the assumptions which may be underlying A's remark and of which he may be quite unaware. He could be assuming that because he is warm, B also feels warm and will welcome the idea of opening a window. He could be assuming that because B is closer to the window, he is the "logical" one to open it and that B will understand and agree with this. He could be assuming that because he means something by his words, B will understand them as A intends them.

Actually, none of these assumptions is *necessarily* warranted. B may be quite comfortable or even chilly with the window closed and thus be offended by A's apparent selfishness. Furthermore, he may fail to see A's logic about B's proximity to the window and instead resent A's "pushing him around." B may even fail to interpret A's words as they were intended. He may, conceivably, hear A's remark as an indictment against B's failure to open the window previously. It is even possible that B may feel that A is not interested in opening a window at all but is sarcastically alluding to B's habits of personal hygiene! B as the receiver, of course, is just as prone to contribute to a misunderstanding influenced as he is by his own assumptions.

Consider these three propositions:

1. Everyone has *assumptions*—certain underlying beliefs, premises, notions, suppositions, rationales, generalizations, principles.
2. Some of these assumptions are *false*—they are not borne out by reality.
3. The individual is partially or, in some cases, totally *unaware* that he is laboring under these fallacious notions. Many of them are

primitive postulates, acquired before the age of reason. They have been semiconsciously learned at best and have never been examined critically.

The third proposition should not be difficult to accept, for does it not stand to reason that most people would not tolerate false assumptions—that they would supplant them with more valid premises? But if one is not *aware* that the assumptions are false or even that he holds such assumptions, what will prompt him to do anything about them? As the 19th-century humorist, Artemus Ward put it: "It ain't the things we don't know that hurt us. It's the things we do know that ain't so."

We are all victims, more or less, of unconsciously holding certain fallacious assumptions which in turn materially, destructively, and *insidiously* affect our encoding and decoding. The frequent result is *miscommunication,* sometimes with grievous consequences.

Assumptions from the language system

Since our concern is expressly with communication, one category of fallacious assumptions, in particular, merits our attention. These are the assumptions we develop partially or largely from our language system. For example, one of these fallacies is that words, rather than being merely labels for things, are somehow inextricably linked with what they represent.[7] This is false, of course, but we do not always behave as if it were. In fact, our reaction to the "thing" is sometimes distinctly colored by its label.

An incident occurred several years ago while the late Professor Irving J. Lee was giving his exceedingly popular course, "Language and Thought," at Northwestern University. Dr. Lee had several graduate assistants who were occasionally given the opportunity to lecture before a class of 200 to 300 undergraduates. On one such occasion an assistant set out to "dramatize" the tendency to react to labels rather than to the object the labels represented. He distributed bits of food which resembled dried biscuit and assured the class that the food was sanitary and nutritious and added that most of them had probably never eaten this type of food before. Each student was to taste the food and decide how much he liked or disliked it. Most students found it relatively tasteless and reported an indifferent reac-

---

[7] This fallacy will be developed more fully in Chapter 13, "'Pointing' and 'Associating.'"

tion. A few said they liked it slightly and even fewer expressed a mild dislike. Not *one* said he liked or disliked it extremely.

The assistant tabulated the results on the blackboard and suggested that perhaps the food would be more tasty with cream and sugar. He added that it was quite inexpensive and readily available. At this point he reached behind his desk and held up a large, distinctly labeled box and said "Just go to your grocer's and ask for —— Dog Biscuits!" The reaction was precisely what he had hoped for—a great deal of groaning, shrieking, laughing, feigned nausea (and some not so feigned) . Whereupon he triumphantly cried out: "Now, just what are you reacting to—those innocuous bits of food—or to the words on this box?!"

Elated by his success, the assistant repeated his "dramatization" in the next term. But the word had spread and students came to expect such things from the course "where they served dog biscuits." Undiscouraged, he changed his tactic. He baked some "special" cookies, passed them out to the class, and tabulated the results. The cookies were sweet and the reactions were unanimously favorable.

"Glad you liked them, I'll give you the recipe," he volunteered, "so you can bake some at home if you wish." The recipe: So much flour, sugar, shortening . . . and two cups of carefully cleaned grasshoppers!

He admitted later that, even had he been able to restore order, he would not have dared to ask: "Now, what are you throwing up about . . . ?!"

The map-territory analogy

For focusing attention on the subtle role language plays in influencing human behavior we are primarily indebted to the late Alfred Korzybski.[8] Korzybski contended that the relation of our assumptions,

---

[8] Alfred Korzybski's *Science and Sanity: An Introduction to Non-Aristotelian Systems and General Semantics* (Lancaster, Pa.: Science Press Printing Co., 1933; in the 4th edition (1959) it is distributed by the Institute of General Semantics, Lakeville, Conn.) is considered the inaugural of the discipline of general semantics. Voluminous, difficult reading for many, but profound, the book's theses have been "translated" and applied by such able writers as J. Samuel Bois, *Explorations in Awareness* (New York: Harper & Row, 1957) ; John C. Condon, Jr., *Semantics and Communication* (New York: The Macmillan Co., 1966) ; S. I. Hayakawa, *Language in Thought and Action* (2d. ed.; New York: Harcourt, Brace & World Co., 1964) and *Symbol, Status, and Personality* (New York: Harcourt, Brace & World Co., 1963) ; Wendell Johnson, *People in Quandaries* (New York: Harper & Row, 1946) and *Your Most Enchanted Listener* (New York: Harper & Row, 1956) ; Irving J. Lee, *Language Habits in Human Affairs* (New York: Harper & Row, 1941) , and *How to Talk with People* (New York: Harper & Row,

unconscious or otherwise, to the phenomena with which they were concerned (people, things, theories, processes, relationships, and so on) is analogous to the relation of maps to the territories they represent. Geographical maps are "pictures," or abstractions, of their territories. Our assumptive maps, similarly, are "pictures" of the "territories" they are used to represent. Man relies on both kinds of maps as guides in his dealings with their respective territories.

But there is an essential difference between our geographical and our assumptive maps. Cartography has advanced to the point that most geographical maps can be followed with great confidence. On the other hand, our assumptive maps are often inadequate and distorted representations of their territories. And we are misled by them because we rely upon them so unquestioningly.

Rapoport used the map-territory analogy to enunciate the basic premises (in part) of general semantics.

A unique peculiarity of the human nervous system is its capacity for symbolizing experience, that is, for "mapping" experience upon a conventionalized language. The "conventionalized" character of language refers to the absence of any "natural" connection between the symbol system and reality. This arbitrary character of language symbols makes language tremendously flexible and makes possible communication and cogitation about absent, past, future, and imagined events.

The flexibility of language plays a dual role. On the one hand, it confers on man a practically limitless potentiality for abstracting, thus for accumulating and transmitting stocks of general knowledge organized into deductive systems (science) and so for controlling and molding nature. On the other hand, since man reacts as readily to symbols as to reality, he stands in constant danger of mistaking verbal constructions of his own making for reality, regardless of whether the former correspond to the latter.

The gradation from sane or un-sane (in extreme cases insane) behavior is reflected in the greater or lesser similarity between the logical structure of man's symbolic interpretation and the objective relations

1952); and Harry L. Weinberg, *Levels of Knowing and Existence* (New York: Harper & Row, 1959). Two journals (*ETC.: A Review of General Semantics*, edited by Thomas Weiss, and the *General Semantics Bulletin*, edited by Charlotte S. Read) publish theoretical and experimental studies concerning or relating to the discipline. Two organizations, the Institute of General Semantics (Lakeville, Conn.), founded by M. Kendig, and the International Society for General Semantics (San Francisco State College), with chapters throughout the world, use Korzybski's formulations as their focal point. Both organizations conduct seminars and workshops.

existing in the world (the degree of correspondence between "map" and "territory") .[9]

Korzybski felt that we are largely *unaware* of the power the structure of our language has upon us. Unconscious of such influence we are in an unlikely position to take action against it. As biologist, J. H. Woodger put it, "Man makes metaphysics just as he breathes, without willing it and above all without doubting it most of the time." And Whorf affirmed the contention.

Natural logic contains two fallacies: First, it does not see that the phenomena of a language are to its own speakers largely of a background character and so are outside the critical consciousness and control of the speaker who is expounding natural logic. Hence, when anyone, as a natural logician, is talking about reason, logic and the laws of correct thinking, he is apt to be simply marching in step with purely grammatical facts that have somewhat of a background character in his own language or family of languages but are by no means universal in all languages and in no sense a common substratum of reason. Second, natural logic confuses agreement about subject matter, attained through use of language with knowledge of the linguistic process by which agreement is attained. . . .[10]

Perhaps this book appears to be at least as much about thinking as it is about communicating. Actually, it is about thinking-communicating, for the two processes are inseparable.

. . . as a man thinks, so does he communicate; as he communicates, so must he think. One cannot separate the ability to communicate from the ability to think clearly and persistently about specific problems. Communication cannot be consistently successful unless it is the product or the facilitation of consistently successful thinking.[11]

SUMMARY

These first five chapters have attempted to prepare a foundation for the book, delineate its scope, and to set out a rationale for its suc-

---

[9] Anatol Rapoport, "Letter to a Soviet Philosopher," *ETC.: A Review of General Semantics*, Vol. 19, No. 4 (February 1963) , pp. 440–41. Reprinted by permission.

[10] Benjamin Lee Whorf, *Language, Thought, and Reality* (Cambridge, Mass.: The Technology Press of the Massachusetts Institute of Technology, 1956) , p. 211. Reprinted by permission.

[11] Lee O. Thayer, *Administrative Communication* (Homewood, Ill.: Richard D. Irwin, Inc., 1961) , p. viii.

ceeding chapters. In these subsequent chapters, we will focus upon the encoding and decoding of a perceiving, need-satisfaction seeking individual communicating in an organizational setting.

The approach to communication here is a psychosemantic one, the basic premises for which can be summarized as follows: Behavior, including communication behavior, is partially the product of one's *sets*. Sets are derived from one's *internal state* which, in turn, is determined by a great many factors including the subtle but important one of one's *language system*. A major contention is that one's language system spawns certain *fallacious,* and often *unconsciously held,* assumptions.[12] Such assumptions lead to sets which in turn pave the way for *miscommunication* and other forms of foolish, immature, dangerous, unsane behavior. Indeed, our chief concern will be with *self-deception* for, in the words of Goethe: "We are not deceived; we deceive ourselves."

Thus, the remaining chapters will explore a number of recurrent, delineable *patterns of miscommunication.* The patterns are not mutually exclusive. Rather they might be considered as so many "handles" with which to grasp and cope with some of the most prevalent and serious anomalies of a complex and vital function—communication.

DISCUSSION QUESTIONS

1. "Experience cannot be transmitted as experience: it must first be translated into something else. It is this something else which is transmitted. When it is 'received' it is translated back into something that resembles experience."—Anatol Rapoport (p. 180)

   Do you agree with the above statement? What are its implications—for communicators? Mass media? Organizational communication? Or any form of communication which goes through a *series* of people?

---

[12] *General Information Bulletin,* No. 6, of the International Society for General Semantics asserts the influence of language:

Nor do we realize how grammar warps our "thinking." When we make sentences, we force symbols (words) into certain set relationships. Yet the things which these symbols represent often have quite different relationships. This happens because our grammar preserves many ancient wrong guesses about the world we live in; such as: similar things may be treated as identical; the "essences" of things never change; parts may be considered without relation to the whole; qualities are properties of "things"; an event has "a cause." Such notions once fit man's knowledge of the world. But our century has seen the birth of the relativity theory and atomic fission. Today, primitive language habits serve only to widen the frightening chasm between our lagging civilization and our leaping technology.

2. Compare the model of communication (pp. 186–87) with those of Berlo, Shannon and Weaver, and Schramm (see footnote 1, p. 179). What are their relative strengths and weaknesses? In what ways are they different, similar? Does their adequacy and validity depend to some extent on what kind of communication experience is represented? Could they be superimposed upon the general behavior model (p. 57)? What are the underlying premises for each model?

3. The issue of *communication complacency:* Do you agree that most people are unrealistically confident about their communication ability? What do you think of the various reasons offered to account for this attitude? Can you suggest others?

4. The Boy Scouts and the "Hydroherpha . . . etc. Patrol" (pp. 183–84): Can literally any nonsense syllable (or polysyllable) become a word? Under what conditions? How do words get to *be* words? Suppose you invent a gadget and contrive a brand new word to represent it. What potential communication problems do you foresee?

5. Regarding Rapoport's reference to the map-territory analogy, do you agree with his assertions about the relationship of language and reality? If his reasoning is essentially valid, in what ways does man profit by possessing language? Similarly, how are his needs thwarted?

ARTICLE

Conditions of success in communication[13]

S. I. HAYAKAWA

The word "semantics" came into modern usage through Michel Breal, who used it as the name of that division of philology concerned with meaning. Hence problems of terminology, problems of definition, and even problems of diction have commonly been thought to be the chief concern of semantics, and even today semantics is presumed to be a discipline concerned solely with words.

It is ironical that such a misconception should exist. From its origins in the "signifies" of Lady Welby in the early years of this century until today, semantics has been in steadfast and systematic revolt against preoccupation with words as such. Lady Welby[14] protested the rote-learning and "barren-verbalism" of educational methods in her day and proposed in their stead a "new discipline of mind" in which words would constantly be related to the nonverbal realities for which they stand. Ogden and Richards[15] found the "meaning of meaning" to lie not in definitions but in observable physical events in the case of scientific language, in psychological events in the case of "emotive" language. P. W. Bridgman[16] in his "operationalism" announced that "The true meaning of a term is to be found by observing what a man does with it, not by what he says about it." Anthro-

---

[13] Abridged from an address presented to the 12th Annual Round Table of the Institute of Languages and Linguistics, Edmund A. Walsh School of Foreign Service, Georgetown University, Washington, D.C., on April 22, 1961.

Reprinted with permission from the *Bulletin of the Menninger Clinic*, Vol. 26, No. 5 (1962), pp. 225–36. Copyright, 1962, by The Menninger Foundation.

[14] Viola Welby, *What Is Meaning?* (London: The Macmillan Co., 1903).

[15] C. K. Ogden and I. A. Richards, *The Meaning of Meaning* (3d ed.; New York: Harcourt, Brace, Inc., 1930).

[16] P. W. Bridgman, *The Logic of Modern Physics* (New York: The Macmillan Co., 1927).

pologists found that "meaning" is to be understood not through dictionaries and glossaries of the tongues under consideration, but through an understanding (preferably through participation) of the lives, habits, and social institutions of the people whose language one wishes to understand. Psychologists after Freud have insisted that the most important components of "meaning" are again not to be found in socially agreed-upon definitions, but in the experiences, extending back to infancy, of the individual. Korzybski,[17] in his general semantics, stressed the study of the evaluative processes of the human nervous system—both the processes that lead to linguistic events and those that result from linguistic events.

As the result of the foregoing and other influences to which I have been exposed, I have become less and less concerned with language as such, and more and more concerned with the totality of that process of human interaction which we know as communication. What are the conditions of success or failure in communication? Or, to put it another way, why do people welcome some communications and reject or ignore other communications? And if our own communications are ignored or rejected, is there anything that can be done about it?

I shall discuss these questions by presenting first a broad theory of human behavior as a framework within which to examine the act of communication.

PRESERVATION OF THE SYMBOLIC SELF

The man in the street accepts Darwin's premise that "self-preservation is the first law of life." The idea of self-preservation, however, fails to take into account many facets of human behavior, so that preachers are fond of pointing out the self-sacrificing behavior of saints and heroes as evidence that naturalistic explanations of human behavior are inadequate. It is not necessary, however, to point to saints or heroes and other exceptional people to show the inadequacy of the idea of "self-preservation." For example, self-preservation obviously has little to do with such behaviors as:

1. The man who works his head off to acquire his tenth million dollars.

---

[17] Korzybski, *Science and Sanity:* . . .

2. The office girl who goes without lunch in order to make payments on a fur coat she cannot afford.
3. The people who try to go over Niagara Falls in a barrel, or who cross the Pacific Ocean in a balsa-wood raft.
4. The people like me who spend $50 or more a year on fishing equipment in order to catch $2.95 worth of bluegills.

Once you grant, however, with Leslie A. White,[18] Ernst Cassirer,[19] Korzybski,[20] and others, that man is a symbolic class of life—once you grant that much of human behavior is symbolic—then the idea of self-preservation can be modified to cover the case of human behavior by a simple restatement, as follows: *The fundamental motive of human behavior is not self-preservation, but preservation of the symbolic self.*

What I call the symbolic self is pretty much the same as what Carl Rogers[21] calls the "self-concept," Andras Angyal[22] calls the "self-organization," and still others call the "self-structure." The law in the form given by Carl Rogers is, first, that "The basic purpose of all activity is the protection, maintenance, and enhancement of the self-concept," and secondly, that "The self-concept or self-structure may be thought of as an organized configuration of perceptions of the self which are admissible to awareness."

In other words, human beings are hopelessly addicted to the processes of abstraction and symbolization, which are the distinguishing features of their survival mechanism. Hence human beings, in addition to abstracting and symbolizing the data of their environment, abstract and symbolize about themselves. Each of us possesses not only a self, but also a self-concept—and the self-concept is not what you are, but what you think you are (Figure 5–3).

Korzybski[23] stated that the relation between words and what they stand for is analogous to the relation between maps and territories. We find that the generalizations in general semantics about the na-

18 L. A. White, "The Symbol: The Origin and Basis of Human Behavior," *Language, Meaning and Maturity*, ed. S. I. Hayakawa (New York: Harper & Row, 1954).

19 Ernst Cassirer, *An Essay on Man* (New Haven, Conn.: Yale University Press, 1944).

20 Korzybski, *Science and Sanity:* . . .

21 Carl Rogers, *Client-Centered Therapy* (Boston: Houghton Mifflin Co., 1951).

22 Andras Angyal, *Foundations for a Science of Personality* (New York: The Commonwealth Fund, 1941).

23 Korzybski, *Science and Sanity:* . . .

FIGURE 5–3

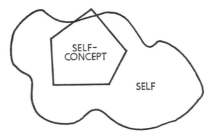

ture of symbolism apply directly to the relations between the self-concept and the self:

1. The map is not the territory. The self-concept is not the self.
2. The map is not all the territory. The self-concept is not all of the self.
3. The map has characteristics not possessed by the territory. For example, conventions of cartography may introduce elements (such as the pinkness of the British Empire) not present in the territory. Furthermore, errors may exist. Similarly in the self-concept, conventions of symbolization (for example, the structure of the language one uses) may introduce structuralizations in the self-concept not present in the self (for example, the division of reason and emotion into separate entities). Furthermore, erroneous notions about the self may be included in the self-concept.

The self-concept, then, is the sum total of the things we feel we know about ourselves, including our past history, our present condition, status, and role, our ideals, our plans for the future, our estimates of our own relationships with others: "I am thin, (or fat)," "I am a good mixer," "I pay my debts promptly," "I am poor at arithmetic," "I shall never be a millionaire," "I am beautiful," "Nobody loves me," "I have less money than Bill, but more brains," "I have less brains than Bill, but more money," "I believe in discipline," "I'm not that kind of a girl," etc. Furthermore, the self-concept is an *organized* configuration of perceptions of the self. This fact is represented in Figure 5–3 where the self-concept is shown as a *regular* geometrical figure, to indicate that we all feel that we make sense to ourselves—that we have some kind of internal organization and integrity—even if to others we seem to make no sense at all. The fact of organization is of enormous importance, because it means that it is difficult for all of us to change one aspect of our beliefs or attitudes without having to rearrange our entire self-organization.

DIFFERENCES OF PERCEPTION

The self-concept, then, is the fundamental determinant of all our behavior. Indeed, since it is an organization of our past experiences and perceptions as well as of our values and goals, it determines the character of the reality we see. Each individual has his own and unique way of extracting meaning from the world about him. For example, an industrial engineer may submit a plan—let us call it Plan X—which has for him the meaning "increased production." He looks expectantly to his colleagues for approval. But to his colleagues, each looking at the plan from his own frame of reference, Plan X can have entirely different meanings: "This plan means no more production than before," "This means that my Plan Y will be ditched if I don't put up a fight," "Plan X reduces my job to being a mere flunky around here," "Plan X is my chance for a promotion," "Plan X may increase production, but who wants that at this time?"

The industrial engineer who proposed Plan X feels that its advantages are so clear and obvious that they ought to be plain to everybody. Encountering unexpected opposition, he is at once tempted to think of his opponents as foolish, stupid, misguided, or willfully obdurate. If, however, we think of the self-concept and the way in which each individual must see the world from his own frame of reference, it is obvious that each person who objects to Plan X objects to it for reasons that make perfectly good sense to him, even if they do not make sense to the industrial engineer. This observation was put in the form of a principle by Donald Snygg and Arthur Combs:[24] "Everything we do seems to be reasonable and necessary at the time we are doing it." They illustrate the principle as follows:

Several years ago one of the authors was driving a car at dusk along a western road. A globular mass about two feet in diameter appeared suddenly in the path of the car. A passenger in the front seat screamed and grasped the wheel, attempting to steer the car around the object. The driver tightened his grip and drove directly into it.

In each the behavior of the individual was determined by his own phenomenal field. The passenger, an Easterner, saw the object in the

[24] Donald Syngg and Arthur Combs, *Individual Behavior* (New York: Harper & Row, 1949).

highway as a boulder and fought desperately to steer the car around it. The driver, a native of the vicinity, saw it as a tumbleweed and devoted his efforts to keeping his passenger from overturning the car.

From the point of view of the driver, the passenger was acting "insanely"; so, from the point of view of the passenger, was the driver. But each was trying only to do what seemed to him at the moment "reasonable and necessary." Each had only his own way of interpreting what he saw, based on his past experiences.

We subscribe to magazines that we agree with because they fortify our self-concept; opposition magazines we find threatening to our self-concept, and therefore distasteful. Whether or not we accept a dinner invitation depends on whether associating with the people who invited us enhances our self-concept. And since the self-concept includes predictions about ourselves, as well as the organization of past experiences, we select or avoid new situations according to our own predictions as to our ability to handle them. If we feel that our organization will be seriously disturbed or threatened by the new situation, we avoid it.

One last point about the self-concept is that it tends to rigidify under threat. If we think of ourselves as "intelligent," and other people, or an unfortunate set of circumstances, offer the implication that we are "unintelligent," we assert our belief in our intelligence with redoubled force. The individual who is unsure of his right to his self-concept tends especially to hold it rigidly. Let us say that there is a salesman whose self-concept is "I am the best salesman in the company." Let us say that the facts are otherwise; several other salesmen are surpassing him. It is possible for such an individual to maintain his self-concept rigidly in spite of mounting evidence, fortifying himself by whatever rationalizations he can think up: "They're giving me the worst territory," "I'd have a terrific record if I could bring myself to descend to the methods some of the other fellows are using," etc. (A diagram of the rigidified self-concept under threat is given in Figure 5–4.)

To return to the problem of communication: at what point do we become deeply concerned about communication? Usually it is at the point when we feel a severe sense of frustration because our message is not getting across. If we are in management, we may say, "Our employees have got to learn. . . ." If we represent the union, we say, "Management has simply got to realize. . . ." If we are parents, we say, "It's high time Wilbur understood. . . ." If we are talking about

FIGURE 5-4

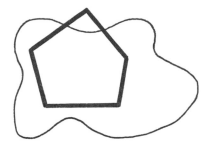

international relations, we say, "The point must be made clear to the Russians. . . ."

This condition of communicative frustration produces similar psychological conditions on both sides. Mr. A has tried to tell something to Mr. B. Mr. B, because he does not like the content of the message as he understands it, or because he does not like the tone of voice in which it was delivered, finds some kind of threat to his self-esteem in the message and resists it—by ignoring it, by arguing back, and often by seeming to twist its meaning in the course of arguing back. Each time Mr. A repeats his message—perhaps getting it down to words of one syllable, perhaps shouting it in a louder tone of voice, or both—Mr. B's resistances increase until his attitude becomes quite rigid.

But Mr. B's resistance implies a criticism of Mr. A's message, and hence of Mr. A himself. Mr. A feels therefore quite threatened by this resistance, and he too becomes rigid. Because Mr. A too has his self-concept, it is much easier for him to think, "This fellow *B* is stupid," than to think, "Maybe there's something wrong with my message or my way of trying to communicate it." Rapidly the situation develops into a "communicative deadlock," in which each is threatened by the

FIGURE 5-5

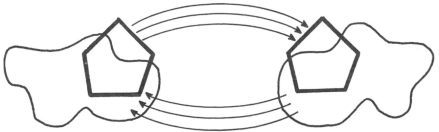

attitude of the other, and therefore each is rigidly defensive of his own values. This condition is easily recognized. Whenever you hear the expression, "Give him an inch and he'll take a mile," you know that there is communicative deadlock. A dramatic example in recent history was the truce negotiation at Panmunjom, where the deadlock continued for months, and where the felt threat on each side was enormous. (Figure 5–5 illustrates communicative deadlock.)

GROUP SELF–CONCEPTS

It is a long and perhaps unjustifiable leap to go from the problems of the individual self-concept to problems of group and national psychology. However, each of us has not only a concept of himself as an individual, but as a member of a group: "I am a member of Rotary (and not of Kiwanis)," "I am a Navy pilot (and not an Air Force pilot)," "I am an American (and not a Russian or a Frenchman)," "I am a Russian (and not an American)." That which is felt as a threat to the group produces many of the same rigidities as threats to the individual self-concept. The depiction in a television series of gangsters as Italians produces a group defensiveness on the part of Italian-American organizations. An angry attack on American policy by a Russian delegate at the United Nations produces a quick response and counterattack from the American delegation. This is because, in one respect, group psychology is not different from individual psychology: whatever sentiments a group may entertain, those sentiments exist within individuals. The old saying, "Love me, love my dog," readily expands itself to wider areas of self-identification: "Love me, love the Air Force," "Love me, love my nation."

Once a condition of mutual threat has been established, which also means a condition of communicative deadlock, there is also established a stereotypic concept of the other fellow, the enemy. The enemy is seen as aggressive, untrustworthy, fiendishly clever, and bent upon our destruction. Defensive measures on one side confirm the fears of the other side, and counterdefensive measures confirm the original defensiveness. Thus the two parties, each acting in such a way as to confirm the worst fears of the other, plunge headlong toward the showdown that neither of them wants. Once this vicious circle is well established, it becomes virtually impossible to break it, because the feelings of threat experienced on both sides both prevent and distort communication. Hence on both sides communications are distorted to fit preconceived stereotypes. Innocuous or even mildly friendly overtures on the part of the United States toward the Soviets are instantly denounced by them as not seriously intended or as stratagems to trick them into an unfavorable position. Meanwhile on our side, the Senate Internal Security Committee denounces the Soviet-American cultural exchanges, including ballet troupes, as part of a "poisonous propaganda offensive."

THE SELF–FULFILLING PROPHECY

The fascinating thing about paranoia, which has been defined as that mental illness in which individuals behave like nations, is the clear operation of the self-fulfilling prophecy. The individual patient who says, "I have no friends; I am surrounded by enemies," believes that he is stating an objective fact. He acts on his assumption and treats everyone, even those who are trying to be friendly, as an enemy —and soon his statement *becomes* true, and he is without a friend in the world. At the international level, too, influential people on both sides of the Iron Curtain have believed the statements, "The Soviet Union is determined to destroy the United States," "American imperialism is determined to destroy the Soviet Union," and have acted on them. They make these statements with the confident objectivity of people making statements in the physical sciences: "There will be snow next winter in Minnesota. We do not know exactly on what day the first snow will come, but it will come, and Minnesota will be blanketed in snow." On both sides of the Iron Curtain, therefore, there are those "crackpot realists" in influential places who are making their paranoic fears come true. And since both sides have nuclear weapons, the world-wide destruction they have dreamed into an imminent possibility will exceed by a hundred thousandfold their wildest fears.

Is there any escaping the destruction with which the world is threatened? Since this is a question involving human relations, any answer we give necessarily involves the self-fulfilling prophecy. If we say no, if we say that our present policy of reliance upon missile build-up and nuclear deterrence is the only possible one, we may as well resign ourselves to our fate. However, if we say yes, if we say that tensions can be relaxed by the improvement of communication, we enhance the possibility of finding solutions. To a large degree the future fate of the world rests in the sum total of our private evaluations: everyone who says that war is inevitable helps to bring the war closer;

everyone who says that it is not inevitable helps, in a tiny but real way, to prevent it from happening.

At this point, I am reminded of something that Alfred Korzybski used to say in his seminars. He would quote from A. E. Housman the famous lines:

> I, a stranger and afraid
> In a world I never made.

Then Korzybski would thunder, "Don't be afraid. With your evaluations you made that world. With other evaluations you can make a different one!" Korzybski, with his long experience in the study of mental illness, saw clearly the degree to which the self-fulfilling prophecy operates in all human affairs, and the extent to which we create the worlds we live in. At the international level, no less than at the private level, the world is the creation of our evaluations.

Of course those who believe that international communication can be improved will agree that cultural exchanges, whether of art exhibitions, agricultural experts, athletic teams, or tourists, should be encouraged. Of course we should be happy about the International Geophysical Year and the successful cooperation of scientists of the world, including those of America and Russia, in that great venture. Also we find gratification in the efforts of Americans, Russians, and other scientists now working cooperatively under international agreement in Antarctica, and strive for other agreements of this kind.

BREAKING THE DEADLOCK

For a paradigm with which to explore the problems raised by the attitudes of mutual paranoia, let us go back to Mr. A and Mr. B. Can the communicative deadlock between Mr. A and Mr. B ever be removed? Of course it can—and that is what psychiatry and clinical psychology are all about. And we can learn something about the unblocking of communication especially from the successful application of psychotherapeutic theories in, for example, business management. An important approach is that which Dr. Carl Rogers[25] calls "nonevaluative listening."

In brief, nonevaluative listening amounts to this: assuming you are Mr. A, and you have tried and tried in vain to convince Mr. B of an idea or proposal, and Mr. B, his defenses thoroughly aroused, dog-

---

[25] Rogers, *Client-Centered Therapy.*

gedly resists, it does no good for you to continue to shout and pound the table. What you must do is something entirely different, namely, temporarily suspend your purposes and listen to Mr. B—and listen nonevaluatively. Such listening means listening without argument or passing judgment, listening fully in order to understand thoroughly how the problem looks to Mr. B and why Mr. B's resistance makes sense to him, given the kind and amount of information he possesses, given the goals for which he is striving.

What happens to Mr. B if you listen nonevaluatively to him is that, no longer confronted with the necessity of countering your arguments, he begins to relax the rigidity of his defenses. His defensive utterances give way to informative utterances. He begins to tone down the absoluteness of his statements, to be less stereotyped and propagandistic in his responses.

Communication being a process of interaction, something also begins to happen to you. Because Mr. B is making less extreme statements, you relax. Having entered empathically into his view of the world, you may succeed in coming to the conclusion that his views, while still unacceptable, at least make a certain amount of sense, given his assumptions. Perhaps this is the turning point in the interactional situation—the point at which you begin to acknowledge that Mr. B is neither dishonest nor insane—and that he seemed so largely because he started with different assumptions and, therefore, different perceptions of the world. I say this is the turning point, because this is the point at which you are willing to admit Mr. B into the human race.

The next possibility is that Mr. B, having been listened to, may now be willing to listen, and to listen nondefensively and, therefore, without distorting your message to fit into his hostile preconceptions of your purposes. And as you state your views, more calmly than you had been stating them earlier, you will moderate the dogmatism of your presentation and further reduce the reasons for his defensiveness.

Then, since both you and Mr. B have tried seriously to listen, you will have received information from him which you formerly did not have; he too will have acquired information which was news to him. In the light of this new knowledge possessed by both of you, both your original proposal and his resistance to it may be obsolete. You jointly are able, at this point, to work out a new scheme which takes into account the entire body of new information—a solution that will be satisfactory to both. This is not compromise, which is a matter of bargaining from fixed positions to one in between, but two-way communication in which both sides acquire new information, so that formerly fixed positions no longer exist, and a resolution is found on new grounds and at different levels. It is this emergence of novelty as the result of communication that makes the students of psychotherapy, the students of group dynamics, the counseling profession, and the general semanticists so hopeful that they may contribute something to the solution of the big problems of conflict resolution that confront us.

LISTENING ACROSS NATIONAL BOUNDARIES

Successful communication is therapeutic in effect, whether psychotherapy is thought of narrowly as between psychiatrist and patient, or broadly as applied to the clearing up of misunderstandings and delusions that becloud relationships between people in normal business and family contacts. In this broad sense of psychotherapy in which no psychiatrist is involved, there is always the question, who is to be the therapist and who the patient? To this question, there is a general answer, namely, that since listening is at the heart of psychotherapy, whoever is able to listen to the other person instead of shouting at him can be the therapist for the other. Whether you are the parent or the child, the employer or the employee, the teacher or the student in a situation of mutual threat, if you have the courage and the firmness and security of internal organization to listen patiently to the other person, even when you feel he is wrong, you can start the therapeutic process rolling.

Perhaps the same principle can be applied to our international communications. Certainly the tensions between America and Russia are such that novel proposals for their relaxation are called for. Hence, I would suggest that instead of shutting our ears to their communications, instead of trying to fit every Soviet pronouncement into our current explanatory stereotypes ("It's all just propaganda"), we should listen seriously to what the Russians are saying in order to understand what it all means.

But how does one nation "listen" to another? Elsewhere[26] I have made the following suggestion:

---

[26] S. I. Hayakawa, "On Communication with the Soviet Union," *ETC.: A Review of General Semantics*, Vol. 17 (1960), pp. 389–400.

We should invite hundreds of Soviet teachers and journalists and parliamentarians and plant managers to come here and explain their way of life, their national purposes, their hopes for the future, their accusations against us, before every college campus, every luncheon club, every church group and public forum in the country. . . . If the Russians are bitter toward us, frustrated by us, or fear us, and if indeed we have no aggressive military designs that they need to fear, let them come and tell us what is on their minds, so that they can get over it. . . . Let us invite them, at our own expense and with no strings attached, to join the perpetual town meeting in which we are all engaged in a free society, and to lay their ideas alongside of ours for comparison and discussion. . . . We have built bombers and missiles of all sizes and none of them has reduced international tensions. Is it not time we tried something different?

The foregoing is only one suggestion as to how one nation can "listen" to another. Psychiatrists and students of social psychology, acquainted as they are with the processes of human communication and interaction, can no doubt think of many other ways in which Americans might listen to the Russians. The essential thing that must be conveyed to the Russians—and this is a matter of actions rather than of words—is the implicit message: "We are trying to understand what makes you think and act as you do." With the establishment of a successful flow of communications from them to us, a pathway is established for later communications from us to them—and this every psychiatrist knows. The aim is thus to start a benign cycle of interactions that might relax existing hostilities, suspicions, and tensions. Like psychotherapy itself, the progress of such a program will be slow, uneven, and marked by discouraging relapses. Nevertheless, it will be worth trying, since the reward of even partial success is the continued postponement, perhaps the avoidance altogether, of thermonuclear war.

Psychiatrists, no less than other social scientists, must emerge from their narrower specialist concerns and contribute what they know about the dynamics of human interaction toward a more informed discussion of national policy. The most urgent call for the services of healers to allay compulsively aggressive behavior and to correct cognitive mistakes comes today not from individual patients, but from human society itself.

Part three

Patterns of miscommunication

6

The inference-observation confusion

Let me begin the first of our patterns of miscommunication by inviting you to test yourself.

Read the following little story. Assume that all the information presented in it is definitely accurate and true. Read it carefully because it has ambiguous parts designed to lead you astray. No need to memorize it, though. You can refer back to it whenever you wish.

Next read the statements about the story and check each to indicate whether you consider it true, false, or "?". "T" means that the statement is *definitely true* on the basis of the information presented in the story. "F" means that it is *definitely false*. "?" means that it may be either true or false and that you cannot be certain which on the basis of the information presented in the story. If any part of a statement is doubtful, make it "?". *Answer each statement in turn, and do not go back to change any answer later and don't reread any statements after you have answered them. This will distort your score.*

To start with, here is a sample story with correct answers:

You arrive home late one evening and see that the lights are on in your living room. There is only one car parked in front of your house, and the words "Harold R. Jones, M.D." are spelled in small gold letters across one of the car's doors.

STATEMENTS ABOUT SAMPLE STORY

1. The car parked in front of your house has lettering on one of its doors.   (T)   F   ?
   (This is a "definitely true" statement because it is directly corroborated by the story.)

2. Someone in your family is sick.   T   F   (?)
   (This could be true and then again it might not be. Perhaps Dr. Jones is paying a social call at your home or perhaps he has gone to the house next door or across the street.)

3. No car is parked in front of your house.   T   (F)   ?
   (A "definitely false" statement because the story directly contradicts it.)

4. The car parked in front of your house belongs to a man named Johnson.   T   F   (?)
   (May seem very likely false, but can you be sure? Perhaps the car has just been sold.)

So much for the sample. It should warn you of some of the kinds of traps to look for. Now begin the actual test. Remember, mark each statement *in order*—don't skip around or change answers later.

THE STORY[1]

A businessman had just turned off the lights in the store when a man appeared and demanded money. The owner opened a cash register. The contents of the cash register were scooped up, and the man sped away. A member of the police force was notified promptly.

STATEMENTS ABOUT THE STORY

1. A man appeared after the owner had turned off his store lights.   T   F   ?
2. The robber was a *man*.   T   F   ?
3. The man who appeared did not demand money.   T   F   ?
4. The man who opened the cash register was the owner.   T   F   ?
5. The store owner scooped up the contents of the cash register and ran away.   T   F   ?
6. Someone opened a cash register.   T   F   ?
7. After the man who demanded the money scooped

---

[1] The story and statements are a portion of the "Uncritical Inference Test," copyrighted, 1955, 1964, 1967, 1972, by William V. Haney. The full-length test is available for educational purposes from the International Society for General Semantics, P.O. Box 2469, San Francisco, California 94126.

up the contents of the cash register, he ran away.   T   F   ?

8. While the cash register contained money, the story
    does *not* state *how much*.   T   F   ?

9. The robber demanded money of the owner.   T   F   ?

10. A businessman had just turned off the lights when
    a man appeared in the store.   T   F   ?

11. It was broad daylight when the man appeared.   T   F   ?

12. The man who appeared opened the cash register.   T   F   ?

13. No one demanded money.   T   F   ?

14. The story concerns a series of events in which only
    three persons are referred to: the owner of the
    store, a man who demanded money, and a member
    of the police force.   T   F   ?

15. The following events occurred: someone demanded
    money, a cash register was opened, its contents
    were scooped up, and a man dashed out of the
    store.   T   F   ?

If you will permit me to withhold the answers for a few pages, I would like to describe a classic study.[2] It was conducted over 50 years ago and has been repeated in many forms since then but always, to the best of my knowledge, the results of the Otto experiment have been corroborated.

The scene is a University of Wisconsin classroom. (See Figure 6–1) A carefully planned incident is about to occur. Of the 75 students present, only four, A, B, C, and D (and the instructor), are "in" on the stunt. At a given signal the following events occur: (1) While the instructor is collecting papers from students in the front row, A suddenly hits B with his fist, and B retaliates by striking A with a book, and the two fall to quarreling very loudly; (2) at the same time C throws two silver dollars into the air, permits them to fall to the floor, and scrambles after them as they roll away from him, and picks them up; (3) the instructor now orders A, B, and C from the room; (4) as he does so, D simply gets up and walks from the room at a normal gait; (5) as A, B, and C are preparing to leave, the instructor walks to the blackboard at the front of the room, glances at his watch, writes "9:45" on the blackboard, erases it, and writes it again; (6) A, B, and C leave the room, and the instructor turns to the class and says, in effect: "You have all seen what has happened, and you know that you

2 M. C. Otto, "Testimony and Human Nature," *Journal of Criminal Law and Criminology*, Vol. IX (1919), pp. 98–104.

FIGURE 6–1

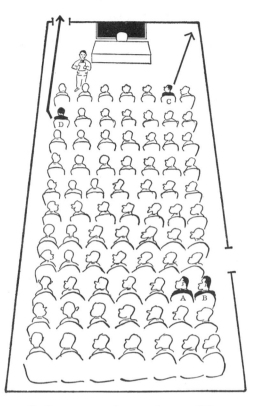

may very well be called upon to give testimony.[3] Let us now take time to write out reports of what we have observed." And with the instructor's assistance the class composes a series of questions to give order to their reports. The following are some of those questions and some of the answers to which these eyewitnesses were willing to testify.

Q: Where was the instructor when the disturbance began?
Twenty-two of the students reported that he was near the front of the room; 20 that he was about in the middle; and 21 that he was in the rear. A number of students scattered all over the room said they would have testified under oath that the instructor was at his (the student's) desk collecting his paper!

---

[3] At this time the university was on a student self-governing basis. This meant that any student disciplinary case, as this incident was to all appearances, would be submitted to a student court and testimony would be taken. In other words, it is most likely that the students saw the situation as quite real and one for which they might very well be asked to appear in court to give testimony.

Q: Where was the instructor and what was he doing when the boys
    left the room?
    Only 5 of the 75 reported the "9:45 business" with any accuracy.
    The attention of the others was obviously fixed elsewhere. How-
    ever, only six said they did not know. The others gave very defi-
    nite testimony. Three said the instructor was holding the door
    open for the students to pass through. One said he was standing
    in the middle of the room muttering, "I'll break this up, or know
    the reason why." Three remembered him sitting dejectedly at his
    desk with his face buried in his hands. The consensus of the re-
    maining students was that he was sitting at his desk nervously
    toying with, variously, the papers he had collected, class cards,
    his watch chain, a piece of chalk, etc. He appeared "as if not
    knowing what to do," and "his face wore an expression of embar-
    rassment and uneasiness."

Q: What did C do?
    You will recall that C had thrown two silver dollars into the air.
    They fell to the floor, and he hurried to pick them up. Some stu-
    dents reported that either A or B, in their fighting, had dropped
    some money; that these coins had rolled to the front of the room;
    and C had scrambled to pick them up. Other students said an
    adjustable desk arm from one of the classroom seats had been
    broken off (and A, incidentally, had tried to poke B with it) dur-
    ing the fighting; the little ratchet-ball inside had fallen out and
    had rolled to the front. It was this ball that C had rushed to pick
    up. The student sitting next to C, ironically enough, insisted he
    had seen a little steel ball come rolling out between C's feet and
    that C grabbed it and put it in his pocket.

Q: How did A, B, and C look as they left the room?
    The reports corresponded directly with the observer's attitude
    toward the instructor's action. If the student felt the instructor
    had been fair and justified in sending the men from the room,
    then they tended to look "embarrassed" and "ashamed." If, how-
    ever, the student thought the instructor too severe, the men
    looked "angry," "injured," and "abused." C's neighbor, who had
    perceived C do nothing more heinous than pocket a steel ball,
    reported that C had looked "very angry," while A and B ap-
    peared "sheepish."

Q: What did D do?
    This question was quite accidental. While the class was deciding
    the questions to be answered for their reports, one student asked:
    "Are we to include the fact that D rushed from the room at the

beginning of the disturbance?" The instructor replied noncommittally: "Please report what you saw as completely as you can, but report no more."

It seems highly likely that, with a vociferous struggle having just been waged in an opposite section of the room, only a few at most would even have noticed D's casual departure. Yet the suggestion of the student's question plus the obvious fact that D was now absent was apparently enough to convince over 85 percent of the students that they *had* seen D leave, and most of them were quite confident about the specific manner in which he left—saying, variously, that he had "rushed," "hurried," "bolted," or "made a wild dash from the room."

Otto, who was concerned with the bearing of this sort of behavior on the taking of legal testimony, seems amply justified in his alarm:

The importance of these facts is obvious. If it is impossible for a witness to reproduce an occurrence as it took place in his presence, even when asked to do so directly after the occurrence; if it is his very nature to demand consistency in such items as he does get, to the point of rejecting some and creating others; if such a thing as sending three men from a room at the same time may act as a suggestion around which is built up what the witness believes himself to have observed concerning them; what are the chances of arriving at the truth under conditions[4] which often obtain where testimony is taken?[5]

It may seem incredible that people could be capable of observing, remembering, and reporting an incident so distortedly—that they could fail so utterly to distinguish between what they had observed and what they only inferred.

THE UNCALCULATED RISK

We need to dig deeper into what we call the inference-observation confusion.

"Taking a calculated risk" is a familiar phrase we ordinarily use to describe a situation in which a person has decided to take an action which may have undesirable consequences—embarrassment, loss of money, injury, and so forth. But we imply that he is *aware* of these

---

[4] Referring to such factors as the time lapse between the observation and the giving of testimony (involving sometimes hours, days, weeks, or even years), the "third-degree" tactics of examining authorities, the leading, confining, and suggestive questions of cross-examining attorneys, and so on.

[5] Otto, "Testimony and Human Nature," *Journal of Criminal Law* . . . p. 104.

potential effects and, furthermore, has *assessed* the likelihood that they will occur. Generally speaking, when one takes a *calculated* risk, he is apt to be in a better position to avoid the hazards or at least to cope with them, should they occur.

The inference-observation confusion, on the other hand, often involves taking *uncalculated* risks. Take this actual traffic accident case,[6] for example.

Diagram *A* shows Driver White halted at a stop sign. Driver Black is approaching the intersection from the south. His right directional signal is blinking. White *assumes* Black is going to turn right at the intersection and, acting on this inference *as if* it were fact, starts to cross the intersection. Black does *not* turn but continues northward and is unable to avoid a costly collision with White (Diagram *B*). The directional signal? Black had intended to turn right into a driveway—50 yards *beyond* the intersection. Who was liable for the personal injuries and property damage?—Usually, White for failing to yield the right-of-way.

FIGURE 6–2

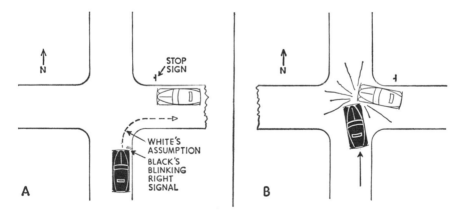

Let us go back and examine White's behavior more closely. We shall presume that he saw Black approaching and that he noted the blinking directional signal. At about this time he must have made his key assumption that Black was going to turn right at the intersection. Somehow in the process, however, *this inference became fused in*

---

6 See William V. Haney, "Are Accident-Prone Drivers Unconscious-Inference-Prone?" *General Semantics Bulletin,* Nos. 20 and 21 (1957). Reprinted in *Traffic Digest and Review,* Vol. 5 (March 1957).

with his observations. Perhaps he forgot that he had, in fact guessed— or perhaps he was never fully aware that he was in the realm of inference. At any rate, his crucial error occurred at the moment he treated the inference *as if* it were not.

It was at this point that he took his *uncalculated risk.* White, in entering the intersection with Black approaching, was taking a very definite risk. But, since he apparently failed to perceive his inference *as an inference*—i.e., as a situation involving a degree of uncertainty —he did not realize the risk he was taking and thus was hardly prompted to calculate its probability.[7]

In sum, the inference-observation confusion apparently occurs as follows: (1) Someone makes an inference, (2) fails to recognize or remember that he has done so, (3) thus does not calculate the risk involved, (4) proceeds to act upon his assumption *as if* it were "certain," and (5) ends by taking an unrecognized and uncalculated risk which may sometimes prove costly, dangerous, or even fatal.

So much for *how* the uncalculated risk occurs. But *why* does it happen and what can be done to *prevent* it?

OBSERVATIONAL AND INFERENTIAL STATEMENTS

Why, after all, does the inference-observation confusion and thus the uncalculated risk happen? Clearly, emotions often play an important role. Consider this incident:

RAZOR-IN-APPLE TALE PROVES HOAX[8]

PHILADELPHIA (AP) —A man was released from jail and six young girls were arrested Wednesday—the result of a Halloween hoax in which the girls said they were given an apple with a razor imbedded in it.

Based on the girls' stories Jack

---

[7] The late Thomas Fansler, of the National Safety Council, described the phenomenon in this manner: "In checking over case histories of traffic accidents, an observer cannot help being impressed with the number of times the idea of suddenness or unexpectedness occurs. After the accident, the driver will report, 'Suddenly the man ran in front of my car,' or 'I expected the other fellow to stop but instead . . .' The inference that may be drawn from this is that there was an *expected* pattern of circumstances in the minds of the drivers and that the change from the *expected* pattern to a 'sudden' or 'unexpected' pattern was partly responsible for the accident." From "The Dynamics of a Traffic Accident," by Thomas Fansler in a Research Memorandum of the National Safety Council (reprinted in the *Traffic Review,* Vol. III, No. 3 [Summer 1949]).

More recently (Newscast, September 7, 1971) Howard Pyle, National Safety Council, attributed 90 percent of traffic accidents to *driver error.*

[8] *The Atlanta Constitution,* Nov. 6, 1969, page 4–C. Reprinted by permission.

Thomas, 52, an unemployed father of three, was jailed Saturday in lieu of $10,000 bail, charged with intent to maim and cruelty to children. He was released from jail Wednesday afternoon.

The six girls admitted Wednesday morning their stories were false after Matthew Blelochi, 44, a guard in the housing project in which they live conducted an investigation of the girls' stories.

Grace Wisotzkey, 12, one of the girls arrested, had told police Thomas had given her an apple with a razor in it.

Under Blelochi's questioning Grace admitted she had gotten an apple with a soft spot from

Thomas, and her friend, Debbie Connors, prodded her into burying the blade in it, then showing it to her mother, police said.

The six girls were, Grace; her sister Carole, 14; Debbie, 13; Jean Hammond, 10; Catherine O'Leary, 10; and Joan Twilley, 11. All were charged with making a false report and conspiracy.

After Thomas was jailed, police said, infuriated neighbors threatened to burn his house.

Municipal Judge Benjamin Segal told the defendant at the time of his arraignment: "They should have whipping posts for people like you."

But emotions constitute only one broad category of variables provoking uncalculated risks. I devoted a lengthy chapter in my Ph.D. dissertation to merely listing and documenting some of the factors which appear to contribute to the inference-observation confusion. They include limited and impaired senses; such physiological conditions as those associated with hunger, thirst, and fatigue, and those incurred with the ingestion of alcohol and narcotics; and a host of psychological factors including emotion and stress, habit and set, values and needs, group and social influences, etc. In a category by itself was a seldom suspected agent: *our language!*

A central theme running through the various *patterns of miscommunication* covered in Part III of this book is that how we think and behave is influenced in no small measure by our language—the linguistic tool by which we reason and communicate.

But what does *language* have to do with the inference-observation confusion? Practically speaking, there are two kinds of declarative statements I can make about what I observe (see, hear, smell, taste, and so forth). Assuming that my vision and the illumination are "normal," I can look at a man wearing a tie and say: "That man is wearing a tie." This is called a *statement of observation* because it corresponds directly to what I have observed. On the other hand, I can look at the same man and say just as confidently: "That man bought that tie." Unless I actually observed him purchasing the tie, this statement is for me a *statement of inference*. I *inferred* he bought the tie because (1) he's wearing it; (2) he looks honest; (3) he appears to be the kind of person who would select his own ties; and so on. I may be right—but I may be wrong. Perhaps someone gave him the tie—or loaned it to him. Perhaps he found it. He may even be the type that prefers to shop after the stores have closed! The point is that, since I did not *observe* him buying the tie, the statement for me is necessarily an inferential one.

Observational and inferential statements are often extremely difficult to distinguish. Certainly the structure of our language offers no indication of their differences. There may be no grammatical, syntactical, orthographical, or punctuational, or pronunciational distinctions between them whatsoever. Moreover, the tones or inflections in which they are uttered may sound equally "certain."

You and I can point to this page and each of us can say: "William Haney wrote this material." Your statement was inferential; mine was observational. Yet the *statements were the same*.

In other words, there is nothing in the nature of our language (nor any other language to my knowledge) that makes it inescapable that we discriminate between inferential and observational statements. It seems reasonable to assume, then, that our failure to distinguish on these *verbal* levels contributes appreciably to the difficulty we have on *nonverbal* levels, namely, our propensity to confuse *inference* and *observation,* per se. Thus, we find it enticingly easy to make inferences and to utter inferential statements with the false assurance that we are dealing with "facts"—and the consequences of acting upon inferences *as if* they were observations are often less than pleasant.

"Mother, I wish I didn't look so flat-chested," said my 15-year-old daughter as she stood before the mirror in her first formal dress.

I remedied the matter by inserting puffs of cotton in strategic places. Then I hung around Mary's neck a string of seed pearls—just as my grandmother had done for my mother and my mother for me.

At midnight her escort brought her home. The moment the door closed behind him Mary burst into tears.

"I'm never going out with him again," she sobbed. "Mother, do you know what he said to me? He leaned across the table and said, 'Gee, you look sharp tonight, Mary. Are those real?' "

"I hope you told him they were," I said indignantly. "They've been in the family for three generations!"

My daughter stopped sobbing. "Oh, the pearls. Good heavens, I'd forgotten all about them."⁹

—Mrs. J. L. H. (*Alabama*)

Lest the reader feel that the inference-observation confusion per-
tains only to teen-age girls and University of Wisconsin students of
1919, let us bring the matter somewhat closer to home. Here are the
answers to the test I trust you took at the beginning of the chapter.

1. ? Do you *know* that the "businessman" and the "owner" are
   one and the same?
2. ? Was there *necessarily* a robbery involved here? Perhaps the
   man was the rent collector—or the owner's son—they sometimes demand money.
3. F An easy one to keep up the test-taker's morale.
4. ? Was the owner a *man?*
5. ? May seem unlikely but the story does not definitely preclude
   it.
6. T Story says the owner opened the cash register.
7. ? We don't know who scooped up the contents of the cash
   register or that the man necessarily *ran* away.
8. ? The dependent clause is doubtful—the cash register may or
   may not have contained money.
9. ? Again, a robber?
10. ? Could the man merely have appeared *at* a door or window
    but did not actually enter the store?
11. ? Stores generally keep lights on during the day.
12. ? Could not the man who appeared have been the owner?
13. F Story says the man who appeared demanded money.
14. ? Are the businessman and the owner one and the same—or
    two different people? Same goes for the owner and the man
    who appeared.
15. ? "Dashed?" Could he not have "sped away" on roller skates
    or in a car? And do we know that he actually left the store?
    We don't even know that he entered it.

CORRECTIVES

An effective technique for avoiding the inference-observation confusion is a two-step procedure:

1. We must be *aware* when we are inferring, as distinguished
   from observing . . . and then

---

⁹ From "Life in These United States," *Reader's Digest,* September 1951. Reprinted
by permission.

2.   We must *calculate* the degree of probability that our inferences are correct.

Step one: Awareness

The critical difficulty with our guesses, suppositions, premises, presumptions, predictions, assumptions, hunches, conjectures—inferences, generally—is not so much that we perform inadequately at Step 2 but rather that we fail at Step 1 and thus never reach 2. For example, if I am *unaware* that "that man bought that tie" is an inference on my part, I am hardly likely to be prompted to assess the probability of my inference, since I don't perceive it as an inference in the first place. That is, I will never ask myself, "How likely is such and such?" if "such and such" has been my observation—*or* an inference I unconsciously consider as my observation.

It was suggested earlier that an important contributor to the confusion of inference for observation was the difficulty that we have in distinguishing *statements* of inference from *statements* of observation. Studies[10] indicate that one *can learn* to make this distinction habitually and thus markedly increase his "inference-awareness."

How, then, does one go about it? Basically, we must internalize the characteristics of statements of observation as distinguished from statements of inference.

Statements of Observation	*Statements of Inference*
1. Can be made only *after* or *during* observation.	1. Can be made at any time.
2. Must stay with what one has observed—must not go beyond. (I observed the man *wearing* the tie—his *buying* it, if he did so, was beyond my observation.)	2. Can go beyond observation—well beyond. We can infer to the limits of our imagination.
3. Can be made only by the observer. (The observational statements of another are still my inferences, assuming that I have not observed what he has.)	3. Can be made by anyone.

---

[10] William V. Haney, "Measurement of the Ability to Discriminate between Inferential and Descriptive Statements," unpublished Ph.D. dissertation, Northwestern

These three requisites of observational statements are vital. You simply do not have a statement of observation if any of these criteria is not satisfied. A fourth pair of characteristics highlights a limitation on rather than a requirement of the statement of observation.

4. Statements of observation only *approach* "certainty."

4. Statements of inference involve degrees of probability.

Anyone who has experienced the fantastic Ames perception demonstrations[11] formerly housed at Princeton University will certainly realize the necessity for the term "approach." We can never get quite "all the way" to certainty. As developed in Chapter 3, our senses are restricted and imperfect, and our perceptions are subject to suggestion and distortion. But in the practical day-to-day world in which most of us live and work, our observations (and our observational statements) come as close to "certainty" as we frail, fallible human beings ordinarily get.

Step two: Calculation

Once I recognize that I am dealing with an inference I am ready for Step 2, the calculation of the risk, i.e., the assessment of the probability that the inference is correct.

Visualize a continuum with an infinite number of gradations. Label one end "the extremely probable," and the other "the extremely improbable." We are constantly going through the process of "pegging our inferences" (provided that we recognize them as such and try to assess their probability) somewhere on this scale. For instance, the inference that the earth will continue to turn on its axis tomorrow seems so *extremely probable* that we feel quite secure in literally "betting our lives" on it. Or we will stake our lives on the *improbability* of the inference that the sun will be destroyed within the week. To return to my inference about the man with the tie—that he bought it—I might peg this guess at the 50–50 mark. I might be willing to wager a quarter that he bought the tie, but probably not a dollar and certainly not five. But suppose in answer to my question the man says in all apparent sincerity: "Yes, I bought the tie."

University, 1953. A précis of the above appeared in *General Semantics Bulletin*, Nos. 16 and 17 (1955). See also my article, "Police Experience and Uncritical Inference Behavior," *General Semantics Bulletin*, Nos. 22 and 23 (1958).

[11] See William H. Ittelson, *The Ames Demonstrations in Perception* (Princeton, N.J.: Princeton University Press, 1952).

This still does not make it an observation for *me*, of course, but his remark may have the practical effect of causing me to change the point on the probability scale. If I know and trust the man, I may now be willing to risk a hundred dollars or even a thousand on the inference. This, then, is the vital process of probability assessment of calculating the risk, but, remember, we must be *aware* of when we are dealing with inferences before we can even enter this phase.

I have a short checklist I carry around in my head to use when I think it is important to distinguish inference and observation. Perhaps you will find it useful, too:

1.   Did I *personally* observe what I am talking or writing about?
2.   Do my observational statements stay with, and not go beyond, my observations?
3.   When I deal with important inferences, do I assess their probabilities?
4.   When I communicate with others, do I label my inferences as such and get them to label theirs?

Not long ago I was discussing this checklist with a group of industrial engineers. Afterward one of the men came up and said: "Am I glad you made that fourth point! That's the core of my problem. I have a man who is constantly giving me his inferences *as if* they were his observations. Maybe he's afraid to tell me they are only guesses, but, in any event, I go upstairs and report them as certainties to my superior—and sometimes they're wrong and I'm in hot water. I think I know now how to deal with this fellow. I'll tell him: 'Look, management doesn't expect us to *know or see* everything, but they do expect us to know the *difference* between what we know and what we're only guessing at.' "

QUESTIONS

Two particular questions sometimes arise when the inference-observation confusion is discussed.

Creativity

What bearing does inference-awareness have on creativity? Wouldn't the rigor required to distinguish inference from observation tend to curtail the imagination?

I see no incompatibility between rigor and creativity. Suppose a policeman observed a motorist racing through a stop light. As the officer gives chase he will very probably be trying to infer the driver's motive in order to determine the *manner* by which to apprehend him. Suppose he assumed the driver was simply in a hurry and felt he could "get away with it." And suppose he fails to recognize this as an inference but blithely treats it as observational. That apparently ends his analysis of the situation and we can only hope that in his interest, at least, his inference is correct.

On the other hand, if he is *aware* and *remains aware* that his first inference was just that—*his first inference*—he is more likely to try to *imagine other possible motives* for the driver's action. Could he be ill or under the influence of drugs or alcohol? Was he preoccupied and unaware that he had seen the light? Is the car out of control, e.g., the accelerator jammed? Is he taking a sick or injured person to the hospital? Is he deliberately flouting the law and egging the officer on? Is he escaping from a felony? And so on.

Aware that he is inferring, the officer will be continuously alert for signs that may help him *calculate* the probability of these various motives and perhaps suggest additional ones. Thus, he will be prepared to deal more *appropriately* with the situation.

The point is that had he confused inference for observation at the outset—had he treated his first inference as observation—he would hardly have been prompted to invent and test the additional alternatives.

Decisiveness

In urging the distinction between inference and observation do I appear to be saying: "Don't take risks. Stay away from inferences. They are dangerous. They only get you into trouble."? Am I advocating analysis paralysis—the sort of academic impotence that George Bernard Shaw scorned when he asserted that "if all the economists in the world were laid end to end, they still wouldn't reach a conclusion"? Nothing could be further from my purpose. In the first place we could not avoid inferences if we tried. We assume incessantly. You and I are assuming that the chairs we are seated on (I am assuming you are sitting on one) will not collapse beneath us. We are assuming that our next inhalation will not be noxious and kill us. When we eat, we make a host of inferences about the source, content, and preparation of the food. Whenever we use the Postal Service we make inferences about the speed and safety of our mail. Whenever we take advice from a doctor, attorney, or cleric and whenever we read a newspaper, magazine, or book (this one included), we make inferences about the credibility of their statements. One might be able to reduce the number of his inferences if he resigned from life and lived in bed as a vegetable. But, even so, he would have to make inferences about those who attended him.

In sum, one *must* deal with inferences. How much does an executive know from *his own direct observation* about his employees, his products, his markets, his competition, his suppliers, his stockholders, the governmental agencies which may regulate his enterprise, his firm's financial status? And to what extent must he rely upon the observations and inferences of others who, in turn, rely upon the observations and inferences of still others, *ad infinitum?*

Inferring, risking is an inescapable part of living in an active world.

We cheerfully trust our lives to total strangers in the persons of locomotive engineers, subway motormen, airplane pilots, elevator boys, steamship captains, taxi drivers, traffic cops, and unhesitatingly consign all our worldly goods to bankers and insurance companies.

I asked a hotel manager, with experience in both Florida and New England, to estimate how many of his patrons turned out to be dead beats. "Oh, a quarter of one percent," he said. If this proportion were as much as 10 percent, society would rock; charge accounts, installment buying, even ordinary banking would be impossible. If it were 25 percent, society would explode. Yet how many of us cherish the delusion that "you can't trust anybody these days"? If you couldn't, it is safe to say you wouldn't be here.[12]

In short, we live in a world of risk; some risks we can avoid, many we cannot or should not avoid. This chapter does not advocate inaction and indecision. The capacity to infer, after all, is essential in the arts and in the sciences. Analysis, problem solving, planning—all involve inference. Think of any creation—a skyscraper, a portrait, an electronic computer, or a picnic; without inferences, none would have been possible.

The point is this: Since we must make inferences anyway, is it not better (1) to be aware that we are making them so that (2) we will

---

[12] Stuart Chase, *Roads to Agreement* (New York: Harper & Brothers, 1951), pp. 43–44.

be prompted to calculate the risk involved? This story of a dining-car waiter makes the point:

It seems a prosperous-looking man walked into the train's diner, sat down, and ordered breakfast. When he finished, he was presented with a check for $1.45. He fished two one-dollar bills out of his wallet and handed them to the waiter. Shortly afterward the waiter returned with his change on a plate—a half-dollar and a nickel. The man gave a grunt of annoyance and pocketed the half-dollar and looked up expecting to see a resentful waiter. Instead the waited grinned widely: "That's all right, sir—I just gambled and lost!"

Aside from miscalculating his "risk," the waiter showed considerable maturity. There is a world of difference between professional and novice "inferencers." The novice goes out to the racetrack, say, and bets his life's savings on what he is completely convinced is a "dead-sure thing." The "pro" may bet the same amount (which he can just as ill afford to lose), but he knows the odds against him. Both may lose their money, but the novice is likely to lose a great deal more than money.

Let me add an important adjunct here. Much of our risk-taking is not of the simple, one-chance, win-or-lose, horse-racing variety. A good deal of it occurs in a process—a flow of events—which can be modified or to which our behavior can be modified in midstream, so to speak. Few of our decisions are intrinsically irrevocable. Take the automobile collision of White and Black, for instance. If sometime during the process, beginning with White's noting of Black and ending with the crash, White had become aware that he was taking a bad risk, there were numerous actions he could have taken to avoid, or at least diminish, the consequences. He might, for example, have speeded up to get through the intersection before Black reached it; sounded his horn or arm-signaled to alert Black of the danger; braked his car sooner; veered off to his right; and so forth. In other words, even a poor decision is not necessarily an injurious one if one keeps himself alerted to the effect of changing circumstances upon his inferences and risk calculations.

The objective, then, is not the *avoidance* but the *awareness* of risking, of inferring. And to suggest the occasional absurdity of *refusing* to risk I pass along this letter which was purportedly written by a corporation attorney.

It seems that the lawyer's company had purchased some land in

Louisiana and was now seeking a loan on it from a federal agency. Before granting the loan the agency asked for a record of the titles to the land. The attorney sent in titles dating back to 1803. The agency's response: "Who owned the land before that?" to which the lawyer replied:

Gentlemen:

Your letter regarding titles in Case #2515619 received. I note that you wish titles to extend further than I have presented them.

I was unaware that any educated man in the world failed to know that Louisiana was purchased from France by the U.S. in 1803.

The title to the land was acquired by France by right of conquest from Spain. The land came into the possession of Spain by right of discovery in 1492 by an Italian sailor named Christopher Columbus, who had been granted the privilege of seeking a new route to India by the then reigning monarch, Queen Isabella.

The good queen, being a pious woman and careful about titles (almost as careful, I might say, as your agency), took the precaution of securing the blessings of the Pope of Rome upon the voyage before she sold her jewels to help Columbus. Now the Pope, as you know, is considered by some as the emissary of Jesus Christ, who is regarded by many to be the Son of God, and God, it is commonly accepted, made the world.

Therefore, I believe, it is safe to presume that God also made that part of the United States called Louisiana. And, I hope to hell you're satisfied.

Very truly yours,

> To recognize what things you know,
>   And what things you do not know—
> This is wisdom.
>   —*Confucius*

DISCUSSION QUESTIONS

1. When one "jumps to a conclusion" what really happens?
2. *Precisely,* what is involved in the inference-observation confusion concept?
3. How can one avoid the inference-observation confusion?
4. How can one help others to avoid taking the uncalculated risk? Without offending them?

5. List five occupations in which inference-awareness would be especially important.

6. List five occupations in which inference-awareness would be unimportant.

7. About inferences—*how* does one go about calculating his risk?

8. Are there limitations to the extent to which one should become inference aware? Could preoccupation with inferences lead to indecision, inaction? To stultification of one's imagination? Explain.

9. Discuss the checklist on page 224. Are there exceptions to these recommendations? Can you make additional recommendations?

10. Describe an incident, possibly involving yourself, in which the inference-observation confusion occurred. Analyze specifically why it occurred, what might have been done to prevent its happening, and what measures would prevent its recurrence.

CASES

56 minutes before Pearl Harbor[13]

HUGH RUSSELL FRASER

My task was to investigate the 56 minutes of warning we had of the Jap air attack on Pearl Harbor, December 7, 1941. What I learned amazed me. I reported every detail to the Assistant Chief Signal Officer—specifically, Maj. Gen. James A. Code.

Now, nearly 17 years later, I can tell that story. The facts, incredible as they are, became a part of my history of the U.S. Signal Corps in World War II. To most Americans who know merely that we had some radar warning of the sneak Jap attack on the "Day of Infamy," the history of those 56 minutes will come as a shock.

Radar could, and did, detect the approach of the Jap air fleet. But not, of course, as it should have been detected, and not as it would have been detected if authorized radar equipment had been installed. Actually, the island of Oahu was to have been ringed with permanent radar-warning installations. It was not. As early as November of the year before, the Corps of Engineers was directed to install six permanent radar-warning sets to be operating around the clock beginning July 1, 1941.

These sets were not installed by July 1. They were not installed by December, nor by December 7. Four mobile radar warning units, mounted in trucks were provided in their place. Regarded generally by the men assigned to them as toys to experiment with, they were in operation only from 4 A.M. to 7 A.M. Why were these hours chosen? Probably it was because those were the three hours out of the 24 when the enemy—any enemy—was most likely to attack. If this was the theory, then it came very close to being 100 percent right!

The Opana mobile radar set, manned by Privates Joseph Lockard and George Elliott, was the one that detected the approach of the

13 *American Mercury*, August 1957, pp. 80–85. Reprinted by permission.

Jap air armada. Singularly enough, it was supposed to be shut down promptly at seven o'clock on the morning of December 7, but, by one of those fortunate accidents of history, the truck coming at that time to take the two men back to base camp and to breakfast was late. So Lockard and Elliott decided to leave the set on until it arrived.

Thus, after 7 A.M., the Opana unit was the only radar unit on the island operating. The other mobile sets, also mounted in trucks, had shut down promptly. One was located at Punaluu on Kahana Bay, 20 miles to the southeast; another on the extreme west side of the island near Makua, and the fourth near Waipahu on the southwest coast, 11 miles west of Pearl Harbor itself.

The Opana unit, which made history, was located about 22 miles due north of Pearl Harbor and about 28 miles northwest of the city of Honolulu. In other words, it was north of the mountains on the island of Oahu, which itself is about 43 miles long and 30 miles wide.

As the seconds after seven o'clock ticked off, Lockard—who kept his eye idly on the machine, noted nothing unusual until, suddenly, at 7:02 A.M., there appeared what he later described as "huge blip of light—bigger than anything I had ever seen before on the set— moving slowly from the extreme left side of the scope to the right. It was, you might call it, a pillar of light. It startled me, for the flight of one plane is represented by a mere dot, several planes a collection of white dots, but here was something different. The whole left side of the scope suddenly took on light!

"My natural reaction," he continued, "was to infer the radar unit was out of order. So I asked the mechanic, Elliott, to check it. He did so in a couple of minutes and reported it was working all right. By then it was 7:04 A.M. Something unusual, I knew, was before my eyes. Elliott thought so, too, although neither of us could imagine what it might be.

"Quickly we plotted it. The calculations were easily made, and it appeared to be definitely a large flight of planes approaching from due North, three points East and about 137 miles away.

"We looked at each other, and Elliott was the first to reach for the phone. At first he couldn't get anybody at the Army Information Center at Fort Shafter. The line was dead. Then he tried another line. It was open, and soon Private Joseph McDonald at the switchboard answered. Tersely, Elliott told him what we were seeing on the scope. McDonald's answer was: 'Well, what do you expect me to do about it? There's nobody around here but me.' Elliott told him to find somebody and then hung up.

"What happened, I learned later, was that there was an officer reading a book in the next room. McDonald had supposed he had gone. He was Lt. Kermit Tyler.[14] McDonald told him what Elliott had reported. Lieutenant Tyler looked up from his book, thought awhile as if to take it all in, then said: 'It's all right, never mind.'

"Joe McDonald then called back and I answered the phone. He told me what Tyler had said. I thereupon insisted on talking to the officer myself. I was a little excited and puzzled and didn't want to let the matter end with McDonald. Joe then asked the lieutenant if he would be good enough to talk to me. The officer then came on the phone and said, 'What is it?'

"I made my reply as brief as possible. 'The scope,' I said, 'indicates a large flight of planes approaching Oahu from due North, three points East, about 137 miles away at the last reckoning.'

"There was a pause for a few seconds, then Tyler said, 'That is probably our B-17's coming in from San Francisco.' I knew there was such a flight coming in, but I knew also those planes would hardly be approaching us from due North.

"At once I made this point clear, and he replied, 'Well, there is nothing to worry about. That is all.' The last words he said with some emphasis and I judged he didn't want to hear anything further about it, so I said: 'All right, sir,' and hung up.

"Meanwhile, somewhat startled by the whole business, although not alarmed, as now the matter was out of my hands, I continued to watch the set. The pillar of light, or 'blip,' as I call it, continued to move steadily from left to right and the truck still had not arrived. At 7:25 A.M. we made a quick computation and the flight of planes, whatever it consisted of was 62 miles out. At 7:39 A.M., just as we heard the truck arriving outside, I made my last computation and the flight was 22 miles away!

"It was at 7:39 A.M. that we closed down the radar unit and climbed into the truck for a long ride back to base. I was still turning over in my mind what we had seen on the scope as the truck

---

[14 A report of the Army Pearl Harbor Board which was published in the *Army and Navy Journal*, September 15, 1945, reads in part: "The Navy was supposed to have detailed officers in the Information Center to be trained as liaison officers, but had not yet gotten around to it. In the Information Center that morning was a Lieutenant Kermit A. Tyler, a pursuit officer of the Air Corps, whose tour of duty thereat was until 8 o'clock. It was Tyler's second tour of duty at the Center and he was there for training and observation, but there were no others on duty after 7 o'clock except the enlisted telephone operator. He was the sole officer there between 7 and 8 o'clock that morning, the rest of the personnel that had made the Center operative from 4:00 to 7:00 had departed." (Reprinted by permission.)]

bounced over the badly rutted road. I said nothing to the driver about it, nor did Elliott—not because we were alarmed but because I knew that what didn't make sense to us would hardly make sense to him.

"After we had been driving about 20 minutes, the driver called our attention to a heavy black pall of smoke that lay on the Pearl Harbor horizon to the South. 'Looks like oil smoke,' he commented. Soon we were hearing what sounded like explosions and even anti-air-craft fire. It was all very puzzling and somebody suggested it was a practice raid on Pearl Harbor.

"However, on we went over the rugged road. Actually, it was only 20 miles back to base camp, but because of the road it took almost 40 minutes. As we hove into view of the camp and the truck slowed down, we saw a lot of soldiers running toward us, shouting questions the words of which I couldn't quite at first make out. Finally, it was plain they were asking, 'What happened?' 'Did you report it?' and the like. I never saw a camp so collectively excited.

"As we started to get out of the truck, a major came elbowing his way through the group of men surrounding us and said, sharply, to us: 'Shut up! Don't say a word! I'll talk to you.'

"With that he took us off to his office and questioned us for 15 minutes. It was not until then I realized the Japs were at that very moment attacking Pearl Harbor, and that what we had seen on the screen was the Jap air fleet approaching.

"Now, as I look back, the position of the flight, the vast number of planes, made sense. I learned later the enemy aircraft carriers had sailed far to the North so that when the planes took the air they would be coming in from an unexpected direction."

Lockard at one point told me that except for the brief questioning by the major on the island of Oahu on the morning of December 7, 1941, I was the first to interrogate him in detail as to those 56 minutes— namely from 7:04. A.M. when Elliott reported the set was not out of order, to the time the first bomb fell on Pearl Harbor.

The tracing of the history of these 56 minutes, however, led me into a further investigation of why the permanent radar sets had not been installed on the island of Oahu by July 1. Here I ran into a curious and amazing story which I tried in vain to have the Congressional Investigating Committee explore.

My investigation disclosed that the colonel in the Corps of Engineers, who was charged with the duty of having these permanent radar sets installed and operated around the clock by July 1, 1941, had spent most of his time in the summer of 1941 drinking. His entire record demonstrates incredible negligence of duty. Not only did he fall down on his job but the toll in lives and ships that we had to pay for his failure was heartbreaking.

I tried to bring my evidence before the committee. To that end I prepared a long memorandum, setting forth the facts as I saw them. I requested that this colonel be summoned and be cross-examined under oath.

To my surprise, the Democratic members of the committee, whom I knew personally and regarded highly, handled my request—made in my capacity as a citizen—as if it was a "hot potato." They not only refused to act on it in any way, or request that he be summoned, but they told me in essence "to forget it"!

Amazed that members of my own party would take this view. I turned to the Republicans. I knew only one personally. He was Representative "Bud" Gearhart of California. Mr. Gearhart read my memorandum carefully and promised to do his best to get the colonel summoned. Later he reported back he had failed, but he had tried his best.

"Why won't they go into this question of radar units?" I asked. "Surely, you know their importance!"

"Yes," he said, "of course. My opinion is that somebody failed and failed terribly, but I ran up against a stone wall. The chairman flatly refused me, and when I asked one of my Democratic friends what was the real reason for what I thought, and still think, was an obvious run-around, he said, 'Look, Bud, you can do what you please and maybe you can get somewhere, but don't forget I'm a Democrat and a loyal one, and I take my orders from my Commander-in-Chief, and my Commander-in-Chief happens to be President of the United States!' "

Tyler Industries, Inc.[15]

Len Williams, manager of the Export Parts order section of Tyler's North European division, was puzzled and troubled. Something had obviously gone sour, but what?

Len had always prided himself on the relaxed, friendly atmosphere

---

15 All names have been disguised.

in the section. Good-natured bantering had been the order of the day and the men would frequently stop by his desk for an informal chat.

Suddenly, things were different. Len hadn't had a "visitor" for over a week and everyone seemed "too busy" with his own affairs for intra-office needling. With the men becoming more taciturn, Len felt himself growing progressively uneasy and unwilling to go out of his way to initiate conversations.

The change had occurred shortly after young Paul Brock had joined the section. But how could there be a connection? Paul seemed eager to learn and gave every indication of wanting to be a good "team player" but the group had clearly not accepted him.

Tyler Industries, Incorporated, was a large multidivision organization headquartered in Cleveland and operating in the Americas, Europe, Africa, the Far East, and Australia. The service functions of the corporation were organized by geographical areas such as the Great Britain division, the North European division, and so on. Some of these functions were located in the regions they served. Others, such as Export Parts, were centralized in Cleveland.

The North European division's Export Parts section consisted of Williams and seven order interpreters. Their eight desks were arranged in a straight line. Williams' desk was at the head of the line and Brock's was second. This desk had been vacated by Lou DeWitt who had just been promoted to chief of another section. Williams assigned the desk to Brock because Paul was new to the corporation as well as to the section and would probably need considerable coaching. Moreover, Len confided to a friend, "I want to avoid that silly desk reshuffling the guys did two years ago when Jack Rosen was promoted out of the section." Coincidentally Rosen had occupied the second desk.

The case of the ledgers[16]

W. C. LOHSE

Alfred Gregory, bank examiner, and his two assistants were making a routine examination of a country bank. The procedure in such bank examinations is to see that all of the various bank ledgers are proved by adding machine to see that they reflect the same figures

---

16 All names have been disguised. Reprinted by permission.

as shown on the bank's statement for that particular day. In examination circles it is customary to refer to the Loan Ledger as a Liability Ledger; Checking Accounts as Commercial Ledgers; and the General Books, in which all entries ultimately arrive and from which the daily statement is made, are called the General Ledger. One of the two assistant examiners had been on the examination force for only two or three months, and as a novice, it became his lot to do the majority of the machine work.

Mr. Gregory and his two assistants, Bill, the recruit, and Mac, the experienced assistant, entered the bank promptly at 7:30 A.M. as Leonard Brace, the cashier and vice president, was opening the bank for business. The examiners' credentials were shown to Brace and the examination proceeded as scheduled. At this point it might be pointed out that no banker is ever aware of when an examination might take place.

GREGORY: "Bill, as soon as you have counted the cash, run the Liability Ledger and then report to Mac."

BILL: "Okay!" Bill was elated because he had been put on his own for the first time.

Bill succeeded in counting the cash and balancing it in a fairly short time, and proceeded to hunt up the Liability Ledger. This bank was considerably different from those Bill had been in before. Here, they kept all the ledgers in one place and they were not labeled. Bill picked up a ledger and proceeded to run it on an adding machine.

Gregory and Mac were working in the Directors' Room, whose open door faced the open door of Brace's office. Bill entered the Directors' Room and went over to Mac with the total he had on his adding machine tape.

BILL: "Here you are, Mac. I ran the Liability Ledger and this is the total that should be on the statement."

MAC (*looking at the statement*): "Boy, you sure goofed. This isn't even close. Run it over again."

BILL: "Okay!"

GREGORY: "Say, Mac, you better have him stick with it; good experience."

Bill returned to his work, tabulated the ledger again, reported to Mac, and was again dismissed as having the wrong total. This procedure was repeated several times more before the morning was over. From where he sat in his office, Brace could see the repeated trips Bill made between Mac and the ledger. At noon, Mr. Gregory explained to Brace that the examiners would have to leave for lunch and since Bill had been unable to strike a balance with the Liability Ledger, the ledger would have to be sealed until they could check it out after lunch.

After lunch the examiners came back to the bank and Bill was sent to Mr. Brace's office to pick up the Liability Ledger that Brace had sealed. Bill returned to the Directors' Room apparently distressed.

GREGORY: "What's the matter, boy?"
BILL: "Boy, I've really messed this up."
GREGORY: "What do you mean?"
BILL: "I have been running the wrong ledger all morning. I was running the Commercial Ledger—no wonder I couldn't balance."
GREGORY: "That's all right, son, no harm done. Here take this Liability Ledger back and run it now."

Bill was passing Mr. Brace's door with the ledger, when Brace called to him.

BRACE: "Wait a minute. I'd like to talk to Mr. Gregory and you fellows."

Bill and Brace walked back to the Directors' Room.

BRACE (*perspiring heavily*) : "Well, I guess the jig's up, Mr. Gregory."
GREGORY (*thinking Brace was joking, as most bankers do with examiners*) : "Yep."
BRACE: "I didn't think that some young fellow would catch me. If I had to be caught I hoped it would be an old-timer like yourself."
GREGORY (*now that it is clear that Mr. Brace is serious*) : "Well, now that we know of this situation, would you please aid us in ascertaining how far it has gone?"

Mr. Brace readily agreed and proceeded to show the examiners where, over the past eight years, he had embezzled $28,000 and the methods used to perpetrate the defalcation. Gregory asked what had given him the idea that the examiners had discovered the defalcation. Mr. Brace said that when he had seen Bill repeatedly going to the Ledger, he figured something was wrong because in all the years that he had been under various examinations, it had never taken an examiner more than an hour to run and balance his ledger.

Brace was subsequently tried and convicted. Despite his family's reimbursement of the major portion of the embezzlement, he was fined $25,000 and sentenced to ten years.

Gregory admitted privately that it was quite unlikely that the defalcation would have been detected by the routine examination.

General Patton and the Sicilian slapping incidents[17]
HENRY J. TAYLOR

> Headquarters Seventh Army
> A.P.O. #758, U.S. Army
> 29th August, 1943

MY DEAR GENERAL EISENHOWER:

Replying to your letter of August 17, 1943, I want to commence by thanking you for this additional illustration of your fairness and generous consideration in making the communication personal.

I am at a loss to find words with which to express my chagrin and grief at having given you, a man to whom I owe everything and for whom I would gladly lay down my life, cause for displeasure with me.

I assure you that I had no intention of being either harsh or cruel in my treatment of the two soldiers in question. My sole purpose was to try and restore in them a just appreciation of their obligation as men and soldiers.

In World War I, I had a dear friend and former schoolmate who lost his nerve in an exactly analogous manner, and who, after years of mental anguish, committed suicide.

Both my friend and the medical men with whom I discussed his case assured me that had he been roundly checked at the time of his first misbehavior, he would have been restored to a normal state.

Naturally, this memory actuated me when I inaptly tried to apply the remedies suggested. After each incident I stated to officers with me that I felt I had probably saved an immortal soul. . . .

> Very respectfully,
> (*Signed*) G. S. PATTON, JR.
> *Lieut. General, U.S. Army*

General D. D. Eisenhower
Headquarters AFHQ
APO #512—U.S. Army

---

17 From the book *Deadline Delayed* by Members of the Overseas Press Club. Copyright, 1947, by E. P. Dutton and Co., Inc., New. Reprinted by permission.

When General Patton gave me a copy of this letter he lay back on the bed in his field-trailer and said, "What does that sound like to you?"

"It sounds to me like only half of the story," I said.

So, first, let's see what actually happened.

Private Charles H. Kuhl (in civilian life a carpet layer from South Bend, Indiana) , ASN 35536908, L Company, 26th Infantry, 1st Division, was admitted to the 3rd Battalion, 26th Infantry aid station in Sicily on August 2, 1943, at 2:10 p.m.

He had been in the Army eight months and with the 1st Division about thirty days.

A diagnosis of "Exhaustion" was made at the station by Lieutenant H. L. Sanger, Medical Corps, and Kuhl was evacuated to C Company, 1st Medical Battalion, well to the rear of the fighting.

There a note was made on his medical tag stating that he had been admitted to this place three times during the Sicilian campaign.

He was evacuated to the clearing company by Captain J. D. Broom, M.C., put in "quarters" and given sodium amytal, one capsule night and morning, on the prescription of Captain N. S. Nedell, M.C.

On August 3rd the following remark appears on Kuhl's Emergency Medical Tag: "Psychoneuroses anxiety state—moderately severe. Soldier has been twice before in hospital within ten days. He can't take it at front evidently. He is repeatedly returned." (*signed*) Capt. T. P. Covington, Medical Corps.

By this route and in this way Private Kuhl arrived in the receiving tent of the 15th Evacuation Hospital, where the blow was struck that was heard round the world.

"I came into the tent," explains General Patton, "with the commanding officer of the outfit and other medical officers.

"I spoke to the various patients, especially commending the wounded men. I just get sick inside myself when I see a fellow torn apart, and some of the wounded were in terrible ghastly shape. Then I come to this man and asked him what was the matter."

The soldier replied, "I guess I can't take it."

"Looking at the others in the tent, so many of them badly beaten up, I simply flew off the handle."

Patton squared off in front of the soldier.

He called the man every kind of a loathsome coward and then slapped him across the face with his gloves.

The soldier fell back. Patton grabbed him by the scruff of the neck and kicked him out of the tent.

Kuhl was immediately picked up by corpsmen and taken to a ward.[18]

Returning to his headquarters Patton issued the following memorandum to Corps, Division and Separate Brigade Commanders two days later:

> Headquarters Seventh Army
> APO #758 U.S. Army
> 5 August, 1943

It has come to my attention that a very small number of soldiers are going to the hospital on the pretext that they are nervously incapable of combat.

Such men are cowards, and bring discredit on the Army and disgrace to their comrades whom they heartlessly leave to endure the danger of a battle while they themselves use the hospital as a means of escaping.

You will take measures to see that such cases are not sent to the hospital, but are dealt with in their units.

Those who are not willing to fight will be tried by Court-Martial for cowardice in the face of the enemy.

> (*Signed*) G. S. PATTON, JR.
> *Lieut. General, U. S. Army*
> *Commanding*

Five days later General Patton, not a medical man, again took matters into his own hands.

He slapped another soldier.

Private Paul G. Bennett, ASN 70000001, C Battery, Field Artillery, was admitted to the 93rd Evacuation Hospital on August 10th at 2:20 P.M.

Bennett, still only twenty-one, had served four years in the Regular Army. He had an excellent record. His unit had been attached to the II Corps since March and he had never had any difficulties until four days earlier when his best friend in the outfit, fighting near by, was wounded in action.

Bennett could not sleep that night and felt nervous. The shells going over "bothered" him. "I keep thinking they're going to land right on me," he said. The next day he became increasingly nervous about the firing and about his buddy's recovery.

---

[18] There Kuhl was found to have a temperature of 102.2° F., gave a history of chronic diarrhea for the past month, and was shown by a blood test to have malaria.

A battery aid man sent him to the rear echelon, where a medical officer gave him some medicine which made him sleep. But he was still nervous, badly disturbed.

On August 10th the medical officer ordered him to the 93rd Evacuation Hospital, although Bennett begged not to be evacuated because he did not want to leave his unit.

General Patton arrived at the hospital that day.

Bennett was sitting in the receiving tent, huddled up and shivering.

Patton spoke to all the injured men. He was solicitous, kind and inspiring. But when he and Major Charles B. Etter, the receiving officer in charge, reached Bennett and Patton asked the soldier what his trouble was, the soldier replied, "It's my nerves," and began to sob.

Patton turned on him like a tiger, screaming at him: "What did you say?"

"It's my nerves," sobbed Bennett. "I can't take the shelling anymore."

In this moment Patton lost control of himself completely. Without any investigation of the man's case whatever, he rushed close to Bennett and shouted: "Your nerves, hell. You are just a . . . coward, you yellow b———."

Then he slapped the soldier hard across the face.

"Shut up that . . . crying," he yelled. "I won't have these brave men here who have been shot seeing a yellow b——— sitting here crying."

Patton struck at the man again. He knocked his helmet liner off his head into the next tent. Then he turned to Major Etter and yelled, "Don't admit this yellow b———, there's nothing the matter with him. I won't have the hospitals cluttered up with these SOB's who haven't got the guts to fight."

Patton himself began to sob. He wheeled around to Colonel Donald E. Currier, the 93rd's commanding Medical Officer. "I can't help it," he said. "It makes me break down to see brave boys and to think of a yellow b——— being babied."

But this was not all. In his blind fury, Patton turned on Bennett again. The soldier now was managing to sit at attention, although shaking all over.

"You're going back to the front lines," Patton shouted. "You may get shot and killed, but you're going to fight. If you don't, I'll stand you up against the wall and have a firing squad kill you on purpose.

"In fact," he said, reaching for his revolver, "I ought to shoot you myself, you———— whimpering coward."

As he left the tent Patton was still yelling back at the receiving officer to "send that yellow SOB back to the front line."

Nurses and patients, attracted by the shouting and cursing, came from the adjoining tent and witnessed this disturbance.

Patton made no initial report of these affairs to his superior, General Eisenhower, who was then in his Headquarters at Tunis on the North African mainland.

"I felt ashamed of myself," General Patton told me, "and I hoped the whole thing would die out."

But an official report by Lieut. Colonel Perrin H. Long, Medical Corps consulting physician, was already on the way to Allied Headquarters through Medical Corps channels.

"The deleterious effects of such incidents upon the well-being of patients, upon the professional morale of hospital staffs and upon the relationship of patient to physician are incalculable," reported Lieut. Colonel Long. "It is imperative that immediate steps be taken to prevent a recurrence of such incidents."

General Eisenhower received this report on August 17th. His communication to General Patton was sent off that night.

In his message, which Patton showed me, the Commanding General told Patton of the allegation, told him that he could not describe in official language his revulsion, informed Patton that he must make, on his own intiative, proper amends to the soldiers involved and take steps to make amends before his whole army.

"This all happened practically on the eve of a new attack in which I had been written in for a large part of the plans, already issued," Patton explained, "and General Eisenhower stated therefore that he would temporarily reserve decision regarding my relief of command until he could determine the effect of my own corrective measures.

"Then Eisenhower did four things: He sent Maj. General John Porter Lucas to Sicily to make an investigation of the charges, sent the Theatre's Inspector General to investigate command relationships in my entire army, sent another general officer to interview the two soldiers and made a trip to Sicily himself to determine how much resentment against me existed in the army.

"Eisenhower's problem was whether what I had done was sufficiently damaging to compel my relief on the eve of attack, thus losing what he described as my unquestioned military value, or whether less drastic measures would be appropriate.

"I went to see both Kuhl and Bennett," Patton continued, "explained my motives and apologized for my actions.

"In each case I stated that I should like to shake hands with them; that I was sincerely sorry. In each case they accepted my offer.

"I called together all the doctors, nurses and enlisted men who were present when the slappings occurred. I apologized and expressed my humiliation over my impulsive actions.

"Finally, I addressed all divisions of the 7th Army in a series of assemblies, the last of which was an address before the 3rd Division on August 30th.

"I praised them as soldiers, expressed regret for any occasions when I harshly treated individuals and offered my apologies as their Commanding General for doing anything unfair or un-American.

"Beyond that, except to leave the Army and get out of the war, I do not know what I could have done."

The man and the desk[19]

F. J. ROETHLISBERGER AND WILLIAM T. DICKSON

The personnel of one of the departments interviewed was moved from one building to another. In the new location, because of lack of space, it was found necessary to seat four people across the aisle from the remainder of the group. It happened that there were three women in the department who were to be transferred to other work. These women were given desks across the aisle so that their going would not necessitate a rearrangement of desks. The fourth person, a man, was given a desk there simply because there was no other place for him to sit. In choosing the fourth person, the supervisor was undoubtedly influenced by the fact that he was older than the rest of the group and was well acquainted with the three women. But, beyond that, nothing was implied by the fact that he was chosen. Now see how this employee interpreted the change in his seating

---

19 *Management and the Worker* (Cambridge, Mass.: Harvard University Press, 1939) , pp. 544–45. Reprinted by permission.

position. He felt that his supervisor evaluated him in the same way in which he evaluated the women. The women were being transferred to other types of work; consequently, he felt that he too would be transferred before long. Two of the women were being returned to jobs in the shop. He felt that he himself might be transferred to the shop; and there was nothing he dreaded more. Having dwelt on speculations like these for a while, the employee recalled with alarm that his name had been omitted from the current issue of the house telephone directory. This omission had been accidental. The house telephone directory, however, constituted a sort of social register. Names of shop people below the rank of assistant foreman were not printed unless they were employed in some special capacity requiring contacts with other organizations. With the exception of typists and certain clerical groups, the names of all office people were listed. The fact that his name had been omitted from the directory now took on new significance for the employee. It tended to reinforce his growing conviction that he was about to be transferred to a shop position. He became so preoccupied over what might happen to him that for a time he could scarcely work.

7

Bypassing

DEFINITION

Belden, West and Bartell[1] was a medium-sized brokerage firm with approximately 95 employees. The accounting department had 17 employees, of whom three were middle-aged women who operated the bookkeeping machines. With the average volume of business, all three were normally finished with their posting about one hour before the usual quitting time.

On February 21st one of the bookkeepers, Elizabeth Morley, phoned in to say she was ill and would be unable to report for duty. The other two pitched in and completed about 75 percent of the absent woman's posting before the normal quitting time. The supervisor then approached one of the bookkeepers, Jane Dover, and said: "Elizabeth just called and said she'll be absent again tomorrow, so the balance of her work [25 percent of her normal work load] will have to be completed the first thing in the morning."

Miss Dover, a very conscientious and somewhat unassertive woman, said nothing. The following morning the supervisor found that Miss Dover had worked until 8:30 P.M. the previous evening to complete Miss Morley's posting. The supervisor had intended that she and the other bookkeeper continue with the remainder of Miss Morley's work in the morning before starting on their own posting.

---

[1] All names have been disguised.

A foreman told a machine operator he was passing: "Better clean up around here." It was ten minutes later when the foreman's assistant phoned: "Say, boss, isn't that bearing Sipert is working on due up in engineering pronto?"

"You bet your sweet life it is. Why?"

"He says you told him to drop it and sweep the place up. I thought I'd better make sure."

"Listen," the foreman flared into the phone, "get him right back on that job. It's got to be ready in twenty minutes."

. . . What [the foreman] had in mind was for Sipert to gather up the oily waste, which was a fire and accident hazard. This would not have taken more than a couple of minutes, and there would have been plenty of time to finish the bearing.[2]

A motorist was driving on the Merritt Parkway outside New York City when his engine stalled. He quickly determined that his battery was dead and managed to stop another driver, a woman. She consented to push his car to get it started.

"My car has an automatic transmission," he explained to her, "so you'll have to get up to 30 to 35 miles per hour to get me started."

The woman smiled sweetly and walked back to her car. The motorist climbed into his own car and waited for her to line up her car behind his. He waited—and waited. Finally, he turned around to see what was wrong.

There was the woman—coming at his car at 30 to 35 miles per hour! The damage to his car amounted to $300!

In each of the preceding instances there was talking and there was listening. There were people "sending" messages and other people "receiving" them. But somehow the communication went awry. The speaker didn't "get through"—the listener didn't "get *him.*" The listener presumably heard the same words that the speaker said, but the communicators seem to have *talked past* one another.

This communication phenomenon is called *bypassing*. Figure 7–1 diagrams the *bypassing* between Sipert and his foreman.

It is evident that the foreman had one meaning for "better clean up around here" and Sipert had another. Their meanings *bypassed* one another without meeting. *Bypassing*, then, is the name for the mis-

---

[2] Quoted from *The Foreman's Letter*, February 8, 1950, published by the NFI, a division of VISION Incorporated, with permission of the editor.

FIGURE 7-1

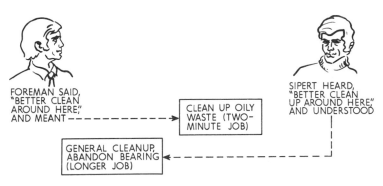

FOREMAN SAID,
"BETTER CLEAN
AROUND HERE,"
AND MEANT – – – – – – – – – ⟶

CLEAN UP OILY
WASTE (TWO-
MINUTE JOB)

SIPERT HEARD,
"BETTER CLEAN
UP AROUND HERE,"
AND UNDERSTOOD

GENERAL CLEANUP,
ABANDON BEARING ⟵ – – – – – – – – – – – ⅃
(LONGER JOB)

communication pattern which occurs when the *sender* (speaker, writer, and so on) and the *receiver* (listener, reader, and so forth) *miss each other with their meanings.*

Same word—different things

Before going on, it should be noted that the three *bypassing* illustrations took the form of some persons "sending" and others "receiving" the *same words* but attributing *different meanings* to them. Miss Dover, for example, heard the *same words* her supervisor had said but interpreted them quite differently from what he had intended. This is a very common type of *bypassing*, but it has an equally prevalent counterpart.

Different words—same thing

Bypassing may occur just as readily when people are using *different words* to represent the *same thing*. I once witnessed with thinly disguised amusement a heated and fruitless argument between my 12-year-old nephew and a Massachusetts soda fountain clerk, only a year or two older. Jimmy, born and reared in Illinois, was visiting the East Coast for the first time.

The conversation went something like this:

JIMMY: Do you have pop?
CLERK: What?
JIMMY: Pop.
CLERK: I don't know what you're talking about.

JIMMY (*scornfully*) : You never heard of pop?

CLERK: No, and neither did you!

JIMMY: Listen, it's that stuff that comes in a bottle—you shake it up and it fizzes out!

CLERK: Oh! You mean a soda!

JIMMY: No! I don't want a soda! (A "soda" where Jimmy lives is made with ice cream, flavoring, and soda water.)

CLERK: Well, then, what *do* you want?

JIMMY: Never mind! You wouldn't have it anyway!

At this point I partially reconciled the two antagonists by suggesting that they were both talking about the same thing. Jimmy, incidentally, finally got his "pop," "soda," "tonic," "minerals," "soft drink," or whatever it is called in your part of the country.

Both types of *bypassing* (same word—different things and different words—same thing) have a common basis, of course. Both involve people missing one another's meanings, and their consequences are equally worthy of consideration.

SOME CONSEQUENCES

Bypassing may occur under such a variety of circumstances that it may be helpful to suggest something of the range of its consequences.

The range of consequences

Bypassing is certainly one of the most prevalent and potentially costly and dangerous patterns of miscommunication in organizations or virtually anywhere else. But bypassing isn't always serious, hazardous, or even important. Much of the time its effects are inconsequential. And at other times its results may be amusing or even hilarious. In fact, much of our humor is based on bypassing. Permit me to make the point with a personal story. It happened on my first day of college teaching years ago. Mustering as much dignity as possible for a neophyte, I walked into the classroom and announced that I was going to seat the class alphabetically. I explained that I had difficulty in associating names with faces, and in seating them alphabetically, "I will get to know you by your seats." You may be quite sure the class bypassed me!

But I was not to have the only red face that day, for 20 minutes later a young, innocent freshman miss rose to describe her initial

campus impressions. She said she was particularly fond of the sere-
nades—when the fraternity boys would come as a group to sing
beneath the girls' dormitory windows. "We girls love it so," she emphasized, "we wish the boys could stay all night!"

Unfortunately, not all bypassings end so delightfully (at least from
the audience's point of view). Bypassings occurring every day in industry, in government, and in homes, result in enormous wastes of
time, money, effort, and tempers. History is full of examples of
bypassing which have led to catastrophes. There is even disturbing
evidence to suggest that a bypassing on a word in the Japanese response to the World War II Potsdam ultimatum may have led to the
dropping of the atomic bombs on Japan and Russia's declaration of
war on Japan—events which have had irrevocable effect upon world
affairs.[3]

Immediate consequences

Before we leave this cursory review of bypassing we should note
that the *immediate* effects of this breakdown in communication generally fall into one or the other of two broad classifications.

Apparent agreement. Most of the bypassing illustrations we
have been considering have had *apparent agreement* as their immediate consequences. That is, the initial result of the bypassing was
such that those involved felt they were in harmony with one another. Sipert and his foreman, Miss Dover and her supervisor, and
the stalled motorist and the woman driver, for example, believed
that they had had an adequate understanding. The bypassing, however, concealed an *actual disagreement* (i.e., the people involved dif-
fered on meanings).

It is acting on the false assurance of agreement which so frequently
leads us into trouble.

Jeannie, 9, called to her mother upstairs: "Mom, may I fix the Easter
eggs?" "Yes, dear," mother called back, "just put three dozen eggs into
the kettle and be sure to cook them for at least 15 minutes."

Jeannie placed the eggs in the largest kettle she could find and filled
it with cold water. Then she set the kettle on the stove and turned on
the gas.

After 15 minutes of eager clock watching, Jeannie removed the eggs

---

[3] William J. Coughlin, "Was It the Deadliest Error of Our Time?" *Harper's Magazine,* March 1953, pp. 31–40.

from the water (which had not yet begun to boil) and set them on the table.

While she was preparing the Easter egg dyes, her brother Tom, 14, walked into the kitchen and picked up an egg. "Are you sure you cooked these long enough?" he asked. "Sure. Exactly 15 minutes, just like Mom said." "Well, okay—say, want to see what a hard head I have?" And with that Tom cracked a very uncooked egg on his head!

Apparent disagreement. But bypassing which conceals *actual agreement* by manifesting *apparent disagreement* can also be disconcerting.

Major Gregory Klimov, for two years an official of the Soviet Military Administration in Occupied Berlin and who later fled to the West, recounts the first meeting of the Allied Control Commission, Economic Directorate. After routine matters had been settled, the head of the American delegation proposed that the first item on the agenda should be: "The working out of basic policy for the economic demilitarization of Germany."

The interpreters now translated the chairman's phrase into Russian as: "Working out the policy of economic demobilization." Another of those borderline cases in linguistics! The English formula had used the word "policy." The interpreters translated this literally into the Russian word "politik," although the English word had a much wider meaning, and the Russian phrase for "guiding principles" would have been a more satisfactory translation.

At the word "politik" General Shabalin sprang up as though stung. "What 'politik'? All the political questions were settled at the Potsdam Conference!"

The American chairman, General Draper, agreed: "Quite correct, they were. Our task is simply to translate the decision into action, and so we have to lay down the guiding policy . . ."

The interpreters, both American and English, again translated with one accord: ". . . 'politik.'"

General Shabalin stuck to his guns: "There must be nothing about politics. That's all settled. Please don't try to exert pressure on me."

"But it's got nothing to do with politics," the interpreters tried to reassure him. "The word is 'policy.'"

"I see no difference," the general objected. "I have no intention of revising the Potsdam Conference. We're here to work, not to hold meetings."[4]

---

[4] Gregory Klimov, *The Terror Machine: The Inside Story of the Soviet Administration in Germany* (New York: Frederick A. Praeger, Inc., 1953), pp. 146–47. Reprinted by permission.

And this futile battle over the awkward word *policy* was the beginning of the first of many long and similar arguments around the conference table.

Whether the immediate consequence of bypassing is an *apparent agreement* or an *apparent disagreement,* the subsequent effect *can* be unpleasant, unproductive, and even fatal. Let us now look into some of the contributing factors of this often troublesome pattern of miscommunication.

THE UNDERLYING MECHANISM

To cope with harmful bypassing we must examine its underlying *mechanism.* Just what happens when people bypass? What kind of thought process occurs which leads to such dangerous and costly miscommunication?

Let us return to the Sipert-foreman incident. They bypassed one another, i.e., missed each other with their meanings. But *why?* Let us presume that neither *intended* to miscommunicate. Certainly the foreman did not use any "big," foreign, or unfamiliar words. Why, then, did the communication go askew?

Suppose we asked Sipert and the foreman what they thought went wrong in their communication. Their responses might follow this pattern:

SIPERT: I was sure I knew what the boss meant. I never thought he was talking about cleaning up the waste.

FOREMAN: I was certain Sipert would understand what I was driving at. It never occurred to me that he would put a different interpretation on my remark.

"I was sure . . . I never thought . . ."; "I was certain . . . It never occurred to me . . ." These men are revealing the key assumption underlying their behavior—the assumption that *"words mean the same to the other fellow as they do to me."*

That is an enormously pervasive assumption. Most of us act on this assumption much of the time—and usually the assumption proves correct. That is, more often than not people *do* interpret our words as we intend—and usually we decode their words appropriately as well. But consistent success sometimes leads to overconfidence and complacency—the ideal attitudes for bypassing.

There are at least two additional reasons for the epidemic prevalence of the assumption. First, it is a highly *enticing* notion. We *want* to feel we are understanding and being understood by the other fellow. Second, the assumption supports our basic egocentrism as evidenced by this passage from Lewis Carroll's *Through the Looking Glass:*

Humpty-Dumpty said: "There's glory for you." "I don't know what you mean by 'glory,'" Alice said. Humpty-Dumpty smiled contemptuously. "Of course you don't till I tell you. I meant, 'There's a nice knock-down argument for you.'" "But 'glory' doesn't mean a 'nice knock-down argument,'" Alice objected. "When I use a word," Humpty-Dumpty said in a rather scornful tone, "it means just what I choose it to mean, neither more nor less."

Few of us are as frank as Humpty, although we are frequently as arrogant. We would not call it "arrogance" (unless we were talking about the other fellow) because we are largely unaware of the prevailing egocentrism which so frequently accompanies our use of words. If a person were to resolve to watch scrupulously his own language use during a 24-hour period, he would almost certainly catch himself talking or listening (writing or reading) dozens of times with the Humpty-Dumpty attitude. He would find himself assuming, "I *knew* what the other person understood or meant simply because that was the way I used or would have used the words."

It is understandable why so much communicating occurs under the influence of such an assumption. But the stark fact remains: The assumption is *not unfailingly valid*—and we have already suggested the scope of consequences of acting unconsciously upon the assumption when it is false.

Digging more deeply we find that the assumption is supported by two pernicious fallacies. One is that words are used in only one way ("the way *I* am using them")—that *words have mono-usage*. The other is that *words have meanings*. I shall attack each of these fallacies for they lie at the foundation of bypassing.

The fallacy that words have mono-usage

The first of the fallacies underlying bypassing is the assumption of mono-usage. The notion that words are used for one and only one meaning is so patently ridiculous that it hardly appears necessary to refute it. Yet so much of our communication seems based on this misconception that I must comment on it.

To begin, let me ask a question: How many words are used in only one way? Excepting certain technological terms, virtually all of our common words (so far as I have been able to determine) are used in more than one way. That is, the words we usually use in our day-to-day communications almost invariably have multi-usage. In fact, for the 500 most commonly used words in our language there is an aggregate of over 14,000 dictionary definitions! Take the word *fast*, for instance:

A person is *fast* when he can run rapidly.
But he is also *fast* when he is tied down and cannot run at all.
And colors are *fast* when they do not run.
One is *fast* when he moves in suspect company.
But this is not quite the same thing as playing *fast* and loose.
A racetrack is *fast* when it is in good running condition.
A friend is *fast* when he is loyal.
A watch is *fast* when it is ahead of time.
To be *fast* asleep is to be deep in sleep.
To be *fast* by is to be near.
To *fast* is to refrain from eating.
A *fast* may be a period of noneating—or a ship's mooring line.
Photographic film is *fast* when it is *sensitive* (to light).
But bacteria are *fast* when they are *insensitive* (to antiseptics).

And note the versatility of *call* in this gripping narrative:

Jim *called* on Joe to *call* him out for *calling* him up at midnight and *calling* him down, but their wives *called* in friends who got the fight *called* off.[5]

If one recognizes the prevalence of *multi-usage* in our language, he will anticipate that words can readily be understood differently by different people. *Parade Magazine* made this point graphically some years ago when it conducted an interesting demonstration. Each of three artists was given a copy of a paragraph from the *Encyclopaedia Britannica*. The paragraph described (words only, no pictures) an animal which purportedly none of the artists had ever seen:

The body is stout, with arched back; the limbs are short and stout, armed with strong, blunt claws; the ears long; and the tail thick at the base and tapering gradually. The elongated head is set on a short, thick neck, and at the extremity of the snout is a disc in which the nostrils

---

[5] The sentence hardly suggests the multi-usages of *call*. Webster's Unabridged lists 40 different definitions for the word. Other kaleidoscopic words: *turn* (54 definitions), *fall* (50), *touch* (46).

open. The mouth is small and tubular, furnished with a long extensile tongue. A large individual measured 6 ft. 8 in. In colour it is pale sandy or yellow, the hair being scanty and allowing the skin to show.[6]

From this purely *verbal* description the artists were asked to draw what they conjured up from the words. The results are shown in Figure 7–2.

The animal (lower right), is an aardvark, or anteater. As bizarre and as diverse as these drawings appear, note one extremely significant point: Each is *a legitimate interpretation* of the paragraph. Note that while a detail may be interpreted *differently,* it is, nevertheless, consistent with *a* common usage of the term. Who can deny, for example, that in each instance the back is "arched," that the ears are "long," or that the tail is "thick at the base and tapering gradually"?

Neologisms. The prevalence of multi-usage in a language is directly related to the extent of the *neologizing* which occurs in that language. When something new appears—an invention, a novel event, a new relationship or combination, and so on—how does it become named? Basically, there are two neological tacks: (1) Invent a new word (word coinage) or (2) use an old word in a different way (usage coinage).

1) WORD COINAGE. The coining of words is a fascinating art. Manufacturers sometimes pay handsome rewards to those who contrive new names which most aptly and appealingly represent their products. Especially impressive are the fabricated labels for the miracle ingredients of some products. Somehow the term suggests a mystique of power, romance, or virtue which even the Federal Trade Commission finds difficult to refute.

A special kind of word coinage is the acronym such as:

RADAR: *R*adio *D*etecting *A*nd *R*anging
SCUBA: *S*elf *C*ontained *U*nderwater *B*reathing *A*pparatus
LASER: *L*ight *A*mplification by *S*timulated *E*mission of *R*adiation
LEM: *L*unar *E*xcursion *M*odule
SNAFU: (The ubiquitous term from World War II) *S*ituation *N*ormal: *A*ll *F*ouled *U*p.[7]

Sometimes words are coined by combining words or parts of words: television, phonevision, motel, teen-ager. Or they are nick-

---

[6] From "Aardvark," *Encyclopaedia Britannica* (1957) p. 4. Reprinted by permission.

[7] *Approximate* translation.

names for longer words such as *fan* which is short for *fanatic* and nincompoop which is a telescoped version of *non compos mentis.* Often common nouns spring from the name of the person who innovated, discovered, or was otherwise associated with the referent.

Earl of Sandwich	Jules Léotard
Lord Cardigan	George Pullman
Lord Raglan	James Watt
Earl of Davenport	Count Ferdinand von Zeppelin
Lord Chesterfield	Antoine Sax
Charles C. Boycott	François-René de Chateaubriand
Rudolph Diesel	Vidkun Quisling
Daniel Fahrenheit	Gaston Chevrolet
Colonel Martinet	Joseph I. Guillotine
Nicolas Chauvin	Etienne de Silhouette

And lest the ladies feel neglected: Amelia Bloomer.

Flowers seem especially beholden to individuals for their names. Among their benefactors:

Michel Bégon	Matthias de l'Obel
Georg Camel	Joel Poinsett
Anders Dahl	Caspar Wistar
William Forsythe	Johann Gottfried Zinn
Alexander Garden	

Our language is occasionally enriched by the proper name of a fictional character becoming a genetic word: *babbitt—quixotic—malapropism—mentor—gargantuan—pollyanna—robot—serendipity.*

2) USAGE COINAGE. The kind of neologism which is more germane to bypassing, however, is that which occurs when a new usage is made of an existing word. But briefly in defense, were it not for usage coinage, puns, sad to contemplate, would be impossible. Thus, we would have been deprived of the delightful liberties taken by the suppliers of names for the colors of the '69 Maverick: *Thanks Vermillion, Hulla Blue, Anti-Establish Mint, Last Stand Custard, Freudian Gilt,* and *Original Cinnamon.* Maverick's marketers opted not to use *Come-and-Get-Me Copper, Gang Green,* and *Statuatory Grape.*

Highlighting the frequency of usage coinage *Life* recently published a list of words which are now being used in ways which are quite different from (and in addition to) the way(s) they were defined less than a decade ago.[8]

---

[8] *Life,* January 23, 1970, p. 28.

acid	demonstration	militant	silo
AFL	dove	Minuteman	soul
Apollo	drop out	moratorium	split
bag	freak	pad	Dr. Spock
black	grass	panther	stoned
blitz	hangup	pig	straight
bread	hawk	pill	topless
brother	head	pot	transplant
busing	joint	Pueblo	trip
Camelot	Sen. McCarthy	rap	turn on
camp	mace	rock	Wallace

This "piling on" of usages moved one anonymous bard to express his frustration in verse:

> Remember when hippie meant big in the hips,
> And a trip involved travel in cars, planes and ships?
> When pot was a vessel for cooking things in,
> And hooked was what grandmother's rugs may have been?
> When fix was a verb that meant mend or repair,
> And be-in meant merely existing somewhere?
> When neat meant well-organized, tidy and clean,
> And grass was a ground cover, normally green?
> When groovy meant furrowed with channels and hollows,
> And birds were winged creatures, like robins and swallows?
> When fuzz was a substance, real fluffy, like lint,
> And bread came from bakeries and not from the mint?
> When roll meant a bun, and rock was a stone,
> And hang-up was something you did with the phone?
> It's groovy, man, groovy, but English it's not.
> Methinks that our language is going to pot.

The *accumulation* of *usages* occurs incessantly in a living language. And if we consider some of the special kinds of usage accumulation we may be alerted to some of the areas of potential bypassing. Among them: (*a*) etymological shifts, (*b*) regionalisms, and (*c*) technical/common usage.

a) *Etymological shifts*.   A great many of our older words have undergone etymological shifts. That is, they have acquired new usages as they have been passed down through time. Some of the usages drop out after a time, but many remain, and the result is often a formidable accumulation of definitions, all of which are operating presently. The word *mess* is a good example. A Latin term, it originally stood for *something sent*. This usage is still reflected in words such as *message, messenger, mission, missile, missive, missionary, emissary, emission, remission,* and so on. Later *mess* came to represent food *sent* from the kitchen to the dining table; then a quantity of soft food (*mess* of porridge) ; then a sufficient quantity of a certain kind of food for a dish or meal (*mess* of peas) . Still later, *mess* referred to the entire dining situation including the people sitting about the dining table (the soldiers were at *mess*) . Finally, *mess* came to denote the various dinnerware, glasses, and dishes with the unfinished food still clinging to them which were piled together in a heap after dinner, and thus represents any general disorganization (what a *mess!*) .[9] We even speak of *emotionally* disorganized people in this way. (Is she a *mess!*)

We have a great knack for using old words in new ways. The words listed on page 257 are among the thousands of words which have acquired new usages during the last several years. Incidentally, I have found that whether one approves of them or not, it is generally wise to keep abreast of these new usages. Recently, my office was chilly, and I walked into my young secretary's office to ask: "Are you cool in here?" "Crazy, man!" she responded gleefully.

The rapidity of the etymological shifts is one reason why learning English is so difficult for foreigners. While they may have mastered the grammar and conventional usages (which remain relatively constant) , they may have trouble keeping up with the ever-changing idiom. Not long ago a student from India enrolled at Northwestern University. On his first day at the university, an American student generously escorted him about the campus, helpfully pointing out the buildings in which the new student would be having classes, the cafeterias, library, and so on. Finally, they returned to the Indian's dormitory room. When the American had seen that the newcomer was comfortably situated, he left with a cheery, "See you later!" The Indian stayed up until 3 o'clock in the morning, for he did not want to be so impolite as to retire when his new friend had obviously promised to return!

A Thailander enrolled at another midwestern university. He eagerly waited for an opportunity to meet the university's president, a renowned scholar. Finally, he was granted an appointment and, with the utmost of humility and solemnity, walked into the presi-

---

[9] Adapted from "Meanings of 'Mess,' " by Dwight Everett Hawkins, *Word Study* (published by G. & C. Merriam Co., Springfield, Mass.), October 1956.

dent's office. He bowed deeply to the president and said: " I am most honored to meet with you, sir. I know that you are a very wise guy."

And sometimes the tables are turned. Copywriters for General Motors discovered that "Body by Fisher" became "Corpse by Fisher" in Flemish. And one U.S. airline learned after a vigorous advertising campaign that their luxurious "rendezvous lounges" were misconstrued. In Portuguese, "rendezvous" denotes a room hired for assignations.

b) <u>*Regional variations.*</u> Word usages <u>vary</u>, not only from time to time but <u>from geographical region to region</u>. Jimmy in his quest for "pop" learned this the hard way. What is a "sweet roll" in some areas is a "bun" in others and a "danish" in still others. "Evening" in some part of the South is the period from noon through twilight. In the rest of the country, however, it generally refers to the period from sunset or the evening meal to ordinary bedtime.

The Pennsylvania Dutch present a special communication problem. These good people speak English all right, but often using a Germanic-type grammar. The results are sometimes quite charming:

"Throw Papa down the stairs his hat."
Girl to her brother chopping wood: "Chonny—come from the woodpile in .' . . Mom's on the table still . . . and Pop's et himself already."

But how would you respond to the pleasant chap, standing in front of you in a line at the post office, who asks: "If a body goes quick out and comes right aways back in again, will he be where he was yet?" And no one will be able to convince the American motorist that the English speak "English."

This summer my wife and I rented a little Morris Minor Saloon and traveled about 3,500 miles in England, Wales and Scotland. Previously I had read the highway regulations, but we were most of the summer learning the British way of addressing the automobile driver and tourist. If we saw a sign ROAD UP, we came to learn that it meant "Road Taken Up" or "Road Repairs Ahead." Near Chepstow we were asked to detour (the British call it DIVERSION) because, said the man who directed us, there had been a BUMP down the road. We could see two cars locked together in a collision.

It is a little shocking to see a sign BENDS FOR ONE-HALF MILE, meaning curves, or DOUBLE BEND, for S-curve. CONCEALED TURNING means "Blind Corner" in England. Near London, you may find a warning DUAL CARRIAGEWAY, meaning "Divided Highway," and at the other end TERMINATION DUAL CARRIAGEWAY, meaning, of course, the end of the divided highway. Instead of "No Passing" the sign reads NO OVERTAKING. When the danger zone is passed, you come to END OF PROHIBITION! You are told not to "Stop" but HALT at highway intersections. If you try to park in a no-parking area, you find a sign NO WAITING.

In town you can get a HACKNEY CARRIAGE just as quickly as you can get a taxi over here. If you want to travel with a trailer, you go down and rent or buy a CARAVAN. You should carry a TORCH with you in your car always, since you might have trouble at night and need a flashlight. If the day is hot, you can stop and get some MINERALS, i.e., cold drinks (though we seldom found them really cold). Sometime during your tour you will need to visit the GENTLEMAN'S HAIRDRESSER (barbershop). As we toured, we POPPED IN at one small hotel after another, either to eat or spend the night, and we learned that the next morning the maid always TURNED THE ROOM OUT to prepare for the next guest.[10]

Small wonder that G. B. Shaw described England and the United States as two great nations separated by the barrier of a common language.

c) _Technical common usage._   Specialists (and almost everyone is a specialist to some degree) tend to develop their own "private language." Salesmen speak of "closure" (the completion of a sale); plumbers of "wiping a joint" (applying molten lead with a pad to join pipes); publishers of "fillers" (short items to fill out columns); television directors of "stretching" (slowing up to consume time); and laundry men of "mangling the wash" (smoothing it by roller pressure). Ordinarily, these specialists use these terms to good effect when communicating with their fellow specialists. Many of these words and phrases, however, are *also* used by the general public, but in quite different ways. Let the technician forget that the outsider is not accustomed to these words in his specialized sense, and the results are likely to be confusing at best.

I learned something of the intricacies of plain English at an early stage in my career. A woman of thirty-five came in one day to tell me that she wanted a baby but that she had been told that she had a certain type of heart-disease which might not interfere with a normal life but would be dangerous if she ever had a baby. From her description I thought at

---

10 Clyde S. Kilby, "Signs in Great Britain," *Word Study,* December 1955. Copyright 1955 by G. & C. Merriam Co., publishers of the Merriam-Webster Dictionaries. Reprinted by permission.

once of mitral stenosis. This condition is characterized by a rather distinctive rumbling murmur near the apex of the heart, and especially by a peculiar vibration felt by the examining finger on the patient's chest. The vibration is known as the "thrill" of mitral stenosis.

When this woman had been undressed and was lying on my table in her white kimona, my stethoscope quickly found the heart-sounds I had expected. Dictating to my nurse, I described them carefully. I put my stethoscope aside and felt intently for the typical vibration which may be found in a small but variable area of the left chest.

I closed my eyes for better concentration, and felt long and carefully for the tremor. I did not find it and with my hand still on the woman's bare breast, lifting it upward and out of the way, I finally turned to the nurse and said: "No thrill."

The patient's black eyes snapped open, and with venom in her voice she said: "Well, isn't that just too bad? Perhaps it's just as well you don't get one. That isn't what I came for."

My nurse almost choked, and my explanation still seems a nightmare of futile words.[11]

Miscommunication is also possible, of course, from specialty to specialty. The dentist's "closure" (the extent to which the upper and lower teeth fit together when the jaw is closed) differs from the salesman's. And the parliamentarian's "closure" (a method for ending debate and securing an immediate vote on a measure) differs from both. Consider the machinist who ordered a tree. "What caliper size do you want?" inquired the nurseryman. "About three or four inches," said the machinist, whose calipers measure *diameters*. The tree man brought a sapling only one inch across, for his calipers measure *circumferences*.

Computers and multi-usage. Because of the multi-usage of English (and many other languages) it is unlikely that computers will replace human translators—at least in the near future. The very precision the computer requires of its inputs severely limits its coping with a highly ambiguous natural language.[12] For example, when asked to interpret the sentence, "Time flies like an arrow," a computer gave two answers: "Check the speed of flies as fast as you can," and "Certain flies have a fondness for an arrow."

And when computerized translation *between* natural languages is

---

[11] Frederic Loomis, M.D., *Consultation Room* (New York: Alfred A. Knopf, Inc., 1939) , p. 47.

[12] In fact, artificial languages such as FORTRAN, ALGOL, and COBOL had to be devised to accommodate the computer.

attempted the problem is compounded. In one test, the computer received in English, "The spirit is willing but the flesh is weak." It is translated into Russian, "The liquor is still good but the meat has gone bad." In an English-Japanese attempt the output was, "Invisible lunatic." The input? "Out of sight, out of mind."

The fallacy that words have meanings

The persistent delusion that words *have* meanings possibly stems from what Irving J. Lee called the "container myth":

> If you think of words as vessels, then you are likely to talk about "the meaning of a word" as if the meaning were *in* the word. Assuming this, it is easy to endow words with characteristics. Just as you may say that one vessel is costlier or more symmetrical than another, you may say that one word is intrinsically more suitable for one purpose than another, or that, in and of itself, a word will have this or that meaning rather than any other. When one takes this view, he seems to say that meaning is to a word as contents are to a container.[13]

He suggested that when one acts upon his unconscious assumption that words *contain* meanings, he is insidiously led to assume that when he talks (or writes) he is handing his listener (or reader) so many *containers* of meanings. If this is the case, the recipient is "bound to get the correct meanings."

Saint Augustine recognized this fallacy almost 15 centuries ago when he argued in his *Christian Instruction* that words do not possess intrinsic meaning. "Rather, they 'have' a meaning because men have agreed upon them."

Words, of course, do not "contain" or "have" meanings. Apart from people using them, words are merely marks on paper, vibrations in the air, raised dots on a Braille card, and so on. Words really do not *mean* at all—only the *users* of words can mean something, with the words they use. This is a sensible enough statement to accept—*intellectually*. Unfortunately, our *behavior* with words very frequently does not abide by it.

But just what *do* words do—or, more precisely, what do people do *with* them? What happens *inside* people as they use words? By way of

---

[13] Irving J. Lee, "On a Mechanism of Misunderstanding," *Promoting Growth toward Maturity in Interpreting What Is Read,* ed. Gray, Supplementary Educational Monographs, No. 74 (Chicago: University of Chicago Press, 1951), pp. 86–90. Copyright, 1951, by the University of Chicago.

examining this internal verbal behavior, perhaps you would respond to the three questions below.

Question one.   In a redwood forest in Northern California stands a huge tree—15 feet in diameter at breast-high level. Clutched to the bark at this level is Super-Squirrel. (Why *Super*-Squirrel will be clear in a moment.) On the opposite side of the tree is a photographer who would like to take Super-Squirrel's picture.

FIGURE 7–3

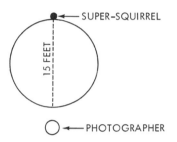

However, when the photographer walks to his right, Super-Squirrel senses the photographer's movement and does the same. When the photographer moves to his left so does Super-Squirrel. No matter how fast or quietly the man moves, Super-Squirrel is a match for him and manages to keep the tree's diameter between them. The photographer decides to back off a mile or two and sneak in from behind, but the uncanny squirrel detects this as well.

A squirrel hunter would suggest throwing a stone or stick to one side of the tree to scare the squirrel around to the other side. And that might work with an ordinary squirrel but this is *Super*-Squirrel! And a *given* in this case is that he keeps the tree's diameter between himself and the photographer at all times.

Another *given:* There is no elevation change such as tree- or mountain-climbing by either Super-Squirrel or the photographer.

The *question:* Can the photographer circle Super-Squirrel?

Question two.   Would you pay $25 for a slightly used but fully functioning Zalunk?

Question three. Does $X + 3 = 5$?

I have no way of knowing your answers but I can report the answers given by over 2,000 people including college students, business and government executives, police administrators, military officers, medical personnel, etc., distributed among 67 groups. Their answers were confined to three choices: "Yes," "No," and "I don't know."

	Yes	*No*	*I don't know*
Question one (Super-Squirrel)....59%	39%	2%
Question two (Zalunk) 11%	32%	57%
Question three (X)............. 5%	2%	93%

Note two aspects about the above figures:

1. The apparent controversy generated by question one in particular. (You might try the Super-Squirrel problem at your next party or coffee break—if you are willing to risk group disintegration!)
2. The rapidly mounting "I don't know" answers and, conversely, the decreasing assurance of answers as we move down through the questions—e.g., 98% positive answers ("yes" or "no") to question one but only 7% to question three.

And yet the three questions share a basic feature. Each contains a key variable and the question cannot be answered "yes" or "no" until that variable is fixed, i.e., defined.

The clearest example is question three. Obviously, the answer is "yes" *if* one fixes the variable X as 2—or "no" if he fixes it as *other than 2*. And perhaps that is why there were so few "yes" or "no" answers. Since the question-asker did not fix the variable for them, people recognized the *active* role they would have to play in fixing it for themselves.

But this was true of the other two questions, too. However, significantly fewer people seemed aware that *they* were the variable-fixers. To say "yes" to the "Zalunk" question, one (unless he were answering facetiously) would presumably have had to fix (define) "Zalunk" as something that was worth $25 to him to own or, at least, to satisfy his curiosity about. To answer "no" would require his defining "Zalunk" as *not* worth $25 to own, etc.

The question with which responders seemed *least* conscious of their roles as variable-fixers was the first. Many steadfastly held that the photographer *could* circle the squirrel and others tenaciously claimed that he could *not*. Put these opposing camps in the same room and observe the decibels rise!

The "yes" responders generally argued that the photographer could walk all the way around the tree. That would cause the squirrel to scamper all the way around it, too, so that the photographer's path would encompass the squirrel's route.

FIGURE 7–4

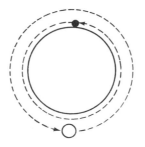

And THAT, according to the "yes-ers," is "circling the squirrel."

"Hardly," the "no" responders retort. "Circling the squirrel requires that the photographer orbit about the squirrel with the latter as the orbit's axis—or at least pass around the back of the squirrel.

FIGURE 7–5

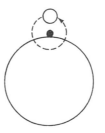

"Since a given in the case prohibits the photographer from being on the same side of the tree as the squirrel (to say nothing of the photographer's passing *through* the tree!), this cannot occur. Thus, the photographer cannot circle the squirrel."

So *either* answer is "correct" depending upon whose definition we accept.

Now why do people quarrel over silly, petty questions like this—and even sillier and pettier ones? Partly because they *think* they are disputing about *facts*—they are not. They are disagreeing about what *name* they will give to those facts. The issue is not a physical but a semantic one.

The cardinal delusion is their belief that *words* have meaning—apart from the people using them. Words are just so many meaningless variables—like "X" and "Y" and "Zalunk"—until someone fixes the *variable,* i.e., chooses to intend or interpret the words in a particular way.

When one assumes that *words* have meaning, he fails to realize the active role the communicator (sender or receiver) plays as a variable-fixer. The communication problem, then, is *not* that people fix variables (i.e., define words) . For we could not communicate otherwise. The problem arises only when (1) the speaker (or writer) fixes a variable one way, (2) the listener (or reader) fixes the variable differently, and (3) each *assumes* the other is or should be fixing it the *same* way.

DELIBERATE BYPASSING

Up to this point we have been presuming that the communicators, regardless of their degree of success or failure, *intended* to understand one another. Clearly, this is not always a warranted assumption. The speaker (or writer) may *desire* to be bypassed. Or the listener (or reader) may just as earnestly contrive to miss meanings. The *motives* of the communicators, therefore, must be considered in any analysis of the factors of a bypassing.

The story is told of the Congressman, running for reelection, who was speaking before a group of constituents. At the conclusion of his prepared talk, a question came from the floor:

"Congressman, you didn't say anything about Social Security. Just how do you feel about Social Security?"

Realizing that his audience was evenly and irreconcilably divided on the issue, he responded with a wink and a knowing smile:

"Don't worry about that subject, my friend—I'm *all right* on that one!"

And *everyone* applauded!

And a certain used car dealer used purposeful bypassing to his advantage with this advertisement: "Money cheerfully refunded in 24 hours if not satisfied." Some wishful-thinking buyers were convinced that they were being offered an unlimited guarantee on their purchase and that it would require only a day for the dealer to refund their money. Weeks (or days) later, when some of the second-hand autos began to break down, expectant owners approached the dealer, who retorted: "The advertisement? Oh, that meant I was giving you a one-day guarantee!"

This is akin to the ad which appeared briefly in a number of newspapers:

HOW TO AVOID THE DRAFT
LEGALLY AND HONORABLY
SEND $1

For his dollar the customer received one word on a card:

ENLIST

For truly "professional" bypassing observe it at the level of international affairs:

Belatedly from the Brussels Fair comes a story of the Russians' genius at the game of semantics—the skillful use of words to conceal facts or pervert meaning.

In the Russian exhibit was their small car, the Ziss. In the U.S. display was an American small car. Somebody got the idea of having a neutral automotive engineer compare the two, point by point, and decide which was the better.

After conscientious checking, the engineer gave his opinion: The American car was the better. The official Russian news agency boastfully reported the matter to the homefolks, thus:

"In comparative tests of Russian and foreign automobiles, the Russian Ziss placed second, while the American car was next to last."[14]

Purposeful bypassing can be used constructively as well. Take the case of a certain labor-management conciliator. The union contract had only a week to run. The union had adamantly refused to discuss terms with management and was preparing to strike. When the con-

---

[14] "Russian Genius" (Editorial), *Chicago Daily News,* April 7, 1959, p. 16. Reprinted by permission.

ciliator asked union officials why they had refused to bargain, he was told: "Why, we want a *substantial* increase [they told him confidentially that this meant 15 to 20 cents per hour], and we're dead sure management won't go along with us, so why waste time?" Nothing the conciliator could say would persuade them to meet with management. Finally, he turned to the company, where he was told in confidence that it was willing to give 5 or 6 cents. "Would you say this would be a 'substantial increase'?" he asked. "It certainly would be," he was assured. He then returned to the union officials and reported that the company was willing to talk in terms of a "substantial increase." With that, he was able to coax the union's representatives to meet with the company's. With his guidance, the two parties were able to reach a compromise in time to avert a strike that neither side wanted.

"Reverend Benson says for you to call later. He just got into the bathtub."

Parade Magazine. Reprinted by permission.

Of course, the *receiver* of communication may bypass intentionally just as readily as the *sender*. Our legal system takes this into account by insisting that a law must be obeyed not merely in accord with its *letter* (words) but with its *spirit* (intent). The law recognizes that the *letter* of even the most cautiously written statute may be subject to willful misinterpretation.

Gobbledygook

Before leaving the area of intentional miscommunication we should consider "gobbledygook." This is the smoke-screen kind of communication which, through the use of technical jargon, involved sentences, and polysyllabic words, seem more calculated to obscure than to inform.

In the pursuit of total organizational flexibility and integrated management mobility, one must consider such factors as systematized transitional capability and synchronized logistical programming as well as parallel reciprocal contingencies. Perhaps, however, the most significant factor of all is the basic balanced policy concept. For after all without optional digital and incremental projections the network is by and large merely a functional second or third generation time-phase continuum.

If that has you reeling it has served its purpose. Impressive, sophisticated—but utterly nonsensical. I composed it from the now famous (infamous?) "Systematic Buzz Phrase Projector" which was purportedly originated in the Royal Canadian Air Force. For aid in constructing your own esoteric prolixities and verbose amphibolies here are the raw materials:

Column 1	*Column 2*	*Column 3*
0. integrated	0. management	0. options
1. total	1. organizational	1. flexibility
2. systematized	2. monitored	2. capability
3. parallel	3. reciprocal	3. mobility
4. functional	4. digital	4. programming
5. responsive	5. logic	5. concept
6. optical	6. transitional	6. time-phase
7. synchronized	7. incremental	7. projection
8. compatible	8. third-generation	8. hardware
9. balanced	9. policy	9. contingency

Simply think of a three-digit number and select the corresponding "buzz words" from the three columns above. For example, 230 produces "systematized reciprocal options," an expression bound to bring instant respect—and confusion.

Gobbledygook leads not so much to miscommunication as to noncommunication. It is often the refuge of the insecure writer (or speaker). (If you can't say it clearly and simply, to paraphrase Jean Sibelius, you don't understand it.) Unsure of what he means or of the reception of his ideas, he—like the proverbial cuttlefish—evades his enemies by disappearing in a cloud of ink.

But whether bypassing be purposeful or not, the pattern of mis-communication is essentially the same and the corrective measures are applicable in either case.

CORRECTIVES

There is no panacea for curing harmful bypassing, but these time-tested techniques can prevent a great deal of it:

1. Be person-minded, not word-minded.
2. Query and paraphrase.
3. Be approachable.
4. Be sensitive to contexts.

Make these techniques *habitual*. Make them your conditioned re-sponse to a communication situation. Consider them as the finely tempered muscles of the athlete. Even after these habits have been established, they must be practiced and strengthened daily.

Be person-minded—not word-minded

The communicator who habitually looks for meanings in the *people* using words, rather than in the *words* themselves, is much less prone to bypass or to be bypassed. He realizes that the important issue in communication is not what the *words* mean, but what the *user* means by them. When an alert communicator talks or writes, he is aware that his listeners or readers may *not* necessarily interpret his words as he means them. When he listens or reads, he is aware that the speaker or writer may have intended the words other than as he is interpreting them at the moment. He recognizes that com-munication involves *variable-fixing* by the sender—*and* by the re-ceiver.

To keep person-minded in his communications he frequently asks himself:

This is what it means to *me*, but what does it, or will it, mean to *him?*
What would I mean if I were in *his* position?
Does my interpretation of his words coincide with his viewpoint (as I see it)?
Are the sender and receiver fixing the variables the *same way?*

Query and paraphrase

Query the speaker or writer.   Some of the best parental advice a child ever receives somehow becomes lost as he grows older. Almost everyone has been told: "If you don't understand the teacher, ask her what she means." But as time goes on, something happens to us. We evidently become too inhibited or proud or embarrassed to ask another person what he means.

A common complaint among my colleagues in college teaching is that students do not ask enough questions in the classroom—the very place where questions should abound![15] It is almost as if we believed that asking a question of a speaker or writer (assuming that circumstances permit) would lead him to doubt our intelligence! Nothing could be farther from the truth. Professors and executives alike indicate that they respect a thoughtful question. To them it indicates interest and a sense of responsibility rather than stupidity.

To be sure, some managers (and teachers) resent questions from subordinates. But more about that later under heading of "approachability."

So, ask questions when:

1.   You don't understand or can't make sense out of what you have heard or read.
2.   You think there may be a legitimate interpretation other than the one which first occurred to you.
3.   You sense something out of alignment—something which doesn't quite mesh with the rest of your knowledge of a situation.

Paraphrase the speaker or writer.   Putting a speaker's or writer's communication into your own words and asking him if he will accept your paraphrasing is one of the oldest, simplest, most useful, and most neglected techniques in communication.

I once observed a fascinating series of business meetings in which the technique of paraphrasing was put to a special use. The meetings involved the regular executive conferences of a certain firm, but a new touch had been added. An outsider was engaged to serve as moderator. The requirements were that he be reasonably intelligent, that

---

[15] Business executives express much the same concern. "What do you have to do to get people to ask questions?" a vice president of a manufacturing firm asks. "If people would only make *sure* they got it straight, we'd save a hundred thousand dollars a year."

he have a good memory for spoken communication, and that he develop the knack of paraphrasing the statement of another *without* embellishments, judgments, deletions, or additions of his own.

This is how it worked. The agenda having been set up previously, the meeting began with the moderator in charge. "Gentlemen," he would say, "the meeting is convened. Who would like to begin?" Some of the men raised their hands, and the moderator recognized, say, Executive A, who then made a statement. Then, *before* anyone else was permitted to speak, the moderator *paraphrased* A's remark. A would now either accept the moderator's rephrasing as accurate (in which case the next person would be permitted to speak) or correct it. In the latter case the moderator would then paraphrase A's correction, which A would either accept or correct, and so on, until A accepted the moderator's paraphrasing *without qualification*.

After A and the moderator agreed on A's communication, any other member was permitted to query or paraphrase what had been said if he were still in doubt about A's meaning.

The procedure sounds laborious, and, indeed, it was for the first few meetings. But after a brief period of practice this group of executives was holding conferences (which had been somewhat notorious for their miscommunications) with startling equanimity and progress. This writer has never experienced group discussions with so few instances of bypassing; moreover, many *potential* bypassings were revealed by the moderator's rewordings. An additional benefit, according to the men involved, was that with the moderator's paraphrasings the speaker was assured that at least one other person in the room understood fully what he was trying to say—a very satisfying and previously infrequent experience!

The meetings, it is true, were somewhat longer[16] than usual, but who can estimate the amounts of time and the money, effort, and nervous tension saved thus by the prevention of miscommunications?

The simple techniques of the query and the paraphrase can be potent defenses against bypassing. But discretion must be exercised. Occasionally a person may go to absurd lengths wherein the techniques seem an end in themselves rather than a means toward clarifying communication.

---

[16] Frequently, of course, B's reaction to A's statement was delayed by the moderator's interposition. For the special value of such delays read pages 498–99.

A Peanuts cartoon a few years ago made the point aptly. It showed Charlie Brown greeting Linus, who was making a snowman in his backyard. The dialogue went approximately like this:

CHARLIE: Hi, Linus. Did you have a good Christmas?
LINUS: What do you mean: "Did I have a good Christmas?"
LINUS: Do you mean did I get a lot of good presents?
LINUS: Or do you mean did I have a good time with all my cousins who came to visit?
LINUS: Or do you mean was it good in a spiritual sense?
LINUS: Or do you mean . . .
CHARLIE: (Sigh)

Be approachable

The responsibilities of the sender. So far we have been discussing the techniques of querying and paraphrasing from the receiver's point of view; that is, how the listener or reader should use them. But communication is a two-way street, with responsibilities at both ends. The sender (speaker, writer) should do his utmost to make querying and paraphrasing possible. He should not only permit it or make himself approachable—he should encourage it, invite it— even, on some occasions, insist on it.

But some people in positions of responsibility are threatened by feedback. They may feel so insecure or poorly versed in their field that they regard a question as a challenge they must ward off. Ironically, the defensiveness of a manager, for example, often leads to even more destructive consequences than those he feared.

For under the best of circumstances most subordinates are somewhat inhibited in dealing with their superiors. Conditioned by past experiences with authority figures and regarding the boss as reward-controller, the subordinate tends to be circumspect in communicating upward. So when a manager deliberately—or unwittingly—becomes *unapproachable,* he virtually assures the strangulation of the channel up to him.

To the extent that communicating up to the boss is perceived as dangerous, painful, embarrassing, or unpleasant the upward flow will be curtailed and filtered. The boss just won't get the bad news until it becomes *so bad* it can no longer be concealed from him— then he *really* has a problem!

A superior who thus contributes to an "approachability gap" between himself and his people is doing a disservice to them, to his organization, and particularly to himself.

A useful daily self-examination:

Am I approachable?[17] Do my people[18] really feel free to query, paraphrase, and, in general, communicate up to me? Have I done everything possible to make their channel to me free and clear—and do I *keep* it that way? Do I make an extra effort to be approachable to more timid, reticent people?[19] Am I *genuinely* receptive to feedback and do I continuously communicate my receptivity to others?

Be sensitive to contexts

> **con-text** \'kän,tekst\ *n -s* [ME, fr. L *contextus* connection, coherence, fr. *contextus,* past part. of *contexere* to weave, join together, fr. *com-* + *texere* to weave — more at TECHNICAL] **1** *obs* **:** the weaving together of words in language; *also* **:** the discourse or writing so produced **2 : the part or parts of a written or spoken passage preceding or following a particular word or group of words and so intimately associated with them as to throw light upon their meaning [verbal context] 3 : the interrelated conditions in which something exists or occurs [situational context]**
>
> *By permission. From Webster's Third New International Dictionary © 1971 by G. & C. Merriam Co., Publishers of the Merriam-Webster Dictionaries.*

Verbal context.   Suppose I overhear two men talking. However, they are so far away the only word I pick up is "plufe." What under the sun did they mean?! The men are drawing closer and now I hear: "Say, Ralph, could you plufe me a dollar? I'll pay it back tomorrow." Then later: "It was raining last night when I landed at O'Hare. So the stewardess plufed me an umbrella, to get from the plane to the terminal."

While I may wonder at that strange word, I am now reasonably confident that I understand what they are saying. But why? No one *defined* "plufe." No one said: "This is what I mean by 'plufe' . . ." I

---

[17] Lest a current or aspiring manager absolves himself too readily—"my people really feel free with me"—let him consider the marked discrepancy between the subordinate's perception of his freedom to communicate up to the boss and boss' perception of that freedom. See: Rensis Likert, *New Patterns in Management,* pp. 41–47.

[18] By "my people" I mean the manager's immediate subordinates—those who report directly to him.

[19] This emphasis on receptivity is not intended to retard the development and maturation of employees. The manager must use discretion to assure an open communication channel without inducing excessive dependence on him by his subordinates.

guessed at what the men meant by this term from the *verbal context* in which it occurred. Using the surrounding words as clues, I zeroed in from an almost unlimited number of possible interpretations to one—a synonym for "loan."

Verbal context is not limited to the accompanying *words* in a sentence but consists of the neighboring sentences, paragraphs, and so on, as well. If you hold up an object and ask: "What's this?" the appropriate response might be "a shirt," "off-white," "$7.50," or "broadcloth," depending upon whether we had been talking about classifications of garments, colors, prices, or fabrics.

It is the *verbal context,* then, that provides the prime body of clues by which others deduce how we are fixing the variables—and vice versa.

Sometimes, however, we are admonished to *reduce* the verbal context—"boil it down," "be concise," "don't camouflage your meaning with excess verbiage."

Pliny the Elder, confessed: "I am writing you at length because I do not have time to write a short letter." And we are reminded that the *Lord's Prayer,* the *Gettysburg Address,* the *Declaration of Independence,* and a recent government directive on cabbage prices required 56, 266, 300, and 26,911 words, respectively. Certainly it is possible to overcommunicate.[20] But an equal if not greater danger lurks in *under*communication which provides such scanty context that bypassing is virtually invited. This memorandum purportedly appeared *briefly* on a federal agency bulletin board a few years ago.

---

[20] Discretion must be exercised especially by the sender, who must avoid unnecessarily long and repetitious communications, for they can be as confusing as if they were intended to deceive.

Dr. George Russell Harrison, dean of the Massachusetts Institute of Technology, recalled this incident:

"A plumber of foreign extraction wrote the National Bureau of Standards and said he found that hydrochloric acid quickly opened plugged drainage pipes and inquired if that was a good thing to use. A scientist at the bureau replied that 'the efficacy of hydrochloric acid is indisputable, but the corrosive residue is incompatible with metallic permanence.'

"The plumber wrote back thanking the Bureau for telling him that hydrochloric acid was all right. The scientist was disturbed about the misunderstanding and showed the correspondence to his boss—another scientist—who wrote the plumber: 'We cannot assume responsibility for the production of toxic and noxious residue with hydrochloric acid and suggest you use an alternative procedure.'

"The plumber wrote back thanking the Bureau for telling him that hydrochloric works fine. Greatly disturbed, the scientists took their problem to the top boss. He broke with scientific jargon and wrote the plumber: 'Don't use hydrochloric acid. It eats hell out of pipes.'" From "Inside Washington" by the Chicago Sun Washington Bureau, *Chicago Sun,* February 17, 1947, p. 10.

Those department heads who do not have the services of full-time secretaries may take advantage of the stenographers in the secretarial pool.

Somehow that reminds me of Groucho Marx' reply to the airline stewardess who informed him that "You can smoke your cigar if you don't annoy the ladies." "You mean there's a choice?" eagerly asked Groucho. "Then I'll annoy the ladies!"

Because of the necessity for conciseness, signs are particularly vulnerable targets for bypassing. Among my "collection":

Sign over a combination gasoline station and diner:

```
┌──────────────────────────────┐
│                              │
│   EAT HERE AND GET GAS       │
│                              │
└──────────────────────────────┘
```

One wonders whether the proprietor was (1) obtuse, (2) banking on others sharing his sense of humor, or (3) issuing a fair warning.

Sign outside a church announcing a forthcoming sermon:

```
┌──────────────────────────┐
│                          │
│   DO YOU KNOW            │
│   WHAT HELL IS?         │
│                          │
│   Come hear our         │
│   new organist.         │
│                          │
└──────────────────────────┘
```

Another church sign:

```
┌──────────────────────────┐
│                          │
│   IF YOU'RE TIRED       │
│   OF SIN - COME IN      │
│                          │
└──────────────────────────┘
```

Penciled beneath: "If you're not—phone 366–5619."

And finally this sign at a power station in Ireland:

> TO TOUCH THESE OVERHEAD
> CABLES MEANS INSTANT DEATH
>
> Offenders will be prosecuted.

Which seems only just for such a shocking offense.

Classified advertisements are another fertile field for inadvertent bypassing. The ad placer, keen on reducing costs, reduces his context:

> Apartment for Rent. View takes in
> 4 counties, 2 bedrooms.

> For Sale: 1969 Cadillac hearse.
> Body in good condition.

> For Sale: Large great dane. Registered pedigree. Will eat anything.
> Especially fond of children.

> Wanted: Man to handle dynamite.
> Must be prepared to travel unexpectedly.

Even grafitti is susceptible. From Norton Mockridge's compendium of some of the more imaginative washroom wall literature, *The Scrawl of the Wild:*

Written on the wall:

> MY MOTHER MADE
> ME A HOMOSEXUAL

Scribbled beneath it:

> If I buy her the wool, will
> she make me one, too?

Quoting out of context. Lifting words or even sentences, paragraphs, and chapters *out of context* is a well-known ploy of propagandists and others who seek to distort communication. This is hardly a new deceit. Witness the circular used by Republicans in the campaign of 1928:

They quoted an article from the presumably unbiased *Encyclopaedia Britannica* (11th ed., Vol. XXVI, p. 392), to show the corruption of Tammany Hall, and the danger of putting a member of the Tammany Society in the presidential chair. They quite failed, however, to quote the very relevant final sentence of the *Britannica* article, namely: "The power of the organization in the state and in the nation is due to its frequent combination with the Republican organization, which controls the state almost as completely as Tammany does the city" [*Nation,* Vol. 127, pp. 438–39].[21]

Some advertisers use similar tactics to their advantage:

The case of the paper filter. Early this year, the *Reader's Digest* furnished grist for another cigaret advertiser's mill. A January *Digest* article —titled "How Harmful Are Cigarets?" was a thoughtful and detailed piece, an objective and factual examination of the effects of smoking. It cited medical and other expert testimony and quoted findings of clinical research and other scientifically developed statistics. The impression it left was that smoking would do no one's health any good, but would not do any serious harm if not carried to excess. The author's own conclusion: "Smoking is a very pleasant, very foolish habit. Most people can indulge in it with no apparent danger. Eight cigarets a day, apparently, harm no normal person." That was the only reference in the entire article to the advisability of smoking only eight cigarets a day. Elsewhere, the article discussed the value of filters. It said using another cigaret as a filter removes 70 percent of the nicotine and using a silicagel cartridge removes 60 percent. It nowhere said anything about the efficacy of paper filters. Further, the nicotine factor was only one of over a half-dozen discussed in the article, and the article seriously questioned the over-all advantage of using filters of any kind ". . . with a filter one is likely to smoke a cigaret until it is shorter than if a filter had not been used—usually 20 percent shorter—and that extra length is the nicotine-filled butt."

Brown and Williamson used this article as a basis for a campaign on its Viceroy filter-tip cigarets. The headline said: "Read January *Reader's Digest* to Find Out Why Filtered Cigaret Smoke Is Better for Your Health." A short bloc of copy said: ". . . if you smoke over eight cigarets a day—you will want to switch . . . to the cigaret which filters your smoke."

The discrepancies are obvious. The *Digest* article did not say that filtered smoking is better for one's health. What it did say about filters had nothing to do with the paper type of filter that Viceroy uses. The reference to smoking eight cigarets a day had nothing to do with anything the article said about using filters.[22]

Returning to the issue of inadvertent bypassing—an answer to the problem of insufficient verbal contexts is, of course, for the sender to provide and/or the receiver to obtain enough related information to determine the intent of the excerpt.

In conclusion, be sensitive to verbal contexts, the surrounding words and sentences which may help to determine the meaning of any word, phrase, or passage. Ask yourself: Is this word, phrase, and so on, taken out of its verbal context? Might I interpret it differently if I knew what went before or after it? Am I giving my receiver sufficient (but not too much) context for him to understand my communication?

Situational context. What lies beyond the context of words and phrases? How does this communication fit into the larger framework of people and happenings? Make a habit of orienting yourself toward the situational context of a situation.

Suppose we reenact the Sipert-foreman case, with one change— Sipert now has a sensitivity about the "bigger picture":

FOREMAN: Better clean up around here.

SIPERT: Okay. (Then moments later after the foreman has left) —Wait a minute! The Boss has me working on this bearing. It's supposed to be a rush-order job. Now he tells me to drop it and clean up my work area. Something is wrong somewhere—I'd better check.

Clearly, if Sipert *had* "checked" (queried or paraphrased), the delay and embarrassment presumably would have been avoided.

Sometimes lack of awareness of the situational context can be even more costly.

Scram-ble!

KEMBLE, England (UPI) — Four Royal Air Force jets were speeding across England Tuesday when the rear pilot radioed: "You are on fire—eject."

---

22 "Advertising Abuses and the Digest," *Tide,* December 15, 1950, pp. 13–14. Reprinted by permission.

Flight Lt. John Rust, 30, bailed
out of one plane.

Flight Lt. Richard Duckett, 27,
bailed out of another.

Rust's plane was on fire. Duckett's wasn't. Both pilots landed un-
injured. Both planes, worth $960,-
000 each, crashed.[23]

Granted the rear pilot should have been more specific but will
Lt. Duckett ever forgive himself for not having asked: "There are
three of us; *which one of us* are you talking to?"

SUMMARY

Bypassing occurs when communicators miss one another's meanings. It may take place when they use the same word to mean different
things or when they use different words to mean the same thing. The
effects of bypassing may range from the trivial and humorous to the
serious and even catastrophic. In general, the immediate consequence
of a bypassing may be either an apparent agreement on meanings
when actually a disagreement exists, or an apparent disagreement
when an actual agreement is the case.

Basically a person bypasses because of the assumption, often unconscious, that words mean the same to the other person as they do
to him. Underlying this assumption are two insidious fallacies. The
first fallacy, that *words have mono-usage,* thrives despite the manifest
multi-usage of so many words in our language. The second fallacy is
that *words HAVE meanings.* This fallacy obscures the fact that words
are not "containers" of meaning but rather they are *variables to be
fixed (defined)* by those who use the words in sending and receiving
messages. In this sense, bypassing occurs when (1) the sender fixes a
variable one way, (2) the receiver fixes it another way, and (3) each
assumes the other is fixing the *same* way. *Deliberate* bypassing was
acknowledged. It is relatively easy to misunderstand or to be misunderstood, if one intends to do so.

Four commonsense but uncommonly used techniques are effective
in curbing bypassing. (1) Be person-minded—not word-minded.
(2) Query and paraphrase. (3) Be approachable. (4) Be sensitive to
contexts (verbal and situational). To be truly effective, these tech-

---

[23] *Chicago Daily News,* December 17, 1969, p. 3. Reprinted by permission.

niques must become deeply imbedded habits which, in a sense, are on the alert even when we are not.

POSTSCRIPT

If everyone at all times practiced the bypassing prevention techniques, the following probably would never have occurred:

Scene: Floor of the United States Senate

Senator Wayne Morse had been denouncing Mrs. Clare Booth Luce. The chivalrous late Senator Everett Dirksen sprang up and with his voice ringing righteous wrath demanded that Morse "stop beating an old bag of bones."

I don't think I would have wanted us to be deprived of that one!

DISCUSSION QUESTIONS

1. If you were looking for a church to join and you were invited to join a church that professed to be based on communistic beliefs, would you:
    a)   Refuse the invitation?
    b)   Report the group to the proper authorities?
    c)   Take some other action? If so, what?
2. Our Constitution states that "all men are created equal," but evidence clearly indicates that babies are born with great variations in mental and physical capacities. Discuss the apparent discrepancy.
3. During a discussion among friends, someone suggests that "more socialistic concepts should be incorporated into our federal government." Then he turns to you and says: "What do you think?" How would you respond?
4. Doing some research on differing socioeconomic classes you spend a couple of weeks in a tiny and remote village in Appalachia. These people refer to their shoes as "holy bibles." How would you respond to this? Why?
5. Precisely what is entailed in "bypassing"?
6. What unconsciously held, fallacious assumptions contribute to it?
7. Why might people find these assumptions attractive?
8. How can one prevent bypassing in his own communication experiences? As sender? As receiver?
9. How can you help others to avoid bypassing without insulting their intelligence?
10. "Our communication would be just as effective if the large sphere in

the sky that shines at night were called 'the sun,' if persons who wear dresses were called 'boys,' and if members of the Republican party were called 'communists.' " How do you respond to this assertion? Why?

11. "Words mean the same to the other fellow as they do to me." Why would communicators make this assumption?

12. The words, "sandwich," "diesel," "bloomers," "magnolia," and "quixotic," have what in common? What was the point of including them in the bypassing chapter? (p. 256)

13. What did G. B. Shaw mean when he defined England and the U.S. as "two great nations separated by the barrier of a common language"? Can you think of analogous situations?

14. What is the principle advantage and limitation of computer languages over natural languages such as English?

15. Give an example of deliberate bypassing. Are there walks of life where deliberate bypassing tends to be practiced? Is deliberate bypassing ever defensible ethically?

16. Discuss the four approaches to minimizing bypassing. Are there limitations to their use?

17. Regarding the "Product Information Program," which picture, Steger's or Robbins', was the more correct? Explain your answer.

18. Describe an incident, possibly involving yourself, in which bypassing occurred. Analyze specifically why it occurred, what might have been done to prevent its happening, and what measures would prevent its recurrence.

CASES

Was there a noise?[24]

In Sweet Esther, Wisconsin, Bert Johnson and Fred Carter were haled into court on a disorderly conduct charge. They had been picked up fighting in a drugstore. When the judge asked them for their story Johnson replied:

"Well, your honor, we're neighbors and Carter, here, told me he was going down to the drugstore—did I want anything. I said I'd go along with him.

"Well, sir, on the way down Carter says: 'I got a puzzle I bet a dollar you can't figure out—suppose lightning strikes a tree in the middle of the forest and the tree falls down. Now, there ain't no animals or birds or insects or people or instruments anywhere near the tree. Was there a noise when it fell?'

"Well, quick as a wink I says: 'Sure there's a noise—it don't matter if people ain't there.' Then Carter gets on one of them superior grins and says: 'I guess you ain't as bright as you think you are—there ain't no noise if nobody can hear it.'"

The two men glared at each other and Johnson continued: "Well, you know how it is, your honor—I'm saying there's a noise and Carter saying there ain't and we start talking louder and louder—one thing leads to another—I guess I gave Carter a little shove—then he took a poke at me—and so on and so on—only by this time we were in the drugstore and I guess we messed the place up a bit."

[*Well, was there a noise when the tree fell? How do others answer this question?*]

---

24 The case is fictitious but is it unrealistic?

The Product-Information Program[25]

The Meridian Corporation is one of the nation's leading manufacturers of television and radio receivers as well as other electronic instruments. It had been the policy of the firm to hold an annual national conference to which its 200 district distributors were invited at company expense. One of the most important events of the convention was the Product-Information Program. This program consisted of a speech coupled with whatever visual aids (motion pictures, sound-slide films, and so on) were appropriate. The purpose of the program was to introduce the new models and to explain their features.

The policy was to provide each distributor with a duplicate set of materials (script, films, recordings, and so on) so that he could stage a similar Product-Information Program for the salesmen in his own district.

To accomplish this, the materials were reproduced 200 times and shipped to the distributors' respective home addresses while they were still in conference. Thus, on returning home they would be able to commence their own Product-Information Program meetings immediately. Beginning the meetings immediately was essential if the salesmen were to be able to capitalize upon the national advertising campaign conducted by the firm simultaneously with the conclusion of the convention.

Daniel Steger, merchandising manager of Meridian, was usually in charge of preparing and presenting the Product-Information Program at the national convention. He would write the script and ordinarily engaged the Raymond Co., a visual aids firm in the city, to prepare his other materials. On this occasion he needed a rather lengthy sound-slide film. A month before the convention, Ted Robbins, a technician from Raymond, and Steger went over the plans for the film in detail. Robbins submitted sketches for each frame, which Steger approved.

Two weeks later Steger phoned Robbins.

S: Say, Robbins, is it too late to add another frame to our film?
R: No, I don't think so—what do you have in mind?
S: Well, this comes between the 16th and 17th frames, so we'll call it frame number 16A. I would like a picture of a stationary core with three or four small dots circling around it—do you get what I mean?

---

[25] All names have been disguised.

R: Sure, I got you—any other changes?

S: No, that'll just about do it.

R: Okay, fine, we'll add 16A and you'll have the finished product the day before the convention.

S: Can't make it any sooner?

R: 'Fraid not—we're swamped already.

S: Okay then—make that change and I'll see you in two weeks.

The sound-slide film was delivered on schedule on the day before the convention. Steger previewed it and when frame number 16A appeared, he stared in amazement. This is what he saw:

FIGURE 7-6

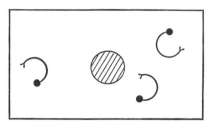

This is what he had in mind when he phoned Robbins two weeks previously:

FIGURE 7-7

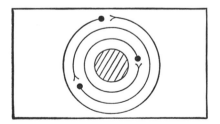

Steger jumped to the phone and demanded that the frame be changed. The Raymond Company assigned a double crew which worked the rest of the day, all of the night, and half of the next morning to replace the 200 sound-slide films and to deliver a copy to a badly shaken Steger, barely in time for him to make his appearance before the convention. The total cost of replacing the films was $1,250.

Jack McGuire[29]

The company I work for is engaged in selling metals to industrial accounts. These metals are steel, aluminum, brass, copper, stainless steel, nickel, Monel and nickel alloys for foundry work, as well as for fasteners (machine screws, washers, nuts, and so on), pipe fittings, rivets, and other items, such as nails, studs, and so forth.

The policy of the company in regard to sales personnel is to hire a man and train him in the plant for about a month to familiarize him with the products sold. The next step is to have him come in the office where he learns office procedure, basic facts about metals, pricing setup, company policy in regard to returned goods and other matters. An important step in this process is listening to a veteran salesman handle customers on the phone, as well as observing how customers who come into the office are handled.

Jack McGuire, a personable young sales trainee, had recently gone through this procedure and was now handling customers by phone. Jack had joined the company immediately after his graduation from high school where he had been an outstanding athlete.

In preface, it should be noted that during an average week a salesman receives about one or two calls wherein the customer has contacted the wrong company or the customer has a misconception about the products handled by the company.

One day McGuire received a call from the purchasing agent of one of our large industrial accounts.

BUYER (*without announcing his company's name*) : "Do you have any track spikes in stock?"

McGUIRE (*with a little chuckle*): "No, I am afraid you called the wrong place. You will have to try a sporting goods house like Dooner's."

BUYER (*angrily*) : "Thank you for the information," and he banged down the receiver.

One week later, our regular salesman, Frank Clifford, called on the account and was confronted by the buyer in an angry manner, "What are you hiring now, wise guys? I called up for track spikes to be used in our scrap metal yard and your salesman told me to go to Dooner's."

---

[26] All names have been disguised. Printed by permission of the author, whose name has been withheld by request.

Clifford explained that the man was new and that it probably was an honest error. Later, Clifford explained to McGuire that what the buyer had wanted were railroad track spikes which are used like steel nails where heavy timber is involved.

Room 406 [27]

It was 4:56 P.M. on Tuesday, January 3, 1967, on the surgical floor of John Randolph Memorial Hospital. Nurse Rhoda Fleming, an efficient woman with 15 years' service in the hospital was in charge of the floor that afternoon. She was making her final check of the rooms prior to the arrival of her relief, who came on at 5:00 P.M. In Room 406 she found that Mr. Henry Youstra, who had undergone surgery the week before, and who had not responded after surgery, had finally died. Mentally, she began to review the procedure on expirations— call a doctor to pronounce death, notify various administrative departments including Admissions and Reception, wrap body, and so forth. Suddenly recalling that she had a 5:15 P.M. dental appointment she decided to ask her relief, who generally arrived early, to handle the procedure.

While depressed with the death, she couldn't suppress a feeling of relief, for bed space was a critical problem at the hospital. She would tell her relief to prepare the room immediately for a new patient. She returned to the floor desk which was located near the elevators. The night nurse, Ann Simmons, had already arrived and was waiting at the desk.

"Anything new, Rho?" she asked.

"406 just died, so that room's all set to go again. I hate to see them go that way, but we can certainly use the space. I'm pressed—will you take over?"

"Sure. How about 411, did you give her her shot yet?"

"No, and you'd better do that soon. Old Doc Anders might be up, and he'd have a conniption if she hadn't had it yet."

"Does the office know that 406 is ready?"

---

[27] All names are disguised. Printed by permission of the author, whose name has been withheld by request.

"No, you can call them after you get things cleaned up."

Nurse Fleming then left, and Nurse Simmons gave 411 her shot and went about her other routine duties. At about 6:30 P.M. Nurse Simmons called the office and told them that room 406 was ready for occupancy, though she had not checked that room herself. She was told that a Mr. Leopold would be down from emergency surgery later on and would be given that bed. She then went on about her duties.

Visitors' hours began at 7:00 P.M. at Randolph Hospital, and as was her custom Mrs. Henry Youstra left home at 6:00 P.M. so as to arrive just at 7:00. Over the weeks of visiting her husband, she had acquired the habit of asking for her visitor's card by the room number, as the cards were issued by room number. The girl at the front desk gave her the card prepared for visitors of Mr. Leopold, and she took the elevator to the fourth floor. Nurse Simmons was at the fourth floor desk when Mrs. Youstra arrived there. Nurse Simmons recognized Mrs. Youstra as a nightly visitor and smiled professionally at her, not recalling which patient she visited, nor looking at the name on the card. Nurse Simmons placed the card in the desk file and Mrs. Youstra went down the hall.

At 8:00 P.M. the end of visiting hours, Nurse Simmons checked each room to see that all visitors had left. In Room 406 she found Mrs. Youstra dead on the floor beside the bed containing her husband's body.

The sturdy corporate homesteader[28]

In a happier time, so a U.S. Chamber of Commerce speaker tells us, the government used the public domain to "give every man a chance to earn land for himself through his own skill and hard work." This is the sturdy homemaker sob with which the air will presently resound when this gentleman's associates get to work on Congress. He may have been thinking of the California redwood forest. It was so attractive a part of the public domain that in this generation we have had to raise millions of dollars from rich men

---

[28] From Bernard De Voto's "The Easy Chair," *Harper's Magazine,* May 1953, pp. 57–58. Reprinted by permission.

and school children to buy back a few acres of it here and there for the public.

Under a measure called the Timber and Stone Act, a homemaker who had his first citizenship papers could buy 160 acres of redwood forest from the government for $2.50 an acre, less than a panel for your living-room costs. Agents of a lumber company would go to a sailors' boarding house on the San Francisco waterfront. They would press a gang of homemakers and lead them to a courthouse to take out first papers. Then they went to a land office and each filed claim to 160 acres of redwood: a quarter-section whose number the lumber company had supplied. At a lawyer's office they transferred to the lumber company the homesteads they had earned by skill and hard work, received $50 for services rendered, and could go back to the boarding house. "Fifty dollars was the usual fee," a historian says, "although the amount soon fell to $10 or $5 and eventually to the price of a glass of beer."

Under this Act four million acres of publicly owned timber passed into corporate ownership at a small fraction of its value, and 95 percent of it by fraud. Under other Acts supposed to "give every man a chance to earn land for himself," enormously greater acreages came to the same end with the sturdy homemaker's help.

The laws stipulated that the homemaker must be in good faith. Erecting a "habitable dwelling" on his claim would prove that he was. Or if it was irrigable land, he had to "bring water" to it, for a homemaker would need water. Under a couple of dozen aliases apiece, employees of land companies or cattle companies would file claim to as many quarter-sections or half-sections of the public domain and after six months would "commute" them, get title to them at $1.25 per acre.

The sworn testimony of witnesses would prove that they had brought water to the claim; there was no reason for the witnesses to add they had brought it in a can. Or the witnesses swore that they had "seen water" on the homestead and so they had, having helped to throw it there cupful by cupful. Or to erect a "twelve by fourteen" cabin on a claim would prove good faith. Homemaker and witnesses neglected to mention that this "habitable dwelling" was twelve by fourteen inches, not feet. Alternatively, a "shingled residence" established that the homemaker intended to live on his claim; or could be created by fastening a couple of shingles to each side of a tent below the ridgepole. Sometimes a scrupulous corporation would build a genuine log cabin twelve by fourteen feet, mount it on wagon wheels, and have the boys drive it from claim to claim, getting the homemaker a lot of public domain in a few hours. In a celebrated instance in Utah the efficiency of this device was increased by always pushing the truck over the corner where four quarter-sections met.

In six months the homemakers, who meanwhile had been punching cows or clerking in town commuted their two dozen parcels of the public domain. They transferred them to their employers and moved on to earn two dozen more quarter-sections apiece by their skill and hard work. Many millions of acres of publicly owned farmland and grazing land thus passed economically into the possession of corporate homemakers. If the corporation was a land company it might get half a million acres convenient to a railroad right-of-way or within a proposed irrigation district. Or a cattle company could thus acquire a hundred thousand acres that monopolized the water supply for miles and so graze a million acres of the public domain entirely free of charge.

Lumber companies could operate even more cheaply. Their employees need not pay $1.25 per acre or wait to commute their claims. They could pay a location fee, say $16 per 320 acres and the company could forthwith clear-cut the timber and let the claims lapse. At twenty cents an acre virgin stands of white or ponderosa pine, Douglas fir, or Norway or Colorado spruce were almost as good as some of the damsites which, our propagandist hopes, will presently be offered to the power companies.

These are typical, routine, second-magnitude land frauds in the history of the public domain out West—to describe the bigger ones would require too much space. Enough that in the golden age of landgrabs, the total area of the public domain proved up and lived on by actual homesteaders amounted to only a trivial fraction of the area fraudulently acquired by land companies, cattle companies, and lumber companies. Among the compelling reasons why the present public-land reserves had to be set aside was the headlong monopolization of the public domain that was threatening the West with peonage. Those reserves were also made to halt the waste of natural resources which the United States had dissipated more prodigally than any other nation. They had to be made so that a useful part of our national wealth could be preserved, developed, wisely managed, and intelligently used in future times. They had to be made so that the watersheds which control the destiny of the West could be safeguarded. But no one should forget for a moment that they were, besides, necessary to prevent Eastern and foreign corporations from taking over the whole West by fraud, bribery, and engineered bankruptcy.

Garnishment policy[29]

The loose credit policies of many retail stores has created a serious problem for many employers. These policies have permitted their employees to extend their credit far beyond their budgeting capabilities. Thus, they become delinquent with their payment contracts. Creditors, to effect repayment of their contracts, resort to legal means of collection. They file wage assignments or garnishments with the individual's employer and by so doing make the employer a collector of indebtedness.

In the Glennon Company[30] the policy regarding garnishments had been to withhold the required amount from the employee's weekly pay check and send a separate check for this amount to the creditor. With delinquencies mounting, the Payroll Department became increasingly burdened by the policy.

Finally, Glennon's board of directors adopted a new policy which complied with the law yet promised to ease the workload of the Payroll Department. Accordingly, the president sent a memo to the Department:

> Effective immediately. Honor assignments of
> wages but do not remit. Hold for full amount
> and make creditor prove claim.

Austin Horlick, a machine operator with an excellent work record, was a victim of the easy credit stores and when he found it impossible to pay all of his obligations as contracted, he skipped payments and became a delinquent on the books of his creditors. It was just a question of time before one or more of them, failing to have their accounts brought to date by credit letters and phone calls, filed wage assignments with his employer.

---

[29] The author's name has been withheld by request.

[30] All names have been disguised.

The Quick Money Loan Company was one of these creditors. Tom Lederer, the Quick Money's manager, called Alan Curland, Glennon's paymaster, to inquire about the status of his assignment. The men were acquainted through many similar contacts.

TOM: Al? Tom, at Quick Money. What is the status of my assignment against Austin Horlick?

AL: Hello, Tom. Just a moment until I check his file. (Pause) You're first, Tom.

TOM: Thanks, Al. Pay days are still Friday, aren't they?

AL: Yes, Tom, but there has been a change in the company policy. I will not be able to send you a payment each week. The new policy is to hold for the entire balance.

TOM: That will be OK, Al. I'll mark my records up for a month and check with you at that time as to the amount you have on hand.

AL: OK, Tom, the plant is working a lot of overtime, so you will probably have about $30 a week held up.

TOM: Thanks, Al. The balance of the account is $171.23. At that rate it will take about six or seven weeks to wipe out the debt. Maybe Horlick will make other arrangements and get a release before then. Thanks again, Al, I'll be talking to you. Goodbye.

AL: Goodbye, Tom.

The following day, George Smith, a co-maker for Austin Horlick, called at the Quick Money Loan Company and made a payment of $100 in exchange for his release from the contract. This payment was made the day after Lederer had talked to Curland. Smith's payment reduced the debt so that the balance could possibly be liquidated by the wage assignment withholdings in three weeks. Lederer marked the record to call Curland again in two weeks to advise him of the correct payoff figure. When the time had elapsed he called Curland.

TOM: Al, Tom Lederer.

AL: Hello, Tom. What's on your mind today?

TOM: The Austin Horlick case. I received a payment on the account from the co-maker and I wanted to give you the payoff figure.

AL: Fine. How much do you need?

TOM: $80.46 will take care of it.

AL: Hold on a minute while I get the file. (Pause) Say, Tom, I can't send you the money yet: we haven't withheld enough.

TOM: How much do you have?

AL: $92.

TOM: That's more than is necessary. I only need $80.46.

AL: The assignment is for $171.23 plus the accruing interest, and that is what I will have to hold for.

TOM: Why? I just told you that I had received a payment from the co-maker and I will only need $80.46.

AL: I'm sorry, Tom, but the policy now is to hold for the entire balance.

TOM: But, Al, the amount has been changed and you will be holding more than will be required.

AL: Can't help it, Tom. I have my orders and I have to comply.

TOM: There is something wrong with that kind of thinking. Hadn't you better call your home office for clarification?

AL: No. They told me what to do and that is what I'm going to do.

TOM: I thought that the company was trying to avoid trouble? This stand is going to cause you to be deluged with law suits.

AL: I know it, but it is out of my hands and from what they have said to me in the past, I'm not going to cross them again. I told them that we would be spending more time in court than before but they don't seem to care. Guess they want to give the legal staff something to do.

TOM: OK, Al, I'll check with you later to see if you can't work something out. I hate to send this to our attorney as it will increase the debt that Horlick has with me. I don't see any reason for him to be penalized because of this foolish misunderstanding.

8

Allness

AN EMPLOYEE: You can't get anywhere around here. What's the use of coming up with any new ideas? They won't listen to you anyway!

HIS SUPERVISOR: My people are automatons—no drive, no ambition, no initiative. They won't move unless I push them!

MOTORIST: Never try to reason with a cop. They're obsessed with their authority!

POLICEMAN: I get fed up taking abuse from the average idiot behind the wheel!

A FATHER: I can't let my son use my tools; he'd ruin them in two seconds![1]

HIS SON: I just *look* at those "precious" tools and Dad blows a fuse!

HAVE YOU NOTICED the tone of finality and absoluteness when people sometimes talk? When they speak, it is almost as if they were declaring: "What I am saying is all there is to say about the subject—there is nothing more." It is hardly a rare characteristic. Stop in at your barber shop or beauty salon, as best suits your gender, and listen to the ease and dispatch with which the intricate problems of national and international affairs are neatly and conclusively solved. Listen to the talking of quarrelers, and you will find a similar note of arro-

---

[1] And he *really would,* dear reader!

gance, of unseemly assurance and know-it-allness—or *allness* as the general semanticist terms it.

Underlying much of this dogmatic, unqualified, categorical, close-minded thinking and communication are two assumptions—both are fallacious and usually held unconsciously by the communicator.

TWO FALSE ASSUMPTIONS

(1) It is possible to know and say everything about something. (2) What I am saying (or writing or thinking) includes all that is important about the subject. These assumptions are so patently ridiculous that it seems pointless to refute them. And yet a considerable proportion of communication is apparently based upon them. Perhaps, as Bois[2] has said, we need to crack through the hard shell of the obvious.

We can go about it this way. Pick up a simple object, say, a piece of schoolroom chalk. Examine it; study it. What could you say about it? You might mention that it is white, small, lightweight, cylindrical, nonedible, inexpensive, a writing instrument, tasteless, hard, smooth, soluble in water, about four inches long, about a third of an inch in diameter, a piece of matter, and related to our national economy. You might add that it is a mineral, usually calcium carbonate, capable of squeaking on a blackboard, brittle, a manufactured product, a schoolroom necessity, used in children's games, a domestic product, powdery when crumbled, likely to soil dark clothing, usually shipped in sawdust or in a protective box, inorganic, and so on, and so on, and so on.

While you might be quite willing to stop talking about the subject, you would not contend that you had said *everything* about it. But just how long would it take to say *everything* about it? A half hour? An hour? Two hours? A day? When we consider the origin of the material, its countless evolutions, and its dynamic atomic structure, it is evident that to say or know *all* about even the simplest object is impossible. This story about Agassiz, the great naturalist, is pertinent:

A scientist, he thought, was a man who sees things which other people miss. . . . One of his students has left an account of how he trained them:

"I had assigned to me a small pine table with a rusty tin pan upon it. . . . Agassiz brought me a small fish, placing it before me with the

---

[2] J. Samuel Bois, *Explorations in Awareness* (New York: Harper & Bros., 1957).

rather stern requirement that I should study it, but should on no account talk to anyone concerning it, nor read anything relating to fishes, until I had his permission so to do. To my inquiry 'What shall I do?' he said in effect: 'Find out what you can without damaging the specimen; when I think that you have done the work I will question you." In the course of an hour I thought I had compassed the fish; it was rather an unsavory object, giving forth the stench of old alcohol. . . . Many of the scales were loosened so that they fell off. It appeared to me to be a case of a summary report, which I was anxious to make and get on to the next stage of the business. But Agassiz, though always within call, concerned himself no further with me that day, nor the next, nor for a week.

"At first, this neglect was distressing; but I saw that it was a game, for he was . . . covertly watching me. So I set my wits to work upon the thing, and in the course of a hundred hours or so I thought I had done much—a hundred times as much as seemed possible at the start. I got interested in finding out how the scales went in their series, their shape, the form and placement of the teeth, etc. Finally, I felt full of the subject and probably expressed it in my bearing; as for words about it then, there were none from my master except his cheery 'Good morning.' At length, on the seventh day, came the question 'Well?' and my disgorge of learning to him as he sat on the edge of my table puffing his cigar. At the end of the hour's telling he swung off and away, saying 'That is not right.'

"It was clear that he was playing a game with me to find if I were capable of doing hard, continuous work without the support of a teacher, and this stimulated me to labor. I went at the task anew, discarded my first notes, and in another week of ten hours a day labor I had results which astonished myself and satisfied him."

After this arduous assignment was over, Agassiz did not praise his pupil . . . but gave him a more difficult task of observation and comparison. This was all the praise the pupil could expect, for it meant: "You are becoming a more competent scientist."[3]

Having established (hopefully to your satisfaction) that we can never know or say *all* about anything, we need to discuss how these fallacious assumptions arise and what can be done to cope with them.

THE PROCESS OF ABSTRACTING

The structure of our language contributes to the problem of *allness.* Just what do we do when we use language—when we talk, write, listen, read, think, and so forth? We abstract. Let me demonstrate

---

[3] From Gilbert Highet, *The Art of Teaching* (New York: Alfred A. Knopf, Inc., 1950), pp. 242–43. Reprinted by permission.

this by first of all listing a few details about a certain person I know. Among many, many other things he is:

a male	red-headed
over 18	a salesman
a husband	a father
a veteran	a human being
a citizen	a car owner
a tax exemption	a taxpayer
a golfer	a bridge player
a Scout leader	a possessor of Civil
a moderate drinker	Rights
a properly registered	an avid detective-story
voter	reader
a churchgoer	a teller of droll jokes
a baseball fan	a "lover" of music, rose
a Rotary member	growing, and swimming
a "hater" of soap	a student of current po-
operas, women driv-	litical campaign issues
ers, and tardy people	a newspaper reader
a consumer	a son

ETCETERA (for I could never list *all* about him) .

Now, what happens when I *say* something about this person? Suppose I say: "He is a good voter." What I am doing, in effect, is calling your attention and mine to *some* details about this person; perhaps to such details as "over 18," "a citizen," "a properly registered voter," "a student of political campaign issues and candidates," and so on. But, at the same time, I am *neglecting* and inducing you to neglect that he is "redheaded," "a husband," "a father," "a veteran," "a car owner," "a golfer," "a churchgoer," and literally thousands of other details that we might have attended to.

This characteristic of language use—this process of focusing-on-some-details-while-neglecting-the-rest—is called *abstracting*. When we talk, write, listen, read, and so on, we are *necessarily* abstracting. However, this is often difficult to remember. And when we are unaware that we are attending to some details about a situation, a person, and so forth, while simultaneously overlooking a host of others, it becomes extremely easy to assume that what we know or what we say is *all* that we really need to know or say. John G. Saxe has depicted the obfuscating property of abstracting on a physical rather than a verbal level in his charming verse about the six blind scholars and the elephant.

It was six men of Indostan
　To learning much inclined,
Who went to see the elephant
　Though all of them were blind
That each by observation
　Might satisfy his mind.

The first approached the elephant
　And, happening to fall
Against the broad and sturdy side,
　At once began to bawl:
"Why, bless me! But the elephant
　Is very much like a wall!"

The second, feeling of the tusk,
　Cried: "Ho! what have we here
So very round and smooth and sharp?
　To me, 'tis very clear,
This wonder of an elephant
　Is very like a spear!"

The third approached the animal,
　And, happening to take
The squirming trunk within his hands
　Thus boldly up he spake:
"I see," quoth he, "The elephant
　Is very like a snake!"

The fourth reached out his eager hand
　And felt about the knee:
"What most this wondrous beast is like
　Is very plain," quoth he:
"Tis clear enough the elephant
　Is very like a tree!"

The fifth who chanced to touch the ear
　Said: "E'en the blindest man
Can tell what this resembles most—
　Deny the fact who can:
This marvel of an elephant
　Is very like a fan!"

The sixth no sooner had begun
　About the beast to grope
Than, seizing on the swinging tail

That fell within his scope,
"I see," quoth he, "the elephant
Is very like a rope!"

And so these men of Indostan
Disputed loud and long,
Each in his own opinion
Exceeding stiff and strong;
Though each was partly in the right,
And all were in the wrong.[4]

Of course, this kind of difficulty is not uncommon even among those of us with 20/20 vision!

ALLNESS DEFINED

Allness, then, is the attitude of one who is unaware he is abstracting and thus assumes that what he says or "knows" is absolute, definitive, complete, certain, all-inclusive, positive, final—and _all there is_ (or at least all there is that is important or relevant) to say or know about the subject. Allness, as banker Alan Perry paraphrased the above definition, is what people have who think they know everything about everything—which is quite annoying to those of us who do!

CRAVING FOR CERTAINTY

Just when the speaker convinces me
Of what he has brilliantly planned,
Just when I bow to his wisdom he says,
"On the other hand—"[5]

This bit of doggerel reminds us of the comfortable feeling of _knowing_, of _being sure_. We may tolerate ambiguity and discontinuity to a certain extent but conversely, in varying degrees, we crave certainty.

"The demand for certainty," wrote Bertrand Russell, "is one that is natural to man, but is nevertheless an intellectual vice."[6] On a

---

[4] By John G. Saxe and printed in Lowrey and Johnson, _Interpretative Reading_ (New York: D. Appleton-Century, Inc., 1942), pp. 44–45.

[5] Arnold J. Zarett, "Ambidextrous," appeared in "Pepper . . . and Salt," _Wall Street Journal_, May 20, 1971, p. 12.

[6] Bertrand Russell, _Unpopular Essays_ (London: George Allen and Unwin, Ltd., 1951), p. 26.

doubtful day propose an outing to your children and note how they insist that you declare whether the day will be fair or foul—and their disappointment when you cannot give a firm answer. The same sort of dogmatism, Russell contended, is demanded, in later life, of "those who undertake to lead populations into the Promised Land."[7]

. . . So long as men are not trained to *withhold judgment in the absence of evidence,* they will be led astray by cocksure prophets, and it is likely that their leaders will either be ignorant fanatics or dishonest charlatans. To endure uncertainty is difficult, but so are most of the other virtues. For the learning of every virtue there is an appropriate discipline, and for the learning of *suspended judgment* the best discipline is philosophy.[8]

But he warned against philosophy teaching no more than skepticism for while the dogmatist may be dangerous the skeptic is ineffectual.

Dogmatism and skepticism are both, in a sense, absolute philosophies; one is certain of knowing, the other of not knowing. What philosophy should dissipate is certainty, whether of knowledge or of ignorance.[9]

Bacon expressed it more succinctly: "Learning teaches how to carry things in suspense without prejudice till you resolve."

The craving for certainty leads easily to oversimplification. Patrick Moynihan, former adviser to President Nixon, on leaving Washington said: "One of our greatest weaknesses as Americans is the habit of reducing the most complex issues to the most simplistic moralisms." As one historian put it, "The essence of tyranny is the denial of complexity."

One top executive cited the urgent need for "complexifiers."

Yesterday—so to speak—the man who could cut through the web of detail and get at the heart of the matter was the hero. He often moved to the top of the organizational ladder. He never seemed to be in doubt!

Now, some of us in my generation used to worry about Adlai Stevenson . . . Adlai seemed so damned indecisive! But *today* we worry more about the person who is *too ready* to fire off an instant decision that solves one problem and creates *twenty* more.

No one welcomes indecision in management . . . The need is not to *agonize,* but to really *analyze*—and to take *intelligent action* . . .

The point is *intelligent action* today must include an understanding

---

7 Ibid.
8 Ibid., p. 27.
9 Ibid.

that a business decision can have political, social, cultural, technological, even religious, as well as economic ramifications. The complex problems of our society which once might have been considered peripheral to business are now *central* to making *intelligent* decisions.[10]

For some the craving for certainty seems essentially motivated by internal insecurities. Others, in fairness, have "omniscience" thrust upon them by the roles they play in society. We dearly *want* the doctors diagnosing our illnesses, the attorneys handling our cases, and the policemen protecting our lives and property to be *right*.

The role imposed upon the physician is particularly relevant here. One psychiatrist analyzes that role as it is initiated during medical training.

The medical student in his freshman year studies as if possessed. In the anatomy class he learns every groove and prominence on the bones of the skeleton as if life depended on it. As a matter of fact, he literally believes just that. He not infrequently says, "I've got to learn it exactly, a life may depend on my knowing that." A consequence of this attitude, which is carefully nurtured throughout medical school, is the development of a phobia: the overdetermined fear of making a mistake.

The development of this fear is quite understandable. The burden the physician must carry is at times almost unbearable. He feels responsible in a very personal way for the lives of his patients. When a man dies leaving young children and a widow, the doctor carries some of her grief and despair inside himself; and when a child dies, some of him dies too. He sees himself as a warrior against death and disease. When he loses a battle, through no fault of his own, he nevertheless feels pangs of guilt, and he relentlessly searches himself to see if there might have been a way to alter the outcome. For the physician a mistake leading to a serious consequence is intolerable, and any mistake reminds him of his vulnerability. Little wonder that he becomes phobic.

The classical way in which phobias are managed is to avoid the source of the fear. Since it is impossible to avoid making some mistakes in an active practice of medicine, a substitute defensive maneuver is employed. The physician develops the belief that he is omnipotent and omniscient, and therefore incapable of making mistakes. This belief allows the phobic physician to actively engage in his practice rather than avoid it. The fear of committing an error in a critical field like medicine is unavoidable and appropriately realistic. The physician, however, must learn to live with the fear rather than handle it defensively through a

10 From an address, "Managerial Effectiveness in an Age of Certainty," by James W. McSwiney, president of the Mead Corporation, given before the Annual MBA Conference, University of Dayton, March 13, 1971.

posture of omnipotence. This defense markedly interferes with his inter-personal professional relationships.

Physicians, of course, deny feelings of omnipotence. The evidence, however, renders their denials mere whispers in the wind. The slightest mistake inflicts a large narcissistic wound. Depending on his underlying personality structure the physician may worry for days about it, quickly rationalize it away, or deny it. The guilt produced is usually exaggerated and the incident is handled defensively. The ways in which physicians enhance and support each other's defenses when an error is made could be the topic of another paper. The feelings of omnipotence become generalized to other areas of his life. A report of the Federal Aviation Agency (FAA), as quoted in *Time* magazine (August 5, 1966), states that in 1964 and 1965 physicians had a fatal-accident rate four times as high as the average for all other private pilots. Major causes of the high death rate were risk-taking attitudes and judgments. Almost all of the accidents occurred on pleasure trips and were therefore not necessary risks to get a patient needing emergency care. The trouble, suggested an FAA official, is that too many doctors fly with "the feeling that they are omnipotent." Thus the extremes to which the physician may go in preserving his self-concept of omnipotence may threaten his own life. This overdetermined preservation of omnipotence is indicative of its brittleness and its underlying foundation of fear of failure.[11]

Is it any wonder that when constantly pressured to fulfill the role people can sometimes be seduced by it? Internally generated or externally imposed, the need for certainty and simplicity leads often to elaborate defense mechanisms which assure that certainty and simplicity. The *allness* attitude, buttressed by its two enticing but false assumptions (see page 295), may be considered as such a mechanism.[12]

MODES OF ALLNESS

More specifically, what sorts of problems does allness contribute to? (The following are intended only to suggest some of the various manifestations of the allness attitude rather than to serve as exhaustive or mutually exclusive categories.)

---

[11] Dr. Leonard I. Stein, "The Doctor-Nurse Game," *Etcetera: A Review of General Semantics,* Vol. 26, No. 2, June 1969, pp. 209–11. Reprinted by permission of the International Society for General Semantics.

[12] For a further discussion of *allness* as a contributor to maladjustment see James G. Snider, "Studies of All-Inclusive 'Conceptualization,'" *General Semantics Bulletin,* No. 36, 1969, pp. 51–55.

Allness will tend to occur:

1. *When one talks, writes (or abstracts in any manner), is* unaware *that he is abstracting, and thus assumes he has covered it all.*

This attitude, which is exemplified by the paired statements at the beginning of this chapter, is epitomized by the expression, "often in error—but never in doubt." This is not to suggest that close-minded people never change their minds but with them it seems to be a process of moving from one state of certainty to another.

Now let us consider what may happen when such abstractors get together!

2. *When two or more people abstract different details from a given situation, are* unaware *that they are abstracting, and thus each assumes that what he "knows" is all.*

The six "students" of the elephant was a case in point, and the almost inevitable consequence of the state of affairs is the rigid drawing of lines and unintelligent, destructive conflict. "Behind every argument," said Justice Louis Brandeis, "is someone's ignorance."

"Letters to the editors" of newspapers and magazines provide abundant examples of this mode of allness. Each letter is, of course, an abstraction—it represents a selection of some details and the omission of others. But so frequently the letter-writer seems *unaware* that he has abstracted—that he has not covered it all. Consider this series of reactions[13] to a *Life* article:

SEXY MOVIES

Sirs:

The name of the photographer who captured that phalanx of Chadron, Neb. "mothers" ("Sexy Movies? Chadron, Neb. Tries Gentle Persuasion," May 30) might well have been Grant Wood, for this is surely American Gothic 1969! I look at these frozen, rigid, closed faces and suddenly for the first time I understand what the youth rebellion is all about.

Sirs:

You have published your all-time champion picture! Those seven women of Chadron! Good old-fashioned Americans mad as hell! More people like these ladies and we would soon be back to normal.

Sirs:

How vile, disgusting, vulgar and completely filled with sin! I refer

---

[13] *Life,* June 20, 1969, p. 22A.

to the small minds of certain people, a few of whom seem to reside in Chadron, Neb. as well as New York, London, Hong Kong. When will they learn that sex, in all of its many forms, is wholesome and normal in every respect?

Sirs:

What our area expected and what it got from LIFE were two different things. Once again the city slickers east of the Hudson have succeeded in labeling the ranchers and rubes of Nebraska as Rip Van Winkles to whom the 20th Century may yet become obvious.

It's nice to see our area get national publicity, and maybe the ladies' approach to the sex movie problem could be copied elsewhere. I just wish that one time someone, somewhere would let the eastern seaboard know that out here on the Great Plains we do hold full membership in the human race. Otherwise, some future Barry Goldwater may do more than just threaten to saw off the Thirteen Colonies.

I had begun to fear these readers would never reconcile their differences when a fifth writer seemed to settle the whole matter.

Sirs:

Thank God for those saviors of morality and decency in Chadron, Neb. It should be quite clear by now that there is a nationwide Communist-supported plot to encourage the moral decay of our youth through sex education in schools and lewd motion pictures featuring perversion and nudity. Besides, if the good Lord wanted us to be photographed running around without any clothes on, we would have been born that way.

How's *that* for unassailable logic!

When one assumes that *his* viewpoint—*his* abstraction—is *the correct* viewpoint, it follows inexorably that all *other* perceptions become quite intolerable. Which recalls a cartoon of a few years ago showing a lady driver and her feminine companion. In front of their car—*six inches* in front of their car—is another car. And the lady driver is saying disgustedly: "Will you look at how close that maniac is driving ahead of us!" As Jonathan Swift said 300 years ago: "It is impossible to reason a man [or woman] out of something he has not been reasoned into."

It is difficult under the best of conditions to concede points of view which differ from our own. Davis has an interesting diagram[14] of how a production expert's perception of a problem tends to differ from that of a sales expert. Each sees his own bailiwick as the central problem area and places differing emphases on what he regards as only related problems.

FIGURE 8-1

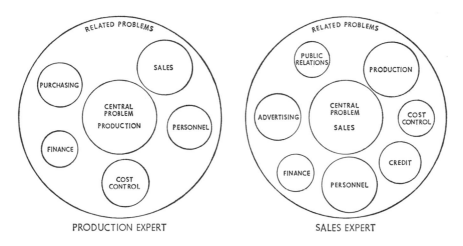

Sometimes when conducting management seminars I ask the executives present to "please raise your hand if you do *not* work in *the key function* of your organization." I have seen very few hands over the years![15] During a recent winter, Washington, D.C. suffered a heavy snowfall and an emergency announcement was made on TV and radio that night: "Only *essential personnel* need report for work tomorrow morning." The next day the agencies reported one of the highest attendance records in history!

---

14 By permission from *Human Relations at Work*, by Keith Davis. Copyright, 1962, McGraw-Hill Book Company.

15 My purpose here is not to discourage pride in or commitment to one's job or to his department. My concern is with destructive provincialism: preoccupation with one's own function to the exclusion of and possible detriment to others. A salesman, for example, might hypo his sales with extravagant promises about the qualities and delivery of the product. The resultant customer complaints could wreak havoc in engineering, production, and service.

3.   *When one evaluates a* group *on the unconscious assumption that his experience with one or a few members holds for all.*

This is still another form of reacting to the abstraction *as if* to the totality. Perhaps the reader is familiar with the literature which appears in Ann Landers' advice column.

Dear Mrs. Landers:

You are wrong when you tell the girls that there is a man shortage. I am 29, have a successful law office and a car. For several years I have tried every conceivable place, including church, to find a girl friend but have had no luck. Many girls marry when they are about 20. They marry men with whom they grew up. Most of the other girls are going steady. I can't even meet young women who are not married or going steady!

I am not quite average looking so women have snubbed me for about 14 years. I now hate all American women and especially USO and Red Cross girls. USO girls snub any man who isn't handsome or doesn't meet their specifications. When Red Cross girls are not on duty they will have nothing to do with enlisted men and date only officers.

My hatred for women now is such that if I saw a woman dying I would not walk a step out of the way to help her. If I handle an eviction suit, a woman tenant gets no break from me. When it is a collection case, if a woman doesn't pay immediately, I have her wages garnisheed even though I know she will lose her job. Why shouldn't I? It looks as though I will have to go to Europe to get a wife.

HOMELY

Dear Sour Grapes:

Better see a psychiatrist, bub, or the little men in white coats will get you. Or go to Europe— who cares?[16]

Admittedly, "Homely's" letter does sound extreme—but then don't some people talk, and think, this extremely on occasion? Supposedly, here is a man who has had *some* unfortunate experiences with *some* members of the opposite gender. But these girls can represent only an infinitesimal fraction of the group. However, "Homely"

---

16 *Chicago Sun-Times,* October 14, 1953. Section 2, p. 4. Reprinted by permission of Ann Landers and Publishers—Hall Syndicate.

Here is another letter to an advice columnist. I include it not because it's relevant to our topic but simply because I couldn't resist it!

I am a girl 11 years old. My mother and big sister keep telling me when I get older there is something they have to tell me. I think I know all about what they are going to tell me. I have heard it from friends. Should I tell my mother and sister now or should I wait awhile?

Debby

Dear Debby:

Tell them now. It's time they knew.

has apparently now forged an all-embracing, unyielding generalization about women which may well constitute a self-fulfilling prophecy. Thus, subsequent relationships with women are likely to continue to be unsatisfactory.

Sidney Harris develops this mode of *allness* more eloquently:

Some weeks ago, I presided as toastmaster at a large luncheon sponsored by the National Conference of Christians and Jews. A few hours later, I flew to New York to visit some friends living in Greenwich Village.

As I taxied into New York from the airport, the relationship between these two events suddenly struck me. To the average mind the phrase "Greenwich Village" conjures up a definite set of images, most of them bad, and most of them false.

To the reader of sensational journals or to the casual tourist, Greenwich Village is a weird neighborhood in lower Manhattan, composed largely of ranting poets, crazy artists, ridiculous perverts and "Bohemians" of the lowest order of depravity.

Actually, this is only a part of the truth and not the larger part. Anyone who has stayed in the Village for more than a few weeks learns that the painters, the poets and the perverts are only the most obvious tenants of the neighborhood.

The great bulk of the population in the Village is made up of substantial citizens living in well-kept homes, with well-tended children, dogs, and back gardens. The houses along 10th St. are charming and almost austerely Early American. Washington Square is bursting with roller skates, softballs and all the springtime signs of bourgeois maternity.

Now, what the ignorant majority thinks of "Greenwich Village" is exactly what it thinks of other races and creeds. It is always the obvious undesirables that, in the public mind, characterize a group or a neighborhood. It is the deplorable habit of human nature to identify any object with its worst attribute.

If a man drinks, we describe him as a "drinker," never adding that he is kind, humorous, brave and truthful. The part we dislike becomes the whole—until we get to know the whole. And, until "brotherhood" among people becomes a reality, we will be as unfair toward other races and creeds as we are in our ignorant and partial judgment of Greenwich Village.[17]

The second to last paragraph smacks a bit of the all-inclusiveness the author himself is condemning. However, the expression, "the

---

[17] "The Village Is Sadly Misjudged," *Chicago Daily News*, April 14, 1954. Reprinted by permission.

part we dislike becomes the whole—until we get to know the whole," is poignant. If I don't like the part am I likely to get to know the whole? Will I not tend to avoid it, to perpetuate my ignorance about it and thus my prejudice against it? Is it a case of knowing what we like—or of *liking what we know and disliking what we don't know?* After all, isn't prejudice, as psychoanalyst Judd Marmor expressed it, "being down on something you're not up on"?

4. *When one becomes closed to the new or different.*

"I can't get *through* to him." "He simply *won't listen.*" "His mind is made up; he *refuses* to be disturbed by facts." Familiar expressions? They are usually directed at a person who appears to have *walled himself in.* His tolerance for the new or different is nil. He seems to have lost—or suppressed—one of man's most distinctive characteristics—his *viability*—his apparently unlimited capacity to *learn,* to *grow psychologically.*

Watch a baby and observe how *natural* it is for him to *learn.* He is constantly reaching, probing, grasping, fingering, testing, looking, tasting, listening. Later his insatiable curiosity, when he becomes agile enough to exploit it, may drive his mother up the walls. But it is graphic evidence of his deeply ingrained drive to *know,* to *discover,* to *grow.*

And yet often by the time he reaches college, or well before, he has lost much of this viability. Why this transformation occurs is too complex a problem to explore in detail here. But let me suggest one way of thinking about the progressive psychological arthritis which seems to afflict many of us to some extent.

As we grow older, more and more of what we learn is actually *re*learning. To learn something new or especially something different *may require that we relinquish something we already hold*—that we discard certain accepted assumptions and cherished beliefs. Initially, this can be an unpleasant, uncomfortable experience. But some people find it a distinctly *threatening* state of affairs. And when one is threatened he usually resorts to some defense mechanism or other. *Allness* can be a particularly effective bastion in the above circumstance.

To the extent that I come to believe genuinely that I know all there is to know—or at least all I need to know—I really need not expose myself to novel, contrary, or disturbing experiences and ideas.

Unfortunately, I must pay a price for my insularity, comforting though it may be: *I do not learn—I cease to grow.* "It is impossible for anyone to begin to learn what he thinks he already knows." Epictetus' 1,900-year-old admonition is still valid. One who thinks he knows—whether he does or not—simply does not have the *motive* to expend the *energy* to do the *growing*—and it *does* take energy to grow psychologically.

And we must *will* to learn—for one cannot *be taught.* Gibran, the Lebanese poet-philosopher, understood that learning was largely an act of the student's volition when he described the province of the teacher:

> If he is indeed wise he does not bid you
>   enter the house of his wisdom,
> But rather leads you to the threshold
>   of your own mind.[18]

All of which suggests that there is an *inverse* relationship between *allness* and *viability.*

FIGURE 8–2

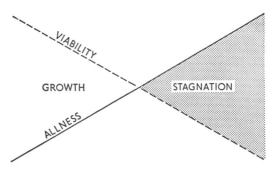

When one's *viability* is high his *allness* is correspondingly low. The gap between them represents the potential for psychological growth. Note, however, that as the allness *increases* the viability *decreases* and the growth potential diminishes until the allness exceeds the viability and now the potential for nongrowth, for psychological stagnation, increases.

This is not to imply that one will live out his life at a *fixed balance*

---

18 Kahlil Gibran, *The Prophet* (New York: Alfred A. Knopf, Inc., 1963, originally copyrighted by Gibran, 1923), p. 55.

between a certain level of viability and a corresponding level of all-ness. Indeed, if one were to plot an average day on the above chart, he might find considerable variation. The key questions: *How much* grey area does he generate? And does it occur at *critical times?* The following might be a typical day in the life of a hopefully atypical student:

FIGURE 8-3

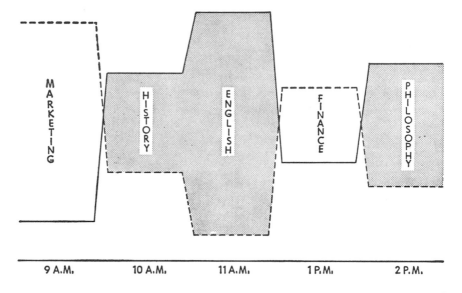

If he were to verbalize his fluctuating attitude, it might sound something like this:

"Marketing—Now there's a field for you! I'm really fascinated by the ways they find out what the public wants to buy and what merchandising techniques are effective and so on. I'm going to be able to *use* this course.

"History—Frankly, this bores me. What is it to know what happened so long ago? Times have changed. Life is different now, so why dig up the dead?

"English—I positively can't stand this! I've had this stuff drilled into me for 12 years. When will they let up? When I go into business, I'll have a secretary writing my letters.

"Finance—This is all right, but it's plenty stiff. Some of it is practical, but a lot of it I'll never use.

"Philosophy—Man, is this stuff up in the clouds! I just hope I can bluff through the exams."

A college student with this much shaded area isn't getting his (or his father's) money's worth out of his education.[19] But there is a more subtle danger here. Aside from the possibility of flunking out, the student is cultivating a pernicious habit. "Getting by" and stagnating can become a way of life. His innermost feeling may be: "If I can just get through this horrible course—or curriculum—and get my degree —or diploma—*then* I'll be free—*then* I'll start to grow![20]

I wish him well but I am not too optimistic about his prospects. Not infrequently, the young person who begins to vegetate as a *matter of course* during college days—or earlier—*continues* to die psychologically more or less the rest of his life. "Anyone who is too old to learn," said Harry Hoskins, has probably *always* been too old to learn." Our habit patterns can be insidious tyrants. "God may forgive us our sins—but our nervous systems *won't!*"

DELIBERATE DECEPTION

Abstracting, to recapitulate, involves simultaneously singling out some details while ignoring the remainder. When one is *unaware* that he is abstracting, he is in danger of unwitting, undesirable allness reactions such as those we have just examined.

However, the *deliberate* and *judicious* selection and suppression of detail *can be* a most cunning device for deception. The *Slovar Inostrannykh Slov* is the Russian dictionary of foreign words. Here is its definition for:

Boy Scout: A member of a bourgeois children's organization having a military-political character in capitalist countries.

A gross slander? Perhaps. But why is it difficult to refute? Let us dissect it.

"bourgeois"?—Admittedly most scouts *are* middle-class kids—but that is because most of the population of "capitalistic countries" is middle-class. The definition gains additional leverage because "bourgeois" is an inflammatory word in Ivan's lexicon.

"military"?—Granted, if being organized into "patrols" and "troops,"

---

[19] An employee with this much shaded area isn't giving his employer his money's worth.

[20] Lest these remarks be construed as pertaining only to college students, let us recognize that we are students all of our lives—or should be. An academic *commencement*, after all, is intended to designate a *beginning*, not an ending.

and having rank, and close-order drill and saluting, and so forth, is "military."

"political"?—Conceded, if pledging allegiance to their nation's flag, and helping to get out the vote (without respect to party or candidate) on election day is "political."

Moreover, the "military-political character" suggests Hitler's youth movement of the '30s, the *Jugendbund,* or Mao's teen-age Red Guard of 1966–67.

The shrewdness of this fallacy lies not in what is said but what is *not.* Where does the definition include the *essence* of scouting—the character building, the "good deed a day," the fitness of body, mind, and spirit, and so forth? These aspects are artfully omitted, for apparently they do not fit the predetermined purpose of the definer.

This is skillful abstracting. If an out and out lie is told about one, he can combat it with the truth. But when a *partial truth* is insinuated as the *whole* . . . How does one respond to: "Is it true that you've stopped using heroin?" without leaving a residue of doubt?

SUMMING UP

Now for a resumé. The rationale of this chapter can be stated as follows:

1. We can never say or know everything about anything.

One of the most tantalizing truths we know is that there is so much we may never know . . . We simply cannot overtake the coy horizons of the sea of unawareness that surround our modest island of perception. On this fact rests securely the conviction that humility is a vital part of wisdom.[21]

2. Thus, when we talk, listen, write, read, think, observe, etc., we *necessarily* abstract—i.e., select some details while omitting the remainder.

Talking is a highly selective process because of the way in which culture works. No culture has devised a means for talking without highlighting some things at the expense of others.[22]

3. However the very process of abstracting can conceal its own nature—that it is a *selection-omission* act.

---

[21] Wendell Johnson, *Your Most Enchanted Listener* (Harper & Brothers, 1956), p. 73.
[22] Edward T. Hall, *The Silent Language* (Garden City, N.Y.: Doubleday and Co., Inc., 1959) , p. 120.

Consider the *tone* of the paired statements at the beginning of this chapter. Does it not suggest the extent to which the speakers were oblivious that they were abstracting?

4. Thus the speaker, listener, etc., has no warning that he or the other fellow is leaving out details and often times the more one leaves out the harder it is to recognize he has left out anything.

I believe it was Bertrand Russell who said: "One's certainty varies inversely with one's knowledge." And four centuries earlier Michel de Montaigne in *Of Divine Ordinances* had written: "Nothing is so firmly believed as what we least know."

This was the trap that Chester Bowles confessed having fallen into.

How easy it would have been to write this book after only three months in Asia! The discoveries were then so fresh and exciting. The problems received were so much more straightforward and uncomplicated, and the issues so clear-cut. Now, back in America after eighteen months as Ambassador to India and Nepal the impression that is strongest is how manifold and complex those issues and problems really are. There are certainly no single or easy answers to the future of Asia, and I feel a deep sense of humility at the thought of putting my views on paper.[23]

5. To be *unaware* that one has abstracted, that he has left out details, that he has not covered everything, is the *ideal condition* for *allness.*

The greatest of all faults is to be conscious of none.

—Thomas Carlyle.

CORRECTIVES

What, then, can we do about our abstracting to correct allness— or better, prevent it from occurring? Stop abstracting—or at least reduce the amount of abstracting we do? The first alternative is impossible—aside from breathing, digesting, and carrying on other autonomic nervous system processes, virtually everything we do involves abstracting in some fashion or other. The second alternative is possible but it could be undesirable. The student, for example, does very little *except* abstract. He listens to lectures, participates in discussions, takes notes, writes research papers, gives oral reports, reads books and articles, takes exams, chooses a major, plans a career.

---

[23] Chester Bowles, *Ambassador's Report* (New York: Harper & Bros., 1954) , p. *ix.*

These activities and hundreds of others inside and outside the classroom require the ability to abstract. In fact, much of his training is calculated to develop and refine his abstracting skills.

And consider people working in organizations. Chances are their *principal value* to their employer are the special kinds of abstracting they do. For example, what does an accountant do? He takes myriads of individual, unorganized data and abstracts from them *meaningful abstractions* such as a profit and loss statement which he and others can use to make important decisions. Imagine carting 30 bushels of raw data into a board of directors' meeting and announcing: "Okay, fellows, here's the information you wanted!'

Generally, the higher a person rises in an organization the more critical his abstracting skills become. Indeed, often one extremely important factor *leading* to his rise is that he had or was developing the abstracting skills required by the more responsible position.

How could a business firm, a government, or any kind of organization *function* if there were not people who could conceptualize, theorize, extrapolate, plan, organize, coordinate, categorize, catalog, codify, generalize, evaluate, analyze, synthetize, and carry on other abstracting processes?

No. The antidote for allness is not the *avoidance* but the *awareness of abstracting.*

Some suggestions:

1. *Develop and maintain a* genuine humility[24]—*a deep conviction that you can never say or know everything about anything.*

Such as the humility displayed by a witness in court while being sworn in:

BAILIFF: Do you swear to tell the truth, the whole truth, and nothing but the truth, so help you God?

WITNESS: Look, if I knew the truth, the whole truth, and nothing but the truth—I would *be* God!

Disraeli said: "To be conscious that you are ignorant is a great first step toward knowledge." Lawrence A. Appley, chairman of the board, American Management Association, holds a similar view with reference to management development:

---

[24] Not in the sense of meekness and self-abasement but in the older usage of the word—*openness to truth.* As such, humility is an antonym for *arrogance, close-mindedness.*

He believes that before the executive can communicate effectively or, in fact, handle any of the other tasks of management, he must first know that he doesn't know. When a man develops the humility to admit that perhaps he doesn't know all the answers after all, then he is ready to begin to learn. It's at this point that management training becomes a wise investment.[25]

Mark Van Doren, Pulitzer Prize poet, feels men distinguish themselves by failure as well as by success:

The fallibility of man, *when man himself sees it,* can be a noble thing. Both the poet and the scientist would do well to look it straight in the face.

Man can afford to be deeply interested in his ignorance—an incurable defect, no matter how we brag of what we know. Those who know most are best aware of their limitations and of the limitations imposed upon all men because they are neither animals nor angels. To recognize these limitations and better yet to honor and respect them is at least to make a kind of sense out of the world. It will never be completely unintelligible to man, if only because he is a part of it, and not the most important part; but the best men have known this best, and their knowledge has made them both proud and humble. They have a right to be proud because they are alone in being able to ask the great question. They have a right to be humble because they are alone in being able to doubt their own best answers.[26]

And *doubting* (of this sort) does not come easily, wrote Anatole France. It is "rare among men. A few choice spirits carry the germ of it in them, but these do not develop without training." Nor without self-effort, John Ruskin would add:

Without seeking, truth cannot be known at all. It can neither be declared from pulpits, nor set down in articles, nor in any wise prepared and sold in packages ready for use. Truth must be ground for every man by himself out of its husk, with such help as he can get, indeed, but not without stern labor of his own.

2. *Recognize that you inescapably abstract (i.e., select and omit details) when you talk, listen, write, read, think, and observe—for when one* consciously *abstracts:*

---

[25] "Is Management Training Worth It?" *Nation's Business,* November 1957, p. 115.

[26] From remarks by Mark Van Doren, at Barnard-Columbia dinner meeting and symposium, May 5, 1959, University Club, Chicago, Illinois. Italics are mine.

. . . he is inclined to evaluate *the* quality *of his abstractions more judiciously—and, if necessary, to* upgrade *their quality.*

 Essayist Leo Rosten regards as shallow and shoddy the abstractions —not of young people in general—but of those who presume to speak for them:

I have read a slew of articles by the young—about their (and our) problems. The writers are bright, articulate, unfailingly earnest. Their grievances, as distinguished from either their knowledge or their reasoning, are often legitimate and moving . . .

There *is* plenty wrong in this muddled, unjust, horrid world. But our problems are outrageously oversimplified by the glib (old *or* young) , and by airy assumptions that money can solve everything, can solve it painlessly, can solve it swiftly . . .

What idealists ignore are the objective *consequences* of their reforms. (Southern farm labor thronged North, into already explosive metropolitan slums, when relief payments were raised there; minimum-wage laws *created* unemployment among those unskilled, dropouts, minorities they tried to help.) [27]

The oversimplifiers notwithstanding, it has taken men thousands of years to acknowledge that no one has all the answers—that the best we can expect from many of our social problems with their subterranean complexities is to reach a teetery compromise which nobody really likes but with which the various interest groups can live.

This is a worn but serviceable kernel of knowledge that one generation should be able to pass along to the next. But so frequently, the "new generation" (my own included, when it was new) seems to become infatuated with its own oversimplifications. And by the time its idealism and realism finally become congruent it has dissipated much of the irreplaceable zeal and energy of youth.

. . . he tends to be more empathic—to sense that the other fellow may not be abstracting as he is.

"Tell me," said the blind man, "what is white like?"
"It's like newly fallen snow," replied his sighted friend.
"Lightweight and damp?"
"No, it is more like paper."
"It rustles then?"

---

[27] If you wish to evaluate the quality of Rosten's abstractions, see: Leo Rosten, "Who Speaks for the Young?" *Look,* May 15, 1970, pp. 16 and 18.

"No, no . . . well . . . it is like an albino rabbit."

"I understand—soft and furry."

. . . he is more prone to be exploratory and innovative; he is less tyrannized by habit, precedent, and tradition.

Chapter 14, "Blindering," develops this aspect of *conscious abstracting.*

3. *Make a habit of adding or at least silently acknowledging the* etcetera *when you abstract.*

Adding the etcetera is an extensional device urged by general semanticists[28] to help keep ourselves aware that we never "cover it all." "The word 'and,' " said William James, "trails along after every sentence. Something always escapes."

Alfred Korzybski went a step further. He arbitrarily defined the *period* (the punctuation mark) as *etcetera.* He said in effect, "When you see a period in my writing or hear one in my talking, please translate it as *etcetera.* It will remind both of us that I have not covered everything."

The important thing about etcetera is that we should think it even when we don't say it. When we make a statement and think of the "and so forth" at the end of it, we show we realize that we have not said all that is possible to say about the subject, that we have uttered an approximation, a fragment, a partiality. The use of etcetera is an exhibition of the consciousness of ignorance, a humility, a sincere modesty.[29]

The point is not to make a festish of conspicuously "etcetering" every statement. This may suggest (sometimes correctly) that one is bankrupt for ideas or further examples.

"Buy my second-hand car. First of all, its depreciation will be nil. Second, personal property taxes on it will be very low if not nonexistent. Third, unlike buying a new car you won't agonize about getting that first dent. *Etcetera, etcetera, etcetera.*" The three *"etceteras"* translated: "I really can't think of a single additional claim for the old hulk but admitting this to you isn't likely to close the deal."

---

[28] So highly regarded is "etcetera" that it is the title of the professional journal published by the International Society for General Semantics.

[29] Leo Lerner, "And So On and So Forth," from "The First Column," *Lerner Newspapers,* September 27, 1955, p. 1.

"Etcetering" can also be used as a ploy to conceal the audacity of the speaker's views. The king of "The King and I" was wont to make the most imperious assertions and then attempt to disclaim any arrogance by vehemently ending the statement with "etcetera, etcetera, etcetera!"

4. *Frequently ask yourself the self-examining question: Do I have an "all-wall"?*

Do I find myself fending off the new or different? After all, I do have the power largely to protect myself from such "disturbing changes."

> Who is so deafe or so blinde as hee
> That *wilfully* will neither heare nor see.
> —*John Heywood* (1546)

CHALLENGING A MYTH

The crux, once again, is the *awareness* of abstracting, not the *avoidance* of it. While extolling the virtues of viability, openmindedness, and flexibility, in no way do I advocate a posture of indecision, diffidence, or vacillation.

Yet there exists a subtle but pervasive myth in our society—that the ability to decide and take action is fundamentally incompatible with the ability to learn, grow, and change. It is as if decisiveness and viability were polar opposites on a single continuum:

DECISIVENESS ⟵————————————————⟶ VIABILITY

Thus, according to this deceit, one could become decisive only at the expense of an open mind. Conversely, one could become open and viable only at the cost of his capacity to act. This is the oversimplification which H. L. Mencken helps to perpetuate:

> It is the dull man
>   who is always sure.
> It is the sure man
>   who is always dull.

The epigram is cute, pithy, and quotable. But it is a fiction.
Why the myth came to be I shall leave to the historians and anthro-

pologists. Perhaps it has something to do with the *action*-orientation of western thought—as distinguished from the passive and contemplative eastern mentality. Is it mere coincidence that so many of our folk heroes have been "men of action," "quick on the draw," "faster than a speeding bullet"?

Be that as it may, the single continuum is simplistic. I submit that decisiveness and viability are independent variables, that a more valid diagram would consist of *two* continua.

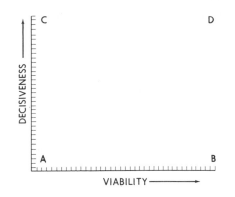

At *A* we see the *vegetable,* at *B* the paralyzed *ineffectual,*[30] at *C* the *impulsive.* The myth suggests that *D* is impossible—and that is why it is a myth. The *D* type orientation is not only possible but mandatory for leaders in our complex organizations.

An old Arabic apothegm is roughly analogous to the chart above.

> He who knows not but knows not that he knows not,
>   he is a fool—shun him.
> He who knows not and knows that he knows not,
>   he is simple—teach him.
> He who knows but knows not that he knows,
>   he is asleep—wake him.
> He who knows and knows that he knows,
>   he is wise—follow him.

---

[30] Some have criticized formal management training for indoctrinating aspiring executives with a *B* orientation:

> Preoccupation with problem solving and decision making in formal management education programs tends to distort managerial growth because it overdevelops an individual's analytical ability, but leaves his ability to take action and to get things done underdeveloped.

J. Sterling Livingston, "Myth of the Well-Educated Manager," *Harvard Business Review,* Jan.–Feb. 1971, p. 82.

Action and viability

The objective, then, is to be able and willing to resolve problems and take action while remaining open to experience. The goal is an attainable but difficult one. "It is hard to be strong and not rash," goes a Japanese proverb.

> The truest courage is always mixed with circumspection; this being the quality which distinguishes the courage of the wise from the hardiness of the rash and foolish.[31]
>
> *—William Jones*

A leader, writes Eisenhower, must constantly make distinctions. "One of his problems is to keep his mind open, to avoid confusing necessary firmness with stubborn preconception or unreasoning prejudice."[32] G. K. Chesterton expressed the thought more trenchantly: "I am firmly convinced that the purpose of opening the mind as in the opening of the mouth is to close it on something solid."

George Counts has confronted the paradox deftly:

There is the fallacy that the great object of education is to produce . . . the individual who adopts an agnostic attitude towards every important social issue, who can balance the pros against the cons with the skill of a juggler, who sees all sides of every question and never commits himself to any, who delays action until all the facts are in, who knows that all the facts will never come in, who consequently holds his judgment in a state of indefinite suspension, and who before the approach of middle age sees his powers of action atrophy and his social sympathies decay. With Peer Gynt he can exclaim:

> Ay, think of it—wish it done—will it to boot,—
> But do it— No, that's past my understanding.

This type of mind also talks about waiting until the solutions of social problems are found, when as a matter of fact there are no solutions in any definite and final sense. For any complex social problem worthy of the name there are probably tens and even scores, if not hundreds, of "solutions," depending upon the premises from which one works. The

---

[31] Quoted in *Forbes*, November 1, 1968, p. 96.

[32] Dwight D. Eisenhower, *Crusade in Europe* (New York: Doubleday & Co., Inc., 1948) , p. 256.

meeting of a social situation involves the making of decisions and the woking out of adjustments. If we wait for a solution to appear like the bursting of the sun through the clouds or the resolving of the elements in an algebraic equation, we shall wait in vain. . . . society requires great numbers of persons who, while capable of gathering, and digesting facts, are at the same time able to think in terms of life, make decisions, and act. From such persons will come our real social leaders.[33]

PROFILE OF VIABLE MEN[34]

VIABLE—capable of living or developing, as viable seeds, physically and psychologically fitted to live and grow.

I know some viable men.

They keep pushing beyond the horizons of what they already know.

They refuse to be stuck in yesterday. They won't even remain rooted in today.

They are teachable.

They keep learning. They continue to see and listen. All their horizons are temporary.

They don't deny today's wisdom—rather, they add dimensions to it.

They have strong beliefs, faith, aspirations, but they know the difference between belief and bigotry—between knowledge and dogmatism.

They are acutely aware of the limits of what they know.

They are more likely to wonder and inquire than to dismiss and deny.

They know a great deal, but they also know that they do not know it all.

I also know some stunted, deadened men.

Their outlooks have been blighted—their interest diminished—their enthusiasm restricted—their sensitivity limited.

They are the old fogies, though they may be young in years.

They strive only to stay where they are.

They see only the dimensions of what has already been explored.

They search with their eyes only for what is old and familiar. They have frozen their views in molds.

They have narrowed the wave lengths.

They are imprisoned in the little community—the little dusty dungeons of their own minds.

They are the conflict carriers.

---

[33] George S. Counts, *Dare the School Build a New Social Order?* New York, The John Day Pamphlets, No. 11, pp. 20–22. Quoted in John T. Wahlquist, *The Philosophy of American Education* (New York: The Ronald Press Company, 1942), p. 79.

[34] This was written shortly before his death in 1955 by Dr. Irving J. Lee, a truly viable man. From Irving J. and Laura L. Lee, *Handling Barriers in Communication* (New York: Harper & Brothers, publishers, 1956), pp. 148–49. Reprinted by permission.

> Not ignorance
> But ignorance of ignorance
> Is the death of knowledge.
> —*Alfred North Whitehead*

DISCUSSION QUESTIONS

1. "The essence of tyranny is the denial of complexity." (p. 300) . What was meant by this?

2. "Dogmatism and skepticism are both, in a sense, absolute philosophies; one is certain of knowing, the other is not knowing. What philosophy should dissipate is *certainty,* whether of knowledge or of ignorance."—Bertrand Russell (p. 300) . Do you agree, disagree? Why?

3. "Prejudice is being down on something you're not up on."—Judd Marmor (p. 308) . Agree? Disagree? Why?

4. Why is it sometimes so difficult to accept or even tolerate viewpoints or abstractions which differ from our own?

5. How best could you teach non-allness to others? How might a supervisor help reduce the allness of one of his subordinates? Vice versa?

6. Precisely what is *allness?* Is it the same as *abstraction?* Explain.

7. What is the relationship, if any, between *allness* and *viability?* Between *allness* and *decisiveness?*

8. Are there any occupations in which *allness* is particularly difficult to avoid? Why?

9. Some people seem to equate *non-allness* and *weakness.* Discuss.

10. Some apparently single-minded leaders, such as Napoleon, Hitler, Stalin, Mao, have been outstandingly effective for varying lengths of time. Discuss them in relation to the allness concept.

11. Describe an incident, possibly involving yourself, in which allness behavior occurred. Analyze specifically why it occurred, what might have been done to prevent its happening, and what measures would prevent its recurrence.

CASES

The kiss and the slap[35]

In a railroad compartment, an American grandmother with her young and attractive granddaughter, a Romanian officer, and a Nazi officer were the only occupants. The train was passing through a dark tunnel, and all that was heard was a loud kiss and a vigorous slap. After the train emerged from the tunnel, nobody spoke, but the grandmother was saying to herself, "What a fine girl I have raised. She will take care of herself. I am proud of her." The granddaughter was saying to herself, "Well, grandmother is old enough not to mind a little kiss. Besides, the fellows are nice. I am surprised what a hard wallop grandmother has." The Nazi officer was meditating, "How clever those Romanians are! They steal a kiss and have the other fellow slapped." The Romanian officer was chuckling to himself, "How smart I am! I kissed my own hand and slapped the Nazi."

[*What do you think of each person's abstractions?*]

Aldermanic election[36]

Allenshire, population 50,000, a suburb of a large city in New England, is largely Republican and predominantly Protestant. Many of its citizens are well-to-do executives and professional people. The per capita income of the suburb is well above the national average.

In a recent aldermanic election Martin J. Stewart, the incumbent Alderman of the 3rd Ward, was opposed by Ronald Green. Stewart's supporters distributed the following leaflet:

---

[35] Alfred Korzybski, "The Role of Language in the Perceptual Processes," *Perception: An Approach to Personality,* Robert R. Blake and Glenn V. Ramsey, eds. Copyright, 1951, The Ronald Press Co. Reprinted by permission.

[36] All names have been disguised.

ALLENSHIRE YOUNG REPUBLICAN CLUB
COMPARE YOUR ALDERMANIC CANDIDATES
Then—VOTE for Alderman Martin J. Stewart—April 7

Alderman Martin J. Stewart	*Ronald Green*
Residence	
212 Grey. Homeowner.	609 Wilson. Homeowner.
Allenshire resident 24 years.	Allenshire resident 8 years.
Family Status	
Married. 2 children, 4 grandchildren.	Married. 2 children.
Occupation	
Businessman. President, National Office Supplies Co.	Lawyer. Partner, law firm of Green, Weisman and Epstein. Former OPA lawyer.
Political Activities	
Assistant secretary, Allenshire Republican Club.	Vice president, Allenshire Democratic Club. Active in last November's campaign for Levine, Democratic nominee for Sheriff.
Local Government Experience	
Alderman the past two years. 12 years on Park District Board without salary. Now president.	None
Civic Activities	
Deacon, First Methodist Church. Charter member, Northwest Allenshire Community Club. Air raid warden during the war. Civilian Defense chairman for Allenshire during the war.	Member, Temple Beth Israel. "Active participant in community and charitable activities."
Endorsements	
Allenshire Young Republican Club. Allenshire Women's Republican Club. 3rd Ward Young Republican Club. 3rd Ward Women's Republican Club. Service as alderman rated very highly in poll of fellow aldermen and city department heads. 3rd Ward Residents for Stewart.	Allenshire Democratic Club. 3rd Ward Independent Citizens for Green. Committee of 100 Nonpartisan 3rd Ward Neighbors.

VOTE APRIL 7   6 AM–5 PM
VOTE FOR ALDERMAN MARTIN J. STEWART

3rd Ward Young Republican Club

Ronald Green's supporters distributed the following leaflet:

Biographical Sketch
of

RONALD GREEN

Candidate for
ALDERMAN—3RD WARD
Allenshire   Election: April 7

Born: [Nearby city], 1914.

Married: One son, 7 years old; one daughter, 6 months old.

Residence: 609 Wilson Avenue, Allenshire (own home). Allenshire resident 8 years.

Education: [Local university], 1936, School of Law, 1938 (Scholarship student—top man in class).

Community and charitable activities:
Participated in community activities such as factory zoning problem in south end of ward, Northwest Allenshire transportation problem, and represented community (without fee) in litigation concerning the Jackson School corner—gasoline station zoning problem. Member of several Allenshire civic, social, and religious organizations; lecturer on municipal, governmental, and legal problems; member, participant, and attorney for charitable organizations.

Experienced educator:
Member of faculty [local university School of Law] since 1947. Presently serving as member of that faculty.

Governmental experience:
Formerly Assistant Regional Attorney, U.S. Government Emergency War Agencies (4 New England states).

Professional experience:
Practicing attorney since 1938. Admitted to practice before state and Federal Courts, U.S. Court of Appeals, and U.S. Supreme Court.

Professional associations:
Member, Allenshire Bar Association; State Bar Association; Federal Bar Association; [list of national and honorary legal fraternities].

[*How do you analyze the two pieces of campaign literature? What are their authors attempting to accomplish? By what techniques?*]

Interview with Miss Winkler[37]

SCHUYLER DEAN HOSLETT

This conversation takes place in the office of Mr. Zurch, director of personnel for an organization employing about 3,500 persons. Miss Winkler has been reported by her supervisors as doing unsatisfactory work; they ask that she be transferred on the basis of a list of charges outlined in a memorandum. Mr. Zurch has sent for Miss Winkler, who enters his office while he is talking to an assistant about another matter. Also present in the office at the time of the interview, but presumably not able to hear the conversation and doing other work, were Mr. Zurch's secretary, his assistant, and the recorder of the interview. Inasmuch as Miss Winkler spoke in a low tone, all of her comments were not audible to the recorder, especially as she became more emotional and finally tearful, but the conversation was substantially as follows:

W: Did you send for me, Mr. Zurch?

Z: Yes, I did; I'll be with you in just a minute. (*Mr. Zurch continues to talk to his assistant for seven minutes. During this time there is considerable confusion in the office, with the telephone ringing often, and with Mr. Zurch becoming more and more concerned over some matter about which he talks loudly, interspersing his rather definite comments with considerable swearing. This, it may be noted, is his usual manner under stress. Mr. Zurch continues*) : Now, look, Miss Winkler (*takes several minutes to look over her file and to talk to his assistant about another matter*) , you remember we talked together in March and at that time B Division was not satisfied, and since you have been with Mr. Newton, and he was not altogether satisfied.

W: He didn't tell me anything like that. (*Speaks in a low, courteous voice.*) He told me after I left that he wanted me back. . . .

Z: Now you have been in C Division and there is a report on your work there. Now Miss Winkler, we take each employee and try to fit her in where she can do the best job. We realize that people sometimes can't get along because of the supervisor, or fellow employees, and we try to make adjustments. (*This comment is given in Mr. Zurch's usual direct and belligerent manner.*) Now you have been in a number of positions. How many have you occupied?

W: (*After thinking a moment*) Four or five.

[37] Reprinted from "Listening to the Troubled or Dissatisfied Employee," *Personnel,* July 1945, pp. 54–56, by permission of the American Management Association.

Z: Do you agree with the comments made in this report? (*Quotes from report before him on the desk.*) "Shows little interest in work and says she doesn't care for filing."

W: (*Miss Winkler's voice is growing husky now and her response is almost inaudible, but she explains that she doesn't like filing, and that she wasn't hired to do that kind of work. She was to be a stenographer.*)

Z: We don't have the work always to everyone's satisfaction.

W: But I wasn't told that was what the job would be.

Z: But we can't give everyone a job he wants . . . (*Interview has turned into something of an argument at this point; Mr. Zurch presents next charge.*) "Deliberately slows down on the job."

W: No, I do not. (*Miss Winkler seems quite incensed at this charge.*)

Z: "Uses business hours to write letters."

W: I did that once.

Z: "Doesn't keep up to date with her work."

W: They put in a new system up there and the supervisor asked me to help with it and I said I would. But I couldn't keep up to date on my own work and do that too. The supervisor asked me to do this at the same time that I had more than enough work of my own to do. (*Though deeply disturbed at these charges, Miss Winkler's responses are direct; by this time, however, she is on the verge of tears.*)

Z: "Leaves fifteen minutes before 12 and returns twenty to twenty-five minutes late."

W: If I went before 12, I returned earlier.

Z: "Uses restroom facilities on 2nd floor instead of 3rd as required by the rules."

W: They were dirty on the 3rd floor.

Z: We can't be in those rooms every minute of the day. When I went in there (*apparently at an earlier complaint*) it wasn't dirty—only a few papers thrown around. It wasn't like any bathroom at home, but it wasn't dirty.

W: I have seen it at times when you couldn't use it.

Z: Why didn't you report it?

W: I did—But that's a petty thing (*i.e., the complaint*).

Z: Yes, but it means five to ten minutes more away from your desk. Listen, Miss Winkler, I think the supervisor doesn't have an ax to grind; maybe all of these things aren't true, but a certain amount is.

W: I did the work I was told to do, but some had to be left over. They expected me to get the mail out, and certain work had to be left.

Z: That's right, but there are those times when you were away from your work. (*Mr. Zurch explains the limitations on the number of persons the organization may hire; that each girl must do her work, or the organization will get behind.*)

W: I still think the charges aren't fair.

Z: Well, tell me, are there any differences between you and Jones *(her immediate supervisor)* ?

W: I'd rather not say.

Z: Don't you get along?

W: Oh, sometimes.

Z: Please tell me the story. . . . *(When apparent there will be no response)* Did you go over this with Miss Counce *(the counselor)* ?

W: *(Miss Winkler replies that she did, but by this time she is crying softly, and the exact words were not heard.)*

Z: We have a reputation of being fair. We try to analyze every factor in a report of this kind. . . . You have been here two years, long enough to know the whole story. . . . Do you think you aren't in the right job?

W: I want to leave the job.

Z: *(In a milder tone)* Now that's not the right attitude. We won't get anywhere that way. Has Mr. Achen *(a higher supervisor)* ever talked to you?

W: Not once.

Z: Has the principal clerk of the department talked to you about it?

W: Yes, once. *(Two sentences not heard.)*

Z: Do you think your work too heavy?

W: I can keep it cleaned up at times, but not all the time. There are days when with dictation, etc., I can't.

Z: Well, why don't we have the job analyzed on a week's basis and see if there is too much for one person.

W: A week wouldn't be right; once I was behind for three weeks.

Z: Honestly, haven't you taken extra time off?

W: No, absolutely not. I've noticed other girls going out when they weren't supposed to, though.

Z: Are you getting along with other employees?

W: Yes.

Z: Well, I'll tell you, you go back upstairs after you get set *(i.e., after she has made repairs on her face because of the crying)*. Do you have any other comment to make?

W: I feel he *(supervisor)* has been very unfair about my slowing down on my work.

Z: All right, O.K., now you stay down until, let's see, it's 3:30 now, until 3:45. I'll call them to expect you at 3:45.

Mr. Zurch's comment after the interview: "This girl comes from a good family and environment and apparently feels that she has a better head than the other workers. Our problem is to get her adjusted. I disagree with this report that she purposely slowed down on the job. The fact that she didn't like filing is nothing against her; we have that trouble all the time. But there is no question that she takes time off. I think 50–60 percent of the charges are correct and the rest is put on for a good story. We'll find that the supervisor hasn't talked to her correctly. She would be a better employee under a girl who could handle her or a smart-looking man. You noted that she was especially indignant at charges of slowing down, but not so indignant on spending extra time out."

Mr. Zurch calls the immediate supervisor and the next higher supervisor into his office to discuss the situation.

Z: What is it all about, this Winkler case?

MR. ACHEN: Her attitude is wrong. She wants to be a stenographer and she was hired as a clerk-typist and there isn't a 100 percent steno job up there. We give her some dictation, but can't give her full time. She doesn't want to do filing.

JONES: She gets behind. (*Telephone call interrupts.*)

MR. ACHEN: She said to someone, "I'll let this filing pile up and just see what happens." I think for the good of the department she should be transferred. (*Another telephone call interrupts.*)

Z: But we can't transfer her all the time.

MR. ACHEN: We spoke to her about the restrooms, but she disregards the rules. We have given her a fair chance.

Z: O.K., thanks a lot. (*Apparently the decision is to transfer Miss Winkler to another department. Mr. Zurch goes off to a meeting.*)

The Hayden Company[38]

The Hayden Company, headquartered in Dayton, Ohio, had numerous divisions in unrelated industries throughout the United States. These divisions for the most part were autonomous in their operations.

Guy Horton was attached to the personnel department in the headquarters office of the Hayden Company. He reported to the personnel director. He served in an advisory capacity and gave assistance in problems of office and laboratory personnel to the office managers in the various divisions of the firm.

---

[38] All names are disguised.

These divisions did not have personnel officers as such, and all recruiting, selecting, and training was carried on through their respective office managers.

An acute problem had arisen in the Memphis division. Because of separations and expanded operations several additional research men would be needed within five to six weeks. The research these men would do would be in the field of farm chemistry and the application of farm products to industry.

Mr. Horton's search to find manpower to fill this need took him to several midwestern universities where he was permitted to look through alumni records and also to talk to graduating seniors who qualified. One of the schools he visited was the Rogers Institute of Technology, an institution with a high scholastic rating.

Horton sent the following report to his superior, relating his experiences at Rogers.

"I visited R.I.T. yesterday morning and was permitted to interview several seniors and also to look at alumni records for candidates for the Memphis Laboratory. The students I talked to gave me a very unfavorable impression, their dress and speech could have been much better. After speaking to a number of them I did not think it worthwhile to interview others. My next step was to seek out the alumni records, and believe me I did not get a great deal of cooperation on this. Some clerk showed me an enormous card file and without further word he left. I leafed through this card file for a while but gave it up as a waste of time. I judged this school as being no more than a trade school and it would be a waste of time to visit it in the future."

Slovar Inostrannykh Slov

The definitions below appear in the *Russian Dictionary of Foreign Words (Slovar Inostrannykh Slov)*. How do you react to them? Why?

Detective literature: A kind of contemporary bourgeois adventure literature—romances, stories, tales devoted to description of "the exploits of detectives defending bourgeois property and the legal order."

Individualism: A bourgeois ideology which puts the egotistical interests of separate personalities in opposition to the interests of society . . .

Internationalism: International class unity and solidarity with the prole-

tarians and the workers of all countries in the struggle for the over-
throw of bourgeois dominance, the destruction of imperialism and the
building of communism in the entire world . . . An example of real
internationalism and a model of the cooperation of peoples in the
U.S.S.R.

Lend-lease: A law passed in 1941 by the U.S.A. Congress for the mutual
transfer or lease of equipment, raw materials, food and other goods to
allied countries during the Second World War. Lend-lease deliveries
brought colossal profits to the large American monopolists.

Lobby: In the U.S.A. the agents of the large bankers and monopolists
having a strong influence in parliamentary circles, lobbying with Con-
gressmen in the interests of monopoly capital as regards the making of
laws.

Police: In capitalist countries these are special administrative organs
made up of armed detachments protecting the bourgeois society and
its order; bourgeois states, being based on police and gendarmerie,
exercise their reactionary power by anti-democratic methods of un-
bridled arbitrary rule directed against the people.

Wall Street: A street in New York on which are located the largest banks,
financial markets, etc. Wall Street is a synonym for the plundering
imperialistic interests of the American financial oligarchy.

9

Differentiation failures I (indiscrimination)

THE FOLLOWING ACCOUNTS may seem quite diverse but they are alike in at least one important respect.

For a camera bug's 50th birthday, a White Plains woman decided to present him with 50 flashbulbs. She knows little about cameras, but she purchased a box camera with a flash attachment for herself at the same time she bought the bulbs. And before wrapping each bulb in gold paper she carefully tested it in the attachment. She was delighted that every bulb "worked," and happily sent them off to her friend—who still hasn't had the heart to tell her the facts of life about cameras.[1]

Grand Falls, N.B., Jan. 9 (AP) —The foamy white waste products of a starch factory looked like snow to Frederick Boucher, 7, so he jumped into an eight foot ditch filled with it. Two classmates on their way home from school with Frederick called for help but by the time rescuers arrived the boy was dead.[2]

The young Negro doctor, fresh from Nashville's Meharry Medical College, learned what he was up against as soon as he started to practice in Sanford, in the heart of Florida's orange-grove country. His first emer-

---

[1] From "Our Town," *Reporter Dispatch* (White Plains, N.Y.) .

[2] *Chicago Sunday Tribune*, January 10, 1954, Part 2, p. 16. Reprinted by permission of the Associated Press.

gency was the case of a woman suffering from what he decided was a ruptured ectopic (outside the womb) pregnancy. When he arrived with the ambulance at the hospital, the head nurse, a white woman, demanded scornfully: "Who told you that you could make a diagnosis?"

Dr. George Henry Starke had to turn his patient over to the white doctor on duty; no Negro was allowed to practice in the biracial hospital. The white doctor let him sit in on the operation, which saved the woman's life, and confirmed Starke's diagnosis. When it was over, the head nurse snapped: "Well, you're the first Negro I ever saw that could make a diagnosis. . . ."[3]

In each case a person failed to discriminate—to separate like things from one another. Whether it was electric bulbs, piles of white material, or Negroes, someone overlooked important differences and saw only similarities. The head nurse, for example, seemed to have had difficulty in differentiating among Negroes. To her they evidently appeared as indistinguishable as the proverbial peas in a pod.

We shall use the term, *indiscrimination*, to represent the behavior which occurs when one fails to recognize variations, nuances, differences; when one is unable or unwilling to distinguish, to differentiate, to separate apparently like things from one another. *Indiscrimination* may be defined, then, as the *neglect of differences,* while *overemphasizing similarities.* It is one of three forms of differentiation failure that we shall examine in this book. Two others, *polarization* and the *frozen evaluation,* are discussed in the next two chapters.

"HARDENING OF THE CATEGORIES"

One of the most troublesome consequences of *indiscrimination* is an evaluational "disease" we might appropriately label "hardening of the categories." Most of us have a penchant for categorizing—for classifying. Show someone something he has never seen before—an unusual butterfly, a peculiar tree leaf, a strange rodent—and one of his first questions is likely to be: "What *kind* is it?" We meet a new person and we are uneasy until we can pigeonhole him—What *is* he? —how is he classified? Is he a salesman, plumber, farmer, teacher, painter? Is he Protestant, Catholic, Jew, atheist? Democrat, Republican, Independent? Lower, middle, upper "class"?

Categorizing, per se, is not undesirable. Under some circumstances, as we shall discuss later, it is quite essential. But we are concerned

---

[3] "Negro in Florida," *Time,* January 19, 1952, p. 71. Reprinted by permission.

here with categorization when the categories become hardened, unyielding, when they tend to deter further analysis and investigation when such would be desirable. Joe White,[4] for example, as an office manager for a meat-packing firm, has developed a category for women workers over 50 years old. "They're insecure, inefficient, ineffectual, and temperamental," he will tell you. Thus, when Mary Grey, 52, a widow, applied for a clerical position, Joe did not even bother to interview her. He knew her "kind." Fortunately, another manager of the company *did* interview her and hired her on the spot. She has since proved to be a stable, energetic, intelligent worker who is likely to give many more years of service than most of the inexperienced, marriage-prone, 18-year-olds Joe tends to hire.

Stereotypes

The word *stereotype* is a useful one for our purposes. Originally a printing term, it stood for a plate which printed the "same" picture, drawing, and so forth, over and over again. Thus a sociological or psychological stereotype is a fixed, conventional image or picture. One who stereotypes applies his image of the group to any individual he assigns to that group. He disregards, consciously or otherwise, any differences or distinctions the individual may have which set him apart from the stereotyped group.

Consider the prevailing stereotype of "poet" in America. Such adjectives as "thin," "effeminate," "meek," "sensitive," "delicate," and "eccentric" may come quickly to mind. The stereotype can exist only so long as the exceptions are suppressed. But the generalized image dissipates when one considers some of our late contemporary poets—for example, warm, wiry Carl Sandburg; barrel-chested former backwoodsman, Lew Sarett; and Robert Frost:

His Vermont neighbors take no special notice of the heavy-set man with the big head of unkempt white hair. Occasionally they meet him on a back-country road, trudging along with an oddly catlike grace, wearing an old blue denim jacket and blue sneakers. They recognize the heavy, big-knuckled hand shaped to ax-helve scythe. Vermonters find nothing outlandish or alarming about Robert Frost.

Neither do U.S. readers, to most of whom the word "poet" still carries a faint suggestion of pale hands, purple passions and flowing ties.[5]

---

[4] The names are fictitious, but the incident actually occurred.

[5] "Pawky Poet," *Time,* October 9, 1950, p. 76. Reprinted by permission.

Of course, stereotypes can be expedient devices at times. Many television, pulp, and movie writers cherish them because they serve as shortcuts to characterizations. Merely depict a lean, lanky, sad-faced Black shuffling through a scene, and you have tapped a familiar mold. His personality and behavior are completely predictable because his writers generally permit no deviations from the established pattern.

The story is told of Metropolitan Opera Company prima donna, Dorothy Kirsten, who was making her debut in motion pictures. Having always worn her hair down, Miss Kirsten was surprised when the studio requested her to change to an upswept coiffure. Reason: "They wanted me to look like a prima donna!" And Hollywood actor John Wayne was given his first opportunity when Director Raoul Walsh decided he measured up to the requirements: "To be a cowboy star, you gotta be six feet three or over; you gotta have no hips and a face that looks right under a sombrero."

And so stereotypes can save time and effort. They obviate any additional analysis or investigation. There is no need to look for *differences*—a stereotype precludes them. Stereotyping permits us to set up neat, well-ordered, and oversimplified categories into which we can slip our evaluations of people, situations, or happenings.

THE BATTLE OF THE CATEGORIES

Few of us go very far in life without having to fight the "battle of the categories." Try to change your line of work, to transfer from one subject major to another in college, to compete for a dramatic role in the school play when you have been classified as an "athlete" or a "campus politician," and you invariably find people resisting your attempt to "break through their categories."

A few years ago a very capable actor committed suicide—why? Apparently out of despondency over being unable to find work. Film executives evidently felt that the public would not accept George Reeves as anyone other than "Superman," a role he had played in television movies for years.

As one hardens his categories, as he habitually goes by stereotypes, he is progressively less able to "search out the differences." His characteristic response to a new person, situation, thing, or idea is to find the "proper category"; slip the object of his attention into the pigeonhole; then he need attend to it no longer. Some persons are terribly uneasy until they can "tack on a label." Is he a union man? A Jew? A Democrat? A Sigma Sigma? An ex-convict? They can relax when they find the "right" tag.

A key danger with *hardened categories* is that the categorizer is prone to evaluate with faulty analogies. Situation (or person) A is new, but seems similar to situation (or person) B. Anxious to do his pigeonholing, the categorizer sweeps A into B's category with the dangerous assumption that the way to behave with respect to A is the way he behaved regarding B.

When his outfit was deactivated Sgt. Vincent Bonura[6] was reassigned to another camp. He reported to his new company commander, Captain Carl Barnes, and the men exchanged salutes.

"At ease, Sergeant, smoke if you like."

"Thank you, sir."

"Well, Sergeant, I want to get the best from every one of my men, so I'll want to check you on all your past experience so I can see best where I can use you. Let's see . . . Bonura. That's Italian, isn't it?"

"No, sir, I'm Sicilian."

"Ooooh, a Sicilian. . . . Well, Sergeant, I've had Sicilians in my outfits before, and I want to get one thing straight. I don't like any troublemakers in my company."

"Sir, I'm not a troublemaker!"

"Don't interrupt me, Bonura!"

"Sorry, sir."

"In France in '45 I had this man. . . . Mazzaro . . . Marzano . . . something like that and from the time he came to me until I got rid of him he gave me nothing but trouble. Now I don't know why you got shipped out of your old outfit. . . ."

"Sir!"

"Sergeant! I don't know why you got shipped out but if you're the hot-headed type I'll make it plenty rough for you around here—and give you plenty of time for cooling off!"

LANGUAGE: A CONTRIBUTING FACTOR

Why do people behave in these irrational, rigid ways we call *indiscrimination?* By definition, it is because they neglect differences and overemphasize similarities. Why, then, do they do so? Fear, greed, insecurity, and other destructive feelings and attitudes undoubtedly play important roles in contributing to indiscrimination.

---

[6] The names have been disguised.

But one factor is especially worthy of attention, not simply because it is important but because it offers a remedial approach to the problem. It constitutes a factor which *can* be altered and thus effect an important change in the outcome. I am speaking of language. We can demonstrate the point if you will study the box in Figure 9–1. Now, before you read any further, make a statement (write it down, speak it aloud, or simply "say" it to yourself) about what you see there.

FIGURE 9–1

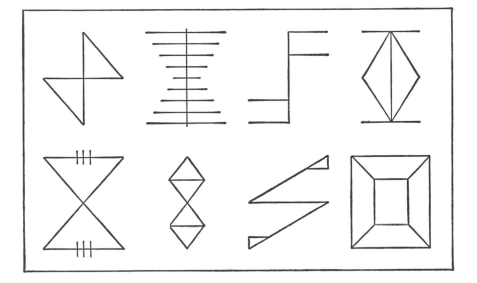

If you responded without too much consideration, the chances are that your statement described how the figures were *alike*. Such phrases as "geometric figures," "straight-line drawings," "patterns," "forms," and so on, are common responses. Our little game illustrates what linguistic specialists have recognized for years, that English-speaking persons find it relatively easy to perceive and to speak in terms of similarities in "reality." We are often more prone to *generalize* than to *differentiate*.

Our propensity to see similarities may be explained partly by the abundance of mass nouns and verbs in our language.[7] We may use the word *wood*, for example, to stand for anything within a myriad of

---

[7] We have no monopoly on general words (or on the ability to generalize). But our language is outstanding in this respect when compared with certain other languages, particularly those of some of the more "primitive" cultures.

objects ranging from a sliver to a giant Sequoia. Consider the enormous variety of fabrics that *cloth* may be used to represent. Think for a moment of the almost infinite variations in form, size, shape, color, and so forth, that such words as *African, furniture, Catholic, student,* and *animal* may be used to represent.

Here is a curious and revealing comparison. In English we can use the word *snow* to refer to a snowflake, a snowball, a flurry, blizzard, avalanche, lightly or heavily falling snow, snow which is dry, wet, caked, loose, compact, shifting, still, and so on. But the Eskimo, astonishingly, has *no one word* for all of these! To be sure, he has a large vocabulary of words for many *specific* forms of snow. But he has no *one general* word, such as our *snow,* for all of them.[8] This is fortunate, in a way, for the Eskimo. With his abundance of specific nouns and a dearth of general nouns, he is led to focus upon the *differences* in his environment. Take the case of snow, for example. The Eskimo has to be constantly on the alert for the *differences* in drift patterns, textures, crust strengths, and so on. If he does not attend to them, he may not provide a full dinner table for his family—he may not even get home to them at all. And so his language which encourages him to perceive *differences,* may be a definite boon in this respect.

Our preponderance of mass verbs is another case in point. We have a large number of verbs which represent, to many foreigners at least, a perplexing variety of actions. *Get, make, do, carry,* and *use* are just a few of these. *Go* is a particularly interesting example. We use this word for going on foot and also for when we are transported as by a vehicle. But the German has no comparable verb. When he *goes* on foot, *gehen* is appropriate. But one does not *gehen* by vehicle. This requires an entirely different verb, *fahren.*

The language of the Navaho Indian goes much further along this line. When he travels by horse, the Navaho simply cannot express the general notion of "going by horseback." His language requires that he specify the speed of the animal whether it be, for example, at a walk, a trot, a gallop, and so forth. Moreover, his language insists upon another kind of dividing the generic process of "going." The Navaho must distinguish between starting to go, going along, arriving at, returning from a point, and so forth. It is not, of course, that

---

8 Lister Sinclair, "Word in Your Ear," *Ways of Mankind,* ed. Walter Goldschmidt (Boston: Beacon Press, 1954), p. 27.

these distinctions *cannot* be made in English but that they *are not* made consistently.[9]

The general nature of the difference between Navaho thought and English thought—both as manifested in the language and also as forced by the very nature of the linguistic forms into such patterns—is that Navaho thought is prevailingly so much more specific, so much more concrete.[10] The nature of their language forces The People to notice and to report many other distinctions in physical events which the nature of the English language allows speakers to neglect in most cases, even though their senses are just as able as those of the Navaho to register the smaller details of what goes on in the external world.[11]

Conversely, it appears that the plethora of general verbs[12] (and nouns) in our language both reflects and encourages our inclination to see the relationships and similarities among phenomena.

The crux of this chapter is that the process of *noting similarities* generally involves the *neglecting of differences*. Recall your reaction to the drawings of a few pages back. When one says or visualizes: "They are all geometrical designs, figures, drawings, and so on," he is calling his attention to the ways in which the units are *alike* and suppressing his cognition of their *differences*. He neglects, for the moment at least, that the second figure, top row, reminds him of a row of telephone poles reflected in water; that the fourth figure, bottom row, is the only rectangle, and so forth.

A language which prompts us to note similarities, then, may tend to discourage us from observing the differences. And the failure to see differences, as we have discussed, may lead to the destructive and dangerous patterns of *indiscrimination*. Let us now examine some of the possible preventives and remedies that we may use in coping with *indiscrimination*.

---

[9] Clyde Kluckhohn and Dorothea Leighton, *The Navaho* (Cambridge, Mass.: Harvard University Press, 1948), p. 201.

[10] Ibid., p. 199.

[11] Ibid., p. 201.

[12] English certainly has no dearth of specific verbs, especially with respect to those aspects of our culture on which we place a great deal of emphasis. Sports is an example in point. These synonyms for the verb "defeat" were gleaned from just one week's scanning of newspaper sports pages:

bash	edge	overtake	slash	stifle	triumph over
batter	mangle	scalp	slaughter	top	trounce
best	massacre	scuttle	slip by	topple	vanquish
blast	maul	shade	smash	trample	wallop
crush	nick	sink	smother	trim	whip
down	nip	skin	squeeze by	trip	whitewash

CORRECTIVES

A difficult aspect in the treatment of *hardened categories* is that the categorizer is usually *unaware* that his stereotypes are affecting his behavior. He becomes so oblivious of his overemphasis on similarities and neglect of differences that he takes the rigidly categorized world of his own making for granted.

Of course, we all carry our sets of categories around with us. You are a rare person if some sort of stereotyped image does not occur to you at the mention of at least some of these terms:

doctors	hippies
Southerners	white-collar workers
divorcees	damn yankees
union officials	management
Blacks	Jews
professors	artists
extremists	teen-agers

But the mere occurrence of conventionalized images to someone does not necessarily make him a chronic stereotyper. One may be quite aware that his generalized image is just that, and often with little or no basis in fact. He says to himself, in effect: "Sure, you mention 'professor' and I think immediately of the pedantic, absent-minded fuddy-duddy, carrying a rolled up umbrella and wearing spats. But that's just the stereotype. Actually, very few of the professors I have known even approach this caricature."

The problem of *indiscrimination* arises when a person is *unaware of* or *unwilling to recognize* his stereotpyes *as such*—when, in other words, his categories become hardened. Thus an approach to the dissolution of stereotypes—to the softening of categories—is to work toward the *awareness* of them. What can one do to alert himself to the influences of stereotypes upon his evaluations and communications?

Become sensitive to differences

Recall that this chapter holds that the overemphasis on similarities with the corresponding neglect of differences leads frequently to stereotyping. In fact, stereotypes cannot exist *without* the neglect of differences. The moment one begins to take differences into account, his stereotypes begin to disintegrate. As one makes a deeply ingrained habit of looking for differences, he approaches a self-awareness which makes possible mature, intelligently discriminating behavior in dealing with people, situations, happenings, relationships, and so forth. "The more we discriminate among," Irving J. Lee said, "the less we will discriminate against."

Internalize the premise of uniqueness. Perhaps the first step toward developing a heightened awareness of differences is to disavow the erroneous notion of "identicalness." No two things have ever been found to be exactly similar in all respects—or even in one respect. Those two pears in the pod are actually quite dissimilar, even to the naked eye, if one observes closely. "Nature" apparently abhors identicalness. No two snowflakes, no two blades of grass, no two grains of sand—no two of anything—have ever been shown to be completely identical. An important technique of identification is based on the presumption that no two fingerprints are exactly the same. Consider that there are presently over 3 billion persons on earth and approximately 10 fingers each and add all the people who have gone before us and are yet to come—it is an astounding presumption. Yet it has never been disproved.

Nor has man contrived two of anything completely identical. A machinist friend tells me that possibly the most precise man-made objects are Johannson blocks. "Jo" blocks are used to check the accuracy of micrometers (extremely exact instruments in themselves). I have seen "Jo" blocks so precise that two of them placed together formed such a close union that a partial vacuum was created and a man found it impossible to pull them directly apart! He had to twist and slide them to separate them. Are "Jo" blocks identical, then? They are incredibly alike—machined within a tolerance of plus or minus two millionths of an inch! But note, these are *tolerances*—that is, even "Jo" block machinists must admit that they can only *approach* identicalness, never attain it.

Because no two of anything have been found to be *absolutely* the *same,* we have a useful premise: *There is always uniqueness; never identicalness.* Thus, if you are deeply convinced that there are *always* differences, you may not be so prone to overlook them. You will be less likely to "disregard the individuality of nature, and substitute a generality which belongs to language."[13]

Index your evaluations. One simple device which has proved suc-

---

[13] A. B. Johnson, *A Discourse on Language* (Utica, N.Y.: William Williams, 1832), p. 10.

cessful in developing the awareness of differences is the *INDEX*. Indexing is hardly a new process. The housewife indexes her recipes; the executive his correspondence; the librarian his papers and books. Each is *separating* items according to the essential differences among them. The habit of *indexing* people, things, situations, and so on, is equally, if not more, useful. The salesman who habitually indexes will react to purchasing agent$_1$ as if he were different from purchasing agent$_2$—he is.

Make a habit of *indexing*. The next time you hear someone (or yourself) making statements such as these below, ask yourself *Which?*

"Union officials are corrupt!"	*Which* officials of *which* unions?
"Women shouldn't be allowed to drive automobiles!"	*Which* women drivers?—and might there be some men you would prohibit?
"Doctors are mercenary!"	*Which* doctors? Would you include your hometown physician? Those who contribute half their time to charity cases? Those who work in laboratories at a fraction of the income they could command?

Doctor$_1$ is different from doctor$_2$, of course, and doctor$_2$ is different from doctor$_3$ and so on. Use the little subscript as a mental exercise, as an habitual memory jogger to call your attention to the differences.

As the next two chapters will describe two other types of *indexing*, we should *index* the *indexes*. To distinguish them, this chapter advocates the use of the *Which* Index.

THE VALUES OF SEEING SIMILARITIES

To digress for a moment, I trust I have not given the impression that one should focus on differences at the *expense* of similarities. The ability to see similarities is essential in generalizing, categorizing, organizing, classifying, arranging, cataloging, and so forth. These activities, in turn, are indispensable in learning, analyzing, problem solving, innovating, decision making, and so on. For example, a child learns about fractions when his teacher shows how the *parts* of a pie, when put together, make a *whole* pie. From this he can *generalize to* (i.e., see the similarities with) fractions of a plot of land or a container of milk. He eventually generalizes to the visualization of "fractions" as an abstract "idea."

Take another case. Suppose a certain businessman plans to build a motel and wants to find the optimum location for it. His basic approach is to analogize—that is, he will look for *similarities* with respect to location among successful existing motels. He may find that they are usually located on major highways within easy access of motorists driving through. Moreover, they tend to be situated on the outskirts of cities, far enough out to avoid high real estate taxes and competition from hotels and yet close enough to utilize the inexpensive urban power and water, and so forth. Thus he may be able to make a wiser decision because he has been able to abstract key similarities out of a myriad of differences among the motels.

Categorization, cataloging, and classifying (all based on seeing the similarities) are imperative in modern business. Imagine the chaos in the offices of the comptroller, the purchasing agent, the production control manager, and so forth, if they were somehow prevented from classifying and organizing the multitudinous data and details with which they deal.

Scientific advance (or progress on any frontier) is intimately related to the perception of similarities. We learn about the unknown largely on the basis of the known. Someone must have been able to generalize from perhaps a rolling log to the notion of a wheel, from a boiling kettle to a steam engine, and from a flying kite, bird, and so on, to the visualization of an airplane.

This chapter hardly proposes to minimize the value of seeing similarities. Our goal is to achieve better-*balanced* perceptions—to see the differences *as well as* the similarities. To accomplish this, most of us need training in looking for differences. Thanks to our formal education, language structure, and so forth, we are already fairly adept at noting the similarities.

SUMMARY

In life there are differences as well as similarities. Our language structure, however, which subtly influences our evaluating and communicating patterns, encourages us to overemphasize the similarities and to neglect the differences. The frequent result is that we may behave in terms of stereotypes (neglect of differences) and react to essentially *different* and *unique* people, situations, and things as if they were "identical" with our self-manufactured stereotypes. One can develop a greater sensitivity to differences by internalizing the premise of uniqueness and by applying the *Which Index* in his evaluations of people, situations, and so forth. The deeply ingrained habit of asking "Which?" will diminish one's tendencies to overgeneralize that so frequently lead to stupid, unsafe, and unsane behavior.

Remember, these are differences which make a difference—take them into account.

DISCUSSION QUESTIONS

1. In "primitive" societies such as Eskimo there tend to be fewer generic words and more specific words, especially for important aspects of their lives. The Trobiand Islanders, for example, have no single word for *yam* but many specific words to denote the yam at its various stages of growth. What are the implications of this? Is it "good" or "bad" that a language has many or few mass words—many or few specific words? Why?

2. "The more we discriminate among, the less we will discriminate against."—Irving J. Lee (p. 341)

   Do you agree? If people lived by this motto would it be an effective attack on bigotry, on racial, ethnic, and sexual inequities? What are the obstacles to promulgating this concept more widely?

3. Almost a century and a half ago A. B. Johnson warned against the tendency to "disregard the individuality of nature, and substitute a generality which belongs to language." (p. 341) What did he mean? Specifically, what should we do to heed his warning?

4. This chapter seems mainly concerned with the tendency to overlook *differences*. But what about the *similarities*? Is there not value in being able to abstract them from a situation, as well?

5. What connection is there between the ability to perceive similarities and *education? Business decisions? Scientific advance? Government?* (See pp. 342–43)

6. Prepare a report on an incident, perhaps involving yourself, in which *indiscrimination* occurred. Analyze *why* it happened, what could have *been done* to prevent or correct this incident, what measures are likely to prevent its *recurrence*.

CASES

The Dixon Company[14]

The Dixon Company, a national restaurant chain, recently found itself short of the cash funds necessary to establish several new restaurants. Albert Bullock, president, instructed Walter Green, the company's 60-year-old treasurer, to enter into negotiations with a local bank for a $600,000 loan. The bank indicated that the loan would be granted provided the company submit a satisfactory audit report by an independent public accounting firm.

Mr. Green requested the public accounting firm of Wilscher and Wunderlich to perform the audit. Edward Thorndike, a partner in W & W, assigned Tom Scott to supervise the audit. Scott, 26, had been with W & W for five years and had proven to be a highly capable Certified Public Accountant although inclined to be somewhat overconfident in his manner.

Within the first few days of the audit Scott uncovered several company accounting policies which were not in agreement with generally accepted accounting principles. After lengthy discussions with Mr. Green, Scott was able to have these exceptions corrected.

During the final week of the audit Scott took another apparent accounting principle variance to Green.

SCOTT: I've got another book adjustment for your approval, Mr. Green.

GREEN: All right, Tom, what is it?

SCOTT: As you know, accounting depreciation principles are based on the theory that certain assets purchased and used in the business produce income. If such an asset is usable over a period of more than one year its cost should be systematically and consistently prorated over its estimated useful life. Thus, each year's income is charged with a proportional part

---

14 All names have been disguised.

345

of the cost of the equipment used to produce such income. I've discovered that while you follow this principle in regard to most assets you do not consistently and systematically depreciate class 10 equipment (dishes, glassware, etc.). In the last three years, you charged off 5 percent, 8 percent, and 3 percent, respectively. If you had followed a correct policy the percentages would all be the same.

GREEN: (*Smiling*) Well, Tom, I've gone along with all your other adjustments but you're off base on this one. I guess you still have a little to learn about the restaurant business.

SCOTT: (*Suddenly flushing with anger*) Why any elementary accounting textbook will tell you you can't vary your depreciation rate policy.

GREEN: You go out and find yourself a modern, up-to-date book on depreciation methods, young man. Then, you will realize you are wrong.

The conversation grew more heated and finally Scott walked angrily from Green's office, saying: "Well, I'm sorry if I can't make you understand this but I'm going to report this to my supervisor and I'm sure we'll have to note this exception in our report to the bank."

Scott phoned Thorndike and reported his disagreement with Green. Mr. Thorndike replied: "Tom, a dish does not *wear* out; its life ends suddenly with a crash. The normal depreciation principle often cannot be applied to a restaurant's class 10 equipment. Variable depreciation rates based on such factors as actual glassware inventory counts or current glassware purchases are acceptable. These factors give some indication of the rate of loss as the result of breakage."

When he had concluded the phone conversation with Scott, Thorndike made this notation in his assignment files: *"If* we get the Dixon job next year we will have to find someone else to handle the field work. Scott seems to have clashed with the company's treasurer."

Full circle[15]

HENRY J. TAYLOR

I travel the whole world, and whenever I come home countless friends ask: "Why do Europeans dislike us Americans so much? Because of our aid? Because America is rich? Why?"

I think we should relax, and worry less about our alleged "failure

---

[15] Copyright, 1956, by The Reader's Digest Assn. Reprinted with permission.

to be loved." For I maintain that *Europeans do not dislike us any more than they dislike each other*. Prove it yourself:

Take a circular trip, country by country. Did you ever find a Scotsman who is on fire with friendliness for the English or the Irish, or vice versa? Cross the Channel. Most British have little more than contempt for the French, and—again—vice versa. The French do not like the Spaniards and, as for liking Italians, many Frenchmen get livid at mere mention of the name. The dislike of Italians, in turn, for Frenchmen, Yugoslavs, Albanians and Greeks is historic; and they have been fighting Austrians for hundreds of years. Austrians, in turn, detest the Czechs and Poles. The Poles detest the Austrians and Czechs.

Go north in the circle. The Norwegians do not like the Swedes. ("You stayed neutral in the war while we fought," say Norwegians. "You would have stayed neutral too if you had not been attacked," reply the outraged Swedes.) The Dutch will tell you there is no excuse for Belgium. ("Northern Belgium should be Dutch. Southern Belgium should be French. Why a Belgium?") The Belgians like neither the Dutch, Danes, nor the French. And as for liking the Germans, from one end of Europe to the other people love the Germans like a bulldog loves a tramp.

I hope we Americans make more friends in Europe, but we are wrong in thinking of ourselves as the special target for European displeasure; wrong in our mystification, wrong in our hurt feelings, and wrong in excessive and futile measures to make ourselves loved by spending money. The fact is, we can easily be too preoccupied with the attitudes toward us of peoples abroad.

What's wrong with the men?[16]

ROME—AP—What's wrong with men, as green-eyed Gianna Maria Canale, Italian film star sees it:

AMERICANS: "They have too many muscles, always thinking of sports and not enough about their women. Besides, they drink too much."

---

16 *Chicago Daily News*, February 12, 1955, p. 36. Courtesy of Associated Press.

ITALIANS: "They are exactly the opposite of Americans. They think only of women, but not in a nice way. They have a one-track mind."

SOUTH AMERICANS: "They resemble Italians."

ENGLISHMEN: "Really too cold to be good."

GERMANS: "They would want to order me around as though they were the commanding officers."

FRENCH: "They lose themselves in too many compliments. Frenchmen talk too much. They're boring."

While waiting for a paragon to come up over her horizon, Miss Canale intends to continue working on pictures and buying valuable paintings, rugs, and antique furniture for her 14-room villa overlooking Rome.

[*What's wrong with Italian film actresses?*]

Wright Cleaners and Dyers, Ltd.[17]

Wright Cleaners and Dyers operated a number of retail branches throughout a large metropolitan area. Many of the older branches were located in neighborhoods which had become economically depressed. A few, such as the store established in Whitesdale six months earlier, were in upper middle-class communities.

Richard Clark, 35, an executive in a rapidly expanding firm, lived in Whitesdale with his wife and two young sons. As Clark left for a short business trip on Monday, he asked his wife to take several of his shirts to Wright's. Mrs. Jackson, sole clerk at the Whitesdale branch, promised Mrs. Clark that the shirts would be ready by Wednesday.

Mrs. Jackson, 61, a widow, had been forced by the death of her husband to obtain employment. She had been working for Wright's for six months—her first job since her marriage in her early twenties. Except for a brief indoctrination period at Wright headquarters, she had spent all of this time at the Whitesdale store.

Clark arrived home late Wednesday night and wasn't expected in the office until Thursday noon. The next morning he drove with his sons to Wright's. He walked into the store with his boys at 8:30 A.M.

---

[17] All names have been disguised.

CLARK: Are my shirts ready yet?

MRS. JACKSON: Do you have your ticket?

CLARK: Ticket? No, I didn't know you had to have one.

MRS. JACKSON: Oh, yes—I can't find your laundry without a ticket number.

CLARK: Well, O.K.—I guess my wife has it at home.

Clark loaded his boys into the car, drove the mile back to his home, picked up the ticket, and returned with his children to Wright's.

MRS. JACKSON: (*after glancing at the ticket number*) Oh, that's not in yet.

CLARK: But my wife said they were promised for yesterday.

MRS. JACKSON: Well, they may have come in this morning, but they would be in large boxes in the back, and it would take an hour to unpack them. You come back in an hour and I'm sure I'll have them ready for you.

CLARK: Why don't you let me help you go through the boxes? This running back and forth is getting ridiculous.

MRS. JACKSON: I can't do that—no one is allowed back of the partition.

At this, Mrs. Jackson walked behind the partition, leaving an exasperated Clark, who decided he could do no more with the situation at this point.

In an hour Clark returned.

MRS. JACKSON: Here are the shirts—I got them out for you. I'm sorry about the delay.

CLARK: If you're sorry, may I assume that you wouldn't like to have this sort of thing happen again?

MRS. JACKSON: Why yes, of course.

CLARK: Well, whose rule is it that no one is allowed to help you sort out the laundry in an emergency?

MRS. JACKSON: The supervisor's—that's a store rule.

CLARK: Then I would suggest that you advise your supervisor, since you are closer to the situation, that this store is in Whitesdale—not in some blighted type of neighborhood. I think you can assume that people are honest here.

MRS. JACKSON: Oh, it isn't a question of honesty. I had a woman in here a couple of weeks ago who went through the cleaning bags hanging on the racks—tearing them open—to find her cleaning.

CLARK: I don't see the similarity—I had the ticket number—nothing would have had to be torn open.

MRS. JACKSON: Well, no one is allowed behind the partition. That's a store rule.

CLARK: I know, and most of the time it's probably a good rule—but don't you suppose there might be an exception—an instance when a rule might be broken?

MRS. JACKSON: No, that's what rules are for. [Mrs. Jackson quickly walks behind the partition].

Later in the day, Clark telephoned Wright's main office and spoke to Anthony Conti, supervisor of stores.

CLARK: Mr. Conti, I didn't feel like doing you people a favor this morning but I'm a little more mellow now. I'd like to tell you about a practice which may lose you customers. [Clark recounted the incident with Mrs. Jackson.]

CONTI: Well, I'll tell you, Mr. Clark—I'll tell you why that happened. You see, we train our girls all alike because we may have to transfer them from one store to another, and so on. Now, we tell them *never* and under *no* conditions to let anyone go back of the partition. And there are two reasons why we tell them this. Now we find that nine times out of ten whenever we get a customer back there fooling around with the cleaning there's going to be confusion. And the second reason is the safety of the girls. You know what I mean—we can't let a man back there with the girls.

CLARK: I know what you mean, but I don't think Mrs. Jackson should have been concerned. She's seen me several times in the store. And I don't exactly dress or look like an escaped convict—besides I had my two little boys with me.

CONTI: Well, you have to have a rule, though—you never know, and those things can happen.

CLARK: Yes, but the probability of their happening in Whitesdale is pretty remote, don't you think?

CONTI: Well, maybe—but rules are rules and we make the girls live up to them.

The Wayland Company[18]

The Wayland Company, a large ore producer with its headquarters offices in New York City, maintained numerous lead, zinc, and feldspar operations. One of its larger feldspar centers was located at Bixby, Utah. Early in the spring, Robert Harris, plant manager at Bixby, flew to New York for an annual meeting with Cal Douglas,

---

18 All names have been disguised.

production manager of the feldspar operations, and Fred Squires, chief cost accountant for Wayland's. Douglas and Squires were located in the New York offices.

The purpose of the meeting was to establish the standard costs[19] of the Bixby plant for the coming fiscal year. Predictions were to be made as to the extent of such expenses as supplies, repair material, repair labor, fuel, and direct and indirect labor. Direct labor[20] costs were by far the largest expenditure in the plant. Direct labor is generally considered a *variable cost*[21] in that it varies directly with the quantity of production. Past experience at Bixby had shown, for example, that the direct labor required for producing one ton of feldspar was approximately one half manhour; for producing two tons, one man-hour, and so on. A measure of the efficiency of the operation could be determined by the extent to which the actual direct labor cost ran above or below this norm. It was the company policy, therefore, to hold the plant manager responsible for maintaining his variable costs, direct labor included, at the lowest feasible level. He was not held responsible, however, for fixed costs, which were beyond his control.

Cal Douglas called the meeting to order and the three men began to go over the standard costs. As the conference reached the topic of direct labor, Fred Squires remarked: "According to our figures the direct labor cost incurred at Bixby should be 98 cents per ton and it should be 100 percent variable cost."

DOUGLAS: I don't think you're taking into consideration the fact that our Bixby plant has recently been organized. A clause in our contract with the union states that five men have to be paid for five hours a day regardless of production. In other words, if Bixby had 100 percent downtime these particular men would have to be paid for five hours for every day of the downtime period, whether it is for one day or for six months! It's my thinking, therefore, that all costs incurred when the plant is not operating should be classified as fixed and not be charged to the plant manager.

HARRIS: Mr. Douglas is correct about our plant being organized and

---

19 "A forecast or predetermination of what costs should be under projected conditions, serving as a basis of cost control, and as a measure of productive efficiency when ultimately compared with actual costs." From Eric L. Kohler's *A Dictionary for Accountants* (New York: Prentice-Hall, Inc., 1952) .

20 Direct labor is that directly related to the product.

21 The obverse of *variable cost,* in accounting terminology, is *fixed cost,* i.e., cost incurred independently of the quantity of production, e.g., rent, property tax, depreciation, insurance, and so forth.

I've got to pay those five men no matter what the production situation is. If their time is classified as variable cost then I would be held responsible for an expenditure over which I have no control. And I certainly agree with Mr. Douglas when he says these should be fixed costs.

SQUIRES: Mr. Harris, you don't seem to realize that what you're asking us to do is contrary to all established cost accounting principles. If we classify any of your plant's direct labor as fixed costs we would incur some serious problems with respect to accounting terminology. Based on my 25 years as a cost accountant this idea would certainly be a radical innovation and in my opinion it just cannot be done.

Cal Douglas, sensing that the meeting had reached an impasse, suggested that they break for lunch. After lunch the conference reconvened and the controversy grew more heated. Finally, Cal Douglas commented: "Gentlemen, it's evident that we have reached a stalemate here. Frankly, we haven't the time to work it out. I think I can see both points of view and I realize that we're asking Fred to act against some established accounting principles but, frankly, I think we must make an exception in this case. We simply must adjust our cost accounting procedure to accommodate our labor problem."

Mr. Squires replied with repressed anger: "Do you realize what repercussions this would lead to? It would change accounting terminology and procedures we've been abiding by for years. Cost accounting, by its nature, has to be consistent from period to period. If we inaugurate this procedure we'll be harming the accuracy of our total plant costing."

On a bus[22]

RUTH LEBOW COGAN

I was doing industrial nursing at the time of this story and if you have ever done industrial work you know you start to work at 8:00 A.M. not five minutes after, and you finish at 4:30 P.M not five minutes earlier.

On this particular evening I had to go to school after work so instead of going home my usual way I caught a Jackson Blvd. bus going

---

[22] Printed by permission of the author.

east. It must have been about twenty minutes to five before I caught the bus since I had to walk a block to catch the bus and had to wait a few minutes before it arrived. The bus reached State St. about five o'clock and it was at this time that I transferred, or tried to, to a north bound bus.

I was carrying an arm load of books and no other packages when I boarded the bus. I handed the driver the transfer and started to move to the back of the bus when the driver called me back. He said, in what appeared to me to be a very accusing voice, that my transfer was an hour overdue, that it was stamped for four o'clock. I told him the other driver must have made a mistake since I had not finished work till four-thirty. At this point he accused me of lying and said I was shopping for an hour and tried to get by with an old transfer. By this time he was shouting and all the people in the bus were intently watching and listening for the outcome. He asked for another fare and seeing there was no future in arguing with him, I opened my purse and found I had no change—only a ten dollar bill. I told the driver I only had a ten dollar bill and asked if he could change it. His face was getting redder and redder and he finally burst out with "I'll change it and give you all your change in silver." By this time I was furious and told him I did not care how he changed it as long as he gave me my change.

At this point he really lost control and blared out that he knew people like me—always trying to cheat the bus lines out of a fare and I didn't pull the wool over his eyes and that he could see through my act. He said he changed his mind, that he would not cash my ten dollars and that I would just have to get off the bus. Under fire of accusations I had no alternative but to get off since technically he was within his rights to refuse to change a ten dollar bill.

The new neighbor[23]

Oak Park, Ill. (pop. 63,175), is one of Chicago's bigger and better suburban bedroom towns, a community which proudly labels itself "the middle-class capital of the world." Its houses are mostly a solid,

23 *Time,* December 4, 1950, pp. 18–19. Reprinted by permission.

two- and three-story type built 20 years ago, and its residents are likewise solid and respectable.

"Did you know a nigger is moving into the neighborhood?" an Oak Park druggist whispered to his customers several months ago. The newcomer to the neighborhood around Chicago and East Avenue was indeed a Negro. He was also one of the nation's ablest chemists. Percy Levon Julian, A.M., Ph.D. (Harvard and the University of Vienna), the only Negro in his class at DePauw University, where he was valedictorian (and a classmate of David Lilienthal), is the highly paid chief of soybean research for Chicago's Gliddon Co. In that job and earlier, Percy Julian, the grandson of an Alabama slave, had made world-famous chemical discoveries. They ranged from processes for the synthetic manufacture of important body-regulating hormones (e.g., testosterone, progesterone) to a foam fire extinguisher which saved many U.S. naval vessels in World War II. But in Oak Park, there were people who attached more importance to the color of a man's skin than to his achievements. The town's only two Negro families lived in the northern section. Julian paid $34,000 for an ornate 15-room house in Chicago Avenue neighborhood and began spending $8,000 more for landscaping and improvements, intending to move his wife and two children in by Christmas. When the news got out, the water commissioner refused to turn on the water until the Julians threatened to go to court. Anonymous telephone callers made threats.

One afternoon last week, after the landscapers and renovators had gone for the day, a dark sedan pulled up at the Julians' house. Two men got out, broke into the house and poured gasoline through all its rooms. They laid a clumsy fuse of surgical gauze to the outside and lit it; it went out. Then they tossed a flaming kerosene torch through a window and drove away. Before the gasoline was ignited, neighbors called firemen and the house was saved.

Percy Julian, a proud, energetic man of 51, stood his ground and served notice that his family would move into the house by New Year's Day. He hired (for $36 a day) a private, round-the-clock guard to patrol the property with bulldog and shotgun. "We've lived through these things all our lives," said Percy Julian. "As far as the hurt to the spirit goes, we've become accustomed to that."

10

Differentiation failures II (polarization)

POLARIZATION MAY BE considered as a special form of indiscrimination, but because of its relevance to what has been happening in our nation and, indeed, in many parts of the world it warrants a separate chapter.

> A college professor may be either a top notch researcher or an excellent teacher; he may not be either but he certainly won't be both.

> Kids these days don't appreciate what they have. Either you sweat for what you get or you'll take it for granted.

> The cops in this precinct are either honest and walking on their uppers or they're grafting and living high.

Perhaps those statements seem a bit jarring. Are such statements less offensive if they are made by people of renown?

> Life is either a daring adventure or nothing.
>
> *—Helen Keller*

> There are but two objects in marriage, love or money. If you marry for love, you will have some very happy days, and probably many very uneasy ones; if for money, you will have no happy days and probably no uneasy ones.
>
> *—Lord Chesterfield*

The world is divided into people who do things and people who get the credit.[1]

The latter statements may be more memorable but they are still oversimplistic. Whether expressed by celebrities or not each of the quotations above perpetrates a *polarization.*

DEFINITION

To define *polarization,* we must distinguish between two kinds of situations which apparently present two, and only two, alternatives. One of these is a genuine dichtomy; the other a false dichotomy.

Contradictories

At any given time and place you will either marry or you will not marry; you will either be arrested for speeding or you will not; you will either receive a pay raise or you will not; you will either make the varsity basketball team or you will not; and so forth. These are authentic dichotomies or *contradictories.* Note their characteristics: (1) *One* alternative *must* occur, but (2) both cannot.[2] Take this statement: "People are either over six feet tall, or they are not." Everyone, at any given time and place, must (1) be in one camp or the other for there is no middle ground, and (2) he cannot be in both camps.

Now, it is quite safe, sound, and sane to make "either-or" statements about *contradictories.* But there is another type of situation about which "either-or" statements and evaluations can be quite misleading and dangerous.

Contraries

Examine this statement: "People are either tall or short." It has the "either-or" form, but it does not involve contradictories, for there *is* middle ground—countless people are *neither* "tall" *nor* "short." And this is the key distinction between contradictories and con-

---

[1] Publisher and wit, Harry Golden also felt there were two kinds of people in the world: Those who insist on dividing the world into two kinds of people and those who don't (!)

[2] Aristotle expressed these requirements as two of his Laws of Thought: (1) Something must be either A or non-A, and (2) nothing can be both A and non-A at the same time and place.

traries. Contradictories involve no middle ground, no other alternatives; contraries do. Moreover, the middle ground may consist of gradations, shadings, degrees—an unlimited number of them in many cases. The temperature of the air around us is a good example—it isn't simply "hot" or "cold." The temperature varies by smooth, continuous changes that we express conveniently in arbitrary steps called *degrees*. Actually, there are an infinite number of gradations between zero and 100 degrees Fahrenheit.

Indeed, it is as if nature abhorred contradictories. According to Berne, "In nature and in the id, there are no opposites which exclude each other."[3] Contradictories appear to be largely man-made. Consider the computer. It operates on the *contradictories* of *open* and *closed*. A given circuit is either open or it is closed. To accommodate this limitation the binary numeral system was adopted. It consists of only *two* numerals—*0* and *1*—to represent *opened* or *closed* circuits. For those who may not be familiar with it the binary system looks like this:

Decimal	Binary	Decimal	Binary	Decimal	Binary
0	0	4	100	8	1000
1	1	5	101	9	1001
2	10	6	110	10	1010
3	11	7	111	11	1011

The decimal "2," then, is not read as "ten" but as one circuit closed, another circuit open.

A simpler example of man-made *contradictories* are the "go—no-go" gauges used in industry to determine *whether or not* an object meets given specifications.

On the other hand consider some of the *contraries masquerading as* contradictories:

Life or death. Precisely when does life begin and when does it end? With abortion legalized in some states and the advent of organ transplants, these are no longer only philosophical questions. They have become vital physiological, legal, and moral issues. For example, when may a heart be transplanted from one person to another? When the donor dies is the oversimplified, black-and-white answer. But *when* does he die? When no pulse or breath can be detected? When no reflex action can be

---

[3] Eric Berne, M.D., *A Layman's Guide to Psychiatry and Psychoanalysis* (N.Y.: Simon & Schuster, 1968) , p. 76.

elicited? When the heart and lungs cease to function? When an irreversible coma is recorded on an encephalograph? In a recent meeting of the American Academy of Neurology one conclusion was clear: There was *no* generally accepted conclusion as to when death comes.[4]

Male or female. As disconcerting as it may be to "male chauvinists" or "women's libbers," there apparently is no 100 percent male or no 100 percent female. Evidently there is "maleness" and "femaleness" in varying degrees in each of us. Again the issue is not merely academic. In the '68 Olympics 11 women athletes were disqualified because analyses revealed that they were *insufficiently* "female" to compete with other women.

Animal or vegetable. As if the foregoing were not disturbing enough, here is yet another old, comfortable oversimplification under attack: the supposed contradictories of animal or vegetable. Where do you put the *euglena* which digests food like an animal and photosynthesizes like a plant? Or where does the *ascidian* fit? It is classified as an animal, yet it produces cellulose, which has been considered a function unique ·to plants.[5]

It seems fair to conclude that most of the important aspects of living involve *contraries.* Health-illness, wealth-poverty, war-peace, loyalty-treason, hero-villan, sanity-insanity, beauty-ugliness, conservative-liberal, intelligence-stupidity, bravery-cowardice, line-staff, investment-speculation, competence-incompetence, mind-body, good-bad, heredity-environment, true-false, honesty-dishonesty, guilt-innocence, and so on, are not simple, either-or matters. But people sometimes deal with these and other contraries in a nonrational way. This behavior has been called *polarization.*

Polarization

Polarization occurs when one, failing to differentiate between them, treats *contraries* as if they were *contradictories;* when one deals with a situation involving gradations and middle ground in strict, either-or *contradictory* terms. I recall quite vividly the intense conflict in a certain midwestern village over the issue of flourine in the

---

[4] Joseph W. Still examines the "life or death" polarization in his article, "Levels of Life and Semantic Confusion," *ETC.: A Review of General Semantics,* Vol. 28, No. 1, March 1971, pp. 9–20.

[5] For a more detailed attack on this spurious dichotomy see: Eugene S. Richardson, Jr., "'Animal' or 'Plant'?" *Chicago Natural History Museum Bulletin,* February 1955, pp. 6–9 and Marston Bates, *Animal Worlds* (London: Thos. Nelson & Sons Ltd., 1963) , pp. 13–14.

town's drinking water. Impressive scientific evidence had been presented to the effect that fluorine in proper proportion to the water markedly reduced dental decay, especially in children. But nothing could persuade the majority of citizens that the fluorine would not be poisonous, and the health measure was voted down.

The fluorine issue involved contraries; it was a matter of gradations. But the majority of the people treated it *as* if they were dealing with contradictories. "Fluorine," they polarized, "is either poisonous or it's safe. We know it's poisonous, so we're not going to have anything to do with it!"

Fluorine is, of course, a deadly poison—*in sufficient quantities.* But medical and dental research had demonstrated that in minute amounts (as with other "poisons," such as iodine, chlorine, and arsenic) it was highly beneficial. It is the failure of some people to see the *graded* uses and effects of flourine that cost the town a valuable health aid.

CONSEQUENCES

Let us examine some of the manifestations and effects of polarization.

Deluding ourselves

Not the least of the negative effects of polarization is that we may deceive ourselves. While the following example may seem extreme, it does illustrate the extent to which one can beguile himself with his own polarizations:

A man of forty consulted a physician by reason of extreme obsessive (either-or) disability; his history showed that he had never contrived to adapt himself to easy association with his fellow-men and women. So far as women were concerned he had a series of reflections which horrified him. In an interview he revealed a classification of all women into contrasting classes—the thin and virtuous, the fat and vicious. He felt that he should marry, and the idea of marriage to any but a thin and virtuous woman was inconceivable. Nevertheless, he was attracted only by fat women, and his few would-be virtuous approaches to thin women had been signally unsuccessful. The alternatives he proposed to himself were fantastic and utterly without warrant in the world of fact. But the endless internal argument that exhausted him was conducted entirely in these terms. For many years his intimate thinking of this important relation had been of this general character.[6]

As bizarre as this unfortunate man's perceptions may have been, are they really much different from the polarizations so many of us practice?[7] I knew an aggressive young man who vowed while in college that his annual income at the age of 30 would be $40,000. Today he is 40—bitter and disillusioned, for he is making "only" $25,000. In his eyes he is a dismal failure.

For several years the comptroller of a big firm, looking forward to his own retirement, had been grooming a man we'll call Smith as his successor. Smith was aware of this plan and worked so successfully toward the goal that he was also being considered as a candidate to step eventually from the comptrollership to the presidency. Then one day he went completely to pieces.

The comptroller asked him sympathetically what was the matter.

"I've just found out," Smith said after some coaxing, "that I've got diabetes."

Examination by a specialist showed that he had only a mild case and that with insulin shots and reasonable care in his diet he would have no trouble. This enabled him to get back to work with much of his old efficiency, but he insisted that he be dropped from consideration as the comptroller's successor.

"Up to now," he explained, "I've hardly been sick a day in my life. Now I'll never again be able to think of myself as healthy."

Smith destroyed his career because he saw health as an absolute. That is, he saw himself as formerly absolutely healthy and now absolutely unhealthy. He had completely obliterated from his mind the possibility of a middle ground.[8]

Another common self-delusion is the false dichotomy of "win-lose." This one seems to plague commercial television in particular. Polls are conducted frequently to estimate the audience size of various programs. These "ratings" often play an important part in destiny of a given series. However, not uncommonly, a series is cancelled largely because it failed to run *first*. For example, *Mr. Novak*, al-

---

6 Elton Mayo, *Some Notes on the Psychology of Pierre Janet* (Cambridge, Mass.: Harvard University Press, 1948), p. 80.

7 Dolliver and Anderson identify four types of debilitating internal conflicts which stem from polarization. See Robert H. Dolliver and Wayne P. Anderson, "Polarities, Perceptions, and Problems," *ETC.: A Review of General Semantics*, Vol. 28, No. 3, September 1971, pp. 293–301.

8 Robert Froman, "How to Say What You Mean," *Nation's Business*, May 1957. Reprinted by permission.

though highly regarded by critics and at least some segments of the public, was dropped. This, despite an audience rating at over 85 percent of that of its chief competitor in the time period. Surely, there is *some* merit in coming in a *good second.*[9]

Deluding others

Polarization may, of course, be used to mislead others. In their famous debates on slavery, Stephen A. Douglas attempted to use polarization to his advantage when he threw apparent contradictories at Abraham Lincoln. Lincoln neatly sidestepped the horns of the false dilemma by exclaiming: ". . . I protest against the counterfeit logic which concludes that because I do not want a black woman for a slave, I must necessarily want her for a wife. I need not have her for either. I can just leave her alone."

Polarization is also a favored ploy for "getting out from under," as per Captain Queeg's stock reply to those who criticized his unreasonably harsh treatment of subordinates: "Well, what do you want me to do—give him a commendation?"[10]

And parents often use it on children for "their own good." A friend of ours thought she had mastered the technique when she would ask her four-year-old: "Which would you rather do first, Johnny, take your bath or brush your teeth?" Johnny, of course, didn't want to do either, but how can you say no to a question like that?

But Johnny learned to retaliate in kind. One day while shopping with his mother, he pulled her over to the toy department and demanded: "What are you going to buy me, Mom, a bicycle or an electric train?"

Among the most effective polarizers in modern history were Adolf Hitler and his Nazi henchmen. "Everyone in Germany," declared Hitler, "is a National Socialist—the few outside the party are either lunatics or idiots."[11] The thesis they so successfully inculcated was that an enemy of the National Socialist party was necessarily an

---

[9] For an analysis of the obstructive role of the "win-lose" polarization in union-management relations, see: Robert R. Blake, "From Industrial Warfare to Collaboration: A Behavioral Science Approach," *General Semantics Bulletin,* Nos. 28 and 29, 1961–62, pp. 49–60.

[10] Herman Wouk, *The Caine Mutiny* (Garden City, N.Y.: Doubleday & Co., Inc., 1951).

[11] *New York Times,* April 5, 1938.

enemy of Germany. "Even if you loved Germany greatly," wrote Hayakawa, "but still didn't agree with the National Socialists as to what was good for Germany, you were liquidated."[12]

The pendulum effect

One of the most destructive consequences of polarization is the *escalating conflict* which might be called the "pendulum effect." Let the pendulum represent one's perception of reality—especially his feelings, attitudes, opinions, and value-judgments about reality. When the pendulum hangs straight down at dead-center, one regards his perception as realistic, virtuous, intelligent, sane, honest, honorable, and so forth. *Key Assertion:* Most of us, under most circumstances, regard *our* pendulum *at or very near dead-center* most of the time.

Enter two friends, Tom and Mike.

1.   Tom makes a statement representing his perception of reality.

2.   Mike's perception differs somewhat from Tom's. Mike is at a critical fork in this process.

3A. Mike may recognize that perceptions, his own included, may be strongly conditioned by past experiences (see Chapter 3). Thus, it is understandable that Tom's perception could differ from his own. *OR* 3B. Mike may regard Tom's statement as representing *reality rather than Tom's perception of reality.*

4A. Unthreatened, Mike may be able to help Tom and himself understand why their perceptions differ. At least he can avoid contributing to a needless, nonconstructive conflict.   4B. Threatened (there can't be *two* realities), Mike may consider that either *his* pendulum has swung off center or—much more likely—that Tom's has. After all, it's either thee or me!

If Tom and Mike should *both* arrive at Stage 4B—each perceives his pendulum at dead-center and the other fellow's pendulum off center—we have the ingredients for the "pendulum effect." Let us dramatize the process. (See Figure 10–1.)

The alternating swings of the pendulum rapidly reach an almost irreconcilable amplitude. The men are clearly at the unreasonable "you are *all* wrong—I am *all* right" stage.

---

[12] S. I. Hayakawa, *Language in Thought and Action* (New York: Harcourt, Brace & Co., Inc., 1949), p. 224.

FIGURE 10–1

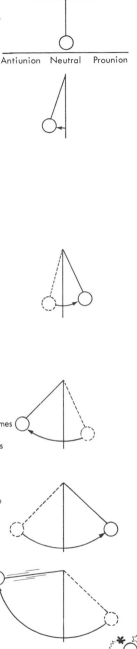

PENDULUM

Antiunion   Neutral   Prounion

SCENE: Two firends are drinking coffee at a restaurant counter. They have just begun to discuss the value of unions, a subject on which both are essentially neutral.

TOM: Did you see the newspaper this morning? That Senate investigating committee is really digging up the dirt. I guess some of these unions are out for what they can get.

(Mike may not be aware of it but he is somewhat threatened by this statement. Confronted with the "thee or me" dilemma he preceives Tom's remark as "off-center." On the conscious level he may be thinking: "I must bring this poor fellow back to reality." So he gives the pendulum a tug —a good one to make sure the pendulum returns to "center.")

MIKE: Now, wait a minute. Sure, there are a few crooked unions--or at least a few crooked officials in them, but most of the unions have been a terrific boost for the workingman.

(Now it is Tom's turn to be alarmed and he adopts the same defense mechanism. However, because of Mike's "good tug," Tom perceives the pendulum as even farther off-center. Obvious remedy —an extra good counter tug.)

TOM: What do you mean, a boost for the workingman? Sure, the unions put more dough in his pockets, but what can he buy with it? Less than when he was getting half the money. And do you know why? Because the money comes from the companies and they get it right back from the workers as consumers with jacked-up prices. And who's scooping up the gravy while all this is going on? The unions!

MIKE: Says who! Don't forget the fat company executives who are raking in a half million or more a year--and with their stock options and delayed salaries and so on-- and don't forget about Uncle Sam's share, either!

TOM: Listen you . . . !

MIKE: Yeah? ! ! . . .

The "alls" in the previous sentence suggest an important element of the pendulum effect. It is the combatants' failure to be *selective.* Faced with a controversial subject they fail to *discriminate among its components*—to identify which aspects they genuinely regard as valid and those which are questionable or could be conceded. Instead they imprison themselves with all-inclusive defenses of their position and blanket indictments of the opposition's.

Often the unconscious assumption is that to concede anything weakens one's position. Lord Acton's advice, however, seems more valid—accede in everything you can, for this strengthens your case for the part you retain.

Sidney Harris, on hearing an argument by two unyielding people about the "the youth problem," was moved to point up the need for discrimination in argumentation:

. . . The attitudes and actions of modern youth are a wonderful illustration of this necessity—to be blindly "for" or "against" what they are saying or doing is stupid and unperceptive, for their motives are as mixed as their conduct.

I like their humanism and their sense that the person must take precedence over the impersonal mechanisms in society—but I dislike their arrogant assumption that institutions and mechanisms are always wrong.

I agree with their feeling that war is a social cancer the world can no longer afford—if it ever could—but I disagree with violent protests that negate the spirit of love and brotherhood and turn them into mere political slogans.

I sympathize with their resentment against educational systems that fail to educate, and must be basically reformed—but I resent their assumption that they should decide what and how they should be taught.

I welcome their sensitivity and their freedom from the emotional constrictions that hang up so many older Americans—but I am fearful that their anti-intellectualism, their know-nothingness, will play right into the hands of the fascists they think they are opposing.

Such a list could be extended by a dozen items, and each of us has an obligation to seek what is good and useful and decent and necessary in the youth movement, and to reject the other elements. But scarcely anyone does this—we are so busy defending or attacking a way of life that is a tangled mixture as if it were a single strand.[13]

The "pendulum effect," then, is the pattern of threat triggering an overreactive defense which, in turn, becomes an even more acute

---

[13] Sidney J. Harris, "Shun Intellectual 'Package Deals,'" *Chicago Daily News,* October 12, 1970, p. 8. Reprinted by permission of Sidney J. Harris and Publishers—Hall Syndicate.

counterthreat, and so on, which progressively drives people into *seemingly* polar positions. They mutually frighten each other into extremities which neither party normally would consider tenable.

The pendulum effect is so pervasive that it is almost a "rhythm" of social affairs. Trace the pattern of an innovation, for example. The new formulation or method, the new science or art, the invention, and so forth, are typically introduced with enthusiasm and often with overstatement. If the claims are too exhuberant, the public (lay or professional) is quite likely to resist. The more resistance, the more frantic become the efforts of the proponents and the pendulum swings in ever greater arcs.

Trouble over innovations is sometimes aggravated by the personality of the discoverer. Discoverers are often men with little experience or skill in human relations, and less trouble would have arisen had they been more diplomatic. The fact that Harvey (discoverer of the circulation of blood) succeeded eventually in having his discovery recognized, and that Semmelweis (discoverer of puerperal fever) failed, may be explained on this basis. Semmelweis showed no tact at all, but Harvey dedicated his book to King Charles, drawing the parallel between the King and realm, and the heart and body.[14]

For examples of the pendulum effect on a more prosaic level, I could not resist these two incidents:

In Marlboro, Md., truck driver John Sanford, Jr., 33, was arrested for doing 50 mph in a 35-mph zone, was then charged with impeding traffic when he refused to drive more than 30 mph in a 50-mph zone on his way to the police station.[15]

Recently a college bookstore in the Northwest was incurring considerable pilferage. To curtail shoplifting, a regulation was imposed requiring students to check their outer coats and bags. A number of students, male and female, entered the bookstore and, by way of protest, checked *everything!*[16] The bare facts speak for themselves.

Polarization in America

Unfortunately, the pendulum effect is not always so innocuous as witness the divisiveness which wracks our nation today.

---

[14] W. I. B. Beveridge, *The Art of Scientific Investigation* (New York: W. W. Norton & Co., Inc., 1950), chap. 9.

[15] *Time*, May 16, 1955, p. 124. Reprinted by permission.

[16] Ralph S. Brown, Jr., "Upholding Professional Standards in the '70s," *American Association of University Professors Bulletin*, Vol. 56, No. 2, p. 119.

. . . two nations between whom there is no intercourse and no sympathy; who are as ignorant of each other's habits, thoughts, and feelings, as if they were dwellers in different planets.

. . . its strength gradually sapped by dissension and division by an incomprehensible blindness in foreign, domestic, and military policy, by the ineptness of its leaders, the corruption of its press, and by a feeling of growing confusion, hopelessness, and cynicism in its people.

No, these are not impressions of present-day America, but they do suggest a precedent for our condition. The first is Disraeli's depiction of 19th-century England. The second is William Shirer's assessment of pre–World War II France.[17] It was to this polarization of right and left, young and old, rich and poor, rather than to inferior military forces, that Shirer attributed France's rapid capitulation to the Nazis.

We may not yet be, in Disraeli's words, two nations but, according to *Time's* essayist, Henry Grunwald, we are in the grip of two views of reality.

In one view of reality, America is under attack from junior barbarians devoid of all respect and patriotism, spoiled by permissive parents and spineless college administrators, misguided by essentially subversive professors and other intellectuals; under attack also from blacks ungrateful for the favors done them and unwilling to work hard enough when crime is so much easier and more tempting. In the other view, America is ruled by a hypocritical Establishment that prates of virtues it does not practice, instead putting profit above all else, fighting an immoral war for material gain and in pursuit of some insane imperialism, and racist to the very marrow of its white bones.

On the one side, law-and-order, honor, country, decency pitted against treason, anarchy, filth, immorality. On the other, freedom, justice, "the people" against entrenched power, blind chauvinism, blood lust and repression. Two visions: two ghastly caricatures: accepted as truths by more and more Americans.

But still far from totally accepted. There are countless gradations between the two visions, and a genuine, tortured desire not to surrender to the extremes.[18]

It is not surprising that some historians contend that we have not been as polarized since the Civil War. How has this come to be? The

---

[17] William L. Shirer, *The Collapse of the Third Republic: An Inquiry into the Fall of France in 1940* (New York: Simon and Schuster, 1969), pp. 11–12.

[18] Henry Grunwald, "Thoughts on a Troubled Eldorado," *Time,* June 2, 1970, p. 18. Reprinted by permission from *Time, The Weekly Newsmagazine,* © Time Inc.

answer would be encylopedic. I will be so bold as to suggest just one contributor to the schisms that beset America. It lies in the ways in which some people *use language* in talking and writing and thinking about Vietnam, racial, ethnic, and sexual inequalities, poverty, labor strife, campus violence, and other problems that confront us.

I submit that people tend to *become* polarized partially because they talk in *polarized terms*. Consider the ubiquitous bumper slogan, "AMERICA—LOVE IT OR LEAVE IT." That has a ring to it and when uttered with sufficient fervor it may tingle the spine. But unfortunately, regardless of the composer's intention, it *can* be an expression of a mindless retaliation against some of the equally mindless criticisms heaped upon our nation. When it is intended or interpreted thusly, it becomes a rank polarization which seems to offer two alternatives: (1) blind faith in and acceptance of the status quo, or (2) give up—and get out.

This was essentially the sentiment expressed in Stephen Decater's famous toast (Norfolk, Virginia—1816) :

> Our country! In her intercourse with foreign nations
> may she always be in the right; but our country, right
> or wrong.

Personally, I prefer Carl Schurz's expression:

> Our country, right or wrong.
> When right, to be kept right;
> When wrong, to put right.
> *—From an address in Congress, 1872.*

So if we must sloganize, perhaps we could adorn our bumpers with a third alternative: AMERICA—STAY AND IMPROVE IT. That may not stimulate the adrenals as much but, it seems to me, it makes eminently better sense. For as Edmund Burke said about England in the 18th Century:

> To make us love our country, our country ought to be
> lovely. To make our country lovely is a task calling for
> the application of intellect to social policy. Let us be
> about it.

The plight of the moderate.   The more divided a society becomes the more difficult it is to remain temperate. One either remains silent, passive, and ineffectual or he speaks out and risks being driven to one or the other of the poles. The distinguished critic, Joseph Wood Krutch, once said: "From experience I have learned that you can't criticize anything without having it supposed that you favor the opposite extreme." Horace warned against this tendency 2,000 years earlier: "When I caution you against becoming a miser, I do not therefore advise you to become a prodigal or a spend thrift."

The plight of the moderate was depicted adroitly a year or so ago in a cartoon showing two men talking. The gist of their conversation:

FIRST MAN: Well, what's your choice—anarchy or repression?

SECOND MAN: What do I get if I choose anarchy?

FIRST MAN: You get crime in the streets, riots, chaos.

SECOND MAN: What do I get if I choose repression?

FIRST MAN: You get law and order, internment camps, censorship, and police brutality.

SECOND MAN: And what do I get if I choose peace, brotherhood among men, and an end to poverty?

FIRST MAN: You get ignored . . . So what's your choice—anarchy or repression?

This was the dilemma to which Senator Margaret Chase Smith addressed herself. A *New York Times* editorial about her Senate speech states in part:

The basic message of the Senator from Maine is that the deep pool of centrist opinion in the country, that essential guarantee against violent political upheavals, is being dangerously shaken. Primarily the threat this time is from the "radical left that advocates and practices violence and defiance of the law."

But beyond that present danger lurks the threat of repression, just beginning to show itself in a governmental defense that is "too extreme and unfair and too repetitive." One feeds on the other. But between the extremes of anarchy and repression, Mrs. Smith has no doubt that the American people, if they feel driven to choose, would take repression in the name of order.

Every present sign makes it plain that she is right. Nor do we doubt that once a national reaction set in against the nihilism and intolerance of the extreme radicals, now so visible in the streets and on television, decent distinctions would tend to disappear. Actually only a few make the campuses of the nation, in the Senator's words, "a rendezvous for obscenity, for trespass, for violence. . . ." But even now their activities are enough, in the eyes of some Americans, to discredit all students, all faculties, all intellectuals.

Many more students, minority groups and radicals—though far from a majority of any of them—are in truth guilty of "refusing to listen while demanding communication." Freedom of speech is scandalously often denied these days, even to people of national stature, by shouting them into silence or even by physically seizing microphones and platforms. And while very few stoop to such stupidity as desecrating the flag, it does not take many instances of such grossness to outrage the feelings of citizens for whom the flag is still a symbol deserving respect.

No one who wants to preserve that civilized discourse without which democracy is unworkable can take issue with Senator Smith's timely warning. We wish only that she had added some notice of the many young Americans today who do know and appreciate what she is talking about and who are working, in increasing numbers within the political system to promote their views on the great issues of the day.

For they know, as she does, that with all its imperfections, the American Constitution has given people the longest span of self-government, of rule subject to popular change, however gradual, in the whole history of the world. That is not something that any of us—left, right or center—should willingly see endangered by anyone else, no matter what his ideology or degree of self-righteousness.[19]

America's viability. Our nation's vitality historically has been its *viability*—its ability and willingness to self-examine, to adjust, to evolve. But we must protect that viability and the system which preserves it from destruction by the polarities of anarchy and suppression. Dwight D. Eisenhower wrote: "We must never confuse honest dissent with disloyal subversion." And Robert Clark, president of the University of Oregon, said:

We ought to distinguish between speech and unlawful action. We ought not to tremble in the presence of ideas which seem to threaten us. We ought to combat them, not with force or coercion, but with reason, and with better ideas.[20]

The danger is that ideas, per se, will be suspect. This is already evident when the hard-hat right and the Yippie-fringe of the left each manifest an authoritarianism which denies even the expression, to say nothing of the examination, of contrary viewpoints.

Fear is ruinous. It compels the fearful to turn to authority, how-

---

[19] "Mrs. Smith's Good Counsel," *The New York Times,* June 3, 1970, p. 40. © 1970 by the New York Times Company. Reprinted by permission.

[20] Quoted in "The Truth Shouldn't Frighten," *Chicago Sun-Times,* August 23, 1970, Sect. 2, p. 11.

ever oppressive, for security. And for the oppressors fear is the fundamental means of control.

Former Attorney General Ramsey Clark recently told the National Students Association that "people who fear dissent will not know the truth." It is, after all, the truth, not fear, which will set us free.

Clearly, our vitality is our viability. Our Constitution is a remarkable document, but even it has been *amended 26*[21] times!

CONTRIBUTING FACTORS

We have defined polarization as the confusing of *contraries* for *contradictories*. We shall now examine some of the reasons for this misevaluation.

Similar grammatical form

Contraries and contradictories are often stated in a similar grammatical form:

You either had coffee this morning or you didn't. (Contradictories)
You are either a coffee fiend or a complete abstainer. (Contraries)

That each is frequently expressed in the ". . . either . . . or" pattern probably accounts for some of the confusion between them.

Neglect of middle ground

A more complex and important reason for polarization is the disregard or avoidance of the shadings and gradations between the extremes. The tendency to neglect the middle ground may be attributed to a number of factors. Most of the important ones fall under the headings of *conditioning* and *expediency*.

Conditioning.   All through life we are *conditioned* to *polarize*. It is altogether possible that our "training" in this respect begins even prenatally. Schilder has a theory about the role of simple motor activities in our conditioning:

It is probable that the charm of thinking in polarities is due to the fact that simple motor attitudes can be expressed in this way. We turn to an object or we turn away from it, we may approach an object or run away

---

[21] As of June 30, 1971.

from it. There are extensor reflexes and flexor reflexes; we master the motions of bending or stretching. We may swallow something or we may spit it out, but these are rather primitive actions and do not lead to a deeper appreciation of the outward world.[22]

Consider, too, our linguistic conditioning. Let me illustrate the point by inviting you to take a little test. First of all, give the opposites of the following words:

white	— _____
good	— _____
polite	— _____
honest	— _____
success	— _____

Simple, wasn't it? Opposites come very readily to mind. But now try the second part of the test: fill in the *gradational terms* between the extremes.

white	— ____ – ____ – gray	— ____ – ____ —	black
good	— ____ – ____ – ____ – ____ – ____ —	bad
polite	— ____ – ____ – ____ – ____ – ____ —	impolite
honest	— ____ – ____ – ____ – ____ – ____ —	dishonest
success	— ____ – ____ – ____ – ____ – ____ —	failure

You probably found this much more difficult. Actually, the cards were stacked against you. There are comparatively few "intermediate terms" in our language. Of course, we have the imprecise, quantifying adjectives and adverbs such as "slightly," "fairly," "medium," "average," "very," "extremely," and so on, but using them requires extra thought and effort, and we frequently neglect them.

The paucity of middle terms tends to encourage polarization. If we cannot say a man is *entirely* honest, it is easiest to classify him at the opposite pole as "dishonest." We disregard the infinite gradations of "honesty" between the poles partially because we lack the quantifying substantive *words* to express them. Recently, a young high-school graduate hanged himself because he had failed by a slim margin to be elected to the National Honor Society. It seemed to make little difference to him that he had been president of his class, that his parents had given him a new convertible as a graduation gift, that he had been awarded a college scholarship, and that he had been ac-

---

[22] Paul Schilder, *Goals and Desires of Man* (New York: Columbia University Press, 1942), p. 211. Reprinted by permission.

cepted by one of the foremost universities in the nation. In his state of depression it was impossible to conceive of anything short of "complete success" as other than "total failure."

There are *many* other factors in our environment which condition us to polarize with ease and alacrity. I shall touch upon just a few of them.

a) THE "TWO-SIDED QUESTION." It seems as if someone is always attempting to temper a heated argument by admonishing: "Now remember, there are two sides to every question!" Our well-meaning friend may actually be more misleading than helpful, for few questions of any importance have only two sides—they are *multi*sided. Are the problems of public school integration, atomic weapons control, or welfare simple pro and con affairs? Or, for that matter, can the problem of choosing a vocation or a mate, of raising children, or of earning a living be solved by a categorical "yes" or "no"? Reporter-columnist Nicholas Von Hoffman stated: "The illusion of objectivity is dead. The old criteria for objectivity are that there are two sides to an argument and both must be reported. This defies the realities of today, where there are 30 or 40 sides to a story."

And yet the "two-sided question" myth is a prevailing one. "Did you hear about the Smiths' breakup? It was all his fault." "No, she was to blame." Could not *both* of them have contributed to the strife and could there not have been factors beyond the control of both—inability to have children, financial difficulties, in-law interference?

To be sure, there are legitimate two-sided questions—in law and in debate, for example. But the charges or resolutions are scrupulously phrased and defined in order to permit positions of "guilty" and "not guilty" (note the avoidance of the contraries "guilty" and "innocent"), "affirmative" and "negative."

b) POPULAR SONGS. One would not have to search long through the lyrics of popular songs to find exhortations to polarize—an influence, unfortunately, that most of us tend to underestimate. Note the utter disregard for gradations in such titles as "All or Nothing at All," "It Must Be Right; It Can't Be Wrong," and so forth.

c) CHEAP FICTION. Whether it occurs in the form of paperback novels, pulp magazines, television, or the movies, cheap fiction is replete with polarization. The "beauty" is breathtaking, while the "beast" is grotesque; the rich are fabulously so, and the poor are penniless; the paragon of honesty invariably clashes with the despicably deceitful.

If there is anything adult about the current rash of "adult" movies it is the avoidance of depicting the "good guy" as insufferably virtuous and the "bad guy" as unrelievedly evil.

d) RESTRICTIVE LAWS.   Laws are sometimes written in either-or, blanket terms. Several years ago the Food and Drug Administration was required to forbid the use of coal tar dies in lipsticks. Under an archaic law an ingested product (ladies evidently consume minute amounts of their lipstick) containing *any amount* of *any toxic material* had to be banned. The industry claimed that a woman would have to eat 100 lipsticks a day for 90 days to suffer any ill effects. Even the FDA admitted that the amount of dye seemed completely harmless, but its hands were tied until the law was changed.

Police officers are often faced with the necessity of modifying the letter of the law. With limited resources they must use discretion in determining the *level of enforcement* which is desirable and feasible.

The State of Illinois has a typically broad statute defining gambling. Under its provisions, the flip of a coin to determine who shall purchase coffee or the playing of penny-ante poker must be considered a violation. As a general policy, the Chicago Police Department devotes its efforts to seeking out gambling activities that are part of an organized operation. We do not devote manpower to ferreting out social card games conducted in the privacy of a home. . . .

The exercise of discretion, on the other hand, suggests that the police are required, because of a variety of factors, to decide overtly how much of an effort is to be made to enforce specific laws. It recognizes that actions short of arrest may achieve the desired goal. It implies that a police officer may decide not to make an arrest even in those situations in which an offense has been committed and both the offender and the evidence are at hand. It tends to portray police officers as something other than automatons.[23]

Expediency.   It is much easier to think of a person as either intelligent or stupid than to rate him more precisely along a continuum of mental ability. It might be considerably simpler for a teacher to "pass" or "fail" his students. But rating them along the range of A–B–C–D–F, percentages, and so on, requires a good deal more consideration and judgment.

And, too, we are often pressured for decisions. We feel we haven't

---

[23] From an address by Herman Goldstein, executive assistant to the superintendent of the Chicago Police Department, given before the Ninth National Institute on Police and Community Relations, Michigan State University, 1963.

the time to investigate and analyze. And we are uncomfortable with the uncategorized, the unresolved—so "if it ain't this, it's gotta be that."

CORRECTIVES

To prevent polarization, habituate these techniques:

1.   Detect the contrary.
2.   Specify the degree—apply the HOW–MUCH INDEX.
3.   Separate the double contraries.
4.   Guard against the pendulum effect.

Detect the contrary

The first step in combating polarization is to detect the *contrary*. But how can one quickly, yet dependably, distinguish it from the *contradictory?* Aristotle's Laws of Thought are 23 centuries old, but, *so far as they apply*, they are still valid and practical.

1.   Something must be either A or non-A.
2.   Nothing can be both A and non-A at the same time and place.

Use them to test an either-or situation.

An employer: "The biggest problem with secretaries is initiative. Some, when they see a job to be done, will always go right ahead and do it without having to be told. But the others—you literally have to lead them by the hand—especially if it involves anything outside of their regular routine."

Which is involved—*contraries* or *contradictories?* To qualify as a contradictory, the situation must measure up to both of Aristotle's requirements. Must a secretary either "always go right ahead and do it" or "be led by the hand"? Hardly; there is abundant middle ground. The situation fails on the first criterion of the contradictory and is, therefore, a contrary.

Specify the degree—apply the how-much index

Having determined that one is dealing with a contrary, the next step is to specify the degree between the extremes. In other words, it is no longer a question of *either-or* but of *how much*.

If a man steals a ten-cent stamp from the office postage supply, we might describe him (or his action) as dishonest—or at least as not honest. If a man steals $100,000 we could say the same thing. But would we not have an obligation to *quantify*—to distinguish the *degree* of dishonesty involved? Do other circumstances influence the *degree of honesty?* Is there a difference between stealing a given amount from a rich man and stealing it from a poor man? Does stealing with the intent of repaying make a difference? What about stealing for a worthy cause?

To a great extent the method of applying the *How-Much Index* depends upon the nature of the contrary and the availability of terms to denote the degrees.

Use a quantitative index when possible. Some objective contraries (e.g., tall-short, light-heavy, hot-cold, large-small, and so forth) lend themselves to a quantifying index. *Time* magazine writers, for example, often use the "telling detail" to specify. "The boy was tall (5 feet 11 inches) for his age (13) . . ."; ". . . a small (annual gross: $300,000) management consulting firm . . ."; ". . . has the largest undergraduate enrollment (18,000) in the state."

Use substantive middle terms when available. Many contraries, of course, cannot be numerically quantified. One cannot describe a person as 89 percent patriotic, 2.3 times more friendly than his neighbor, or $1/4$ ill. But some contraries do have a supply of substantive middle terms which may be helpful in specifying approximate degrees between the poles. The following adjectives, by no means as precise and as nonoverlapping as inches, pounds, or miles per hour, may suggest some of the gradations and nuances along the "beautiful-ugly" continuum:

agreeable	drab	grisly
attractive	dreadful	grotesque
beauteous	elegant	gruesome
becoming	exquisite	handsome
bonny	fair	heavenly
charming	fetching	hideous
coarse	frightful	homely
comely	ghastly	horrible
cute	glamorous	horrid
dazzling	good-looking	ill-favored
devastating	gorgeous	loathesome
divine	graceless	lovely

monstrous	presentable	revolting
nondescript	pretty	uncomely
ordinary	radiant	unprepossessing
passable	ravishing	unseemly
piquant	repugnant	unsightly
plain	repulsive	well-favored
pleasing	resplendent	winsome

Use quantifying terms. Certainly, words such as "very," "slightly," "moderately," "extremely," "generally," "seldom," "average," "fairly," "often," "medium," and so forth, do not approach the specificity of the numerical indexes, but they are obviously superior to the absence of quantification. Remove the quantifying terms, "most" and "generally," from the statement below, and note how much more harsh, unyielding, and "either-or-ish" it becomes:

Most American educators agree that the elective system in our colleges and high schools leads generally to an aimless nibbling at knowledge, or to excessive specialization.

Separate the double contraries

The *compound* polarization merits special consideration. Actually, it involves mistaking double (or multiple) contraries for single contradictories. This bit of doggerel epitomizes a common *compound* polarization:

Girls at college
Are of two strata:
Those with dates
And those with data.[24]

The old "beautiful-but-dumb" cliché. The counterpart for males: "All brawn and no brain." Both notions are not only fallacious, but some evidence indicates that if there is a correlation between physical and intellectual superiorities it is a positive rather than a negative one.

But let us return to the double contraries—how can we deal with them? The first step is to cut them down to size—to separate the contraries and work on them individually. Suppose we take the "brawn-brain" fable. Expanded, it would appear: People are either brainy (and puny) or brawny (and stupid). It is immediately clear that

---

24 Richard Armour, *Reader's Digest,* January 1952, p. 20. Reprinted by permission.

there are two "continua" involved—intelligence and strength. We can now proceed to specify degrees on each of them with the *How-Much Index* as before. Graphically, our double value-determining might be expressed as shown in Figure 10–2.

FIGURE 10–2

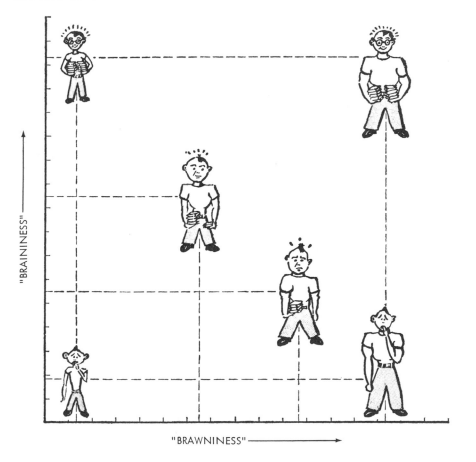

Lest the foregoing treatment appear a bit frivolous, consider these compound polarizations:

There are two kinds of doctors; Those who are dedicated; those who are dollar-conscious.[25]

Is it not more likely that most doctors are some degree of both?

---

[25] Attributed to a high-ranking officer of a national service and fraternal organization.

And what do you make of the executive's evaluation in the incident below?

Eugene R. Lang,[26] 51, a foreman at the Rugge Company was recently dismissed from the firm. Lang had been with Rugge for 18 years. Wayne S. Finley, president, gave this reason for Lang's dismissal: "He revealed his position as pro-Communist by his many outspoken attacks on Senator [Joseph] McCarthy and his wonderful work."

Combining contraries. Compound contraries, then, are misleading when (1) they are treated as contradictories and (2) they are falsely correlated. But sometimes contraries *are* related—and useful information can be expressed by combining them. This is provided they are dealt with *as contraries* rather than as contradictories.

The Weather Bureau has done this in devising the Temperature-Humidity Index (THI). What is important to most of us is not how cold or hot or how humid or dry the weather will be, but how comfortable *we* will be. A temperature of 85 degrees Fahrenheit sounds warm but the THI tells us that at a 25 percent relative humidity the day will be reasonably comfortable. The THI tells us that a more moderate 75 degrees will be rather unpleasant if it is accompanied by a humidity over 60 percent.

More recently the Bureau has combined the contraries of temperature and wind velocity to give us the Wind-Chill Index. 10 degrees above zero coupled with a brisk breeze can be decidedly more uncomfortable and dangerous than 10 degrees below zero on a calm day.

Guard against the pendulum effect

One can minimize the pendulum effect or at least his contribution to it if he is mindful of two of its key characteristics:

Perceptions are conditioned. Recognize that perceptions in the area of value judgments, feelings, opinions, and the like are conditioned by experience. Thus there is no need to be dismayed if the other fellow's perceptions do not happen to coincide with your own. If you perceive no threat in the differences between you, you can dampen the pendulum effect because you will be less prompted to talk and act in ways which threaten the other person. Recall it is the ever-increasing *mutual* threats that keep the pendulum swinging in a widening arc. This, feels Bayard Rustin, a leading civil rights figure,

---

[26] All names with the exception of Senator McCarthy's have been disguised.

is a prime danger in the racial equality issue: "As you get black backlash in response to white backlash the intensity of white backlash increases. We're in trouble because one backlash reinforces the other."

The complexity of issues.   Controversial issues are generally
highly complex. Because they are multifaceted it is highly unlikely
that any one viewpoint will be 100 percent valid. Be wary, therefore,
of blanket positions (no pun intended). One can prevent or ameliorate the pendulum effect if he analyzes the issues, carefully selecting
aspects to be conceded and specifying the nuances and gradations
between the polarities.

SUMMARY

Polarization tends to occur when contraries (situations involving
graded variations, middle ground) are treated *as if* they were contradictories (strictly either-or affairs).

We may be forced by habit to think in polarities, but this is only a
habit without regard for the real structure of things . . . If one observes
carefully enough, true opposites are not found. Thinking in opposites is
only a hasty oversimplification.[27]

Moreover, we may be misled not only by our own polarizations but
by the purposeful or unintentional polarizations of others.

One of the most destructive forms of polarization is the "pendulum
effect"—the escalation of conflict. It thrives on overreactions. Re-
grettably, the easiest, the most dramatic, and the most infantile response to opposition is absolute counter-opposition. Such polarization
in America has become a commonplace but it is nonetheless a clear
and present threat. Whether suppression or anarchy or sanity will
prevail is yet to be seen. But one cannot but agree with William
Buckley's admonition: "Reason may not save us; but the absence of
reason will not save us."

The factors contributing to polarization include the similar grammatical form of contradictories and contraries and, more importantly,
our propensity to neglect the middle ground. Conditioning and ex-
pedience are among the influences accounting for the latter.

Polarization tends to be reduced when one develops habits, first, of
distinguishing contraries from contradictories and, second, of specifying the degree (applying the How-Much Index). In the case of

---

[27] Paul Schilder, *Goals and Desires of Man.*

compound polarizations the initial step is to separate the contraries. Then the gradations can be specified on each continuum.

The vicious pendulum effect can be dampened if we can recognize differing perceptions as products of differing conditionings and if we can acknowledge that in complex issues literally no one (including ourselves) has *the one* complete and unassailable viewpoint.

EPILOGUE

On May 8, 1970, a few days after the tragic deaths of several Kent State University students, the International Communication Society adopted a resolution. I believe it is a most fitting epilogue to this chapter.

The members of the International Communication Association share the sorrow and dismay of others at the deaths at Kent State University this week. The Association cannot afford to be indifferent to violence as a means of resolving conflict or to the resulting tragedies.

In a divided society, opportunity for expression and dissent must be guarded zealously. We believe that many of those who demonstrate do so because they genuinely believe that the established channels of communication are ineffective or blocked to them.

We believe that violence is perpetuated by *escalating confrontation and retaliation* in the absence of effective lines of communication. Society needs to develop new means of expressing conflict, because decision by violence derogates rational processes and constitutional rights.

While lack of communication is not a necessary and sufficient cause of violence and polarization in our society, we believe that establishing effective lines of communication and understanding between dissident groups is necessary to achieve a better means of living together.

Accordingly, the International Communication Association encourages its members to bring their professional competence and expertise to bear on the problems of achieving a tolerant and just society. Specifically, we encourage our members to devote research and theoretical energies to the problem of understanding obstacles to communication between groups in society, developing in these groups a commitment to rational decision-making through communication and understanding and appreciating each others' motives and humanity.

Therefore, the Eighteenth Convention of the International Communication Association wishes to go on record as approving this resolution and further resolves that papers prepared in accordance with the preceding principles be presented to the annual convention in 1971 at a special session devoted to Research on Communication as an Alternative to Violence.[28]

DISCUSSION QUESTIONS

1. "Faced with tremendous increases in applicants, should colleges stiffen admissions requirements or expand facilities?" How do you feel about this?

2. What cases in the *polarization* chapter as well as in other chapters seem to involve the "pendulum effect"?

3. Give ten examples of true contradictories and ten involving contraries.

4. "Modern logic has abandoned one of Aristotle's most basic principles: the law of the excluded middle, meaning that a statement must either be true or false. In the new system a statement may have three values: true, false, or indeterminate. A close analogy to this system in the legal field is the Scottish trial law, which allows three verdicts—guilty, not guilty or not proven."—John Pfeiffer (*Scientific American*) quoted in Harry Maynard "How Can We Say What We Mean?" *Dateline '62*, Vol. 6, No. 1, April 13, 1962, p. 29.
   How do you react to the above?

5. Precisely what is *polarization?* What contributes to it? How can it be prevented?

6. What is the *pendulum effect?* What are its "mechanics"—i.e., how does it occur? Remedies?

7. Was there any polarization involved in the "General Patton and the Sicilian Slapping Incident" case (Chapter 6)?

8. The "Craving for Certainty," which was discussed in Chapter 8—does it have any bearing on polarization?

9. "Be contented and you'll live longer."
   "Don't be contented—or you'll stagnate."

   "War is coming—because there have always been wars."
   "War isn't coming—because neither side can win it and knows it."

   "Think big—for you have to spend money to make money."
   "Watch your pennies—and the dollars will take care of themselves."

   "An objective test doesn't let you express yourself."
   "An essay test is so vague you don't know what's expected."

   Your reaction?

---

[28] Reprinted by permission. Italics are mine.

10. "What we tragically fail to recognize is that extremism is always a symptom of failure in the feedback process of an institution, and not a cause of anything in itself."

—Sydney J. Harris

How do you feel about the above statement? Why?

11. "I divide all readers into two classes: those who read to remember, and those who read to forget."

—William Lyon Phelps

How do you react to that statement? Why?

12. What pendulum effects do you see occurring today in your community? In our nation? In the world?

13. "In nature and in the id, there are no opposites which exclude each other."

—Eric Berne

Do you agree?

14. "Life or death" and "male or female"—list and discuss other "contraries masquerading as contradictories." For example: "mind or body," "heredity or environment."

15. What is the "plight of the moderate"? Can one be a centrist and still be effective?

16. In addition to the THI Index and the Wind-Chill Index, what other combinations of contraries are useful?

17. Describe an incident, possibly involving yourself, in which polarization occurred. Analyze specifically why it occurred, what might have been done to prevent its happening, and what measures would prevent its recurrence.

CASES

Deadly force[29]

The use of deadly force in effecting the arrest of an alleged felon is a serious problem to the police officer and can place him in the position of judge and jury. He must at times decide the guilt or innocence of a person in a split second which ordinarily could take a court months of contemplation to decide.

Ralph Rogers, an officer for less than a month, was patrolling his post on foot. Suddenly, he saw a man sprinting from a store with a woman chasing after him, screaming, "Stop that robber!" The man was running toward an idling automobile. Another man was at the wheel, evidently waiting for the runner. The officer realized that he could not possibly overtake the fleet runner and considered for a moment his terrible dilemma. He decided against shooting, and the man scrambled into the car which was already starting to move—a screech of tires and the car turned a corner and was out of sight.

The lady, breathless, ran up to the officer. She was furious. "Why didn't you stop him!" she snarled. "You could have shot him easily! He stole $700 from me!"

The officer's face grew crimson. "Look, lady," he choked, "what could I do? If I had shot and killed him I could have been tried for murder or manslaughter."

"But he robbed me of $700! Don't you have the right to shoot a robber?"

"Yes—but I didn't *know* he was a robber when I was chasing him. Maybe you don't know this but if he had stolen less than $15 that would be petty larceny and he would not be classified as a felon. That means that if I had killed the guy I could be tried for murder or manslaughter.

---

[29] All names have been disguised. Printed by permission. The author's name has been withheld by request.

"So, do you see the position I'm in? If I shoot and possibly kill a man I am liable for a serious offense. If I let him get away I'm the goat. Don't worry, lady, you won't be the only one I get hell from. The chief is going to have plenty to say and so are the newspapers! What a law we have when you're damned if you do—and damned if you don't!"

Evans and Borne[30]

Evans and Borne was a partnership with branches in four cities, New York, Chicago, Boston, and Los Angeles. Each branch was supervised by a vice president. The firm was an investment banking firm which participated in securities underwritings and also acted as a dealer and agent in the sale or purchase of securities. The company had been rapidly increasing its business volume during the last five years and currently employed 400 persons.

Due to this expansion the accounting department had been responsible for an ever-increasing amount of record-keeping. (The department also maintained an interoffice account which was necessary because each branch office kept its own accounting records.) Management decided that a consulting firm ought to look into the possibility of a basic change in procedure. Such a firm was engaged and, after a study of several weeks, submitted the following recommendation:

Evans and Borne has arrived at a point in its operation where a decision must be made as to whether to continue operations under the present system or to install an electronic accounting system. We recommend the latter.

The consulting firm was discharged and the president, James L. Borne, called in his executive committee (the four vice presidents) to discuss the recommendation. After about an hour's discussion of the pros and cons of the two alternatives, Mr. Borne, well known for his decisiveness, rose and spoke enthusiastically.

Judging from our talking here we are just about unanimously agreed that the electronic system is for us. I feel the same way. The growth of

---

30 All names are disguised. Reprinted by permission.

our business alone convinces me that a year from now we will have no choice. The size and complexity of our operation will force us into electronic accounting. And so I firmly feel that not only should we go into the new system but that we should do so immediately. As you know these new machines are a tremendous investment and I want them to start paying off just as soon as possible. So, what do you say? Shall we get into electronics as soon as possible?

The system was installed within three months. It was quite evident within the first month that the company had gone in over its head. There had not been time to train personnel adequately and tempers flared continuously.

The turmoil in the accounting department was such that management was seriously considering discarding the system. But by this time the company had been irrevocably committed to it; there would be no turning back. It was almost a year before the department was restored to order.

Les enragés[31]

DAPHNE DU MAURIER

"The National Convention declares Louis Capet, last King of the French, guilty of conspiracy against the liberty of the nation, and of attempting to undermine the safety of the State.

"The National Convention decrees that Louis Capet shall suffer the death penalty."

There was not a home throughout the country, during January of '93, where the case was not argued, for or against the King. Robespierre had stated the matter with his usual clarity, when he declared in December before the Convention, "If the King is not guilty, then those who have dethroned him are."

There were no two ways about it. Either it was right to depose the monarch for summoning the aid of foreign powers against the State, or it was wrong. If right, then the monarch had been guilty of treason and must pay the penalty. If wrong, then the National Convention

---

31 *The Glassblowers* (New York: Doubleday & Co., Inc. Copyright 1963 by Daphne du Maurier) , pp. 238–39. Reprinted by permission.

must dissolve, ask pardon of the monarch, and capitulate to the enemy.

"You cannot go against Robespierre's logic," said my brother Pierre. "The Convention must either accuse the King, or accuse itself. If the King is absolved, it is tantamount to saying the Republic should never have been proclaimed, and the country must lay down its arms against Prussia and Austria."

"Who cares about l-logic?" answered Michel. "Louis is a t-traitor, we all know it. One sign of weakness on the p-part of the Convention, and every aristocrat and p-priest in the country will be rubbing their hands with j-joy. They should g-guillotine the lot."

"Why not send the royal family into exile? Wouldn't that be punishment enough?" I asked.

A groan went up from my two brothers, and my husband too.

"Exile?" exclaimed Pierre. "And let them use their influence to win more support for their cause? Imagine the Queen in Austria, for example! No, imprisonment for life is the only solution."

Michel gestured with his thumb towards the ground. "One answer, and one only," he said. "As long as those p-people live, above all that woman, they're a menace to s-security."

Two factions[32]

A problem of undeniable importance lies within the confines of the police department for which I work. I think that I can safely say that it has directly involved a large percentage of the members of this department and, moreover, its effect has been felt by every citizen of our city.

The problem originated years ago, but instead of diminishing with time it has grown to be a complex and difficult situation. This problem is now evidenced by open dissension and strife within the ranks of those employed around me.

Approximately 10 years ago, the city's police administration tolerated gambling and the illegal sale of liquor (bootlegging) to a considerable extent. In all probability, this tolerance was the result of

---

[32] Printed by permission. The author's name has been withheld by request.

some political pressures plus the desires of a few corrupt people who were interested, not in better government, but in building large bank accounts.

This state of affairs continued unchallenged for several years until a group within the department began to develop. About 25 or 30 officers, headed by 4 or 5 recognized leaders of no great rank, held a few informal meetings. They decided that all illicit forms of entertainment in the city would be closed. It was clear that some of the officers were motivated largely by public spiritedness while others joined the group because they had been excluded from the group receiving graft money and privileges.

Thereupon, this group (with the exception of a few who agreed in theory but would not shoulder direct responsibility) began to act. In groups and simultaneously, they entered establishments, effected some arrests, and closed the doors to further operation. These officers, for the most part, made these raids and arrests while on off-duty time.

Immediately, attempts were made to conciliate the two factions, but they failed. The consequences were not long in coming. The leaders of the "Vigilante" group were fired upon the provisions that they had been acting without authority, due to the fact that they were not actually on duty, nor did they have their supervisor's consent to act.

Within the police department, the remaining "Vigilantes" were met with both hatred and sympathy and a wide crack soon appeared within the organization.

Almost at once, the dismissed members began suit to regain their positions and after a year's legal debate, full reinstatement plus salary reimbursement was ordered. All of the men resumed their positions with the department.

Perhaps this solved their respective problems but it certainly was of no value with respect to the enmities created in the rank and file. In fact, the flames were fanned to the point where everyone was placed in an impossible situation—he must either associate with one group or another or be disliked by both.

These two factions, the "Vigilantes" and the "Anti-Vigilantes," have been at great odds since that date. Men refuse to speak to one another and open condemnations are the rule. Politics play a larger and larger part in the organizational structure of the department. The Public Safety Commissioner (an elective position) if favorable to one faction will immediately, upon taking office, assign favored positions to his group and thus relegate the "out-group" members who had been holding these positions to more or less menial stations. It should be quite evident how this constant displacement of key personnel depreciates the value of our organization and also should show quite clearly that the breach in ranks grows deeper with each change.

Many new men have been added to our department since the trouble originated, and a large percentage of them have been drawn into the struggle. I cite my own experiences as an example: One of my best friends in the city happens to have been an active leader of the "Vigilante" group. Our friendship is based almost entirely on mutual interests outside our field of work, namely fishing and hunting, but because of my association with him, many say I am a sympathizer of the "Vigilante" faction. I have lost several friends who say that because I enjoy this man's company, I am a believer in his theories and a backer of his principles.

Upon the completion of my probationary period, I was told that it would be impossible for me to be a "fence-sitter," in other words, that I would be forced to declare my sympathies for one group or another. I laughed then because I could not see why my choice of friends should be based on such damned foolishness. But I am no longer laughing for it has affected my working conditions and even threatens any future chance for advancement or promotion. This much has happened to me and, of a certainty, it is happening and has happened to many others.

11

Differentiation failures III (the frozen evaluation)

THIS CHAPTER deals with a third form of failure to differentiate. The previous two chapters were concerned with the necessity for indexing on a "horizontal" basis—that is, the need for differentiating among people, circumstances, attitudes, objects, and so forth, at *a given time*. The present chapter calls for a "vertical" sort of indexing, to take into account the way a person, a situation, a "thing," and so on, *changes* with time.

THE CASE OF FRANK

I want to tell you about a personable man you would probably like and respect. Frank, to give him a name, began life with two strikes against him. To make a long, sordid story short, an alcoholic, violent-tempered father, the frequent absence of a mother who was forced to work away from home, and the influence of a gang of young toughs which Frank joined at 13 were sufficient to turn him into a brash, cynical, externally callous adolescent. After numerous scrapes he finally got into serious trouble in 1941. Caught stealing a car at 18, he was sentenced to two years in prison. Actually, the sentence was a fortunate development for Frank. Appalled by the grimness of prison life, his brashness quickly dissolved. Under the skillful guidance of the prison chaplain and a social therapist, Frank was beginning to gain insights about himself at the time of his release. With 11 months off for good behavior, Frank felt he had paid his debt to society—but there were those who did not agree. On his return home, his father cursed him and forbade him at first to enter the house, ironically, for bringing shame to the family's name. Some of the neighbors openly mocked him as he walked down the street; others pointedly ignored him. He tried to find work, but, even with an abundance of wartime jobs, no one would hire anyone with his record. Frank was understandably relieved when he was drafted a few months later.

He sank gratefully into anonymity, but even in the Army there were incidents, as, for example, the time an officer's footlocker had been burglarized. Frank, though innocent, was the first to be called in for questioning. But, on the whole, Frank's three years in the Army were helpful. It gave him time to think. He could now see how his environment had almost driven him into crime. He began to go to church, where he found solace and encouragement and resolved firmly to salvage the rest of his life.

When the war ended Frank received an honorable discharge and returned home. His father had died during the war. His brothers and sisters had all married, and three of them had moved away. A fourth lived in the family house with his wife and two children, and Frank's mother lived with them.

It was now over five years since Frank had stolen the car, but many had still not forgotten. There was no more open taunting, but many of the neighbors seemed cool and distant. Finding a job, too, was difficult. It became painfully clear that his record still followed him. Once he lied about his prison sentence and was hired—only to be fired under embarrassing circumstances a week later when he was found out. Police drove up to his home twice during his first month at home to take him into headquarters for questioning about auto thefts.

Finally, Frank moved to another section of the city, and life began to improve. A kindly man hired him as a mechanic's apprentice in his garage. Three years later with steady pay increases he married. Today, he is the likable manager of the garage, has a lovely wife and two lively youngsters. He still visits his mother from time to time, but he much prefers to have her come to his home. The old neighborhood hasn't forgotten the old Frank.

Frank has been the victim of a special form of failure to differentiate: the *frozen evaluation*. Some people made evaluations about the "Frank of 1941." The "Frank of 1973" is virtually another person, but the evaluations have remained unchanged—frozen.

Not all *frozen evaluations,* of course, are as poignant and enduring as those concerning Frank. I was recently the delighted[1] target of one. Hurrying for an appointment, I was fortunate enough to find the one remaining parking space in the area. The space was the one nearest to the corner. Thirty minutes later when I returned, the car in the space behind mine had left and a woman was trying energetically but ineptly to park between my car and the one in the third space from the corner. As I unlocked my door, the woman leaned out and proceeded to upbraid me most indecorously for failing to park in the second space, thus depriving her of the corner space, a much easier space in which to park! In her frustration she had unconsciously frozen her evaluation of the parking situation. She had assumed, in other words, that the now vacant second space was also empty at the time I had parked!

The parking incident was an example of an evaluation made in the present and frozen to apply inappropriately to the past—a sort of "retroactive" frozen evaluation. The obverse—evaluations which are indiscriminately spread over the future without respect for change, as in the case about Frank—can also have undesirable consequences. Universities, hospitals, and other institutions which receive stipulated bequests and gifts are sometimes hamstrung by this kind of *frozen evaluation.* Several decades ago an eastern college was willed $200,000 —a very considerable gift, especially in those days. The donor, an ardent railroader, decided that the industry would *always* flourish, as indeed it did at the time he wrote his will. Thus he stipulated that his gift was to be invested in 10 particular railroad stocks in prescribed amounts. The investment was to remain undisturbed. Only the dividends were to be used by the college. A foolproof plan, reasoned the benefactor: the college would have a continually increasing endowment with commensurate dividends. Unfortunately, his prediction was faulty. As the years passed, most of the railroads on the list met with difficult times, and a few failed. The college, unable to react to changing economic conditions, could only sit by helplessly and watch the investment shrink to a fraction of its original value.

When one unconsciously (or perhaps deliberately) spreads an

---

[1] "Delighted" only because I felt the incident would be an apt illustration for this chapter.

evaluation over the future and/or over the past, then, *disregarding changes* in whatever he is judging (a person, group, situation, and so on) , we say that he has frozen his evaluation. Some of our most destructive *frozen evaluations* are those we make about ourselves. Take this case of self-imposed torment, for example:

An attractive girl, aged 17, came to the attention of a certain clinic as a voluntary case. For several years her parents had been concerned over the abnormal shyness which she exhibited in the presence of young men or boys. In the presence of members of the opposite sex she would blush violently and lapse into a nervous silence after a few stammered remarks. Her behavior was arrogant when she was with girls of her own age, and at least confident in the presence of adult women.

The medical findings were negative. . . . The social investigation revealed nothing in the home environment at the moment which would seem to be responsible for her mental condition. But social investigation did yield the significant fact that her shyness had developed quite suddenly three years before. The parents had no explanation to offer as to the possible cause of the condition.

The psychologist talked with the girl in a friendly and informal manner. In the course of the conversation it was observed that, while she discussed sports and school activities quite freely, she would invariably become emotional when the subject of boys was mentioned. . . .

Little by little the following story came out: Three years before at a children's party the girl had been playing with some boys. In some manner she caught her fingers in a door when it was slammed shut. This caused the child such extreme pain that she became ill and vomited. The incident was quickly forgotten by everybody but the little girl herself, to whom it remained a crushing misfortune. Although she tried not to think of it, the bitter memory was always there to be reinstated by the presence of boys![2]

THE ASSUMPTION OF NONCHANGE

The frozen evaluation seems to occur most frequently when one somehow assumes *nonchange.* Suppose John Brown, as a freshman, failed one of my courses mainly through negligence and irresponsibility. And suppose someone comes to me four years later and asks my appraisal of Brown, whom I have neither seen nor heard of since. I can very confidently say, "Oh, Brown is a poor student," *if* I assume

---

[2] From *Psychology and Life,* third edition by Floyd L. Ruch. Copyright, 1948, by Scott Foresman and Company, Chicago. Reprinted by permission.

John has *not* changed. But how reliable is this assumption? I think you will agree that I might be doing Brown a great disservice with my obsolete evaluation.

This leads to a much broader question: How dependable is the general premise of *nonchange*—the assumption which appears to underlie so many of our frozen evaluations? Actually, the notion that there is rest, pause, cessation, and so on, is a pernicious, yet prevailing, fallacy.

On every stratum we can observe, or at least presume, process. Everywhere about us we can see evidences of incessant change—of aging, of wearing out, of growing, of eroding, of regenerating, of decaying, and so forth. Even the "solid" earth undergoes perpetual change. Aside from dramatic changes such as earthquakes and volcanic eruptions and the slower ravages (wind, rain, glacial movements, and so on), the surface of the earth is in continuous motion.

The land surfaces of the world are no more in a state of absolute quiet than its water surfaces. Minute waves called microseisms are continuously moving through the rocks over the entire surface of the earth as can be seen by examining a sensitive seismograph record obtained in any part of the world.[3]

And on submicroscopic levels, modern-day physicists postulate, there is never-ceasing change. This "inert" book you are reading is presumed to be composed of infinitesimal particles whirling about at the speed of light—the "mad dance of electrons," as Korzybski called it.

Changes in people

And people change—often imperceptibly, sometimes markedly. Infants become children, adolescents, young adults, middle-aged, and finally elderly people, experiencing gradual, sometimes abrupt, changes beyond enumeration. The periods in which people live change, too. Consider the attitude shifts of "the public." In 1922, for example, *Good Health* published an article which typified current public opinion about smoking:

Tobacco benumbs all the finer sensibilities. That's why men smoke. A man who loves his wife and children is lonely when away and misses the

---

[3] Frank Neumann, *Earthquake Investigation in the United States,* Special Publication No. 282 (rev. [1953] ed., U.S. Department of Commerce, U.S. Coast and Geodetic Survey), p. 32.

home folks. He smokes, and at once his loneliness is gone. Tobacco fills the place of home and family. It kills the fine sentiment that made him long for the home fires and the familiar faces.

The smoker's business is not prospering. He is worried. He ought to find out the cause and remove it. He smokes instead. He is no longer worried. All is well. But the business fault is not corrected. More business enterprises have run aground in a fog bank of tobacco smoke than have been wrecked by hard times or business panics. Tobacco is an enemy of business as well as of morals. . . .

The college "smoker" is a devil's den, a snare which has lured many thousands of promising young men to mental and moral ruin. The smoking room is sister to the saloon and must be eliminated along with its iniquitous relative, if civilization is to be saved from the demoralization which threatens it.[4]

Contrast this with the public's attitude years later! In 1962 with eight out of ten men and one out of three women smoking, the *nonsmoker* was almost an oddity! Public acceptance of smoking was so strong, in fact, that, despite numerous grave warnings by health authorities that lung cancer and other serious diseases are likely to be related to smoking, annual tobacco sales (500 billion cigarettes and 6 billion cigars) were the highest in history! Now public attitude is changing once again. Increasingly the smoker is being considered not as a moral leper but as a witless self-destructionist—even a threat to the health of others who inhale his "second-hand" smoke.

Our attitudes about dress are equally transient. This mandate on beach apparel was rigorously enforced in 1925 by the Wilmette (Illinois) Park District:

For women, blouse and bloomer suits may be worn, with or without skirts, with or without stockings, providing the blouse has one-quarter arm sleeve, or close fitting arm-holes and providing the bloomers are full and not shorter than four inches above the knee.

Men's suits must have skirt effect or shirt worn outside of trunks, except when flannel knee pants with belt are worn. The trunks must not be shorter than four inches above the knee, and the shirt must not be shorter than two inches above the bottom of the trunk.

Changes in business

One of the most dynamic aspects of American life is business. Fluctuation is the rule. Booms and busts, sellers' markets and buyers' mar-

---

[4] "The Immorality of Smoking," *Good Health,* December 1922.

kets, inflations and deflations—nothing stands "still" for very long. The television market is a dramatic example. Twenty-five years ago 7- and 10-inch sets were being snapped up at high prices. Fifteen years ago, in TV-saturated areas, dealers were driven to considerable lengths to move their merchandise. One offered a 21-inch set for $100, no down payment. He did a brisk business, but only because of his special enticement: a no-interest $500 loan went with each set! His advertisement: "Pay off your doctor and grocer bills; buy shoes for the kids; make payments on your house, car, and appliances—and have TV, too!" Five years ago color TV and manufacturers found it impossible to keep up with the demand. Today the industry faces intense competition with foreign imports—principally, Japanese. And tomorrow?

In summary, if there is anything *constant* about the world and the people in it, it is the *constant change* they undergo.

The influence of language

It seems strange that such a palpable fallacy as the notion of non-change may persist. Let us examine the role that language may play in nurturing this insidious assumption.

Language and thought are intimately related. As Lister Sinclair expressed it:

> . . . But always we begin by speaking as we think, and end by thinking as we speak. Our language is an expression of our culture, shaped by the way we are brought up; and on the other hand, the way we are brought up is shaped by our language.[5]

Trace back to the roots of our language and you will discover many clues as to why we talk—and *behave*—as we do. The basic form and structure of the English language were laid down in ancient Greece. Now consider what life must have been like then—comparatively slow, static, and unchanging. Not much written history to read to get a sense of process. To us the average Athenian's life would seem quite placid—one day very much like any other.

Consider, then, that our language was spawned from this relatively constant society. Is it any wonder that they created a language which reflected their static existence? The result is that, although we live in an enormously more dynamic environment, we still use a language

---

[5] Lister Sinclair, "A Word in Your Ear," *Ways of Mankind*, ed. Walter Goldschmidt (Boston: Beacon Press, 1954), p. 24.

which strongly implies nonchange, rest, and permanence—thus we are enticed to overlook change.

Note how incredibly easy it is in our language to speak or write (or listen or read) without taking "time" into account. Read each of the paragraphs below and decide the date line of each. After you have dated all three, read the answers which follow:

POPE CONDEMNS USE OF NEW "HORROR" WEAPONS

Vatican City—Prompted by widespread fears that new weapons of mass destruction might wipe out Western civilization, the Pope today issued a bull forbidding their use by any Christian state against another, whatever the provocation.

Date_____

MORAL ROT ENDANGERS LAND, WARNS GENERAL

Boston—The head of the country's armed forces declared here today that if he had known the depth of America's moral decay he would never have accepted his command. "Such a dearth of public spirit," he asserted, "and want of virtue, and fertility in all the low arts to obtain advantages of one kind or another, I never saw before and hope I may never be witness to again."

Date_____

"UNITE OR DIE," U.S. STATESMAN WARNS EUROPEAN

Philadelphia—Only by uniting immediately into one great state can Europe end the wars and trade struggles that are destroying her, the grand old man of American politics declared here today. The sole solution, he declared, is for Europe to call at once a constitutional convention which would "combine all her different states and kingdoms into one federal union."

Date_____

Perhaps you will agree that these paragraphs *could* apply to contemporary affairs. According to the author,[6] however, they referred to (1) "Pope Innocent II in 1139; the weapon was neither germ warfare nor the hydrogen bomb"; (2) "George Washington, in 1775"; (3) "Benjamin Franklin, who urged a union of Europe on the American model in 1787."

---

6 Willard R. Espy, "Say When," *This Week,* July 13, 1952. Reprinted from *This Week* magazine. Copyright, 1952, by the United Newspapers Magazine Corporation.

And therein lies an important inadequacy of our language system —the prevailing failure to specify time:

Hollywood's legion of columnists, correspondents and reporters crowded into the Beverly Hills Hotel last week for movie journalism's traditional big night. It was the annual award-to-actors banquet put on by *Photoplay*, venerable pioneer (founded in 1911) of movie magazines. Master of Ceremonies Ronald Reagan, president of the Screen Actors Guild, rose for his polite remarks about *Photoplay*, then astounded the journalists with a diatribe against the "irresponsible press" of Hollywood. . . .

The *Daily News* made its own unjournalistic retort four days later. For a story headlined EX–ACE JAILED ON A CHARGE OF BANK ROBBERY, the *News* dug up an old picture of Reagan talking to one Byron Kennerly, an ex-Air Force officer who had been arrested on a charge of robbing an East Los Angeles bank. (Reagan had posed with Kennerly nine years before, when the airman was technical advisor on one of Reagan's pictures.) [7]

This letter-to-the-editor containing a tongue-in-cheek speech might be merely good fun if it did not so closely resemble some *actual* political oratory. Note the author's ridiculous but artful implication that, had the Republicans remained in power, there would have been no technological change:

Voters! Think Back! Recall the days of Horrible Herbert! Take, for example, such a commonplace item as your family car of 1932 and compare it to the one which 20 years of Democratic administration has brought you.

Did your dilapidated Republican car have automatic shift or overdrive—I ask you—did it? No! It took the good old Democrats to bring those things to you! Did your Republican car have air conditioning, or push-button window lifts, or crash-pad dash, or torque conversion, or Hollywood wheels? Of course not!

All of those things came to your car during the progressive Democratic administration! And in truth, voters, had the Republicans been in power all these years, you would still have 30 by 3 high-pressure tires on your Model T!

Make this test, if you doubt the progress which Democratic foresight has brought—go to a used-car lot and you'll find you can buy the best car ever put out under a Republican administration for 25 bucks! That in

---

[7] *Time*, February 26, 1951, p. 56. Reprinted by permission.

itself is proof of the improvements which the Trumanvelt forces have provided!

So don't let them take it away! Scan your ballot carefully! Maybe somebody will be running on the Whig ticket. If so, and he's elected, history will be rolled back 100 years! Sure, it will! They'd come out and take out your telephone, your lights, your radio, and you'd be forced to wear a beaver hat and grow a spade-shaped beard! Please, Mr. Voter, you don't want to grow a spade-shaped beard, do you?[8]

And speaking of politics, a national magazine once published statements to the effect that all the presidents through Franklin D. Roosevelt in their combined 156 years of administration took from the public only $248 billion. Harry Truman, on the other hand, in his six years took $260 billion!

The statements may not have been intentionally deceptive, but they were certainly misleading. The obvious implication was that Mr. Truman's administration had been incredibly extravagant. Specifically (and to spare you the arithmetic), Mr. Truman received 27 times more tax dollars per year than that required by the average pre-Truman president.

All of this, of course, is based on the *frozen evaluations* that "a dollar is a dollar" and "an administration is an administration." If we sidestep these misevaluations, we will get a rather different picture. Consider these among the extenuations:

1. The value of the dollar has greatly diminished over the years. The dollar at the time of the magazine's statements (1951), for example, was only half the value of the 1939 dollar.
2. Much of Truman's expenditures were inevitable and due to an evolution in the responsibilities of the federal government.
    a) Our population had grown tremendously—a 30,000 percent increase since 1790. Governing our nation had become correspondingly more expensive.
    b) The *nature* of the administration had changed. Over the years the federal government had come to play a greater and greater role in the national economy. This role required bureaus and personnel—and money.
    c) The character of our government in world affairs had changed. Only recently had we become a leader fighting (and spending) for *world* freedom.

---

[8] *Chicago Dialy News*, August 8, 1952, p. 8.

3. World War II, the most costly in history, was fought during F.D.R.'s time, but much of it was *paid* for during Truman's.
4. And let us not forget the extraordinary expenses of the Korean War, the national remobilization, and the rehabilitation of half the world.

CORRECTIVES

The previous two chapters described the need for discriminating among people, qualities, traits, and so forth, *without* regard for time differences. The current chapter calls for *time* differentiation. Let me say this a little differently.

The *frozen evaluation* was defined as a judgment set in concrete— an evaluation which remained constant and inflexible despite changes in its object. The basic problem, therefore, is to keep one's evaluation in pace with past and future changes in the person, situation, and so forth—whatever it is that he is evaluating. When the object changes, then the evaluation ought to change correspondingly. How can we accomplish this? How can we keep from freezing our evaluations and how can we "thaw" those already frozen?

Internalize the premise of change

Substitute the conscious premise of *change* for the unconscious notion of *nonchange*. Believe firmly in the process nature of man, of situations, of things, and so forth, and you will be more likely to keep your evaluations *up to date*.

Apply the when index

A very simple, yet effective, device for implementing the awareness of change is the *When Index*. Using the *When Index* is simply assigning a *date*. For example, the following Associated Press release appeared in 1950:

WILLIAMS SIGNS WITH RED SOX FOR
RECORD BASEBALL PAY OF $125,000

Boston, Feb. 7 (AP)—Ted Williams, the Red Sox slugger, today signed the highest salaried contract

in baseball history—for an estimated $125,000.

Babe Ruth's $80,000 salary in
1930 and '31 was tops in the old
days.[9]

At first glance Mr. Williams seems to have fared considerably better
financially than Mr. Ruth. But the Foundation for Economic Education, Inc., made a revealing analysis by *When-Indexing* (i.e., dating)
the purchasing power of the take-home dollar.

FIGURE 11-1

DOLLAR SALARIES

This is a comparison of
Ruth's and Williams'
dollar salaries.

TAKE-HOME PAY

But after federal in-
come taxes, this is a
comparison of their
take-home pay.

WHAT THE TAKE-
HOME WILL BUY

Inflation has shrunk
the buying power of
the dollar since 1931,
so Williams' real take-
home pay is only a
little over half of
Ruth's—57%.

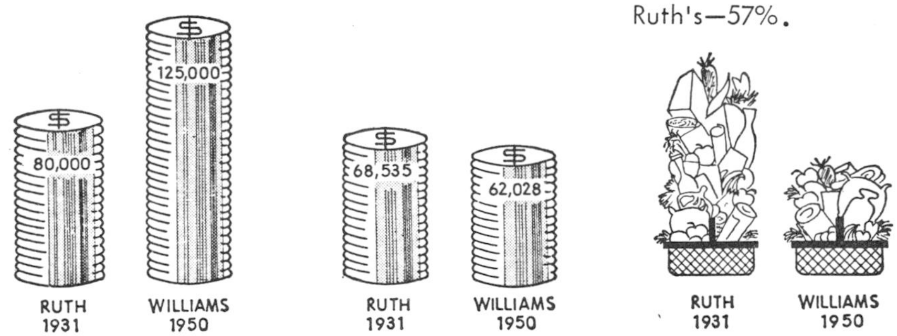

80,000	125,000	68,535	62,028		
RUTH 1931	WILLIAMS 1950	RUTH 1931	WILLIAMS 1950	RUTH 1931	WILLIAMS 1950

If Ted Williams were to have as much buying power in 1950 as Babe Ruth
had in 1931, he would have to be paid $327,451.

To update this illustration: In 1972 the Atlanta Braves paid a
record $200,000 to Henry Aaron. His take-home pay was a still im-
pressive $87,020. But considering the cost of living index those in-
flated dollars would have bought Aaron only 40 percent of Ruth's

---

9 Appeared in *The New York Times,* February 8, 1950. Reprinted by permission of
the Asociated Press.

market basket! To equal the Babe's purchasing power, Hank would have required an income of over \$600,000.

The *When Index* (which may be expressed as a mental or even explicit superscript, e.g., the U.S.^{1973} is not the U.S.^{1967}) is a reminder of the process nature of life. It reminds us of the constant flux that is characteristic of the world. It is such a versatile little tool that the following three brief cases will only suggest its usefulness:

THE CASE OF RICHARD ROE[10]

Richard Roe embezzled \$10,000 in 1963 and was soon apprehended, convicted, and sentenced. Roe in 1973 has served his term. Roe ^{1973} is not Roe ^{1963}. There are bound to have been changes. But this does not mean that a prospective employer does not have the right to investigate Roe thoroughly before hiring him. Indeed, it would be imprudent, usually, to fail to do so. But no employer, it seems to me, has the *moral* justification to *refuse* to hire him *without* an investigation. To dismiss Roe summarily as an undated "ex-convict" may not only deprive the employer of an able worker but, more importantly, it may contribute to Roe's destruction as a useful citizen.

THE CASE OF EUGENE PLONKA

Eugene Plonka, 40 . . . fell 25 feet to his death from a second-story fire escape door in the Cameron Can Machinery Company. . . .

Police believed Plonka, an assembler, was unaware when he stepped from the door that the fire escape had been removed for repairs. Employees said Plonka frequently spent his "rest break" on the fire escape.[11]

Even a structure as seemingly unchangeable as a fire escape is not always the same. "Fire escape ^{yesterday}" is not "fire escape ^{today}." Had Mr. Plonka ingrained the habit of *When Indexing,* he would have been prompted to *look* before stepping out onto a fire escape which was not there.

THE CASE OF DAVID

Six-year-old David had had his experiences with inoculations, so his mother was not too surprised that he protested vigorously when she told him he was to receive a polio shot the following afternoon.

"David," she countered, "I know how you feel, and I am willing to make a bargain with you. Now, the shot is not going to hurt you today or tomorrow morning, is it?" "No," he admitted. "And it isn't going to hurt

---

[10] Fictitious.

[11] *Chicago Daily News,* December 12, 1953, p. 12. Reprinted by permission.

when we leave the house and while we are driving to the doctor's office?"
"No." "And it isn't going to hurt when we are sitting in the waiting room,
reading the comic books?" "No." "Or when the doctor rubs your arm with
alcohol and gets the hypodermic ready?" "No." "Then there would be no
sense in crying or yelling at any of these times, would there?" "No, I guess
not." "But it *will* hurt when he sticks the hypodermic into your arm,
right?" "Yes!" "Well, young man, *at that time* you may yell your head off!"

David agreed, and when the inoculation actually occurred, a relaxed
David considered the prick hardly worth yelling about, and his *When
Indexing* had spared him needless anxiety.

Try this sort of *When Indexing* on yourself the next time you make
a dental appointment or anticipate some other unpleasant experience. A wise old professor of mine expressed his feeling about anxiety
a little differently: "I'm never late until I get there!"

SUMMARY

A *frozen evaluation* is one which is spread unconsciously (or perhaps deliberately) over the future and/or over the past, without regard for change. The effects of the *frozen evaluation* may take on a
great variety of forms, not the least serious of which are those which
have to do with our evaluations of ourselves. Evidently, underlying
most *frozen evaluations* is the assumption of *nonchange*—a fallacious
and often unconsciously held notion that there is rest, permanence,
constancy. A simple device, the *When Index,* reminds us to take
change into account in our evaluations—to distinguish among time^1,
time^2, time^3, and so on.

DISCUSSION QUESTIONS

1. What do "indiscrimination," "polarization," and "frozen evaluation"
    have in common? How are they distinguished?
2. The "Case of Frank" (pp. 389–91) is about a man who found it diffi-
    cult to live down his past. Do you know of anyone who has resigned
    himself to others' frozen evaluations of him? Under what conditions
    is this most likely to happen?
3. ". . . But always we begin by speaking as we think, and end by think-
    ing as we speak . . ."—Lister Sinclair (see p. 395) . What are the im-
    plications of this statement? If we were to improve our language sys-
    tem would this improve our thinking? What are the practical limita-
    tions on improving or changing a language system?

4. Why is it possible in English and in many other languages to talk and write "datelessly"—i.e., to make declarative statements, for example, without specifying the time to which these statements apply?

5. The "Case of David" suggests a way of using the When Index to minimize anxiety over future events. What do you think of this notion? Is there positive value in worry—especially if such concern helps us to prevent or avoid or cope with a problem?

6. Report upon an incident, perhaps involving yourself, in which *frozen evaluations* played a role. Why did the incident occur? What could have been done to prevent or correct the situation? What measures could prevent a recurrence of such frozen evaluations?

CASES

Ordeal in London[12]

Subtract 8 days, 23 hours, and 31 minutes from 29 days, 15 hours, and 7 minutes.

If HMFL spells JOHN in a particular code, how does that code work?

Four men, Smith, Robinson, Jones, and Brown, all grow vegetables. All four grow lettuce. All but Smith and Robinson grow potatoes. Smith and Brown grow cabbages. Robinson grows peas. Which two vegetables does Robinson grow? Which two does Smith grow? Which man grows potatoes, lettuce, cabbage, but no peas?

For $2\frac{1}{2}$ hours, one day last week, 32,000 little Londoners, aged $10\frac{1}{2}$ to $11\frac{1}{2}$, sat at their school desks puzzling over such questions as these. Their puzzlement was fierce, as if they thought their very lives depended on their answers. In their estimate of the seriousness of the test, the young Londoners were pretty much right.

The examinations they were taking were the awesome "selection tests"—Britain's new way of finding out just what sort of secondary education each child should have. If he does well, he will win a coveted "place" in one of the "grammar" schools, and there he will get a solid academic education that may eventually lead him to a university. If he does not do so well, he will be sent to a "central" or "secondary technical" school where he will spend more time on vocational training. The bottom 60 percent of the children will end up in a "secondary modern" school. There, formal academic training is at a minimum.

The selection system started in 1944, when the British government decided that every child should get a free secondary education. Before that, parents paid the bill, and most children merely stayed on in elementary schools until they could legally drop out at 14. Now all chil-

---

[12] *Time*, February 4, 1952. Reprinted by permission.

dren must go on to secondary school at eleven. Since too few grammar schools exist, the government has had to set up a rigid system of selection. But by last week, as the London exams fell due, some Britons were asking whether the system is really worthwhile.

Teachers were willing to admit that the tests could winnow out the bright and the quick. But they still did not pick out the hard-working or the talented. They gave no quarter to the late bloomers, made no allowances for children who happened to be overwrought during the exam. Cried one parent last week: "The test gets the child so worked up. My Patricia went out of the house white as a sheet, and couldn't eat any breakfast." Added another: "It's terrible to think that what a boy does at eleven will govern his whole life."

Money troubles[13]

The money market can be treated in the same way as any commodity market. In general, when the supply of money is plentiful, its price (which is the rate of interest) will be lower than when its supply is short. This however, is only part of the story, since it is widely known that federal controls on money supply are in force. This incident arose out of the changing price on money. As a farm loan appraiser for an insurance company's mortgage loan department, I am charged with several duties. Perhaps the most important of these is the recommendations of new loan business.

In April of 1966, money supplies were diminishing significantly and mortgage money was becoming scarce. Those of us in the field were aware of the tighter money market, but no policy change in regard to interest rate was issued from the Home Office. In my own case, I had two farm loan applications on my desk, to be submitted at the then prevailing interest rate of 5 percent. These would be sent to the office for approval as soon as the appraisal report was completed and as soon as proper credit checks were made. The following day I mailed these cases into the office and made assurances to the applicants that their cases would be approved.

In that same day's mail a memorandum was received stating that

---

[13] Printed by permission of the author, whose name has been withheld by request.

"all farm loan applications must be submitted at a 5½ percent interest rate, effective as of the date of this memorandum."

The two loan applications that were submitted at 5 percent were committed and mailed to the applicants bearing at 5½ percent rate. Both applicants were very unhappy with the change in their applications. They felt they had been "double-crossed." There is no question that the company and I lost considerable goodwill not only with these people but with many of their friends to whom they complained about our treatment of them.

The "good old days"[14]

Mike and I walked down the road to Mollie and Bill's last night to see if they'd like to play a game of Scrabble, but Bill wasn't in the mood for Scrabble—he was hopping mad about a $27 bill he had received from a plumber for a small job in the house—"that wouldn't have cost a third as much in the Good Old Days." Mollie merely laughed at him and said, "Serves you right—if you weren't so lazy you would have done the job yourself."

Then Mike aired his latest gripe about the cost of some minor repairs to his car last month and the sloppy way it was done. "All a workman today thinks of is his pay check—he has no pride in his work—once it's out of his hands he doesn't care how soon it falls apart—"

So then we all got into the game and enjoyed a Complain Session about "Labor" in general. We all agreed that such household equipment as refrigerators, stoves, washing machines, vacuum cleaners, etc. are not made as well as they used to be. Neither the materials nor the workmanship are in them. Nothing seems to be made to LAST any more. "Including children's toys," says I—thinking of all the broken plastic toys around the house already since Christmas.

But Mollie, who is a very fair-minded person, felt that even though all this may be true—still, we wouldn't want to go back to the so-called "Good Old Days" of our grandparents. So she went to the book-

---

14 *Wilmette Life,* January 17, 1957. Reprinted by permission of Lloyd Hollister, Inc., publishers.

case and found a little printed card—brittle with age. "I want to read this to you," she said. "These are the rules given each new employee —my father was one—way back in the 80's, by what is now one of Chicago's largest department stores. Listen to this and I don't think you'll wonder why Labor rebelled:—

Store must be swept and counters and base shelves and show cases dusted. Lamp trimmed, filled and chimney cleaned; pens made; doors and windows opened; a pail of water and a scuttle of coal must be brought in by each clerk before breakfast.

Store must not be opened on the Sabbath Day unless absolutely necessary and then only for a few minutes.

Any employee who is in the habit of smoking Spanish cigars, getting shaved at a Barber Shop, going to dances and other such places of amusement will most certainly give his employer reason to be suspicious of his integrity and all around honesty.

Each employee must pay not less than $5 per year to the Church and must attend Sunday School every Sunday.

Men employees are given one evening a week for courting purposes, and two if they go to prayer meeting regularly.

After 14 hours of work in the store, leisure time must be spent in reading good literature.

Nobody said anything for a minute after Mollie finished reading. I guess we were all trying to digest this form of dictatorship. Then Mike said, "Well, I guess that does it! And I thought we were getting too much regimentation in the past few years. Looks like we're just beginning to know what freedom is."

John Lundy[15]

John Lundy, 40, had been a press operator with the Romaine Company for over 15 years. For the past four years he had operated mechanical forming presses. His most frequent job was making top and bottom caps for water heater jackets. His raw material was a sheet of 18 to 20 gauge cold-rolled steel. The sheet was 8 feet long, 2 feet wide, and weighed about 10 pounds. The procedure was to grasp the sheet with a suction cup, slide it on rollers to a stop at which the first two

---

[15] All names are disguised.

feet of the strip were properly positioned under the press. He would then press two buttons simultaneously which caused the machine to press down with a force of 100 tons, forming the cap.[16] The press would rise automatically, whereupon John reached under with both hands and lifted and removed the cap and placed it on his stack of finished pieces. He then moved the next two feet of sheet under the press and repeated the process. Thus, he made four caps from each strip.

The job was on incentive. Lundy had perfected his techniques to a high degree and was regarded as an excellent worker.

One day, the press suddenly malfunctioned. John had pressed the buttons, the press descended and rose, and he started to reach for the cap. Without warning, the press descended a second time and Lundy narrowly escaped serious injury. Cautiously, he tried the machine again and it double-hit again. He called Frank Torgeson, his foreman, and complained about the press. Torgeson immediately ordered the machine shut down and called maintenance. In the meantime, he assigned Lundy to a similar press nearby.

Three hours later two maintenance men arrived, briefly discussed the machine with the foreman, and set to work. They suspected that a faulty connection in the machine's electrical system permitted a second cycle. Accordingly, they climbed to the top of the press, about 18 feet above the floor and called to John: "Hey, Lundy, do you want to come over here and go through an operation so we can see what's happening from up here?"

"Okay," John replied and walked to the press. He cupped the sheet, slid it into place, and pressed the buttons. The press descended and John reached under for the cap—the press re-cycled and his right hand was severed at the wrist.

---

[16] The buttons were positioned at eye level and spread apart in such a way as to require the use of both hands to operate them, thus protecting the operator's hands from injury as the press descended.

12

Intensional orientation I
(a general statement)

THIS CHAPTER will not deal with a specific pattern of communication difficulty. The purpose here is to describe and discuss a general orientation toward the relationship between words and what we use them to stand for—between "the map" and "the territory." In the two following chapters we shall examine a number of forms of misevaluation and miscommunication to which this orientation can lead.

One way to define the *intensional* (the *s* is inten*t*ional) *orientation* is to show it in action.

THE GRAHAM UNIVERSITY TAX CASE[1]

Graham is a large private university located in Allyn, a pleasant suburb. For years, town-gown relations had been quite amicable except for one point of friction—taxation.

Graham held two types of exemption from real estate taxation. Exemption$_1$ concerned its educational property, i.e., property used directly for educational purposes, such as classrooms, libraries, administration buildings, dormitories, athletic fields, and so on. No one quarreled over this exemption, however, for it was granted to all schools and colleges in Allyn.

Exemption$_2$, on the other hand, covered Graham's investment

---

1 The names have been disguised; otherwise the details are factual.

properties. These were real estate holdings which were *not* directly used for educational purposes, although the income from them was. It was around this exemption that the friction revolved. Interest in the issue waxed and waned, but there was always an underlying current of resentment among many of the townspeople. It was generally believed that the university's exemption had removed a sizable portion of the suburb's real estate from the tax rolls, thus increasing the taxation on the individual's property.

The debate became especially heated during election years. One aldermanic candidate, for example, published a statement in the *Allyn Times* to the effect that Graham's exemption$_2$ was depriving Allyn of tax revenue from 6 percent of its area and 10 percent of its assessed value. Other published statements, letters to the editor, and so on, contended that the exemption covered as much as 50 percent of Allyn's real estate.

And there were citizens who supported the exemption. "So what if we have to pay more taxes," they argued, "isn't it worth it? Graham has put Allyn on the map, made us a cultural center. Moreover, Graham's thousands of students contribute to the economic health of the community with their purchases in Allyn."

And so the discussing and the contending and the arguing continued until the *Times* decided to do something about it. It hired competent real estate taxation specialists to determine the status of tax exemptions in Allyn. After a comprehensive survey the specialists submitted their report: 16 percent of the total of Allyn's real estate was tax exempt. This included not only Graham's property, educational and investment, but that of the other colleges, private and public schools, the churches, the municipal buildings, the libraries, the hospitals, the parks, and so forth. The subject of debate—Graham's investment property—constituted only one half of 1 percent of Allyn's real estate!

The friction disappeared almost immediately. Even the most ardent disputants admitted: "If that's all it amounts to—it's hardly enough to fuss about."

INTENSION AND EXTENSION

The Graham case involved a problem which was approached in two vitally different ways. For years people had been verbalizing, theorizing, speculating about Graham's exemption$_2$. They talked, they discussed, they disputed. The more they talked about the problem, the farther they seemed to move away from *it*. They became so absorbed in their own personal *maps of the territory* that it became increasingly difficult for them to examine *the territory itself*. They were *intensionally oriented*—more concerned, that is, with the feelings, thoughts, suppositions, beliefs, theories, etc., *"inside* their skins" than with the life facts *outside*.

Finally, the *Allyn Times* took a radically different tack. "Look," said the publisher, "all this *talking* about the problem has only succeeded in aggravating the situation. Let's quit *talking* for once and go out and do some *looking*—let's go out and *see* just what this exemption amounts to." The publisher's "stop talking and start looking" approach is characteristic of the *extensional orientation*.

One is *oriented intensionally* when he is predisposed to become absorbed with the map and to neglect the territory. This tendency is epitomized in this charming fable of the recession of 1957–58.

A Man Lived by the Side of the Road . . .
. . . and sold hot dogs.
He . . . had no radio.
He had trouble with his eyes, so he had no newspaper.
But he sold good hot dogs.
He put up a sign on the highway, telling how good they were.
He stood by the side of the road and cried: "Buy a hot dog, mister." And people bought.
He increased his meat and bun orders, and he bought a bigger store to take care of his trade.
He got his son home from college to help him. But then something happened.
His son said: "Father, haven't you been listening to the radio? There's a big depression on. The international situation is terrible, and the domestic situation is even worse."
Whereupon his father thought: "Well, my son has been to college. He listens to the radio and reads the papers, so he ought to know."
So, the father cut down his bun order, took down his advertising sign, and no longer bothered to stand on the highway to sell hot dogs.
His hot-dog sales fell almost overnight.
"You were right, son," the father said to the boy. "We are certainly in the middle of a great depression."[2]

---

[2] From a Quaker State Metals Co. advertisement, courtesy of *Newsweek* (February 24, 1958), p. 77.

Extensional orientation, on the other hand, is the predisposition to inspect the territory *first*—and *then* to build verbal maps to *correspond with it.* One of the greatest extensionalists in history was Galileo. Time and again he refused to be governed by the revered maps—the theories and postulates—of his time and went instead to observe the "territory" for himself. The Aristotelian Law of Falling Bodies was one of these unquestioned maps. Postulated more than 19 centuries before, it held that the velocity of falling bodies was directly proportional to their weight—a notion consistent with the prevailing theory of gravitation. But Galileo had to *see* for himself and proceeded to the Tower of Pisa, where he exploded the "Law" and started the world thinking about a new theory of gravity.

INTENSIONALITY: SOME MANIFESTATIONS

Basically, one behaves *intensionally* when he responds to his "maps" (his feelings, imaginings, visualizations, formulations, attitudes, theories, preconceptions, evaluations, inferences) *as if* he were responding to the territory (objects, people, happenings, relationships, things, and so on) . Trouble tends to come when the map is an inadequate representation of the territory. Take the case of a young southern soldier in World War II. Seriously wounded at the front, the unconscious boy's life hung in the balance. He desperately needed a transfusion, but blood of his unusual type was unavailable, and there was scant hope of acquiring some in time. Fortunately, a Negro in a neighboring battalion heard about the boy's condition and volunteered for a transfusion. His blood type was suitable; the transfusion was made, and the young soldier's life was saved. On the road to recovery several days later, the young Southerner was told of the Negro who had given his blood. The boy became almost uncontrollable with fear and rage. He was overwhelmed by a life-long delusion that the Negro's blood in his veins would change the color of his skin and even alter the shape and size of his lips and nose, the texture of his hair, and so forth.

Instead of reacting to the territory, a situation in which he was generously given lifesaving blood, the young man responded in terms of his fallacious map.

To a greater extent than most of us are aware we are conditioned to react *intensionally* by the phenomena of our environment. Society's customs, traditions, norms, mores, and so on, are maps—sometimes spurious ones—which become so ingrained in us that we often treat them as territories.

I can still recall the hubbub a few years ago when a college professor married a woman who had attended one of his courses a year before. The man, an exceptional scholar and teacher, was 40, and his lovely and intelligent bride was 32. Though entering matrimony relatively late in life, they were obviously well suited to each other, and their marriage has since proved eminently successful.

This was the territory, but some people paid more attention to their specious maps. One newspaper headlined the wedding story with a ridiculous, cradle-snatching implication: "Teacher Marries Pupil." Many readers, largely ignorant of the facts of the situation, raised their eyebrows, clucked their tongues, and some even wrote letters of protest to the college president. They had become so distraught at the imagined violation of a social taboo that they were hardly able or willing to examine the territory behind their fallacious maps.

Sometimes we behave *intensionally* because we want to. It is a relief, occasionally, to escape to our inner self-made worlds. There is value in daydreams, movies, television, novels, and so forth, when they serve as *temporary* safety valves. There is danger, however, when the world of make-believe becomes accepted as real. Children are perhaps the most susceptible. A mother caught her seven-year-old son pouring ground glass into the family stew. He wanted to see if it would "really work" as it had with the characters in a television play he had seen.[3] Another youngster accidentally hung himself while attempting to free himself from a trick knot from which a comic book hero had escaped.[4] And still another boy caused a $100,000 warehouse fire by using a clever incendiary made of a burning cigarette inserted in a book of matches. He had learned the trick from a movie.

But some adults are almost as prone to delude themselves—to react to faulty or fictional maps as if they were the actual territories. Milton Caniff, originator of the comic strip, "Terry and the Pirates," tells of the time one of the characters, "Hot Shot Charlie," was sent to the United States for a period. Always a precisionist, Caniff depicted him as quartered at an actual apartment in Boston. One day

---

[3] Norman Cousins, "The Time Trap," *Saturday Review of Literature,* December 24, 1949, p. 20.

[4] "Tell Hanged Boy's Boast He Could Do Escape Trick," *Chicago Sun-Times,* January 15, 1955, p. 4.

the strip showed "Hot Shot" receiving a cable with the apartment's address clearly visible on the wire. The next panels showed him packing and leaving for overseas.

A day or so later Caniff received an urgent request from the apartment-house owner. "Please print a block in your comic strip," he pleaded, "and explain that there is no vacancy at ———— St.!" The poor man had been deluged with eager inquiries about "Hot Shot's vacant apartment!"

And Bing Crosby gives an amusing illustration of the undeniable effect of another kind of map, the motion picture:

> I'd heard of the public identifying actors and actresses with roles, but this was the first time I'd got the full treatment myself. Not long after *Going My Way* was released, I attended a dinner party at the home of my friend Jack Morse. Before dinner, cocktail canapés and hors d'œuvres were served, among them toasted frankfurters on toothpicks. They were served by a gray-haired, motherly-looking maid from the Ould Sod. It happened to be Friday, and when I absent-mindedly took one of the frankfurters, I thought she'd have a stroke. "Holy Mother! Father Crosby!" she burst out, "you're not going to eat one of those!" Obviously she was subconsciously thinking of me as the priest I'd played, and the fact that "Father O'Malley" would eat a meat canapé on Friday upset her.
>
> The other guests collapsed with laughter, and she retreated in confusion to the kitchen. I was a little confused myself.[5]

Unfortunately, the impact of the motion picture and other forms of entertainment is not always so delightful. Their chief danger to our children and young people, writes Sidney J. Harris, is not immorality, as many fear, but "the totally false impression of love, marriage and adult relations in general":

> A child cannot so easily be corrupted by "dirtiness" as he can be seduced by romanticism. Young people usually laugh at "sexy" movies; but they lap up romantic ones with credulous ecstasy. And this is the basic betrayal of the film-makers.
>
> Most pictures end just where life itself begins—with the romantic clinch and the march up the marriage aisle. "They lived happily ever after" is a more dangerous line than any of the sadism and sensuousness to be found in a "tough" picture.
>
> What creates most of the devastation and despair among young adults is not their tendency toward immorality but their lack of emotional prepa-

---

5 Bing Crosby as told to Pete Martin, *Call Me Lucky* (New York: Simon & Schuster, Inc., 1953), pp. 186–87. Reprinted by permission.

ration for living. Fed during their formative years on the romantic pap of the film, the serial story, the radio and TV play, they are woefully unequipped to deal with the reality of marriage and social pressures of all sorts.

They always see the lovers laughing and kissing; they never see the quarrels and conflicts that are inevitable between any two personalities. They are "enchanted" by romantic pictures; but the terrible thing about enchantment is that it must inevitably come to an end.[6]

But the most pathetic victims of the celluloid chimera are perhaps some of the stars themselves. Living in the fanciful world created by press agents and celebrity-worshippers, their maps become tragically out of phase with life facts. The too frequent results are emotional breakdowns, broken marriages, and suicides.

Generally speaking, *intensionality* is most likely to lead to undesirable consequences (1) when one's map *inadequately* represents the territory and (2) when he is *unaware* that he is responding to his map rather than to the territory.

Every medical student knows that the length of the small intestine is 22 feet or thereabouts, for his textbook has taught him so. But Dr. Betty Underhill has revealed this "map" as a dangerous fallacy. In 100 autopsies she found that men's intestines ranged from 16 to 25 feet 9 inches, women's from 11 feet to 23 feet 6 inches. Differences such as these, she asserted, can be life-and-death matters in surgery.[7]

CORRECTIVES

As the problem *of intensional orientation* has been stated only generally, at this point we can offer only general advice for dealing with it. We shall reserve for the next two chapters the task of defining *intensionality* in its more specific forms and of offering techniques for preventing or diminishing their consequences.

The basic advice is to *"get extensional."* Develop the "show me" or "let me see" attitude. Develop a healthy distrust of preconstructed maps—go to the territory, look, observe, explore, probe, examine— *then* make your maps. This is the tenor of the homey advice World Court Justice John Bassett Moore once gave the late radio-television

---

[6] Sidney J. Harris, "Calls False Romance Worst Film Offense," *Chicago Daily News,* March 3, 1954, p. 14.

[7] From *Time,* December 5, 1955, p. 65.

commentator, Edward R. Murrow: "When you meet men of great reputation, your judgment of them will be greatly improved if you view them as though they were in their underwear."

Extensionality is the *sine qua non* of the scientist. He makes hypotheses (tentative maps), yes, but usually on the basis of previous observation of the territory, and then he checks them against the territory again—and again—and again. If the map matches the territory, well and good; but if it does not, he alters his map or discards it and builds another, and another, until it adequately represents the territory.

This is the scientific attitude, the territory-first-then-map approach; but surely there is great need for it beyond the confines of the laboratory.

SUMMARY

Intensional orientation is a general term for the tendency to be guided primarily, if not exclusively, by one's maps rather than by the territory. Trouble, confusion, and danger are most likely to occur (1) when the map *inadequately* represents the territory and (2) when the individual is *unaware* that he is dealing with the map rather than with the territory.

The basic technique for preventing or minimizing the injurious effects of *intensional orientation*, simply stated, is to develop an *extensional orientation*—a readiness to seek out the territory rather than a willingness to be mesmerized by one's often fallacious maps. *Extensionality*, in short, is the propensity to "look first—then talk."

DISCUSSION QUESTIONS

1. *Intensional orientation* can sometimes lead to harmful, unintelligent, even self-destructive behavior. However, are there not circumstances when such an orientation would be harmless—even desirable?
2. What are the conditions when *intensional orientation* would be considered undesirable?
3. Report on an incident, perhaps involving yourself, in which *intensional orientation* played a role. Why did the incident occur? What could have been done to prevent or correct the situation? What measures could prevent a recurrence of similar incidents?

CASES

The Continental Electric Company[8]

The following statement is by Howard Teal, manager of the Man-dota plant of the Continental Electric Company, regarding a problem he had had with an assembly line. The line consisted of 35 women working on precision electrical parts.

TEAL: Two years ago during the summer, five women working at about the middle of the assembly line began to complain of severe itching and of welts on their arms and legs. The welts resembled mosquito bites, but the women insisted these were not mosquito bites. They said that bugs were crawling from the assembly table and biting them. The women sat at the assembly table with their backs to heavily screened windows. No mosquitoes could possibly have come in from the outside.

Well, we finally called in an exterminator, who spread all sorts of insecticides around the room. Things were fine for a few days, but then the women began complaining again. The exterminator came back every three weeks, but that didn't seem to help. By the end of the summer, 11 women had registered complaints. The unrest subsided in the fall.

With the coming of hot weather last year, the complaints began once more. This time, 15 women insisted they were being bitten. Finally, in July, they threatened to walk off the job. I immediately called in a dermatologist, who examined the employees. He told them they were not being bitten and that the whole thing was in their imaginations.

The women became angry, and the complaints became more pro-

8 All names and organizational designations have been disguised. Northwestern University cases are reports of concrete events and behavior, prepared for class discussion. They are not intended as examples of "good" or "bad" administrative or technical practices. Copyright, 1958, by Northwestern University. Reprinted by permission.

nounced. So back came the exterminators. After a few days, the complaints began anew.

The employees claimed they had seen little green bugs crawling around their work areas. There were a few insects, small enough to get in through the screen—the things one finds on trees during the summer. I know they don't bite, but I wasn't going to argue with the women. Instead, I had the exterminators back a few more times until the fall season started.

Then, as before, the complaints ceased.

This year, the hot weather set in about May 15, and so did the unrest in the assembly room. Some 20 to 25 women were now convinced they were being bitten by insects around the assembly table. Even my supervisor began to itch.

I then visited Dr. Jay, an entomologist at the university. He suggested I have the employees collect insects from the assembly room, put them in jars, and send them to him for analysis. Many employees in the assembly room collected insects with zeal. I might add that assembly line efficiency dropped somewhat. When the collection had been completed, I delivered our specimens to Dr. Jay. After a careful analysis, he concluded that none of the insects brought to him for analysis would bite human beings. But the complaints continued.

Dr. Jay decided to visit the plan. Upon arrival, he took off his shirt, rolled up his trousers, and sat at the assembly table for a long time. He was not bitten once. He then interviewed several complaining employees and let each tell her own story. He suggested they might themselves be bringing in insects from the outside. The women insisted they were being bitten at work because the symptoms occurred only in the plant.

Dr. Jay then submitted a highly technical report with the scientific terms for each type of insect he had analyzed. The report suggested that these insects did not normally bite and listed various physiological causes of itching. He suggested that the welts could have been caused by intense scratching due to itching sensations brought about by perspiration or by psychological causes. I posted his report on the bulletin board for all the employees to read.

At Dr. Jay's suggestion, I painted two ordinary 150-watt bulbs purple and secured them to the floor at each end of the assembly line. The lights gave the appearance of ultraviolet ray. As far as the employees were concerned, that was exactly what they were. They were and are still unaware of what I did.

Throughout June, July, August, and September, after installation of the lights, we had only two minor complaints of employees being bitten while on the assembly line.

The "Water-American"[9]

At my first admission into this printing-house I took to working at press, imagining I felt a want of the bodily exercise I had been us'd to in America, where presswork is mix'd with composing. I drank only water; the other workmen, near fifty in number, were great guzzlers of beer. On occasion, I carried up and down stairs a large form of types in each hand, when others carried but one in both hands. They wondered to see, from this and several instances, that the *Water-American*, as they called me, was *stronger* than themselves, who drank *strong* beer! We had an alehouse boy who attended always in the house to supply the workmen. My companion at the press drank every day a pint before breakfast, a pint at breakfast with his bread and cheese, a pint before breakfast and dinner, a pint at dinner, a pint in the afternoon about six o'clock, and another when he had done his day's work. I thought it a detestable custom; but it was necessary, he suppos'd, to drink *strong* beer, that he might be *strong* to labor. I endeavored to convince him that the bodily strength afforded by beer could only be in proportion to the grain or flour of the barley dissolved in the water of which it was made; that there was more flour in a pennyworth of bread, and therefore, if he would eat that with a pint of water, it would give him more strength than a quart of beer. He drank on, however, and had four or five shillings to pay out of his wages every Saturday night for that muddling liquor; an expense I was free from. And thus these poor devils keep themselves always under.

"Get off Route 25, young man"[10]

CHARLES F. KETTERING

My home is in Dayton, Ohio, and I was a friend of the Wright family and learned to fly on the very early Wright airplanes. Their

[9] From *The Autobiography of Benjamin Franklin* (New York: D. C. Heath & Co., 1908). Reprinted by permission.

[10] *Colliers,* December 3, 1949, pp. 13–14. Reprinted by permission.

first flight was on the 17th of December, 46 years ago. Everyone was perfectly sure that it was a crazy thing to try. The undertakers moved into Kitty Hawk with a number of caskets because they thought the Wrights would kill themselves.

When they made those first three flights on December 17, 1903, they wired their sister that they had succeeded, that they were very happy, and that they should be home for Christmas.

She thought it was a world-shaking event, so she very excitedly called a Dayton newspaper on the telephone. She rang and rang and rang. The newspaper boys were playing pinochle, but finally one of them answered.

He said, "Yes?"

She said, "This is Katherine Wright speaking," and very excitedly read the telegram.

He said, "Good. Glad to hear the boys are going to get home for Christmas," and hung up the telephone.

The newspaperman said to the others: "Nobody's going to catch me on that, because it has been proved mathematically that a heavier-than-air machine can't fly."

I had a friend who was the research and development man for one of the British railroads. He came to this country to deliver a commencement adddress at a technical university. After the address he came to Detroit to see our laboratories.

"Ket," he said, "when you were over in London last year you told me some things you fellows were doing with Diesel locomotives and you lied to me."

I said, "Not intentionally."

"But," he said, "you told me you were running these locomotives about a hundred miles an hour."

I said, "We are."

"And that you were taking power on the front wheels; that is, the wheels that are ahead."

I said, "We are."

He said, "I have the formulas in my portfolio that say you can't do that."

I said, "For Heaven's sake, don't let the locomotive know about it."

I said to him, "I won't argue with you at all." I took the telephone, called Chicago and got him transportation from Chicago to Denver, and flew him to Chicago to make the connection. He made the trip to Denver, where I had him ride part way on the Diesel engines.

He stopped in to see me on his way back. He was returning to England. I said, "I didn't expect to see you again. Did you ride that locomotive?"

"Yes," he said.

"Did it go a hundred miles an hour?"

"It did."

"Well," I said, "that's the reason I didn't expect to see you back. Maybe you forgot to take the portfolio with the equations in it."

He said, "The thing that amazes me is why we could be so one hundred percent wrong."

I said, "You weren't wrong. You didn't start in right."

The two of us got out his formulas. He wasn't talking about our locomotive at all. Our locomotive uses an ordinary truck like a street car's. He was talking about a locomotive with a rigid frame which would normally have a small-wheel lead truck in front of it.

I said, "What's the use of using mathematics on one kind of thing and then applying it to another which is in no way related? It isn't even a second cousin to it."

When we first put self-starters on automobiles I attended a meeting of the American Institute of Electrical Engineers. They asked me if I would make a little talk on the self-starter, and I did.

One fellow got up and said, "No wonder you made your self-starter work; you profaned every law of electrical engineering."

I didn't profane any fundamental laws of electrical engineering. All I did was make the starter work. Those laws had nothing whatever to do with self-starters; they were written for something entirely different.

As I said before, my home is in Dayton, and we have had our laboratories for years in Detroit, which is several hundred miles away. I keep my home in Ohio and drive back and forth weekends.

Some of the people who work with me also drive between Dayton and Detroit. One said, "I understand you drive from here to Dayton in four and one-half hours."

I said, "I can do that once in a while, depending on traffic."

He said, "I don't believe it."

I said, "But I do it."

He said, "I'm a much better driver than you are, and I can't do it."

I said, "I'm going down Friday. Why don't you ride along with me?"

So we rode into Dayton in about four and one-half hours, or a little more, and he said, "Hell, no wonder you can do it. You didn't stay on Route 25!"

Now, Route 25 is the red line that is marked on all the maps between Detroit and Dayton. If you are a stranger, that's the road you should take. It never occurred to my colleague that you could take any other road on either side of Route 25. There's a lot of country on either side of it; in fact, half the earth is on each side of it. . . .

The trials of Galileo

Galileo is perhaps most widely known and remembered for his astronomical studies. Early in life he became a convert to the Copernican ideas, ideas that conflicted with the medieval conception of the universe as established by Ptolemy. Ptolemy declared that the earth was an immovable sphere, fixed in the center of the universe, with the sun and the stars revolving about it. For many centuries the Ptolemaic system was almost undisputedly accepted. Not only did it seem to agree with the perception of the senses but it was also in harmony with the homocentric doctrine of theology, which recognized man as the principal object of divine concern. The entire universe was conceived as having been created to serve man's needs. Hence it was but natural to regard the earth, the abode of man, as the center of the universe. . . .[11]

It was not until he made a number of discoveries by means of the telescope that he boldly championed Copernicanism. Apprised that a contrivance had been invented in the Dutch Netherlands by which distant objects could be made to appear much nearer and larger, he set to work and soon constructed a telescope, becoming the first scientist to apply it to astronomical observation. With the new instru-

---

[11] From *Europe from the Renaissance to Waterloo* by Robert Ergang (New York: D. C. Heath & Co., 1939). Reprinted by permission.

ment Galileo made a number of important discoveries. He found that the moon, instead of being self-luminous, owed its light to reflection; also he proved its surface was deeply furrowed by valleys and mountains. The latter discovery shattered the Aristotelian idea that the moon was a perfect sphere, absolutely smooth. Especially noteworthy was Galileo's discovery of the four satellites of Jupiter, whose revolutions confirmed by analogy the Copernican explanation of the solar system. Galileo also perceived movable spots on the disc of the sun, inferring from them the sun's axial rotation and by analogy the rotation of the earth on its axis.

After making his discoveries with the telescope Galileo could not restrain his enthusiasm for the Copernican system. So persistent were his activities in behalf of it and so unsparing was his ridicule of its opponents that the Church, which still adhered to the Ptolemaic theory, became alarmed. In 1615 he was ordered by the Inquisition to desist from further advocacy of the doctrine "that the earth moves around the sun and that the sun stands in the center of the world without moving from east to west." Galileo submitted, and for the next sixteen years remained silent. Meanwhile, however, he was writing the great work of his life, which he published in 1632 under the title *Dialogue Concerning the Two Chief Systems of the World.* The main reason for his choice of a dialogue between three persons as the medium for his thought was probably a desire to avoid committing himself openly. The work presented overwhelming proof of the Copernican theory. When it was examined by the ecclesiastical authorities, Galileo was immediately summoned to appear before the Inquisition at Rome. Near seventy and broken in spirit, he was forced in the presence of the full Congregation to abjure on his knees the doctrines defined as contrary to the Holy Scriptures. The oath of recantation read in part, "I Galileo Galilei . . . swear that with honest heart and in good faith I curse and execrate the said heresies and errors as to the movement of the earth around the sun and all other heresies and ideas opposed to the Holy Church; and I swear that I will never assert or say anything either orally or in writing, that could put me under such suspicion." A story has it that after he recited the abjuration Galileo muttered under his breath, "Eppur si muove (But it [the earth] does move)." Though the legend is unsupported by historical evidence, it indicates the value of the renunciation which was obtained under duress and expresses the general belief as to what went on in Galileo's mind.

The last years of his life Galileo devoted to the study of **dynamics,** publishing in 1636 his famous *Dialogues on Motion,* a consolidation of his earlier work on the subject. This book not only laid the foundation for the study of mechanics but specifically served as the preliminary work for Newton's laws of motion. Soon after publishing it Galileo became blind and also partially deaf. Yet he continued to work until his death on January 8, 1642, at the age of seventy-eight. Many historians of science regard Galileo as the founder of experimental science. His investigations of nature discredited dependence upon accepted authority, particularly upon Aristotle. Galileo's fight for the Copernican system did much to promote its acceptance and win supporters for it.[12]

"They don't do it our way"[13]

DR. INA TELBERG

"What the Distinguished Lady Representative has just suggested proves that women can be more than decorative—they can also be useful."

With this jovial remark, a United States Delegate looked at his Soviet Colleague in the Population Commission of the United Nations and awaited a smile of response. None came. The Russian sat stiff and unsmiling. In Russia there are no jokes about women drivers or women delegates, so beloved by the Americans. The Russian conception of courtesy, therefore, forbade the Soviet Delegate to do anything but freeze into a silent disapproval. The well-meaning American attempt to find common ground by means of a joke thus increased, rather than decreased, the psychological distance between the two delegations. . . .

ONE MAN'S MEAL . . .

One of the most deeply rooted, and largely unconscious, features of any culture is what the psychologists call the *time perspective.*

---

[12] Ibid., 1954 edition. Reprinted by permission.
[13] Reprinted by permission from *UNESCO Courier,* May 1950.

Within the United Nations, at least three different time perspectives operate.

"Gentlemen, it is time for lunch, we must adjourn," announces the Anglo-Saxon chairman, in the unabashed belief that having three meals a day at regular hours is the proper way for mankind to exist.

"But why? We haven't finished what we were doing," replies—in a puzzled manner that grows rapidly more impatient—an Eastern European Delegate, in whose country people eat when the inclination moves them and every family follows its own individual time-table.

"Why, indeed?" placidly inquires the Far Eastern representative, hailing from a country where life and time are conceived as a continuous stream, with no man being indispensable, with no life-process needing to be interrupted for any human being, and where members of electoral bodies walk in and out of the room quietly, getting a bite to eat when necessary, talking to a friend when pleasant; but where meetings, theatre performances, and other arranged affairs last without interruption for hours on end, while individuals come and go, are replaced by others, meditate or participate as the occasion requires, without undue strain, stress, or nervous tension.

As one or the other group persists in its own conception of the time perspective, as the Anglo-Saxons demand that the duration of meetings and conferences be fixed in advance and that meals be taken regularly at fixed hours, and as the Russians sit irritated and the Latins puzzled and the Secretariat frantic—as this condition continues, mutual friction grows, murmurs of "unreasonableness" are heard around the room; and, when the issue under discussion is an important one, overt accusations are hurled across the room of "insincerity," "lack of a serious approach to the problem," and even "sabotage."

IRONY OR POETRY

Another frequent source of irritation, rooted deeply in the cultural differences among nations, is the *length and the style of oration.*

The Latins are usually accused of unnecessary length and of equally unnecessary flights of poetic fancy. The Russians are disliked both for the length of their speeches and for the irony and sarcasm of the speeches' content. The utilization of irony in political speeches is a long-standing tradition of *public oratory in Russia.* It has nothing to do with the Soviet Government. Mr. Vishinsky, for example, most noted for this type of oration, was born, trained, and had had considerable success as trial lawyer and political orator, long before the establishment of the Soviet Government.

It was in November 1946, that I was flown to Lake Success from the Nuremberg Trials. I was tired, sleepy, and a stranger to the United Nations. On November 15th Vishinsky was delivering his now-famous veto speech in the Political Committee at Lake Success. A regular interpreter failed, and I was rushed to the microphone in the middle of the speech. I remember how my voice trembled when I first began to speak. I knew that I was on the air, and that many of my friends in America and England were listening. In a few minutes, however, I lost every trace of self-consciousness as Mr. Vishinsky's Russian carried me away by its sheer beauty, force, and richness of expression. Latin quotations, Russian proverbs, even Shakespearian poetry, were utilized for the purposes of his attack on the British and the American positions.

Next day I was startled by the press reactions. I myself even received some fan mail: a couple of letters that denounced me as a Communist for having interpreted the speech with such fervor, and another one that praised me for same. I realized then how unnecessarily vitriolic, aggressive, and offensive the address was when translated: in fact, how ill-adapted was the Russian oratorical style to delivery in a foreign tongue. It was not the language itself, however, that was the obstacle. It was the tradition behind the language; what I have since learned to call *speech etiquette.*

SETTLING A "GRAVE" ISSUE

The Latins, on the other hand, far from employing sarcasm, prefer to sprinkle their speeches with a liberal amount of poetic imagery, metaphysical expressions, and literary allusions.

During the General Assembly meetings in Paris, a Latin-American delegate pleaded for the inclusion of the phrase, "from the cradle to the grave," in the Article of the Declaration of Human Rights dealing with social security. He wanted to insure that a worker, or rather, a citizen, should be covered by measures of social protection in just that manner: from the cradle to the grave. He meant precisely, literally, what he said.

"Such phrases have no place in a serious document," pronounced a Western European delegate.

"But the Declaration should be beautifully worded," argued another Latin delegate.

"It's a legal document—not a poem," muttered a Benelux member.

A member of the United States Delegation whispered darkly into a neighbor's ear:

"Why not 'from womb to tomb'? At least it rhymes!"

Before the final text of the Article was settled upon, several other poetical versions were suggested. Some others, quite unprintable, shortly made the rounds of the corridors outside the conference rooms. . . .

THE ORIGIN OF MAN

Life itself is prized differently in different cultures. To die of peaceful old age is the ideal life pattern in some parts of the world. Death for a country or an ideal is the desirable social behavior in others. Nowhere have these differences been made so manifest as in the drafting of the Declaration of Human Rights.

"Man is of divine origin, endowed by nature with reason and conscience," argued several Latin-American delegates.

"All life is of divine origin, not only human life," a representative of a Buddhist state murmured gently. *"Is it not vanity to attribute divine origin to human life alone?"*

"Man is not divine. He is rooted in the very land he tills, in the soil that bred him," once stated an Eastern European Delegate from a preponderantly agricultural area. The Soviets suggested tactfully that science had reservations on the whole subject. The Anglo-Saxon bloc, evidently not quite definite on the subject of human divinity, kept still.

CONFUSION OVER CHINA

Humour relief is not infrequently provided by the very cultural differences that are usually so productive of misunderstandings.

On one occasion, a misunderstanding was particularly startling:

"Gentlemen, gentlemen, let us not act in this matter like an elephant in a china shop!"

As this remark was being rendered from the Russian into English, a language in which the Chinese Delegate was following proceedings, he promptly raised his hand.

"*Mr. Chairman, I should like the Soviet Delegate to explain just what China has to do with his objections.*"

"*Mr. Chairman, I said nothing whatever about China. The Chinese Delegate must have misunderstood.*"

"*Mr. Chairman, I distinctly heard my country mentioned. I request an explanation.*" . . .

Making glamor sell glamor[14]

At a fashion show in Houston, Texas, not long ago, the commentator matter-of-factly began her pitch: "Gown by Ceil Chapman, body by Slenderella."

Six years ago, nobody would have known what she was talking about. Today, thousands of women know. Last year they haunted Slenderella reducing salons to gross more than $12 million (at $2 a throw) for Slenderella International, founded and headed by Lawrence L. Mack, 38, of Stamford, Connecticut.

Mack is living evidence that in a plush economy, the sizzle counts for more than the steak. If the steak is rather thin, the sizzle gains importance. What Slenderella offers is more a state of mind than a product. . . .

His sales objective has been twofold: To take the curse off the unsavory reputation that some reducing concerns had earned in the past, and to build up a steady flow of repeat customers. To do this, Mack called into play every psychological tactic in his book.

His pitch is to underplay the reducing angle. "We are in the figure proportioning business, not reducing," he says. He isn't much interested in the woman who has become grossly overweight; "She needs a doctor," he says. "We sell dress sizes. If a woman once wore a size 10 or 12, and now needs a 14, that's the lady we like to help."

The typical Slenderella patron, he says, is pretty intelligent; she's in her 30s, with a child or so; she's about 15 pounds overweight; she once had a good figure and is smart enough to want it back.

---

14 *Business Week*, August 11, 1956. Reprinted by permission.

Three Ply—The "treatment" consists of three items. Key to it is a muscle-toning table, developed, Mack says, at a Midwestern university. Then there's diet—Slenderella prefers to call it a "menu," which the company is smart enough to require the client's own doctor's O.K. on. The doctor invariably approves it, says Mack, because it's a good basic diet, high in protein, low in carbohydrates.

The third ingredient is a mint wafer to provide minerals and vitamins. On these again Mack calls psychology into play. The patron is asked to eat one mint five times a day. The dose could just as well have been one wafer, five times more potent. But the repetitions serve to keep the woman's mind on her job.

Aura of Respectability—Obviously, there's nothing here that a woman couldn't do on her own if she would. How, then, do you parlay a mechanical table, a menu, and some mint tablets into a business that is expected to gross $20 million this year?

With the cardinal need of establishing an aura of social respectability, Slenderella salons themselves are a show-case. The decor is tasteful, the lighting subtle; Muzak lulls the client. Mack still places stress on the fact that the system involves no personal massaging, that the customer gets her passive exercise fully clothed. . . .

The flag, the anthem, and a four-letter word

THE FLAG[15]

Eugene B. Colin, 46, a Skokie advertising executive, used an American flag to teach his night school class something about semantics, but learned something himself in the process.

Colin was served Tuesday night with a warrant charging him with desecrating a flag in the presence of his 15 adult pupils at Niles North Twp. High School September 30. He said he was only trying to illustrate the flag's semantic properties.

Colin said he held a small flag in his hand for about 30 minutes while he explained to his students that its real value lay in which it meant to them. Otherwise, he told them, it was cloth made up into stripes and stars of various colors.

---

[15] "Teacher Learns More About Flag," *Chicago Sun-Times,* October 16, 1968, p. 2. Reprinted by permission.

Then, he said, he placed it on the floor in front of him. And that was the trouble.

"If anything, it certainly was a case of poor judgment," Colin said later. "I don't think I'm second to anyone in my reverence for everything this country stands for," he continued. "I just wanted to illustrate that the value of a thing is what we impute to it."

What the students imputed to the placing of the flag on the floor was something else. A report of the incident was given to the Skokie police, who obtained the warrant from Judge Harold W. Sullivan of the Circuit Court's Skokie Branch.

Colin, who lives at 9331 N. Forest View in the suburb and who receives no salary for his teaching, said he didn't know he had done anything wrong in placing the flag on the floor.

School officials, he said, had told him that most of the class wanted him to continue teaching, but he wasn't sure how many of them would support him when his case comes up in the court October 29.

THE ANTHEM[16]

On a Saturday evening in December, 1941, shortly after Pearl Harbor, I had a dinner date with another graduate student. We went to a restaurant which had a small dance floor at the end of the room farthest from the entrance and which employed a small orchestra on week-ends. We sat at the table next to the dance floor.

During an intermission three young men in Navy uniforms, who occupied a table near us and who had each downed several drinks from the bar since our arrival, went out on the dance floor and began an impromptu floor show. Their horseplay included several apparently unintentional sprawls on the floor and the "emcee's" speech came out as "Laszh'n'szhen'lemen," etc. Suddenly one of them seized a trumpet from the deserted orchestra stall and began playing a wavering but recognizable version of "The Star-Spangled Banner." With his two companions following, he began a stumbling parade up and down the dance floor. By the time the trumpeter had reached the second or third bar of the anthem, everybody in the restaurant had risen to his feet—except my escort. When I realized that he had remained seated, I sank back down into my own chair. One of the men in uniform stopped, looked at us, and called "Shtan' up! Shtan' up!"

---

16 By Alma Johnson Sarett. Reprinted by permission.

but we remained silent and seated. After they had returned to their table, my escort said, "I will not take part in dishonoring a symbol of my country." Shortly afterward, we rose to leave. As we made our way the length of the room to the door, it seemed to me that all talk ceased and that the eyes that followed us were filled with hostility and suspicion.

A FOUR–LETTER WORD[17]

In a suburban courtroom just north of Detroit last week, a high school teacher named Nancy Timbrook clutched a shredded Kleenex as she defended her actions before a judge. She admitted that she had, as charged, written a four-letter variant of the word "to copulate" on her classroom blackboard.

PROSECUTOR: Didn't you know that it was an unfit word to use in front of children?

MRS. TIMBROOK: That's what I was trying to teach—that it was indecent and immoral. It's always made me sick every time I've seen it. I've seen it every day in the (school) john. I wanted to stop it.

PROSECUTOR: Did you know that writing that word was a crime?

MRS. TIMBROOK: I didn't know I was doing anything that would send me to jail.

JUDGE: Ignorance is no excuse.

MRS. TIMBROOK: Perhaps I should have studied law instead of literature.

While the four-letter word under discussion has become commonplace in the works of many modern novelists, its use is far from accepted in high school English classes. Any teacher who makes it the theme of a classroom exercise can expect a strong reaction—if not from the students themselves, at least from their parents. Which is what happened to Mrs. Timbrook, 36, a truck driver's wife and the mother of nine children, who teaches at Lamphere High School in Madison Heights, Mich.

Led by God. The incident took place last month after Patrick Eady, 32, a social studies teacher at Lamphere, invited two college-age youths who are members of a local left-wing group called the White Panthers to address his students. Their talk was freely sprinkled with the provocative verb (or noun, or adjective, depending on how it is

[17] "English Lesson," *Time*, March 28, 1969, pp. 69 and 72. Reprinted by permission.

used). News of the highly unusual lesson spread quickly through the school. Annoyed by the students' snickering, Mrs. Timbrook decided to discuss the word in class the very next day. She printed the word on the blackboard for each of her four English classes and asked each what it meant. "I was led to do that by God," Mrs. Timbrook, a deeply religious woman, later recalled. "I didn't know what I was going to do until I walked into the classroom."

For the most part, the students merely giggled and answered that the word meant "sexual intercourse." But many of the 42,000 residents of the town questioned Mrs. Timbrook's divine inspiration. She insisted that her lecture's purpose was to prove that the word was "devoid of life and love." Nevertheless, parents besieged the superintendent of schools with irate phone calls and, at hastily convened meetings, vilified Mrs. Timbrook as a "whore" and a "disgrace to womankind."

Eady was fired from his job. When Mrs. Timbrook was given nonteaching duties in the superintendent's office, other teachers boycotted the school for a full day. Then one father, Police Lieutenant William Sloan brought criminal charges against Mrs. Timbrook and Eady. Both were arrested on a state charge—"depraving the morals of children." Mrs. Timbrook was also charged with violating a local ordinance that forbids the writing of "indecent and immoral language."

In court Judge Edward Lawrence conceded that her motive had been a moral one. But he was not inclined to minimize her offense. "People may commit murder in the heat of passion," he said, "but that doesn't excuse murder. People may write obscenity for various reasons, but that doesn't excuse obscenity." While the state charge against her was dropped, Mrs. Timbrook pleaded guilty to violating the local ordinance. She faces penalties of up to 90 days in prison and $500 fine at her sentencing next month. Eady, who comes to trial next month, is not likely to get much more sympathy.

13

Intensional orientation II
("pointing" and "associating")

A DEPARTMENT STORE manager once received a shipment of high-quality handkerchiefs and, in an experimental mood, placed half of them in a pile at one end of a sales counter with a sign: "Fine Irish Linen—50¢ Each." He stacked the other half at the opposite end of the counter with a sign: "Nose Rags—3 for 25¢." The "Irish Linens" outsold the "nose rags" five to one!

A delicatessen operator performed somewhat the same sort of "experiment" with some first-rate cheese. He cut two large wedges from the same round and placed them in his showcase. One wedge he labeled "Imported English Cheddar," and the other, "Smelly Cheese." The former, at twice the price, far outsold the latter.

And Haldeman-Julius, publishers of the little five-cent "Blue Books," discovered years ago that changing titles may have a salutary effect on sales:

Title	No. of Copies Sold*
Markheim	100
Markheim's Murder	7,000
The Mystery of the Iron Mask	100
The Mystery of the Man in the Iron Mask	11,000
The Art of Controversy	100
How to Argue Logically	30,000
Fleece of Gold	6,000
Quest for a Blond Mistress	50,000

* During equal periods of time.

433

It is obvious that the way we react to the *words* by which things are called can affect very considerably the way we react to the *things* themselves. You will recall from Chapter 5 that the students in Dr. Lee's classes responded quite differently to the foods they were eating *after* they were told that the foods were "dog biscuits" and "grasshopper cookies."

One way of understanding how our response to words can affect our evaluations of things is to recognize the versatility of language use. Among other uses, we employ and react to words as *pointers* which call attention to something. We use and react to them also as *evokers* of associations.

Suppose you and I are riding through the country and I see a small pool of water and say, "Look at that swimming hole over there." My words may serve the purpose of a pointing finger and call your attention to the pool that you might otherwise have missed.

But if you happen to associate certain memories, experiences, and feelings, pleasant or otherwise, with the phrase "swimming hole," then it is entirely possible that my words would "stir" you up a bit. Moreover, they might suggest to you a great deal beyond the physical pool to which I was referring.

For convenience, we will use the terms *pointing* and *associating,* respectively, to represent these two functions of language. However, we must guard against the artificial dichotomy that words are used *either* as pointers *or* as associators. They are ordinarily used and reacted to as both. The situation is a case of double contraries.

Take the term "sulfuric acid." (See Figure 13–1.) For A, who has never studied chemistry and is not especially acquainted with the words in any other context, the term may have little pointer or associator value; for B, whose face was once badly burned when someone threw sulfuric acid at him, the words might usually have great associator value but perhaps comparatively little pointer value; C, a chemist, may ordinarily use and react to the term with largely pointer value and practically no associator value; and so forth.

Theoretically, depending upon the individual, time, place, verbal context, and other circumstances, one may use or react to a given word or phrase with values anywhere along the infinitely graded double continua.

Even though our terms *pointers* and *associators* imply a fallacious polarization, they provide a useful distinction for describing and coping with serious patterns of miscommunication. I shall henceforth

FIGURE 13-1

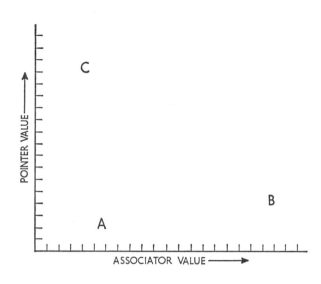

use the words in quotes to remind the reader of the multivalued and interrelated sense in which I am intending them. Let the quotation marks remind us also that *people* (not words) do the "pointing" and "associating" with words.[1]

It is clear that when people "send" and "receive" them, words may have many functions; "pointing" and "associating" are prominent among them. The crux of this chapter, then, is that, *when communicators forget or are unaware that both* "*pointing*" *and* "*associating*" *are usually involved in communication, confusion, misunderstanding, and other kinds of trouble may readily occur.*

The failure to recognize the "pointing-associating duality" of language may lead to several patterns of miscommunication. Three prevalent and troublesome forms are the "*pointing-associating*" *confusion*, "*name-calling*," and "*associative*" *bypassing*.

THE "POINTING–ASSOCIATING" CONFUSION

The commonest experience of deluding ourselves with words occurs when we confuse the "associating" and "pointing" functions. We

---

[1] The reader has probably assumed that I am deliberately refraining from using the words *denotations* and *connotations*. These terms have come to suggest so strongly a polarized view of language use that it seemed advisable to avoid them.

often react to the associations evoked in us by the label *as if* we were reacting to what the label was "pointing" to—the object itself. Most Americans shudder at the prospect of eating rattlesnake meat or snails or French fried grasshoppers. Is it because they dislike the taste? Hardly, for most have never eaten these foods, which, incidentally, are regarded as delicacies in some parts of the world. It is obvious that they are reacting not to the foods themselves but to their *names* and to the associations they have for the names. Consider whether you would not be somewhat more favorably disposed toward a "sirloin steak" than toward a slice of "dead cow," even though both labels "point" to the same piece of meat.

Euphemisms and dysphemisms

To *euphemize* is to substitute an inoffensive, mild, or pleasant "associator" for one which may produce an opposite reaction. When one euphemizes, he figuratively "puts a good face" on something. Calling a liquor store a "package store" or "party store" does not change the store, its contents, or its function, but it may soften the *impression* for many. The *dysphemism* is the counterpart of euphemism. It puts a "bad face" on the thing. Calling the same establishment a "booze store" still doesn't change the store, but it may change the way some people feel about it.

There are many occasions when euphemisms or dysphemisms, used judiciously, may serve good purposes—or at least expedient ones. When consoling a friend who has just lost someone near, you would almost certainly use "passed away" rather than "croaked" or "kicked the bucket." And surely it is kinder to refer to a thin woman as "on the slender side" than as "skinny" or "spindly." More appealing titles for people's jobs, as one wit pointed out, may also have their value:

Yesterday	*Today*	*Tomorrow* *
Typewriter	Stenographer	Visual transcriptionist
Bookkeeper	Comptroller	Tax avoidance researcher
Garbageman	Sanitary engineer	Excess materials manager
Telephone girl	Switchboard operator	Audio connection supervisor
Head clerk	Office manager	Coffee break coordinator

* Harold Coffin, from "Look on the Lighter Side," ed. Gurney Williams, *Look*, August 21, 1956, p. 116. Reprinted by permission of the author and *Look* magazine.

On the other hand, a man running for election might not be reluctant to use dysphemisms in describing his determined, liberal intellectual opponent as "that stubborn, radical, egghead." Your children and mine may be equally energetic, but if I don't happen to like you, I may prefer to describe yours as "wild" and my own as "active." Your wife may be a "gabby gossip," but mine is an "enthusiastic conversationalist." And, while my home may have that "lived-in look," yours is just "shabby."

One of the most acute dangers of euphemisms-dysphemisms and, in general, of reacting to "associators" as if they were "pointers" is that we tend to lose sight of the "things" being represented. We become so mesmerized by the *name* that the "thing" becomes obscured. On some campuses the *name* of one's sorority or fraternity apparently looms very large in extracurricular matters. Fraternity men have told me that the dating of sorority women of other than the "better" houses is frowned upon by their brothers. Ironically, the "Eta Byta Pi" label on a girl sometimes seems a more important criterion for date selection than the unique characteristics and qualities of the girl herself. But is this behavior less rational than voting a straight party ballot without any apparent concern for the qualifications of the individual candidates? Speaking of politics, have you heard of the Democratic nomination for treasurer in a Michigan county a few years ago? Democrats discovered that they had nominated a T. Edward Aho, 52, an inmate of a state mental hospital! Aho, an unemployed worker, was not prominent in the county, but his Finnish name had vote appeal in the Finnish-dominated county. Similarly, a certain city ward, predominantly Scandinavian, voted a Mr. Jenson into a minor office. It was only after the election that most of the voters realized Mr. Jenson was a black man!

There are many who readily capitalize upon our tendency to react to "associators" as if they were "pointers." You would find some of the most skillful of them writing advertising copy. With deft pens poised, these word-magicians sift through hundreds of words to find the term or phrase most likely to elicit quickly the desired response to their products. They overlook few possibilities for word appeal. In the automobile industry, for example, even the car's colors are verbally glamorized. It is no longer possible to buy a "black" or a "red" or a "green" or a "blue" auto. But you can get one in "Onyx Black," "Carnival Red," "Fern Mist Green," "Ginger Glow," "Calypso

Coral," or "Burgundy Fire." My personal prize goes to the inventor of the name for a certain yellow color that one manufacturer used a few years ago. To me, at least, the color was a bilious gray-yellow, reminiscent of dusty mustard. Its name—the stroke of a master—was "Sunglo!"

Classified advertisers are generally not as adept as their distant cousins in the agencies, but they too contrive studiously to find the "right word." The favorite terms for describing a house for sale, according to a survey of 8,000 ads in eight major United States daily newspapers, were "cute," "a cutie," "adorable," "exquisite," "elegant," "a dandy," "magnificent," "glamorous," "spic and span," "clean as a pin," "a rare find," and a "real bargain." A farm was seldom a "farm" but a "rural hideaway," a "rustic retreat," or a "secluded estate." There were few "jobs" in the Help Wanted columns, but "openings" and "positions" were plentiful. A lost dog was frequently the "pet of an invalid grandmother" or belonged to a "heartbroken little girl." Dogs for sale were advertised variously as "love that money can't buy," "darlings," "cuddlies," and "swell pets." Possibly the most refined touch of all was the term for a bitch with a litter of pups—she was listed as a "matron."

Even the farmer who was busily building an unusual structure on his "east forty" had a flair for "associators." "What's it going to be?" asked a neighbor. "It all depends," was the reply. "If I rent it, it's a pastoral lodge—if I don't, it's a cowshed." And if you happen to write restaurant menus, you had better watch your "associators," for they determine to some extent how much you can charge for the food.

IT ALL DEPENDS ON WHERE YOU EAT*

Hamburger	$0.50
Salisbury Steak	1.00
Chopped Tenderloin Steak	1.50
Charcoal-Broiled Chopped Tenderloin Steak	2.50
Prime Tenderloin Steak, Charcoal Grilled (Chopped)	3.50
Du Bœuf Haché Grillé au Charbon de Bois	4.50

* Carl H. Nilson, from "Look on the Light Side," ed. Gurney Williams, *Look*, July 10, 1956, p. 83. Reprinted by permission of the author and *Look* magazine.

Lest it appear that euphemizing and dysphemizing are merely "playing with words," I submit that a key issue in a continuing controversy is whether an abortion should be considered as "killing a human being" or "terminating a pregnancy."

"NAME CALLING"

There is a species of the "pointing-associating" confusion which merits special attention. It concerns the "associating" labels which people apply to one another and to themselves. The "names" we call others or by which we are called can profoundly influence our evaluations and behavior.

The double burden

The child's retaliation, "Sticks and stones may break my bones, but names can never hurt me," is unfortunately only half correct. Names *can* hurt us, even more grievously, on occasion, than "sticks and stones."

Consider the youngster who survives polio with a withered leg. The physical pain of walking and the psychic pain of watching other children run may be as nothing compared with the burden of a thoughtlessly imposed nickname such as "Limpy" or "Gimpy." Or consider the youngster scarred by acne. His disfigured face is a sufficient trial, but a label such as "Scarface" may well double his burden.

Adults are not exempt from carrying a double burden. A psychologist who serves as an employee counselor with a manufacturing firm recently described the case of a young, intelligent, and attractive stenographer who came to him for help. Until recently she had been considered by her supervisor to be a superior employee, but during the last few months she had grown nervous and irritable. Her work began to deteriorate, and her supervisor finally recommended that she speak with the counselor. He learned that the young woman had been divorced three years previously but seemed to have made a satisfactory adjustment. In recent months, however, her social life was more than she could bear. Breaking down, she sobbed: "I've dated four men in the last year, and in each case things were going fine until my boyfriend found out I had been married. Two of them dropped me like a hot potato, and the other two began taking such liberties that I had to drop them. Why don't men give divorcees a chance to start over? Look, I'm decent and I intend to stay that way but they make it pretty rough."

Living up to the labels

This young woman was resisting her "name," but this is not always the case. People, often unconsciously, tend to *live up to their labels*. I shall never forget an experience in a group dynamics course in college. There were about 20 in the class, and we met twice weekly in two-hour discussion sessions. Our basic purpose was to study group dynamics by observing the dynamics of our own group. Along about the sixth week, one member of the group made a statement to this effect: "It has occurred to me that certain people in this group tend to play certain roles. I have noticed that whenever someone is being picked on, Kathy will step in to defend him—she's sort of a protector of the underdog. And when we begin to argue and the tension begins to build, have you noticed that it's often Bill who tries to relax us with a comical remark? And Don usually backs anyone who wants a change—he's 'Mr. Progressive!' " He continued to categorize three or four other members. The group responded with some chaffing of the "underdog protector," "the jokester," and so on, and the subject was forgotten—apparently. But, as the weeks went on, it became obvious that some of those labeled were portraying their "roles" in and out of season! Kathy was defending underdogs more vehemently than ever; Bill was joking more than ever—even when there were no tensions to be broken, and so forth.[2]

Unhappily, living up to one's labels can have far graver consequences. Consider this statement from a social worker's file:

I got a reputation as the town's bad girl. Sure, I did some of the things they said I did. But not until I had been blamed for a lot of things not my fault. After that I didn't care.

The double burden has become so oppressive for adolescents in trouble that authorities have been moved to speak out against such incriminating labels as "juvenile delinquent." Joseph Lohman, sociologist and, for four years, sheriff of Cook County, Illinois, has said: "The name juvenile delinquent . . . sets the young person apart and may motivate further misbehavior." Mrs. Newton P. Leonard, president of the National Congress of Parents and Teachers (PTA), a few years ago, exhorted her nearly 9 million members to discard the label. "Juvenile delinquents, so-called, are children in trouble, children in conflict—with the law, with society, with themselves," she said. "The last thing they need is to be branded with a dehumanizing label and a matching set of attitudes from members of the community."

---

[2] In fact, their role playing was so rigid that this was virtually the only *kind* of behavior they were able or willing to portray.

Living down the labels

Living *up* to one's labels may result in irrational and tragic behavior, but the consequences of living them *down* can be equally foolish and dangerous. For instance, a Claremont, California, youth became so embarrassed when he failed his driver's license test that, to prove himself to his ridiculing friends, he stole a car and drove it—to Philadelphia! But, for a more poignant example, consider the case of a 17-year-old who stabbed a 14-year-old boy to death. A typical attack-by-bully incident? If one were to look behind the glaring headlines, he would find a very different kind of explanation. He would discover the story of a life in torment—the story of a boy pathetically small for his age, frail since infancy, a boy prevented by malnutrition from entering school until he was 8, a boy now 17 who weighed only 90 pounds and stood 4 feet 11 in his shoes. One could see the image of a lad taunted by his playmates with the stinging labels of "Half-pint," "Short-stuff," and "Peanut."

Pink-cheeked Adrian Konecki, 17, twirled in the witness chair today as he told a jury in Judge Pope's court how he stabbed a friend to death after being called a "runt."

Adrian weighs 90 pounds and his victim, Michael Bucsko, 8600 Houston Ave., though three years younger weighed 140. . . .

On the fateful day, the boy said, he went to church, then sought out friends in a bowling alley, then started home and encountered "Mickey" Bucsko and Thomas Karczewski, 14, (5 feet 11, 135 pounds) . . . .

"They said they'd been drinking and using toothpaste to cover it up. Mickey sneered, 'You can't drink, you runt!' I said, 'Say that again.' He did, and asked, 'You wanta make something out of it?'

"I said 'Yes' and slapped him. Mickey started for me and Tommy went to the side. I backed up and pulled my knife."

The weapon was a three-inch switchblade knife which Adrian said he found in a vacant lot and used to open boxes in the grocery store where he works.

He went on: "They were bigger than me and I thought they were gonna jump me and beat me up. I hadda use something to protect myself. He kept coming and I stabbed him."

His feet swinging clear of the floor, Adrian kept staring at the jurors with interest but without emotion. His face clouded as he suddenly recalled his tormentors also had called him an imp, a weasel, and "wimpy."[3]

---

[3] Elgar Brown, "Boy Tells Jurors He 'Had to Kill'," *Chicago's American,* September 19, 1957, p. 5. Reprinted by permission.

Positive labels

These sobering illustrations of the possible consequences of living up to or of living down one's labels should not suggest that such behavior is *necessarily* negative and destructive in its effect. On the contrary, labels may sometimes have definite positive influence. I am firmly convinced that a fair share of the "good" in people is derived from the "good" that was *expected* of them as children. Many a child, I am confident, has become an honest, responsible, generous adult partly, if not largely, because others, notably his parents, teachers, and playmates, *expected* such qualities of him and *communicated* their anticipations to him. By making clear to a child that you know he is truthful and that you genuinely trust him, you are implicitly, if not explicitly, labeling him as a "truth-teller," and chances are that he will live up to the label. It is the genuine high expectation (which implies trust, confidence, respect) of the other which, after all, is the cornerstone of Theory Y (see Chapter 2).

But even positive labels may be dangerous. Unrealistic positive labels may entice one to overreach his capabilities and thus lead to frustration, disillusionment—even tragedy. Consider the case of the young man described in the *polarization* chapter, who, on the eve of his high school graduation, was found hanged in his attic. An outstanding personality, the boy had been president of his class, active in school affairs. He had just been accepted for enrollment by one of the nation's leading universities and had been given a new convertible by his proud parents. What could conceivably have driven him to suicide? Authorities uncovered a probable reason: He had missed being elected to the National Honor Society by a fraction of a point. His self-image (his self-labels, if you will) and this overwhelming "failure" were evidently irreconcilably polarized in his tortured mind.

"ASSOCIATIVE" BYPASSING

The "pointing-associating duality" of language offers still another possibility for communication difficulty. An earlier chapter described *bypassing* as the miscommunication pattern whereby people miss one another with their meanings. We were concerned with words which were being used and reacted to as primarily "pointers." It is now pertinent to discuss the tendency of people to miss one another's *"associative"* meanings.

"Associative" bypassing becomes possible:

1. When the sender (speaker, writer, and so on) assumes that, because he intends his words as merely "pointers," they will necessarily have little or no "associative" value for his receiver (listener, reader, and so forth) :

In the earlier years of commercial aviation a stewardess would warn her passengers: "We're flying through a *storm*. You had better fasten your *safety* belts; it will be less *dangerous*." She might have intended nothing more than merely "pointing" with her words, but you may be sure the novice passengers "associated" a great deal more. Today, stewardesses are trained to elicit pleasant and secure associations with: "We're flying through some *turbulence* now; please fasten your *seat* belts—you will be more *comfortable*." Even so perfection still eludes us—not long ago a vivacious young stewardess strayed from the "script" to announce gaily that we were to land soon: "Folks, please fasten your seat belts; we'll be hitting the ground in just a few minutes."

2. When the receiver interprets words as largely or solely "pointers," whereas the sender intended them to be "associative."

If you have ever complained: "Oh! You take things so literally," you have probably been involved in this sort of *"associative"* bypassing. It is the pathetic miscommunication which occurs when the young lady vainly tries to encourage her shy date with "Johnny, I'm cold." Whereupon her gallant escort whips off his jacket and slips it around her shoulders. She had wanted the jacket, all right, but with Johnny's arms still in the sleeves!

This is the pattern, too, of sarcasm which fails. A sales manager was busily preparing for a trip which was to take him away from the office for the day. He called his filing clerk, pointed to a small pile of correspondence, and instructed: "Please file these letters." And, hoping to jar her from her usual lethargy, he added wryly: "Be sure to take all day with the job!" She did.

3. When the communicator (sender or receiver or both) assumes that words have the *same* "associative" value for the other fellow as they have for him.

Illustrative is the case of the hospital patient who was awaiting major surgery. He was toying with breakfast as he worried about the operation. Suddenly a nurse appeared at his door, noticed the barely touched food, and blithely said: "Better eat—*while you can!*" The poor man immediately assumed the worst. But the nurse had only meant to imply that the food service attendant would soon pick up the breakfast tray!

A POSSIBLE MISUNDERSTANDING

If in discussing these particular pitfalls of language I have given the impression that "associators" are "bad" or that they are to be avoided or abolished, I have not intended to. In the first place, "associating" is not a "thing" which can be destroyed. It is a function of words, and it has no existence apart from *people* using and reacting to words. As long as people have "imaginations," as long as they have the agility to leap beyond the immediate objects of their senses, there will be "associating." And let us be everlastingly grateful for it. The world would be unbearably prosaic without humor (an enormous portion of which is based upon association) and without poetry, drama—literature, in general—which is designed to elicit rich associations from us. "I love you" (among the most highly "associative" phrases in our culture) would be just so many flat, commonplace words if the sender and receiver were not able to transport themselves beyond mere "pointers."

Are we not sometimes the poorer for having cast out "associators"? Consider that in Victorian times only horses *sweated,* men *perspired,* and women—why they merely *glowed!*

No, this chapter has not been calculated to annihilate "associators" (even if it were possible). And certainly there has been no intention of debasing or minimizing their value and usefulness. On the other hand, it is clear that there are occasions when it is important, even imperative, to be *aware* of when "associators" are being used and to know how to cope with them. It is for these purposes that the following corrective measures are offered.

CORRECTIVES

It is the major thesis of this chapter that words can be used and reacted to both as "pointers" and as "associators." When communicators forget, ignore, deny, or, for any reason, are unaware of this "duality," patterns of miscommunication become possible which may lead to confusion and trouble. Among these patterns are the *"pointing-associating"* confusion, *"name calling,"* and *"associative"* bypassing. The suggestions which follow should be helpful in recognizing and dealing with these patterns.

The "pointing-associating" confusion

Make a habit of distinguishing between labels and "things." Living and communicating with labels as we do, we are frequently enticed to accept them as the "things" they represent. Communicators must be wary of reacting to labels as if they were more than representations (and often misleading representations, at that). In this vein, give Mrs. Haney credit for a sensible adjustment to what had been a distinctly distasteful task for her. As a child it was occasionally her lot to fish the potato peelings, carrot scrapings, and assorted remains from the dinner dishes out of the sink. This was referred to in the family as "cleaning out the garbage," a chore (and phrase) which distressed her to the point of nausea. At Girl Scout camp a year or so later, she gained an insight. There the girls were instructed to scrape the "leftover food" off their plates. On returning home, she discovered she could remove the "garbage" from the sink with scarcely a qualm so long as she reminded herself that it was "leftover food" she was touching.

Remember, the map is *not* the territory; words are *not* that which they are being used to represent. Ask yourself: "Am I responding to the *object* or to the *association* I have for its *name?*"

Don't permit the label to obscure the "product." Develop the extensional habit of looking "behind" labels to see the "product" more clearly. Manufacturers who assume that consumers usually look beyond the labels have sometimes paid for their overconfidence. Several years ago a new chocolate dessert topping came on the market. The product was tasty and inexpensive, but many customers adamantly refused to try it, apparently because they were unable or unwilling to look beyond its rather descriptive name—"Goop!"

Some companies, however, learn the lesson less painfully. "Mrs. Japp's Potato Chips" had been distributed throughout greater Chicago for sometime before World War II. But shortly after Pearl Harbor sales began to sag. It didn't take Mrs. Japp (a Danish name) long to find the answer and change the name to "Jay's Potato Chips." The product has prospered ever since.

It came as no great surprise to the sports world that the National League Cincinnati Baseball Club in the era of congressional investigations of Communists changed its name from "Reds" to "Redlegs." This, incidentally, was the same word-wise organization which felt "bleachers" was a somewhat unattractive name for its uncovered stands. Since 1954 the stands have been known as the "Sun-Deck," and its patrons are permitted to wear beach costumes. For night games—miracle of miracles—it becomes the "Moon-Deck!"

Another convincing illustration of the role that a label plays in the acceptance of its product occurred several years ago when Hopalong Cassidy was riding into fame and fortune on millions of television screens. It happened at the time that a certain Boston restaurant, catering to families, was featuring a children's-size meat potpie. But the kids were recalcitrantly uninterested until a bright young assistant manager clapped a new label on the potpies. With the menu featuring the "Hopalong Casserole," the kitchen was unable to keep up with the demand!

"Name calling"

The basic advice is to recognize "names" for what they are—merely tags, often inaccurate, and always incomplete representations of the flesh-and-blood persons to whom they are appended. Remember that the labels in themselves are utterly powerless and meaningless. It is our *reactions* to the labels of others (and to our own) that can have profound effects on our evaluations and behavior. It is tempting for those who do the labeling and for those who are labeled to assume that the labels are valid and complete.

More specifically, if the labels assigned to you are negative and unfavorable, refuse to live up to them, to resign yourself to them. Resist them, contradict them with your behavior (actions are usually more convincing than words). But, on the other hand, avoid overreacting to them and assuming a manner or characteristic which is equally or more objectionable than the trait originally labeled. If your labels are positive, recognize that they may serve as a beneficial stimulant, but be wary of overreaching your capacities.

If you are doing the labeling, if label you must, be careful in your selection of "tags." Negative labels are seldom useful and often dangerous, while positive labels are often, but not invariably, beneficial. If you want someone to be honest, let *him* know you genuinely trust him.

"Associative" bypassing

"Associative" bypassing occurs when communicators miss one another with their "associative" meanings. As such, "associative" bypassing is similar to bypassing (the missing of "pointer" meanings), and the reader is encouraged to review the correctives section in Chapter 7, "Bypassing."

But, in addition, remember:

1. Words to which you "associate" little or nothing may be highly "associative" for the other person:

Labor contract negotiators have learned to be alert to some of the "red-flag" words which upset the other party. In meeting with company representatives, union negotiators, for example, refrain from mentioning the union "demand" and substitute union "proposal" when softer associations seem in order. They find, too, that discussions with management in terms of what "your employees want" rather than what "the union (or 'we') wants" are often carried on with more equanimity and objectivity.

2. Words "associating" a great deal to you may "associate" little or nothing to the other person—they may merely *"point"* for him:

Before making his final decision on a proposal to move to new offices, the head of a large company called his top executives for a last discussion of the idea. All were enthusiastic except the company treasurer, who insisted that he had not had time to calculate all the costs with accuracy sufficient to satisfy himself that the move was advantageous. Annoyed by his persistence, the chief finally burst out:

"All right, Jim, all right! Figure it out to the last cent. A penny saved is a penny earned, right?"

The intention was ironic. He meant not what the words denoted but the opposite—forget this and stop being petty. For him this was what his words connoted.

For the treasurer "penny saved, penny earned" meant exactly what it said. He put several members on his staff to work on the problem and, to test the firmness of the price, had one of them interview the agent renting the proposed new quarters without explaining whom he represented. This indication of additional interest in the premises led the agent to raise the rent. Not until the lease was signed, did the agency chief discover that one of his own employees had, in effect, bid up its price.[4]

3. Your receiver (or sender) may not be "associating" with his words as you are:

Employed by a tool and die works, a young engineer was assigned to study the plant's production procedures in general and to devise im-

---

[4] From Robert Froman, "Make Words Fit the Job," *Nation's Business*, July 1959, p. 78. Reprinted by permission.

provements. Tool and die men are the aristocracy of factory workers, and their foremen are of correspondingly high standing. The engineer was aware of this and took great care to show respect.

. When he found one department where he thought he could make considerable improvement, he first set about making friends with the workmen and their foreman. Once he had gained their acceptance he got the foreman to call the men together so that he could outline his plans to the whole group. Because he thought that several of the men might resist change, he sought to allay their fears by saying:

"Of course, at this stage what I'm proposing is only an experiment." . . .

The men not only dragged their heels but actively sabotaged his attempted innovations. Finally, the foreman went to the production manager. The gist of his complaint was that the engineer was trying to use him and his men as "guinea pigs."

You may be tempted to dismiss this as an unthinking reaction on the part of the men. But it was the engineer who sought to communicate something to them, not they to him. He wanted to make them feel that he was proposing only tentative changes which would not become permanent unless they proved successful.[5]

DISCUSSION QUESTIONS

1. "Euphemisms" and "dysphemisms" are sometimes used to deceive others. What can be done to combat such forms of misrepresentation since they are usually not direct contradictions of truth?
2. On the other hand, what should be the rights of advertisers, public relations people, editorialists, lawyers, salesmen, writers, and others who rely largely upon words to accomplish their purposes?
3. Do you agree that only *half* of the "sticks and stones" expression is true? Why?
4. Recalling the illustration of students living up to their labels in the group dynamics course: What can be gained or lost by such labeling?
5. What are the pros and cons of "positive labeling"?
6. What are the pros and cons of "associators"?
7. Report upon an incident, perhaps involving yourself, in which "pointing"-"associating" confusion (or "name calling" or "associative" by-passing) was involved. Why did the incident occur? What could have been done to prevent or correct it? What measures would tend to prevent its recurrence?

[5] Ibid., pp. 76–77.

CASES

Galvanized sheets[6]

From 1940 to 1953 the manufacturers of galvanized sheeting were experimenting with new methods of galvanization. The object was to develop a process which would be quick, inexpensive, and yet would coat sheeting in such a manner that it could be bent sharply without the galvanizing peeling off. One firm, the Ewell Company, finally developed a process which met these qualifications.

Their method was to manufacture sheeting in a continuous roll in order that it could be galvanized as it rolled through the galvanizing pit. The sheeting was then cut to specifications.

The company felt it had a superior product but decided upon a marketing test as a precautionary measure. A few salesmen in certain pilot territories were instructed to begin selling the new products to their customers, i.e., sheet metal shops, ventilating firms, and so forth. Since no trade name had as yet been selected, the salesmen were told to refer to the new product as "continuous roll galvanized sheets."

Customer reaction ranged from apathy to resistance. The salesmen returned to the plant and complained that the average customer had a firm conviction that the "rolling process"[7] would flatten out the galvanizing to the point that it would be too thin to withstand severe bends without peeling.

The salesmen tried in vain to explain that the "continuous roll" of their new galvanizing process didn't really involve "rolling" in the *thinning* sense at all. The reports were disturbing, but Ewell, convinced of the superiority of its product, decided to gamble. The continuous roll process was adopted throughout the plant. The product

---

[6] All names have been disguised.

[7] "Rolling" in the metals industries generally referred to the process of thinning strips of metal as they passed between sets of rollers. The rollers exerted great pressure on the strips and literally squeezed them down into thinner gauges.

was trademarked "Flex-tite" in the hope that it would offset prejudices. Production began in full swing while management crossed its
fingers and waited.

Within two years it was obvious that the gamble had paid off. The
company, now producing "Flex-tite" exclusively, had doubled its
total sales of galvanized sheeting.

Case of the growing boy[8]

Even in maturity, long-leggy (6 foot 6 inches) Clarence E. Mc-
Vey, 49, a carpenter of Graham, N.C. (pop. 5,000) could not forget
the misery of his school days. He had grown so fast that he towered
above all his classmates, was so gangling and awkward that he became
the butt of their jokes. He swore that his five-year-old son David, already over four feet tall, would never have to suffer from the family
curse of being "too big for his age."

Just to make sure, he decided last fall to start David in school a
year early, even though North Carolina law forbids pupils to enter
before they are six. At first, no one was the wiser, and David became
one of the best pupils in the first grade. Then one day someone told
David's dreadful secret.

The teacher asked Clarence McVey to take five-year-old David out
of school. McVey flatly refused. A few weeks later, the county school
board made the same request, but McVey still refused. Last week,
when he ignored a formal order from North Carolina's Tenth District Superior Court to keep David at home, he was hauled off to jail.
Said McVey: "I'll stay here and rot before I take little David out of
school." This week, there he stayed—and David stayed in school.

Seek to change name of Cicero[9]

Cicero town officials have decided that they just can't bury Al
Capone.

---

8 *Time,* April 9, 1951. Reprinted by permission.

9 *Chicago Sun-Times,* September 14, 1952, p. 3. Reprinted by permission.

"He's been gone 30 years, he was here only six months and yet our town still is burdened by his reputation," said town attorney Nicholas Berkos.

To help lay the Capone legend to rest, the members of the town board will meet Monday night to hear arguments pro and con on changing the name of their town. They feel that a new name may erase the old black marks.

After the meeting, citizens of Cicero will circulate petitions to urge the name change. If more than half of the voters in the last election approve it, the name will be changed after a search to discover if there are any similarly named places in the state.

Most prominently mentioned as new names for the old town are Electra—to mark the place as a center of the electrical industry—and Normandy—reminiscent of a beachhead and a brave, new start.

"We have one of the lowest crime rates in the country," Berkos said. "Juvenile delinquency here is non-existent."

"And yet a kid from Cicero can't get into a fraternity or a sorority at a college because of the town's reputation. Real estate value is held down because of the unearned bad repute."

"No politician can get elected to any job outside if he's from Cicero. People everywhere think we're just a bunch of hoods. Maybe a name change will help."

Opponents of the plan to change the town's name contend it would be a cowardly act and feel sure that they can live down the dark associations with the word Cicero in time.

"We're not trying to force the thing," Berkos said. "If more than half of the people don't want to change the name, then Cicero still will be Cicero."

Sticks and stones . . .[10]

Despite the child's defiant jingle, names hurt more than sticks or stones: a man can more easily bear an attack on his body than an offense to his feelings, and will remember an insult long after he has forgotten an injury.

—*Sidney Harris*

---

[10] All items except the Harris quotation are from *Time* and are reprinted with permission.

Live wire.   In Christchurch, New Zealand, haled into court on a charge of using foul language to a telephone operator, an angry subscriber countercharged that the girl "just laughed and laughed" after he obliged her by spelling his name: Montmorency de Villiers.

Any other name.   In Calgary, Alta., George and Rosie Big Belly asked the Provincial Secretary what could be done for them under the provisions of "The Change of Name Act."

Typo.   In Philadelphia, when *Inquirer* Columnist Frank Brookhouser reported that Hubert B. Wolfeschlegelsteinhasenbergerdorff had registered to vote in the November elections, Hubert wrote in indignantly to say that a "u" had been left out: his name was Wolfeschlegelsteinhausenbergerdorff.

In Washington, Mrs. Alben Barkley told reporters that she did not like to be addressed as "The Veepess": "Somehow or other it sounds like a snake. I guess I connect it with the word viper. I'd really much rather be called Mrs. Veep."

In New Haven, Conn., Yale Graduate Student Edmund D. Looney petitioned the superior court for permission to change his name, claimed that it might interfere with the practice of his future profession—psychiatry.

Tired of living in Snake Den.   Johnston, R.I. residents of Snake Den Rd. complained to the City Council of the "frightful" name of their street. The council ordered the name changed to "Belfield Dr."

Southern hospitality.   In Birmingham, when the judge asked him what the initials stood for, Juryman W. J. Weaver recalled: "My mother and daddy had eleven daughters in a row. They decided to call me Welcome John."

The manatee[11]

The flesh of the manatee is light-colored and tastes much like fresh pork. It is such excellent eating that the animal was in danger of being exterminated by the settlers and tourists. Kirk Monroe related how he had introduced a bill in the legislature in which he left out its common names and put in only the scientific one, *Trichechus*

---

[11] From *The World Grows round My Door* by David Fairchild (New York: Charles Scribner's Sons, 1947), p. 64. Reprinted by permission.

latirostris, a bill which made the penalty for killing one $500. The measure hung fire until the last day of the session. Then one senator got up and declared:

"If there is a beast with any such name as that in the State of Florida it ought to be protected." Everyone agreed with him, and the manatee became a protected animal.

The four goals of labor[12]

. . . *Fortune* staged an informal experiment—and of a type the reader can easily try out on his associates. A cartoon chart of "The Four Goals of Labor" was clipped from a C.I.O. newspaper and photostated. A new legend, however, was attached at the bottom: "From June 3 N.A.M. Newsletter." Twenty C.I.O. members were then shown the ad and asked if they thought it was a fair presentation of labor's goals. Four grudgingly said it was and two couldn't make up their minds. The remaining fourteen damned it as "patronizing," "loaded," "paternalistic," "makes me want to spit." . . .

Prestige foods[13]

"Prestige foods," attractively packaged fruits, fowl, meats, and so forth, have found widespread favor as business gifts. The foods are generally of high quality and even more highly priced. The gift is invariably accompanied by a piece of sales literature. The following were sent with a smoked pheasant and a box of apples, respectively.

SMOKE DREAMS COME TRUE

Rembrandt stewed over his canvas—a regular fuss-budget about deep, rich browns. Stradivari swooned over a violin, working for a tone of pure gold. But they weren't in it with the way *we* toil, turning out our smoked bird masterpieces.

---

[12] From "Is Anybody Listening?" *Fortune,* September 1950, p. 82. Reprinted by permission.

[13] All names have either been disguised or omitted.

Wild life is pampered on our rolling wooded acres. Birds are urged to gorge on the fat of the land. To the plumpest we award the great adventure of the smokehouse and the great wide world, where they make mouths water and gladden hearts.

This succulent creature is ready to eat. It's been slowly smoked over fragrant hickory embers. Lazy little plumes of smoke sealed in the sweet juices, turned the outside crackly brown. We firmly believe you can't get such happy flavor anywhere else.

This bird will keep approximately two or three weeks in the refrigerator. (Hsst! Or a year in a freezer with the wrapper left on. But who's that Spartan?)

Hints for Serving

How to Slice. With any smoked bird it's gourmet-wise (not stingy) to slice it wafer thin. That lets your lucky palate savor every delicious smoky morsel. A good sharp knife will do the trick.

Getting Het up, Whole. If—instead of eating your bird cold, just as it comes—you have a yen to try it hot, here's how. Put it in a roaster with some good strong chicken broth or consomme. Use a moderate oven and baste conscientiously.

Wonderful Canapes. Here's where a smoked bird really preens itself. Try slivers of the tender smoked meat on little squares of fresh buttered toast—goldly brown and fragrant. Top with a dab of horse radish, or better yet, our very own Dippin' Gravy.

Or mince some of the smoked meat and add to softened, well seasoned cream cheese. Spread on crisp crackers.

Or serve thin slices of smoked meat with snowy rings of Bermuda onion on rounds of buttered rye.

Or carry out your own inspirations. This bird can't *help* being delicious!

Fancied Up

Smoked Bird à la King. And we really mean regal. Use your favorite Chicken à la King recipe, substituting whatever smoked bird you're blessed with. Just before serving add a good stiff dose of Sherry or Madeira.

Smoked Bird Rarebit. Nestle slices of smoked bird between pieces of hot buttered toast. Cover with strips of brisk sharp cheese and slide under the broiler till the cheese starts to burble and run. Serve at once.

Smoked Bird and Scrambled Eggs. Mince the meat and add to slightly beaten eggs. Cook in double broiler, stirring thoughtfully.

Smoked Bird Salad. Toss some savory bird shreds in with your favorite mixed salad—crisp greens, dewy tomatoes, shivery cucumbers. Let it glisten with good French dressing and rejoice in a mite of Roquefort.

Glorious Leftovers

Never, *never* throw out that precious carcass till it's worked magic! Would you toss out platinum? Would you discard diamonds?

'Tis wonderful—that carcass—in soup, beautiful soup. And that goes for the glittering white bones of the most greedily denuded. Try simmering that exposed frame in a kettle of Split Pea Soup. Serve in man-size soup plates, spiked with Sherry. O tempora! O mores! And the same for Black Bean or Lentil.

Greetings From
Sparkling Brook[14]
California

Dear Epicure:—

These "Golden Globe" Apples were sent to you at the request of the person whose name appears on the address label.

They are grown solely by me, in a little hidden valley in the Sierra Nevada Mountains of California. Your donor is able to send them to you through having acquired a Preferred Share in the fruits of my orchard.

When I first found this valley, over twenty years ago, it was an abandoned homestead—so forlorn that folks poked fun at me, and said: "What are you going to raise, Joe—sagebrush or rabbit weed?"

But here I had found one old apple tree, with a heavy crop on it. And a native of these parts told me that every fall, for twenty-five years, he had helped himself to apples from it. "Hmm," I thought, "a natural apple spot if there ever was one."

So here I planted a dozen different kinds of apples—including a new one, recently discovered growing wild on a mountain side. And this new one turned out to be just the apple this little valley was waiting for.

Here our golden California sun gives its flesh and skin a golden tinge. Here our cold mountain nights develop its fruit sugars, and make it so crisp that every bite crackles. Here the volcanic ash in the soil gives it a tang no other apple has. And here the pure mountain

---

[14] All names have been disguised.

springs from which its growth is watered fill it with a cider-like juice which is nature's true champagne.

Because this "Golden Globe" Apple is a luxury fruit which can be gotten nowhere else, apple lovers all over America now send to me for it. If, after eating these, you would like information on my various packs, and Preferred Rights to them, I will be glad to send it.

Sincerely yours,
Joe Wilson

Flight from scorn[15]

—A TALE OF 2 BOYS

Oklahoma City— (AP) —A 13-year-old Enid (Okla.) boy didn't like being called "fatty" by his schoolmates.

Five months ago, Dean Roberts weighed 105 pounds—not too hefty for his 5-foot-5 frame, but in his own mind, just a bit too chunky. He decided to reduce and practically stopped eating.

At first, his parents thought nothing of it. But when his weight dropped to 62 pounds, they took him to a hospital.

Finding no glandular trouble, doctors ordered him fed through tubes. He gained 10 pounds in five days.

Then the story came out. He had been worried about being teased.

Now he's up to 74 pounds and doctors have let him go back home for another crack at Mom's good home cooking.

———

Schoolmates at Maryville Academy, Des Plaines, teased Orville Culp about his eyes.

Orville, 11, has one brown eye and one blue eye.

The boys at Maryville got to calling him "old brown and blue eyes," Orville told police.

On Monday, Orville couldn't take it any longer. He ran away.

But two nights of sleeping under porches on the Near West Side were even worse than the teasing.

So Orville gave himself up Wednesday night to Warren Ave. police. He was turned over to juvenile authorities pending his return to Maryville, a home and school for dependent children.

———

15 *Chicago Daily News,* August 8, 1954, p. 10. Courtesy of Associated Press.

McCall College[16]

McCall College is a small eastern liberal arts college. For many years its theatre department had enjoyed an excellent and well-deserved reputation among the student body and faculty and among the community in which the college was located. The theatre department presented eight or nine plays yearly, the season beginning in October and ending in May. Each play was presented for six performances— one each night from Wednesday through Sunday and a matinee on Saturday. The average attendance over the years had been gratifyingly high, 85 percent of capacity, ranging from 60 to 65 percent to frequent standing-room-only audiences.

Last year the Theatre's director, Doug Lawson, decided that for one of the midseason productions he would present a collection of excerpts from several plays rather than one single play. The theme was to portray the changes in theatrical production from classic Greece up to the 20th century. He titled the production, accurately enough, *Theatre Styles Review*, and chose excerpts from Euripides' *Hippolytus*, representing the classic Greek theatre; *Everyman* (medieval morality play) ; Shakespeare's *Midsummer Night's Dream* (16th century) ; Molière's *The Would-Be Gentleman* (17th century) ; Sheridan's *School for Scandal* (18th century) ; Stowe's *Uncle Tom's Cabin* (19th-century melodrama) ; Ibsen's *Ghosts* (19th-century realism) ; and Wilde's *The Importance of Being Earnest* (19th-century comedy of manners) .

Lawson designed the sets and carefully rehearsed the cast. After several weeks of hard work everyone from Lawson to the student curtain-puller eagerly anticipated the audience reaction.

Finally, on opening night Lawson peeked through the act curtain to "count the house." The auditorium was virtually empty! It seemed incredible. The weather was typically unpleasant for February, but audiences had turned out on much more inclement nights. No one could think of a competing attraction in town that night and yet there they were— (or weren't!) —an audience of only 20 percent capacity!

But the show must go on—and so it did, admirably. The sparse audience thoroughly enjoyed the presentation, and Lawson, despite his disappointment with the size of the audience, was justifiably

---

16 All names have been disguised.

proud of his company. He had rarely seen an opening night at McCall so brilliantly and flawlessly executed.

After the performance the director, cast, and crew sat down together to ponder. The only possible answer, everyone agreed, must lie in freakish chance. It just happened, someone offered, that everyone decided, for one reason or another, that he would attend on some night other than the first. But just wait, some promised bravely, we'll have overflow crowds the rest of the week!

But there were no overflow crowds. To be specific, the audiences ranged between 20 and 35 percent of capacity. Lawson was stunned. Didn't people like the excerpt format? He had had good audience reactions to it on several previous occasions. Were the performances poor? Certainly his own judgment and the demonstrably appreciative audiences precluded this as a reason. What then? Lawson called his company together and began:

As you all know we have just had the greatest attendance flop in the 15 years I have been here. Now why? Don't tell me the audiences, what there were of them, didn't love it. And you people did marvelously. Now the purpose of this meeting is to decide what went wrong, correct it, and run the show again in May. I gambled with it once and lost but I'm just stubborn enough, and confident enough of my product, to gamble again. Now, what went wrong?

Several suggestions for minor changes in dialogue, business, and sets were made. Someone suggested that the title might be changed. Lawson invited the group to think of a better name. Some suggestions: *Lagniappe, Grease Paint Review, Sex through the Ages, Euripides Goes Wilde, 2600 Years of Grease Paint.* Finally, *Athens to Broadway* was selected, and the production was repeated during a week in May.

The attendance soared to the old standard. The audiences ranged from 70 to 85 percent of capacity during the six performances.

The bright young man

Bob Elgin, a district manager, had long considered the company's management training program inadequate and felt he had a responsibility to supplement company sponsored trainees with the development of management potential people from the "ranks." Such was the case when he hired Bruce Gorman, recently discharged from the Army, for an office position in one of his plants.

Bruce immediately asserted himself and was not hesitant about offering suggestions for improvement and criticism for areas he felt were not up to par. Bob took an immediate liking to Bruce and proposed him for acceptance into the company sponsored management training program. Bob's request was denied, primarily because Bruce lacked a college education and because of the personnel interviewer's evaluation of Bruce as having a "cocksure" attitude.

Exercising his prerogative Bob decided to put Bruce through the training program at the district's own expense.

Bob and Bruce developed considerable rapport and, with the management trainer's guidance, Bruce progressed rapidly. When the opening arose Bob was able to "sell" Bruce to higher management as a plant manager.

Bruce was so elated that he told Bob that in his new assignment he would break all existing records—and proceeded to do so. One of the boasts Bruce made to Bob was that he would reach a credit currency of 70 percent his first month. The plant under the previous manager had never exceeded 55 percent currency. Bruce's first month's credit currency was 68.9 percent.

Bob was delighted. He immediately dispatched a congratulatory memo to Bruce, inserting a good-natured "needle" about his missing his prediction by a hair:

To: B. N. Gorman
From: R. L. Elgin
Subject: Credit Currency Report

> 68.9 percent is not 70 percent but what else can I expect from a "green" manager. Here's hoping you do better this month.

A week later Bob visited Bruce's plant for the first time since the credit currency report. He entered Bruce's office to find him hard at work at papers strewn about his desk.

Bob said jocularly: "That's mighty fine impersonation of a hard worker!"

Startled, Bruce looked up and retorted sharply: "I thought I'd have more than one month to prove my worth!"

14

Intensional orientation III (blindering)

A GOOD WAY to get the essence of this chapter under your skin is to make an earnest effort to solve this problem:

FIGURE 14-1

Objective: To draw through all nine of the dots.
Restrictions:

1. Start with your pencil on any one of the dots.
2. Draw four straight lines without removing your pencil from the page.
3. You may cross over lines but you may not repeat them, i.e., trace back on them.

Most people have difficulty with the problem because they unconsciously add a fourth restriction—one which renders the problem insoluble.

Did you perceive the nine dots as a *square?* (Figure 14–4, left)

Most people in our culture would see it as such.[1] But did you then proceed to restrict your drawings of lines to the boundaries of *your* square? Did you assume that you could not draw *beyond?*

If you did (and most of us would), you were, of course, severely hampering your progress toward a solution. Once you remove the *self-imposed restriction,* the solution comes easily (Figure 14–4, right).

The nine-dot puzzle illustrates one of the key difficulties in problem solving—one's tendency to restrict his view of the problem. Clearly, one of the most important reasons why the problem solver restricts his perception of a problem grows out of his *definition* of the problem. (Most people define or think of the problem above as the "nine-dot *square.*") David A. Levine, while a mathematician for the National Advisory Committee for Aeronautics at Langley Memorial Laboratories, Virginia, found that an inaccurate term for a phenomenon apparently misguided even a scientist who was studying it:

I began to notice semantic flaws in certain theory. The one particular problem I was interested in at the time dealt with what is called "boundary layer theory." According to the vernacular of the science when an airfoil, like the wing of an airplane passes through the air, the air does not slip over the surface of the wing. The air right next to the wing surface sticks to the surface thus forming a layer or blanket of sluggish, slow-moving air as opposed to the swiftly flowing stream farther out from the wing. The picture this brings to mind is something like this:

FIGURE 14–2

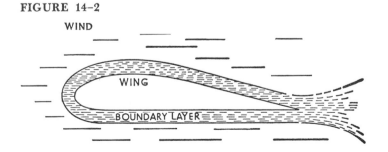

WIND

WING

BOUNDARY LAYER

---

[1] Evidently people in some cultures fail to perceive such connecting lines and would see, in this case, simply an aggregate of isolated dots. See Dorothy Lee's discussion of the Trobriand Islanders' nonlineal apprehension of reality, "Lineal and Nonlineal Codifications of Reality," *ETC.: A Review of General Semantics,* Vol. 8, No. 1 (Autumn 1950), (published December 1950).

The boundary layer apparently forms a *discrete* blanket or layer over the wing surface according to this picture.

Upon examining the *mathematics* of the boundary layer I got a similar but vitally different picture. According to the mathematics the air stuck to the wing surface, but did not form a sluggish *layer,* but a sluggish *region.* This mathematical picture looks something like this:

FIGURE 14–3

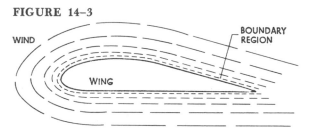

There is a vital difference in the two pictures. A boundary *layer* implies a *discrete blanket* with a definite defining thickness. A boundary *region* implies a *continuous,* nondiscrete sluggish *region* which has no definite thickness.

Of course this is well-known, old-hat stuff to aeronautics men, but the point is I found one scientist had *unconsciously assumed* a discrete layer because of the incorrect symbolism, boundary *"layer."*[2]

In short, the *words* we use to define a problem or situation may act as *blinders* (not unlike a horse's blinders or blinkers which prevent distractions from the side) and thus restrict us in our approach to the problem or situation.

FIGURE 14–4

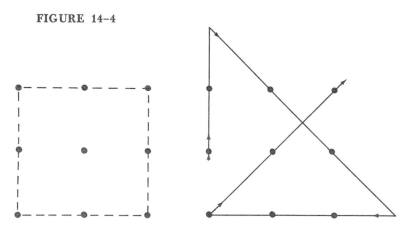

---

[2] David A. Levine, "A Student's Progress Report on Some Applications of Korzybskian Methodolgy," *General Semantics Bulletin,* Nos. 10 and 11 (Autumn-Winter 1952–53), p. 65. Reprinted by permission of the Institute of General Semantics.

SOME CONSEQUENCES

Roughly speaking, *blinders* may lead to two broad kinds of consequences. *Blindering* may (1) delay or impede solutions and (2) lead to solutions which are undesirable.

Delayed solutions

If you are still in the mood for puzzles, try this one.[3] Two cyclists are separated by 30 miles of straight, flat road. They begin pedaling toward each other simultaneously. At the same time, a fly takes off from the handlebars of one of the cyclists, flies to the second, turns instantaneously, flies back to the first, and so on. The fly continues to make these alternating flights as the cyclists continuously decrease the distance between themselves. Finally, the fly is smashed between the cyclists as they collide. Both cyclists were traveling at 15 miles per hour and the fly at 40—all at constant rates of speed. The problem: what is the total distance of the fly's flight, i.e., how far did the fly fly? (Don't read farther until you have tried to work out the problem for yourself.)

If you arrived at an incorrect answer or at no answer at all, or at the correct answer in more than 15 seconds, something must have impeded your progress. Examine the assumptions you made about the problem. Did your reactions fall into one or more of the categories below?

1. "The problem is difficult. It requires computation—paper and pencil work."
2. "The problem is incomplete. I don't have all of the necessary data."
3. "The problem is silly. I won't waste my time and energy."
4. The technicality finder: "A fly couldn't fly that fast." "How could the fly turn instantaneously—he would lose some speed."

Probably underlying each of these expressions (although only the first admits it) is the assumption that the problem is *complex.* Once one *defines* a problem as complex, he is more likely to search (if he

---

[3] From Stuart Chase, *Guides to Straight Thinking* (New York: Harper & Bros., 1956).

searches at all) for an answer by using complex techniques, for example, by computing the sum of the decreasing distances of the fly's individual flights.

The problem, however, is quite simple—*if one defines it as such.*
The cyclists are 30 miles apart and pedaling at 15 miles per hour.
They will thus collide in one hour. The fly which travels at 40 miles
per hour will thus have flown 40 miles.

I admit that I *helped* you to blinder yourself by asking "How *far*
did the fly fly?" thus focusing attention on distance and away from
time. Had the question been "How long did the fly fly and, therefore,
how far?" the correct answer would probably have come much more
rapidly and easily.

The phenomenon of *blindering* as a factor in impeding progress is
suggested by M. W. Ball:

> Oil men, through some queer quirk of herd psychology, have been
> great respecters of political boundaries. When oil is found in a state they
> are likely to search that state with enthusiasm and thoroughness, ignor-
> ing areas of equal promise just over the state line. Perhaps this explains
> why no oil was produced in New York until five years after its discovery
> in Northern Pennsylvania. . . .[4]
>
> Down in Texas, close to the southeast corner of New Mexico, the year
> that saw Maljamar discovered saw the discovery of the Hendricks field,
> one of the great fields of the West Texas Permian basin. The field was
> scarcely more than a stone's throw south of the New Mexico border, on
> a structural feature that obviously extended into New Mexico, yet for
> nearly three years the state line stopped the oil men cold.[5]

The Electra story.   It would be difficult to find a more poignant
example of blindering contributing to a tragic delay in problem solving than that of the ill-fated Electra.

On September 29, 1959, a Lockheed Electra flying over Buffalo,
Texas, crashed, killing all 34 aboard. Why had it crashed was a mystery. The weather had been clear and calm. No planes or rockets were
reported in the region. The pilot had reported no difficulties a few
minutes previous.

The tragedy touched off one of the most extensive aviation acci-

---

[4] From *This Fascinating Oil Business,* by Max W. Ball, copyright, 1940, used by
special permission of the publishers, The Bobbs-Merrill Co., Inc., p. 342.

[5] Ibid., pp. 358–59.

dent investigations in history. Before it was over it had involved hundreds of engineers, pilots, and government investigators.

The investigation was intensive, extensive, expensive—and for six months almost completely futile. The Lockheed and Civil Aeronautics Board investigators had made the blindering assumption "that the Electra was a sound mechanism and had presumed that the Buffalo crash was caused by some inexplicable distortion of a basically solid plane."[6]

The engineers who designed the Electra's advanced, low-drag, high-speed wing had every reason to congratulate themselves at the time the plane was certificated on August 22, 1958. Their thin, stubby airfoil was not only enormously efficient but enormously strong. It satisfied every standard laid down by the government during a severe test program.[7]

A terrible price had to be paid for this blindering—for this delay in solving the problem. On March 17, 1960, another Electra with 63 aboard plummeted into soft earth near Tell City, Indiana.

The CAB investigating team excavated 10 feet of dirt before they discovered what had happened to the plane: the 104-foot fuselage and all its contents—including 10,000 pounds of human flesh—had compressed into a cylinder of broken metal only 35 feet high as it came to rest underground. The masked investigators in glistening plastic gloves and aprons who removed this awful debris from the hole were seized with an overwhelming sense of horror, pity and physical revulsion as they worked. Those who had been concerned with the earlier Electra crash found themselves saying, "Maybe if I had been a little smarter. . . ."[8]

The circumstances of the crash suddenly made it impossible to continue to assume that the Electra was a basically sound plane.

Now, the investigators concentrated on the design of the plane itself. And finally an answer came.

As long as the Electra's outboard nacelles retained the stiffness for which they had been designed, the plane was safe and sound. But *if* the struts and braces inside the nacelle structure cracked or otherwise loosened, and *if* the wing was jolted hard by air turbulence or by a sudden pull-up, and *if* the plane was moving at high speed at the time, a curious chain reaction effect could be induced. Both the Electra's big, square-

---

[6] "Brilliant Detection in Jet-Age Mystery," *Life*, Vol. 49, no. 4, July 25, 1960, p. 81.
[7] Ibid., p. 78.
[8] Ibid., p. 82.

bladed propeller and its turbine engine turn at high speeds—the prop makes 1280 revolutions and the turbine 13,820 revolutions a minute. Thus, when running, they comprise a huge gyroscope with all the same odd reactions to disturbance that children discover in toy gyroscopes at Christmas. When the sudden jolt caused the wing to flex and agitated a nacelle, this whole package of spinning metal, which projects far out in front of the leading edge of the wing, would begin wobbling in its mount, like a pointed forefinger with its tip describing a small circle.

The odds against this motion doing anything more than dampening or soothing the initial movement of the wing itself were enormous. But in the Electra the oscillating wing and the swirling power plant suddenly began "exchanging energy." Each deformation of the flexing wing forced the turbine to wobble more wildly. Every increase in the engine's wobble, in turn, fed new violence back into the fluctuation of the wing. As the wing's leading edge was twisted alternately upward and downward by this process, airflow added still more impetus to its movement. In a very few seconds with all these tremendous forces working on it in lethal rhythm like a fat man jumping harder and harder on a springboard, the wing would snap off as though it were made of glass. The mystery—in the opinion of Lockheed, of the FAA, and of the airlines involved—was finally solved.[9]

Yes, finally solved (we hope) but at what a price for a blindered delay.

Blinder names.   One cannot help wondering how long progress has been retarded by the assignation of inappropriate names. How much time was lost and how many lives were squandered by the term *malaria?* Contracted from the Italian words *mala aria* ("bad air"), it perpetuated the erroneous notion that the disease was caused by the bad air of the swamps. And how long were the properties of *oxygen* concealed because of its misleading name? Oxygen stems from the Greek terms for acid-producer—but, unfortunately, oxygen does not produce acid! And how many bright and willing scientists were inhibited from even dreaming of the possibility that the *atom* (from the Greek for *indivisible) could* be split largely because its *name* said it could *not* be divided?

Undesirable solutions

Blindering may not only retard or prevent the finding of appropriate, constructive solutions, but it may steer us toward improper, un-

---

[9] Ibid., p. 88.

intelligent, even dangerous, solutions. As an analyst for an insurance company, Benjamin Lee Whorf was solely concerned at first with the physical factors in fires and explosions, e.g., defective wiring, presence or lack of air spaces between metal flues and woodwork, and so forth. But he soon began to notice certain *human* factors as well. He found that the way people defined or labeled a situation greatly influenced their behavior toward it. For example, he found that people tended to be extremely cautious around what they called "gasoline drums." Great care was taken to prevent smoking or striking matches in their vicinity. But when the drums were emptied and were thus now labeled *"empty* gasoline drums," caution was thrown to the winds. Cigarettes were smoked with abandon because the situation was now *defined* as safe. Ironically, the "empty" drums were *full* of gasoline vapors, and one spark could be sufficient to explode them—an enormously more dangerous circumstance than when they contained the liquid gasoline.[10]

Among other similar incidents, Whorf cited the case of the tannery drying room:

A drying room for hides was arranged with a blower at one end to make a current of air along the room and thence outdoors through a vent at the other end. Fire started at a hot bearing on the blower, which blew the flames directly into the hides and fanned them along the room, destroying the entire stock. This hazardous setup followed naturally from the term "blower" with its linguistic equivalence to "that which blows," implying that its function necessarily is to "blow." Also its function is verbalized as "blowing air for drying," overlooking that it can blow other things, e.g., flames and sparks. In reality a blower simply makes a current of air and can exhaust as well as blow. It should have been installed at the vent end to draw the air over the hides, then through the hazard (its own casing and bearings) and thence outdoors.[11]

CORRECTIVES

It is obvious that blindering may be a serious hindrance in business, education, government, science, even in our personal lives. How,

---

[10] From "The Name of the Situation as Affecting Behavior," by B. L. Whorf. Published in "The Relation of Habitual Thought and Behavior to Language," in *Language, Culture, and Personality: Essays in Memory of Edward Sapier,* ed. Leslie Spier *et al.* (Menasha, Wis.: Sapir Memorial Fund, 1941). This article, with the exception of the following incident involving the "blower," is reproduced in the "Cases" section following this chapter.

[11] Ibid.

then, can we cope with it? How can we eliminate it or at least minimize its destructive influence? The following suggestions are offered:

Remember, defining = neglecting

Blindering may be described as the process of narrowing one's perception, of channeling one's vision of a situation, problem, phenomenon. These restrictions are frequently introduced by the verbal (and
nonverbal) *definitions* that he assigns to the situation, and so on. *To
define* is "to mark the limits of boundaries of." Thus, when I define
the chair I am sitting on as a "piece of office furniture," I am setting
up certain restrictions. I am calling attention to those attributes my
chair has in common with other "office furniture," such as that it is
usually found indoors, in offices (rather than in homes or on lawns),
that it is largely utilitarian (as opposed to decorative), and so forth.
At the same time, however, my definition is neglecting a host of other
aspects which my chair does *not* share with "office furniture" in general. My definition *distracts* attention from a myriad of details unique
to my chair—among them, its specific colors, weight, textures of the
plastic and steel surfaces, tensile strengths of the various materials,
style, molecular structure, cost, resale value, and origins of materials.
In short, the process of defining inevitably involves the excluding of
some (actually, most) details.

The crux is that, while it is unavoidable that definitions neglect
aspects, it is nevertheless essential that we *do* define, delimit, categorize, classify, organize our data and experience. The practical implication, therefore, is that it is dangerous to *forget* that defining by
its function is a process of restricting and neglecting. Remember in
other words, that you are abstracting.

Does my definition blinder me?

Hunt[12] reports an interesting experiment conducted with college
students. One group was confronted with the problem of removing a
ping-pong ball from the bottom of an upright rusty pipe. They were
not to change the position of the pipe in any way. In the room were a
hammer, pliers, rulers, soda straws, pins, and a bucket of dirty water.

---

[12] Morton M. Hunt, "How to Overcome Mental Blocks," *Mayfair,* December 1956.

After several futile attempts with the various "tools" to fish the ball out, they struck upon the idea of pouring the dirty water into the pipe and floating the ball up.

A second group of students was given the same problem, but with one change. Instead of the bucket of dirty water, a large pitcher of clear ice water, surrounded by crystal goblets, and set on a clean table cloth, was placed in the room. They never solved the problem. In this case they defined the water as *drinking water*—and their definition blindered them from other possible uses.

The same phenomenon is illustrated by the popular scissors and strings experiment. The experimenter hangs two strings from the ceiling as in Figure 14–5. The objective is to tie the two ends together as in Figure 14–6. The strings are far enough apart, however, that the performer cannot quite reach string *B* while holding *A,* or reach *A* while holding *B* (Figure 14–7) . He is now given one instru-

FIGURE 14–5   **FIGURE 14–6**   **FIGURE 14–7**

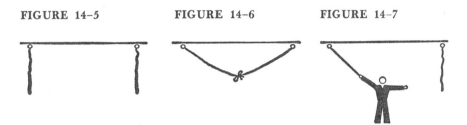

ment with which to solve the problem—a pair of scissors. Some individuals promptly snip off a length from one string and tie it to the other. The addition permits them to move closer to where the end *was,* but, alas! they find that the shorter string is now too high for them (Figure 14–8) .

Their definition of scissors as a "cutter" inhibits their thinking of it as anything else. A pair of scissors, after all, is also a *length,* and ty-

FIGURE 14–8

ing it to the end of one of the strings might have given the additional length necessary to reach the second string. It is also a *weight,* and tying it to a string which could then be set in motion as a pendulum would be an effective solution for the problem (Figure 14–9).

FIGURE 14–9

It may be exceedingly helpful on occasion to ask one's self: "Am I blindering myself, restricting my approach to the problem by my definition, my 'sizing-up' of the problem?"

How to recognize our blinders

This is the crux, of course. How can one cope with his blinders if he does not recognize that he is being blindered? We laugh at the old wives' tales of yesteryear, but is it not possible that unwittingly we still accept a good many chimeras as valid? Consider the alumnus who returned to visit his old physics professor. After looking over some of the examination papers the old gentleman was grading, he was prompted to remark: "Why, professor, these are the same questions I had when I was a student 20 years ago!" Whereupon the old man smiled indulgently and said: "Yes, the *questions* are the same, but the *answers* are different now!"

Is it not true that the answers of today often become the problems of tomorrow? Reflect on the tremendous resistance against William Harvey's discovery of the circulation of blood. His findings contradicted "the prevailing beliefs that the blood ebbed and flowed in the vessels, that there were two sorts of blood and that the blood was able to pass from one side of the heart to the other."[13]

Harvey was fearful that the news of his discovery would not find receptive ears, and his fears were well founded. He suffered ridicule

---

[13] W. I. B. Beveridge, *The Art of Scientific Investigation* (New York: W. W. Norton & Co., Inc., 1950), p. 103.

and abuse, and his practice suffered considerably. It required 20 years of ceaseless struggle before his discovery became accepted.

Are there any practical, day-to-day techniques which will help us to uncover and eliminate our blinders? Here are a few that are often useful:[14]

1. ***Talk with an outsider.***   There are times when all of us have difficulty "seeing the forest for the trees." We become so immersed with a problem that we become quite unable to see it from other vantage points. One of the chief values of an outside consultant to a business institution is the freshness of outlook he brings with him. As a dispassionate observer, unencumbered with the minutiae of problems, he is often able to suggest views and insights that have eluded men closer to the situation. The Bell System Laboratories deliberately assign a new man to a research team from time to time in order to get the benefit of his naïveté, his ignorance, if you will. He is often able to stir up the thinking of the scientists who have been at the problems longer and thus prompt them to arrive at new and better approaches.

But the outsider need not always be a professional or even well versed with a particular problem area. Often a wife, a friend, a parent, even a child, can help one see a problem in a new light. And not infrequently, as in nondirective counseling, the very process of explaining the problem to another, of making the effort to get someone else to see his problem, helps one to break through his self-created encasements.

2. ***Kill "killer phrases."***   This apt coinage is by Charles H. Clark of Autonetics, Inc., who has compiled a list of phrases which squelch a new idea before it has a chance to be examined. "Let's be practical," "We've never done anything like that," and "The customers won't stand for it" are examples. Granted, some suggestions prove to be worthless or worse. But some, ridiculous or impractical at first hearing, may have a gold nugget in them—something which, if combined with other ideas, might prove exceedingly useful. The point is that the killer phrase will decapitate the infant idea before anyone has had the opportunity to dig for its gold, to give it a fair appraisal.

3. ***Brainstorm with a group.***   Brainstorming, an idea-generating technique which swept the nation a few years ago, acquiring many

---

[14] Suggested by Morton M. Hunt, "How to Overcome . . . ," *Mayfair.*

advocates and not a few antagonists, has definite blinder-finding potential. The rules of the game are quite simple. A group of people meet to make suggestions relevant to a given problem area. The goal is quantity—not quality—the more ideas, the better. No one evaluates or censures their worth. Only afterward are the ideas sifted through for possible pearls. The key antiblindering feature of brainstorming is the interpersonal excitement and stimulation generated among the group. Mr. A may say something that sets off Miss B and Mr. C, who in turn mention something that triggers ideas from D, E, and F, and so on. The upshot is that ideas may appear that might never have occurred to the same people working as solitary thinkers.

However, brainstorming is not without its own blindering dangers. Without skilled leadership, the flow of ideas may get started down one relatively narrow channel—one idea merely pressing another deeper into this specialized rut. Good leadership can guide the ideas through a more comprehensive and useful area.

4. Start anywhere—but start.   How many times have you tackled a creative project and had difficulty in beginning? Perhaps it was a term paper, an essay, or a report, and the main heading or the lead sentence simply did not come, regardless of your efforts to grind it out. I have wasted hours, I am embarrassed to say, because I could not begin a chapter or an article or even a paragraph in a way that satisfied me. I have discovered at this late date what others have known for years—that it is rarely *necessary* to begin at the *beginning*. The important thing is to start—start anywhere, middle, end, but *start*. Often when I start *where I can make a start,* I come back to the beginning, and the chapter title or the lead line, or whatever it was that had me blocked, falls into place.

5. Break the tension cycle.   Sometimes you find yourself working on a problem, making reasonable headway, when suddenly there's a brick wall. You are blocked, stymied. Most people back off a few feet and run headlong at the wall to butt it down. It doesn't give, so they try it again—and again—and again. Ironically, the more frustrated one becomes in attacking problems, the tenser he becomes. The more tense, the more fixated, the less insight—the less likelihood of noticing that there may be other ways of dealing with a brick wall, perhaps of going over, under, or around it. And thus the tension cycle, one of the most effective deterrents to problem solving to which man is subject, takes over.

There are several ways to break the tension cycle—leaving the area of frustration, learning to relax physically the individual members of the body, participating in an unrelated activity, and so on. The last is my favorite. If I find myself stymied in my work and beginning to grow tense, I shift to another area of the same work. If this is not effective, I pull out of my desk a list of previously planned short-term and reasonably agreeable tasks. Then I spend 20 minutes taking a book to the library—or out of the library, or answering a letter, or reorganizing my bookshelves, or just taking a walk around the block. When I return to my original work, I am invariably more relaxed, and quite often I can now see a solution to the problem that I had not noticed before. Regardless of what you call it—intuition, subconscious, what-have-you—there *does* appear to be something working inside of us even if we are not fully aware of it, and often it works more efficiently when we are not consciously holding the reins.

Deadlines

One of the greatest sources of personal tension in our modern world is the well-known deadline. But the relationship between deadline tension and blindering is not always clear. How is it that some people seem to work well under "deadline pressure" while others go to pieces? Part of the confusion may lie in the ambiguity of "deadline." There are at least three types of deadlines.

1. *Those that are externally imposed and unavoidable.* Some people, such as newsmen, work with these deadlines hanging over them constantly. Evidently they accommodate themselves to the pressure of time and work with great efficiency and surprising ease. For most of us, however, unavoidable deadlines are rare occurrences. Most of our deadlines are of the latter two kinds.

2. *Those that are self-imposed.* Among individuals who tend toward perfectionism there is the inclination to set up arbitrary deadlines for themselves. Before long, the deadlines seem to become quite demanding, and the tension cycle is likely to set in. Self-imposed deadlines may be helpful stimulators and guides, so long as we recognize them as such; but if we let them take on the guise of externally imposed unavoidable deadlines, we are inviting tension and blindering.

3. *Those that are created through procrastination.* There must be students who do not procrastinate, but they seem to have successfully avoided my classes. These deadlines actually exist, of course, but

better planning could have made them less formidable. But advice of this sort is usually futile, for procrastinators usually rationalize that they work better under pressure anyway—and perhaps they do. Like the newsmen, they have had a great deal of experience under these conditions!

Perhaps the best overall antidote for blindering is expressed by the motto of the Air University, "Proficimus more irrenti," usually translated as "Progress unhindered by tradition." Major General M. K. Deichelmann phrased it more pragmatically as "Stay loose, boy— stay loose."

DISCUSSION QUESTIONS

1. Precisely what is *blindering?* How does it occur? Why? What are its potential dangers? What measures help to prevent or correct it?
2. How many *blinder* names or phrases (see p. 467) can you think of?
3. The tension cycle was described as a cyclical process of frustration leading to direct attack on the blockage which in turn increases frustration which in turn leads to more fixated attacks, and so on. How can one know when he is withdrawing gracefully or giving up too easily?
4. Does "blindering" seem to be related to other concepts in the book?
5. Report upon an incident, perhaps involving yourself, in which *blindering* occurred. *How* and *why* did it occur? What could have prevented it or ameliorated its consequences? What measures could prevent its recurrence?

CASES

The Rawley Company[15]

The Rawley Company, manufacturers of custom-made metal forming machinery, had been in business for over half a century. It was
located in a large midwest city and employed approximately 100 persons. Executives of Rawley had become aware that their company
sales had fallen considerably short of its production capacity. Stimulated by the company's president, James Howe, a dynamic man with
an inquiring mind, the firm decided to approach the problem
through the cooperative efforts of a group of persons to be known as
the Sales Council.

The Sales Council was to be composed of representatives of various
departments of the firm, some of which were not conventionally concerned with sales. The representatives and their departments included:

James Howe, *president* (designer, engineer, sales)
Donald Brewster, *vice president* (assistant general manager, manager
  of sales)
Raymond Prescott, *treasurer*
Clifford Carlin, *assistant vice president* (production manager)
Ralph Goodwin, *assistant vice president* (warehouse manager)
Arthur Howard, *assistant sales manager*
Chester Green, *eastern sales*
Fred Lemec, *charge of machinery orders*
Russell Thurston, *engineer and salesman*

The Sales Council was to operate on the basic assumption that ultimately every employee was directly or indirectly related to the sale of
the company's products. Consequently, the combined thinking of rep-

---

15 All names have been disguised. Printed by permission of the author, whose name
has been withheld by request.

resentatives of these various sections might produce helpful suggestions for their common objective, increased sales.

In order to expedite the meetings of the Sales Council a professor of interpersonal communication from a local university was called in to act as moderator. It was felt that he should act as disinterested chairman whose primary responsibility was simply to help the members of the group to understand one another as clearly and as accurately as possible. Specifically, he was to repeat and/or paraphrase the statement of each speaker immediately after the speaker had finished making it. This was to give the speaker the feeling that at least one person understood what he had tried to communicate. Furthermore, all other members were to have the opportunity to agree or to disagree with the accuracy of the moderator's restatement of the speaker's statement until, theoretically, everyone was satisfied that he had understood the speaker.

Shortly before the first Sales Council meetings were to be held, some of Rawley's executives and the professor met for an orientation session in a conference room in a nearby restaurant. The meeting was to explain to the professor what the Sales Council was, what its objectives were, and what the professor's role as moderator was to be.

After each executive present had expressed his view of these points the professor, David Wilson, asked to have the floor.

WILSON: Gentlemen, I'd like to try to sum up what I think you have been saying about the Sales Council so that you can tell me if you think I understand you. As I get the picture you are proposing an experiment in group problem solving. Casting this approach in my own frame of reference this is going to be essentially a group—something like the conventional classroom situation—in which the lines of communication are directly between teacher and students and only indirectly from student to student. . . .

HOWE [acting as chairman, breaks in]: I see heads shaking in disagreement, Dave. Ralph?

GOODWIN: Dave, I don't like your analogy. This is not going to be a classroom situation at all. The moderator isn't supposed to act as an autocrat. He's trying to achieve the cooperation and communication of the group at a high level. . . .

WILSON: I think you're right about the analogy being a poor one, but I only used it to describe the direction of the communication lines as I see them in the Sales Council. . . .

CARLIN: No offense meant, Dave, but you can't presume to act the role of a teacher, the subject-matter expert. You don't have the company background for it.

Ten minutes later.

WILSON: Now, getting specifically to the role of the moderator. . . . The way I get it he is to listen to Speaker A, filter through his personality and background what he thinks A has said and express it to the group. . . .

GOODWIN: You don't filter anything. Your job is to repeat what A has said.

CARLIN: Well, he's to *paraphrase* what A has said so that A will know that at least one person has understood him.

WILSON: I get that, but how can I possibly relay a man's statement, other than through the sheer repetition of his exact words, unless I interpret, size up what he has said. In other words isn't it inevitable that I filter what comes to me through my own nervous system, my personality, my background?

GOODWIN: Filtering is changing the substance you are conveying—that isn't your job.

CARLIN: You don't *filter*—you *reflect* what has been said.

WILSON: Perhaps "filter" has been a bad figure of speech but even in reflecting the other fellow's statement, must I not determine his meaning for myself—and how can I size up his meaning unless I relate his words to my own unique frame of experience?

At this point dinner was announced, and the subject was dropped.

The name of the situation as affecting behavior[16]

B. L. WHORF

There will probably be general assent to the proposition that an accepted pattern of using words is often prior to certain lines of thinking and forms of behavior, but he who assents often sees in such a statement nothing more than a platitudinous recognition of the hypnotic power of philosophical and learned terminology on the one hand or of catchwords, slogans, and rallying-cries on the other. To see

---

16 From "The Relation of Habitual Thought and Behavior to Language," in *Language, Culture, and Personality: Essays in Memory of Edward Sapir*, ed. by Leslie Spier, et al. (Menasha, Wis.: Sapir Memorial Fund, 1941) , pp. 75–77. Reprinted by permission.

only thus far is to miss the point of one of the important interconnections which Sapir saw between language, culture, and psychology. . . . It is not so much in these special uses of language as in its constant ways of arranging data and its most ordinary every-day analysis of phenomena that we need to recognize the influence it has on other activities, cultural and personal.

I came in touch with an aspect of this problem before I had studied under Dr. Sapir, and in a field usually considered remote from linguistics. It was in the course of my professional work for a fire insurance company, in which I undertook the task of analyzing many hundreds of reports of circumstances surrounding the start of fires, and in some cases, of explosions. My analysis was directed toward purely physical conditions, such as defective wiring, presence or lack of air spaces between metal flues and woodwork, etc., and the results were presented in these terms. Indeed it was undertaken with no thought that any other significances would or could be revealed. But in due course it became evident that not only a physical situation *qua* physics, but the meaning of that situation to people, was sometimes a factor, through the behavior of the people, in the start of the fire. And this factor of meaning was clearest when it was a *linguistic meaning,* residing in the name or the linguistic description commonly applied to the situation. Thus around a storage of what are called "gasoline drums" behavior will tend to a certain type, that is, great care will be exercised; while around a storage of what are called "empty gasoline drums" it will tend to be different—careless, with little repression of smoking or or tossing cigarette stubs about. Yet the "empty" drums are perhaps the more dangerous, since they contain explosive vapor. Physically the situation is hazardous, but the linguistic analysis according to regular analogy must employ the word "empty," which inevitably suggests lack of hazard. The word "empty" is used in two linguistic patterns: (1) as a virtual synonym for "null and void, negative, inert," (2) applied in analysis of physical situations without regard to, e.g., vapor, liquid vestiges, or stray rubbish, in the container. The situation is named in one pattern (2) and the name is then "acted out" or "lived up to" in another (1) ; this being a general formula for the linguistic conditioning of behavior into hazardous forms.

In a wood distillation plant the metal stills were insulated with a composition prepared from limestone and called at the plant "spun limestone." No attempt was made to protect this covering from excessive heat or the contact of flame. After a period of use the fire below one of the stills spread to the "limestone," which to everyone's great surprise burned vigorously. Exposure to acetic acid fumes from the stills had converted part of the limestone (calcium carbonate) to calcium acetate. This, when heated in a fire decomposes, forming inflammable acetone. Behavior that tolerated fire close to the covering was induced by use of the name "limestone," which because it ends in "stone" implies noncombustibility.

A huge iron kettle of boiling varnish was observed to be overheated, nearing the temperature at which it would ignite. The operator moved it off the fire and ran it on its wheels to a distance, but did not cover it. In a minute or so the varnish ignited. Here the linguistic influence is more complex; it is due to the metaphorical objectifying (of which more later) of "cause" as contact or the spatial juxtaposition of "things"—to analyzing the situation as "on" versus "off" the fire. In reality the stage when the external fire was the main factor had passed; the overheating was now an internal process of convection in the varnish from the intensely heated kettle, and still continued when "off" the fire.

An electric glow heater on the wall was little used, and for one workman had the meaning of a convenient coat-hanger. At night a watchman entered and snapped a switch, which action he verbalized as "turning on the light." No light appeared, and this result he verbalized as "light is burned out." He could not see the glow of the heater because of the old coat hung on it. Soon the heater ignited the coat, which set fire to the building.

A tannery discharged waste water containing animal matter into an outdoor settling basin partly roofed with wood and partly open. This situation is one that ordinarily would be verbalized as "pool of water." A workman had occasion to light a blow-torch nearby, and threw his match into the water. But the decomposing waste matter was evolving gas under the wood cover, so that the setup was the reverse of "watery." An instant flare of flame, ignited the woodwork, and the fire quickly spread into the adjoining building. . . .

Beside a coal-fired melting pot for lead reclaiming was dumped a pile of "scrap lead"—a misleading verbalization, for it consisted of the lead sheets of old radio condensers, which still had paraffin paper between them. Soon the paraffin blazed up and fired the roof, half of which was burned off.

Such examples, which could be greatly multiplied, will suffice to show how the cue to a certain line of behavior is often given by the analogies of the linguistic formula in which the situation is spoken of, and by which to some degree it is analyzed, classified, and allotted its place in that world which is "to a large extent unconsciously built up on the language habits of the group." And we always assume that the linguistic analysis made by our group reflects reality better than it does.

You get what you want[17]

ROBERT FROMAN

A little more than a year ago the maker of a popular kitchen gadget for mixing waffle batter, milk shakes, and such decided to improve on his product. He put engineers to work designing a new model more powerful than the old and almost completely noiseless. When the redesigning was completed, at a cost of thousands of dollars, he invested more thousands in retooling part of his plant.

Several months later the first of the new models reached the retail stores. And there most of them remained. You, the members of the great buying public, simply weren't interested.

Much disturbed, the manufacturer sent out investigators to learn why. They returned with a flabbergasting answer.

"Darn' thing doesn't seem to have any power," one potential purchaser who had changed his mind summed it up for all. "Doesn't make any noise."

And that was that. The manufacturer had to withdraw the new models and rebuild them so that they made a little more noise. That was the way you wanted them, so that was the way they had to be. Attempting to argue with you in such matters, once you have made up your minds, leads only to bankruptcy court. . . .

There are occasions when you react most unexpectedly, but you still have your way. Early automobile fog lights had amber-colored lenses on them. Some years later the Westinghouse Electric Corporation brought out a more powerful fog light and used a clear lens.

You weren't interested. By then fog lights meant amber lights to

---

[17] From the article of the same name, in *Colliers*, April 17, 1951. Reprinted by permission of the author.

you. Westinghouse tried an advertising campaign, pointing out that its clear lens produced the same road-hugging light pattern as the amber and had other advantages. The campaign failed almost completely. Today, the company sells four fog lamps with amber lenses for every one with a clear lens, though it has to charge more for the amber.

The United States Rubber Company has had a somewhat similar experience with inner tubes. Before World War II the tubes were made of natural rubber and were red in color. During the war natural rubber inner tubes disappeared and were replaced by gray, synthetic butyl tubes. Many of you automatically assumed that the synthetic tubes were inferior and, as soon as natural red rubber became available again after the war, began clamoring for tubes made of it.

Actually, says U.S. Rubber, butyl tubes hold air 10 times longer and are more resistant to tearing than those made of natural rubber. What's more, the red tubes' price is considerably higher, because natural rubber costs more than butyl. . . .

In many similar matters you adamantly resist any change whatsoever. Over the years, for instance, would-be innovators in the manufacture of playing cards have attempted such novelties as replacing the usual effigies of king, queen and jack with photographs of such personalities as Babe Ruth, Lana Turner and Jimmy Durante. Any who went so far as to invest money in such an endeavor probably lost every penny of it. You like the faces of playing cards the way they are, and that's that. . . .

Some problems which result from your demands are quite irrelevant to the basic nature and purpose of the products concerned. When synthetic detergents first went on the market for household use in the thirties, they proved excellent for many washing purposes. Huge advertising and publicity campaigns broadcast this news far and wide. You were sufficiently impressed to give the detergents a trial, but you weren't very enthusiastic.

The puzzled manufacturers turned to the market researchers. You just didn't know, the latter found, whether detergents were as good as they were supposed to be.

Why not? the researchers wanted to know. Didn't they do a good clearning job?

Well, that might be, you temporized. But the stuff didn't make suds. You had got used to the idea that the more suds a soap produced, the better job it did.

So back went the detergents to the laboratories. If you wanted suds, the chemists had to find a way of making detergents produce them. And they finally turned up a sudsing agent which could be blended into the detergents without interfering with their action. It convinced you, and sales soared. . . .

Occasionally, you grow downright capricious in your demands. When the makers of foam rubber first adapted the material for pillows, they made them as soft as possible on the theory that the whole purpose of a pillow is softness. But many of you objected. You like "hard" pillows. So the manufacturers made some firmer, some more yielding.

The result was confusion compounded. When those of you who like your pillows soft found foam-rubber ones which were firm, you took the notion that *all* pillows of this material were too hard for you. You finally drove The Dayton Rubber Company, which makes Kool-foam pillows, to desperate measures. The company has adapted the Goldilocks story and now puts out a Baby Bear pillow labeled very soft, a Mama Bear pillow which is medium soft and a Papa Bear pillow which is quite firm.

At the opposite extreme from items on which you make such outrageous demands are those about which you don't know very clearly what you want. Automobile manufacturers spend millions every year to coax from you a few hints on what you expect of a car. But they have found that you can be oddly equivocal about what you want. When you consider a car in the abstract you say one thing. But when you set out to buy one, you often do the opposite.

One company's questionnaire, for instance, lists 10 general automobile features such as dependability, economy, comfort and appearance, and asks which you consider the most important. You nearly always put dependability or economy near the top of the list and appearance near the bottom. But when you buy a car, say the dealers, appearance almost always seems to be your chief and sometimes your only concern. And you can be contradictory about appearance. When asked about chrome trimming, most of you say the less the better. But when the chrome on a new model is cut down, its sales drop precipitately.

One of the most elaborate systems for trying to sound you out on a new product is the General Electric Company's Consumer Advisory Council. This is composed of 2,000 families scattered all over the country and representing every income group and cities of all sizes. Usually, GE first asks these people what they think of a new idea, then, if they like it, sends them samples to try out.

What makes this arrangement so useful is that odd, unpredictable quirks constantly turn up in your reactions to new products. When GE decided to try a foot pedal for opening the door of its refrigerator, one member of the council had a singular complaint: "I don't like foot pedals," she announced. "My cat thinks he's people. He'll sit on it and open the door to cool off."

So before General Electric put refrigerators so equipped on the market, it designed the pedal to take more pressure than cats or other house pets could apply.

Perhaps the oddest of all your quirks is your occasional insistence on being hoodwinked. Champagne labeling is a case in point. Both United States producers and importers have entered a sort of half-open conspiracy with you not to call things by their right names.

What lies behind this is that most people who drink champagne like it to taste fairly sweet. But there's a general belief that a true champagne connoisseur wants it to taste dry. Naturally, most people who drink it want to think of themselves as connoisseurs. So the champagne men label their product "Brut"—which means absolutely dry—when very little sweetening has been added, "Dry" when it's a bit sweeter and sometimes "Extra Dry" when it's sweetest.

Along the same line is your frequent refusal to believe in a new product until it is dramatized for you. Such dramatizing is one of the chief functions of industrial designers like Raymond Loewy.

Not too long ago a new client turned up at Loewy's office. He was the maker of a device for automatically cooking and vending hot dogs and hamburgers. When a customer inserted a coin, the wrapped sandwich dropped into view, was cooked from the inside out electronically in a little over a minute and was then ready to eat.

The machine worked perfectly, did everything it was supposed to do. But most people flatly refused to believe in it. On being questioned they admitted that the sandwiches were delivered hot and seemed to be cooked. But, said the customers, they couldn't *see* anything happening. So they suspected some trickery. Loewy's solution was simple. He installed orange-red lights which glowed while the sandwich cooked. They had nothing to do with the cooking process, but they convinced you that something was happening.

The Roberts Machine Company[18]

Roberts Machine Company was a medium-size firm which produced various types of shop machines—lathes, punch presses, drill presses, milling machines, and so forth. The sales department held a dinner meeting every other month. After dinner, in a hotel private dining room, Gordon Swift, sales manager, conducted a business meeting. The October meeting was attended by Swift, Al Rockland, assistant sales manager, and 11 salesmen, 6 of whom had more than 15 years of service with Roberts. Also present was James Jacobs, sales manager of Electro-Products, Inc., manufacturers of electrical components for home appliances. Jacobs was a personal friend of Swift and known to most of the men. He had been invited to observe the meeting. Swift had previously sat in on one of Jacobs' sales conferences.

The purpose of the meeting was to review a proposed new method for communicating product information to Roberts' dealers, using a phonograph record to accompany the firm's catalog. The dealer, in his own shop or home, could play the record as he leafed through the Roberts catalog. Swift felt the pictures and copy of the catalog alone did not communicate adequately the sales appeal of their product line. The record, in his words, "added another dimension to product communication."

Swift opened the meeting by explaining the purpose of the catalog-record technique and asked each salesman to play the role of a dealer as he listened to the record. The salesmen leafed through the catalog as the record called attention to certain advantages of each item.

When the record ended, Swift asked for comments. Most of the men contributed to the informal discussion which followed. Mr. Jacobs did not participate.

Pros and cons of the technique were discussed; most of the men seemed to agree that the catalog-record idea was basically sound—a way of communicating to the dealer in two media, visually and aurally. A few wondered if it might be too difficult for a man to listen, look at pictures, and read text at the same time.

---

[18] All names and organizational designations have been disguised. Northwestern University cases are reports of concrete events and behavior, prepared for class discussion. They are not intended as examples of "good" or "bad" administrative or technical practices. Copyright, 1958, by Northwestern University. Reprinted by permission.

There was some disagreement about whose voice should be used on the record. Several felt a professional announcer should do the job; the majority preferred Mr. Swift as narrator. One of the salesmen suggested that the sales manager's voice would add a note of warmth and make the process seem more personal than the colder media of catalogs, pamphlets, and newsletters.

Some thought the record increased the accuracy of the communication—the emphasis and inflection of the narrator's voice would help convey information more precisely than the written word alone. One man wondered if the average dealer would have facilities for playing the record. Others felt almost every home had a 33⅓-rpm record player these days.

After discussion had continued for some 30 minutes, one of the younger salesmen, Ed Knoll, commented: "As long as we're talking about dealer communication, I think we could capitalize on the visual angle, too. I wonder if we couldn't take some film clips of several of our machines in action."

There was an audible groan from several other salesmen—one brought up another topic, and the subject of film clips was not resumed. Jacobs was puzzled about the apparent indifference and negative reactions to the film clip idea.

While not strictly relevant to the catalog-record proposal, Jacobs thought the idea might have potential value for Roberts' overall sales program. The Roberts machines were intricate. Motion shots of machines in action could show what words and still pictures could not possibly convey. Moreover, Jacobs had always considered Knoll a bright, hardworking young man, who had shown drive and imagination during his three years with the firm. But Jacobs remained silent as the meeting continued for another hour.

At nine o'clock, Swift said:

Well, gentlemen, I think we've kicked this around long enough, and I appreciate your comments. Al and I will get our heads together next week, and we'll let you know whether or not we decide to go ahead with the catalog-record idea.

But right now, I'd like to hear what our friend, Jim Jacobs, has to say about the performance we put on for him. He's been sitting here soaking it all in. Any reactions, Jim?

JACOBS: You're right, Gordon, I have been soaking it all in, which is a bit unusual for me. I'm usually running the show rather than watching it—and I certainly appreciate your invitation. I'd like to do this more often.

Now, if you don't mind, Gordon, I wonder if I could impose upon you and your men for about three minutes.

SWIFT: Go right ahead, Jim. Got something cooked up?

JACOBS: Well, in a way. You men all know how enthusiastic Gordon is about the subject of communication. And most of you know that I feel pretty much the same way. Gordon and I have spent hours at a stretch talking about the problems of communication in business. Heaven only knows we've got them in our plant—and in my own department, too. Now, there was one point in this meeting that particularly interested me. You all recall that remark of Ed Knoll's about film clips? Well, I wonder if you'd oblige me by writing a short sentence or two about your reaction to Ed's comment. Don't bother to sign your name.

Each salesman wrote a brief note and passed it to Jacobs, who said: "Thank you very much, gentlemen. You might be interested in what I'm up to. Frankly, it's just a little experiment I thought of while I was sitting with my ears open for a change—instead of my mouth. I really don't know what to expect from it.

"But Gordon is giving me a lift home, so I imagine you'll be getting a feedback through him."

"Fine, Jim," Swift replied, "this might be interesting at that. And now, unless anyone has anything else to add, let's adjourn the meeting."

Swift began talking with several salesmen at the door while others were collecting their papers and getting their coats. Jacobs walked over to Knoll and said: "Ed, I wonder if you would tell me just what you had in mind with that film clip idea?"

KNOLL: Well, Mr. Jacobs, I thought we could shoot a short film on our own—probably wouldn't run more than 20 dollars. I have a 16-mm camera, and if the company would buy the film and let me rig up a few lights—

JACOBS: Were you suggesting that the film would be coordinated with the record?

KNOLL: Oh, no—it would be entirely apart from the catalog and record. It would be just another way of communicating with our dealers and their customers, too. Our machines are too big, too expensive, and there are too many models for our dealers to stock the complete line. The film would be a way of showing our machines in actual operation.

Jacobs thanked Knoll and joined Swift, who was waiting to drive him home. As they rode, Jacobs read the statements aloud. There were 11 of them:

COST!!![19]

Oh, no! Not the movie boys again!

That isn't the kind of thing we can afford to do now.

Coupled with the record and review of the catalog, the film would be a sharp idea.

Necessity of having a projector and screen besides a phonograph—too much apparatus.

Completely irrelevant in terms of a critique of the record idea.

The idea is for catalogs and records to be sent out and heard. If they are going to show movies, you don't need catalogs.

Vision with the record sounded like a good idea.

A sound film would be better than a film with a separate record.

Book, voice, and pictures—too much to absorb.

That's all we need—another unusable film!

Flies, typhoid, and publicity[20]

It was while I was working at the Memorial Institute that an opportunity came for me to bring my scientific training to bear on a problem at Hull House. (My efforts in the baby clinic could not be called scientific.) This was in the fall of 1902, when I came back from Mackinac to find Chicago in the grip of one of her worst epidemics of typhoid fever. At that time the water, drawn from the lake, was not chlorinated; the only precaution taken against dangerous pollution was to make daily cultures of samples from the different pumping stations and the next day, when the cultures had had time to develop, publish the results and tell the public whether or not to boil water. It was assumed that housewives would look up these instructions every day, and act accordingly, but the actual result was that

---

[19] Swift told Jacobs that the Roberts Company had an unpleasant, costly experience with a product film prepared by a film production firm. The film had cost $12,000 and for various reasons had never been used.

[20] From *Exploring the Dangerous Trades* by Alice Hamilton, M.D. (Boston: Little, Brown & Co., 1943). Reprinted by permission.

typhoid was endemic in Chicago and periodically it reached epidemic proportions. On this particular occasion Hull House was the center of the hardest-struck region of the city—why, nobody knew. Miss Addams said she thought a bacteriologist ought to be able to discover the reason.

It was certainly not a simple problem. The pumping station which sent water to the Nineteenth Ward sent it to a wide section of the West Side, the milk supply was the same as that for neighboring wards. There must be some local condition to account for the excessive number of cases. As I prowled about the streets and the ramshackle wooden tenement houses I saw the outdoor privies (forbidden by law but flourishing nevertheless), some of them in backyards below the level of the street and overflowing in heavy rains; the wretched water closets indoors, one for four or more families, filthy and with the plumbing out of order because nobody was responsible for cleaning or repairs; and swarms of flies everywhere. Here, I thought, was the solution of the problem. The flies were feeding on typhoid-infected excreta and then lighting on food and milk. During the Spanish–American War, when we lost more men from typhoid fever than from Spanish bullets, Vaughan, Shakespeare, and Reed had made a study of conditions in camps—open latrines, unscreened food—which led them to attribute an important role in the spread of typhoid fever to the house fly. That was what started the "Swat the fly" campaign.

Naturally, my theory had to be put to the test, so, with two of the residents to help me, Maude Gernon and Gertrude Howe, I went forth to collect flies—from privies and kitchens and filthy water closets. We would drop the flies into tubes of broth and I would take them to the laboratory, incubate the tubes, and plate them out at varying intervals. It was a triumph to find the typhoid bacillus and I hastened to write up the discovery and its background for presentation before the Chicago Medical Society This was just the sort of thing to catch public attention: It was simple and easily understood; it fitted in with the revelations made during the Spanish War of the deadly activities of house flies, and it explained why the slums had so much more typhoid than the well-screened and decently drained homes of the well-to-do.

I am sure I gained more kudos from my paper on flies and typhoid than from any other piece of work I ever did. Even today I sometimes hear an echo of it. In Chicago the effect was most gratifying; a public inquiry resulted in a complete reorganization of the Health Department under a chief loaned by the Public Health Service, and an expert was put in charge of tenement-house inspection. But unfortunately my gratification over my part in all this did not last long. After the tumult had died down I discovered a fact which never gained much publicity but was well-authenticated. My flies had had little or nothing to do with the cases of typhoid in the Nineteenth Ward. The cause was simpler but so much more discreditable that the Board of Health had not dared reveal it. It seems that in our local pumping station, on West Harrison Street, near Halsted, a break had occurred which resulted in an escape of sewage into the water pipes and for three days our neighborhood drank that water before the leak was discovered and stopped. This was after the epidemic had started. The truth was more shocking than my ingenious theory, and it never came to light, so far as the public was concerned. For years, although I did my best to lay to rest the ghosts of those flies, they haunted me and mortified me, compelling me again and again to explain to deeply impressed audiences that the dramatic story their chairman had just rehearsed had little foundation in fact.

15

Undelayed reactions

OUR CULTURE tends to place a premium on the "man of action," the "quick thinker." And, to be sure, there are circumstances when the "snap" decision is to be desired over the delayed response or no action at all. On the other hand, the consequences of some undelayed, unreasoned reactions have ranged from mild embarrassment to some of the greatest catastrophes in history. Consider the tragic phenomenon of panic. Take the famous Iroquois Theatre fire (Chicago, 1903), for example. It is generally conceded that a considerable portion of the terrible death toll (almost 600) could be attributed to the crush of fear-crazed persons who jammed the exits.

Doors, windows, hallways, fire escapes—all were jammed in a moment with struggling humanity, fighting for life. Some of the doors were jammed almost instantly so that no human power could make egress possible. Behind those. in front pushed the frenzied mass of humanity. Chicago's elect, the wives and children of its most prosperous business men and the flower of local society, fighting like demons incarnate. Purses, wraps, costly furs were cast aside in that mad rush. Mothers were torn from their children, husbands from their wives. No hold, however strong, could last against that awful indescribable crush. Strong men who sought to the last to sustain their feminine companions were swept away like straws, thrown to the floor and trampled into unconsciousness in the twinkling of an eye. Women to whom safety of their children was more than their own lives had their little ones torn from them and buried under the mighty sweep of humanity, moving onward by intuition rather

490

than through exercise of thought to the various exits. They in turn were swept on before their wails died on their lips—some to safety, others to an unspeakably horrible death.[1]

Veteran writer Ben H. Atwell, an eyewitness, gave testimony of the senseless loss of lives:

Piled in windows in the angle of the stairway where the second balcony refugees were brought face to face and in a death struggle with the occupants of the first balcony, the dead covered a space fifteen or twenty feet square and nearly seven feet in depth. *All were absolutely safe from the fire itself when they met death,* having emerged from the theatre proper into the separate building containing the foyer. In this great court there was absolutely nothing to burn and the doors were only a few feet away. There the ghastly pile lay, *a mute monument to the powers of terror. . . .*

To that pile of dead is attributed the great loss of life within. The bodies choked up the entrance, barring the egress of those behind. Neither age nor youth, sex, quality or condition were sacred in the awful battle in the doorway. The gray and aged, rich, poor, young and those obviously invalids in life lay in a tangled mass all on an awful footing of equality in silent annihilation.[2]

If that calamity seems remote, consider the more recent Cocoanut Grove nightclub fire:

To a week already overcrowded with gruesome news pictures from the war, Boston added a terrible climax of civilian tragedy on Saturday night (Nov. 28) when more than 400 people[3] lost their lives in a fire at a midtown night club. It was the worst U.S. disaster of its kind since the 1903 Iroquois Theatre fire in Chicago.

A thousand merrymakers were packed in the Cocoanut Grove celebrating football victories and "getting away from the war" at 10:15 P.M. when the floor show was scheduled to start. A bus boy struck a match to see how to screw a light bulb back into its socket. A tinsel palm tree nearby caught fire and havoc took the stage. The guests' mad headlong rush for the two inadequate exits ended by completely clogging all escape. *More than the flames and stifling smoke, it was the hysteria and panic of the screaming, clawing crowds which piled up the dead like a dam.* One

---

[1] *Chicago's Awful Theatre Horror* by the Survivors and Rescuers (Chicago: Memorial Publishing Co., 1904) , p. 36.

[2] Ibid., pp. 41–42. Italics are mine.

[3] A subsequent article ("After Cocoanut Grove," *Atlantic Monthly*, Vol. 171, No. 3 [March 1943], pp. 55–57) totaled the fatalities at just under 500, the hospitalized at 250.

chorus boy kept his head in the pandemonium, directing entertainers to the safety of an adjacent roof through a second story window.[4]

Panic, of course, is not exclusively a group phenomenon. The individual may experience "solo panic" which can lead to destructive consequences. I am looking at a newspaper clipping which tells of a businessman who was dozing as his commuter train carried him home. The train stopped at the station just below his own and started up again, awakening the man. Startled and thinking he was missing his station, the man dashed out the forward door of the coach. He stumbled and fell under the train, and its wheels cut off his feet at the ankles. He was taken to a hospital, where authorities said his condition was critical.[5]

Riots, lynchings, and many other forms of mob or individual violence or inaction[6]—unsanity, in any case—are almost invariably earmarked by irrational, impulsive behavior.

THREE CLASSES OF BEHAVIOR

The question is: How is it possible that normally civilized, law-abiding, peaceful, sane, and adult persons sometimes act like fear-crazed or enraged animals? How can humans, collectively or individually, "lose their heads" or "fly off the handle" and, as a consequence, effectively contribute to the harm and destruction of themselves and of others? A way of approaching the problem is to compare three broad classifications of human behavior.

I. Reflex responses

Shine a light into someone's eyes and watch his pupils contract. Draw a pointed instrument across the sole of his foot and note the reaction of his toes. Tap his knee just below the patella and watch his lower leg jerk. These simple reactions are called *reflex responses*. Involving no "thinking," they are uncontrolled (and largely uncontrollable), direct and immediate responses of the organism to stimuli.

---

[4] "Boston Holocaust," *Life*, December 7, 1942, © Time Inc., p. 44. Reprinted by permission. Italics are mine.

[5] "Leaps Off Train, Loses Feet," *Chicago Sun-Times*, September 23, 1954, p. 66.

[6] See Meerloo's discussion of "Frozen Panic" in Joost A. M. Meerloo, M.D., *Patterns of Panic* (New York: International Universities Press, Inc., 1950), pp. 28–30.

II. Voluntary responses

Now ask the same person to spell his full name backward, to multiply 43 by 9, and to estimate your weight. Assuming that he had had no special preparation for these tasks, his responses will have the opposite characteristics of reflexes. They will involve some "thinking"; they will be delayed, controllable (and controlled), responses.

III. Reflexlike responses

Compare these two forms of behavior with a third:

We enlisted men were at bat in a hotly contested baseball game with our officers, when a private hit what looked like a single to short right field. Instead of stopping at first, however, he foolishly started a wild dash for second. Realizing, then, that he couldn't make it, he scrambled back toward first. Now he was being chased in a rundown between the lieutenant playing first and the colonel playing second.

It looked like a sure out, but just as the lieutenant flipped the ball back to the colonel, the private snapped to attention, saluting the colonel. . . . The colonel snapped a salute back—and muffed the catch.[7]

The colonel's reaction appears to be a cross between a reflex response and a voluntary response. Like a reflex, his reaction was undelayed, uncontrolled, and apparently involved little or no thought. On the other hand, it resembled a voluntary response, in that his action was controllable (*albeit* largely uncontrolled in this instance). In short, his response *could* have been delayed, controlled, and premeditated—in other words, it *could* have been a voluntary response, but years of conditioning and habit militated against it. A reflexlike response, then, may be considered a *potential* voluntary reaction which, through habit, panic, conditioning, surprise, and so on tends to resemble reflexes.

Useful reflexlike responses. Reflexlike responses often begin as conscious, voluntary actions. One learns to drive a car, play a musical instrument, type, throw a baseball, and so forth, quite consciously and perhaps laboriously at first. But with repetition these actions became so habituated that they may be carried on with virtually no conscious control. Our capacity for learning these responses is invaluable

---

[7] Cpl. Bill O'Brian in *True,* quoted in *Reader's Digest,* May 1958, p. 166. Reprinted by permission of Fawcett Publications, Inc.

to us. Consider driving an automobile. If the driver had to maintain conscious control of his steering, braking, accelerating, and so on, he might have considerable difficulty in coping with, say, the added complexity of the car in front stopping quickly. One simply does not have the time, under these conditions, to decide with due pre-meditation that he must slow up or stop his car (and to do this he must take his foot off the accelerator), that he must put it on the brake, that he must press the brake pedal hard enough to stop in time but not hard enough to skid his car into oncoming traffic, that he must be looking for possibilities of steering around the stopped car, that he must take into account the actions of the drivers behind and beside him, and so forth. If he is an experienced driver, he has so thor-oughly habituated many of these actions that he will perform them without prethought and therefore will have time and concentration for coping with the less familiar aspects of the situation. A good typ-ist, for example, is unaware of the specific movements of her fingers. In fact, if she began to *will* that certain fingers strike certain keys, her rate would fall off markedly, and her errors would probably increase. If a punch-press operator had to make conscious decisions before stamping each piece, you can imagine the decrease in his productivity. In short, there is a great deal to be said for properly trained reflexlike responses.

Dangerous reflexlike responses.   There are occasions, however, when reflexlike responses can lead to trouble. There was, for ex-ample, the incident of the rookie police officer who was assigned to night duty in a downtown shopping district. He was making his rounds, checking the rear doors of the shops, when he found the door of a furniture store unlocked. He swung the door open and noticed with a start that the figure of a man loomed in the darkness inside. The officer quickly went for his gun and was dismayed to see the "other man" go for his. The policeman *immediately* pulled his re-volver and fired—and the "man" disappeared amid the sound of shat-tering glass. Upon investigating, the young officer discovered that he had destroyed a $95 mirror!

Most of us might argue that we would have done the same thing as the embarrassed rookie—and so we might, for we would have been "rookies," too. But veteran policemen tell us that the situation could have been handled more skillfully. They say that they have learned from experience to suspect immediately the possibility of a mirrored image. They say that there are ways of weaving, ducking, and dodging—while reaching for one's gun—which (1) make one a difficult target if the "man" should turn out to be actually there and (2) permit a check on the suspected mirror. Of course, if the other "man" *doesn't* weave, duck, and dodge as you do, you may have a problem on your hands! But, the veterans insist, you are usually in a better position to cope with it.

The undelayed, unthinking response can sometimes have far graver consequences than minor property damage and embarrassment. These tragedies might be appropriately labeled "The Quick and The Dead."

ALBANY, TEX.— (UP) —A schoolgirl raced for her life trying to get off a railroad trestle as the freight train bore down on her Friday. But she stumbled and was killed, sheriff Jack Moberley reported Saturday.

Margie Dell Macon, 12, became frightened when she felt the trestle vibrate as the train rumbled onto it with its brakes on. She started to run. Her sister, Barbara, 14, remained where she was—crouched on the edge of the trestle. The train didn't touch her. . . .[8]

Fear of a snake crawling along the roadside cost the life of a 6-year-old boy.

Romeo Ramos was killed Wednesday when he darted into the path of an oncoming car at Wilke and Kirchoff Rds. in Arlington Heights.

His brother Roel, 11, told the police he and Romeo were walking along the shoulder of the road when they spotted the snake. He said Romeo, afraid, ran onto the road.

Police said the snake apparently was one of the harmless "grass snake" type.

Isadore J. Valente, 35, of Elmwood Park, driver of the car, was not held by police.[9]

THE PROBLEM OF UNDELAYED REACTIONS

The problem of undelayed reactions does not, of course, involve true reflexes which, for the most part, consist of harmless and often self-protective[10] behavior. Nor are we concerned with properly trained and habituated reflexlike actions which increase one's efficiency in

---

[8] "Girl Races Train on Trestle, Dies," *Chicago Daily News,* December 18, 1954, p. 1. Courtesy of United Press.

[9] "Auto Kills Boy Fleeing from Snake," *Chicago Daily News,* July 8, 1954, p. 43. Reprinted by permission.

[10] As in the case of the gagging reflex, pupillary contractions and dilations, eye winks, and so forth.

repetitive tasks and facilitate his handling of unusual situations, as in driving an automobile, as previously discussed.

The undelayed reactions which are of concern here are those which *can* and *ought* to be delayed, controlled, and premeditated. If the girl on the trestle, for example, had delayed for a moment, as her sister apparently did, and considered possibilities other than a headlong, panic-stricken rush from the train, she might be alive today.

The correctives which follow, then, apply to the reflexlike responses which, in the interest of saving tempers, time, energy, money, and lives, could and ought to be delayed, conscious, voluntary responses.

CORRECTIVES

Instantaneous action—rarely necessary

First of all, let us recognize that very few emergencies require an immediate action. This chapter has cited numerous examples of critical circumstances ranging from a policeman's reflection in a mirror to the unforgettable Iroquois Theatre fire. In no case was immediate, unthinking response necessary. In fact, in every case, had those involved delayed their reactions for even a moment to "size up" the situation, the consequences might have been a good deal happier.

The habit of delay

Bishop Samuel Fallows, on the aftermath of the Iroquois Theatre catastrophe, wrote:

Let every safeguard that human ingenuity can devise be furnished and yet there always remains the personal element to be taken into account. Habitual practice of self-control in daily life will help give coolness and calmness in times of peril. Keeping one's head in the ordinary things prevents its losing when the extraordinary occurs.[11]

The *"habitual practice of self-control in daily life"* is precisely what is advocated here. Frequently practice the technique of delaying your response, if only for an instant. It is especially helpful to discipline one's self under "semiemergency" circumstances. If, for example, someone makes a remark which seems offensive, resist the impulse to respond—instead, let your *initial* reaction be *delay*. Give yourself time to size up the situation—Did he really mean that? Will

---

[11] *Chicago's Awful Theatre Horror,* p. xv.

it be wise to retaliate in kind? What are his reasons for saying it? Could he be only joking? Hadn't I better give him a chance to clarify this? Chances are with you that your delayed reactions will be appreciably more intelligent, mature, and, in the long run, effective than your impulsive response would have been. The point is not simply to "count to 10" but to *size up the situation—to analyze, get more data, look for other alternatives, date, index, distinguish inferences from observations—while doing so.*

Since many of our harmful, overquick responses are vocal, a friend has developed the habit of clenching a pen or pencil crosswise in his teeth when the urge to "pop off" comes upon him. While the wear and tear on the writing instrument may be considerable, this little technique not only reminds him of the wisdom of delaying but rather effectively inhibits the verbal outburst!

Advance preparation for emergencies

The best general provision for emergencies is the deeply ingrained habit of delay-while-sizing-up, but more specific preparation is often possible. Generally speaking, an emergency *is* an emergency because it involves circumstances which are unexpected, unfamiliar, and with which we feel unprepared or unable to cope. To the extent that the circumstances are anticipated and made familiar and to the extent that we are equipped to cope with them, they are no longer overwhelming crises. Training for combat is an excellent example of this. The recruit spends weeks going through many of the activities of warfare, firing his rifle, throwing grenades, forced hikes with full field pack, bayonet drill, crawling through the infiltration course,[12] and so on. The object is to acquaint him with as many of the aspects of combat as possible, in order that the actual experience will not seem overpoweringly complex and terrifying.

Speech training is another good example of advance preparation for "emergencies." The beginning speaker is advised to familiarize himself in advance, insofar as he can, with the components of the speaking situation. He is urged, for example, to master the speech (in many cases this will require committing the ideas and their connectives, [not the exact wording] to memory) ; to learn in advance what

---

[12] The infiltration course is a simulated battlefield. The trainee crawls 50 yards or so under barbed wire, with a brace of machine guns firing real bullets a few inches above his head. As an added fillip, charges explode sporadically throughout the field, showering him with grit or mud, as the case may be.

he can about the audience (size, age, sex, interests, prejudices, and so on) ; to know the purpose of the occasion, the topics of any previous and subsequent speakers, and the role his own talk will play; to acquaint himself with the physical aspects (acoustics, arrangement of audience, position of speaker's stand, lighting, and so forth) . In short, one becomes able to cope with difficult and critical situations to the extent that he has predicted, prepared for, and controlled factors in advance.

Anticipate the undelayed responses of others

So far, we have been concerned with measures one can take to encourage his own delayed reactions. Let us now consider how to deal with the harmful undelayed responses of others. First of all, it should be recognized that the tendency to react overquickly varies from individual to individual, and *within* the individual, from time to time. In other words, *index* and *date* the other fellow's propensity to fly off the handle. While Sam seemed to stand up under pressure last week, there is no guarantee that he will be as serene now.

Second, if you anticipate a potential flareup, use the most "snap reaction-proof" medium of communication possible. For example, it is extremely easy for a man who loses his temper on the telephone to cut you off in an instant and proceed to act foolishly and destructively. A memo or letter, under some circumstances, with no chance of immediate feedback from the other person or possibility of control on your part, may be even worse. But a face-to-face communication gives you a chance to see the storm clouds forming and to forestall them. And even if the other fellow does "blow his top," you are *there* to help him regain his composure.

Third and most important, don't match the other fellow's undelayed response with one of your own. As sorely tempting as it may be at times, mutual overquick reactions may make reconciliation considerably more difficult. And, after all, if you are right, you can afford to keep your temper; if you are wrong, you can't afford to lose it.

A group technique

In the chapter on *bypassing* I described a special conference technique.[13] While the clarification of communication among the partici-

---

13 See pp. 271–72.

pants was the prime objective, an important by-product emerged. The executive meetings of this particular firm characteristically had been marred by frequent angry exchanges among the conferees. But not long after the installation of the "moderator system" it became evident that something had happened—the outbursts had disappeared. In fact, the meetings moved along with amazing tranquility. The reason was soon apparent. The system required the moderator to paraphrase a speaker's remark *before* anyone else was permitted to respond. It was clear that this necessary delay, plus the likelihood of clarifying the communication, forced the quick responder to delay, to reconsider his response! And when he was finally allowed to speak, he was invariably more cool-headed and objective than he would have been, had he been permitted to respond immediately.

And perhaps there is a moral in this experience for the individual as well as for the group. If you feel you disagree or disapprove of what someone has just said, *take the time* to make sure you understand him correctly. This can have at least three salutary effects. You may find that you *have* misunderstood and are not actually in disagreement; your attempt to understand will tend to communicate respect for the other person, and he may be likely to return the consideration; and, finally, the delay may have given you both time to be more intelligent and reasonable in your differing.

DISCUSSION QUESTIONS

1. "Our culture tends to place a premium on the man of action, the quick thinker." (p. 490)
   Do you agree with that assertion? If so, why is it so? Are other cultures similarly action-oriented?

2. Regarding the "group technique" (pp. 498–99) : Will this delaying technique have any undesirable effects upon the group's activity? Might it slow progress to the point of boredom and apathy? Will any creativity be lost in the process? Will discussants be less candid if they realize they are to be paraphrased?
   On the other hand, what are the positive features of the technique?

3. Report upon an incident, perhaps involving yourself, in which an undesirable, undelayed reaction occurred. *How* and *why* did it occur? What were its consequences? How might it have been prevented? What measures might prevent its recurrence?

CASES

The Logan Company[14]

The Logan Company, a manufacturer of television and radio receiver sets, employed some 2,000 persons. The firm, which had been privately owned for over 30 years, had been sold to a large electronics holding corporation four years earlier but retained substantially the same management after the sale. Following three unsatisfactory years, the president of Logan retired. The holding corporation installed Eric Stone as general manager; he was from outside the firm but within the holding company. Stone was given the rank of vice president, although he carried out the functions of the president, an office now vacant. He made many changes in the upper and middle management levels, including the product-line managers. The current situation, then, may be said to be one of flux and readjustment.

Among the responsibilities of the industrial engineering department was the supervision of the installation of production lines as new products or changes in products were introduced. One of these was a new conveyor assembly line for television tuners. Formerly the tuners had been assembled by conventional bench assembly methods, with workers compensated on an individual incentive basis. Many employees had expressed dissatisfaction with the new methods, complaining that their take-home pay had been markedly reduced.

Ray Edwards, 35, six years with Logan, was the industrial engineer in charge of installing the tuner conveyor line. He found on Tuesday that it was necessary to adjust the pace of the conveyor in order to train assemblers. He realized that the product-line manager, Fred Peterson, who had joined the firm two months earlier, was under

---

14 All names have been disguised. Printed by permission of the author, whose name has been withheld by request.

considerable pressure to increase tuner production. So he phoned Peterson at 11 A.M. to discuss the intended adjustment but was unable to reach him. As he waited for Peterson to return his call, Edwards reviewed four alternatives for timing the change:

1. Have Logan's maintenance men make the adjustment after work hours that day. To Edwards this did not appear to be a happy choice, since it would require overtime pay at time and a half for the maintenance workers. This pay would be charged against the industrial engineering department. The department's budget for such expenses was already strained for the fiscal period.
2. Wait until Saturday (a nonworking day) and have maintenance men make the installation. Their overtime pay would then be charged to the miscellaneous budget. While this would entail no loss of production time or employee pay and would relieve the industrial engineering department of overtime charges, the delay in installing the change would interfere with operator training.
3. Have the salesman of the adjustment equipment make the change during work hours. Since he would be paid by his own firm, the expense would not be charged to the industrial engineering budget. However, tuner production would be shut down, and workers would not be paid during the shutdown period.
4. Have the salesman start to make the change during the lunch period. Edwards favored this plan because it would not only remove the burden of overtime pay from his department's budget, but would require a minimum of shutdown time and loss of worker pay. However, Edwards wanted to inform Peterson that the change might take longer than the lunch period.

Peterson had spent the morning in conference in the office of the vice president in charge of manufacturing, Roy Sheldon. Also present was Tom Flynn, manager of the industrial engineering department, to whom Edwards reported. Flynn, 38, had 13 years of service with the company. At 12:45 P.M., as Peterson left Sheldon's office, he was stopped by Miss Larson, Sheldon's secretary, who gave him Edwards' message, which had been relayed to her by Peterson's secretary.

Peterson immediately picked up the phone on Miss Larson's desk and called Edwards.

PETERSON: Ray, I understand you called—just got the note.
EDWARDS: [The fourth alternative was now no longer possible, because

the assemblers' lunch period had ended.] Yes, Fred—we're going to have to regulate the tuner line. As you know, it has been going too fast for the girls.

PETERSON: Yeah? (*Suspiciously*.)

EDWARDS: Well, we've purchased some new gearing that should do the trick of slowing down the line. Now, as to whom to make the change, I have a few ideas to sound out with you.

PETERSON: Shoot.

EDWARDS: First, we could have the maintenance men do the job tonight. Frankly, I'm opposed to this, and so is Flynn. Their time would be charged to us, and we're up to the hilt right now in overtime charges. I don't think Tom would stand for it. So I thought—.

[*Click!*] Peterson had hung up. He charged angrily back into Mr. Sheldon's office and, in the presence of Sheldon, proceeded to upbraid Tom Flynn for trying to shut down his production line in order to avoid overtime costs.

The Mid-Western Telephone Company[15]

The general staff of the Mid-Western Telephone Company decided upon a revision in the company's billing procedure. Formerly, billing machine symbols had appeared on four portions of the bill. The change consisted in using symbols on only one section of the bill. Thus, it was necessary to have three sets of symbols removed from each of the firm's billing machines.

Late Friday afternoon Charles Liska of the general staff notified the United Office Machine Company, who serviced the machines, to send out a repairman at the beginning of the week to remove the unneeded symbols. Liska then instructed Ted Jennings of the division staff to notify the district heads and supervising accountants of each of the districts of the change. Each of the supervising accountants was to have relayed the information to the supervisor under him.

These lines of communication are charted below:

---

15 All names have been disguised. Printed by permission of the author, whose name has been withheld by request.

FIGURE 15–1

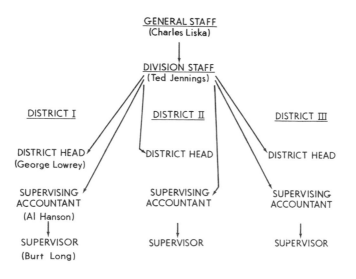

Jennings tried to contact George Lowrey, the district head in District I, and was unable to reach him. Jennings then called Al Hanson, supervising accountant in District I, and gave the message to him and requested him to notify Burt Long, the supervisor whose unit was involved.

At the time he was called, Hanson was wrestling with a production problem and was several hours behind schedule. He did not take any notes and forgot to contact Long.

Monday morning the repairman walked into Long's unit and told him that he was there to remove something but he was hazy on whether he was to remove all of the symbols or only some of them from the machines. Long, who had not been contacted about the matter, tried to call Hanson, but he was not at his desk. Long then called Mr. Lowrey to ask him what to do. Hanson happened to be in Lowrey's office when Long's call came in. Lowrey, knowing nothing of the situation, told Hanson that Long was asking what to do about symbols on the billing machines. He asked if Hanson could handle the situation.

Hanson flushed with embarrassment as he suddenly recalled his failure to pass Jennings' message to Long. He vaguely remembered something about the removal of symbols but because he felt Lowrey

was already holding him responsible for his current production problem he dreaded admitting his error in the presence of his superior.
He clutched the phone and told Long that all of the symbols were to
be removed. He silently resolved to stop the repairman and check
with Jennings as soon as he left Lowrey's office. Unfortunately, the
district head began a prolonged discussion of Hanson's production
difficulty. Hanson became so preoccupied with Lowrey's remarks that
the symbols matter slipped his mind. Meanwhile Long relayed Hanson's instruction to the repairman who proceeded to remove all of the
symbols.

Some time later in the morning, Jennings, following up to see if
the work had been done, discovered what had happened. Upon checking with the United Office Machine Company, he was told that the
correct symbols could be replaced at $35 per machine and that the
machines would have to be brought into the shop for the replacement.

The end result was that the 10 machines of the unit were taken out
of production for several days and that a cost of $350 was necessary
for the replacement of the symbols.

"You did that on purpose!"[16]

Before the war it was customary to allow civilians aboard Navy
ships during visiting hours on Sunday. The Saratoga, which was an-
chored in the San Pedro–Long Beach area, attracted a lot of these
visitors, and usually they found its decks as steady as their own front
porches. Occasionally, however, a freak wind would raise swells behind the breakwater, and if these swells hit the Saratoga broadside,
she would roll most heartily. When this happened, the visitors were
loaded into running boats and taken quickly ashore.

One stout matron was so resentful at having her visit cut short in
this way that the officer of the deck had to have her escorted to the
accommodation ladder in order to get her off on the last visitors'
boat. This ladder is simply a set of open steps leading down the side
of the ship from the deck to a small platform near the water, from

---

16 *Saturday Evening Post,* May 1, 1948. Reprinted by permission of the author,
Captain Marcus A. Peel, U.S.N.

which the visitors step into the shoregoing boats. The O.D. carefully cautioned the lady to stay off this platform until he gave the word, but she was too angry to pay attention. Head high, she stepped briskly down to the platform and waited for the boat.

Meanwhile the Saratoga had completed its swing in one direction and was rolling back. The platform started down, hit the water; the O.D. shouted another warning, but by this time the chill harbor water was well above the woman's ankles.

Gasping with surprise and indignation, she glared up at the helpless O.D. "You young whippersnapper!" she roared. "You did that on purpose!"

Your eyes can deceive you[17]

ARTHUR BARTLETT

George Smith got home from a date with his girl about midnight. His mother was not at home. Probably she was out playing cards with friends, George thought. That had been her favorite recreation ever since her divorce, when George was six. Working all day in the candy factory, she liked to relax in the evenings. Now that George was 20, and working, and had a girl to occupy his attention, she often stayed out fairly late. So George went up to his own front room, undressed, got into bed and lay there reading the newspaper.

A bus stopped across the street, and George pulled aside the window shade and looked out. Under the street light, he could see his mother descending from the bus. A tall, heavy-set man got out behind her. The bus moved on. George was about to drop back on his pillow when his startled eyes stopped him. The man was reaching for his mother, trying to put his arms around her. George saw her push at him and try to step back off the curb; saw him grab her again and start pulling her towards him.

George leaped out of bed, pulled on his trousers and rushed down the stairs to the front door. Across the street, the man was still attempting to embrace his mother and she was struggling against him. George dashed to the rescue. Clenching his fist as he ran, he leaped

[17] Reprinted by permission from the *American Weekly*, © 1951, by Hearst Publishing Company, Inc.

at the man and punched with all his strength, hitting him squarely on the jaw. The man toppled backward and uttered a groan as his head hit the sidewalk. Then he lay there, still.

What happened next filled George with utter confusion. Dropping to her knees beside the unconscious man, his mother looked up at him with anguish in her eyes. "George," she cried, "what have you done? This is Howard Browser. . . . Howard, the candymaker at the factory . . . the man who asked me to marry him." . . .

The boy stared at his mother across the crumpled figure on the pavement. "He wasn't attacking you?" he demanded, dully.

"Of course not," she told him. "We'd been out together all evening. He brought me home. He wanted a good-night kiss, that's all. I was just teasing him."

An ambulance took Howard Browser to the hospital, but he never regained consciousness. He died the next day. George Smith spent that night in a jail cell.

The authorities finally decided not to prosecute. George, the investigation proved, didn't know Browser; had never seen him before. He had honestly thought that what he saw was a man attacking his mother.

But he had been misled by what he saw. His imagination exaggerated the evidence presented by his own eyes and converted it into something that wasn't true at all. As a result he had killed his mother's suitor. . . .

Take the case of Matthew J. Flaherty, a Boston policeman, some years ago. Shortly after being appointed to the force, Matt Flaherty took a bride and they moved into their own home on Newcastle Road. Eleanor Flaherty loved the house, but she was nervous about being alone in it at night, waiting for Matt to come home from his late tour of duty. Every little noise made her think that there was someone in the house or trying to get in. When Matt got home she was usually so upset that he would search the whole house, from cellar to attic, though smiling at her fears.

"No burglars," he would assure her, "except in your pretty little head."

Still, he couldn't help feeling anxious. If anyone really were prowling around his house while he was away nights. . . .

One night—they had been living in the house about two months then—he made the usual fruitless search and went to bed. But he had hardly dropped off to sleep, it seemed, when he woke with a start.

What had awakened him? Naturally, his first thought was of a prowler. Listening tensely, he heard a sound—the creaking of a floor board—on the other side of the closed bedroom door. Quietly, he reached for his gun and eased himself up in bed.

Sure enough, the door began to push open. Somebody was coming right into the room.

"Who's there?" Matt Flaherty yelled, taking careful aim. There was no answer but a startled gasp and he started shooting. It was too dark to see the figure beyond the half-opened door, but whoever it was fell with a thump to the floor.

Then Matt turned on the light. That was when he realized, for the first time, that Eleanor was not there in the bed beside him.
She was lying just outside the door, dead.

[*Is it our* EYES *which deceive us?*]

Torment in a neighborhood[18]

WALTER B. SMITH

What made James Lee, the Chinese laundryman, go berserk?

Why did he shoot three men, two of them police, then try to fight off 150 more cops before falling with a bullet wound through the skull?

Lying Saturday in County Hospital, his head throbbing and his left ankle shackled to the bed frame, Jimmy Lee gave his explanation of why he did it.

"I was scared," he said.

He was scared, he said, because he thought the three men had come to beat him up and perhaps take his money because he had slapped a boy.

And he slapped the boy, Lee said, because he finally had become fed up with the way neighborhood kids in general tormented him with squirt guns, name-calling, door-banging and other mischief.

The furious gun battle took place just a week ago in Lee's laundry at 2705 Diversey.

The city was shocked—the more so because such violence is so rare among Chicago's law-abiding Chinese.

---

[18] *Chicago Daily News,* February 13, 1954, p. 3. Reprinted by permission.

Today two of Lee's victims are dead—detectives Jeremiah Lucey and Roman C. Steinke.

The third victim, truck driver Steven Malenk, 40, father of the slapped boy, has recently been discharged from a hospital.

The 42-year-old Lee has a sewed-up hole in his head where a bullet went right through. Doctors expect him to recover, but he may be paralyzed for life.

Lee started the shooting when the two policemen went to the laundry with Malenk to arrest Lee on a warrant charging assault.

The warrant stemmed from an incident three nights earlier when Lee had slapped Malenk's son Steve Jr., 11.

For months, Lee said, neighborhood kids had badgered him. Sometimes they spit on the floor, sometimes they threw things, sometimes they called him obscene names.

On the evening of Feb. 3, Lee said, the Malenk boy and a companion were heckling him. (The boys say they were just looking in the window.)

Lee chased them and caught Steve, slapping him.

Soon afterward Steve came back to the laundry with his father. Lee said the truck driver threatened him and they struggled. The laundryman admits he batted Malenk with a flatiron, breaking his wrist.

Malenk went to the Shakespeare police court next day and got the warrant charging Lee with assault.

Lee said he did not know about that when the officers came to get him last Saturday. Why didn't he go along peacefully to the police station?

"I was scared," Lee said. "All I knew was that these three men were coming to get me and wanted me to pay them $125. I thought they were going to beat me up."

He said he did not know that the men with Malenk were police. They wore civilian clothes.

"All I could think of was to shoot first."

The mention of $125 apparently was a misunderstanding of the policemen's statement that Lee would have to post $125 bail at the police station.

Lee said he kept the pistol and shotgun with which he fought the police as protection against burglars.

He lived alone at the laundry. He has no relatives in Chicago.

Lee told his story twice. First it was in halting English to a *Daily News* reporter. Then it was in Chinese to the Rev. Philip Lee, no relation, who is pastor of the Chinese Christian Union Church at 23rd St. and Wentworth.

The wounded man's chief worry was about his laundry. The Rev. Mr. Lee assured him that arrangements would be made with a Chinese friend to see that the customers get back their shirts.

The clergyman said Chinese welfare organizations were making plans to give Lee the help he needs.

Lee said he was brought to America in 1914, at the age of 2. After three years in New Jersey he was brought to Chicago, where he has lived ever since.

He said he had had his laundry at the Diversey address for six years, but that the trouble with the youngsters did not start until last September.

An inquest into the death of Detective Lucey has been continued to March 9.

*   *   *

James Lee died two-and-a-half months later from his wounds. A newspaper account included the following:

Lee said he went berserk because he was afraid the officers were going to beat him up. However, a fingerprint check showed Lee was sought as an Army deserter, and police said that might have been the reason he feared arrest.

Dyer Public Relations, Inc.[19]

Ralph Stewart, staff writer for a business magazine with large, national circulation, was talking with Mr. Dyer for the second time in early March. He had already recorded Mr. Dyer's account of the formation and development of Dyer Public Relations, Inc., as well as his personal history. Now, to round out his prospective article, he needed further information about others in the firm.

Robert Dyer was cooperative and said, "If you uncover anything

---

19 All names and organizational designations have been disguised. Northwestern University cases are reports of concrete events and behavior, prepared for class discussion. They are not intended as examples of "good" or "bad" administrative or technical practices. Copyright, 1964, by Northwestern University. Printed by permission.

constructive about how our communications and human relations are functioning, we'd be grateful—especially me. If it doesn't come up naturally, I suggest you probe and hear what we now call the 'Office Boy Incident.' Our people know you're here, and I've requested them to be frank in their interviews with you."

Dyer Public Relations, Inc., had been founded 14 years earlier in a large West Coast city by Mr. Dyer—a driving, ambitious, dynamic young man with seemingly inexhaustible energy. The company became a nationally recognized firm, grossing over $2 million annually. Dyer, Inc., employed approximately 40 persons. A partial organization chart appears at the end of the case (Figure 15–2).

In addition to Mr. Dyer, the following persons were involved in the "Office Boy Incident":

Mark Taylor—47, treasurer, joined Dyer 13 years earlier. Mr. Taylor also maintained a private accounting practice. He had a working agreement with Mr. Dyer that he would spend approximately half his time on the Dyer accounts and the other half on his own practice. These percentages were never adhered to rigidly. Some months, Mr. Taylor spent more than 50 percent of his time on Dyer affairs; some months, less. This had been an established arrangement between the two men, and both seemed satisfied with its operation.

William Frey—27, held a Ph.D. in industrial psychology. He was in charge of personnel services, including testing and placement for clients and the Dyer staff. Frey had been with the Dyer firm for two years. His predecessor, Kenneth Elson, had served as director of personnel services and as office manager. When Dr. Frey assumed the personnel responsibilities, Mrs. Lane became office manager.

Miriam Lane—26, was office manager of the firm and personal secretary to Mr. Clawson. She had six years' service with Dyer and had been office manager for the past two years. The firm's general clerical work flowed across her desk. She assigned it to secretaries who were not already busy with duties for their immediate supervisors. She had direct responsibility for the work of Russell Harmon, office boy.

Russell Harmon—21, office boy, a university student majoring in business management, had been working approximately 30 hours per week with Dyer for the past year.

THE OFFICE BOY INCIDENT

Over the past several months, because of tax deadlines and other financial problems, Mark Taylor had been devoting considerably more than 50 percent of his time to the Dyer firm. He was attempting to clear up a few personal affairs before leaving on a business trip for Dyer. He handed a typed letter about his professional fraternity to the bookkeeper, Arlene Roney, telling her to have 25 copies made. Miss Roney had been with the firm some two weeks and knew little of the firm's procedures. She knew that reproduction work was done by the office boy, Russell Harmon. She also knew the firm owned a photocopying machine but was unaware that the company also had an offset duplicator.[20] She assumed the letter was to be photocopied, called to Harmon as he was passing her desk, and handed the letter to him. She said, "Mr. Taylor would like 25 copies of this."

Harmon had just been told by Frey to deliver several packages to an office building across town. He glanced at the letter, realized that in its present form (without mat) he could only photocopy it, a job requiring 15 to 20 minutes, and said, "I can't do that now. I've got to run an errand. If I get back in time, I could do it before closing time, but I doubt if I can make it that soon. Guess it'll have to wait until tomorrow."

Miss Roney felt she could do no more about the situation and placed the letter on her desk. A few minutes later, Mr. Taylor approached her. "Did Russell run off those copies of the letter yet?"

Miss Roney answered, "No, he said he didn't have time now and probably couldn't do it until tomorrow."

Taylor, visibly angered, immediately stalked to Mr. Dyer's office. "Say, Bob, I know this is my personal work, but I would think I could get a little cooperation from the personnel around here—especially when you consider the amount of time I've been putting in for you."

DYER: What do you mean? What kind of cooperation?

TAYLOR: Why, Harmon just refused to run off 25 copies of a personal letter for me.

DYER [Considerably disturbed]: Where is he? We'll just see what the hell's going on here!

Dyer walked to Mrs. Lane's desk in the main office and demanded loudly, "Where is Harmon?"

MRS. LANE: Why—I don't know. I imagine he's out on an errand for Dr. Frey (*pointing toward Frey's office*). He's been sending Russell to the Weber Building, on the other side of the city.

---

[20] The two machines served different purposes. The photocopy machine could reproduce a few copies quickly without the material having to be retyped on a stencil or mat. However, the offset duplicator was faster and less expensive when a quantity of copies was required.

Mr. Dyer turned and strode into Frey's office. "Why can't Harmon do this work for Mark?"

Frey was nonplussed. This was the second time that day that Mr. Dyer had appeared to hold him personally responsible for the conduct of persons over whom, in his opinion, he had no authority. Earlier in the day, Dyer had come to him with complaints about errors in the work of the secretaries. Moreover, Frey had noticed through the glass partition of his office that Mrs. Lane had apparently directed Mr. Dyer to him. He was suddenly angered with Dyer's accusations and Mrs. Lane's "buck-passing" and snapped, "I don't know! Harmon doesn't work for me! He works for Lane!"

Mr. Dyer stamped out of Frey's office and headed for his own. As he passed Mrs. Lane's desk, he shouted, "When Harmon comes back, tell him I want to see him!"

Mrs. Lane was incensed with Frey. She assumed he had sent Mr. Dyer back to her. She got up and followed Mr. Dyer into his office. "Do you have to make a scene about this?" she asked. Mr. Dyer slammed his office door behind Mrs. Lane and himself and said, "Who in the hell does Russell Harmon think he is? If Harmon refuses to work for Mark Taylor, he can just get this rear end out of this office!"

Mrs. Lane: What's this all about?

Mr. Dyer: Mark brought something to Harmon to reproduce, and Harmon refused to do it. I want to see this kid, now!

Mrs. Lane: I'll find out from Russell about this.

Dyer: *I'll* ask him!

Mrs. Lane returned to her desk. Shortly afterward, Mr. Dyer, who had an outside appointment, left the office for the day. Harmon returned just before quitting time. When told of the incident, Harmon was bewildered. He felt betrayed by Dr. Frey, who had not, in his words, "stuck up" for him by telling Mr. Dyer that he was on an errand. He remarked about Miss Roney to a friend, "I was never even introduced to the girl, and it looks like she's trying to cut me down. Why, I don't even know her!"

Mrs. Lane questioned Harmon about the affair and said she would explain everything to Mr. Dyer in the morning.

By coincidence, Dr. Frey, Mrs. Lane, and Russell Harmon were scheduled to work overtime that evening. Harmon was still disturbed. Dr. Frey saw him talking to Mrs. Lane at the water cooler and went out to join them.

HARMON: What I can't understand is why Mr. Taylor didn't come to me. I could have explained everything, and the whole thing could have been prevented. But, boy! I guess I'm in the soup now. I want to see Mr. Dyer. It doesn't seem fair that he should only hear one side of the story.

FREY: Speaking about "sides of the story," maybe you would be interested in mine. [Frey proceeded to recount how Mr. Dyer had charged into his office and upbraided him for Harmon's conduct.]

MRS. LANE: If you ask me, I'm the gal with the responsibility. I've got to see Mr. Dyer first thing tomorrow morning.

The three continued to compare their versions of the "Office Boy Incident." Dr. Frey and Mrs. Lane were able to reconcile their suspicions of one another, although neither offered a formal apology to the other. Harmon, however, still felt upset. He told the others that nothing could clear up the situation until he had a chance to explain the matter directly to Mr. Dyer, which he planned to do the first thing the following day.

Early the next morning, Mrs. Lane explained the confusion to Mr. Dyer. At first, he became angry with Mr. Taylor for not giving him the complete account of the affair and said, "That's poor communication. If Mark is having trouble with his girl, I'll give him a pamphlet on how to communicate!"

Later, he grew aggravated with himself and finally became contrite: "I'm sorry—that's one of my failings. I should be able to control myself." Stewart was told that Mr. Dyer frequently made this sort of statement after a flare-up.

When Russell Harmon reported to work, he walked to Mrs. Lane's desk.

HARMON: Is Mr. Dyer in yet?

MRS. LANE: Well, yes, but the situation is all cleared up.

HARMON: Would it be all right if I saw him? I'd like to explain the thing to him.

MRS. LANE: Russell, I don't think you should do that. He knows that you weren't to blame, and I really think you should let the thing blow over.

After assurances from Mrs. Lane that he was "in the clear," Harmon decided to let the matter drop.

Several employees told Stewart that Mr. Clawson was out of town at the time of the incident. One of them added, "It probably wouldn't have made any difference if he had been here."

FIGURE 15-2

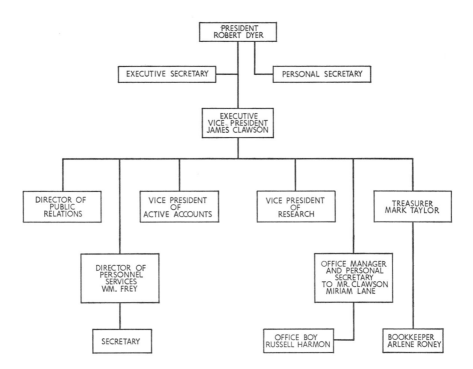

* The chart does not fully express the working relationships within the firm. Mr. Dyer frequently communicated directly with Mr. Taylor, the two vice presidents, and Mrs. Lane. Each of these also communicated directly with Dyer. Dyer also worked directly with Dr. Frey and the public relations director. These two men, however, rarely initiated direct relations with Mr. Dyer.

Part four

Overview
and bibliography

16
Overview

WE HAVE been examining human communications (the encoding and decoding phases, in particular) as they are influenced by assumptions held by the communicators involved. Some of these assumptions are destructive and troublesome because (1) they are false and imply an inadequate, distorted view of the world and (2) the communicator is usually unaware that his evaluations and communications are being influenced by them. Under these conditions, patterns of misevaluation and miscommunication are prone to occur and recur. Before summarizing the patterns we have considered, let us review Chapters 1 through 5, which laid the foundation for our examination of communication.

INTRODUCTION

Chapter 1 emphasized that human communication is a vital but complex and challenging process. Despite prodigious progress in the technical aspects of message transmission, storage, and reception, we still have much to learn about what happens *inside people* as they engage in communication.

The book's focus was to be on these latter aspects—the subtle, subjective, internal phenomena of human communication.

The organization of the book was described and the special role of the cases appended to the chapters was recommended as a means toward internalizing the contents of the chapters.

ORGANIZATIONAL CLIMATE
AND COMMUNICATION

Chapter 2 delineated a basic setting for communication behavior —the organization. An organization consists of a number of interdependent people who require coordination if their individual efforts are to serve most effectively the organization's objectives. Moreover, organizations are growing larger and more complex. They are challenged to respond to ever greater demands from society and especially from their own members. In consequence, the organization requires greater communication competence on the part of its managers and key personnel than ever before in history.

We then examined the overall aura or atmosphere of the organization, suggesting that a high-trust—high-performance cycle was desirable in the interests of both the individual and the organization. Conversely, a low-trust–low-performance cycle was to be prevented or, if already in effect, broken. McGregor's Theory Y, with a policy of *appropriate* trust coupled with personal development, seemed a tenable approach. The *integration* of individual and organizational goals appeared to be a sound objective.

PERCEPTION AND COMMUNICATION

Chapter 3 was the first of two chapters which focused on the individual. The basic premise of the chapter was that people respond not *directly* to reality but to their *perceptions* of reality. One's unwillingness or inability to internalize this truism can readily lead him to defensive and self-destructive behavior. The frame of reference construct was offered as a means for obviating the world-is-as-I-see-it presumption which insidiously sets the stage for unconstructive conflict. The self-image is an especially potent factor in determining the breadth and clarity of one's "frame."

The key to the situation appears to be the development of openness and the willingness to permit one's self-image to be changed in the direction of greater validity. Having clarified his own frame of reference one is eminently more able to assess accurately the frames of reference of others. By so doing he will be more able to understand them, predict their responses, and communicate with them.

MOTIVATION AND COMMUNICATION

In Chapter 4 we were still concerned with the individual but as a need-satisfying organism whose *needs influenced his perceptions* and thus his behavior (including his communication behavior). We agreed with Demosthenes: "The easiest thing of all is to deceive one's self; for what a man wishes he generally believes to be true." We explored several classifications of needs in order to determine a basis for understanding and predicting the behavior of others—mandatory skills for effective communicators.

THE PROCESS OF COMMUNICATION

Chapter 5 focused on the individual's *communication behavior* and presented a model of the communication process—encoding, transmitting, medium, receiving, decoding. We stressed encoding and decoding as the most subtle, least understood, and most neglected phases of the process. The insidious role of fallacious, unconsciously held assumptions was underscored. Such assumptions contribute to recurrent patterns of miscommunication—a consideration of some of the most troublesome of which constitutes the remainder of the book.

INFERENCE–OBSERVATION CONFUSION

The *inference-observation confusion* occurs when one somehow acts upon his inference *as if* it were his observation. In essence he takes a risk without being aware that he is taking one and is off guard, therefore, against the possibility that his inference is erroneous. The situation is not unlike that of walking downstairs in the dark—of striding off the last step, "certain" that you had reached the floor level!

One of the key reasons we often find it easy to accept inference for observation is that our *statements* of inference can be readily confused with *statements* of observation. That is, there is nothing in the nature of our language (grammar, spelling, pronunciation, syntax, and so on) which inescapably distinguishes between them. Thus the habit of differentiating *statements* of inference from *statements* of observation should go far in training one's acuity for distinguishing between inferences and observations on nonverbal levels.

Accordingly, a two-step procedure for coping with the inference-observation confusion was suggested:

> Step One—Be aware when inferring (largely by internalizing the characteristics of observational statements as distinguished from inferential statements).
>
> Step Two—Calculate the probability that the inference is correct.

Finally, it was argued that creativity and decisiveness are not incompatible with inference-awareness. Creativity can be facilitated when one is conscious of inferring. And the quality of decisions can be enhanced by inference-awareness.

The issue is not the *avoidance* of inferring (risk-taking) but the *awareness* of it.

BYPASSING

Bypassing occurs when communicators miss one another with their meanings—either by using the same word while meaning different things or by using different words while meaning the same thing. Resulting in false disagreements (or agreements), bypassings can sometimes be innocuous, even humorous. But on other occasions they can be significantly more costly and destructive.

Immediately underlying bypassing is the supposition that "words mean the same to the other fellow as they do to me." This belief, in turn, is supported by two insidious fallacies: that words have *mono-usage;* that words *have meanings.*

To guard against unintentional bypassing (deliberate bypassing was acknowledged), the communicator can supplant these assumptions with two others which represent much more adequately the relation between words and meanings: (1) most words, with the exception of some technical terms, are used in *more* than one way; (2) meanings exist not in words but only in the *people* who speak, hear, write, and read them; the people, who *fix the variables*—i.e., assign meanings to words.

Querying, paraphrasing, being approachable, and remaining alert to contexts, verbal and situational, are ways of implementing these premises.

ALLNESS

Allness is a sort of evaluational "disease." It occurs when one unconsciously assumes that it is possible to know and to say everything about something; that what he is saying (or writing or thinking) covers *all* there is (or all that is important) about the subject. The assumption is manifestly fallacious, and yet it is an extremely difficult one to dislodge if one does not recognize that he is inevitably and continuously abstracting.

To abstract is to select some details of a situation while neglecting all others. We abstract when we observe (see, hear, smell, and so on), talk, listen, write, read, think, and so forth.

When one fails to realize that he is abstracting, i.e., leaving out details, he is in distinct danger of believing that he has left out nothing—nothing of consequence, at any rate. Arrogance, intolerance of other viewpoints, and closed-mindedness are very frequent consequences of such false assurances.

Allness is encouraged by the craving for certainty—the intolerance of uncertainty, if you will—which afflicts all of us (*all* of us?) in some degree.

If one were to intensify his awareness of abstracting and thus avoid allness, he should:

1. Cultivate the humility to concede that he can never say or know everything about anything.
2. Recognize that abstracting is inevitable when he talks, listens, etc., for then he would be more likely . . .
   —to assess and perhaps improve the quality of his abstractions.
   —to be empathic.
   —to be creative and less inhibited by past practices.
3. "Remember the ETC.," a simple, yet effective device.
4. Free himself from the insularity of an "all-wall."

The essence of this chapter is not the *avoidance* but the *awareness* of abstracting. Accordingly, it was asserted that decisiveness and viability *are* compatible.

DIFFERENTIATION FAILURES

I. Indiscrimination

Indiscrimination occurs when one fails to recognize *differences* among the similarities. The frequent result is that one reacts to blacks, policemen, politicians, businessmen, Jews, and so forth, as if they were all identical—or at least enough alike to preclude any important differences. But people, situations, happenings, things, theories, and so forth, are unique. No two of anything are totally identical. And often there are differences which make a difference. The basic device for warding off dogmatic, unreasonable indiscriminations is the *Which Index*—black$_1$ is not the *same* as black$_2$, and so on.

II. Polarization

Polarization is the result of the confusion of *contraries* (situations involving graded variations, middle ground, alternatives) for *contradictories* (strict either-or, no-middleground affairs). It is the tendency to evaluate and communicate in black-and-white terms when shades of gray would be more appropriate.

An escalating conflict (the "pendulum effect") occurs when polarizers drive each other into extreme positions. This pattern of miscommunication is dangerous enough on the interpersonal level but on national and international levels it can be catastrophic.

Polarization can be prevented or at least diminished if we learn to distinguish contraries from contradictories and to apply the *How-Much Index*.

To cope with the pendulum effect, it is helpful to regard differing perceptions as the consequence of differing conditioning and to concede that in complicated problems no one (including ourselves) has *the one* complete and incontestable solution.

III. The frozen evaluation

The frozen evaluation generally occurs when one assumes nonchange. It tends to happen when one unconsciously believes that the way it (a person, a process, a situation, an object, and so on) is now is the way it has always been—or always will be. This can be a troublesome and dangerous premise because literally nothing (especially human beings) remains the same. Perhaps the only constant aspect about the world in which we live is its inconstancy.

We can keep ourselves alert to the process nature of life by habitually *When Indexing* (dating) our thoughts and statements. Man$_1$ [1963], after all, is not the same as Man$_1$ [1973].

INTENSIONAL ORIENTATION

I. A general statement

The chapter on intensional orientation did not deal with a specific pattern of miscommunication but rather with a general approach to "reality." One is *intensionally oriented* when he goes primarily, if not solely, by his "maps" (verbal and otherwise) of the "territory" rather than by the "territory" itself. An intensional parent, for example, would be guided by hazy memories of his own childhood, by the theories in Sunday supplement articles, and, by various child-rearing notions and nostrums of his generation to the virtual exclusion of his firsthand observations of the behavior of his child.

Intensional orientation invites trouble, confusion, and conflict because (1) often one's "maps" (his child-care theories and notions, for example) inadequately and fallaciously represent the "territory" (the flesh-and-blood child's feelings and behavior) and (2) one may be *unaware* that he is dealing primarily with these "maps" and not with the respective "territories" they represent. He may thus be led to react to the "territory" inappropriately, unintelligently, and even dangerously.

An examination of the map alone gives no information about the correspondence between it and the territory it is supposed to represent. Therefore, sanity and incessant reality-testing go hand in hand.[1]

The basic remedy for diminishing the destructive effects of intensional orientation is to "get extensional." That is, develop a readiness to go out and examine the "territory" rather than be content to be deluded by one's often spurious "maps." The byword of extensionality is to "look first—then talk."

II. "Pointing" and "associating"

Among the ways we use words are these: (1) simply to point to, or call attention to, what we are representing by the words and (2) to evoke associations (memories, feelings) for what we are referring to. "Jail," for example, may be used to point, figuratively, to the physical structure where prisoners are housed. But it may also be used to elicit an emotional response, as when one is threatened with "jail."

When one is unaware that words may be used for these dual purposes, there is the possibility of a number of miscommunication patterns, including the "pointing-association" confusion (the tendency for one to respond to the associations evoked in him by words *as if* he were responding to what was being represented by the words); "name calling" (the tendency for one's evaluation of a

---

[1] Anatol Rapoport, "Letter to a Soviet Philosopher," *ETC.: A Review of General Semantics,* Vol. 19, No. 4, February 1963, p. 141.

person to be influenced by the "associative" labels which have been applied to that person) ; and "associative" bypassing (the tendency for communicators to miss each other's "associative" meanings) .

III. Blindering

One's definition (i.e., his interpretation, size up, perception, appraisal, and so on) of a problem greatly influences his attempts at solving the problem. But a definition is inevitably an abstraction, a leaving out of details. If, then, in defining a problem, one is unaware that he is leaving out details (especially if they are important or vital details), he is in danger of becoming blindered—of unconsciously permitting his narrowed perception to restrict his attack on the problem. The basic correctives are (1) to remember that definitions inevitably involve the exclusion of details (perhaps crucial ones) and (2) to recognize and remove one's blinders. How to do the latter was discussed more specifically in the chapter.

UNDELAYED REACTIONS

Some undelayed reactions, such as reflex responses, are largely unavoidable, harmless, and even self-protective. Others, such as many reflexlike responses, may be highly useful when they have been properly conditioned and employed—the numerous actions of driving an automobile, for example. But some reflexlike responses—for instance, those manifested in fear and rage—are often destructive in their consequences. It is the latter which should be controlled if we are to avoid contributing to the harm of ourselves and others.

In some respects this was the key chapter of the book. Whereas the other chapters recommended various techniques, habits, and devices for avoiding and correcting the patterns of misevaluation and miscommunication, this chapter urged the basic setting for using them—the habit of delay-while-evaluating before action.

*   *   *

Our basic corrective methods, then, have been to suggest techniques for becoming (and remaining) *aware* of the insidious assumptions that influence our evaluation and communication and, second, to recommend the substitution of new, more adequate premises.

To implement these premises, I have suggested a number of valuational habits as substitutes for, or modifications of, some existing habits. Let the reader be cautioned, however. The firm, enduring acquisition of these deceptively "simple" habits will not come easily. They will require practice and persistence. The experience will not be unlike that of the person who for years has typed with two fingers and who is now learning the touch system of 10-finger typing. He may become discouraged, for his efficiency may decrease *at first*. But eventually he will develop a typing facility of which he had never thought himself capable.

With cultivation, then, these evaluational habits (Which, When, and How-Much Indexing; remembering the ETC.; querying and paraphrasing; distinguishing inference from observations; and so forth) can become "second-nature" conditioned responses that will pay handsome rewards in terms of more intelligent, safe, productive, and mature communicative behavior.

Bibliography

A bibliography
on communication,
organizational behavior,
and related areas

COMMUNICATION, ORGANIZATIONAL
BEHAVIOR

Ackoff, Russell L. "Towards a Behavioral Theory of Communication," *Management Science*, Vol. 4 (1958), pp. 218–34.

Adler, Mortimer. "Challenges of Philosophies in Communication," *Journalism Quarterly*, Vol. 40, No. 3 (Summer 1963).

Allen, Robert. "Communicative Skills and Applied Imagination," *Journal of Communication*, Vol. 8, No. 3 (Autumn 1958), pp. 137–41.

Aranguien, J. L. *Human Communication.* London: World University Library, 1967.

Argyris, Chris. *Integrating the Individual and the Organization.* New York: John Wiley & Sons, Inc., 1964.

———. *Interpersonal Competence and Organization Effectiveness.* Homewood, Ill.: Dorsey Press, 1962.

———. *Personality and Organization.* New York: Harper & Row, Publishers, 1957.

———. *Understanding Organizational Behavior.* Homewood, Ill.: Dorsey Press, 1960.

Armstrong, T. O. "Developing Effective Supervisor-Employee Communication," *Personnel*, Vol. 27 (July 1950), pp. 70–75.

Athos, Anthony G., and Coffey, Robert E. *Behavior in Organizations: A Multidimensional View.* Englewood Cliffs, N.J.: Prentice-Hall, 1968.

Ayer, A. J.; Haldane, J. B. S.; et al. *Studies in Communication.* London: Martin Secker & Warburg, 1955.

Babcock, C. Merton. *The Harper Handbook of Communications Skills*. New York: Harper & Row, Publishers, 1957.

Bales, Robert F. "Communication in Industry," *Harvard Business Review* (March–April, 1954) pp. 44–50.

———. *Personality and Interpersonal Behavior*. New York: Holt, Rinehart and Winston, Inc., 1970.

Barlow, Walter G. "Measuring the Effectiveness of Communication," *Key Problems in Human Relations*. American Management Association General Management Series, No. 181. New York, 1956.

Barnlund, Dean C. (ed.). *Interpersonal Communication: Survey and Studies*. Boston: Houghton Mifflin, 1968.

Bass, B. M. *Leadership, Psychology, and Organizational Behavior*. New York: Harper & Row, Publishers, 1960.

———, and Deep, Samuel D. *Studies in Organizational Psychology*. Boston: Allyn and Bacon, Inc., 1972.

Batten, Joe D. "Bare Knuckle Management or Fist-in-Glove Management?" *Factory* (October 1965), pp. 104–5.

Beller, Arlyn J., and Beller, Ronald. "Toward a Theory of Organization Communication: Consideration in Channel Selection," *The Journal of Business Communication*, Vol. 5, No. 2 (Winter 1967), pp. 5–21.

Benjamin, Robert E. "Communication Barriers between Employee and Employer," *Journal of Communication*, Vol. 3 (1953), pp. 124 ff.

Bennett, W. E. "Communication in Industry," *Journal of Communication*, Vol. 2, No. 2 (1952), pp. 38 ff.

Bennis, Warren G. "Leadership Theory and Administrative Behavior: The Problem of Authority," *Administrative Science Quarterly*, Vol. 4 (December 1959), pp. 259–301.

———; Schein, Edgar H.; Berlew, David E.; and Steele, Fred I. (eds.). *Interpersonal Dynamics: Essays and Readings on Human Interaction*. Homewood, Ill.: Dorsey Press, 1964.

Bergen, G. L., and Haney, W. V. *Organizational Relations and Management Action*. New York: McGraw-Hill Book Co., 1966.

Berlo, David K. *The Process of Communication*. New York: Holt, Rinehart & Winston, Inc., 1960.

Bernem, Eric. "Concerning the Nature of Communication," *Psychiatric Quarterly*, Vol. 27 (1953), pp. 185–98.

Bingham, W. V., and Moore, B. V. *How to Interview*. New York: Harper & Row, Publishers, 1959.

Blair, Claude M. "The Challenge of Technology in Communication," *Journalism Quarterly* (Special Supplement to Summer Issue, 1963).

Borden, George A. *An Introduction to Human Communication Theory*. Dubuque, Ia.: Wm. C. Brown Co., 1971.

Borman, Ernest G.; Howell, William S.; Nichols, Ralph G.; and Shapiro, George L. *Interpersonal Communication in the Modern Organization*. Englewood Cliffs, N.J.: Prentice-Hall, Inc., 1969.

Brown, Floyd H. "Management Use of Employee-Attitude Surveys," *Journal of Communication*, Vol. X, No. 2 (June 1960), pp. 95–99.

Bruner, Jerome S.; Goodnow, Jacqueline T.; and Austin, G. A. *A Study of Thinking*. New York: John Wiley & Sons, Inc., 1967.

Burling, Temple. "Aids and Bars to Internal Communication," *Hospitals*, Vol. 28 (November 1954).

Burnett, Verne. "Management's Tower of Babel," *Management Review* (June 1961), pp. 4–11.

Campbell, D. T. "Systematic Error on the Part of Human Links in Communication Systems," *Information and Control*, Vol. 1, 1958, pp. 334–69.

Campbell, James H., and Helper, Hal W. (eds.). *Dimensions in Communication*. Belmont, Calif.: Wadsworth Publishing Co., Inc., 1965.

Carter, Robert M. (ed.). *Communication in Organizations*. Detroit: Gale Research Co., 1972.

Cartier, Francis A., and Harwood, K. A. "On Definition of Communication," *Journal of Communication*, Vol. 3 (1953), pp. 71 ff.

Cases in Business Administration: Intercollegiate Bibliography, published and distributed on behalf of the Intercollegiate Contributors and the American Association of Collegiate Schools of Business. Vol. 1. Boston: Harvard Business School, Division of Research, 1957————. See especially cases listed under "Human Aspects of Administration."

Chase, Stuart. *Power of Words*. New York: Harcourt, Brace & World, Inc., 1954.

————. *Roads to Agreement*. New York: Harper & Row, Publishers, 1951.

Cherry, Colin. *On Human Communication*. New York: Technology Press of Massachusetts Institute of Technology Press and John Wiley & Sons, Inc., 1957.

Costello, T., and Zalkind, S. *Psychology in Administration*. Englewood Cliffs, N.J.: Prentice-Hall, Inc., 1963.

Crane, Edgar. *Marketing Communications*. New York: John Wiley & Sons, Inc., 1965.

Crocker, Lionel. "The Employer as a Communicator," *Journal of Communication*, Vol. 6, No. 4 (Winter 1956), pp. 162–66.

Crowley, Thomas W.; et al. *Modern Communication*. New York: Columbia University Press, 1962.

Cutlip, Scott M., and Center, Allen H.   *Effective Public Relations*. 4th ed. Englewood Cliffs, N.J.: Prentice-Hall, 1971.

Dahle, Thomas L.   "An Evaluation of Communication Skills Training," *Journal of Communication*, Vol. 9, No. 3 (September 1959), pp. 127–30.

―――.   "Transmitting Information to Employees: A Study of Five Methods," *Personnel*, Vol. 31 (November 1954), pp. 243–46.

Dance, Frank E. X. (ed.).   *Human Communication Theory: A Book of Readings*. New York: Holt, Rinehart & Winston, Inc., 1966.

―――.   "A Planned Communication Campaign for Businessmen," *Kansas Business Review*, Vol. 15 (November 1962)

Dandeneau, Richard J.   "How to Set Up an Employee Communications Program," *Management Methods*, Vol. 9, No. 3 (December 1955).

Darnell, Donald K.   "Toward a Reconceptualization of Communication," *The Journal of Communication*, Vol. 21 (March 1971), pp. 5–16.

Davis, Keith.   "Evolving Models of Organizational Behavior." *Academy of Management Journal*, Vol. 11, No. 1 (March 1968), pp. 27–38.

―――.   *Human Relations at Work*. 3d ed. New York: McGraw-Hill Book Co., 1967.

―――.   "Making Constructive Use of the Office Grapevine" in *Human Relations in Management* (eds. I. L. Heckmann, Jr. and S. G. Huneryager), pp. 334–46. Cincinnati: South-Western Publishing Co., 1960.

―――.   "Studying Communication Patterns in Organizations," *Studies in Personnel and Industrial Psychology* (ed. Edwin A. Fleishman), Homewood, Ill.: Dorsey Press, 1961.

―――.   "Success of Chain-of-Command Oral Communication in a Manufacturing Management Group," *Academy of Management Journal*, Vol. 11, No. 4 (December 1968), pp. 379–87.

―――, and Scott, William G.   *Readings in Human Relations*. New York: McGraw-Hill Book Co., 1964.

Davitz, Joel R., and Davitz, Lois Jean.   "Correlates of Accuracy in the Communication of Feelings," *Journal of Communication*, Vol. 9, No. 3 (September 1959), pp. 110–17.

Dee, James P.   "Oral Communication in the Trade Union Local," *Journal of Communication*, Vol. 10, No. 2 (June 1960), pp. 77–85.

Deutsch, Karl W.   "On Communication Models in the Social Sciences," *Public Opinion Quarterly*, Vol. 16, No. 3 (Fall 1952).

Deutsch, M.   "Trust and Suspicion," *Journal of Conflict Resolution*, Vol. 2 (1959), pp. 265–79.

Dimock, Hedley G.   "Improving Communication Skills through Training," *Journal of Communication*, Vol. 11, No. 4 (September 1961), pp. 149–56.

Dooher, M. Joseph, and Marquis, Vivienne. *Effective Communication on the Job*. Rev. ed. New York: American Management Association, Inc., 1963.

Dover, C. J. "An Analysis of Interpretative Communication Management," *Journal of Communication*, Vol. 8, No. 3 (Autumn 1958), pp. 99–105.

———. *Effective Communication in Company Publications*. Chicago: The Bureau of National Affairs, Inc., 1959.

———. "The Three Eras of Management Communication," *Journal Communication*, Vol. 9, No. 4 (December 1959), pp. 168–72.

Dubin, Robert. *Human Relations in Administration*. 2d ed. New York: Prentice-Hall, Inc., 1961.

Eisenson, Jon; Auer, J. Jeffrey; and Irwin, John V. *The Psychology of Communication*. New York: Appleton-Century-Crofts, 1963.

Elbing, Alvar O. *Behavioral Decisions in Organizations*. Glenview, Ill.: Scott, Foresman, 1970.

Emmert, Philip, and Brooks, William D. *Methods of Research in Communication*. Boston: Houghton Mifflin Co., 1970.

Employee Communication: Executive Summary. New York: General Electric.

Employee Communications for Better Understanding. Rev. ed. New York: National Association of Manufacturers.

Feinberg, Mortimer R. "Performance Appraisal and Executive Morale," *Management Review*, Vol. 50 (June 1961), pp. 25–31.

Festinger, Leon; et al. "Study of Rumor: Its Origin and Spread," *Human Relations*, Vol. 1 (August 1958).

Filley, Alan C., and House, Robert J. *Managerial Process and Organizational Behavior*. Glenview, Ill.: Scott, Foresman, 1969.

Fisk, George (ed.). *The Frontiers of Management Psychology*. New York: Harper & Row, Publishers, 1964.

Fleishman, E. A. *Studies in Personnel and Industrial Psychology*. Homewood, Ill.: Dorsey Press, 1961.

Flippo, Edwin B. *Management: A Behavioral Approach*. Boston: Allyn and Bacon, Inc., 1970.

Freedman, William A. "A Study in Communication," *Journal of Communication*, Vol. 9, No. 1 (March 1959), pp. 27–31.

Froman, Robert. "How to Say What You Mean; Business Communication." *Nation's Business*, Vol. 45 (May 1957), pp. 76–78.

———. "Make Words Fit the Job," *Nation's Business*, Vol. 47 (July 1959), pp. 76–79.

"Fundamentals of Communications," *Management Record*, National Industrial Conference Board (September 1954).

Gardner, Burleigh B., and Moore, David G.   *Human Relations in Industry.*
4th ed. Homewood, Ill.: Richard D. Irwin, Inc., 1964.

Gellerman, Saul W.   *The Management of Human Relations.* New York: Holt,
Rinehart & Winston, Inc., 1966.

Gerber, George.   "Toward a General Model of Communication," *Audio-
Visual Communication Review,* Vol. 4 (Summer 1956).

Giffin, Kim, and Patton, Bobby R.   *Basic Readings in Interpersonal Communication.* New York: Harper and Row, 1971.

———— and ————.   *Fundamentals of Interpersonal Communication.* New York:
Harper and Row, 1971.

Glenn, Edmund S.   "Interpretation and Intercultural Communication,"
ETC: A Review of General Semantics, Vol. 15, No. 2 (Winter 1957–58).

————.   "Meaning and Behavior: Communication and Culture," *The
Journal of Communication,* Vol. 16, No. 4 (December 1966).

Glover, John Desmond, and Hower, Ralph M.   *The Administrator: Cases on
Human Relations in Business.* 4th ed. Homewood, Ill.: Richard D. Irwin,
Inc., 1963.

Goetzinger, C. S., and Valentine, M. A.   "Communication Channels,
Media, Directional Flow, and Attitudes in an Academic Community,"
Journal of Communication, Vol. 11, No. 1 (March 1961), pp. 23–26.

————, and ————.   "Communication Patterns, Interactions, and Attitudes of Top-Level Personnel in the Air Defense Command," *Journal of
Communication,* Vol. 13, No. 1 (March 1963), pp. 54–57.

Goyer, Robert S.   "Communication, Communicative Process, Meaning:
Toward a Unified Theory," *Journal of Communication,* Vol. 20, No. 1
(March 1970), pp. 4–16.

————.   "Communication Process: An Operational Approach," in *Perspective On Communication* (Larson, C., and Dance, F. X., eds.), Milwaukee,
Wis.: University of Wisconsin, 1968.

Greenberg, Joseph H.   *Language, Culture, and Communication.* Stanford, Calif.:
Stanford University Press, 1971.

Guest, Robert H.   *Organizational Change: The Effect of Successful Leadership.*
Homewood, Ill.: Richard D. Irwin, Inc. and The Dorsey Press, 1962.

Haire, Mason.   "Psychological Problems Relevant to Business and Industry," *Psychological Bulletin,* Vol. 56 (1959), pp. 169–94.

————.   *Psychology in Management.* 2d ed. New York: McGraw-Hill Book
Co., 1964.

Hampton, D. R.; Summer, C. E.; and Webber, R. A.   *Organizational
Behavior and the Practice of Management.* Glenview, Ill.: Scott, Foresman,
1968.

Haney, William V.   "A Comparative Study of Unilateral and Bilateral

Communication," *Academy of Management Journal*, Vol. 7, No. 2 (June 1964), pp. 128–36.

————. "Serial Communication of Information in Organizations" (eds. Sidney Mailick and Edward H. Van Ness), *Concepts and Issues in Administrative Behavior*. Englewood Cliffs, N.J.: Prentice-Hall, Inc., 1962, pp. 150–65. Reprinted in *ETC: A Review of General Semantics*, Vol. 21, No. 1 (March 1964), pp. 13–29.

Heckmann, I. L., and Huneryager, S. G. *Human Relations in Management*. 2d ed. Cincinnati: South-Western Publishing Co., 1967.

Heider, F. *The Psychology of Interpersonal Relations*. New York: John Wiley & Sons, Inc., 1958.

Hersey, Paul, and Blanchard, K. H. *Management of Organizational Behavior*. Englewood Cliffs, N.J.: Prentice-Hall, 1969.

Hodge, Billy J., and Johnson, Herbert J. *Management and Organizational Behavior*. New York: John Wiley and Sons, Inc., 1970.

Human Relations. Quarterly, Vol. 1 (1947.48————).
"Human Relations: Where Do We Stand Today?" (Thomas G. Spates, "Human Relations: How Far Have We Come?"; Peter F. Drucker, "Human Relations: How Far Do We Have to Go?"; Chris Argyris, "Human Relations: A Look into the Future"), *Management Record* (March 1959).

Indik, B. P.; Georgopoulos, B. S.; and Seashore, S. E. "Superior-Subordinate Relationships and Performance," *Personnel Psychology*, Vol. 14 (1961), pp. 357–74.

Jackson, Jay M. "The Organization and Its Communication Problem," *Advanced Management*, Vol. 24 (February 1959), pp. 17–20.

Janis, I. L., and Feshbach, S. "Effect of Fear-Arousing Communications," *Journal of Abnormal and Social Psychology*, Vol. 48 (January 1953), pp. 78–92.

Janis, Jack Harold (ed.). *Business Communication Reader*. New York: Harper & Row Publishers, 1959.

Johannsen, James R., and Edmunds, Carolyn Y. *Annotated Bibliography on Communication in Organizations*. La Jolla, Calif.: Western Behavioral Science Institute, 1962.

Johnson, F. Craig, and Klare, George R. "General Models of Communication Research: A Survey of the Developments of a Decade," *The Journal of Communication*, Vol. 11, No. 1 (March 1961), pp. 13–26.

Johnson, Kenneth G. "Understanding the Communication Process," *Extension Insights*. Newsletter of the University of Wisconsin Extension Division, Madison, Wisconsin.

Johnson, Wendell. "The Fateful Process of Mr. A Talking to Mr. B," *Harvard Business Review*, Vol. 31 (January 1953), pp. 49–56.

Kegel, Charles H., and Stevens, Martin. *Communication: Principles and Practice*. Belmont, Calif.: Wadsworth Publishing Co., Inc., 1959.

Kelly, Joe. *Organizational Behavior*. Homewood, Ill.: Richard D. Irwin, Inc., 1969.

Knowles, W. H. "Human Relations in Industry: Research and Concepts," *California Management Review*, Vol. 1 (1958), pp. 87–105.

Knudson, Harry R., Jr. *Human Elements of Administration*. New York: Holt, Rinehart & Winston, Inc., 1963.

Kolasa, Blair J. *Introduction to Behavioral Science for Business*. New York: John Wiley and Sons, Inc., 1969.

Kornhauser, A. "Observations on the Psychological Study of Labor-Management Relations," *Personnel Psychology*, Vol. 14 (1961), pp. 241–49.

Krech, David; Crutchfield, Richard; and Ballachey, E. L. *Individual in Society*. New York: McGraw-Hill Book Co., 1962.

Kuriloff, Arthur H. "An Experiment in Management—Putting Theory *Y* to the Test," *Personnel*, Vol. 40 (November 1963), pp. 8–17.

Kyle, Aileen L. "Employee Commitment to Company Goals," *Management Record* (September 1962), pp. 2–10.

Larson, C., and Dance, F. E. X. (eds.). *Perspectives on Communication*. Milwaukee, Wis.: University of Wisconsin, 1968.

Lawrence, Paul R. "How to Deal with Resistance to Change," *Harvard Business Review* (May–June 1954).

————; Seiler, John A.; et al. *Organizational Behavior and Administration*. 2d ed. Homewood, Ill.: Richard D. Irwin, Inc., 1965.

Leavitt, Harold J. *Managerial Psychology*. Rev. ed. Chicago: University of Chicago Press, 1964.

————. "Unhuman Organizations," *Harvard Business Review*, Vol. 40 (July 1962), pp. 90–98.

————, and Bass, B. M. "Organizational Psychology," *Annual Review of Psychology*, Vol. 15 (1964), pp. 371–98.

————, and Pondy, Louis R. (eds.). *Readings in Managerial Psychology*. Chicago: The University of Chicago Press, 1964.

Lee, Irving J. *Customs and Crises in Communication*. New York: Harper & Row, Publishers, 1954.

————. *How to Talk with People*. New York: Harper & Row, Publishers, 1952.

————. "Procedure for 'Coercing' Agreement," *Harvard Business Review*, Vol. 32, No. 1 (January 1954), pp. 39–45.

————, and Lee, Laura L. *Handling Barriers in Communication*. New York: Harper & Row, Publishers, 1957.

Leeseberg, D. G. "Management's Dilemma—Theory 'X' v Theory 'Y,' *The Chicago Purchaser* (August 1966), pp. 30–34.

Likert, Rensis. *The Human Organization, Its Management and Value.* New York: McGraw-Hill, 1967.

———. *New Patterns in Management.* New York: McGraw-Hill Book Co., 1961.

Lippitt, Gordon L.; This, Leslie E.; and Bidwell, Robert G. *Optimizing Human Resources.* Reading, Mass.: Addison-Wesley, 1971.

Longnecker, Justin G. *Principles of Management and Organizational Behavior.* 2d ed. Columbus, Ohio: Charles E. Merrill Pub. Co., 1969.

Loomis, J. L. "Communication, the Development of Trust, and Cooperative Behavior," *Human Relations,* Vol. 12 (1959), pp. 305–15.

McCroskey, James C.; Larson, Carl E.; and Knapp, Mark L. *An Introduction to Interpersonal Communications.* Englewood Cliffs, N.J.: Prentice-Hall, 1971.

McGregor, Douglas. "The Human Side of Enterprise," *Adventure in Thought and Action.* (Proceedings of the 5th Anniversary Convocation of the School of Industrial Management, Massachusetts Institute of Technology, April 9, 1957).

———. *The Human Side of Enterprise.* New York: McGraw-Hill Book Co., 1960.

McLuhan, Marshall. *Understanding Media.* New York: McGraw-Hill Book Co., 1964.

McMurray, Robert N. "Are You the Kind of Boss People Want to Work For?" *Business Management,* Vol. 28 (August 1965), pp. 59–60.

McNair, Malcolm P. "Thinking Ahead, What Price Human Relations?" *Harvard Business Review,* Vol. 35, No. 2 (March–April 1957).

Macrorie, Ken. *The Perceptive Writer, Reader, and Speaker.* New York: Harcourt, Brace & World, Inc., 1959.

Maier, Norman R. F., et al. *Communication in Organizations.* Ann Arbor: Foundation for Research on Human Behavior, 1959.

———. *Superior-Subordinate Communication.* New York: American Management Association, Inc., 1961.

Mambert, W. A. *The Elements of Effective Communication.* Washington, D.C.: Acropolis Books, 1971.

Mandell, Milton M., and Duckworth, Pauline. "The Supervisor's Job: A Survey," *Personnel,* Vol. 31 (March 1955), pp. 456–62.

Marrow, Alfred J. *Making Management Human.* New York: McGraw-Hill Book Co., 1957.

Maslow, Abraham H. *Eupsychian Management.* Homewood, Ill.: Richard D. Irwin, Inc. and The Dorsey Press, 1965.

————. *Toward a Psychology of Being.* Princeton, N.J.: D. Van Nostrand Co., Inc., 1962.

Mayo, Elton. *The Human Problems of an Industrial Civilization.* Boston: Harvard Business School, Division of Research, 1945.

————. *The Social Problems of an Industrial Civilization.* Boston: Harvard Business School, Division of Research, 1945.

Megginson, Leon C. *Personnel: A Behavioral Approach to Administration.* Rev. ed. Homewood, Ill.: Richard D. Irwin, Inc., 1972.

Mehling, Reuben. "A Study of Nonlogical Factors of Reasoning in the Communication Process," *Journal of Communication,* Vol. 9, No. 3 (September 1959), pp. 118–26.

Mehrabian, A., and Reed, H. "Some Determinants of Communication Accuracy," *Psychological Bulletin,* Vol. 70 (1968), pp. 365–81.

Mellinger, Glen D. "Interpersonal Trust as a Factor in Communication," *Journal of Abnormal and Social Psychology,* Vol. 52 (May 1956).

Menninger, William C., and Levinson, Harry. *Human Understanding in Industry: A Guide for Supervisors.* Chicago: Science Research Associates, Inc., 1956.

Merrihue, Willard V. *Managing by Communication.* New York: McGraw-Hill Book Co., 1960.

Miller, George A. *The Psychology of Communication: Seven Essays.* New York: Basic Books, 1967.

Moser, George V. "How Not to Influence People," *Management Record* (March 1958).

Murray, Elwood. "How an Educator Looks at Industrial Activities in the Field of Communication," *Journal of Communication,* Vol. 6, No. 2 (1956), pp. 51–55.

Nafziger, Ralph O., and White, David M. *Introduction to Mass Communications Research.* Baton Rouge, La.: Louisiana State University Press, 1958.

National Industrial Conference Board. *Behavioral Science: Concepts and Management Application.* New York, 1969.

Newman, John B. "Communication: A Dyadic Postulation," *Journal of Communication,* Vol. 9, No. 2 (June 1959), pp. 51–58.

Nilsen, Thomas R. "Some Assumptions That Impede Communication," *General Semantics Bulletin,* Nos. 14 and 15 (Winter–Spring 1954).

Parker, John P. "Some Organizational Variables and Their Effect upon Comprehension," *Journal of Communication,* Vol. 12, No. 1 (March 1962), pp. 27–32.

Parry, John. *The Psychology of Human Communication*. London: University of London Press, 1967.

Pepinsky, H. B.; Weick, K. E.; and Riner, J. W. *Primer for Productivity*. Columbus, O.: Ohio State University Research Foundation, 1964.

Peters, Raymond W. *Communication within Industry*. New York: Harper & Row, Publishers, 1950.

Petrullo, L., and Bass, B. M. *Leadership and Interpersonal Behavior*. New York: Holt, Rinehart & Winston, Inc., 1961.

Pfeiffer, J. William, and Jones, John E. *A Handbook of Structured Experiences for Human Relations*, Vols. I, II, III. Iowa City, Ia.: University Associates Press, 1969, 1970, 1971.

Pigors, Paul. "Communication in Industry: A Cure of Conflict?" *Industrial and Labor Relations Review* (July 1953).

————; Myers, Charles A.; and Malm, F. T. *Management of Human Resources: Readings in Personnel Administration*. New York: McGraw-Hill Book Co., 1964.

Platt, James H. "What Do We Mean, 'Communication'?" *Journal of Communication*, Vol. 5, No. 1 (1955), pp. 21–26.

Porter, Donald E.; Applewhite, Philip B.; and Misshavk, Michael J. (eds.). *Studies in Organizational Behavior and Management*. 2d ed. Scranton, Pa.: Intext Educational Publishers, 1971.

Public and Employee Relations Research Service. *Leadership Style and Employee Morale*. New York: General Electric, 1958.

Read, W. H. "Some Factors Affecting the Accuracy of Upward Communication at Middle Management Levels in Industrial Organizations." (Doctoral dissertation, University of Michigan, 1960).

Redding, W. Charles, and Sanborn, George (eds.). *Business and Industrial Communication: A Source Book*. New York: Harper & Row, Publishers, 1964.

Redfield, Charles E. *Communication in Management*. Rev. ed. Chicago: University of Chicago Press, 1958.

————. "Communication: The Lifestream of Every Organization," *Harvard Office Management*, Vol. 18 (March 15, 1957).

Research Group in Psychology and the Social Sciences. *The Technology of Human Behavior*. Washington, D.C.: Smithsonian Institution, 1960.

Richard, James E. "A President's Experience with Democratic Management," *Occasional Paper Series*, No. 18. Chicago: Industrial Relations Center, University of Chicago, 1960. Abstracted in *The Executive* (November 1960).

Roethlisberger, Fritz J. "The Administrator's Skill: Communication," *Harvard Business Review*, Vol. 31 (November 1953), pp. 55–62.

————. "Barriers to Communication between Men," *Northwestern University Information*, Vol. 20, No. 25 (April 21, 1952).

————. "The Foreman: Master and Victim of Double Talk," *Harvard Business Review*, Vol. 23 (1945), pp. 283–98.

————. "Human Relations in Industry: A Problem of Communication," *General Semantics Bulletin*, Nos. 14 and 15 (Winter–Spring 1954).

————. *Management and Morale.* Cambridge, Mass.: Harvard University Press, 1952.

————, and Dickson, William J.   *Management and the Worker.* Cambridge, Mass.: Harvard University Press, 1950.

————; Lombard, George F. F.; and Ronken, Harriett O.   *Training for Human Relations.* Harvard Business School, Division of Research, 1954.

Rosenfeld, J. M., and Smith, M. J.   "The Emergence of Management Theory *Z*," *Personnel Journal*, Part I (October 1965) and Part II (November 1965).

Ross, A. M., and Hartman, P. T.   *Changing Patterns of Industrial Conflict.* New York: John Wiley & Sons, Inc., 1960.

Ruesch, J., and Bateson, G.   *Communication: The Social Matrix of Society.* New York: W. W. Norton & Co., Inc., 1951.

————, and Kees, Weldon.   *Nonverbal Communication.* Berkeley, Calif.: University of California Press, 1956.

Saltonstall, Robert.   *Human Relations in Administration.* New York: McGraw-Hill Book Co., 1959.

Sayles, Leonard R.   *Managerial Behavior.* New York: McGraw-Hill Book Co., 1964.

————, and Strauss, George.   *Human Behavior in Organizations.* Englewood Cliffs, N.J.: Prentice-Hall, Inc., 1966.

Schachter, Stanley, and Burdick, Harvey.   "A Field Experiment on Rumor Transmission and Distortion," *Journal of Abnormal and Social Psychology*, Vol. 50, No. 3 (May 1955).

Schein, Edgar H.   *Organizational Psychology.* Englewood Cliffs, N.J.: Prentice-Hall, Inc., 1965.

Schmidt, W. H., and Tannenbaum, R.   "Management of Differences," *Harvard Business Review*, Vol. 38, No. 6 (November 1960), pp. 107–15.

Schramm, Wilbur.   "How Communication Works" in *The Process and Effects of Mass Communication* (ed. W. Schramm). Urbana, Ill.: University of Illinois Press, 1954.

————. "Mass Communication," *Annual Review of Psychology*, Vol. 13 (1962), pp. 251–84.

————, and Roberts, Donald F.   *The Process and Effects of Mass Communication.* Rev. ed. Urbana, Ill.: University of Illinois Press, 1971.

———— (ed.).   *The Science of Human Communication.* New York: Basic Books, Inc., Publishers, 1963.

Schutte, William, and Steinberg, Erwin. *Communication in Business and Industry*. New York: Holt, Rinehart & Winston, Inc., 1960.

Schutz, William C. *FIRO: A Three-Dimensional Theory of Interpersonal Behavior*. New York: Holt, Rinehart & Winston, Inc., 1960.

————. "The Interpersonal Underworld," *Harvard Business Review* (July–August 1958).

Scott, William E., and Cummings, Larry L. *Readings in Organizational Behavior and Human Performance*. Rev. ed. Homewood, Ill.: Richard D. Irwin, 1973.

Scott, William G. *Human Relations in Management*. Homewood, Ill.: Richard D. Irwin, Inc., 1962.

————. *Organization Theory: A Behavioral Analysis for Management*. Homewood, Ill.: Richard D. Irwin, Inc., 1967.

————, and Mitchell, Terrence R. *Organization Theory: A Structural and Behavioral Analysis*. Rev. ed. Homewood, Ill.: Richard D. Irwin, Inc., 1972.

Secord, P. F., and Blackman, C. W. *Social Psychology*. New York: McGraw-Hill Book Co., 1964.

Seiler, John. *Systems Analysis in Organizational Behavior*. Homewood, Ill.: Richard D. Irwin, Inc., 1967.

Sereno, Kenneth K., and Morlensen, C. David. *Foundations of Communication*. New York: Harper and Row, 1970.

Sexton, R., and Staudt, V. "Business Communication: A Survey of the Literature," *Journal of Social Psychology*, Vol. 50 (1959), pp. 101–18.

Shannon, C., and Weaver, W. *The Mathematical Theory of Communication*. Urbana, Ill.: University of Illinois Press, 1949.

Simpson, R. L. "Vertical and Horizontal Communication in Formal Organizations," *Administrative Science Quarterly*, Vol. 4 (September 1959), pp. 188–96.

Singer, T. E. R. (ed.). *Information and Communication Practice in Industry*. New York: Reinhold Publishing Corp., 1958.

Smith, A. G. (ed.). *Communication and Culture, Readings in the Codes of Human Interaction*. New York: Holt, Rinehart & Winston, Inc., 1966.

Smith, Henry Clay. *Psychology of Industrial Behavior*. 2d ed. New York: McGraw-Hill Book Co., 1964.

Solomon, Arthur. *Interpersonal Communication: A Cross-Disciplinary Approach*. Springfield, Ill.: Charles C. Thomas, Publisher, 1970.

Sondel, Bess. *Communication: A Field Theory*. Chicago: University of Chicago Press, 1958.

Stagner, Ross. *The Psychology of Industrial Conflict*. New York: John Wiley & Sons, Inc., 1956.

Steinberg, Charles S.   *The Communicative Arts.* New York: Hastings House, 1971.

Stieglitz, Harold.   "Barriers to Communications," *Management Record*, National Industrial Conference Board, Vol. 20 (January 1958), pp. 2–5.

Strauss, George, and Sayles, Leonard.   *Personnel: The Human Problems of Management.* Englewood Cliffs, N.J.: Prentice-Hall, Inc., 1960.

Sutermeister, Robert.   *People and Productivity.* New York: McGraw-Hill Book Co., 1963.

Tannenbaum, A. S.   "Control in Organizations: Individual Adjustment and Organizational Performance," *Seminar on Basic Research in Management Controls.* Stanford, Calif.: Stanford University Press, 1963.

Tannenbaum, Robert; Wechsler, Irving R.; and Massarik, Fred.   *Leadership and Organization: A Behavioral Science Approach.* New York: McGraw-Hill Book Co., 1961.

Tarr, J. C.   "Improving Communication in the Air Force," *Journal of Communication*, Vol. 9, No. 2 (June 1959), pp. 77–82.

Thayer, Lee O.   *Administrative Communication.* Homewood, Ill.: Richard D. Irwin, Inc., 1961.

———.   *Communication and Communication Systems: In Organization, Management and Interpersonal Relations.* Homewood, Ill.: Richard D. Irwin, 1970.

Thompson, Wayne N.   *Fundamentals of Communication: An Integrated Approach.* New York: McGraw-Hill Book Co., 1957.

Toward Understanding Men. Topeka, Kan.: Menninger Foundation, Division of Industrial Mental Health, 1956.

Vardaman, George T.   *Effective Communication of Ideas.* New York: Van Nostrand Reinhold Co., 1970.

———, and Halterman, Carroll C.   *Managerial Control through Communication.* New York: John Wiley & Sons, Inc., 1968.

———; ———; and Vardaman, Patricia Black.   *Cutting Communications Costs and Increasing Impacts.* New York: John Wiley and Son, Inc., 1970.

Vroom, Victor H.   "Industrial Social Psychology," *Handbook of Social Psychology.* Vol. II, 2d ed., Lindzey, G., and Aronson, E. (eds.) Reading, Mass.: Addison-Wesley, 1968.

Watzlawick, Paul; Beavin, Janet H.; and Jackson, Don D.   *Pragmatics of Human Communication.* New York: W. W. Norton, 1967.

Webb, Wilse B.   "Elements in Individual-to-Individual Communication," *Journal of Communication*, Vol. 7, No. 3 (Autumn 1957), pp. 119–24.

Weick, Karl E.   *The Social Psychology of Organizing.* Reading, Mass.: Addison-Wesley, 1969.

Weiss, E. B.   "A Revolution in Communication," *Marketing Insights* (November 14, 21, 28, 1966; December 5, 1966; and January 16, 23, 1967).

Weissenberg, Peter. *Introduction to Organization Behavior*. Scranton, Pa.: Intext Educational Publishers, 1971.

Westley, Bruce H., and MacLean, Malcomb S., Jr. "A Conceptual Model for Communications Research," *Audio-Visual Communication Review*, Vol. 3, No. 1 (Winter 1955).

Whyte, William F. *Men at Work*. Homewood, Ill.: Richard D. Irwin, Inc., 1961.

––––––. *Organizational Behavior: Theory and Applications*. Homewood, Ill.: Richard D. Irwin, Inc., 1969.

––––––. *Pattern for Industrial Peace*. New York: Harper & Row, Publishers, 1951.

Whyte, William H., and the Editors of *Fortune*. *Is Anybody Listening?* New York: Simon and Schuster, Inc., 1952.

Wickesberg, A. K. "Communication Network in the Business Organization Structure," *Academy of Management Journal*, Vol. 11, No. 3 (September 1968), pp. 253–62.

Wiener, Norbert. *The Human Use of Human Beings*. Boston: Houghton Mifflin Co., 1950.

Wiksell, Wesley. *Do They Understand You?* New York: The Macmillan Co., 1960.

Wood, Roy V.; Yamauchi, Joanne S.; and Bradac, James J. "The Communication of Meaning Across Generations," *The Journal of Communication*. Vol. 21 (June 1971), pp. 160–69.

Zaleznik, Abraham, and Moment, David. *The Dynamics of Interpersonal Behavior*. New York: John Wiley & Sons, Inc., 1964.

Zelko, Harold P. *Management-Employee Communication in Action*. Cleveland: Howard Allen, Inc., Publishers, 1957.

––––––. "Trends in Oral Communication Training in Business and Industry," *Journal of Communication*, Vol. 12, No. 2 (June 1962), pp. 106–16.

ORGANIZATION, MANAGEMENT

Albers, Henry H. *Principles of Organization and Management*. 3d ed. New York: John Wiley & Sons, Inc., 1969.

Allen, Louis. *The Management Profession*. New York: McGraw-Hill Book Co., 1964.

Barnard, Chester I. *The Functions of the Executive*. Cambridge, Mass.: Harvard University Press, 1938.

Bass, Bernard M. *Organizational Psychology*. Boston: Allyn & Bacon, Inc., 1965.

––––––, and Leavitt, H. J. "Experiments in Planning and Operating," *Management Science*, Vol. 9, No. 4 (1963), pp. 574–85.

Beckhard, Richard. *Organization Development: Strategies and Models.* Reading, Mass.: Addison-Wesley, 1969.

Bellows, Roger; Gilson, Thomas Q.; and Odiorne, George S. *Executive Skills: Their Dynamics and Development.* Englewood Cliffs, N.J.: Prentice-Hall, Inc., 1962.

Bennis, Warren G.; Benne, Kenneth D.; and Chin, Robert. *The Planning of Change.* Holt, Rinehart & Winston, Inc., 1961.

Blake, Robert Rogers. *Corporate Excellence Through Grid Organization Development.* Houston: Gulf, 1968.

Blau, P. M., and Scott, W. R. *Formal Organizations.* San Francisco: Chandler Publishing Co., 1962.

Campbell, J.; et. al. *Managerial Behavior, Performance and Effectiveness.* New York: McGraw-Hill, 1970.

Champion, John M., and Bridges, Francis J. *Critical Incidents in Management.* Rev. ed. Homewood, Ill.: Richard D. Irwin, Inc., 1969.

Clough, D. J. *Concepts in Management Science.* Englewood Cliffs, N.J.: Prentice-Hall, Inc., 1963.

Cooper, W. W.; Leavitt, H. J.; and Shelly, M. W., II. *New Perspectives in Organization Research.* New York: John Wiley & Sons, Inc., 1964.

Cyert, R. M., and March, J. G. *A Behavioral Theory of the Firm.* Englewood Cliffs, N.J.: Prentice-Hall, Inc., 1963.

Dale, Ernest. *Management: Theory and Practice.* New York: McGraw-Hill Book Co., 1965.

Dalton, M. "Managing the Managers" in *Some Theories of Organization* (eds. A. H. Rubenstein, and C. J. Haverstroh). Homewood, Ill.: Richard D. Irwin, Inc., 1960.

Donnelly, James H., Jr.; Gibson, James L.; and Ivancevich, John M. *Fundamentals of Management: Functions, Behavior, Models.* Homewood, Ill.: Richard D. Irwin, Inc., 1971.

———; ———; and ——— (eds.). *Management: Selected Readings.* Homewood, Ill.: Richard D. Irwin, Inc., 1971.

Drucker, Peter Ferdinand. *The Effective Executive.* New York: Harper & Row, 1967.

———. *Managing for Results.* New York: Harper & Row, Publishers, 1964.

———. *The Practice of Management.* New York: Harper & Row, Publishers, 1954.

Etzioni, Amitai. *A Comparative Analysis of Complex Organizations: On Power, Involvement, and Their Correlates.* New York: The Free Press, Division of The Macmillan Co., 1961.

——— (ed.). *Complex Organizations: A Sociological Reader.* New York: Holt, Rinehart & Winston, Inc., 1961.

————. *Modern Organizations*. Englewood Cliffs, N.J.: Prentice-Hall, Inc., 1964.

Flippo, Edwin B. *Management: A Behavioral Approach*. 2d ed. Boston: Allyn and Bacon, Inc., 1970.

French, J. R. P., Jr. "The Effects of the Industrial Environment on Mental Health: A Theoretical Approach," *American Psychologist*, Vol. 15 (1960).

French, Wendell, and Hellriegel, Don. *Personnel Management and Organization Development*. Boston: Houghton Mifflin, 1971.

Goulder, Alvin (ed.). *Studies in Leadership*. New York: Harper & Row, Publishers, 1960.

Haire, Mason (ed.). *Modern Organization Theory*. New York: John Wiley & Sons, Inc., 1959.

———— (ed.). *Organization Theory in Industrial Practice*. New York: John Wiley & Sons, Inc., 1962.

Jay, Antony. *Management and Machiavelli*. New York: Holt, Rinehart, & Winston, 1968.

Jennings, Eugene E. *An Anatomy of Leadership*. New York: Harper & Row, Publishers, 1960.

Johnson, Rossall J. *Executive Decisions*. 2d ed. Cincinnati: South-Western Publishing Co., 1970.

Jones, Manley Howe. *Executive Decision Making*. Rev. ed. Homewood, Ill.: Richard D. Irwin, Inc., 1962.

Jucius, Michael I. *Personnel Management*. 7th ed. Homewood, Ill.: Richard D. Irwin, Inc., 1971.

Kahn, R. L.; Wolfe, D. M.; Quinn, R. P.; Snoek, J. D.; and Rosenthal, R. A. *Organizational Stress: Studies in Role Conflict and Ambiguity*. New York: John Wiley & Sons, Inc., 1964.

Katz, Daniel, and Kahn, Robert L. *The Social Psychology of Organization*. New York: Wiley, 1967.

Koontz, Harold, and O'Donnell, Cyril. *Management: A Book of Readings*. 3d ed. New York: McGraw-Hill Book Co., 1972.

————. *Principles of Management*. 5th ed. New York: McGraw-Hill Book Co., 1972.

Latané, Henry A.; Mechanic, David; Strauss, George; Strother, George B.; and Leavitt, Harold J. (eds.). *The Social Science of Organizations*. Englewood Cliffs, N.J.: Prentice-Hall, Inc., 1963.

Leavitt, H. J. "Recent Concepts in Administration," *Personnel Psychology*, Vol. 13 (1960), pp. 287–94.

————, and Whisler, T. L. "Management in the 1980's," *Harvard Business Review*, Vol. 36 (1958), pp. 41–48.

Lippitt, Gordon L. *Organization Renewal: Achieving Viability in a Changing World*. New York: Appleton, 1969.

Litterer, Joseph. *The Analysis of Organizations*. Englewood Cliffs, N.J.: John Wiley & Sons, Inc., 1965.

———— (ed.). *Organizations: Structure and Behavior*. 2d ed. Vols. 1 & 2. New York: John Wiley & Sons, Inc., 1969.

McFarland, Dalton E. *Management: Principles and Practice*. 3d ed. New York: The Macmillan Co., 1970.

McGregor, Douglas. *The Professional Manager*. New York: McGraw-Hill, 1967.

Mailick, Sidney, and Van Ness, Edward H. (eds.). *Concepts and Issues in Administrative Behavior*. Englewood Cliffs, N.J.: Prentice-Hall, Inc., 1962.

March, James G. *A Handbook of Organizations*. Skokie, Ill.: Rand McNally & Co., 1965.

————, and Simon, H. A. *Organizations*. New York: John Wiley & Sons, Inc., 1958.

Mee, John F. *Management Thought in a Dynamic Society*. New York: New York University Press, 1963.

Megley, John E. "Management and the Behavioral Sciences: Theory Z." *Personnel Journal*, Vol. 49, No. 5 (May 1970), pp. 216–21.

Metcalf, H. C., and Urwick, L. (eds.). *Dynamic Administration. The Collected Papers of Mary Parker Follett*. Bath, England: Management Public Trust, 1941.

Moore, Franklin G. *Management: Organization and Practice*. New York: Harper & Row, Publishers, 1964.

———— (ed.). *A Management Sourcebook*. New York: Harper & Row, Publishers, 1964.

Myers, M. Scott. *Every Employee a Manager*. New York: McGraw-Hill Book Co., 1970.

Newman William H. *Administrative Action*. 2d ed. Englewood Cliffs, N.J.: Prentice-Hall, Inc., 1963.

————; Summer, Charles E., Jr.; and Warren, E. Kirby. *The Process of Management*. 3d ed. Englewood Cliffs, N.J.: Prentice-Hall, Inc., 1972.

Odiorne, George. *Personnel Administration by Objectives*. Homewood, Ill.: Richard D. Irwin, 1971.

Parkinson, C. N. *Parkinson's Law, and Other Studies in Administration*. Boston: Houghton Mifflin Co., 1957.

Peter, Lawrence. *The Peter Prescription*. New York: Morrow, 1972.

————. *The Peter Principle*. New York: Morrow, 1969.

Pfiffner, John M., and Sherwood, Frank P. *Administrative Organization*. Englewood Cliffs, N.J.: Prentice-Hall, Inc., 1960.

Pigors, Paul, and Myers, Charles A. *Personnel Administration.* 6th ed. rev. New York: McGraw-Hill Book Co., 1969.

Reddin, W. J. *Managerial Effectiveness.* New York: McGraw-Hill, 1970.

Rubenstein, Albert H., and Haberstroh, Chadwick J. (eds.). *Some Theories of Organization.* Homewood, Ill.: Richard D. Irwin, Inc., 1960.

Schein, Edgar H. *Process Consultation: Its Role in Organization Development.* Reading, Mass.: Addison-Wesley, 1969.

Schull, Fremont A., and Delbecq, Andre L. *Selected Readings in Management.* Homewood, Ill.: Richard D. Irwin, Inc., 1962.

Simon, H. A. *Administrative Behavior.* 2d ed. New York: The Macmillan Co., 1957.

Simonds, Rollin H.; Ball, Richard E.; and Kelley, Eugene E. *Business Administration: Problems and Functions.* Boston: Allyn & Bacon, Inc., 1962.

Summer, Charles E., Jr., and O'Connell, Jeremiah J. *The Managerial Mind.* Rev. ed. Homewood, Ill.: Richard D. Irwin, Inc., 1968.

Suojanen, Waino W. *The Dynamics of Management.* New York: Holt, Rinehart & Winston, Inc., 1966.

Terry, George R. *Principles of Management.* 5th ed. Homewood, Ill.: Richard D. Irwin, Inc., 1968.

Thompson, V. W. *Modern Organization: A General Theory.* New York: Alfred A. Knopf, Inc., 1961.

Tosi, H. L., and Carrol, J. S. "Management Reaction to Management by Objectives," *Academy of Management Journal,* Vol. 11, No. 4 (December 1968), pp. 415–26.

Townsend, Robert. *Up the Organization.* New York: Knopf, 1970.

Wadia, Maneck S. *Management and the Behavioral Sciences: Text and Readings.* Boston, Mass.: Allyn and Bacon, Inc., 1968.

Wasmuth, William J.; et al. *Human Resources Administration: Problems of Growth and Change.* Boston: Houghton Mifflin, 1970.

PERCEPTION

Allport, F. H. *Theories of Perception and the Concept of Structure.* New York: John Wiley & Sons, Inc., 1955.

Bartley, S. Howard. *Principles of Perception.* New York: Harper & Row, Publishers, 1958.

Blake, R. R., and Ramsey, G. V. (eds.). *Perception: An Approach to Personality.* New York: The Ronald Press Co., 1951.

Beardslee, David C., and Wertheimer, Michael. *Readings in Perception.* Princeton, N.J.: D. Van Nostrand Co., Inc., 1958.

Bender, I. E., and Hastorf, A. H. "On Measuring Generalized Empathic

Ability (Social Sensitivity)," *Journal of Abnormal and Social Psychology*, Vol. 48 (1958), pp. 503–06.

Broadbent, Donald E. *Perception and Communication.* New York: Pergamon Press, Inc., 1958.

Bronfenbrenner, U. "Toward an Integrated Theory of Personality" (eds. R. R. Blake, and G. V. Ramsey), *Perception: An Approach to Personality.* New York: The Ronald Press Co., 1951.

Brouwer, Paul J. "The Power to See Ourselves," *Harvard Business Review*, Vol. 42 (November 1964), pp. 156–62.

Bruner, Jerome S. "Social Psychology and Perception" in *Readings in Social Psychology* (eds. E. Maccoby; T. M. Newcomb; and E. L. Hartley). 3d ed. New York: Holt, Rinehart & Winston, Inc., 1958.

————, and Krech, David. (eds.). *Perception and Personality.* New York: Greenwood Press, 1966.

Cline, V. B., and Richards, J. N., Jr. "Accuracy of Interpersonal Perception—A General Trait?" *Journal of Abnormal and Social Psychology*, Vol. 60 (1960), pp. 1–7.

Cronbach, L. J. "Processes Affecting Scores on 'Understanding of Others' and 'Assumed Similarity,'" *Psychological Bulletin*, Vol. 52 (1955), pp. 177–93.

Crow, W. J. "Effect of Training on Interpersonal Perception," *Journal of Abnormal and Social Psychology*, Vol. 55 (1957), pp. 355–59.

Dearborn, D. C., and Simon, H. A. "Selective Perception: A Note on the Departmental Identifications of Executives," *Sociometry*, Vol. 21 (1958), pp. 140–44.

Ferullo, Robert J. "The Self-Concept in Communication," *Journal of Communication*, Vol. 13 (1963), pp. 77–86.

Feshbach, S., and Singer, R. "The Effects of Fear-Arousal and Suppression of Fear upon Social Perception," *Journal of Abnormal and Social Psychology*, Vol. 55 (1957), pp. 283–88.

Festinger, L. *A Theory of Cognitive Dissonance.* Evanston, Ill.: Row, Peterson, 1957.

Frenkel-Brunswik, Else. "Personality Theory and Perception" in *Perception: An Approach to Personality* (eds. R. R. Blake and G. V. Ramsey). New York: The Ronald Press Co., 1951.

Frye, R.; Cassens, F. P.; and Vegas, O. V. "Learning Set as a Determinant of Perceived Cooperation and Competition," *American Psychologist*, Vol. 19 (1964).

Gibb, Jack R. "Defense Level and Influence Potential in Small Groups," in *Leadership and Interpersonal Behavior* (eds. L. Petrullo, and B. M. Bass), pp. 66–81. New York: Holt, Rinehart & Winston, 1961).

————. "Defensive Communication," *Journal of Communication*, Vol. 11, No. 3 (September 1961), pp. 141–48.

————. "Sociopsychological Processes of Group Instruction," in *The Dynamics of Instructional Groups* (ed. N. B. Henry), pp. 115–35. 59th Yearbook of the National Society for the Study of Education, Part 2, 1960.

Haire, M., and Grunes, W. F. "Perceptual Defenses: Processes Protecting an Original Perception of Another Personality," *Human Relations*, Vol. 3 (1958), pp. 403–12.

Harrison, R. L. "Workers' Perceptions and Job Success," *Personnel Psychology*, Vol. 12 (Winter 1959), 619–25.

Hirst, R. J. *The Problems of Perception*. New York: The Macmillan Co., 1959.

Horney, Karen. *Neurosis and Human Growth: The Struggle Toward Self-Realization*. New York: W. W. Norton & Co., Inc., 1950.

Ittleson, William. *The Ames Demonstrations in Perception*. Princeton, N.J.: Princeton University Press, 1952.

Jourard, Sidney M. *The Transparent Self*. New York: D. Van Nostrand, 1964.

Klein, G. S. "The Personal World Through Perception" in *Perception: An Approach to Personality* (eds. R. R. Blake and G. V. Ramsey). New York: The Ronald Press Co., 1951.

Lawler, E. E., and Porter, L. W. "Perceptions Regarding Management Compensation," *Industrial Relations*, Vol. 3 (1963), pp. 41–49.

Livingston, J. Sterling. "Pygmalion in Management," *Harvard Business Review*, Vol. 47, No. 4 (July–August 1969), pp. 81–89.

Luft, J. "Monetary Value and the Perception of Persons," *Journal of Social Psychology*, Vol. 46 (1957), 245–51.

Porter, L. W. "Differential Self-Perceptions of Management Personnel and Line Workers," *Journal of Applied Psychology*, Vol. 42 (1958), pp. 105–09.

————. "Job Attitudes in Management. I. Perceived Deficiencies in Need Fulfillment as a Function of Job Level," *Journal of Applied Psychology*, Vol. 46 (December 1962), pp. 375–84.

————. "Self-Perceptions of First-Level Supervisors Compared with Upper Management Personnel and with Operative Line Workers," *Journal of Applied Psychology*, Vol. 43 (1959), pp. 183–86.

————. "A Study of Perceived Need Satisfactions in Bottom and Middle Management Jobs," *Journal of Applied Psychology*, Vol. 45 (1961), pp. 1–10.

————, and Ghiselli, E. E. "The Self-Perceptions of Top and Middle Management Personnel," *Personnel Psychology*, Vol. 10 (1957), pp. 397–406.

Rogers, C. R. *Client-Centered Therapy*. Boston: Houghton Mifflin Co., 1951.

————. "Communication: Its Blocking and Its Facilitation," *Northwestern University Information*, Vol. 20, No. 25, pp. 9–15.

————. "A Theory of Therapy, Personality, and Interpersonal Relationships, as Developed in the Client-Centered Framework" in *Psychology: The Study of a Science, Vol. 3 Formulations of the Person and the Social Context* (ed. Sigmund Koch). New York: McGraw-Hill Book Co., 1959.

Rosenbaum, M. E.   "Social Perception and the Motivational Structure of Interpersonal Relations," *Journal of Abnormal and Social Psychology*, Vol. 59 (1959), 130–33.

Sebald, H.   "Limitations of Communication: Mechanisms of Image Maintenance in Form of Selective Perception, Selective Memory, and Selective Distortion," *The Journal of Communication*, Vol. 12, No. 3 (September 1962), pp. 142–49.

Smith, H. C.   *Sensitivity to Perception.* New York: McGraw-Hill Book Co., 1966.

Solley, C. M., and Murphy, G.   *Development of the Perceptual World.* New York: Basic Books, Inc., Publishers, 1960.

Taft, R.   "The Ability to Judge People," *Psychological Bulletin*, Vol. 52 (1955), pp. 1–23.

Tagiuri, R., and Petrullo, L. (eds.).   *Person Perception and Interpersonal Behavior.* Stanford, Calif.: Stanford University Press, 1958.

Vroom, V. H.   "*The Effects of Attitudes on Perception of Organizational Goals,*" *Human Relations*, Vol. 13, No. 3 (1960), pp. 229–40.

————. "Projection, Negation, and the Self Concept," *Human Relations*, Vol. 12, No. 4 (1959), pp. 335–44.

Weaver, C. H.   "Measuring Point of View As a Barrier to Communications." *Journal of Communication*, Vol. 7, No. 1 (Spring 1957), pp. 5–13.

————. "The Quantification of the Frame of Reference in Labor-Management Communication," *Journal of Applied Psychology*, Vol. 42 (1958), pp. 1–9.

Zalkind, S. S., and Costello, T. W.   "Perception: Some Recent Research and Implications for Administration," *Administrative Science Quarterly*, Vol. 7 (September 1962), pp. 218–35.

MOTIVATION, FRUSTRATION, COGNITIVE DISSONANCE

Adams, J. S., and Rosenbaum, W. B.   "The Relationship of Worker Productivity to Cognitive Dissonance About Wage Inequities," *Journal of Applied Psychology*, Vol. 46 (June 1962), pp. 161–64.

Allport, G. W.   "The Functional Autonomy of Motives," *The Nature of*

Personality: Collected Papers. Reading, Mass.: Addison-Wesley Publishing Co., Inc., 1950.

Belcher, David W. "Toward a Behavioral Science Theory of Wages," *Journal of the Academy of Management,* Vol. 5, No. 2 (August 1962), pp. 102–16.

Boulding, Kenneth. *Conflict and Defense: A General Theory.* New York: Harper & Row, Publishers, 1962.

Chung, Kae H. "Developing a Comprehensive Model of Motivation and Performance," *Academy of Management Journal,* Vol. 11, No. 1 (March 1968), pp. 63–73.

Clark, J. V. "Motivation in Work Groups: A Tentative View," *Human Organization,* Vol. 19, No. 4 (1960–61), pp. 199–208.

Cofer, Charles N., and Appley, Mortimer H. *Motivation: Theory and Research.* New York: John Wiley & Sons, Inc., 1964.

Dalton, Gene W., and Lawrence, Paul R. *Motivation and Control in Organizations.* Homewood, Ill.: Richard D. Irwin, Inc., 1971.

Ericson, Richard F. "Rationality and Executive Motivation," *Journal of the Academy of Management,* Vol. 5, No. 1 (April 1962), pp. 7–23.

Ewing, David W., and Fenn, Dan H., Jr. *Incentives for Executives.* New York: McGraw-Hill Book Co., 1962.

Festinger, Leon A. "The Motivating Effect of Cognitive Dissonance in *Assessment of Human Motives*" (ed. G. Lindzey), pp. 65–86. New York: Holt, Rinehart & Winston, Inc., 1958.

———. *A Theory of Cognitive Dissonance.* Stanford, Calif.: Stanford University Press, 1962.

Gellerman, Saul W. *Management by Motivation.* New York: American Management Association, 1968.

———. *Motivation and Productivity.* New York: American Management Association, Inc., 1963.

Hall, D. T., and Nougaim, K. E. "An Examination of Maslow's Need Hierarchy in an Organizational Setting," *Organizational Behavior and Human Performance,* Vol. 5, No. 1 (February 1968), pp. 12–35.

Herzberg, Frederick. "One More Time: How Do You Motivate Employees?" *Harvard Business Review* (January–February 1968), p. 59.

———. *Work and the Nature of Man.* Cleveland: The World Publishing Company, 1966.

———; Mausner, B.; and Snyderman, B. *The Motivation to Work.* 2d ed. New York: John Wiley & Sons, Inc., 1962.

House, R. J., and Wigdor, L. A. "Herzberg's Dual-Factor Theory of Job Satisfaction and Motivation," *Personnel Psychology,* Vol. 20, No. 4 (Winter 1967), pp. 369–389.

Huxley, Aldous. "Human Potentialities," *Bulletin of the Menninger Clinic*, Vol. 25, No. 2 (March 1961), pp. 54–55.

Klein, G. S. "Cognitive Control and Motivation" in *Assessment of Human Motives* (ed. G. Lindzey). New York: Holt, Rinehart & Winston, Inc., 1958.

Lewin, Kurt. *A Dynamic Theory of Personality*. Trans. Donald K. Adams and Karl E. Zener. New York: McGraw-Hill Book Co., 1935.

McClelland, David C. "Business Drive and National Achievement," *Organization and Human Behavior* (ed. G. D. Bell). Englewood Cliffs, N.J.: Prentice-Hall, Inc., 1967.

———; Atkinson, J. W.; Clark, R. A.; and Lowell, E. L. *The Achievement Motive*. New York: Appleton-Century-Crofts, 1953.

——— (ed.). *Studies in Motivation*. New York: Appleton-Century-Crofts, 1955.

McGregor, Douglas. *Leadership and Motivation* (eds. Warren G. Bennis and Edgar H. Shein). Cambridge, Mass.: Massachusetts Institute of Technology Press, 1966.

Maier, N. R. F. *Frustration*. New York: McGraw-Hill Book Co., 1949.

Maslow, Abraham H. *Motivation and Personality*. 2d ed. New York: Harper & Row, Publishers, 1970.

Munn, N. L. *Psychology: The Fundamentals of Human Adjustment*. 4th ed. Boston: Houghton Mifflin Co., 1961.

Myers, M. S. "Who Are Your Motivated Workers?" *Harvard Business Review* (January–February 1966).

Patton, Arch. *Men, Money, and Motivation*. New York: McGraw-Hill Book Co., 1961.

Schachter, Stanley. *Psychology of Affiliation*. Stanford, Calif.: Stanford University Press, 1959.

Skinner, B. F. *Science and Human Behavior*. New York: Macmillan Co., 1953.

Slater, C. W. "Some Factors Associated with Internalization of Motivation Towards Occupational Role Performance." (Doctoral dissertation, University of Michigan, 1959).

Stagner, R. "Motivational Aspects of Industrial Morale," *Personnel Psychology*, Vol. 11 (Spring 1958), pp. 64–70.

Vroom, Victor H. "Ego–Involvement, Job Satisfaction, and Job Performance," *Personnel Psychology*, Vol. 15 (Summer 1962), pp. 159–77.

———. *Work and Motivation*. New York: John Wiley & Sons, Inc., 1964.

Whyte, William F. *Money and Motivation*. New York: Harper & Row, Publishers, 1955.

Young, Paul T. *Motivation and Emotion.* New York: John Wiley & Sons, Inc., 1961.

Youngberg, C. F. X.; Hedberg, R.; and Baxter, B. "Management Action Recommendations Based on One vs. Two Dimensions of a Job Satisfaction Questionnaire," *Personnel Psychology,* Vol. 15 (1962), pp. 145–50.

Zaleznik, A.; Christensen, C. R.; and Roethlisberger, F. J. *The Motivation, Productivity, and Satisfaction of Workers: A Prediction Study.* Boston: Harvard Business School, Division of Research, 1958.

COMMUNICATION PROCESSES

Speaking

Anderson, Kenneth E. *Persuasion: Theory and Practice.* Boston: Allyn and Bacon, 1971.

Baird, A. Craig, and Knower, Franklin H. *General Speech.* 3d ed. New York: McGraw-Hill Book Co., 1963.

Barker, Larry L., and Kibler, Robert J. (eds.). *Speech Communication Behavior: Perspectives and Principles.* Englewood Cliffs, N.J.: Prentice-Hall, 1971.

Bosmajian, Haig A. *Readings in Speech.* 2d ed. New York: Harper and Row, 1971.

Brandes, Paul D., and Smith, William S. *Building Better Speech.* New York: Noble & Noble, Publishers, Inc., 1964.

Brigance, W. N. *Speech—Its Disciplines and Techniques in a Free Society.* 2d ed. New York: Appleton-Century-Crofts, 1961.

Bryant, Donald, and Wallace, Karl. *Oral Communication.* 3d ed. New York: Appleton-Century-Crofts, 1962.

Capp, Glenn R. *Basic Oral Communication.* Englewood Cliffs, N.J.: Prentice-Hall, Inc., 1971.

Clevenger, Theodore, Jr., and Matthews, Jack. *Speech Communcation Process.* Glenview, Ill.: Scott, Foresman and Co., 1971.

Crocker, Lionel. *Business and Professional Speech.* New York: The Ronald Press Co., 1951.

Cronkhite, Gary. *Persuasion: Speech and Behavioral Change.* Indianapolis: Bobbs-Merrill Co., 1969.

Dance, Frank E. X., and Larson, Carl. *Speech Communication: Functions, Modes and Roles.* New York: Holt, Rinehart and Winston, 1972.

Dickens, Milton. *Speech: Dynamic Communication.* 2d ed. New York: Harcourt, Brace & World, Inc., 1963.

Gibson, James W. *Speech Organization—A Programmed Approach.* San Francisco: Rinehart Press, 1971.

Gilman, Wilbur E.; Aly, Bower; and White, Hollis L. *The Fundamentals of Speaking.* 2d ed. New York: The Macmillan Co., 1964.

Hance, Kenneth G.; Ralph, David C.; and Wiksell, Milton J. *Principles of Speaking.* Belmont, Calif.: Wadsworth Publishing Co., Inc., 1962.

Howell, Wm. S., and Bormann, Ernest G. *Presentational Speaking for Business and the Professions.* New York: Harper and Row, 1971.

Huston, Alfred D.; Sandberg, Robert A.; and Mills, Jack. *Effective Speaking in Business.* Rev. ed. Englewood Cliffs, N.J.; Prentice-Hall, Inc., 1955.

Jeffrey, Robert C., and Peterson, Owen. *Speech: A Text with Adapted Readings.* Scranton, Pa: Harper & Row, 1971.

Jensen, J. Vernon. *Perspectives on Oral Communication.* Boston: Holbrook Press, 1970.

Keltner, John W. *Interpersonal Speech Communication: Elements and Structures.* Belmont, Calif.: Wadsworth Publishing Co., Inc., 1970.

McBurney, James H., and Wrage, Ernest J. *The Art of Good Speech.* New York: Prentice-Hall, Inc., 1953.

Martin, Howard H., and Anderson, Kenneth E. *Speech Communication: Analyses and Readings.* Boston: Allyn and Bacon, 1971.

Martin, John M. *Business and Professional Speaking.* New York: Harper & Row, Publishers, 1956.

Martin, Robert C.; Robinson, Karl F.; and Tomlinson, Russell C. *Practical Speech for Modern Business.* New York: Appleton-Century-Crofts, 1963.

Minnick, Wayne C. *The Art of Persuasion.* 2d ed. Cambridge, Mass.: Riverside Press, 1968.

Monroe, Alan. *Principles and Types of Speech.* 5th ed. Chicago: Scott, Foresman, 1962.

Murray, Elwood. *Integrative Speech: Speech-Communications in Human Management.* Denver: University of Denver Press, 1949.

Nichols, Ralph G., and Lewis, Thomas R. *Listening and Speaking.* Dubuque: William C. Brown Company, Publishers, 1954.

Oliver, Robert T., and Cortright, Rupert L. *Effective Speech.* 5th ed. New York: Holt, Rinehart & Winston, Inc., 1970.

———; Zelko, Harold P.; and Holtzman, Paul D. *Communicative Speech.* New York: Holt, Rinehart & Winston, Inc., 1962.

Phillips, David C. *Oral Communication in Business.* New York: McGraw-Hill Book Co., 1955.

Robinson, Karl F., and Lee, Charlotte. *Speech in Action.* Glenview, Ill.: Scott, Foresman, Inc., 1965.

Ross, Raymond S. *Speech Communication: Fundamentals and Practice*. 2d ed. Englewood Cliffs, N.J.: Prentice-Hall, Inc., 1970.

Sandford, W. P., and Yeager, W. H. *Principles of Effective Speaking*. 6th ed. New York: The Ronald Press Co., 1963.

Sarett, Lew; Foster, William Trufant; and Sarett, Alma Johnson. *Basic Principles of Speech*. 3d rev. ed. Boston: Houghton Mifflin Co., 1958.

Smith, Raymond G. *Speech-Communication: Theory and Models*. New York: Harper and Row Publishers, 1970.

Stedman, William. *A Guide to Public Speaking*. Englewood Cliffs, N.J.: Prentice-Hall, Inc., 1971.

Stewart, Charles J. (ed.). *On Speech Communication*. New York: Holt, Rinehart & Winston, 1972.

Tacey, William S. *Business and Professional Speaking*. Dubuque, Ia.: Wm. C. Brown Co., 1970.

Thompson, Wayne N. *Modern Argumentation and Debate: Principles and Practices*. New York: Harper and Row, 1971.

Verderber, Rudolph. *The Challenge of Effective Speaking*. Belmont, Calif.: Wadsworth Publishing Co., 1970.

Weaver, A. T., and Ness, O. G. *The Fundamentals and Forms of Speech*. Rev. ed. New York: The Odyssey Press, Inc., 1963.

————, and ————. *An Introduction to Public Speaking*. New York: The Odyssey Press, Inc., 1961.

Weldon, Terry A., and Ellingsworth, Huber W. *Effective Speech Communication: Theory in Action*. Glenview, Ill.: Scott, Foresman, 1970.

Zelko, Harold P. "Practical Training in Effective Speaking," *Journal of the American Society of Training Directors* (January 1958).

————, and Dance, Frank E. X. *Business and Professional Speech*. New York: Holt, Rinehart & Winston, Inc., 1965.

Writing

Adelstein, Michael E. *Contemporary Business Writing*. New York: Random House, Inc., 1971.

Aurner, R. *Effective Communications in Business*. 5th ed. Cincinnati: South-Western Publishing Co., 1967.

Berenson, Conrad, and Colton, Raymond. *Research and Report Writing in Business and Economics*. New York: Random House, 1970.

Bromage, W. C. *Writing for Business*. Ann Arbor, Mich.: G. Wahr Co., 1964.

Brown, Leland. *Communicating Facts and Ideas in Business*. 2d ed. Englewood Cliffs, N.J.: Prentice-Hall, Inc., 1970.

Cloke, Marjane, and Wallace, Robert. *The Modern Business Letter Writer's Manual.* Garden City, N.Y.: Doubleday and Co., Inc., 1969.

Comer, David B., III, and Spillman, Ralph R. *Modern Technical and Industrial Reports.* New York: G. P. Putnam's Sons, 1962.

Devlin, Frank J. *Business Communication.* Homewood, Ill.: Richard D. Irwin, Inc., 1968.

———. *Progress Guide and Workbook for Business Communication.* Homewood, Ill.: Richard D. Irwin, Inc., 1968.

Egleson, Janet Frank. *Design for Writing.* Beverly Hills, Calif.: Glencoe Press, 1970.

Estrin, H. A. (ed.). *Technical and Professional Writing: A Practical Anthology.* New York: Harcourt, Brace & World, Inc., 1963.

Gaum, Carl G.; Groves, Harold F.; and Hoffman, Lyne S. *Report Writing.* New York: Prentice-Hall, Inc., 1965.

Godfrey, J. W., and Parr, G. *The Technical Writer.* New York: John Wiley & Sons, Inc., 1959.

Hay, Robert D. *Written Communications for Business Administrators.* New York: Holt, Rinehart, & Winston, Inc., 1965.

Himstreet, W. D., and Baty, W. M. *Business Communications.* 3d ed. Belmont, Calif.: Wadsworth Publishing Co., Inc., 1969.

Janis, J. Harold. *Writing and Communicating in Business.* New York: The Macmillan Co., 1964.

Jones, W. Paul. *Writing Scientific Papers and Reports.* 6th ed. Dubuque: William C. Brown Co., 1971.

Keithley, Erwin M., and Thompson, Margaret H. *English for Modern Business.* 2d ed. Homewood, Ill.: Richard D. Irwin, Inc., 1972.

Leiskar, Raymond V. *Business Communication: Theory and Application.* Rev. ed. Homewood, Ill.: Richard D. Irwin, Inc., 1972.

———. *Report Writing for Business.* 3d ed. Homewood, Ill.: Richard D. Irwin, Inc., 1969.

Lindauer, J. S. *Writing in Business.* Riverside, N.J.: The Macmillan Co., 1971.

McLaughlin, T. J.; Blum, L. P.; and Robinson, D. E. *Communication.* Columbus, Ohio: Charles E. Merrill Books, Inc., 1964.

Mandel, Siegfried. *Writing for Science and Technology.* New York: Dell, 1970.

Menning, J. H., and Wilkinson, C. W. *Communicating through Letters and Reports.* 5th ed. Homewood, Ill.: Richard D. Irwin, Inc., 1972.

Murphy, Herta A., and Peck, Charles E. *Effective Business Communication.* New York: McGraw-Hill Book Co., 1972.

Parkhurst, C. C. *Business Communications for Better Human Relations.* Englewood Cliffs, N.J.: Prentice-Hall, Inc., 1961.

Perrin, Porter G.   *Writer's Guide and Index to English.* 3d ed. Glenview, Ill.: Scott, Foresman, 1959.

Robinson, David M.   *Writing Reports for Management Decisions.* Columbus, O.: Charles E. Merrill, 1969.

Schultz, H., and Webster, R. G.   *Technical Report Writing.* New York: David McKay Co., Inc., 1964.

Shurter, Robert L., and Williamson, J. Peter.   *Written Communication in Business.* 3d ed. New York: McGraw-Hill Book Co., 1971.

————; ————; and Broehl, Wayne G., Jr.   *Business Research and Report Writing.* New York: McGraw-Hill Book Co., 1965.

Schutte, W., and Steinberg, Erwin R.   *Communication in Business and Industry.* New York: Holt, Rinehart & Winston, Inc., 1962.

Sigband, Norman B.   *Communication for Management.* Glenview, Ill.: Scott, Foresman, 1969.

————.   *Effective Report Writing, For Business, Industry, and Government.* New York: Harper & Row, Publishers, 1960.

Sklare, Arnold B.   *Creative Report Writing.* New York: McGraw-Hill Book Co., 1964.

Smart, W. K.; McKelvey, L. W.; and Gerfen, R. C.   *Business Letters.* 4th ed. New York: Harper & Row, Publishers, 1957.

Strong, E. P., and Weaver, R. G.   *Writing for Business and Industry.* Boston: Allyn & Bacon, Inc., 1962.

Strunk, W., and White, E. B.   *The Elements of Style.* 2d ed. New York: The Macmillan Co., 1972.

Tichy, H. J.   *Effective Writing.* New York: John Wiley and Sons, Inc., 1967.

Turner, Rufus P.   *Technical Report Writing.* San Francisco: Rinehart Press, 1971.

Ulman, Joseph N., and Gould, Jay R.   *Technical Reporting.* 3d ed. New York: Holt, Rinehart & Winston, Inc., 1972.

Van Hagan, Charles E.   *Report Writer's Handbook.* Englewood Cliffs, N.J.: Prentice-Hall, Inc., 1961.

Vardaman, Patricia Black.   *Forms for Better Communication.* New York: Van Nostrand Reinhold, 1970.

Weeks, F. W. (ed.).   *Readings in Communication from Fortune.* New York: Holt, Rinehart & Winston, Inc., 1961.

Weisman, Herman M.   *Basic Technical Writing.* Columbus, O.: Charles E. Merrill Books, Inc., 1962.

————.   *Technical Correspondence.* New York: John Wiley and Sons, 1968.

Wilcox, Sidney W.   *Technical Communication.* Scranton, Pa.: International Textbook Co., 1962.

Wilkinson, C. W.; Menning, J. H.; and Anderson, C. A. *Writing for Business.* 3d ed. Homewood, Ill.: Richard D. Irwin, Inc., 1960.

Winfrey, Robley. *Technical and Business Report Preparation.* 3d ed. Ames, Ia.: Iowa State University Press, 1962.

Wolseley, Roland E. *Critical Writing for the Journalist.* Philadelphia: Chilton Books—Educational Division, 1959.

Listening

Barbara, Dominick A. *The Art of Listening.* Springfield, Ill.: Charles C. Thomas, Publisher, 1966.

————. *How to Make People Listen to You.* Springfield, Ill.: Charles C. Thomas, Publisher, 1971.

Barker, Larry L. *Listening Behavior.* Englewood Cliffs, N.J.: Prentice-Hall, Inc., 1971.

Bird, Donald E. "Bibliography of Selected Materials about Listening," *Education* (January 1955).

————. "Teaching Listening Comprehension," *Journal of Communication,* Vol. 3 (1953), pp. 127 ff.

Carter, Raymond. "Listening Improvement Training Programs in Business and Industry in the United States." (M.A. thesis, University of Kansas, 1963).

Connelly, J. Campbell. *A Manager's Guide to Speaking and Listening.* New York: American Management Association, 1967.

Duker, Sam. *Listening Bibliography.* New York: Scarecrow Press, Inc., 1964.

————. *Listening: Readings.* Metuchen, N.J.: Scarecrow Press, Inc., 1966.

————, and Petrie, C. R., Jr. "What We Know About Listening: Continuation of a Controversy." *The Journal of Communication,* Vol. 14, No. 4 (December 1964), pp. 245–52.

Education, Vol. 75 (January 1955). Entire issue deals with listening.

Erickson, Allen G. "Can Listening Efficiency Be Improved?" *Journal of Communication,* Vol. 4, No. 4 (Winter 1954), pp. 53 ff.

Hayakawa, S. I. "The Task of the Listener," *ETC.: A Review of General Semantics,* Vol. 7, No. 1 (Autumn 1949).

"Is Anybody Listening? Business Must Start Doing More Listening Itself," *Fortune,* Vol. 42 (September 1950), pp. 77–83.

Johnson, Wendell. "Do You Know How to Listen?" *ETC.: A Review of General Semantics,* Vol. 7, No. 1 (Autumn 1949).

Keller, Paul W. "Major Findings in Listening in the Past Ten Years," *The Journal of Communication,* Vol. 10, No. 1 (March 1960), pp. 29–38.

Nichols, Ralph G. "Listening Is a 10-Part Skill," *Nation's Business* (July 1957).

——, and Lewis, Thomas R. *Listening and Speaking.* Dubuque, Iowa. William C. Brown Company, Publishers, 1954.

——, and Stevens, Leonard A. *Are You Listening?* New York: McGraw-Hill Book Co., 1957.

——, and ——. "If Only Someone Would Listen," *Journal of Communication,* Vol. 8, No. 1 (Spring 1957), pp. 8 ff.

——, and ——. "Listening to People," *Harvard Business Review* (September–October 1957), pp. 85–92.

Phifer, Gregg. "Propaganda and Critical Listening," *Journal of Communication,* Vol. 3 (1953), pp. 38 ff.

Rogers, Carl R., and Farson, Richard E. *Active Listening.* Chicago: Industrial Relations Center, University of Chicago, 1955.

Strong, Lydia. "Do You Know How to Listen?" *Management Review,* Vol. 44 (August 1955), pp. 530–35.

Toussaint, Isabella H. "A Classified Summary of Listening, 1950–1959," *The Journal of Communication,* Vol. 10, No. 3 (September 1960), pp. 125–34.

Zelko, Harold P. *How to Be a Good Listener.* New York: Employee Relations, Inc., 1958.

——. "An Outline of the Role of Listening in the Communication Process," *Journal of Communication,* Vol. 4 (1954), pp. 71 ff.

Reading

Bache, Walter Burke. *Educator's Guide to Personalized Reading Instruction.* Englewood Cliffs, N.J.: Prentice-Hall, Inc., 1961.

Duker, Sam. *Individualized Reading.* Springfield, Ill.: Charles C. Thomas, 1971.

Fries, C. C. *Linguistics and Reading.* New York: Holt, Rinehart & Winston, Inc., 1963.

Grebanier, Bernard D. N., and Rector, Seymour. *College Writing and Reading.* New York: Holt, Rinehart & Winston, Inc., 1959.

Guiler, Walter S., and Raeth, Claire J. *Developmental Reading.* Philadelphia: J. B. Lippincott Co., 1958.

Harris, A. J. *How to Increase Reading Ability.* 4th ed. New York: David McKay Co., Inc., 1962.

Hildreth, Gertrude. *Teaching Reading: A Guide to Basic Principles and Modern Practices.* New York: Holt, Rinehart & Winston, Inc., 1958.

Lefevre, Carl A. *Linguistics and the Teaching of Reading.* New York: McGraw-Hill Book Co., 1964.

Miller, Lyle L.   *Maintaining Reading Efficiency*. New York: Holt, Rinehart & Winston, Inc., 1959.

Sheldon, William D., and Braam, Leonard S.   *Reading Improvement for Men and Women in Industry*. Syracuse, N.Y.: Syracuse University Press, 1959.

Smith, Nila Banton.   *Read Faster and Get More from Your Reading*. New York: Prentice-Hall, Inc., 1958.

Spache, G. D.   *Toward Better Reading*. Champaign, Ill.: Garrard Publishing Co., 1963.

————, and Berg, Paul C.   *Faster Reading for Business*. New York: Thomas Y. Crowell Company, 1958.

Strong, Ruth M.   *Diagnostic Teaching of Reading*. New York: McGraw-Hill Book Co., 1964.

————; McCullough, Constance M.; and Traxler, Arthur E.   *Problems in the Improvement of Reading*. 3d ed. New York: McGraw-Hill Book Co., 1961.

Tinker, Miles A.   *Bases for Effective Reading*. Minneapolis: University of Minnesota Press, 1965.

Witty, Paul A.   *How to Improve Your Reading*. Chicago: Science Research Associates, 1963.

PROBLEM SOLVING, DECISION MAKING, CREATIVITY

Bruner, J. S.; Goodnow, J. J.; and Austin, G. A.   *A Study of Thinking*. New York: John Wiley & Sons, Inc., 1956.

Clark, Charles H.   *Brainstorming*. Garden City, N.Y.: Doubleday & Co., Inc., 1958.

Corson, J. J.   "Innovation Challenges Conformity," *Harvard Business Review*, Vol. 40, No. 3 (1962), pp. 67–74.

Dunnette, M. D.; Campbell, J.; and Jaastad, K.   "The Effect of Group Participation on Brainstorming Effectiveness for Two Industrial Samples," *Journal of Applied Psychology*, Vol. 47 (1963), pp. 30–37.

Hoffman, L. R.   "Conditions for Creative Problem-Solving," *Journal of Psychology*, Vol. 52 (1961), pp. 429–44.

Hyman, R.   "Creativity and the Prepared Mind: The Role of Information and Induced Attitudes" in *Widening Horizons in Creativity* (ed. C. Taylor). New York: John Wiley & Sons, Inc., 1964.

Maier, N. R. F.   *Problem-Solving Discussions and Conferences*. New York: McGraw-Hill Book Co., 1963.

Meadow, A.; Parnes, S. J.; and Reese, H.   "Influence of Brainstorming Instructions and Problem Sequence on a Creative Problem-Solving Test," *Journal of Applied Psychology*, Vol. 43 (1959), pp. 413–16.

Morgan, John S. *Improving Your Creativity on the Job.* New York: The American Management Association, 1968.

Newall, A. N.; Shaw, J. C.; and Simon, H. A. *Elements of a Theory of Human Problem-Solving.* Santa Monica, Calif.: The Rand Corp., 1957.

Osborn, Alex F. *Applied Imagination: Principles and Procedures of Creative Thinking.* New York: Charles Scribner's Sons, 1953.

Parnes, S. J. "Effects of Extended Effort in Creative Problem Solving," *Journal of Educational Psychology,* Vol. 52 (June 1961), pp. 117–22.

Simon, H. A. *The New Science of Management Decision.* New York: Harper & Row, Publishers, 1960.

———. "Theories of Decision-Making in Economics and Behavioral Science," *American Economics Review,* Vol. 69 (1959), pp. 253–83.

Smith, E. E., and Kight, S. S. "Effects of Feedback on Insight and Problem-Solving Efficiency in Training Groups," *Journal of Applied Psychology,* Vol. 43 (1959), pp. 209–11.

Stein, Morris I., and Heinze, Shirley J. *Creativity and the Individual.* New York: The Free Press, Division of the Macmillan Co., 1960.

Weisskopf-Joelson, E., and Eliseo, T. S. "An Experimental Study of the Effectiveness of Brainstorming," *Journal of Psychology,* Vol. 45 (1961), pp. 45–49.

GROUP PROCESSES: GROUP DYNAMICS, DISCUSSION, CONFERENCE

Allen, Louis A. "The Problem-Solving Conference," *Developing Executive Skills.* New York: American Management Association, Inc., 1958.

Bales, Robert F. "In Conference," *Harvard Business Review* (March–April 1954).

———. *Interaction Process Analysis.* Reading, Mass.: Addison-Wesley Publishing Co., Inc., 1950.

———. "Small Group Theory and Research," in *Sociology Today: Problems and Prospects* (eds. Robert K. Merton; *et al.*). Basic Books, Inc., Publishers, pp. 293–305, 1959.

Barnlund, Dean C., and Haiman, Franklyn, S. *The Dynamics of Discussion.* Boston: Houghton Mifflin Co., 1960.

Blake, R. R., and Mouton, J. S. *Group Dynamics—Key to Decision-Making.* Houston: Gulf Publishing Co., Book Div., 1961.

Bonner, Hubert. *Group Dynamics: Principles and Applications.* New York: The Ronald Press Company, 1959.

Braden, Waldo W., and Brandenburg, Earnest. *Oral Decision Making; Principles of Discussion and Debate.* New York: Harper & Row, Publishers, 1955.

Brilhart, John K. *Effective Group Discussion.* Dubuque, Iowa: Brown, 1967.

Brown, C. S., and Cohn, T. S. (eds.). *The Study of Leadership.* Danville, Ill.: The Interstate Printers & Publishers, Inc., 1958.

Cartwright, Dorwin. "Social Psychology and Group Processes," *Annual Revue of Psychology,* Vol. 8 (1957), pp. 211–36.

————, and Zander, Alvin (eds.). *Group Dynamics.* 3d ed. New York: Harper & Row, Publishers, 1968.

Cohen, A. M.; Bennis, W. G.; Wolkon, G. H. "The Effects of Changes in Communication Networks on the Behavior of Problem Solving Group," *Sociometry,* Vol. 25 (1962), pp. 177–96.

Cohen, D.; Whitmyre, J. W.; and Funk, W. H. "Effect of Group Cohesiveness and Training Upon Creative Thinking," *Journal of Applied Psychology,* Vol. 44 (1964), pp. 319–22.

Collins, Barry E., and Guetzkow, Harold. *A Social Psychology of Group Processes for Decision-Making.* New York: John Wiley & Sons, Inc., 1964.

Cortright, Rupert, and Hinds, George. *Creative Discussion.* New York: The Macmillan Co., 1959.

Deutsch, M. "Some Factors Affecting Membership Motivation and Achievement Motivation in a Group," *Human Relations,* Vol. 12 (1959), pp. 81–95.

Fiedler, Fred E. *Leader Attitudes and Group Effectiveness.* Urbana, Ill.: University of Illinois Press, 1958.

Fisher, B. Aubrey. "Communication Research and the Task-Oriented Group," *The Journal of Communication,* Vol. 21 (June 1971), pp. 136–49.

Gergen, Kenneth J. *The Psychology of Behavior Exchange.* Reading, Mass.: Addison-Wesley, 1969.

Gibb, J. R. *Factors Producing Defensive Behavior Within Groups.* Final Technical Report, Contract Nonr. 1147 (03). Boulder, Colo.: University of Colorado Press, 1956.

Golembiewski, Robert T. *The Small Group.* Chicago: University of Chicago Press, 1962.

Guetzkow, Harold (ed.). *Groups, Leadership, and Men.* Pittsburgh: Carnegie Press, 1951.

Gulley, Halbert. *Discussion, Conference, and Group Process.* New York: Holt, Rinehart & Winston, Inc., 1960.

Harnack, R. Victor, and Fest, Thorrel B. *Group Discussion Theory and Techniques.* New York: Appleton-Century-Crofts, 1964.

Hoffman, L. R., and Smith, C. G. "Some Factors Affecting the Behavior of Members of Problem-Solving Groups," *Sociometry,* Vol. 23 (1960), pp. 273–91.

Homans, George. *The Human Group*. New York: Harcourt & Row, Publishers, 1950.

————. *Social Behavior: Its Elementary Forms*. New York: Harcourt & Row, Publishers, 1961.

How to Lead Discussions. Leadership Pamphlet No. 1. Chicago: Adult Education Association of the U.S.A.

Keltner, John. *Group Discussion Processes*. New York: Longmans, Green & Co., 1957.

Lakin, Martin. *An Encounter with Sensitivity Training*. New York: McGraw-Hill Book Co., 1970.

————. "Group Sensitivity Training: Uses and Abuses," *ETC.: A Review of General Semantics*, Vol. 28, No. 2 (June 1971), pp. 291-12.

Lee, Irving J. *How to Talk with People*. New York: Harper & Row, Publishers, 1952.

Lippitt, Ronald. "Methods for Producing and Measuring Change in Group Functioning: Theoretical Problems," *General Semantics Bulletin*, Nos. 14 and 15 (Winter–Spring 1954).

Loney, Glenn M. *Briefing and Conference Techniques*. New York: McGraw-Hill Book Co., 1959.

McBurney, James H., and Hance, Kenneth G. *Discussion in Human Affairs*. New York: Harper & Row, Publishers, 1950.

Maier, Norman R. F. *Problem-Solving Discussions and Conferences*. New York: McGraw-Hill Book Co., 1963.

————. *Problem Solving and Creativity in Individuals and Groups*. Belmont, Calif.: Brooks/Cole Publishing Co., 1970.

Moulder, M. "Communication Structure, Decision Structure, and Group Performance," *Sociometry*, Vol. 23 (1960), pp. 1-14.

Phillips, Gerald M. and Erickson, Eugene C. *Interpersonal Dynamics in the Small Group*. New York: Random House, 1970.

Potter, David, and Andersen, Martin P. *Discussion: A Guide to Effective Practice*. 2d ed. Belmont, Calif.: Wadsworth Pub. Co., 1970.

Rogers, Carl. *Carl Rogers on Encounter Groups*. New York: Harper and Row, 1970.

Schein, E. H., and Bennis, W. G. *Personal and Organizational Change Through Group Methods*. New York: John Wiley & Sons, Inc., 1965.

Shaw, Marvin. *Group Dynamics: The Psychology of Small Group Behavior*. New York: McGraw-Hill Book Co., 1971.

Thelen, Herbert A. *Dynamics of Groups at Work*. Chicago: University of Chicago Press, 1954.

Thibault, John W., and Kelley, Harold H. *The Social Psychology of Groups*. New York: John Wiley & Sons, Inc., 1959.

Training Group Leaders. Leadership Pamphlet No. 8. Chicago: Adult Education Association of the U.S.A.

Understanding How Groups Work. Leadership Pamphlet No. 4. Chicago: Adult Education Association of the U.S.A.

Zelko, Harold P. *Successful Conference and Discussion Techniques*. New York: McGraw-Hill Book Co., 1957.

RELATED STUDIES

General Semantics

Berman, Sanford I. *Understanding and Being Understood*. San Diego: The International Communication Institute, 1965.

Bois, J. Samuel. *The Art of Awareness*. Dubuque: William C. Brown Co., Publishers, 1966.

———. "Executive Training and General Semantics," *General Semantics Bulletin*, Nos. 14 and 15 (Winter–Spring 1954).

———. *Explorations in Awareness*. New York: Harper & Row, Publishers, 1957.

Bontrager, O. R. "Some Possible Origins of the Prevalence of Verbalism," *Elementary English*, Vol. 28 (February 1951), pp. 94–104.

Brown, Roger W. *Words and Things*. New York: The Free Press, Division of the Macmillan Co., 1958.

Chase, Stuart. *Danger! Men Talking*. New York: Parent's Magazine Press, 1969.

Chisholm, Francis P. *Introductory Lectures on General Semantics*. Lakeville, Conn.: Institute of General Semantics, 1944.

Condon, John C., Jr. "Bibliography of General Semantics," *ETC.: A Review of General Semantics*. Part I: Vol. 20 (May 1963), pp. 86–105; Part II: Vol. 20 (September 1963), pp. 312–39; Part III: Vol. 21 (March 1964), pp. 73–100; Part IV: Vol. 22 (March 1965), pp. 59–86.

———. *Semantics and Communication*. New York: The Macmillan Co., 1966.

Decker, John P. "A Human Engineering Approach to Conflict," *ETC.: A Review of General Semantics*, Vol. 28, No. 2 (June 1971), pp. 191–200.

ETC.: A Review of General Semantics. Quarterly. San Francisco: International Society for General Semantics, San Francisco State College.

Exton, William, Jr. "Semantics of Industrial Relations," *Personnel*, Vol. 26, No. 6 (May 1950).

Fleishman, Alfred. *Sense and Nonsense: A Study in Human Communication*. San Francisco: International Society for General Semantics, 1971.

Froman, Robert. "How to Say What You Mean; Business Communication," *Nation's Business*, Vol. 45 (May 1957), pp. 76–78.

————. "Make Words Fit the Job," *Nation's Business*, Vol. 47 (July 1959), pp. 76–79.

————. "Prevent Short Circuits When You Talk," *Nation's Business*. Vol. 51 (January 1963), pp. 88–89.

————. "Test Your Judgment," *Nation's Business*, Vol. 50 (January 1962), pp. 66–69.

————. "Words Can Block Success," *Nation's Business* (September 1961), pp. 36 ff.

General Semantics Bulletin. A periodic publication of the Institute of General Semantics, Lakeville, Conn.

Glenn, Edmund S. "Semantic Difficulties in International Communication," *ETC.: A Review of General Semantics*, Vol. 9, No. 3 (Spring 1954).

Haney, William V. "The Uncritical Inference Test: Research and Applications," *General Semantics Bulletin*, Nos. 28 and 29 (1961).

————. "The Uncalculated Risk," (motion picture) Beverly Hills, Calif.: Round Table Films, Inc., 1971.

Hayakawa, S. I. "How Words Change Our Lives," *Saturday Evening Post*, Vol. 231 (December 27, 1958), pp. 22–23.

————. *Language in Thought and Action*. 2d ed. New York: Harcourt, Brace & World, Inc., 1964.

————. *Language, Meaning, and Maturity*. New York: Harper & Row, Publishers, 1954.

————. "The Meaning of Semantics," *New Republic*, Vol. 99 (August 2, 1939), pp. 354–57.

————. "New Techniques of Agreement," *Colgate Lectures in Human Relations*. Hamilton, N.Y.: Colgate University, 1950.

————. (ed.). *Our Language and Our World*. New York: Harper & Row, Publishers, 1959.

————. *Symbol, Status, and Personality*. New York: Harcourt, Brace & World, Inc., 1963.

————. *The Use and Misuse of Language*. New York: Fawcett World Library: Crest, Gold Medal & Premier Books, 1962.

Johnson, Wendell. *People in Quandaries*. New York: Harper & Row, Publishers, 1946.

————. *Your Most Enchanted Listener*. New York: Harper & Row, Publishers, 1956.

————; et al. "Studies in Language Behavior," *Psychological Monographs*, Vol. 56 (1944).

Kendig, M. (ed.). *Papers from the Second American Congress on General Semantics*. Lakeville, Conn.: Institute of General Semantics, 1943. Some 80 papers on theoretical aspects and practical application: Wide-ranging considerations from aesthetics to finance, reading-readiness to journalism.

Keyes, Kenneth S. *How to Develop Your Thinking Ability.* New York: McGraw-Hill Book Co., 1950.

Korzybski, Alfred. "General Semantics," *The American People's Encyclopedia.* Vol. 9. Chicago: Spencer International Press, 1948.

———. *Manhood of Humanity* (1921). Lakeville, Conn.: Institute of General Semantics, 1950.

———. "The Role of Language in the Perceptual Process" in *Perception: An Approach to Personality* (ed. R. R. Blake, and G. V. Ramsey). New York: The Ronald Press Co., 1951.

———. *Science and Sanity: An Introduction to Non-Aristotelian System and General Semantics* (1933). Lakeville, Conn.: Institute of General Semantics, 1948.

———. *Time-Binding: The General Theory.* (Two Papers, 1924–26.) Lakeville, Conn.: Institute of General Semantics, 1949.

———, and Kendig, M. *Foreword: A Theory of Meaning Analyzed.* General Semantics Monographs, No. 3. Lakeville, Conn.: Institute of General Semantics, 1942.

Lee, Irving J. *How Do You Talk about People?* Freedom Pamphlet. New York: Anti-Defamation League of B'Nai B'Rith.

———. *Language Habits in Human Affairs.* New York: Harper & Row, Publishers, 1941.

———, and Lee, Laura L. *Handling Barriers in Communication.* New York: Harper & Row, Publishers, 1957.

Minteer, Catherine. *Understanding in a World of Words.* San Francisco: International Society for General Semantics, 1970.

Morain, Mary (ed.). *Teaching General Semantics.* San Francisco: International Society for General Semantics, 1969.

Nilsen, Thomas R. "Some Assumptions That Impede Communication," *General Semantics Bulletin,* Nos. 14 and 15 (Winter–Spring 1954).

Rapoport, Anatol. *Fights, Games, and Debates.* New York: Harper & Row, 1960.

———. "Letter to a Soviet Philosopher," *ETC.: A Review of General Semantics,* Vol. 19, No. 4 (February 1963).

Thayer, Lee O. (ed.). *Communication: General Semantics Perspectives.* New York: Spartan Books, 1970.

Wagner, Geoffrey. *On the Wisdom of Words.* Princeton, N.J.: D. Van Nostrand Co., 1968.

Weinberg, Harry L. *Levels of Knowing and Existence.* New York: Harper & Row, 1959.

Whyte, William Foote. "Semantics and Industrial Relations," *Human Organization*, Vol. 8, No. 2 (1949), pp. 4–10.

Williamson, Merritt A. "Communication Problems (in four parts)—(1) Inference-Observation Confusion; (2) 'Bypassing'; (3) Know It Allness; and (4) Indiscrimination." *Research . Development*, Vol. 18, No. 12 (December 1967), pp. 46, 48, 50; Vol. 19, No. 1, 2, & 3 (January 1968), pp. 48, 50, 51 (February 1968), pp. 34, 36; and (March 1968), pp. 36, 38, 40.

Other related studies

Allport, Gordon W. *Pattern and Growth in Personality*, New York: Holt, Rinehart & Winston, Inc., 1961.

———, and Postman, Leo. *The Psychology of Rumor*. New York: Holt, Rinehart & Winston, Inc., 1947.

Anshen, Ruth Nanda (ed.). *Language: An Enquiry into Its Meaning and Function*. New York: Harper & Row, Publishers, 1957.

Attneave, Fred. *Applications of Information Theory to Psychology*. New York: Holt, Rinehart & Winston, Inc., 1959.

Bar-Hillel, Yehoshua. *Language and Information*. Reading, Mass.: Addison-Wesley Publishing Co., Inc., 1964.

Berelson, Bernard, and Steiner, G. A. *Human Behavior: An Inventory of Scientific Findings*. New York: Harcourt, Brace & World, Inc., 1964.

Birdwhistell, Ray L. *Kinesics and Context: Essays on Body Motion Communication*. Philadelphia: University of Pennsylvania Press, 1970.

Black, Max (ed.). *The Importance of Language*. Englewood Cliffs, N.J.: Prentice-Hall, Inc., 1962.

Brown, Roger. *Social Psychology*. New York: The Free Press, Division of The Macmillan Co., 1965.

———. *Words and Things*. New York: The Free Press, Division of The Macmillan Co., 1958.

Bruner, J. S.; Goodnow, J. J.; and Austin, G. A. *A Study of Thinking*. New York: John Wiley & Sons, Inc., 1956.

Burke, Kenneth. "What Are the Signs of What?" *Anthropological Linguistics*, Vol. 4, No. 6 (1962), pp. 1–23.

Carroll, John B. "Communication Theory, Linguistics, and Psycholinguistics," *Review of Educational Research*, Vol. 28 (1958), pp. 79–88.

———. *Language, Thought, and Reality: Selected Writings of Benjamin Lee Whorf*. New York: John Wiley & Sons, Inc., 1956.

Chase, Stuart. *Guides to Straight Thinking*. New York: Harper & Row, Publishers, 1956.

Dean, Leonard F., and Wilson, Kenneth G. (eds.). *Essays on Language and Usage*. New York: Oxford University Press, 1959.

Dewey, John. *How We Think*. Boston, D. C. Heath & Co., 1933.

Dexter, Lewis Anthony, and Manning, David (eds.). *People, Society, and Mass Communications*. New York: The Free Press, Division of The Macmillan Co., 1964.

Eisenberg, Abne M., and Smith, Ralph R., Jr. *Non-Verbal Communication*. Indianapolis, Ind.: The Bobbs-Merrill Co., Inc., 1972.

Fodor, Jerry A.; and Katz, Jerrold J. *The Structure of Language*. Englewood Cliffs, N.J.: Prentice-Hall, Inc., 1964.

Francis, W. Nelson. *The Structure of American English*. New York: The Ronald Press Co., 1958.

Garvin, Paul L. (ed.). *Natural Language and the Computer*. New York: McGraw-Hill Book Co., 1963.

George, A. L. *Propaganda Analysis: A Study of Inferences Made from Nazi Propaganda in World War II*. Evanston, Ill.: Row, Peterson & Co., 1959.

Greenberg, Joseph H. *Language, Culture and Communication*. Stanford, Calif.: Stanford University Press, 1971.

Hall, Edward Twitchell. *The Silent Language*. Garden City, N.Y.: Doubleday, & Co., Inc., 1959.

Happe, Bernard F., and Kaminsky, Jack. *Logic and Language*. New York: Alfred A. Knopf, Inc., 1956.

Harris, Robert T., and Jarrett, James L. *Language and Informal Logic*. New York: Longmans, Green & Co., 1956.

Henle, Paul (ed.). *Language, Thought, and Culture*. Ann Arbor Paperbacks, 1965.

Hockett, Charles F. *A Course in Modern Linguistics*. New York: The Macmillan Co., 1958.

Huff, Darrell. *How to Lie with Statistics*. New York: W. W. Norton & Co., Inc., 1954.

Ittelson, William. *The Ames Demonstrations in Perception*. Princeton, N.J.: Princeton University Press, 1952.

Jacobs, N.J. *Naming Day in Eden: The Creation and Recreation of Language*. New York: The Macmillan Co., 1959.

Johnson, Alexander Bryan. *The Meaning of Words*. New York: Harper & Row, Publishers, 1854. Now available in an edition published by John Winston Chamberlin, Milwaukee, Wis.

Kelley, Earl. *Education for What Is Real*. New York: Harper & Row, Publishers, 1947.

Kluckhohn, Clyde. *Mirror for Man*. New York: McGraw-Hill Book Co., 1949.

Larrabee, Harold. *Reliable Knowledge*. Boston: Houghton Mifflin Co., 1945.

Lawson, Chester A. *Language, Thought, and the Human Mind*. East Lansing, Mich.: Michigan State University Press, 1958.

Leary, William G. and Smith, James S. (eds.). *Thought and Statement*. New York: Harcourt, Brace & World, Inc., 1960.

Lee, Irving J. *The Language of Wisdom and Folly*. New York: Harper & Row, Publishers, 1949.

Levinson, Harry. *Emotional Health in the World of Work*. New York: Harper & Row, Publishers, 1964.

————; Price, C.; Muden, K.; Mandl, H.; and Solley, C. *Men, Management, and Mental Health*. Cambridge, Mass.: Harvard University Press, 1962.

Maccoby, E.; Newcomb, T. M.; and Hartley, E. L. (eds.). *Readings in Social Psychology*. 3d ed. New York: Holt, Rinehart & Winston, Inc., 1958.

McLuhan, Marshall. *Understanding Media: The Extensions of Man*. New York: McGraw-Hill Paperbacks, 1965.

Martin, John L. *International Propaganda: Its Legal and Diplomatic Control*. Minneapolis: University of Minnesota Press, 1958.

Martin, R. M. *Truth and Denotation: A Study in Semantical Theory*. Chicago: University of Chicago Press, 1958.

Menninger, Karl A. *The Human Mind*. New York: Alfred A. Knopf, Inc., 1945.

Miller, G. A. *Language and Communication*. New York: McGraw-Hill Book Co., 1951.

Morris, Charles. *Signs, Language, and Behavior*. New York: Prentice-Hall, Inc., 1946.

Ogden, C. K., and Richards, I. A. *The Meaning of Meaning*. New York: Harcourt, Brace & World, Inc., 1952.

Oliver, Robert T., and Barbara, D. A. *The Healthy Mind in Communion and Communication*. Springfield, Ill.: Charles C. Thomas, Publisher, 1962.

Preston, George H. *Psychiatry for the Curious*. New York: Holt, Rinehart & Winston, Inc., 1940.

Rapoport, Anatol. *Science and the Goals of Man: A Study in Semantic Orientation*. New York: Harper & Row, Publishers, 1950.

Reis, Samuel. *Language and Psychology*. New York: Philosophical Library, Inc., 1959.

Rokeach, Milton. *The Open and Closed Mind*. New York: Basic Books, Inc., Publishers, 1960.

Ruesch, Jurgen. *Disturbed Communication*. New York: W. W. Norton & Company, Inc., 1957.

————. "The Role of Communication in Therapeutic Transactions," *The Journal of Communication*, Vol. 13, No. 3 (September 1963), pp. 132–39.

————. *Therapeutic Communication*. New York: W. W. Norton & Company, Inc., 1961.

Russell, Bertrand. *Human Knowledge*. New York: Simon and Schuster, Inc., 1948.

Sapir, Edward. "Language," *Encyclopedia of the Social Sciences*. Vol. 14.

Sinclair, L. (ed.). "A Word in Your Ear," *Ways of Mankind*. Boston: Beacon Press, 1954.

Skinner, B. F. *Verbal Behavior*. New York: Appleton-Century-Crofts, 1957.

Smith, Alfred G. (ed.). *Communication and Culture*. New York: Holt, Rinehart & Winston, Inc., 1966.

Tabori, Paul. *The Natural Science of Stupidity*. Philadelphia: Chilton Books—Educational Division, 1959.

Thurman, Kelley (ed.). *Semantics*. Boston: Houghton Mifflin Co., 1960.

Toffler, Alvin. *Future Shock*. New York: Random House, 1970.

Toulmin, Stephen E. *The Uses of Argument*. New York: Cambridge University Press, 1958.

Ullman, Stephen. *Semantics: An Introduction to the Science of Meaning*. New York: Barnes & Noble, Inc., 1962.

Werkmeister, W. H. *An Introduction to Critical Thinking*. Chicago: Johnson Publishing Co.—Book Division, 1948.

Wertheimer, Max. *Productive Thinking*. (rev. by Michael Wertheimer). New York: Harper & Row, Publishers, 1959.

Whorf, Benjamin. *Language, Thought, and Reality*. Cambridge, Mass.: The Technology Press, Massachusetts Institute of Technology, 1956.

Wiener, Norbert. *The Human Use of Human Beings*. Boston: Houghton Mifflin Co., 1950.

Indexes

Index to Cases and Articles

Index